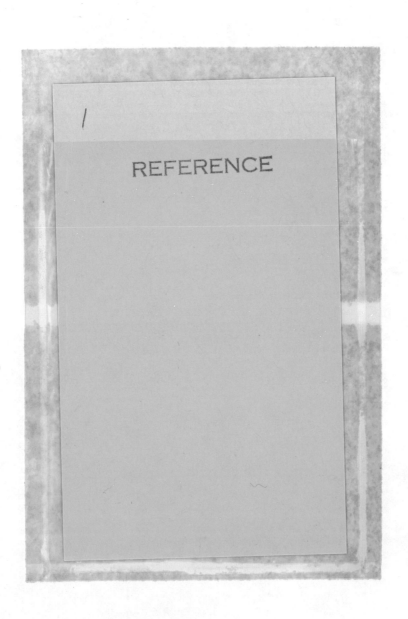

POETRY INDEX
ANNUAL
1982

POETRY INDEX
ANNUAL
1982

A Title, Author, and Subject
Index to Poetry in Anthologies

Prepared by
THE EDITORIAL BOARD
GRANGER BOOK CO., INC.

GRANGER BOOK CO., INC.
GREAT NECK, NEW YORK

Copyright © Granger Book Co., Inc. 1982

International Standard Book Number 0-89609-223-2

Manufactured in the U.S.A.

CONTENTS

PREFACE

The POETRY INDEX ANNUAL has been developed to provide access to the preponderance of anthologized poetry which is not indexed anywhere.

Standard works, such as *Granger's*, are selective in scope and do not endeavor to index other than the most generally accessible anthologies; they are not cumulative: each new edition adds only some new anthologies and generally eliminates those no longer in print. While the excellence of such references is acknowledged, they do not serve the broader and more specialized needs of many users.

The POETRY INDEX ANNUAL is the first and only work to systematically index *all* poetry anthologies as they are published. Being cumulative, each annual edition will complement and supplement the preceding issues; no superseding editions will be published. Taken together, the annual editions will form an ongoing and comprehensive title, author, and subject index to anthologized verse.

This 1982 edition, covering anthologies published in 1981, is the inaugural volume in the series.

EXPLANATORY NOTES

Each anthology indexed is referred to by a short alphabetical symbol. The complete title of the anthology and other publishing information is contained in the Key to Symbols of Works Indexed section which follows.

Each of the poems collected in each anthology is fully indexed for title, author, and subject. Where it is determined, however, that the full indexing of a work is not appropriate, the anthology is listed in the Key to Symbols with an asterisk, and is printed in the title, author, and subject entries in full capitalization.

Publication Dates. The actual publication date of a book is sometimes difficult to ascertain; copyright dates, announced dates, and other such indicia are not always reliable. In determining the inclusion dates for the POETRY INDEX ANNUAL, the copyright date will be the rule of thumb, although it will not be inflexibly applied. Accordingly, some anthologies copyrighted in 1981 which were not available for this edition are omitted but will be included in the next issue; likewise, 1980 anthologies which were made available in 1981 are indexed in this volume.

Arrangement. The filing is alphabetical word by word (e.g. "my world" precedes "myself"). Articles at the beginning of titles are retained but disregarded in the alphabeting; otherwise articles have alphabetical value. The alphabeting is stringently applied: all words are listed as spelled (e.g. "Mr." is filed as such and not as "Mister"). Numbers precede letters, and capital letters precede lower case letters. Punctuation is not disregarded in filing.

Entries. Entries are of three types: title, author, and subject. Each entry is complete in itself and each contains the anthology symbol wherein the poem is located; cross reference is not required. As this is a dictionary index, all entries are filed together in one alphabetical sequence. Where two different type entries are identical (as where the title of a poem is the same as the name of a subject), the order of listing is: title, author, subject.

1. *Title Entry* This entry contains the title of the poem, its author, and the symbol of the anthology in which it is located. The first word of the title is printed in bold face. If only a portion of the poem is contained in the anthology, the abbreviation "sels" follows the title. Limericks are generally entered under "Limerick" followed by the first line.

2. *Author Entry* Author, title, and anthology symbol are given in this entry. The author's name is printed in bold face. The title is always indented four spaces on the next line; where there is more than one poem by an author, each additional poem begins a new line similarly indented. Where more than one line is required for a poem, any succeeding line is indented an additional two spaces.

There is no author entry for anonymous poems. Translators are listed in addition to authors when the translation itself is deemed important. The name by which a poet is listed generally is the best known writing name, whether a pseudonym, married, or legal name; it is not necessarily the name used in the source anthology or that which

EXPLANATORY NOTES

appears on the title page of the poem. This reconciliation of the various forms of an author's name prevents unncessary duplication and confusion. Cross references from variant forms are made to the main author entry.

In collaborative poems, such as Japanese renga and Chinese linked verse, only the first or most prominent poet is indexed.

Chinese and Japanese poets' names are rendered in traditional fashion: family name first, given name second. The romanization of Chinese names generally follows that of the source anthology, either Wade-Giles or Pinyan. Exception is made for prominent poets widely known by their Wade-Giles name form, such as Tu Fu (Du Fu in Pinyan). In such cases reconciliation to the Wade-Giles system is undertaken to promote uniformity and to obviate confusion and duplication; cross reference from the Pinyan form to the main entry is provided.

3. *Subject Entry* Title, author, and anthology symbol are also given in this entry. The subject name is printed in bold face.

While some subjects, such as Love are so universal a theme of poetry as to be excluded from some indexes, they are included here when they are the main theme of a poem.

Users may want to consider the title of a poem in locating subjects, but they should be cautioned that this is often an unreliable methodology.

KEY TO SYMBOLS OF
WORKS INDEXED

BlS   Black Sister: poetry by black American women, 1746-1980. *Erlene Stetson, ed.* (c.1981) Indiana University Press

BrBD   Breakfast, Books, & Dreams: a day in verse. *Michael Patrick Hearn, ed.* (c. 1981) Frederick Warne

BuAC   Burning Air and a Clear Mind: contemporary Israeli women poets. *Myra Glazer, ed.* (c.1981) Ohio University Press

ByM   By Myself. *Lee Bennett Hopkins, ed.* (c.1980) Thomas Y. Crowell

CoP   Contemporary Polish Poetry, 1925-1975. *Nadeline G. Levine.* (c.1981) Twayne Publishers

DoNG   Do Not Go Gentle: poems on death. *William Packard, ed.* (c.1981) St. Martin's Press

DuD   Dusk to Dawn: poems of night. *Helen Hill, Agnes Perkins, & Aletha Helbig, eds.* (c.1981) Thomas Y. Crowell

EeBC   Eerdmans Book of Christian Poetry. *Pat Alexander, comp. Veronica Zundel, ed.* (c.1981) William B. Eerdmans

EvIm   The Evil Image: two centuries of Gothic short fiction and poetry. *Patricia L. Skarda and Nora Crow Jaffe, eds.* (c.1981) New American Library

FoFS   Four French Symbolist Poets: Baudelaire, Rimbaud, Verlaine, Mallarme. *Enid Rhodes Peschel, ed. & tr.* (c.1981) Ohio University Press

FreS   French Symbolist Poetry: an anthology. *John Porter Houston and Mona Tobin Houston, eds. & trs.* (c.1980) Indiana University Press

FroA   From A to Z: 200 contemporary American poets. *David Ray, ed.* (c.1981) Swallow Press

FroC   From the Country of Eight Islands: an anthology of Japanese poetry. *Hiroaki Sato and Burton Watson, eds. & trs.* (c.1981) University of Washington Press

GrAC   The Great Age of Chinese Poetry: the High T'ang. *Stephen Owen.* (c.1981) Yale University Press

HaAP   The Harper Anthology of Poetry. *John Frederick Nims, ed.* (c.1981) Harper & Row

HoA   The Hopwood Anthology: five decades of American poetry. *Harry Thomas and Steven Lavine, eds.* (c.1981) University of Michigan Press

KEY TO SYMBOLS OF WORKS INDEXED

KEY TO SYMBOLS OF WORKS INDEXED

POETRY INDEX
ANNUAL
1982

A-Apple pie. Unknown. IlTH
A-apple pie. Walter De La Mare.
    MiRN

Aardvarks
    Alicia aardvark. Patricia Viale
    Wuest. StPo

The **Abbess** of Whitby. Grace
    Schulman. StPo
Abeita, Luci
    Honest John's seven idols pawn
        shop. ReE
    Squash blossom shit and heishi
        horrors. ReE
Abel. Else Lasker-Schuler. VoWA
Abide with me. Henry Francis
    Lyte. WBP4
Abishag. Jakov Fichman. VoWA
Abishag writes a letter home.
    Itzik Manger. VoWA
Abortion
    Filth. Jean Lorrain (Paul
        Deval). FreS
    The lost baby poem. Lucille
        Clifton. BlS
    The mother. Gwendolyn Brooks.
        BlS
    Period piece. Bruce Berlind.
        FroA
Abou Ben Adhem. Leigh Hunt. WBP4
About her & about him. Miriam
    Oren. BuAC
About the cows. Roger Pfingston.
    FroA
About to leave Yi-feng Temple.
    Ling-yi. GrAC
Abraham. Delmore Schwartz. VoWA
Abraham. Edwin Muir. EeBC
Abraham. Stephen Mitchell. VoWA
Abraham. Eisig Silberschlag.
    VoWA
Abraham
    Abraham and Isaac. Else
        Lasker-Schuler. VoWA
    Abraham in Egypt. Howard
        Schwartz. VoWA
    Abraham. Delmore Schwartz. VoWA
    Abraham. Edwin Muir. EeBC
    Abraham. Eisig Silberschlag.
        VoWA
    The story of Abraham and Hagar.

    Edna Aphek. VoWA
Abraham Sutskever. Seymour
    Mayne. VoWA
Abraham and Isaac. Else
    Lasker-Schuler. VoWA
Abraham and Sarah. Itzik Manger.
    VoWA
Abraham in Egypt. Howard
    Schwartz. VoWA
Abrahams, Dawn
    Be what you are. YoVA
Abramovitch, Henry
    Psalm of the jealous god. VoWA
Absalom. Zerubavel Gilead. VoWA
Absalom
    Absalom. Zerubavel Gilead. VoWA
    Another poem on Absalom. Nathan
        Yonathan. VoWA
Absalom and Achitopel, sels.
    John Dryden. HaAP
Abse, Dannie
    Song for Dov Shamir. VoWA
    Tales of Shatz. VoWA
Absence. Unknown. WBP3
Absence. Frances Anne Kemble.
    WBP3
Absence of noise Presence of
    sound. Olga Broumas. TeMP
Absence. See Separation
Absent star. Quinton Duval. FroA
Absolute Zero (temperature)
    Approaching absolute zero.
    Joyce Peseroff. TeMP
Academic curse: an epitaph.
    Wesli Court. TyW
Accident at Three Mile Island.
    Jim Barnes. FroA
The **accident** has occurred.
    Margaret Atwood. LiHE
An **accomodating** lion. Tudor
    Jenks. IlTH
An **account** of a visit... Ts'en
    Shen. GrAC
The **ache** of marriage. Denise
    Levertov. LiHE
Achilles
    The shield of Achilles. Wystan
        Hugh Auden. HaAP
Acoma. William Oandasan. ReE
Acomb, Stanford K.
    Painted men. YoVA
Acquainted with the night.
    Robert Frost. HaAP
The **act.** William Carlos
    Williams. SlW
The **act** of love. Robert Creeley.
    HaAP
Acting and Actors
    The end of the play. William
        Makepeace Thackeray. WBP4

Thespian in Jerusalem. Myra
  Glazer (Schotz). VoWA
Ada
  Lines ("From fair
    Jamaica's.."). BlS
  Lines ("My spirit leans..."").
    BlS
  To the memory of J. Horace
    Kimball. BlS
  Untitled ("Oh, when...earthly
    tenement"). YoVA
Adam and Eve
  Adam and Eve at the garden
    gate. Marsha Pomerantz. VoWA
  Adam in love. Stephen Mitchell.
    VoWA
  Adam lay ibounde. Unknown .
    HaAP
  Adam's dream. Howard Schwartz.
    VoWA
  The begetting of Cain. Hyam
    Pultzik. VoWA
  Cain's song. Donald Finkel.
    VoWA
  Earth. Mark Mitchell. YoVA
  Eve's song in the garden. Lynn
    Gottlieb. VoWA
  Eve. Jakov Fichman. VoWA
  The first wedding in the world.
    Joel Rosenberg. VoWA
  The fortunate fall. Alfred
    Alvarez. VoWA
  Four. Chaya Shenhav. BuAC
  From the dust. Elaine Dallman.
    VoWA
  The good beasts. Willis
    Barnstone. VoWA
  Imperial Adam. Alec Derwent
    Hope. HaAP
  Like weary trees. Jacob
    Glatstein. VoWA
  Never again would birds' song
    be...same. Robert Frost. HaAP
  An old story. Rena Lee. VoWA
  Paradise lost, sels. John
    Milton. WBP4
  Paradise. Chana Bloch. VoWA
  Scrawled in pencil... Don
    Pagis. VoWA
Adam and Eve at the garden gate.
  Marsha Pomerantz. VoWA
Adam in love. Stephen Mitchell.
  VoWA
Adam lay ibounden. Unknown. HaAP
Adam's curse. William Butler
  Yeats. SlW
Adam's death. Gabriel Levin.
  VoWA
Adam's dream. Howard Schwartz.
  VoWA

Adam, Jean
  There's nae luck about the
    house. WBP2
Adams, Sarah Flower
  Father, thy will be done! WBP4
Addams, Charles
  The Charles Addams Mother
    Goose. TrWB
Adderly, Julian ("Cannonball")
  Cannon arrested. Michael S.
    Harper. FroA
Addio a la mamma. Noe Jitrik.
  VoWA
Addison, Joseph
  The spectator, sels. WBP4
Addison, Joseph (about)
  How did they fume, and
    stamp,and roar.... Alexander
    Pope. TyW
Adieu, adieu! my native shore.
  George Gordon,6th Baron
  Byron. WBP3
Adieu, farewell earth's bliss.
  Thomas Nashe. HaAP
Adirondack Mountains
  Home. Maurice Kenny. ReE
Adler, J.
  Song of the times. OnCP
Adlestrop. Edward Thomas. HaAP
The **admiral's** daughter. E.G.
  Burrows. HoA
Admirals all. Henry Newbolt. MTS
Adolescence. Dennis Schmitz.
  FroA
Adrian, Roman C.
  Bel woman. ReE
  Happening. ReE
Adrift. David Newton. YoVA
Advertising
  The personals. Alan Feldman.
    TeMP
Advice. Yehuda Amichai. VoWA
Advice. William Dunbar. WBP1
Advice. Gwendolyn B. Bennett.
  BlS
Advice
  Blind children. Claire Dugan.
    YoVA
  Death threat. Rainie Kunde.
    YoVA
  I have a big favor to ask you,
    brothers. Zishe Landau. VoWA
Advice from old age. Ryan
  Synovec. YoVA
Advice to a girl. Thomas
  Campion. WBP2
Advice to children. Carolyn
  Wells. IlTH
Advice to grandsons. Unknown.
  IlTH

Advice to my son. J. Peter
    Meinke. LiHE
Ae fond kiss before we part.
    Robert Burns. WBP3
Aella: a tragical interlude,
    sels. Thomas Chatterton.
    HaAP--WBP2
Aeschylus
    Prometheus, sels. WBP3
Afar in the desert. Thomas
    Pringle. WBP3
An affair. Paula Cordier. YoVA
Affaire d'amour. Margaret Wade
    Deland. WBP2
"Affluence-define it as."
    Hezutsu Tosaku. FroC
Africa and Africans
    Cape Coast castle revisited. Jo
    Ann Hall-Evans. BlS
    Early loses: a requiem. Alice
    Walker. BlS
    Return. Johari M. Kunjufu. BlS
    Seduction. Jo Ann Hall-Evans.
    BlS
    To the Rt Hon William..., sels.
    Phillis Wheatley. BlS
After. Philip Levine. VoWA
After Shiki. Larry Eigner. FroA
After Sunday dinner we uncles
    snooze. John Ciardi. HoA
After Verlaine. Anselm Hollo.
    FroA
After a time. Catherine Davis.
    LiHE
After an eclipse of the sun.
    Eugene Heimler. VoWA
After apple-picking. Robert
    Frost. LiHE
After death. Sir Edwin Arnold.
    WBP3
After fish. Linda Hogan. ReE
After great pain, a formal
    feeling comes. Emily
    Dickinson. HaAP--LiHE
After her death. Anne Stevenson.
    HoA
After my death. Hayim Nachman
    Bialik. VoWA
After our war. John Balaban.
    FroA
After reading Nelly Sachs. Linda
    Pastan. VoWA
After spending all day at
    the..Museum... Alan Britt.
    FroA
After summer. Philip Bourke
    Marston. WBP3
After the Ch'ing-ming
    Festival...
    Liu-Ch'ang-ch'ing. GrAC

After the fair. Thomas Hardy.
    HaAP
After the flood. Arthur Rimbaud.
    SlW
After the raiders have gone.
    Yuan Chieh. GrAC
After the rain. Stanley Crouch.
    LiHE
After the sea-ship. Walt
    Whitman. MTS
After the surprising
    conversions. Robert Lowell.
    HaAP
After the war. Hayim Naggid.
    VoWA
The aftermath. William Carlos
    Williams. FroA
Afternoon
    Nantucket. William Carlos
    Williams. HaAP--SlW
Afternoon's angel. Seymour
    Mayne. VoWA
Afterword. Nishiwaki Junzaburo.
    FroC
The Aga Kahn. Steve Orlen. TeMP
Again. Daryl Lynn Stewart. YoA
Again my fond circle of doves.
    Baxter Hathaway. HoA
again you slept with mr no man.
    Yona Wallach. BuAC
Against education. Charles
    Churchill. TyW
Against parting. Natan Zach.
    VoWA
Against priests who live with
    concubines. Euricius Cordus.
    ReLP
Against winter. Elaine
    Feinstein. VoWA
Agatha. Alfred Austin. WBP3
Agatha. Remy de Gourmont. FreS
Agathias Scholasticus
    Time's revenge. WBP3
Age. Tomioka Taeko. FroC
Age. Marya Mannes. FroA
The age of dreams. Eloi de
    Grandmont. MoVT
The age of wisdom. William
    Makepeace Thackeray. WBP2
Aging. Ingrid Schulz. YoVA
Aging
    Age. Tomioka Taeko . FroC
    Age. Marya Mannes. FroA
    The approach of age. George
    Crabbe. WBP3
    Autumn bank songs XV, sel. Li
    Po . GrAC
    Change of life. Constance
    Urdang. VoWA
    The descent. William Carlos

Williams. HaAP
Early spring, writing my
feeling. Ch'ing-chiang . GrAC
Easy does it. Henry Chapin.
FroA
Fall letter. Dave Kelly. FroA
Generations. Moishe Steingart.
VoWA
"I look into my glass." Thomas
Hardy. HaAP
Myself departin. Takahashi
Mutsuo . FroC
Next day. Randall Jarrell. HaAP
Not going with it. Zali
Gurevitch. VoWA
Penelope, unweaving. Patricia
Celley Groth. StPo
Portrait. Madeline Mason. StPo
Rivers grow small, sels.
Czeslaw Milosz. CoP
Song for the white hai. Liu
Hsi-yi . GrAC
Time's reveng. Agathias
Scholasticus . WBP3
To a lady. John James Piatt.
WBP2
Toward myself. Leah Goldberg.
VoWA
Agnes. Jean Moreas. FreS
Agnes, Saint
The Eve of St. Agnes. John
Keats. HaAP--WBP3
Saint Agnes. Alfred, Lord
Tennyson. WBP4
Agnew, Edith
"Los Pastores." PoCh
The agony of victory. John
Morretti. YoVA
Agrius
Silva II: Agrius. George
Buchanan. ReLP
Ah, sun-flower! William Blake.
HaAP
Ahasuerus. Joseph Roth. VoWA
Ai
Pentecost. TeMP
Aiken, Conrad
Doctor's row. HaAP
The things. HaAP
Aiken, Joan
John's song. DuD
Night landscape. DuD
Rhyme for night. DuD
The aim. Charles G. D. Roberts.
WBP4
Ain't I a woman? Sojourner
Truth. BlS
Ainslee, Hew
The Ingle-side. WBP1
Air. Tomaz Salamun. VoWA

The air. Mary Jahnke. YoVA
Air. I. Amiri Baraka (LeRoi
Jones). SlW
Air
Free gift. Tony Mancuso. HoWM
Memory air. Charles Dobzynski.
VoWA
Air Raids
The buzz plane. Robert Francis.
TyW
Still falls the rain. Edith
Sitwell. EeBC--ShBa
Air Travel
Flight 539. John Malcolm
Brinnin. HoA
A San Diego poem:
January-February 1973. Simon
J. Ortiz. ReE
Silver flight. Douglas Morris.
YoVA
Air Warfare
The death of the ball turret
gunner. Randall Jarrell.
HaAP--LiHE
The air vision. Jakov van Hoddis
(H.Davidson). VoWA
Aji. Gary Bolick. YoVA
Aka. Frederick Eckman. FroA
The Akedah. Matti Megged. VoWA
The Akedah. Aliza Shenhar. VoWA
Akenside, Mark
Song ("The shape alone let
others prize.") WBP2
Akera Kanko
Autumn wind. FroC
Year end. FroC
Akerman, Lucy E.
Nothing but leaves. WBP4
Akers, Elizabeth
Little feet. WBP1
Rock me to sleep. WBP1
The telltale. WBP2
Aki, Prince
Song ("My wife is far away.")
FroC
Akiba. Muriel Rukeyser. VoWA
Akiba
Akiba. Muriel Rukeyser. VoWA
Akwesasne. Maurice Kenny. ReE
Al Capone in Alaska. Ishmael
Reed. TyW
Alabaster, William
Sonnet 56. ShBa
Sonnet 62. ShBa
Sonnet 66. ShBa
Alas! 'tis very sad to hear.
Walter Savage Landor. TyW
Alba. Ezra Pound. HaAP--SlW
The albatross. Charles
Baudelaire. FoFS

Albatross
      The albatross. Charles
            Baudelaire. FoFS
Albert Einstein. Carolyn Pintye.
      StPo
Alberti, Rafael
      Landing. NiR
Alcestis. Maura Stanton. TeMP
The alchemical cupboard. Asa
      Benveniste. VoWA
Alciat, Andrea
      Epigram: an almond tree. ReLP
Alcock, Mary
      A receipt for writing a novel.
            EvIm
Alcohol. See Drinks & Drinking
Alcon
      Eclogue: Alcon. Baldassaro
            Castliglione. ReLP
Alderson, D.F.
      Montezuma. IlTH
Aldis, Dorothy
      Ice. RoRF
Aldrich, James
      A death-bed. WBP3
Aldrich, Thomas Bailey
      Alec Yeaton's son. MTS
      Baby Bell. WBP1
      Palabras carinosas. WBP2
Alec Yeaton's son. Thomas Bailey
      Aldrich. MTS
Aleph. Stuart Z. Perkoff. VoWA
The aleph bet. Fay Lipschitz.
      VoWA
Alexander and Campaspe, sels.
      John Lyly. WBP2
Alexander, Cecil Francis
      Burial of Moses. WBP4
Alexis, here she stayed. William
      Drummond. WBP2
Alger (trans.), William R.
      The parting lovers. WBP3
Alicia aardvark. Patricia Viale
      Wuest. StPo
Alienation
      In the last flicker of the
            sinking sun. Peretz Markish.
            VoWA
      You ask me what it means.
            Giovanni Giudici. NeIP
Aliens, sels. Georgia Douglas
      Johnson. BlS
Aliger, Margarita
      House in Meudon. VoWA
      To a portrait of Lermontov.
            VoWA
      Two. VoWA
Alison. Unknown. HaAP
All day we've longed for night.
      Sarah Webster Fabio. BlS

All is God's. Jakov de Haan.
      VoWA
All night long. Nina Cassian.
      VoWA
All the dirt that's fit to pot.
      Vita C. Ungaro. StPo
All this so tasteless and
      threatening. Yona Wallach.
      BuAC
"All through the night". Ryokan.
      FroC
All's well that ends well, sels.
      William Shakespeare. WBP3
Allegory. Paul Verlaine. FoFS
Allen, Joseph Baneth
      Common knowledge. YoVA
Allen, Minerva
      In the lodge where no one
            lives. ReE
      Returning from/scouting for
            meat. ReE
Allen, Paula Gunn
      Hoop dancer. ReE
      Ikce wichasha. ReE
      Rain for ke-waik bu-ne-ya. ReE
      Snowgoose. ReE
      Tucson: first night. ReE
Alley, Jennifer
      As the sea dries up. YoVA
Allingham, William
      Among the heather. WBP2
      The dirty old man. WBP3
      Half-waking. WBP1
      Lovely Mary Donnelly. WBP2
Allston, William
      Boyhood. WBP1
Almi, A.
      Everywhere. OnCP
The almighty Thor. Lamont Jones.
      HoWM
Almond Trees
      Epigram: an almond tree. Andrea
            Alciat. ReLP
Almond, Kimberly Diane
      Colorado. YoVA
Almost beyond the churches of
      men. Armando Jaramillo. YoVA
Alone. Itzik Manger. OnCP--VoWA
Alone. Lisa Smith. YoVA
Along the field as we came by.
      Alfred Edward Housman. HaAP
Alonzo the Monk and Fair
      Imogine. Matthew Gregory
            Lewis. EvIm
The alphabet. Karl Shapiro. VoWA
Alphabet
      A-Apple pi. Unknown . IlTH
      The aleph bet. Fay Lipschitz.
            VoWA
      Aleph. Stuart Z. Perkoff. VoWA

The alphabet came to me. Jerome
  Rothenberg. VoWA
The alphabet. Karl Shapiro.
  VoWA
Gimel. Stuart Z. Perkoff. VoWA
Hai. Stuart Z. Perkoff. VoWA
The alphabet came to me. Jerome
  Rothenberg. VoWA
An alphabet of questions.
  Charles Edward Carryl. IlTH
Alquit (Eliezer Blum), B.
  The light of the world. VoWA
  Wandering chorus. VoWA
Alta
  I don't have no bunny tail on
  my behind. TyW
Alterman, Nathan
  Poem about your face. VoWA
  The spinning girl. VoWA
  Tammuz. VoWA
  This night. VoWA
  To the elephants. VoWA
Alvarez, Alfred
  A cemetery in New Mexico. VoWA
  Dying. VoWA
  The fortunate fall. VoWA
  Mourning and melancholia. VoWA
Amalek. Friedrich Torberg. VoWA
Amazing, beauteous change!.
  Philip Doddridge. WBP4
Amber child. John Lukas. YoVA
The ambiguous dog. Arthur
  Guiterman. IlTH
Ambition
  Birdless countr. Shimazaki
  Toson . FroC
The ambitious mouse. John
  Farrar. MiRN
American Revolution
  Concord hymn. Ralph Waldo
  Emerson. HaAP
American rhymes. Nicolas
  Guillen. NiR
An American thought. Carl
  Gingras. YoVA
Amerson, Hiram
  Time. YoVA
Amichai, Yehuda
  Advice. VoWA
  God has pity on kindergarten
  children. VoWA
  I am a leaf. VoWA
  I am sitting here. VoWA
  I think of oblivion. VoWA
  In the old city. VoWA
  Jerusalem, port city. VoWA
  Lament. VoWA
  Lay your head on my shoulder.
  VoWA
  Not like a cypress. VoWA

Of three or four in a room.
  VoWA
On the Day of Atonement. VoWA
On the wide stairs. VoWA
Shadow of the old city. VoWA
Since then. VoWA
Sodom's sister city. VoWA
The town I was born in. VoWA
Amichai, Yehuda (about)
  Yehuda Amichai. Seymour Mayne.
  VoWA
Amir, Aharon
  Nothingness. VoWA
Amis, Kingsley
  Shitty. TyW
Ammons, Archie Randolph
  The constant. HaAP
  Cut the grass. HaAP
  Life in the boondocks. HaAP
  Mechanism. HaAP
  Model. FroA
  Room conditioner. TeMP
  Self-projection. FroA
  Winter saint. TyW
"Among a thousand clouds..."
  Han-shan. LuL
Among iron fragments. Tuvia
  Ruebner. VoWA
Among school children. William
  Butler Yeats. HaAP
Among so many concerns, sels.
  Tadeusz Rozewicz. CoP
Among the heather. William
  Allingham. WBP2
Among the pine trees. Moshe Dor.
  VoWA
Amoretti: LXVIII. Edmund
  Spenser. EeBC--HaAP
Amorosi, Ray
  Note in a sanitorium. FroA
Ample make this bed. Emily
  Dickinson. DoNG
Anath. Haim Guri. VoWA
The anatomie of the world, sels.
  John Donne. ShBa
Ancestors. Harold Schimmel. VoWA
The ancestors. Anita Barrows.
  VoWA
Ancestry. See Heritage
Anchor. Maruyama Kaoru. FroC
An ancient custom. Anatoly
  Steiger. VoWA
The ancient law. Andre Spire.
  VoWA
Ancient murderess night. Anna
  Margolin (R. Lebensboim).
  VoWA
Ancient music. Ezra Pound. TyW
Ancient of days. Anthony Rudolf.
  VoWA

Ancient stirring, sels. Ch'ang
    Chien. GrAC
The ancient temple of Hsiang Yu.
    P'an Shu. GrAC
And I love you. Penny Ward. YoVA
And I too was in Arcady, sels.
    Tadeusz Rozewicz. CoP
And death shall have no
    dominion. Dylan Thomas. DoNG
And did those feet in ancient
    time. William Blake. HaAP
And doth not a meeting like
    this. Thomas Moore. WBP1
And if I did, what then?. George
    Gascoigne. HaAP
And if I don't return?. Edwin
    Castro. NiR
And in that drowning instant.
    A.M. Klein. VoWA
"And it is Christ, like a
    sailor". Max Elskamp. FreS
And now you're ready... James
    Vincent Cunningham. TyW
And on my return. Haim Guri.
    VoWA
And that will be heaven.
    Evangeline Paterson. EeBC

...And the old women gathered.
    Mari Evans. BlS

And the silver turns into night.
    Nathan Yonathan. VoWA
And though I liked not the
    religion. Sir Nicholas
    Throckmorton. ShBa
And yet. Kadya Molodovsky. VoWA
Anders, Lois-Long
    John Smith. StPo
    Large order. StPo
Anderson, Alexander
    Cuddle doon. WBP1
Anderson, Jack
    The invention of New Jersey.
    TyW
Anderson, Susan Mae
    I am a drifter. YoVA
    Those days of depression. YoVA
Andres. Fernando Gordillo. NiR
Andres, Dan
    Girls. YoVA
Andrew's bedtime story. Ian
    Serraillier. DuD
Andromache

The swan. Charles Baudelaire.
    FoFS
Andy-Diana DNA letter. Andrew
    Weiman. HaAP
Anecdote of a jar. Wallace
    Stevens. SlW
Anecdote of the prince of
    peacocks. Wallace Stevens.
    SlW
The angel Michael. Anath Bental.
    VoWA
The angel and the clown. Vachel
    Lindsay. PrVo
The angel in the house, sels.
    Coventry Patmore. WBP2
The angel of patience. John
    Greenleaf Whittier. WBP3
The angel's whisper. Samuel
    Lover. WBP1
Angela Davis. Alice S. Cobb. BlS
Angelina Runs-Against. Marnie
    Walsh. ReE
Angelou, Maya
    My Arkansas. BlS
    On diverse deviations. BlS
    Sepia fashion show. BlS
    Still I rise. BlS
    Woman me. BlS
Angels. Richard Burns. VoWA
Angels
    Afternoon's angel. Seymour
    Mayne. VoWA
    The angel and the clown. Vachel
    Lindsay. PrVo
    Angels in the house. Jerred
    Metz. VoWA
    The angels' song. Edward
    Hamilton Sears. WBP4
    Document d'osieaux: document of
    bird. Takiguchi Shuzo . FroC
    God's language. Ruth Fainlight.
    VoWA
    Jacob and the angel. Stephen
    Mitchell. VoWA
    Lame angel. Donald Finkel. VoWA
    Love calls us to...things of
    this world. Richard Wilbur.
    HaAP
    The ministry of angels. Edmund
    Spenser. WBP4
    Of angels. E.L. Mayo. FroA
    Our angels. Howard Schwartz.
    VoWA
    Reversibility. Charles
    Baudelaire. FoFS
    The two angels. John Greenleaf
    Whittier. WBP4
    When the angels are exhausted.
    Yona Wallach. VoWA
Angels in the house. Jerred

Metz. VoWA
The **angels'** song. Edward
Hamilton Sears. WBP4
Anger
A cloud in trousers, sels.
Vladimir Mayakowsky. SlW
Do not go gentle into that good
night. Dylan Thomas.
LiHE--TyW
Anger of Cupid. Helen Denniston.
YoVA
Angeriano, Girolamo
Of his love Caelia. ReLP
Anima mundi, sels. R.M. Milnes
(Lord Houghton). WBP4
Animal nonsense. Unknown. IlTH
Animal song. Alfredo Giuliani.
NeIP
The **animals**. Edwin Muir. EeBC
Animals. J. Ashby-Sterry. IlTH
Animals
Animal nonsens. Unknown . IlTH
Birds of a feathe. Mother Goose
. MiRN
The carnivoristicous ounce.
Mrs. M.E. Blake. IlTH
The catipoce. James Reeves.
IlTH
The Chimera. Alfred Mombert.
VoWA
Eden's courtesy. Clive Staples
Lewis. EeBC
The friendly beast. Unknown .
PoCh
Hymn to joy. Julia Cunningham.
PoCh
Jabberwocky. Lewis Carroll
(C.L. Dodgson). IlTH
Old Noah's ar. Unknown . IlTH
Struggling at the kill. Shlomit
Cohen. BuAC
The witnesses. X.J. Kennedy.
PoCh
Words from an old Spanish
carol. Ruth Sawyer. PoCh
Animals are passing from our
lives. Philip Levine. TyW
Anne Rutledge. Edgar Lee
Masters. DoNG--HaAP
Anne and the field mouse. Ian
Serraillier. MiRN
The **Anniad**. Gwendolyn Brooks.
BlS
Anniversary. Giancarlo Majorino.
NeIP
Anniversary. Daniel Weissbort.
VoWA
The **anniversary**. John Donne.
HaAP
Anniversary poem...Cheyennes who

died... Lance Henson. ReE
The **annoyer**. Nathaniel Parker
Willis. WBP2
Annunciation over the shepherds,
sels. Rainer Maria Rilke.
PoCh
Annus mirabilis, sels. John
Dryden. MTS
Anonymous tragedy. Donnelle
Gerling. YoVA
Another day. Michelle Dawn
Ferguson. YoVA
Another day, another time.
Denise L. Gastil. YoVA
Another fan. Stephane Mallarme.
FoFS
Another grace for a child.
Robert Herrick. EeBC
Another mother and child.
Joe-Ann McLaughlin. FroA
Another poem on Absalom. Nathan
Yonathan. VoWA
Another voice. Paolo Volponi.
NeIP
Another year. Unknown. HaAP
The **answer**. Unknown. WBP4
Answer. Leah Goldberg. VoWA
Answer to Master Wither's
song... Ben Jonson. WBP2
Answer to Voznesensky &
Evtushenko. Frank O'Hara. HoA
An **answer** to another persuading
a lady... Katherine Philips.
HaAP
Answerers. William Stafford.
TeMP
answering a late call. Muriel
Fath. StPo
Anthem for doomed youth. Wilfred
Owen. HaAP
Anthracite. Bartolo Cattafi.
NeIP
Anthropology & Anthropologists
Indian anthropologist.... Wendy
Rose. ReE
Anti-Semitism
Anti-nostalgia. Henryk
Grynberg. VoWA
Everywhere. A. Almi. OnCP
Softly let us all vanish. Zishe
Landau. OnCP
Today the Nazis forces marched.
Melech Ravitch (Z.K.
Bergner). OnCP
Anti-nostalgia. Henryk Grynberg.
VoWA
Antigone
Antigone and Oedipus. Henrietta
Cordelia Ray. BlS
Antigone and Oedipus. Henrietta

Cordelia Ray. BlS
Antipatros
Fortune-tellers say I won't
last long. DoNG
Never again, Orpheus. DoNG
Antiquity
"With my books closed again..."
Stephane Mallarme. FoFS
Antony and Cleopatra. William
Haines Lytle. WBP3
Ants. Lewis Hyde. FroA
Ants
Ants. Lewis Hyde. FroA
Departmental. Robert Frost.
LiHE
Anxiety. Rigoberto Perez Lopez.
NiR
Anxiety. Rigoberto Lopez Perez.
NiR
Anxiety pastorale. Ted Schaefer.
FroA
anyone lived in a pretty how
town. Edward Estlin Cummings.
HaAP
Anzai Hitoshi
Hitomaro. FroC
Random thoughts on the
Shinkokinshu... FroC
Village hairdresser. FroC
Warbler. FroC
Winter evening. FroC
Apart from oneself. Alejandra
Pizarnik. VoWA
Apfel, Shulamit
Bedouin woman. BuAC
A big woman screams out her
guts. BuAC
Mad Rosalinde. BuAC
Aphek, Edna
Sarah. VoWA
The story of Abraham and Hagar.
VoWA
Aphrodite. Shlomit Cohen. BuAC
Aphrodite
Aphrodite. Shlomit Cohen. BuAC
Myth on Mediterranean Beach:
Aphrodite... Robert Penn
Warren. HaAP
Apocalpyse. Jean Lipkin. VoWA
Apocalyse
Burnt debris. Thomas Sessler.
VoWA
A song on the end of the world,
sels. Czeslaw Milosz. CoP
Apocrypha. Stanley Moss. VoWA
Apollinaire, Guillaume
The hermit. FreS
It's raining. SlW
The little car. SlW
Prayer ("When I was just a

little mite"). MoVT
Sea of land. MoVT
Ties. MoVT
Zone. SlW
Apology for E.H.. William
Hathaway. FroA
Apparently with no surprise.
Emily Dickinson. LiHE
Apparition. Stephane Mallarme.
FoFS
An **appeal** to cats...business of
love. Thomas Flatman. HaAP
An **appeal** to my countrywomen.
Frances E.W. Harper. BlS
Appendix to the Anniad.
Gwendolyn Brooks. BlS
Apple Trees
Hurricane. Patricia Viale
Wuest. StPo
Apple pie
A-apple pie. Walter De La Mare.
MiRN
Apple trees apple trees apple
trees. Nelo Risi. NeIP
Appleman, Philip
Memo to the 21st century. TeMP
Apples
After apple-picking. Robert
Frost. LiHE
Application. Grace Schulman.
StPo
The **approach** of age. George
Crabbe. WBP3
Approaching absolute zero. Joyce
Peseroff. TeMP
Approaching the canvas. Kathleen
Spivack. TeMP
Apres. Arthur Joseph Munby. WBP3
April
At April. Angelina Weld Grimke.
BlS
"Hear how in April near the
acacias." Arthur Rimbaud.
FoFS--FreS
April inventory. William DeWitt
Snodgrass. LiHE
Aquaintance. Janet G. Rice. YoVA
Arakida Moritake
Pine resin, sels. FroC
Arauz Mairena, Jose
A song for Pedro J. Chamorro,
sels. NiR
Archilochos. John Tagliabue.
FroA
Ardans, Ted
i was once told how. YoVA
if i was born on this bed. YoVA
(kill the flowers) put
words.... YoVA
Are the children at home?.

Margaret E. M. Sangster. WBP3

Arellano, Jorge Eduardo
In Rivas, Nicaragua. NiR
Nightmare and/or reality. NiR

Argentarios, Marcus
Dead, they'll burn you up....
DoNG

Argument against metaphor. Gad
Hollander. VoWA

The **argument** of his book. Robert
Herrick. HaAP

Ariadne
Theseus and Ariadne. Robert
Graves. HaAP

Arima (640-658), Prince
Pitying himself...the execution
place. FroC

Arise and be aware. Angie Britt.
YoVA

Ariwara no Narihira
Eighteen tanka. FroC

Arkansas
My Arkansas. Maya Angelou. BlS

Armadillos
Limerick:" .an arch armadillo."
Carolyn Wells. IlTH

Armies
The army. Hagiwara Sakutaro.
FroC

Arms and letters. Alvaro
Gutierrez. NiR

Arms and the boy. Wilfred Owen.
HaAP

The **army**. Hagiwara Sakutaro.
FroC

Arnett/Gogisgi, Carroll
Early song. ReE
Homage to Andrew Jackson. ReE
The old man said: two. ReE
Powwow. ReE
Roadman. ReE
The story of my life. ReE
Tlanuwa. ReE
wwohali. ReE

Arnold, Matthew
Desire. WBP4
Dover Beach. LiHE--MTS
Empedocles on Etna, sels. TyW
The forsaken merman. MTS
The good shepherd with the kid.
WBP4
Growing old. LiHE
Requiescat. WBP3
The scholar-gypsy. HaAP
To Marguerite-continued. MTS

Arnold, Matthew (about)
The Dover bitch. Anthony Hecht.
LiHE

Arnold, Sir Edwin
After death. WBP3

Pearls of the faith, sels. WBP3
The secret of death. WBP3

The **arrival**. Ernesto Cardenal.
NiR

Arriving. Gabriel Preil. VoWA

Arriving at a new poem... David
Curry. PrVo

Arriving at the frontier on a
mission. Wang Wei. GrAC

Arroyo, Francisco
The battle in my mind. YoVA

Ars Poetica. Archibald MacLeish.
HaAP--LiHE

Ars poetica. Adam Wazyk. VoWA

Arson and Arsonists
To Cynthia. Sir Francis
Kynaston. HaAP

Art
Canto XLV. Ezra Pound. TyW
Common knowledge. Joseph Baneth
Allen. YoVA
Drawing. Roy Fuller. MiRN
Persian miniature. Jane Shore.
TeMP
A study in terro. Tamura
Ryuichi . FroC

Art in America. Theodore Weiss.
StPo

Art of poetry. Paul Verlaine.
FoFS--FreS

The **art** of poetry. Marcus
Hieronymus Vida. ReLP

Art thou poor...? Thomas
Dekker. HaAP

Art thou weary? John Mason
Neale (trans.). WBP4

Art thou weary?. Saint Stephen
the Sabaite. WBP4

Art-flower. Tristan Corbiere.
FreS

Arthurian Legend
Good King Arthu. Unknown . WBP1
Sir Galahad. Alfred, Lord
Tennyson. WBP4
Sir Launcelot and Queen
Guinevere. Alfred, Lord
Tennyson. WBP2

The **artificer**. Patricia E. Fann.
YoVA

An **artistry** of happiness. Judy
Ellen Mills. YoVA

As I am my father's. Rose
Drachler. VoWA

As I lay upon a night. Unknown.
ShBa

As I rode out. Unknown. ShBa

"**As** I was standing in the
street". Unknown. IlTH

as is the sea marvelous. Edward
Estlin Cummings. MTS

As long as... Unknown. NiR
As one put drunk into the
    packet-boat. John Ashbery.
    HaAP
As sand. Natan Zach. VoWA
As slow our ship. Thomas Moore.
    WBP3
As snow fell. Matt Braunstein.
    YoVA
As spring the winter. Anne
    Dudley Bradstreet. EeBC
As the sea dries up. Jennifer
    Alley. YoVA
As yesterday was washed away.
    Laurie Campbell. YoVA
As you came from the holy land.
    Sir Walter Ralegh. HaAP
As you like it, sels. William
    Shakespeare. WBP2
As you like it, sels. William
    Shakespeare. WBP3
Asante sana, te te. Thadious M.
    Davis. BlS
Ascension Day
    The disciples after the
    Ascension. Arthur Penrhyn
    Stanley. WBP4
Ascription. Charles G. D.
    Roberts. WBP4
Ash-glory. Paul Celan. VoWA
Ashbery, John
    As one put drunk into the
    packet-boat. HaAP
    He. SlW
    The instruction manual.
    HaAP--SlW
    Mixed feelings. HaAP
    Our youth. SlW
    The painter. SlW
Ashby-Sterry, J.
    Animals. IlTH
Ashes of roses. Elaine Goodale
    Eastman. WBP3
Ashford, Stacey
    Don't let it end. YoVA
    Where do I begin? YoVA
Ashkelon. Anthony Rudolf. VoWA
Asia
    Shark. Kaneko Mitsuharu . FroC
Ask me no more. Thomas Carew.
    HaAP
Askenazy, Ludvik
    The wall. VoWA
Askew, Anne (Kyme)
    The balade...made & sange in
    Newgate. PaW
    The fight of faith. WBP4
Asleep, asleep. Lucy A. Bennett.
    WBP3
Aspatia's song. Francis

Beaumont. HaAP
Aspects of the sea. Sharon
    Watson. YoVA
Assassinations and Assassins
    Anxiety. Rigoberto Lopez Perez.
    NiR
    Kayanerenhkowa. Ernesto
    Cardenal. NiR
    Last will and testament.
    Rigoberto Lopez Perez. NiR
    To David Tejada Peralta. David
    Macfield. NiR
Assaulted earth VI. Jean Orizet.
    MoVT
Assaulted earth III. Jean
    Orizet. MoVT
Astraea
    A dialogue betweene two
    shepheards, sels. Mary S.,
    Countess of Pembroke. PaW
Astronomy and Astronomers
    When I heard the learn'd
    astronomer,sels. Walt
    Whitman. HaAP-LiHE
Astrophel and Stella, sels. Sir
    Philip Sidney. WBP3
Astrophel and Stella, sels. Sir
    Philip Sidney. HaAP
Asya
    Celan. VoWA
    The deer. VoWA
    A grain of moonlight. VoWA
    My strawlike hair. VoWA
    My true memory. VoWA
    Pause a moment. VoWA
At 6 and 11. Maria Cardenas.
    YoVA
At April. Angelina Weld Grimke.
    BlS
At Dante's grave. Ezra Zussman.
    VoWA
At God's command. Joseph Rolnik.
    VoWA
At Melville's tomb. Hart Crane.
    HaAP--MTS
At Shoraku-ji in Omi, first poem
    (1568). Kishun Ryuki. FroC
At Shoraku-ji in Omi, first poem
    (1591). Kishun Ryuki. FroC
At Staufen. Michael Hamburger.
    VoWA
At a fragrance of plums. Matsuo
    Basho. FroC
At arm's length. Shirley
    Bossert. FroA
At dawn. Patrick Michael Hearn.
    BrBD
At dawn the Virgin is born. Lope
    de Vega. PoCh
At first I was given centuries.

boatswain. MTS
This lunar beauty. SlW
The unknown citizen. LiHE
The wanderer. SlW
Audisio, Gabriel
Rhapsody on rain. MoVT
The stars. MoVT
Auerbach, Ephraim
Grey uncles. OnCP
Seismograph. VoWA
Auf wiedersehen. James Russell
Lowell. WBP3
August. Joseph L. Concha. ReE
August on sourdough, a visit...
Gary Snyder. SlW
Augustine, Saint
The ladder of Saint Augustine.
Henry Wadsworth Longfellow.
WBP4
A passage in the life of Saint
Augustin. Unknown . WBP4
Auld Robin Gray. Lady Anne
Barnard. WBP3
The **auld** folks. Andrew Park.
WBP1
The **auld** house. C. Oliphant,
Baroness Nairne. WBP1
Auld lang syne. Robert Burns.
WBP1
Aunt Phillis's guest. William
Channing Gannett. WBP3
Aunt Sue's stories. Langston
Hughes. DuD
Aunts
The Aga Kahn. Steve Orlen. TeMP
Vickie Loans-Arrow, 1971.
Marnie Walsh. ReE
Aurora (mythology)
Hymn to the dawn. Marcantonio
Flaminio. ReLP
Lusus XXXVII. Andrea Navagero.
ReLP
Auschwitz from Columbo. Anne
Ranasinghe. VoWA
Auslander, Rose
Father. VoWA
Hasidic Jew from Sadagora. VoWA
In Chagall's village. VoWA
Jerusalem. VoWA
The lamed-vov. VoWA
My nightingale. VoWA
Passover. VoWA
Phoenix. VoWA
Auster, Paul
Covenant. VoWA
Hieroglyph. VoWA
Scribe. VoWA
Song of degrees. VoWA
Austin (trans.), Sarah Taylor
The passage. WBP3

Austin (trans.), Mary
Song of a man...to die in a
strange land. ReE
Austin, Alfred
Agatha. WBP3
Austin, William
Chanticleer. EeBC
The **author's** apology. T. Carmi.
VoWA
The **author's** resolution, in a
sonnet. George Wither. WBP2
Autobiography. Belinda J.
Braley. YoVA
Autobiography. Don Pagis. VoWA
Autobiography, sels. Jim Barnes.
ReE
Autobiography: Hollywood.
Charles Reznikoff. VoWA
Automobiles
A car can be a toy. Douglas
Hartley. YoVA
Car. Ron Simon. YoVA
Cars. Kevin Beasely. YoVA
A drag race. Dale Mayfield.
YoVA
The low-backed car. Samuel
Lover. WBP2
Mad like a bull when hit
unexpectedly. Mark W. Unruh.
YoVA
The poppy. Cid Corman. HoA
Put aside and forgotten. Frank
Alexander Rossi. YoVA
Spring sunday on Quaker Street.
Tom Bass. FroA
Three car poems. Richard Jones.
FroA
Autumn. Angela Van Gemert. YoVA
Autumn. Sheila Troutman. YoVA
Autumn. Itzik Manger. VoWA
Autumn. Albert Giraud. FreS
Autumn. Bonny Elifritz. YoVA
Autumn. John Clare. HaAP
Autumn
The autumn is beginning. Ruan Ji.
LuL
Autumn song. Paul Verlaine.
FoFS--FreS
Autumn song. Stephen
Stepanchev. FroA
Autumn. Albert Giraud. FreS
Autumn. Angela Van Gemert. YoVA
Autumn. Itzik Manger. VoWA
Autumn. John Clare. HaAP
Autumn. Sheila Troutman. YoVA
Binge. Ellen L. Kisthardt. StPo
A compendium of good tanka.
Furiwara no Teika . FroC
Fall. Chris Patterson. YoVA
Indian summer. Jennifer Rogers.

YoVA
Lament of monotonous autumn.
Jules Laforgue. FreS
"Lost face of summer." Vita C.
Ungaro. StPo
Of autumn. Veronica Porumbacu.
VoWA
"Put on mourning, October..."
Adolphe Rette. FreS
The pyre of my Indian summer.
Mani Leib. VoWA
Seventy-eight tanka. Princess
Shikishi. FroC
Sixth (6th) state. Mary C.
Colver. StPo
A song of fall. Karen Elizabeth
Patterson. YoVA
Soon autumn. Tachihara Michizo.
FroC
Three poets at Yuyam. Botange
Shohaku . FroC
To autumn. John Keats. HaAP
Twenty-four tanka. Minamoto no
Sanetomo. FroC
View of the wind. Tu Fu . GrAC
The wet month. Henry Bataille.
FreS
Autumn ("On the morning that a
typhoon"). Nishiwaki
Junzaburo. FroC
Autumn ("The bandaged rain...")
Tamura Ryuichi. FroC
Autumn 1942, sels. Julian
Przybos. CoP
Autumn bank songs XV, sels. Li
Po. GrAC
Autumn day. Keng Wei. GrAC
Autumn evening on the great
lake. Wang Ch'ang-ling. GrAC
The autumn is beginning. Ruan
Ji. LuL
Autumn meditations, sels. Tu Fu.
GrAC
An autumn morning in Shokoku-ji.
Gary Snyder. HaAP
Autumn music. Gabriel Preil.
VoWA
Autumn night: to Ch'iu Tan. Wei
Ying-wu. GrAC
Autumn song. Stephen Stepanchev.
FroA
Autumn song. Paul Verlaine.
FoFS--FreS
An autumn song for Ch'ang-hsin
Palace. Wang Ch'ang-ling.
GrAC
Autumn wind. Akera Kanko. FroC
Autumn-strewn ground. Charles
Van Lerberghe. FreS
Aux Italiens. Owen Meredith

(Earl Lytton). WBP2
Avant, Lori Susan
Friction. YoVA
It hurts! YoVA
Avarice
The pardoner's tale. Geoffrey
Chaucer. HaAP
Avenue Y. Anita Barrows. VoWA
Aviation and Aviators
Litany of the planes. Pablo
Antonio Cuadra. NiR
Avison, Margaret
Hiatus. HaAP
A lament ("A gizzard and some
ruby...") HaAP
Water and worship: an open-air
service... HaAP
The avocado pit. Carl Rakosi.
FroA
Awakening. Washington Gladden.
WBP3
Away with the old. David Newton.
YoVA
Axioms. Gad Hollander. VoWA
Ay patria. Otto Rene Castillo.
NiR
Ayton, Sir Robert
Woman's inconstancy. WBP3
Azazel
Lament for Azazel. Francis
Landy. VoWA
Azuma uta & Sakimori no uta: 25
sels. Unknown. FroC

Baal Shem Tov (Israel Eliezer)
The strange guest. Itzik
Manger. VoWA
Babcock, N.P.
The stranger cat. IlTH
Babi Yar. Lev Ozerov. VoWA
Babi Yar, Ukraine
Babi Yar. Lev Ozerov. VoWA
The babie. Jeremiah Eames
Rankin. WBP1
Babies
The angel's whisper. Samuel
Lover. WBP1
The bab. Kalidasa . WBP1
The babie. Jeremiah Eames
Rankin. WBP1
Baby Bell. Thomas Bailey
Aldrich. WBP1
Baby Louise. Margaret Eytinge.
WBP1
Baby May. William Cox Bennett.
WBP1
Baby Zulma's Christmas carol.

Augustus Julian Requier. WBP1
The baby. George MacDonald.
    WBP1
Bedtime. F.R. Erskine (Earl of
    Rosslyn). WBP1
Bitter sweet, sels. Josiah
    Gilbert Holland. WBP1
Children. Walter Savage Landor.
    WBP1
A cradle hymn, sels. Isaac
    Watts. WBP1
Cradle song ("Sleep, little
    baby.") Unknown . WBP1
Erotopaegnia, sels. Edoardo
    Sanguineti. NeIP
Etude realiste. Algernon
    Charles Swinburne. WBP1
The hanging of the crane, sels.
    Henry Wadsworth Longfellow.
    WBP1
The happy hour. Mary Frances
    Butts. WBP1
Laus infantium. William Canton.
    WBP1
A little child's hymn. Francis
    Turner Palgrave. WBP1
Little feet. Elizabeth Akers.
    WBP1
Mother and child. William
    Gilmore Simms. WBP1
The mother's sacrifice. Seba
    Smith. WBP1
The motherless bairn. William
    Thom. WBP1
No baby in the house. Clara G.
    Dolliver. WBP1
On a child who lived one
    minute. X.J. Kennedy. HoA
On an infant. Samuel Taylor
    Coleridge. WBP4
On the death of an infant. Dirk
    Smits. WBP1
On the picture of an infan.
    Leonidas of Alexandria . WBP1
Our wee White Rose. Gerald
    Massey. WBP1
Philip, my king. Dinah Maria
    Mulock Craik. WBP1
The princess, sels. Alfred,
    Lord Tennyson. WBP1
She came and went. James
    Russell Lowell. WBP1
Silent baby. Ellen Bartlett
    Currier. WBP1
To my infant son. Thomas Hood.
    WBP1
Weighing the baby. Ethel Lynn
    (E.E. Beers). WBP1
The baby. Sir William Jones
    (tr.). WBP1

The baby. Kalidasa. WBP1
The baby. George MacDonald. WBP1
Baby. Tammy Slaughter. YoVA
Baby Bell. Thomas Bailey
    Aldrich. WBP1
Baby Louise. Margaret Eytinge.
    WBP1
Baby May. William Cox Bennett.
    WBP1
Baby Zulma's Christmas carol.
    Augustus Julian Requier. WBP1
"Baby and I/Were baked in a
    pie". Unknown. IlTH
Baby's shoes. William Cox
    Bennett. WBP1
Babylon revisited. I. Amiri
    Baraka (LeRoi Jones). TyW
Bachar, Eli
    A dawn of Jaffa pigeons. VoWA
    Houses, past and present. VoWA
    Room poems. VoWA
Back into the garden. Sarah
    Webster Fabio. BlS
Bacon, Sir Francis
    The world. WBP3
Bacsi, Mike
    Make-up. YoVA
    Touch me. YoVA
Baczynski, Krzysztof Kamil
    The poet's wedding, sels. CoP
    To my parents, sels. CoP
    White magic, sels. CoP
Badger. John Clare. HaAP
Badgers
    Badger. John Clare. HaAP
    The catch. Brewster Ghiselin.
    HaAP
Baer, Bonnie
    The rain. YoVA
Bagman O'Reilly's curse. Les A.
    Murray. TyW
Baguio, Philippines
    Waiting for God. Harry
    Roskolenko. FroA
Bailey, Philip James
    Death in youth. WBP3
    Festus, sels. WBP3
    Festus, sels. WBP4
    Youth and love. WBP1
The bailiff's daughter of
    Islington. Unknown. WBP2
Baillie, Joanna
    Song ("The bride she is
    winsome...") WBP2
Baker, Alison
    Custer (1). FroA
    Custer (2). FroA
Baker, George Augustus
    Thoughts on the commandments.
    WBP2

Baker, Josephine
  So many feathers. Jayne Cortez.
    BlS
Bakers
  Of a painter and a baker.
    Theodore de Beze. ReLP
Balaban, John
  After our war. FroA
The balade...made & sange in
    Newgate. Anne (Kyme) Askew.
    PaW
Balestrini, Nanni
  But we'll make another one.
    NeIP
  De cultu virginis. NeIP
  The fugitive's apologue. NeIP
  In this manner. NeIP
  The instinct of
    self-preservation. NeIP
  Tape mark. NeIP
  Without tears for the roses.
    NeIP
Ballad ("He did not kill.")
    Jacob Glatstein. OnCP
A ballad ("The night was
    clear.") Kelli McFarland.
    YoVA
Ballad of Aeradrel. Karen
    Westerfield. YoVA
The ballad of Dead Men's Bay.
    Algernon Charles Swinburne.
    MTS
The ballad of an oysterman.
    Oliver Wendell Holmes. MTS
The ballad of bouillabaisse.
    William Makepeace Thackeray.
    WBP1
Ballad of luna, luna. Federico
    Garcia Lorca. SlW
Ballad of peach blossom spring,
    sels. Wang Wei. GrAC
Ballad of the hoppy-toad.
    Margaret Walker. BlS
The ballad of the holy evening
    bread. Itzik Manger. OnCP
Ballad of the morning streets.
    I. Amiri Baraka (LeRoi
    Jones). SlW
A ballad of trees and the
    Master. Sidney Lanier.
    EeBC--WBP4
A ballad of trees and the
    master. Sidney Lanier. WBP4
Ballad of youth. Li Po. GrAC
A ballad upon a wedding, sels.
    Sir John Suckling. WBP2
A ballad...going down to the
    store, sels. Miron
    Bialoszewski. CoP
Ballade des belles milatraisses.

  Rosalie Jonas. BlS
Ballantine, James
  Ilka blade o' grass keps its
    ain...dew. WBP3
Ballet
  Ballet under the stars. Robert
    Stewart. FroA
Ballet under the stars. Robert
    Stewart. FroA
Balloons. Loretta Pierce. YoVA
Balloons. Bryan Darr. YoVA
Balloons
  Balloons. Bryan Darr. YoVA
  Balloons. Loretta Pierce. YoVA
  The death balloon. Patricia
    Goedicke. FroA
  The secret. Sonya M. Michlin.
    HoWM
  Went up a year this evening!
    Emily Dickinson. HaAP
Ballowe, James
  Illinois coalscapes. PrVo
Balshemtov, Yisroel (about)
  The holy Balshemtov. Zishe
    Landau. OnCP
  Saint Balshemtov. Itzik Manger.
    OnCP
Baltimore, Maryland
  Incident. Countee Cullen. LiHE
Bamboo. Hagiwara Sakutaro. FroC
Bamboo
  Bambo. Hagiwara Sakutaro . FroC
  Bamboo grass. Unknown. FroC
  Bamboo isle. Ch'ien Ch'i., GrAC
  On a snowy night.. Sugawara no
    Michizane . FroC
Bamboo & Oak. Miyazawa Kenji.
    FroC
Bamboo grass. Unknown. FroC
Bamboo isle. Ch'ien Ch'i. GrAC
Banim, John
  Soggarth aroon. WBP4
The banks o' Doon. Robert Burns.
    WBP3
The banks of a river. Abraham
    Sutskever. VoWA
Banks, George Linnaeus
  What I live for. WBP4
Banquets
  At the prefectural library in
    the rai. Wei Ying-wu . GrAC
Bantista, R.M.
  Waiting to be born. ReE
Banus, Maria
  Eighteen. VoWA
  Gift hour. VoWA
Bar Mitzvah. Isaac Goldemberg.
    VoWA
Bar Mitzvahs
  Bar Mitzvah. Isaac Goldemberg.

VoWA

Baraka (LeRoi Jones), I. Amiri
Air. SlW
Babylon revisited. TyW
Ballad of the morning streets.
SlW
Cold term. SlW
A poem for black hearts. SlW
Red light. SlW
Reprise of one of A.G.'s best
poems! TeMP
Song form. SlW
Barbara's land - May, 1974.
Geary Hobson. ReE
Barbauld, Anna Letitia
Life. WBP3

The mouse's petition. MiRN

Praise to God. WBP4
The Sabbath of the soul. WBP4
Barbers
Limerick:"..a barber of Kew."
Cosmo Monkhouse. IlTH
Barbor, Carolyn
We met/and we were friends.
YoVA
Barcelona, Spain
Dream of Barcelona: my ancient
world. Takahashi Mutsuo. FroC
Barclay (trans.), Alexander
Of hym that togyder wyll
serve... WBP4
The **bard**, sels. Thomas Gray. TyW
The **bare** facts. Elizabeth
Cook-Lynn. ReE
The **barefoot** boy. John Greenleaf
Whittier. WBP1
Baring-Gould, Sabine
Child's evening hymn. WBP1
Barker, Edward D.
Go sleep, ma honey. WBP1
Barker, George
Pacific sonnets, sels. MTS
Barker, Ginger D.
Momma's song. YoVA
Barks, Coleman
Finger of necessity. TyW
Barlow, George
The old maid. WBP2
Barlow, Sumner
City expendables. StPo
The **barn**. Seamus Heaney. HaAP
Barnard, Lady Anne
Auld Robin Gray. WBP3
Barnard, Mary
The solitary. FroA
Barnes, Jim
Accident at Three Mile Island.
FroA

Autobiography, sels. ReE
Descent to Bohannon Lake. FroA
The last chance. ReE
Lost in sulphur canyons. ReE
Notes for a love letter from
mid-America. ReE
Old soldiers home at
Marshalltown, Iowa. FroA
Wolf hunting near Nashoba. ReE
Barnes, William
Musings. HaAP
The wife a-lost. HaAP
Barnett, Anthony
The book of mysteries. VoWA
Celan. VoWA
Cloisters. VoWA
Crossing. VoWA
A marriage. VoWA
Barns
The barn. Seamus Heaney. HaAP
Lamplighter barn. Myra Cohn
Livingston. RoRF
Barnstone, Aliki
A letter from the hotel. FroA
Barnstone, Willis
Gas lamp. VoWA
The good beasts. VoWA
Grandfather. VoWA
Miklos Radnoti. VoWA
Paradise. VoWA
Rooftop. FroA
The worm. FroA--VoWA
Baron, Mary
For an Egyptian boy, died c.
700 B.C.. HoA
Letters for the New England
dead. HoA
Barr, Amelia Edith
The bottom drawer. WBP3
Barrax, Gerald William
Christmas 1959 et cetera. PoCh
A **barren** area. Hagiwara
Sakutaro. FroC
Barren the landscape, sels.
Christian Santos des Praslin.
NiR
Barrington, Patrick
I had a hippopotamus. IlTH
Barrows, Anita
The ancestors. VoWA
Avenue Y. VoWA
Bars fight, August 28, 1746.
Lucy Terry. BlS
Barton, Bernard
Not ours the vows. WBP2
Baseball. Mark Van Overschelde.
YoVA
Baseball
Baseball. Mark Van Overschelde.
YoVA

Cobb would have caught it.
Robert Fitzgerald. HaAP
Notes to Joanne, LXI. John F.
Kerr. ReE
The opposite field. Dabney
Stuart. TeMP
Basia: I. Ioannes Secundus
(Everaerts). ReLP
Basia: VII. Ioannes Secundus
(Everaerts). ReLP
Basia: XIII. Ioannes Secundus
(Everaerts). ReLP
Basinger, Sherri
Old house on the hill. YoVA
Basketball
The agony of victory. John
Morretti. YoVA
Twenty-eight to twenty (28 to
20). Scott Moore. YoVA
Bass, Tom
Spring sunday on Quaker Street.
FroA
Basse, William
A memento for mortality. HaAP
The bastard from the bush. Henry
Lawson. TyW
Bat. David Herbert Lawrence.
HaAP
Bat-Miriam, Yocheved
Distance spills itself. VoWA
The monasteries lift gold
domes. VoWA
Bataille, Henry
Villages. FreS
The wet month. FreS
Bates, Arlo
On the road to Chorrera. WBP2
Bats
Bat. David Herbert Lawrence.
HaAP
The end of the weekend. Anthony
Hecht. HaAP
The battle in my mind. Francisco
Arroyo. YoVA
The battle of Zion Canyon.
Shelly Qualls. YoVA
Baudelaire, Charles
The albatross. FoFS
The beacons. FoFS
The cat. FoFS
The clock. FoFS
Condemned women. FoFS
Correspondences. FoFS
The cracked bell. FoFS
Duellum. FoFS
Evening harmony. FoFS
Exotic perfume. FoFS
The former life. FoFS
Head of hair. FoFS
Invitation to the voyage. FoFS

The jewels. FoFS
Lethe. FoFS
Lovers' wine. FoFS
Meditation. FoFS
Music. FoFS
Parisian dream. FoFS
A phantom. FoFS
Reversibility. FoFS
The self-torturer. FoFS
The seven old men. FoFS
Spleen ("I am like the
king...") FoFS
Spleen ("I have more
memories...") FoFS
Spleen ("When the low, heavy
sky...") FoFS
The swan. FoFS
To the reader. FoFS
The vampire. FoFS
The voyage. FoFS
Baudelaire, Charles (about)
Charles Baudelaire's tomb.
Stephane Mallarme. FoFS
Bauhuysen, Bernhard van
Divine love. ReLP
Epigram: "You have as many
qualities..." ReLP
Bavarian gentians. David Herbert
Lawrence. HaAP--SlW
Baxter, Richard
Lord, it belongs not to my
care. EeBC
The baying yearning of the norse
horn. John Reinke. YoVA
The bayonet and the needle.
Eliezer Steinbarg. VoWA
Be still. Mani Leib. OnCP
Be what you are. Dawn Abrahams.
YoVA
Be'er, Hayim
Love song ("In the light of the
moon.") VoWA
The sequence of generations.
VoWA
Tabernacle of peace. VoWA
Beaches. See Seashore
The beacon. Nicole Drassel (N.
Lessard). MoVT
The beacons. Charles Baudelaire.
FoFS
The bean eaters. Gwendolyn
Brooks. BlS--HaAP
Bear. Peter Blue Cloud. ReE
Beard, Lori Lynn
Santa does his thing. YoVA
Bears
"A cheerful old bear at the
zoo." Unknown . IlTH
"Fuzzy Wuzzy was a bear."
Unknown . IlTH

Meeting a bear. David Wagoner.
  HaAP
Beasely, Kevin
  Cars. YoVA
  Love. YoVA
  Success. YoVA
Beasley, Etta Marie
  Love letter. YoVA
  You can't stop now. YoVA
The **beast** that rode the unicorn.
  Conny Hannes Meyer. VoWA
Beatty, Pakenham
  When will love come? WBP2
Beaumont, Francis
  Aspatia's song. HaAP
  On the tombs in Westminster
    Abbey. WBP3
Beautiful dead leaf. Takamura
  Kotaro. FroC
Beautiful sleeper. Danny Logan.
  YoVA
Beautiful snow. James M. Watson.
  WBP3
Beauty. Edward, Baron
  Hovell-Thurlow. WBP2
Beauty
  Beauty. Edward, Baron
    Hovell-Thurlow. WBP2
  A budget of paradoxes. John
    Martley. WBP2
  Daybreak. Sir William Davenant.
    WBP2
  Dirce. Walter Savage Landor.
    HaAP
  Disdain returned. Thomas Carew.
    WBP2
  "Drink to me only with thine
    eyes" Ben Jonson. WBP2
  The girl of Cadiz. George
    Gordon,6th Baron Byron. WBP2
  Give place, ye lovers. Earl of
    Surrey (Henry Howard). WBP2
  Hero and Leander, sels.
    Christopher Marlowe. WBP2
  Hymn to intellectual beauty.
    Percy Bysshe Shelley. HaAP
  I died for beauty. Emily
    Dickinson. DoNG
  "I have cupped in my hands..."
    David Newcomb. HoWM
  I sit and wait for beauty. Mae
    V. Cowdery. BlS
  Januar. Nishiwaki Junzaburo .
    FroC
  Lovely Mary Donnelly. William
    Allingham. WBP2
  Lullaby ("Lay your sleeping
    head...") Wystan Hugh Auden.
    HaAP
  The merchant of Venice, sels.

  William Shakespeare. WBP2
  Merciles beautee. Geoffrey
    Chaucer. HaAP
  The might of one fair fac.
    Michaelangelo Buonarotti .
    WBP2
  My lad. Dante Alighieri . WBP2
  Nude descending a staircase.
    X.J. Kennedy. HoA
  O, fairest of rural maids.
    William Cullen Bryant. WBP2
  Ode on a Grecian urn. John
    Keats. HaAP--LiHE
  An opal. Ednah Procter Clarke
    Hayes. WBP2
  The portrait. Thomas Heywood.
    WBP2
  Prostration. David Semah. VoWA
  The rape of the lock, sels.
    Alexander Pope. WBP2
  Riddle of night. Jiri Mordecai
    Langer. VoWA
  Rosalynd. Thomas Lodge. WBP2
  "She is not fair to outward
    view." Hartley Coleridge.
    WBP2
  "She walks in beauty, like the
    night." George Gordon,6th
    Baron Byron. WBP2
  A song ("Ask me no more where
    Jove...") Thomas Carew. WBP2
  Song ("The shape alone let
    others prize.") Mark Akenside.
    WBP2
  Song ("When from the sod the
    flowerets.") Walther von der
    Vogelweide . WBP2
  Sonnet CVI. William
    Shakespeare. WBP2
  Sonnet CXXX. William
    Shakespeare. HaAP--LiHE
  Sonnet XVIII. William
    Shakespeare. HaAP--LiHE
  Sprin. Meleager . WBP2
  To Dianeme. Robert Herrick.
    WBP2
  To Helen. Edgar Allan Poe. WBP2
  To a lady admiring herself...
    Thomas Randolph. WBP2
  To roses in the bosom of
    Castara. William Habington.
    WBP2
  To the Princess Lucretia.
    Torquato Tasso. WBP2
  The triumph of Charis. Ben
    Jonson. WBP2
  Twelfth night, sels. William
    Shakespeare. WBP2
  A violet in her hair. Charles
    Swain. WBP2

Vision of a fair woma. Unknown WBP2

A vision of beauty. Ben Jonson. WBP2

Whenas in silks my Julia goes. Robert Herrick. WBP2

The **beauty** of the ship. Walt Whitman. MTS

Beaver skin. Antonio Porta. NeIP

Because I could not stop for death. Emily Dickinson. EeBC--HaAP

Because I could not stop for death. Emily Dickinson. DoNG--SlW

Beddoes, Thomas Lovell
Bona de mortuis. TyW
Bury him deep. TyW
Dream-pedlary. HaAP

Bedell, David
Poetastery. YoVA

Bedouin love-song. Bayard Taylor. WBP2

Bedouin woman. Shulamit Apfel. BuAC

Bedtime. F.R. Erskine (Earl of Rosslyn). WBP1

Bee! I'm expecteding you. Emily Dickinson. SlW

Beechhold, Henry F.
A note to Mr. Frost. StPo
Un chien Andalou. StPo
Vermeer recalled. StPo

Beer drops. Melba Joyce Boyd. BlS

Beer-Hofmann, Richard
Lullaby for Miriam. VoWA

Beers (see Ethel Lynn), E.E.

Bees
Bee! I'm expecting you. Emily Dickinson. SlW
How doth the little busy bee. Isaac Watts. WBP1
A look at a bee. Leah Goldberg. BuAC

Before the anaesthetic. Sir John Betjeman. EeBC

Before the feast of Shushan. Anne Spencer. BlS

"**Before** this high hall had collapsed". Tu Fu. GrAC

"**Before** you depart/Pale morning star". Paul Verlaine. FoFS

The **begetting** of Cain. Hyam Pultzik. VoWA

The **beggar.** Thomas Moss. WBP3

Beggar song. Unknown. FroC

Beggars
The ballad of the holy evening bread. Itzik Manger. OnCP

Beggar son. Unknown . FroC

The **beggar.** Thomas Moss. WBP3

Death ("This evening the fatal...") Gregoire Le Roy. FreS

"Done begging...." Ryokan. FroC

"Finished begging..." Ryokan. FroC

Proud beggarman. Jane St. John. YoVA

Beginning. David Rokeah. VoWA

A **beginning** and an end. Edouard Roditi. VoWA

Beginning of love. Tanikawa Shuntaro. FroC

Beginning to end. Mike Evans. YoVA

Beginnings. Erez Biton. VoWA

The **beginnings,** sels. Rudyard Kipling. TyW

Begonias
Diagram. James F. King. StPo

Behave yoursel' before folk. Alexander Rodger. WBP2

Behind the shadow. Ellen L. Kisthardt. StPo

Behind the smoke stained glass. Saundra Lyn Hendon. YoVA

Behle, Elissa
Endurance. YoVA
Escape. YoVA

Behn, Harry
A Christmas carol. PoCh
Christmas morning. PoCh

Being a teenager. Lisa M. Thorn. YoVA

being to timelessness as it's to time. Edward Estlin Cummings. HaAP

Beker, Ruth
Don't show me. VoWA

Bel woman. Roman C. Adrian. ReE

A **belated** violet. Oliver Herford. WBP1

Believe me, if all those endearing... Thomas Moore. WBP2

Bell, Charles G.
Two families. FroA

Bell, Marvin
Coralville, in Iowa. FroA
The extermination of the Jews. VoWA
Getting lost in Nazi Germany. VoWA
He said to. TeMP
The Israeli Navy. VoWA

The **bell-founder,** sels. Denis Florence MacCarthy. WBP1

Bella and the golem. Rossana
    Ombres. VoWA
Bellg, Albert
    Raincoats for the dead. FroA
    Watertower. FroA
Belli, Gioconda
    God said. NiR
    It's been months, my daughter.
      NiR
    Operation Eagle Z. NiR
    Strike. NiR
    There is no holding
      back...victory, sels. NiR
    They followed me. NiR
    The time I haven't seen the
      blue sky. NiR
    To Commander Marcos. NiR
    Until we're free. NiR
    We begin by loving and
      compromise, sels. NiR
    We'll be new. NiR
    What are you Nicaragua? NiR
Belloc, Hilaire
    Henry King, who chewed bits of
      string... IlTH
    Lines for a Christmas card. TyW
    Lines to a don. TyW
    Matilda. IlTH
    On a politician. TyW
Bells
    Before the anaesthetic. Sir
      John Betjeman. EeBC
    The chimes of England. Arthur
      Cleveland Coxe. WBP4
    Christmas bells. Henry
      Wadsworth Longfellow. EeBC
    The cracked bell. Charles
      Baudelaire. FoFS
    Curfew must not ring to-night.
      Rose Hartwick Thorpe. WBP2
    In memoriam, sels.. Alfred,
      Lord Tennyson. ShBa
    The sound of bells. Pierre
      Reverdy. MoVT
Bells for John Whiteside's
    daughter. John Crowe Ransom.
    HaAP--LiHE
Ben Bolt. Thomas Dunn English.
    WBP1
ben Yeshaq, Yosef Damana
    The rusted chain. VoWA
Ben plays hide & seek in the
    deep woods. Geoff Hewitt.
    FroA
Ben-Yitzhak, Avraham
    Blessed are those who sow
      and...not reap. VoWA
    I didn't know my soul. VoWA
    Psalm ("There are very few
      moments"). VoWA

Benches
    White public benche. Hagiwara
      Sakutaro . FroC
Benedicite. John Greenleaf
    Whittier. WBP1
Benedicte, what dreamed I this
    night? Unknown. HaAP
Benedicti, George
    Memory's epitaph to Sir Philip
      Sidney. ReLP
Benediction. Myra Sklarew. VoWA
Benediction. William Freedman.
    VoWA
Benjamin, Park
    The old sexton. WBP3
Bennett, G.
    The time for prayer. WBP4
Bennett, Gwendolyn B.
    Advice. BlS
    Fantasy. BlS
    Hatred. BlS
    Heritage. BlS
    Secret. BlS
    Song ("I am weaving a song of
      waters"). BlS
    To a dark girl. BlS
    To usward. BlS
Bennett, John
    Pentecost. EeBC
Bennett, Lucy A.
    Asleep, asleep. WBP3
Bennett, William Cox
    Baby May. WBP1
    Baby's shoes. WBP1
    The worn wedding-ring. WBP2
Bental, Anath
    The angel Michael. VoWA
    Jerusalem in the snow. VoWA
Bental, Anath (about)
    Anath. Haim Guri. VoWA
Benveniste, Asa
    The alchemical cupboard. VoWA
Beranger, Pierre-Jean de
    The old vagabond. WBP3
Berckes, Bonnie
    Reviewing footsteps. YoVA
Berg, Stephen
    Desnos reading the palms of
      men... VoWA
Berger, Suzanne E.
    Mornings. TeMP
Bergner (see M.Ravitch), Z.K.

Berlind, Bruce
    Fragment. FroA
    Period piece. FroA
Bermudas. Andrew Marvell. MTS
Bermudez, Horacio
    The guerrilla fighters. NiR
Bernard of Cluny (Morlaix)

De contemptu mundi, sels. WBP4
Praise of the celestiral
    country. WBP4
Bernhardt, Suzanne
In a dream ship's hold. VoWA
The unveiling. VoWA
Bernos de Gasztold, Carmen
The prayer of the donkey. PoCh
The prayer of the mouse. MiRN
Berrigan, Daniel
Handicapped. FroA
Berryman, John
The dream songs, sels. HaAP
Lauds. HaAP
Sonnet 37. HaAP
Bessie Dreaming Bear, 1960.
    Marnie Walsh. ReE
The **best** dance hall in Iuka,
    Mississippi. Thomas Johnson.
    FroA
The **best** of two worlds. Wendy
    Taddio. YoVA
Beth Shaul, Israel
To Xanadu, which is Beth Shaul.
    Arye Sivan. VoWA
Bethune, George Washington
It is not death to die. WBP3
Betjeman, Sir John
Before the anaesthetic. EeBC
Christmas. EeBC
The heart of Thomas Hardy. TyW
Late-flowering lust. TyW
A subaltern's love-song. HaAP

A **better** resurrection. Christina
    Georgina Rossetti. EeBC
Better to spit on the whip....
    Colette Inez. TyW
Bettinus, Marius
The Blessed Virgin offers
    violets... ReLP
"**Betty** Botta bought some
    butter." Unknown. IlTH
Between life and death.
    Frantisek Gottlieb. VoWA
Between the world and me.
    Richard Wright. LiHE
Between walls. William Carlos
    Williams. SlW
Between-. Tomioka Taeko. FroC
Bevans, Neal
Promise me. YoVA
A straight answer. YoVA
Beware. Henry W. Longfellow
    (trans.). WBP1
The **bewildered** ones. Arthur
    Rimbaud. FoFS
Beyond memory. Monny de Boully.
    VoWA
Beyond the smiling and the

weeping. Horatius Bonar. WBP3
Beyond words. Robert Frost. TyW
Beze, Theodore de
Description of virtue. ReLP
Of a painter and a baker. ReLP
Bialik, Hayim Nachman
After my death. VoWA
Footsteps of spring. VoWA
I didn't find light by
    accident. VoWA
I scattered my sighs to the
    wind. VoWA
My song. VoWA
Place me under your wing. VoWA
The sea of silence exhales
    secrets. VoWA
Summer night. VoWA
When the days grow long. VoWA
Bialoszewski, Miron
A ballad...going down to the
    store, sels. CoP
Gray eminences of rapture,
    sels. CoP
In romance with the concrete,
    sels. CoP
Lu. He.'s story, sels. CoP
Rodowod gory odosobnienia,
    sels. CoP
Self-verified, sels. CoP
Bible (about)
The book of God. Horatius
    Bonar. WBP4
The letters of the book. Rose
    Drachler. VoWA
Mother's Bible. Susan Zielke.
    YoVA
My mother's bible. George Pope
    Morris. WBP1
A riddle. Cynthia Ozick. VoWA
Bible-New Testament
The book of revelation, sels.
    DoNG
St. Luke, sels. PoCh
Bible-Old Testament
Job, sels. MTS
Psalm CIV, sels. MTS
Psalm CVII, sels. MTS
Psalm LXXVII, sels. MTS
The psalms of David, sels. DoNG
Bicycles and Bicycling
A simple pleasure. Scott Van
    Klaveren. YoVA
Bidermann, Jacob
The blessed Magdalene
    weeping... ReLP
The scourge reddened...blood of
    Jesus. ReLP
Big grave creek. Cid Corman. HoA
Big talk. Yen Chen-ch'ing. GrAC
A **big** woman screams out her

guts. Shulamit Apfel. BuAC
BigEagle, Duane
  Flowers of winter: four songs.
    ReE
  My father's country. ReE
  My people. ReE
  Oklahoma boyhood. ReE
  What eagle saw in the west. ReE
Bigger, Duff
  "The comedian said it." FroA
  "It is when the tribe is gone."
    FroA
Bill and Joe. Oliver Wendell
    Holmes. WBP1
Billington (ed.), Ray Allen
  LIMERICKS HISTORICAL AND
    HYSTERICAL. LiHA
Billy in the darbies. Herman
    Melville. HaAP
Billy, Jacques de
  Sonnets spirituels, sels. ReLP
The **binding of Isaac.** Itzik
    Manger. OnCP
Binge. Ellen L. Kisthardt. StPo
Binni the meshuggener. Danny
    Siegel. VoWA
Binyon, Laurence
  John Winter. MTS
Biographical note. Gabriel
    Preil. VoWA
Biography. Jacob Glatstein. OnCP
Biography. Leonel Rugama. NiR
Bion
  I dreamt I saw great Venus.
    WBP2
Birch Trees
  Birches. Robert Frost. LiHE
Birches. Robert Frost. LiHE
Bird cage. Hector de
    Saint-Denys-Garneau. MoVT
The **bird of night.** Randall
    Jarrell. DuD
Bird song. Betsy Rosenberg. VoWA
A **bird's nest.** Erez Biton. VoWA
Bird, Bessie Calhoun
  Proof. BlS
Bird-window-flying. Tess
    Gallagher. TeMP
Birdless country. Shimazaki
    Toson. FroC
Birds
  Bird cage. Hector de
    Saint-Denys-Garneau. MoVT
  Bird song. Betsy Rosenberg.
    VoWA
  The birds (Czechoslovakian
    carol). Unknown. PoCh
  Birds in the wood. Unknown.
    HaAP
  The cage. Avner Treinin. VoWA

The dark birds. Bert Meyers.
    VoWA
December 22, 1977. Harold
    Littlebird. ReE
Dialogue with Herz. Antonio
    Porta. NeIP
"The great bird flies." Li Po .
    GrAC
I point out a bird. Quinton
    Duval. FroA
Listen to the bird. Laya
    Firestone. VoWA
"Perfect rainbow arc." Kitty
    Druck. StPo
Redwings. William Heyen. TeMP
Sea dreams, sels. Alfred, Lord
    Tennyson. WBP1
Sea-change. John Masefield. MTS
Shira. Howard Schwartz. VoWA
Siege at Stony Point. Horace
    Gregory. FroA
Subnarcosis. Andrea Zanzotto.
    NeIP
The tidbit and the clodder baw.
    Ellen De Haan. YoVA
Untitled journe.
    Goweitduweetza(Veronica
    Riley) . ReE
White bird. Matti Megged. VoWA
The windhover. Gerard Manley
    Hopkins. EeBC--HaAP
The **birds** (Czechoslovakian
    carol). Unknown. PoCh
Birds are drowsing on the
    branches. Leah Rudnitsky.
    VoWA
Birds in the wood. Unknown. HaAP
Birds of a feather. Mother
    Goose. MiRN
Birds' Nests
  A bird's nest. Erez Biton. VoWA
Birrell, Sharon
  Christmas. YoVA
Birth. Constance Urdang. VoWA
Birth. Grace Raymond (Anne
    Stillman). WBP1
Birth. Amir Gilboa. VoWA
Birth
  The birth in a narrow room.
    Gwendolyn Brooks. BlS
  Birth. Amir Gilboa. VoWA
  Birth. Constance Urdang. VoWA
  Birth. Grace Raymond (Anne
    Stillman). WBP1
  Blessing of the firstborn.
    Howard Schwartz. VoWA
  Celebration: birth of a colt.
    Linda Hogan. ReE
  Eve's birth. Kim Chernin. VoWA
  First days. Tuvia Ruebner. VoWA

WBP4

Blackmore, Richard Doddtridge
  Reunited love. WBP2
Blackmur, Richard P.
  Half-tide ledge. MTS
The **blacksmiths.** Unknown. TyW
Blacksmiths and Blacksmithing
  Swarte-smeked smithes.. Unknown
    HaAP
  The village blacksmith. Henry
    Wadsworth Longfellow. WBP1
  With my God, the Smith. Uri Zvi
    Greenberg. VoWA
Blake, Mrs. M.E.
  The carnivoristicous ounce.
    IlTH
Blake, William
  Ah, sun-flower! HaAP
  And did those feet in ancient
    time. HaAP
  The chimney sweeper. LiHE
  The clod and the pebble. EeBC
  A cradle song. ShBa
  The divine image. EeBC
  Europe, sels. ShBa
  The four Zoas, sels. TyW
  The garden of love. HaAP--LiHE
  Gates of paradise, sels. HaAP
  The lamb. EeBC--ShBa
  London. HaAP
  Mock on, mock on, Voltaire,
    Rousseau. HaAP
  On another's sorrow. EeBC
  The piper. WBP1
  A poison tree. HaAP
  A poison tree. LiHE--TyW
  Songs of experience, sels. HaAP
  To the muses. HaAP
  The tyger. HaAP--LiHE
  When Sir Joshua Reynolds died.
    TyW
Blamire, Susanna
  The siller croun. WBP2
  What ails this heart of mine?
    WBP3
Blanchard, Laman
  The mother's hope. WBP1
Bland (trans.), Robert
  Home. WBP1
  Time's revenge. WBP3
Bland, Jean
  It's a secret. YoVA
  Love. YoVA
Blank reflections. Tommy
    Dameron. HoWM
Blank verse for a fat demanding
    wife. Jim Lindsey. TyW
Blaustein (Bluwstein), Rachel
  My dead. VoWA
  My white book of poems. VoWA

  Perhaps. BuAC--VoWA
  Rachel. VoWA
  Revolt. VoWA
The **bleached** ruffled leaves.
    Richard Cromwell. YoVA
The **blessed** Magdalene weeping...
    Jacob Bidermann. ReLP
The **Blessed** Virgin offers
    violets... Marius Bettinus.
    ReLP
Blessed are they that mourn.
    William Cullen Bryant. WBP3
Blessed are they. Rossiter
    Worthington Raymond. WBP3
Blessed are those who sow
    and...not reap. Avraham
    Ben-Yitzhak. VoWA
"**Blessed** is the land where
    Sons..." Thomas Lodge. PaW
Blessing. Melvin Wilk. VoWA
Blessing of the firstborn.
    Howard Schwartz. VoWA
Blessings. Linda Hogan. ReE
Blessings
  Benediction. Myra Sklarew. VoWA
  Benediction. William Freedman.
    VoWA
Blest as the immortal gods.
    Ambrose Phillips (trans.).
    WBP2
Blest as the immortal gods.
    Sappho. WBP2
Blighted love. Lord Strangford
    (trans.). WBP3
Blighted love. Luis de Camoens.
    WBP3
Blind. Israel Zangwill. WBP3
"**Blind** Mori..." Ikkyu Sojun.
    FroC
Blind children. Claire Dugan.
    YoVA
The **blind** leading the blind.
    Lisel Mueller. TeMP
Blind, Mathilde
  The dead. WBP3
  The mystic's vision. WBP4
  A parable. WBP1
Blindness
  On his blindness. John Milton.
    EeBC--HaAP
  Samson Agonistes, sels. John
    Milton. WBP3
  Sonnet to Cyriack Skinner. John
    Milton. WBP3
  Splendor. Shin Shalom. VoWA
  Three blind mic. Mother Goose .
    MiRN
  Turn blind. Paul Celan. VoWA
Bloch, Chana
  Noah. VoWA

Paradise. VoWA
The sacrifice. VoWA
Yom Kippur. VoWA
Blocked by winds on the Pien
    River. Meng Yun-ch'ing. GrAC
Blood. Nina Cassian. VoWA
Blood
    Blood. Nina Cassian. VoWA
    Missing dates. William Empson.
    HaAP
Blood and feathers. Jacques
    Prevert. MoVT
Blood, Henry Ames
    The song of the Savoyards. WBP3
Bloody brother, sels. John
    Fletcher. WBP3
Bloomfield, Terri
    What is to be. YoVA
The blossoming of a soul.
    Dalynne Bunting. YoVA
Blow Gabriel. Blind Gary Davis.
    DoNG
Blowe, Vicki
    To: my boyfriend. YoVA
Blue Cloud, Peter
    Bear. ReE
    Fire/rain. ReE
    For rattlesnake. ReE
Blue blaze trail. James F. King.
    StPo
Blue collar. Robert Pregulman.
    YoVA
Blue eyes. John Keats. WBP2
Blue heaven. David Kirkpatrick.
    YoVA
Blue owl song. Alfred Kittner.
    VoWA
Blue stones. Larry Lewis. TeMP
Blue-jay January. Jean S.
    Harrison. StPo
Blumenthal-Weiss, Ilse
    A Jewish child prays to Jesus.
    VoWA
Bly, Robert
    Black pony eating grass. FroA
    The fallen tree. TeMP
    The hatred of men with black
    hair. TyW
Boating on Yeh Creek. Meng
    Hao-jan. GrAC
Boats and Boating
    Blocked by winds on the Pien
    Rive. Meng Yun-ch'ing . GrAC
    Boating on Yeh Cree. Meng
    Hao-jan . GrAC
    Drifting at White Dragonhole,
    sel. Ch'ang Chien . GrAC
    The drunken boat. Arthur
    Rimbaud. FoFS--FreS
    Eaton's boatyard. Philip Booth.

TeMP
Evening view from a boat. Meng
    Hao-jan.   GrAC
A Mei-p'i lake son. Tu Fu .
    GrAC
Mid-current song. Ts'ui Kuo-fu.
    GrAC
Rowing in turns. David Swanger.
    TeMP
Sailing on Jo-yeh Creek in
    sprin. Chi-wu Ch'ien . GrAC
Tanka ("At Nikitatsu...")
    Princess Nukada. FroC
A terrestrial cuckoo. Frank
    O'Hara. SlW
When the ex-Empress Jito...
    Takechino Kurohito . FroC
Boats in a fog. Robinson
    Jeffers. MTS
Bobbitt, Mark
    Painting of an underground
    river. HoWM
Bobby. Kevin Hansen. YoVA
Bobo the clown. JoCarol Lacy.
    YoVA
Bodecker, N.M.
    John. RoRF
Bodenstedt, Frederich M. von
    Unchanging. WBP3
Body. Valerie Worth. FroA
Body (human)
    Air. Tomaz Salamun. VoWA
    And now you're ready... James
    Vincent Cunningham. TyW
    A dialogue between body and
    soul. Andrew Marvell. HaAP
    Festival of the blin. Ishigaki
    Rin . FroC
    Fine body. Josephine Clare.
    FroA
    from Janie. Faye Kicknosway.
    TeMP
    Her true body. Jerred Metz.
    VoWA
    His body. Sandra McPherson.
    TeMP
    "I am exploring through
    the...body." Laura Hite. HoWM
    One writing against his pric.
    Unknown . TyW
    Saints lose back. Nancy
    Willard. HoA
    "Thought this body, I know."
    Kino Sadamaru . FroC
The body is like roots
    stretching. Charles
    Reznikoff. VoWA
Boer War
    Drummer Hodge. Thomas Hardy.
    HaAP

The man he killed. Thomas
   Hardy. HaAP
Boetsch, Charles E.
   Faces/Friends, laughter. YoVA
   The spring snow trickled. YoVA
Bogan, Louise
   Cassandra. HaAP
   Old countryside. HaAP
Bogan, Marty
   The crowning of Madeline. YoVA
   Drops of love. YoVA
Bogin, George

   Troopship for France, War II.
      FroA
   The visitor. FroA
Bohemia
   My Bohemian life. Arthur
      Rimbaud. FoFS
Boimwall, Rachel
   At night. VoWA
   Diaspora Jews. VoWA
   Lifelong. VoWA
   Round. VoWA
Bold white face. Sara Tollefson.
   YoVA
Bolick, Gary
   Aji. YoVA
Bolin, Debbie
   Understanding. YoVA
   Untitled. YoVA
Bolton, Sarah Knowles
   Her creed. WBP4
A bomb. Shelly Qualls. YoVA
Bombs
   Lament. Yehuda Amichai. VoWA
Bomze, Nahum
   City of light. VoWA
   Pshytik. VoWA
Bona de mortuis. Thomas Lovell
   Beddoes. TyW
Bonar, Horatius
   Beyond the smiling and the
      weeping. WBP3
   The book of God. WBP4
Bonar, Horatus
   The master's touch. WBP4
Bonds. Kathy Johnson. YoVA
Bone poem. Nancy Willard. HoA
Bone, Adolfo Baez
   Epitaph for...Adolfo Baez Bone.
      Ernesto Cardenal. NiR
   Zero hour. Ernesto Cardenal.
      NiR
Bonefons, Jean
   Pancharis: I. ReLP
   Pancharis: XVI. ReLP
   Pancharis: XXIV. ReLP
Boner, John Henry
   The light'ood fire. WBP1
Bones. Carl Sandburg. MTS

Bones. Frederick Morgan. FroA
Bonnefoy, Yves
   The same voice, always. MoVT
   A stone. MoVT
   Threats of the witness, sels.
      MoVT
The bonnie broukit bairn.
   Christopher Murray Grieve.
   HaAP
Bonny Barbara Allan. Unknown.
   LiHE
Bonsignor (see V.Larbaud), C-M

The book of "Che". Leonel
   Rugama. NiR
The book of God. Horatius Bonar.
   WBP4
The book of mysteries. Anthony
   Barnett. VoWA
The book of revelation, sels.
   Bible-New Testament. DoNG
The book rises out of the fire.
   Edmond Jabes. VoWA
Books and Reading
   The collection. Jolene Nickell.
      YoVA
   The dictionary. Andrea Long.
      YoVA
   An experience and a moral.
      Frederick Swartwout Cozzens.
      WBP2
   For Gabriel. Laya Firestone.
      VoWA
   Gas from a burner. James Joyce.
      TyW
   if everything happens that
      can't be done. Edward Estlin
      Cummings. LiHE
   Mortalities memorandum, sels.
      Rachel Speght. PaW
   Reading books, sel. Rai San'yo.
      FroC
   Six small songs for a silver
      flute. Barry Spacks. TeMP
   A study of reading habits.
      Philip Larkin. TyW
   To the reader...friendly to
      poetrie. Anne (Edgcumbe)
      Trefusis. PaW
   Whodunit. Florence Trefethen.
      StPo
   With a book at twilight. Jakov
      Steinberg. VoWA
The boomerang. Adriano Spatola.
   NeIP
Booth, Philip
   Eaton's boatyard. TeMP
   Rout. FroA
Booth, Sherrie
   For you. YoVA

Jackie. YoVA
Boots and Shoes
Baby's shoes. William Cox
Bennett. WBP1
A cartload of shoes. Abraham
Sutskever. VoWA
My mother's shoes. Rayzel
Zychlinska. VoWA
Shoeless Man II. Gladys
Cardiff. ReE
The shoeless man. Gladys
Cardiff. ReE
Borders. Marieve Rugo. TeMP
Borders
At the un-national monument...
William Stafford. HaAP
Bore! bore! bore!. Gayle Lea.
YoVA
Boredom
The dream songs, sels. John
Berryman. HaAP
Hothouse ennui. Maurice
Maeterlinck. FreS
"In the endless ennui/Of the
meadowland." Paul Verlaine.
FoFS
Spleen ("I am like the
king..."). Charles
Baudelaire. FoFS
To the reader. Charles
Baudelaire. FoFS
Borenstein, Emily
Life of the letters. VoWA
Borgia, Lucretia
On seeing a hair of Lucretia
Borgia. Walter Savage Landor.
HaAP
Boris was bad enough. Robert
Kraus. TrWB
Bossert, Shirley
At arm's length. FroA
Botange Shohaku
Three poets at Yuyama. FroC
Bothwell, James Hepburn, Earl
Sonnets to Bothwel. Mary Queen
of Scots . PaW
Bottled. Helene Johnson. BlS
The bottom drawer. Amelia Edith
Barr. WBP3
Botton, Isaac de
Desire. VoWA
Bourbon, Nicolas
Elegy: the poet
mourns...Francis... ReLP
Epigram: to Hans Holbein
painter... ReLP
Song ("The sparrow that was
beautiful "). ReLP
To his mistress. ReLP
Bourdillon, Francis W.
Light. WBP2

Bourgeoisie
How beastly the bourgeois is-.
D.H. Lawrence. TyW
Middle-class autumn. Douglas
Shearer. YoVA
Bowers, Bonnie
A last cry for truth. YoVA
The bowls are empty. Leonel
Rugama. NiR
Bowman, Jackie
Together forever. YoVA
Bowman, Scott
"I am snow." HoWM
Bowring (trans.), Sir John
God. WBP4
Bowring, Sir John
From the recesses of a lowly
spirit. WBP4
Boy Scouts
Robert's Rules of Order. Robert
Peterson. FroA
The **boy** Urashima of Mizunoe.
Takahashi Mushimaro. FroC
The **boy** and coyote. Simon J.
Ortiz. ReE
The **boy** of summer. Barney Bush.
ReE
Boy on the bus. Lee Bennett
Hopkins. ByM
The **boy** stood in the
supper-room. Unknown. IlTH
Boy trash picker. Jim Howard.
FroA
Boyd, Gloria
The weary dancers. YoVA
Boyd, Mark Alexander
Venus and Cupid. HaAP
Boyd, Melba Joyce
Beer drops. BlS
Sunflowers and Saturdays. BlS
Why? BlS
Boyhood. William Allston. WBP1
The **boys.** Roberto Uriarte. NiR
The **boys.** Oliver Wendell Holmes.
WBP1
Boys. See Youth
Brack, Janet
The seasons. YoVA
What a strange place this is!
YoVA
Bradley, Brenda
My friend. YoVA
My land. YoVA
Bradstreet, Anne Dudley
As spring the winter. EeBC
A letter to her husband... HaAP
To my dear and loving husband.
HaAP
Bradstreet, Anne Dudley(about)

Letters for the New England
    dead. Mary Baron. HoA
The **braes** were bonny. John
    Logan. WBP3
Brahma. Ralph Waldo Emerson.
    HaAP--WBP4
Brahman
    Brahma. Ralph Waldo Emerson.
    HaAP--WBP4
Brainard, John Gardiner C.
    I saw two clouds at morning.
    WBP2
Brainstorm. Howard Nemerov. HaAP
Braley, Belinda J.
    Autobiography. YoVA
    The intruder. YoVA
Brandt, Sebastian

    Of hym that togyder wyll
    serve... WBP4
Braunstein, Matt
    As snow fell. YoVA
    Running. YoVA
The **brave** man. Wallace Stevens.
    SlW
Bread
    The ballad of the holy evening
    bread. Itzik Manger. OnCP
    Evening bread. Jacob Glatstein.
    VoWA
The **bread** of our affliction.
    Martin Grossman. VoWA
Break of day in the trenches.
    Isaac Rosenberg. VoWA
Break, break, break. Alfred,
    Lord Tennyson. WBP3
Break, break, break. Alfred,
    Lord Tennyson. HaAP--MTS
Breakfast. Beltran Morales. NiR
Breakin' up. Robin Nobles. YoVA
Breaking off from waiting.
    Clarisse Nicoidski. VoWA
The **breasts** of the queen...,
    sels. Stanislaw Grochowiak.
    CoP
"**Breath** of spring..." Ryokan.
    FroC
The **breeze** comes filling the
    valley. Miyazawa Kenji. FroC
Brenan, Joseph
    Come to me, dearest. WBP3
Brenner, Raya
    Raya Brenner. Pinhas Sadeh.
    VoWA
Breshears, Rusty
    The unliberated woman. YoVA
Breton, Nicholas
    I would I were an excellent
    divine. WBP4
    Phillida and Corydon. WBP2
Briar Rose. Anne Sexton. EvIm

Bricks
    I am a brick. Patrick Tolliver.
    HoWM
The **brides.** Alec Derwent Hope.
    HaAP
The **bridge** of sighs. Thomas
    Hood. WBP3
The **bridge,** sels. Hart Crane.
    HaAP
Bridgeport, Ohio
    In response to a rumor....
    James Wright. TyW
Bridges
    "I'd never dare to walk across."
    Gelett Burgess. IlTH
    Ku-feng, sel. Li Po . GrAC
Bridges (M.A.De Vere),Madeline

    The spinner. WBP3
Bridges(M.A.De Vere), Madeline
    Friend and lover. WBP1
Bridges, Robert
    Triolet ("All women born...")
    TyW
    'The unillumined verge'. WBP3
    Who has not walked upon the
    shore. MTS
Bridges, Robert Seymour
    So sweet love seemed. WBP2
Bridges, Robert
    The evening darkens over. HaAP
    A passer-by. MTS
Brief letter to my wife. Ricardo
    Morales Aviles. NiR
Brief thaw. Ralph J. Mills
    (Jr.). PrVo
Bright star! Would I were
    steadfast... John Keats.
    HaAP--WBP3
Bring in the wine. Li Po. GrAC
Brinkman, Laura
    Our love is like spring. YoVA
Brinnin, John Malcolm
    Carmarthen bar. HoA
    Flight 539. HoA
    Hotel paradiso e commerciale.
    HoA
    Saul, afterward, riding east.
    HoA
Britt, Alan
    After spending all day at
    the..Museum... FroA
    Serenade. FroA
Britt, Angie
    Arise and be aware. YoVA
    Race of doom. YoVA
Broad bean. Matsuo Basho. FroC
Broadax. Nishiwaki Junzaburo.
    FroC
Brocaded sash. Fuzoku Uta. FroC
Brock, Edwin

Five ways to kill a man. LiHE
The **Brockton** murder:...out of Wm
　　James. Knute Skinner. TyW
Brodsky, Joseph
　　Etude. VoWA
　　A Jewish cemetery near
　　　Leningrad. VoWA
　　Monument to Pushkin. VoWA
　　Pilgrims. VoWA
　　To a tyrant. VoWA
　　Verses on accepting the world.
　　　VoWA
Brody, Alter
　　A family album. VoWA
　　Ghetto twilight. VoWA
　　Lamentations. VoWA
Broke loose. Linda Kozusko. StPo
The **broken** home. James Merrill.
　　HaAP
Bronte, Charlotte
　　Retrospection. EvIm
　　Rochester's song to Jane Eyre.
　　　EvIm
Bronte, Emily
　　I am the only being whose doom.
　　　TyW
　　Last lines. EeBC
　　No coward soul is mine. EvIm
　　R. Alcona to J. Brenzaida. EvIm
　　Remembrance. HaAP
　　Song ("The linnet in the rocky
　　　dells"). HaAP
Bronze tablets! John F. Kerr.
　　ReE
Brooke, Rupert
　　A channel crossing. MTS
　　The fish. MTS
　　The soldier. DoNG
Brooklyn Bridge
　　The bridge, sels. Hart Crane.
　　　HaAP
Brooks (M.del Occidente),Maria
　　Song of Egla. WBP3
Brooks (trans.), Charles T.
　　Max and Maurice, sels. WBP1
Brooks, Gwendolyn
　　The Anniad. BlS
　　Appendix to the Anniad. BlS
　　The bean eaters. BlS--HaAP
　　The birth in a narrow room. BlS
　　The children of the poor, sels.
　　　LiHE
　　The mother. BlS
　　Otto. PoCh
　　A penitent considers...coming
　　　of Mary. PoCh
　　The rites for cousin Vit. HaAP
　　The sundays of Satin-Legs
　　　Smith. LiHE
　　We real cool. HaAP

Brooks, Phillips
　　O little town of Bethlehem.
　　　WBP4
The **brookside**. R.M. Milnes (Lord
　　Houghton). WBP2
The **broom**,. the shovel, the
　　poker... Edward Lear. IlTH
A **brother**. Angela Romano. YoVA
Brother. Mary Ann Hoberman. IlTH
Brother Baptis' on woman
　　suffrage. Rosalie Jonas. BlS
Brother and sister. Lewis
　　Carroll (C.L. Dodgson). IlTH
Brother of my heart. Galway
　　Kinnell. FroA
The **brother-in-law**. Larry Rubin.
　　TyW
Brotherhood
　　Fraternal exhortation. Raul
　　　Javier Garcia. NiR
　　The knot. Tom Clark. HoA
Brothers. Don Pagis. VoWA
Brothers and Sisters
　　Absent star. Quinton Duval.
　　　FroA
　　Brother and sister. Lewis
　　　Carroll (C.L. Dodgson). IlTH
　　A brother. Angela Romano. YoVA
　　Brother. Mary Ann Hoberman.
　　　IlTH
　　Drinking wine with Yoshiyuki..
　　　Ryokan . FroC
　　Let her have it. William Cole.
　　　BrBD
　　My brother was silent. Amir
　　　Gilboa. VoWA
　　My brother. Julie McAdams. YoVA
　　The older brother. Pablo
　　　Antonio Cuadra. NiR
　　The opposite field. Dabney
　　　Stuart. TeMP
　　Pictures of memory. Alice Cary.
　　　WBP1
　　Plain, humble letters. David
　　　Vogel. VoWA
　　Sister Zahava. Edith Bruck.
　　　VoWA
　　Sisters. Patty Corbett. YoVA
　　To her sister misteris A.B.,
　　　sels. Isabella Whitney. PaW
　　Twenty hokk. Mukai Kyorai .
　　　FroC
　　The twins. Henry Leigh. IlTH
Broumas, Olga
　　Absence of noise Presence of
　　　sound. TeMP
Brown, Joseph Brownlee
　　Thalatta! Thalatta! WBP3
Brown, Korey
　　I am a raindrop. HoWM

Brown, Susan
  He understands. YoVA
Brown, Thomas (Tom)
  "I do not like thee, Doctor
    Fell" TyW
Brown, Thomas Edward
  My garden. EeBC
Browne, William
  My choice. WBP2
  On the Countess Dowager of
    Pembroke. HaAP
  Welcome, welcome, do I sing.
    WBP2
The **brownies'** joke book. Palmer
  Cox. TrWB
Browning (tr.), Elizabeth B.
  Prometheus, sels. WBP3
Browning, Elizabeth Barrett
  Comfort. WBP3
  The cry of the human. WBP4
  De Profundis. WBP3
  Hopeless grief. WBP3
  Lord Walter's wife. HaAP--WBP2
  Mother and poet. WBP3
  Patience taught by nature. EeBC
  A portrait. WBP1
  The prospect. WBP4
  The romance of the swan's nest.
    WBP1
  The sleep. WBP3
  Sonnets from the Portuguese,
    sels. WBP2
  Sonnets from the Portuguese,
    sels. HaAP
  Tears. WBP3
  Two sayings. WBP4
Browning, Elizabeth B. (about)
  To Edward Fitzgerald. Robert
    Browning. TyW
Browning, Robert
  The bishop orders his tomb...
    HaAP
  Epilogue. WBP4
  Evelyn Hope. WBP3
  Herve Riel. MTS
  Home-thoughts, from the sea.
    MTS
  In a gondola. WBP2
  Love ("Such a starved bank of
    moss"). WBP2
  Love among the ruins. HaAP
  My last duchess. HaAP--LiHE
  Parting at morning. MTS
  Pippa passes, sels. WBP4
  Pippa's song. EeBC
  Porphyria's lover. HaAP
  Prospice. DoNG--WBP3
  Rabbi Ben Ezra. WBP4
  Soliloquy of the Spanish
    cloister. TyW

To Edward Fitzgerald. TyW
  A toccata at Galuppi's. HaAP
Bruadar and Smith and Glinn.
    Unknown. TyW
Bruchac, Joseph
  Coots. FroA
  Elegy for Jack Bowman. ReE
  Ellis Island. ReE
  First deer. ReE
  The geyser. ReE
  The Narrows. FroA
  Open. FroA
  The remedies. ReE
  Three poems for the Indian
    steelworkers. ReE
Bruck, Edith
  Childhood. VoWA
  Equality, father! VoWA
  Let's talk, mother. VoWA
  Sister Zahava. VoWA
  Why would I have survived?
    VoWA
Brudne, Eva
  A farewell ballad to poppies.
    VoWA
  Memento vivendi. VoWA
Brueghel, Pieter
  The dance. William Carlos
    Williams. HaAP
Brumbaugh, Robin
  Fingers of war. YoVA
Brussels. Arthur Rimbaud. FreS
Brussels, Belgium
  Brussels. Arthur Rimbaud. FreS
  Brussels: simple frescoes. Paul
    Verlaine. FreS
Brussels: merry-go-round. Paul
  Verlaine. FoFS--FreS
Brussels: simple frescoes. Paul
  Verlaine. FreS
Bryant, Duane
  Forget. YoVA
Bryant, Kathie
  Memories. YoVA
  The time has come. YoVA
Bryant, William Cullen
  Blessed are they that mourn.
    WBP3
  The conqueror's grave. WBP3
  The future life. WBP4
  A hymn of the sea. MTS
  O, fairest of rural maids. WBP2
  Thanatopsis. WBP3
  To a waterfowl. EeBC
Buber, Martin
  The fiddler. VoWA
  I and thou, sels. VoWA
Buchanan, George
  Epithalamium...Mary Queen of
    Scots... ReLP

Epithalamium..marriage Mary
   Queen Scots. ReLP
Love. ReLP
Silva II: Agrius. ReLP
Buchanan, Robert
   The little milliner. WBP2
Buchlyvie. Unknown. TyW
Buckley, Debby
   Misty lady. YoVA
   Romance? - Romance! YoVA
Buddha and Buddhism
   Climbing Pien-chuen Templ. Wang
      Wei . GrAC
   God's measurements. Laurence
      Lieberman. TeMP
   A new spring at Yi-fen. Ling-yi
      . GrAC
   Songs: 32 songs from the Ryojin
      Hish. Unknown . FroC
   Words of oblivion and peace.
      Gabriel Preil. VoWA
A **budget** of paradoxes. John
   Martley. WBP2
Bueno, Susan
   There once was a boy named
      Timmy. YoVA
   Tin soldi/ers stand. YoVA
Building a person. Stephen Dunn.
   FroA
The **building** of the ship, sels.
   Henry Wadsworth Longfellow.
   MTS
Buildings. Myra Cohn Livingston.
   RoRF
Buildings. Daniela Gioseffi.
   FroA
Buildings
   Buildings. Myra Cohn
      Livingston. RoRF
   On the sixth floor. Bartolo
      Cattafi. NeIP
Bukowski, Charles
   A love poem for all...women I
      have known. TeMP
Bulls
   A misunderstanding. Kitty
      Druck. StPo
   Superbull. Harold Witt. FroA
Bulwer-Lytton, Edward, Baron
   When stars are in the quiet
      skies. WBP2
Bunting, Basil
   Gin the goodwife stint. TyW
Bunting, Dalynne
   The blossoming of a soul. YoVA
   Life. YoVA
Bunyan, John
   The pilgrim's song. EeBC
   The shepherd boy's song. EeBC
Burdette, Robert Jones

When my ship comes in. WBP3
Burgess, Gelett
   "I love to go to lectures."
      IlTH
   "I wish my room had a floor."
      IlTH
   "I'd never dare to walk across."
      IlTH
   "If people's heads were not so
      dense." IlTH
   "If the streets were filled
      with glue." IlTH
   The little father... IlTH
   "My feet thay haul me round the
      house." IlTH
   "My house is made of graham
      bread." IlTH
   "The proper way to leave a
      room." IlTH
   "The roof it has a lazy time."
      IlTH
   Table manners-II. IlTH
   Table manners-I. IlTH
Burial of Moses. Cecil Francis
   Alexander. WBP4
Burleson, Marcie L.
   One of many. YoVA
   Prisoner. YoVA
The **burning** Babe. Robert
   Southwell. HaAP--ShBa
Burning Bush
   Purity. Hayim Lenski. VoWA
   Twelve lines about the burning
      bush. Melech Ravitch (Z.K.
      Bergner). VoWA
The **burning** bush. Norman
   Nicholson. EeBC
Burning drift-wood. John
   Greenleaf Whittier. MTS
Burning sand of Sinai. Nelly
   Sachs. VoWA
The **burning** trees were
   limitless. Jane Dulin. YoVA
Burns, Richard
   Angels. VoWA
   Mandelstam. VoWA
Burns, Robert
   Ae fond kiss before we part.
      WBP3
   Auld lang syne. WBP1
   The banks o' Doon. WBP3
   Comin' through the rye. WBP2
   The cotter's Saturday night.
      WBP1
   The day returns, my bosom
      burns. WBP2
   Duncan Gray cam' here to woo.
      WBP2
   Elegy on Captain Matthew
      Henderson. WBP1

Epigram on Elphinstone's
translation.... TyW
Epitaph on James Grieve,Laird
of Boghead. TyW
Green grow the rashes O. WBP2
Highland Mary. WBP3
Holy Willie's prayer. TyW
I love my Jean. WBP3
John Anderson, my jo. WBP2
Let not woman e'er complain.
WBP2
My wife's a winsome wee thing.
WBP2
O, my luve's like a red, red
rose. WBP3
O, saw ye bonnie Leslie? WBP3
Oh wert thou in the cauld
blast. HaAP
A red, red rose. LiHE
To Mary in heaven. WBP3
To a mouse. HaAP
To a mouse. MiRN--LiHE
To the unco guid. WBP4
The toad-eater. TyW
Whistle, and I'll come to you,
my lad. WBP2
Burnshaw, Stanley
House in St. Petersburg. VoWA
Isaac. VoWA
Talmudist. VoWA
Burnt. Boris Slutsky. VoWA
Burnt debris. Thomas Sessler.
VoWA
Burroughs, John
Waiting. WBP3
Burroughs, Margaret Goss
Black pride. BlS
Everybody but me. BlS
Only in this way. BlS
To soulfolk. BlS
Burrows, E.G.
The admiral's daughter. HoA
Dear country cousin. HoA
Hidden valley. HoA
Burt, Della
A little girl's dream world.
BlS
On the death of Lisa Lyman. BlS
Spirit flowers. BlS
Bury him deep. Thomas Lovell
Beddoes. TyW
Bury me in America. Arno Karlen.
FroA
Bus. Ronald Rogers. ReE
Busby, whose verse no piercing
beams.... Richard Moore. TyW
Busch, Wilhelm
Max and Maurice, sels. WBP1
Bush, Barney
The boy of summer. ReE

Daylight no longer comes. ReE
Powwow/and I am in your. ReE
The business life. David
Ignatow. TyW
Buskirk, Patti
Moon light. YoVA
Busses
Boy on the bus. Lee Bennett
Hopkins. ByM
Bus. Ronald Rogers. ReE
Dream. Carol Coyle. YoVA
Oriental wonder. Heather
Wiegand. YoVA
The red fox. Marnie Walsh. ReE
The school bus. Larry Eigner.
FroA
The bustle in a house. Emily
Dickinson. HaAP
But we'll make another one.
Nanni Balestrini. NeIP
Butcher shop. Charles Simic.
TeMP
Butchers
Butcher shop. Charles Simic.
TeMP
Friday lunchbreak. Gregory Orr.
TeMP
Butler, Samuel
Hudibras, sels. WBP4
Butter yellow kitchen. Patricia
Viale Wuest. StPo
Buttercups
On some buttercups. Frank
Dempster Sherman. WBP2
The butterflies. Lisa Sattler.
YoVA
Butterflies
The butterflies. Lisa Sattler.
YoVA
Butterfly. David Herbert
Lawrence. SlW
Sixty-four tank. Saigyo . FroC
The will to live. Mekeel
McBride. TeMP
The butterfly. Pavel Friedmann.
VoWA
Butterfly. David Herbert
Lawrence. SlW
Buttocks
Ode ("Old tumbril rolling with
me..."). X.J. Kennedy. TeMP
Butts, Mary Frances
The happy hour. WBP1
Buying a shop on Dizengoff. Erez
Biton. VoWA
The buzz plane. Robert Francis.
TyW
"By cool Siloam's shady rill".
Reginald Heber. WBP1
By the fireside. Lucy Larcom.

WBP1

By the sea. Christina Georgina
    Rossetti. MTS
By the water. Emile Verhaeren.
    FreS
By the waters of Babylon.
    Benjamin Fondane (Fundoianu).
    VoWA
Bye baby bother. Florence M.
    ("Stevie") Smith. TyW
Byrd, William
    A carol for Christmas day. ShBa
    Lulla la, lulla lulla lullaby.
    ShBa
Byrom, John
    A hymn for Christmas day. ShBa
    My spirit longeth for thee.
    EeBC
Byron in Greece. Norman Rosten.
    HoA
Byron, George Gordon,6th Baron
    Adieu, adieu! my native shore.
    WBP3
    Childe Harold's pilgrimage,
    sels. MTS
    The destruction of Sennacherib.
    HaAP
    Divine comedy, sels (trans.).
    WBP2
    Don Juan, sels. MTS
    Don Juan, sels. HaAP--TyW
    The dream. WBP3
    The dying gladiator. DoNG
    Epitaph ("Posterity will ne'er
    survey"). TyW
    Farewell to his wife. WBP3
    The giaour, sels. WBP3
    The girl of Cadiz. WBP2
    Hebrew melodies, sels. WBP2
    In the first year of freedom's
    second.... TyW
    Maid of Athens, ere we part.
    WBP3
    Manfred. EvIm
    A picture of death. WBP3
    "She walks in beauty, like the
    night" WBP2
    So we'll go more a-roving. HaAP
    Stanzas for music. HaAP
    Stanzas written on the road...
    WBP2
    "'Tis time this heart should be
    unmoved." WBP3
    Who killed John Keats? TyW
    Written after swimming..Sestos
    to Abydos. MTS
Byron, George G.,Baron (about)
    Byron in Greece. Norman Rosten.
    HoA
Byzantium. William Butler Yeats.

HaAP
Byzantium
    Byzantium. William Butler
    Yeats. HaAP
    Sailing to Byzantium. William
    Butler Yeats. HaAP--LiHE

Ca' the yowes. Isabel Pagan.
    WBP2
Cabala
    The Kabbalist. Deborah Eibel.
    VoWA
    Modern Kabbalist. Marcia Falk.
    VoWA
    Safed and I. Molly Myerowitz
    Levine. BuAC--VoWA
Caedmon
    Caedmon's hymn. EeBC
Caedmon (about)
    The Abbess of Whitby. Grace
    Schulman. StPo
Caedmon's hymn. Caedmon. EeBC
Caelica, sels. Fulke Greville
    (Lord Brooke). HaAP
Caesar and the flesh. Ernesto
    Mejia Sanchez. NiR
Cafe in Warsaw. Allen Ginsberg.
    HaAP
The cage. Avner Treinin. VoWA
Cain and Abel. Itzik Manger.
    OnCP
Cain and Abel
    Abel. Else Lasker-Schuler. VoWA
    Autobiography. Don Pagis. VoWA
    Brothers. Don Pagis. VoWA
    Cain and Abel. Itzik Manger.
    OnCP
    Near. Abba Kovner. VoWA
Cain's song. Donald Finkel. VoWA
Cain, John
    At the nursing home. FroA
Cairel, Becky
    Together. YoVA
Cajina Vega, Mario
    Placard. NiR
Calam, Richard
    So misunderstood. YoVA
    Spring fever. YoVA
Caledonia. Colleen J. McElroy.
    BlS
Calico pie. Edward Lear. IlTH
California
    The Californians. Theodore
    Spencer. TyW
California poem. Sandie Nelson.
    ReE
The Californians. Theodore

The **cancer** cells. Richard
    Eberhart. HaAP
Candle. Jacob Isaac Segal. VoWA
Candles
    A song for candles. Armando
        Jaramillo. YoVA
The **cane-bottomed** chair. William
    Makepeace Thackeray. WBP1
"A **canner**, exceedingly canny."
    Carolyn Wells. IlTH
Cannon arrested. Michael S.
    Harper. FroA
Cannon, Edward
    An unsuspected fact. IlTH
Canoes and Canoeing
    Lullaby ("The long canoe").
        Robert Hillyer. DuD
The **canonization**. John Donne.
    HaAP
Cantata. Marlys Weber. YoVA
Canterbury Cathedral, England
    In Canterbury Cathedral. E.W.
        Oldenburg. EeBC
The **Canterbury** tales, sels.
    Geoffrey Chaucer. TyW
The **Canterbury** tales, sels.
    Geoffrey Chaucer. MTS
Canto 17. Lois Marie Harrod.
    StPo
Canto I, sels. Dante Alighieri.
    DoNG
Canto II. Ezra Pound. HaAP
Canto LXXXI, sels. Ezra Pound.
    HaAP
Canto XLV. Ezra Pound. TyW
Canto XXII, sels. Dante
    Alighieri. DoNG
Canton, William
    Laus infantium. WBP1
A **cantor's** dream before...High
    Holy Days. Martin Robbins.
    VoWA
Cantrell, Theresa
    Slowly meeting God. YoVA
Cape Coast castle revisited. Jo
    Ann Hall-Evans. BlS
Capri, Italy
    Shepherd in Capr. Nishiwaki
        Junzaburo . FroC
Caprice. William Dean Howells.
    WBP2
The **captain**. Alfred, Lord
    Tennyson. MTS
Captain Jones' invitation.
    Philip Freneau. MTS
The **captain** stood on the
    carronade. Frederick Marryat.
    MTS
Captured. Courtney Strang. YoVA
Car. Ron Simon. YoVA

A **car** can be a toy. Douglas
    Hartley. YoVA
Carbery (Anna MacManus), Ethna
    Thinkin' long. WBP3
Cardenal, Ernesto
    The arrival. NiR
    Epigram ("Haven't you
        read...") NiR
    Epigram ("The National
        Guard...") NiR
    Epigram XIX. NiR
    Epigram XXXII. NiR
    Epitaph for Joaquin Pasos. NiR
    Epitaph for...Adolfo Baez Bone.
        NiR
    Journey to New York, sels. NiR
    Kayanerenhkowa. NiR
    Lights. NiR
    The meaning of Solentiname. NiR
    National song. NiR
    Oracle on Managua. NiR
    The peasant women of Cua. NiR
    Somoza unveils the statute of
        Somoza.... NiR
    You wake up to cannon fire. NiR
    Zero hour. NiR
Cardenas, Maria
    At 6 and 11. YoVA
    Two hundred five/math. YoVA
Cardiff, Gladys
    Combing. ReE
    Fish dock-Port Townsend. ReE
    How my cousin was killed. ReE
    Indian dancer. ReE
    Long person. ReE
    Moving camp too far. ReE
    Nilla northStar. ReE
    Shoeless Man II. ReE
    The shoeless man. ReE
The **careless** gallant. Thomas
    Jordan. HaAP
The **cares** of a caretaker.
    Wallace Irwin. IlTH
Carew, Thomas
    Ask me no more. HaAP
    Disdain returned. WBP2
    Give me more love or more
        disdain. WBP2
    A song ("Ask me no more where
        Jove...") WBP2
Carey, Alice
    My creed. WBP4
Carey, Henry
    The contrivances, sels. WBP2
    A maiden's ideal of a husband.
        WBP2
    Sally in our alley. WBP2
Cargoes. John Masefield. MTS
Carleton, Will
    Out of the old house, Nancy.

WBP1
Over the hill to the
poor-house. WBP3
Carman, Bliss
The joys of the road. WBP1
Spring song. WBP1
Carman, Sherry
The past. YoVA
Carmarthen bar. John Malcolm
Brinnin. HoA
Carmi, T.
The author's apology. VoWA
The condition. VoWA
Carnegie (Earl Southesk),James
Kate Temple's song. WBP2
Carnivals
At the carnival. Anne Spencer.
BlS
Jenny the juvenile juggler.
Dennis Lee. BrBD
The **carnivoristicous** ounce. Mrs.
M.E. Blake. IlTH
Carol ("He came all so still").
Unknown. PoCh
A **carol** for Christmas day.
Francis Kinwelmersh. ShBa
A **carol** for Christmas day.
William Byrd. ShBa
Carol of the brown king.
Langston Hughes. PoCh--ShBa
Carol of the three kings.
William Stanley Merwin. PoCh
Caroline, Queen of England
On Queen Caroline's deathbed.
Alexander Pope.
Carpenter, Janice A.
Shining like paned glass. YoVA
Carpenters
The walrus and the carpenter.
Lewis Carroll (C.L. Dodgson).
IlTH--WBP1
Carper, John

The moon is round. HoWM
Carr, Aaron
Solar systems. ReE
A **carriage** from Sweden. Marianne
Moore. HaAP
Carroll (C.L. Dodgson), Lewis
Brother and sister. IlTH
The crocodile. IlTH
Father William. IlTH
Jabberwocky. IlTH
The mad gardener's song. IlTH
Mouse's tail. MiRN
A sea dirge. MTS
The tale of the mice. MiRN
The walrus and the carpenter.
IlTH--WBP1
The white knight's ballad. HaAP
Carrousels

Brussels: merry-go-round. Paul
Verlaine. FoFS--FreS
Carruth, Hayden
Contra mortem. TeMP
My dog Jack. FroA
A paragraph. FroA
Privation. FroA
Carry me off. Henri Michaux.
MoVT
Carryl, Charles Edward
An alphabet of questions. IlTH
The camel's lament. IlTH
Cars. Kevin Beasely. YoVA
Carter, Bob
The lonely crowd. YoVA
Tomorrow. YoVA
Carter, Russell Gordon
Jungle incident. IlTH
Carter, Sydney
The faith came first. EeBC
A **cartload** of shoes. Abraham
Sutskever. VoWA
Cartouche: the sign of the king.
Marian J. Darling. StPo
Cartwright, William
On a virtuous young
gentlewoman... HaAP
Carver, Raymond
Luck. TeMP
Cary (trans.), Henry Francis
The divine comedy, sels. WBP4
The fairest thing in mortal
eyes. WBP3
Cary, Alice
Pictures of memory. WBP1
A spinster's tale. WBP2
Cary, Elizabeth (Tanfield)
Mariam, fairie queene of Jewry,
sels. PaW
Cary, Phoebe
Nearer home. WBP4
Casimir the Great; King-Poland

It kindles all my soul. WBP4
Casimoro three times over.
Ricardo Morales Avila. NiR
Cassandra. Louise Bogan. HaAP
Cassandra
Cassandra. Louise Bogan. HaAP
Cassian, Nina
All night long. VoWA
Blood. VoWA
Cripples. VoWA
Like Gulliver. VoWA
Self-portrait. VoWA
Cassou, Jean
Consequence. MoVT
Second ballad. MoVT
The **castaway.** William Cowper.
MTS
Castelete, Rachael

Three little mice (or Six....
Mother Goose . MiRN
Catsius (Kats), Jacobus
Motto-death is like a mask...
ReLP
Cattafi, Bartolo
Anthracite. NeIP
Black thread. NeIP
Darkness. NeIP
On the sixth floor. NeIP
Something precise. NeIP
Tabula rasa. NeIP
Vulnerability. NeIP
Wingspan. NeIP
Cattails. Debbie Farrar. YoVA
Cattle
Cattle show. Christopher Murray
Grieve. HaAP
The quiet-eyed cattle. Leslie
Norris. PoCh
Cattle show. Christopher Murray
Grieve. HaAP
Catullus #3, sels. Caius
Valerius Catullus. DoNG
Catullus, Caius Valerius
Catullus #3, sels. DoNG
Get you to the hell.... TyW
Homeward bound. WBP1
Caucasus
Commerce in the Caucasu.
Ishihara Yoshiro . FroC
Causley, Charles
"Quack!" said the billy-goat.
RoRF
Cecilia, Saint
Saint. Stephane Mallarme. FoFS
A song for St. Cecilia's Day.
John Dryden. HaAP
The **ceiling.** Theodore Roethke.
IlTH
Celan. Anthony Barnett. VoWA
Celan. Asya. VoWA
Celan, Paul
Ash-glory. VoWA
Cello entry. VoWA
Corona. VoWA
Death fugue. VoWA
Hut window. VoWA
In Egypt. VoWA
In Prague. VoWA
Just think. VoWA
Over the three nipple-stones.
VoWA
Psalm ("No one kneads us
again..."). VoWA
A speck of sand. VoWA
Tenebrae. VoWA
Turn blind. VoWA
Zurich, zum Storchen. VoWA
Celan, Paul (about)

Celan. Anthony Barnett. VoWA
In memoriam Paul Celan. Gad
Hollander. VoWA
A letter to Paul Celan in
memory. Jerome Rothenberg.
VoWA
Celebration. Menke Katz. MiRN
The **celebration.** Robert Mezey.
FroA
Celebration
The confetti thrown by many a
hands. Kathy Sears. YoVA
Celebration: birth of a colt.
Linda Hogan. ReE
The **celestial** surgeon. Robert
Louis Stevenson. EeBC
Cellars
In the cellar. Josiah Gilbert
Holland. WBP1
In the cellars. Jiri Gold. VoWA
Cello entry. Paul Celan. VoWA
Cemeteries
Anniversary. Daniel Weissbort.
VoWA
At the Jewish cemetery in
Prague. Oscar Levertin. VoWA
The boomerang. Adriano Spatola.
NeIP
Chelsea churchyard. Ralph J.
Mills (Jr.). FroA
Cool tombs. Carl Sandburg. HaAP
The drunken stones of Prague.
David Scheinert. VoWA
During Prince
Takechi's...enshrinement..
Kakinomoto no Hitomaro . FroC
During Princess
Asuka's...Enshrinement..
Kakinomoto no Hitomaro . FroC
Elegy written in a country
churchyard. Thomas Gray.
HaAP--LiHE
The emmigrant lassie. John
Stuart Blackie. WBP3
The English cemetery. Franco
Fortini. NeIP
God's-acre. Henry Wadsworth
Longfellow. WBP3
Grasses. Ralph J. Mills (Jr.).
FroA
Grave at Cassino. Noah Stern.
VoWA
The grave of Sophocle. Simmias
. WBP3
Graveyard by the sea. Thomas
Lux. TeMP
The graveyard road. Tom
McKeown. HoA
Greenwood cemetery. Crammond
Kennedy. WBP3

Ikce wichasha. Paula Gunn
   Allen. ReE
In an old Jewish cemetery,
   Prague, 1970. Edward Lowbury.
   VoWA
The Indian burying ground.
   Philip Freneau. HaAP
The Jewish Cemetery at Newport.
   Henry Wadsworth Longfellow.
   HaAP
The Jewish cemetery. Cesar
   Tiempo (Israel Zeitlin). VoWA
A Jewish cemetery near
   Leningrad. Joseph Brodsky.
   VoWA
Old Jewish cemetery in Worms.
   Alfred Kittner. VoWA
On a grave at Grindelwald.
   Frederic William Henry Myers.
   WBP3
On the tombs in Westminster
   Abbey. Francis Beaumont. WBP3
The pilgrimage to Testou. Ryvel
   (Raphael Levy) . VoWA
The Quaker graveyard. Silas
   Weir Mitchell. WBP3
Rainy Mountain Cemetery. N.
   Scott Momaday. ReE
Reflections on visiting the
   grave... Ann Plato. BlS
The relic. John Donne. HaAP
Scared. Jack Forbes. YoVA
Sleepy hollow. William Ellery
   Channing. WBP3
Teika, a No play. Komparu
   Zenchiku. FroC
Thirty tanka. Fujiwara no
   Shunzei. FroC
To my father. Susannah Fried.
   VoWA
The unquiet grav. Unknown .
   HaAP
The unveiling. Suzanne
   Bernhardt. VoWA
A cemetery in New Mexico. Alfred
   Alvarez. VoWA
The Cenci, sels. Percy Bysshe
   Shelley. TyW
Cendrars (F. Sauser), Blaise
   Prose of the Transsiberian,
   sels. MoVT
Censorship. John Ciardi. TyW
Censorship
   Letter to a librarian. Irving
   Layton. TyW
   When you read this poem. Pinkie
   Gordon Lane. BlS
Central America. Pablo Neruda.
   NiR
A century of epigrams, sels.

James Vincent Cunningham.
   HaAP
Cerberus. H.L. Van Brunt. FroA
Ceremonies for Christmas, sels.
   Robert Herrick. PoCh
Ceremony. Johari M. Kunjufu. BlS
Ceremony. Kattie M. Cumbo. BlS
Cereus
   The night-blooming cereus.
   Robert Hayden. HoA
Ceylon. Nishiwaki Junzaburo.
   FroC
Ch'ang Chien
   Ancient stirring, sels. GrAC
   Drifting at White Dragonhole,
   sels. GrAC
   Written on the Meditation
   Garden... GrAC
Ch'ang-an, China
   The roads of Ch'ang-an, sel.
   Ch'u Kuang-hsi . GrAC
   Sightseeing on a winter da.
   Wang Wei . GrAC
Ch'en Tzu-ang
   Observing the past on Chi Hill,
   sels. GrAC
Ch'ien Ch'i
   Bamboo isle. GrAC
   Egret returning in evening.
   GrAC
   Kingfisher with fish in beak.
   GrAC
   Sending off Inquest Judge
   Yuan... GrAC
   Written on the cottage wall...
   GrAC
Ch'ing-chiang
   Early spring, writing my
   feelings. GrAC
   Setting out early from
   Hsia-chou. GrAC
Ch'u Kuang-hsi
   Climbing the Stupa in the
   Temple...,sels. GrAC
   Drifting on East Creek of Mao
   Mountain. GrAC
   Eight various responses to farm
   life,sel. GrAC
   Farm life. GrAC
   The fisherman. GrAC
   The roads of Ch'ang-an, sels.
   GrAC
   The song of the fisherman. GrAC
   Wang Chao-chun. GrAC
Chadwick, John White
   The rise of man. WBP4
   The two waitings. WBP3
Chaet, Eric
   A letter catches up with me.
   VoWA

Yom Kippur. VoWA
Chagall, Marc
  Epithalmion. Grace Schulman.
    FroA
  In Chagall's village. Rose
    Auslander. VoWA
  Painting. A.C. Jacobs. VoWA
Chagrin. Isaac Rosenberg. VoWA
Chain. Lorde Audre. BlS
A **chaine** of pearle, sels. Diana
    Primrose. PaW
Chairs
  The cane-bottomed chair.
    William Makepeace Thackeray.
    WBP1
  In romance with the concrete,
    sels. Miron Bialoszewski. CoP
  The old arm-chair. Eliza Cook.
    WBP1
  Reflections. Bubba Lloyd. YoVA
  Self-verified, sels. Miron
    Bialoszewski. CoP
  The table and the chair. Edward
    Lear. IlTH
Chalfi, Abraham
  My father. VoWA
  The one who is missing. VoWA
Chalfi, Raquel
  A childless witch. VoWA
  Life a field waiting.
    BuAC--VoWA
  Lunatics. BuAC
  Tel Aviv beach, Winter '74.
    BuAC
  Tiger-lily. BuAC
  A witch cracking up. BuAC
  A witch going down to Egypt.
    VoWA
  A witch without a cover. BuAC
The **chambered** Nautilus. Oliver
    Wendell Holmes. MTS
Chambers of Jerusalem. Yehuda
    Karni. VoWA
Chamorro, Pedro Joaquin
  Barren the landscape, sels.
    Christian Santos des Praslin.
    NiR
  A song for Pedro J. Chamorro,
    sels. Jose Arauz Mairena. NiR
Chandra, G.S. Sharat

  In praise of blur. FroA
Chang Chiu-ling
  Climbing a tall building...
    GrAC
Chang Yueh
  Composition in drunkenness.
    GrAC
Chang, Tarah Ting-pei
  Fiddler. YoVA
Change

As the sea dries up. Jennifer
    Alley. YoVA
East Coker. Thomas Stearns
    Eliot. HaAP
Change of life. Constance
    Urdang. VoWA
The **changed** cross. Mrs. Charles
    Hobart. WBP3
Changes. Sheila Stauffer. YoVA
Changing the children. Maxine
    Kumin. StPo
A **channel** crossing. Rupert
    Brooke. MTS
Channel firing. Thomas Hardy.
    HaAP
Channing, William Ellery
  Sleepy hollow. WBP3
Chanticleer. William Austin.
    EeBC
Chanukah
  Hanukah. Jakov de Haan. VoWA
Chapin, Henry
  Easy does it. FroA
  Helpmate. FroA
  A quality of air. FroA
  Threes. FroA
Chapman, George
  Sonnet ("Muses, that sing
    Love's..."). WBP2
Chapman, Peggy
  I dared. YoVA
Chapman, Sheryl
  Lost dreams. YoVA
Char, Rene
  The Epte Woods. MoVT
  The wind on leave. MoVT
Character. Darlene Jo Kellison.
    YoVA
The **character** of Holland, sels.
    Andrew Marvell. TyW
Charity. See Service
The **Charles** Addams Mother Goose.
    Charles Addams. TrWB
Charles Baudelaire's tomb.
    Stephane Mallarme. FoFS
Charles I, King of England
  Fames roule, sels. Mary Fage.
    PaW
  The vows. Andrew Marvell. TyW
Charles II, King of England

  Absalom and Achitopel, sels.
    John Dryden. HaAP
  The secular masque, sels. John
    Dryden. HaAP--ShBa
Charles IX, King of France
  Paean our chant triumphal...
    Jean Dorat. ReLP
Charlie Machree. William J.
    Hoppin. WBP2
Chassidim

Hasidic Jew from Sadagora. Rose
    Auslander. VoWA
The morning prayers of...Rabbi
    L.Yitzhok. Phyllis Gottlieb.
    VoWA
The **chastened** clown. Stephane
    Mallarme. FoFS
Chateaubriand (F.Auguste),Vis.

    Jeune fille et jeune fleur.
      WBP3
Chato, Bernadette
    Mickey. ReE
    Shighan-the Navajo way. ReE
    To Nilinigii. ReE
Chattahoochee trip. Mark Fearer.
    YoVA
A **chattel** to freedom. Janet G.
    Rice. YoVA
Chatterton, Thomas
    Aella: a tragical interlude,
      sels. HaAP--WBP2
    Minstrel's marriage song. WBP2
    Minstrel's song. WBP3
    The resignation. WBP4
Chaucer, Geoffrey
    The Canterbury tales, sels. MTS
    The Canterbury tales, sels. TyW
    Hyd, Absolon, thy gilte tresses
      clere. HaAP
    Merciles beautee. HaAP
    Now welcom, somer. HaAP
    The pardoner's tale. HaAP
"A **cheerful** old bear at the
    zoo". Unknown. IlTH
Chelsea churchyard. Ralph J.
    Mills (Jr.). FroA
Cheney, John Vance
    The happiest heart. WBP1
Chernin, Kim
    Eve's birth. VoWA
Cherokee invocation. Raven Hail.
    ReE
Cherries. Lucien Stryk. TeMP
Cherry. Hagiwara Sakutaro. FroC
Cherry Trees
    Cherr. Hagiwara Sakutaro . FroC
    Dawn cherrie. Hezutsu Tosaku .
      FroC
    Loveliest of trees, the cherry
      now. Alfred Edward Housman.
      HaAP
The **cherry** tree carol, sels.
    Unknown. PoCh--ShBa
Cherrylog Road. James Dickey.
    HaAP
Chess
    The chess-board. Owen Meredith
      (Earl Lytton). WBP2
    The game of chess. Marcus
      Hieronymus Vida. ReLP

The game. Jolene Nickell. YoVA
Song for General Cha. Ts'en
    Shen . GrAC
The waste land. Thomas Stearns
    Eliot. HaAP
The **chess-board.** Owen Meredith
    (Earl Lytton). WBP2
Chesterton, Frances

    How far is it to Bethlehem?
      PoCh
Chesterton, Gilbert Keith
    The donkey. EeBC
    The happy man. EeBC
    Lepanto. MTS
The **chestnut** casts his
    flambeaux, sels. Alfred
    Edward Housman. TyW
Chi gate, sels. Kao Shih. GrAC
Chi-wu Ch'ien
    Sailing on Jo-yeh Creek in
      spring. GrAC
Chia Chih
    On first arriving at Pa-ling.
      GrAC
    Out of the passes. GrAC
    The white horse. GrAC
Chiao-jan
    Cold mountain. GrAC
    "I don't like foreign
      languages..." GrAC
    "I hide my heart and not my
      deeds." GrAC
    On the topic "Stone bridge
      stream." GrAC
    Playful poem. GrAC
    Red pine. GrAC
    Song of the soaring hawk. GrAC
    Spontaneous poem I. GrAC
Chickens. Geoff Hewitt. FroA
Chickens
    Chickens. Geoff Hewitt. FroA
    When Mama plucks the chickens.
      Kate Dodson. YoVA
The **child** in the garden. Henry
    Van Dyke. WBP1
A **child** is born. Ulla Jonsson.
    YoVA
The **child** is the mother. Gloria
    C. Oden. BlS
Child of Europe, sels. Czeslaw
    Milosz. CoP
A **child** of my choice. Robert
    Southwell. EeBC
The **child** who cried. Felice
    Holman. ByM
Child's evening hymn. Sabine
    Baring-Gould. WBP1
Child's game. Judson Jerome. DuD
The **child's** marvel. Julie
    Cumberland. YoVA

"A **child/against** the light".
   Georges Linze. MoVT
Childe Harold's pilgrimage,
      sels. George Gordon,6th Baron
      Byron. MTS
Childers, Mark
   The greatest wisdom. YoVA
   Self-delusion. YoVA
Childhood. Rainer Maria Rilke.
   SlW
Childhood. Edith Bruck. VoWA
Childhood memory. Susan
   Henderson. YoVA
A **childless** witch. Raquel
   Chalfi. VoWA
Children. Christy Lombardozzi.
   YoVA
Children. Sandra Hilton. YoVA
The **children**. Charles M.
   Dickinson. WBP1
Children. Walter Savage Landor.
   WBP1
Children. Rogena Orndorff. YoVA
Children and Childhood
   Among school children. William
      Butler Yeats. HaAP
   Are the children at home?
      Margaret E. M. Sangster. WBP3
   The barefoot boy. John
      Greenleaf Whittier. WBP1
   The bewildered ones. Arthur
      Rimbaud. FoFS
   Boris was bad enough. Robert
      Kraus. TrWB
   Boyhood. William Allston. WBP1
   The child's marvel. Julie
      Cumberland. YoVA
   "A child/against the light."
      Georges Linze. MoVT
   Childhood. Rainer Maria Rilke.
      SlW
   Children when they're very
      sweet. John Ciardi. IlTH
   The children's hour. Don
      Johnson. TeMP
   The children. Charles M.
      Dickinson. WBP1
   Children. Christy Lombardozzi.
      YoVA
   Children. Rogena Orndorff. YoVA
   Children. Sandra Hilton. YoVA
   Christmas is really for the
      children. Steve Turner. EeBC
   Cruel Frederic. Unknown . IlTH
   Crystal pieces. Ron Simon. YoVA
   Cutting out a dress. Dennis
      Schmitz. TeMP
   Days were great as lakes. David
      Vogel. VoWA
   Death of a son. Jon Silkin.

   VoWA
   Double-barrelled ding-dong-bat.
      Dennis Lee. BrBD
   Dunce song 6. Mark Van Doren.
      DuD
   Eleven. Archibald MacLeish.
      HaAP
   The endless wall. Lisa Dunn.
      YoVA
   The English struwwelpeter,
      sels. Heinrich Hoffmann. WBP1
   Epilogue ("I too was a little
      child"). Joseph Eliya. VoWA
   Expectation. Aliza Shenhar.
      VoWA
   For Arthur Gregor. Edward
      Field. FroA
   For Lori Tazbah. Luci
      Tapahonso. ReE
   For an Egyptian boy, died c.
      700 B.C.. Mary Baron. HoA
   For the children who
      died..smallpox...Ryokan .
      FroC
   Foreign children. Robert Louis
      Stevenson. WBP1
   The four Zoas, sels. William
      Blake. TyW
   Freddy. Dennis Lee. BrBD
   The gambols of children. George
      Darley. WBP1
   The happy family. John Ciardi.
      DuD
   I think of oblivion. Yehuda
      Amichai. VoWA
   if i was born on this bed. Ted
      Ardans. YoVA
   In the pitch of the night. Lee
      Bennett Hopkins. ByM
   Josephine. Alexander Resnikoff.
      IlTH
   Kristen Diane. Scott Van
      Klaveren. YoVA
   Letty's globe. Charles Tennyson
      Turner. WBP1
   Little Bell. Thomas Westwood.
      WBP1
   Little goldenhair. Mrs. F.
      Burge Smith. WBP1
   The lost heir. Thomas Hood.
      WBP1
   Luck. Raymond Carver. TeMP
   Marina. Thomas Stearns Eliot.
      MTS
   Mr. Nobod. Unknown . IlTH
   My little girl. Samuel Minturn
      Peck. WBP1
   Neglected child. Anthony
      Pressley. YoVA
   Nikki-Rosa. Nikki Giovanni. BlS

Nilla northStar. Gladys
    Cardiff. ReE
Nokondi (the helpless
    creature). Hengenike Riyong.
    VooI
Our childhood spilled into our
    hearts. David Vogel. VoWA
Over all the roof tops. Reuben
    Iceland. OnCP
Papuan folk songs, sel. Unknown
    . VooI
Poets seven years old. Arthur
    Rimbaud. SlW
Polly. William Brightly Hand.
    WBP1
A portrait. Elizabeth Barrett
    Browning. WBP1
Probity. David Swanger. FroA
Proof. Leslie Ullman. FroA
Retrospection. Charlotte
    Bronte. EvIm
Schoolyard rimes, sels. Dennis
    Lee. BrBD
Science for the young. Wallace
    Irwin. IlTH
Seven times four. Jean Ingelow.
    WBP1
Shock-headed Peter. Unknown.
    IlTH
Sister Bernardo. Heather Wilde.
    FroA
A souvenir from childhood.
    David Dietzen. YoVA
The spring of my life, sel.
    Kobayashi Issa . FroC
The story of little
    suck-a-thumb. Heinrich
    Hoffmann. IlTH
There was a little girl. Henry
    Wadsworth Longfellow. WBP1
Three years she grew in sun and
    shower. William Wordsworth.
    HaAP--WBP1
To Alpha Dryden Eberhart...
    Richard Eberhart. TeMP
To Hartley Coleridge. William
    Wordsworth. WBP1
To J.H.. Leigh Hunt. WBP1
To a child during sickness.
    Leigh Hunt. WBP1
To my child. Abraham Sutskever.
    VoWA
Under my window. Thomas
    Westwood. WBP1
Under the shawl. Rose Drachler.
    VoWA
We are seven. William
    Wordsworth. WBP1
We tried to tell you at
    different times. Beth Lewis.

YoVA
When I was nine. Raymond
    Roseliep. FroA
Where knock is open wide.
    Theodore Roethke. HaAP
Why? Melba Joyce Boyd. BlS
Willie Winkie. William Miller.
    WBP1
The witch in the glass. Sarah
    Morgan Bryan Piatt. WBP1
Children of Auschwitz. Naum
    Korzhavin. VoWA
The **children** of the poor, sels.
    Gwendolyn Brooks. LiHE
Children when they're very
    sweet. John Ciardi. IlTH
Children's Games
    Child's game. Judson Jerome.
        DuD
    A good play. Robert Louis
        Stevenson. WBP1
    Jumping rope. Shel Silverstein.
        BrBD
    The land of counterpane. Robert
        Louis Stevenson. WBP1
    The land of story-books. Robert
        Louis Stevenson. WBP1
    A merry gam. Unknown . IlTH
    The unseen playmate. Robert
        Louis Stevenson. WBP1
The **children's** carol. Eleanor
    Farjeon. PoCh
The **children's** church. James
    Freeman Clarke (trans.). WBP1
The **children's** church. Karl
    Gerock. WBP1
The **children's** hour. Don
    Johnson. TeMP
Children's song. Arye Sivan.
    VoWA
Chills. Mark Mitchell. YoVA
Chimaera. Jean Moreas. FreS
Chimaera. See Chimera
The **Chimera**. Alfred Mombert.
    VoWA
Chimera
    "The high hall and its funereal
        doors" Adolphe Rette. FreS
The **chimes** of England. Arthur
    Cleveland Coxe. WBP4
Chimney Sweepers
    The chimney sweeper. William
        Blake. LiHE
    Sootie Joe. Melvin B. Tolson.
        FroA
The **chimney** sweeper. William
    Blake. LiHE
Chimneys. Stanislaw Grochowiak.
    CoP
Chimneys

Scott. PoCh

Mary, Mother of Christ. Countee Cullen. PoCh

The mice celebrate Christmas. Alf Proysen. MiRN

Mice in the hay. Leslie Norris. PoCh

Midnight in Bonnie's stall. Siddie Joe Johnson. PoCh

More sonnets at Christmas. Allen Tate. ShBa

My favorite time of year. Maxine Jones. YoVA

The Nativity of our Lord. Christopher Smart. HaAP--ShBa

The Nativity. Clive Staples Lewis. EeBC

The nativity. Henry Vaughan. ShBa

The new Nutcracker Suite, sels. Ogden Nash. PoCh

New heaven, new war. Robert Southwell. ShBa

New prince, new pomp. Robert Southwell. ShBa

"Now Christmas is come." Unknown. PoCh

O simplicitas. Madeleine L'Engle. EeBC

An ode on the birth of our Saviour. Robert Herrick. ShBa

Ode: on the morning of Christ's nativity. John Milton. ShBa

On the morning of Christ's nativity. John Milton. WBP4

Otto. Gwendolyn Brooks. PoCh

The oxen. Thomas Hardy. HaAP--PoCh

Paradise regained, sels. John Milton. PoCh

Patapan. Bernard De la Monnoye. PoCh

A penitent considers...coming of Mary. Gwendolyn Brooks. PoCh

The perfect gift. Edmund Vance Cooke. PoCh

Phantasus: I, 8. Arno Holz. PoCh

A poor child's Christmas. Angie Wright. YoVA

The prayer of the donkey. Carmen Bernos de Gasztold. PoCh

The quiet-eyed cattle. Leslie Norris. PoCh

Santa Claus and the mouse. Emilie Poulsson. MiRN

Santa Claus. Walter De La Mare. PoCh

The second coming. William Butler Yeats. LiHE--ShBa

She sang, dear song, lullay. Unknown   ShBa

The shepherd who stayed. Theodosia Garrison. PoCh

Shepherd's song at Christmas. Langston Hughes. PoCh

The shepherds. Henry Vaughan. ShBa

"Sing hey! Sing hey!" Unknown. PoCh

Sonnets at Christmas. Allen Tate. HaAP

Spider. Norma Farber. PoCh

St. Luke, sel. Bible-New Testament . PoCh

The stable cat. Leslie Norris. PoCh

Those last, late hours of Christmas Eve. Lou Anne Welte. PoCh

Three holy kings from Morgenland. Heinrich Heine. PoCh

The three kings. Ruben Dario. PoCh

Three songs of Mary, sels. Madeleine L'Engle. PoCh

To Noel. Gabriela Mistral. PoCh

The true Christmas. Henry Vaughan. ShBa

Tryste Noel. Louise Imogen Guiney. WBP4

The twelve days of Christmas. Unknown. PoCh

Under the mistletoe. Countee Cullen. PoCh

Unto us a son is given. Alice Meynell. EeBC

Village. Juan Ramon Jimenez. PoCh

A visit from St. Nicholas. Clement Clarke Moore. PoCh--WBP1

Wassail, wassail, wassail, sing we. Unknown.   ShBa

We three kings of Orient are. John H. Hopkins. PoCh

What cheer? Unknown. ShBa

Wind in the willow, sels. Kenneth Grahame. PoCh

The witnesses, sels. Clive Sansom. PoCh

The witnesses. X.J. Kennedy. PoCh

Words from an old Spanish carol. Ruth Sawyer. PoCh

Christmas 1959 et cetera. Gerald William Barrax. PoCh

Christmas at sea. Robert Louis
    Stevenson. MTS
Christmas bells. Henry Wadsworth
    Longfellow. EeBC
Christmas bells, sels. Henry
    Wadsworth Longfellow. PoCh
A Christmas carol, sels.
    Stanislaw Grochowiak. CoP
A Christmas carol, sels.
    Christina Georgina Rossetti.
    PoCh--ShBa
A Christmas carol. Algernon
    Charles Swinburne. ShBa
A Christmas carol. Robert
    Herrick. PoCh--ShBa
A Christmas carol. Harry Behn.
    PoCh
A Christmas childhood. Patrick
    Kavanaugh. PoCh
A Christmas hymn. Alfred Domett.
    WBP4
A Christmas hymn. Richard
    Wilbur. PoCh
"Christmas is coming. The
    geese...fat". Unknown. PoCh
Christmas is really for the
    children. Steve Turner. EeBC
Christmas lights. Valerie Worth.
    PoCh
Christmas morning. Elizabeth
    Madox Roberts. PoCh
Christmas morning I. Carol
    Freeman. PoCh
Christmas morning. Harry Behn.
    PoCh
Christmas nonsense. Thomas P.
    Vilbert. YoVA
Christmas ornaments. Valerie
    Worth. PoCh
A Christmas package: no. 7.
    David McCord. PoCh
A Christmas package: no. 8.
    David McCord. PoCh
A Christmas prayer. George
    MacDonald. PoCh
A Christmas scene. Thomas
    Osborne Davis. WBP2
The Christmas tree. Peter
    Cornelius. PoCh
Christopher, Saint
    Saint Christopher. Dinah Maria
    Mulock Craik. WBP4
Christus consolator. Rossiter
    Worthington Raymond. WBP3
Chronabery, Patty
    Watermelon/Plump, juicy. YoVA
The chronicle. Abraham Cowley.
    WBP2
Chugan Engetsu
    Atami. FroC

The church porch, sels. George
    Herbert. WBP4
Church-monuments. George
    Herbert. HaAP
Churches
    At the church gate. William
    Makepeace Thackeray. WBP2
    A cathedral. Stanislav Vinaver.
    VoWA
    The children's church. Karl
    Gerock. WBP1
    The church porch, sels. George
    Herbert. WBP4
    The Greater Friendship Baptist
    Church. Carole C. Gregory.
    BlS
    London churches. R.M. Milnes
    (Lord Houghton). WBP3
    Shoan Temple. Takamura Kotaro.
    FroC
Churchill, Charles
    Against education. TyW
Chysanthemums
    For Murasaki. Josephine
    Jacobsen. FroA
Ciardi, John
    After Sunday dinner we uncles
    snooze. HoA
    Censorship. TyW
    Children when they're very
    sweet. IlTH
    The happy family. DuD
    In place of a curse. HoA
    In the hole. HoA
    Minus one. HoA
    What someone said when he was
    spanked.... RoRF
Cincinnati, Ohio
    The dear ladies of Cincinnati.
    Anne Stevenson. HoA
Cinderella. Fareedah Allah (Ruby
    Saunders). BlS
Circles
    A circular cry. Edmond Jabes.
    VoWA
A circular cry. Edmond Jabes.
    VoWA
The circumcision. Linda Zisquit.
    VoWA
The circumstance and the word.
    Fernando Gordillo. NiR
Circus
    Large order. Lois-Long Anders.
    StPo
Circus connection. Lexie
    Donaldson. YoVA
A circus dancer. Celia Dropkin.
    VoWA
Cisneros, Sandra
    I the woman. PrVo

A **clear** midnight. Walt Whitman.
     HaAP
Clemo, Jack
     Christ in the clay-pit. EeBC
     The winds. EeBC
"Clenched against winter".
     Martha W. McKenzie. StPo
Cleopatra. William Wetmore
     Story. WBP2
Cleopatra
     Antony and Cleopatra. William
          Haines Lytle. WBP3
     Cleopatra. William Wetmore
          Story. WBP2
Clephane, Elizabeth Cecilia
     The lost sheep. WBP4
Clergy
     Against priests who live with
          concubines. Euricius Cordus.
          ReLP
     Bagman O'Reilly's curse. Les A.
          Murray. TyW
     The bishop orders his tomb...
          Robert Browning. HaAP
     Deacon Morgan. Naomi Long
          Madgett. BlS
     Holy Willie's prayer. Robert
          Burns. TyW
     How to hide Jesus. Steve
          Turner. EeBC
     Last came, and last did go.
          John Milton. TyW
     Lycidas. John Milton.
          HaAP--WBP3
     On the site of a mulberry
          tree.... Dante Gabriel
          Rossetti. TyW
     The pastor's reverie.
          Washington Gladden. WBP4
     The priest. Ephraim Mikhael.
          FreS
     Soggarth aroon. John Banim.
          WBP4
     The two rabbis. John Greenleaf
          Whittier. WBP4
Cleveland, John
     The rebel Scot. TyW
     Upon the death of Mr. King...
          HaAP
Cliches
     A clash with cliches. Vassar
          Miller. FroA
     I don't know. Terri Reeves.
          YoVA
Clifford, Carrie Williams
     The black draftee from Dixie.
          BlS
Clifton, Lucille
     The lost baby poem. BlS
     Miss Rosie. BlS

My mama moved among the days.
     BlS
Climbing Hsien Mountain with
     others. Meng Hao-jan. GrAC
Climbing Kasuga Field. Yamabe no
     Akahito. FroC
Climbing Mount Kagu... Emperor
     Jomei (593-641). FroC
Climbing Pien-chuen Temple. Wang
     Wei. GrAC
Climbing a tall building...
     Chang Chiu-ling. GrAC
Climbing the Stupa in the
     Temple...,sels. Ch'u
     Kuang-hsi. GrAC
Climbing the tower. Wei Ying-wu.
     GrAC
Climbing to Camphor Pavilion...
     Meng Hao-jan. GrAC
Climbing to the heights of
     Pao-yi Temple. Wei Ying-wu.
     GrAC
Cline, Rae
     Oh breeze. YoVA
The **clock**. Charles Baudelaire.
     FoFS
Clocks. Malka Locker. VoWA
Clocks
     Bold white face. Sara
          Tollefson. YoVA
     Clocks. Malka Locker. VoWA
     Hickory, dickory, dock. Mother
          Goose . MiRN
     Oh, no! Mary Mapes Dodge. IlTH
     On the porch of the antique
          dealer. Paul Ramsey. FroA
     The watch. May Swenson. HaAP
The **clod** and the pebble. William
     Blake. EeBC
Cloisters. Anthony Barnett. VoWA
"**Close** your gate fast...". Wang
     Wei. GrAC
The **closed** system. Larry Eigner.
     VoWA
The **clothes**. Rayzel Zychlinska.
     VoWA
Clothing and Dress
     The clothes. Rayzel Zychlinska.
          VoWA
     Cutting out a dress. Dennis
          Schmitz. TeMP
     A first-rate equation. Luciano
          Erba. NeIP
     John. N.M. Bodecker. RoRF
     A new dress. Rachel Korn. VoWA
     On a girdle. Edmund Waller.
          WBP2
     Sedoka: 13 sedok. Unknown .
          FroC
     Six small songs for a silver

flute. Barry Spacks. TeMP
Upon Julia's clothes. Robert
  Herrick. HaAP
Wilhelmina Mergenthaler. Harry
  P. Taber. IlTH
Cloud game. Clarissa Watts. YoVA
A cloud in trousers, sels.
  Vladimir Mayakowsky. SlW
The clouded pounce. Martha W.
  McKenzie. StPo
Clouds. Peggy Grup. YoVA
Clouds. Debbie Farrar. VoYA
Clouds
  Cloud game. Clarissa Watts.
    YoVA
  "Clouds are the ornaments of
    sky..." Jie Zi Yuan Hua Zhuan.
    LuL
  Clouds. Debbie Farrar. VoYA
  Clouds. Peggy Grup. YoVA
  Even if. Rachel Fishman. VoWA
  I'm a cloud. Dwana Thomas. HoWM
  Overcast. Pierre Reverdy. MoVT
  The prefectural engineer's
    statement... Miyazawa Kenji .
    FroC
  Sandia crest. Ronald Rogers.
    ReE
  Under restless clouds. Hanny
    Michaelis. VoWA
  Volcano clouds: parting. Ts'en
    Shen   GrAC
  When the maiden of Hijkata was
    cremated. Kakinomoto no
    Hitomaro . FroC
"Clouds are the ornaments of
  sky..." Jie Zi Yuan Hua
  Zhuan. LuL
Clouds on the mountain. Mei
  Yao-chen. LuL
Clough, Arthur Hugh
  Come home, come home! HaAP
  Despondency rebuked. WBP3
  In a lecture-room. WBP4
  The latest decalogue. HaAP
  Natura naturans. HaAP
  Qua cursum Ventus. MTS--WBP3
  Qua cursum ventus. MTS--WBP3
  Where lies the land to which
    the ship..? MTS
Clouts, Sydney
  Firebowl. VoWA
  Of Thomas Traherne & the pebble
    outside. VoWA
  The portrait of Prince Henry.
    VoWA
  The sleeper. VoWA
The clown. Sandra Sanford. YoVA
The clown. Paula Guarino. YoVA
The clown. Jackie Pierce. YoVA

Clowns
  The angel and the clown. Vachel
    Lindsay. PrVo
  Bobo the clown. JoCarol Lacy.
    YoVA
  The chastened clown. Stephane
    Mallarme. FoFS
  Circus connection. Lexie
    Donaldson. YoVA
  The clown. Jackie Pierce. YoVA
  The clown. Paula Guarino. YoVA
  The clown. Sandra Sanford. YoVA
  My secret with the clown.
    Krystal Siler. YoVA
Cloys, Mona
  Destiny. YoVA
Clumsiness
  Sir Smasham Uppe. Emile Victor
    Rieu. IlTH
CoBabe, Emily
  Quiet, dear quiet. YoVA
Coal. Lorde Audre. BlS
Coal
  Anthracite. Bartolo Cattafi.
    NeIP
  Illinois coalscapes. James
    Ballowe. PrVo
Coal-liquefaction
  One plant for man-made oi. Ono
    Tozaburo . FroC
Coatsworth, Elizabeth
  The mouse. MiRN
  The open door. DuD
Cobb would have caught it.
  Robert Fitzgerald. HaAP
Cobb, Alice S.
  Angela Davis. BlS
  The searching. BlS
Cocanougher, Cindy
  Daybreak. YoVA
The cock. Ewa Lipska. VoWA
The cock crows. Unknown. FroC
Cocks
  The cock crow. Unknown . FroC
  I have a gentil cock. Unknown.
    HaAP
  On a cock at Rochester. Sir
    Charles Sedley. TyW
Coconut. Mario Satz. VoWA
The coconut. Shimazaki Toson.
  FroC
Coconuts
  The coconu. Shimazaki Toson .
    FroC
  Coconut. Mario Satz. VoWA
Coda. David Meltzer. VoWA
Codish, Edward
  A juggle of myrtle twigs. VoWA
  Yetzer ha Ra. VoWA
Coffin, Robert P. Tristram

Cows are coming home in Maine.
 DuD
Coggins, Nora
 "The wall." YoVA
 "The wheat field." YoVA
Cohen, Leonard
 Story of Isaac. VoWA
Cohen, Shlomit
 Aphrodite. BuAC
 Drawing of a woman. BuAC
 The impossible is no hindrance.
  BuAC
 The same dream. VoWA
 So abruptly. BuAC
 Struggling at the kill. BuAC
 An unraveled thought. VoWA
 Wife of Kohelet. BuAC--VoWA
Cohoe, Grey
 Tocito visions. ReE
Cold
 "In the mountain's shadow."
  Ryokan . FroC
 In this room it is cold.
  Victoria Guerica. YoVA
 "Though I lie here." Ryokan .
  FroC
Cold Food Festival. Han Hung.
 GrAC
Cold air, numb fingers. Patrick
 Crosson. YoVA
Cold creek. Maurice Kenny. ReE
The cold heaven. William Butler
 Yeats. HaAP
Cold mountain. Chiao-jan. GrAC
Cold term. I. Amiri Baraka
 (LeRoi Jones). SlW
The coldness. Jon Silkin. VoWA
Cole, James
 The wheel. FroA
Cole, Joanna
 Driving to the beach. ByM
Cole, William
 Let her have it. BrBD
 Sneaky Bill. IlTH
Coleman, Elliott
 Sirens. FroA
 Winter over nothing. FroA
Coleman, Horace
 A black soldier remembers. FroA
 Remembrance of things past.
  FroA
Coleman, Jerome
 "I fell in paradise" HoWM
Coleridge, Hartley
 "She is not fair to outward
  view." WBP2
Coleridge, Mary Elizabeth
 I saw a stable. EeBC--PoCh
 There. EeBC
Coleridge, Samuel Taylor

Christabel. EvIm
Cologne. TyW
The exchange. WBP2
Frost at midnight. HaAP
The good great man. WBP3
Hymn, before sunrise... WBP4
Kubla Khan. HaAP
Love. WBP2
On an infant. WBP4
On my joyful departure
 from...Cologne. TyW
The rime of the ancient
 mariner. HaAP--MTS
The rime of the ancient
 mariner. HaAP
Wallenstein, sels. WBP4
Youth and age, sels. WBP1
Coles (trans.), Abraham
 Stabat Mater Dolorosa. WBP4
The collar. George Herbert. HaAP
The collection. Jolene Nickell.
 YoVA
Collections and Collectors
 Relics. David Wagoner. FroA
Collins, J.R.
 On being high. YoVA
 You are mine. YoVA
Collins, Mortimer
 The two worlds. WBP4
Collins, Robin
 Letters of my father. YoVA
 Ms. L. YoVA
 When you rise. YoVA
Collins, William
 Ode to evening. HaAP
 Ode, written in...1746. HaAP
A colloquy with Gregory on the
 balcony. Howard Moss. FroA
Collyer, Diane
 Life. YoVA
Cologne. Hilde Domin. VoWA
Cologne. Samuel Taylor
 Coleridge. TyW
Cologne, Germany
 Cologne. Hilde Domin. VoWA
 Cologne. Samuel Taylor
  Coleridge. TyW
 On my joyful departure
  from...Cologne. Samuel Taylor
  Coleridge. TyW
Colombia, South America
 Four Christmas carols, sels.
  Cheli Duran (trans.). PoCh
Color
 Picture 4. Tiffany Peters. HoWM
 A rainy day. Trent Conrad. HoWM
 What is color? Sheri Neb. YoVA
Colorado. Kimberly Diane Almond.
 YoVA
Colorado

Connubial life. James Thomson.
    WBP2
The conqueror's grave. William
    Cullen Bryant. WBP3
Conrad. Antoni Slonimski. VoWA
Conrad, Joseph
    Conrad. Antoni Slonimski. VoWA
Conrad, Trent
    A rainy day. HoWM
Conscience. Melech Ravitch (Z.K.
    Bergner). VoWA
Conscience
    Conscience and remorse. Paul
        Laurence Dunbar. WBP4
    Conscience. Melech Ravitch
        (Z.K. Bergner). VoWA
    Found wanting. Emily Dickinson.
        WBP4
    The private theater. Nelo Risi.
        NeIP
    Satire XIII, sel. Juvenal.
        WBP4
    A woman killed with kindness,
        sels. Thomas Heywood. WBP4
Conscience and remorse. Paul
    Laurence Dunbar. WBP4
Consequence. Jean Cassou. MoVT
Consider the lilies. Dorothy
    Donnelly. HoA
Considering the bleakness.
    Moishe Leib Halpern. VoWA
The conspiracy. LeAnnette
    Donahey. YoVA
Constancy. Unknown. WBP2
Constancy. Sir John Suckling.
    WBP2
The constant. Archie Randolph
    Ammons. HaAP
"Contemplating the law..."
    Ikkyu Sojun. FroC
Contentment
    Art thou poor...? Thomas
        Dekker. HaAP
    The changed cross. Mrs. Charles
        Hobart. WBP3
    Compensation. Christopher
        Pearse Cranch. WBP3
    Despondency rebuked. Arthur
        Hugh Clough. WBP3
    If we knew. May Riley Smith.
        WBP1
    Pippa's song. Robert Browning.
        EeBC
    Quiet, dear quiet. Emily
        CoBabe. YoVA
    Something beyond. Mary Clemmer
        Ames Hudson. WBP3
    Sonnet ("While yet these
        tears..."). Louise Labe. WBP3
    Take the world as it is.

        Charles Swain. WBP1
    To myself. Paul Fleming. WBP3
    Why thus longing? Samuel
        Winslow Sewall. WBP4
Contoski, Victor
    The suicides of the rich. FroA
Contra mortem. Hayden Carruth.
    TeMP
Contreras, Eduardo
    To Commander Marcos. Gioconda
        Belli. NiR
The contrivances, sels. Henry
    Carey. WBP2
The convergence of the twain.
    Thomas Hardy. MTS
Conversation. Rose Fyleman. MiRN
Conversation. Gyorgy Raba. VoWA
Conversation
    La tienda. Carol Lee Sanchez.
        ReE
    So misunderstood. Richard
        Calam. YoVA
Conversation with the prince,
    sels. Tadeusz Rozewicz. CoP
Conversation with a countryman.
    Antoni Slonimski. VoWA
Conversations. Luci Tapahonso.
    ReE
(Conversations #4). Carol Lee
    Sanchez. ReE
(Conversations #1). Carol Lee
    Sanchez. ReE
(Conversations #2). Carol Lee
    Sanchez. ReE
The conversion of Saint Paul.
    John Keble. WBP4
Cook, Eliza
    Ganging to and ganging frae.
        WBP2
    The old arm-chair. WBP1
Cook-Lynn, Elizabeth
    The bare facts. ReE
    Jesus saves or Don't ask me to
        join AA... ReE
    The last remarkable man. ReE
    When you talk of this. ReE
Cooke, Edmund Vance
    The perfect gift. PoCh
Cooking and courting. Unknown.
    WBP2
Cool tombs. Carl Sandburg. HaAP
Coolidge (Sarah Woolsey),Susan
    When. WBP4
Coolie. Yoshioka Minoru. FroC
Cooper, James Fenimore
    My brigantine. MTS
Cooperative council. Takamura
    Kotaro. FroC
Coots. Joseph Bruchac. FroA
Coots

Coots. Joseph Bruchac. FroA
Coralville, in Iowa. Marvin
  Bell. FroA
Corbett, Patty
  Sisters. YoVA
Corbiere, Tristan
  Art-flower. FreS
  Epitaph ("He killed himself
    with ardor.") FreS
  The ill-starred flower. FreS
  Letting the pack run. FreS
  Litany of sleep. FreS
  Pariah. FreS
  Time ("Alms for the hunting
    highwayman.") FreS
  To a suckling satirist. FreS
  To the eternal madame. FreS
  To the memory of Zulma. FreS
Cordier, Paula
  An affair. YoVA
Cordoba. Asher Mendelssohn. VoWA
Corduś, Euricius
  Against priests who live with
    concubines. ReLP
  Epigram: on doctors. ReLP
Corinna's going a-Maying. Robert
  Herrick. HaAP--LiHE
Corman, Cid
  Big grave creek. HoA
  I promessi sposi. HoA
  The poppy. HoA
  Three tiny songs. HoA
Cormorants
  Carmarthen bar. John Malcolm
    Brinnin. HoA
  The common cormoran. Unknown.
    IlTH
Corn
  Laughing corn. Carl Sandburg.
    PrVo
Corneille, Pierre
  Polyeucte, sels. WBP2
Cornelius, Peter
  The Christmas tree. PoCh
Cornwall (B.W. Procter), Barry
  Life. WBP3
  A petition to time. WBP1
  The poet's song to his wife.
    WBP2
  Sit down, sad soul. WBP4
  Softly woo away her breath. WBP3

Corona. Paul Celan. VoWA
Corpman, Izora
  The photos from summer camp.
    FroA
The corpse of a cat. Hagiwara
  Sakutaro. FroC
Correspondences. Charles

Baudelaire. FoFS
Corruption
  Daisy Fraser. Edgar Lee
    Masters. HaAP--PrVo
Cortez, Jayne
  Grinding vibrato. BlS
  In the morning. BlS
  Orange chiffon. BlS
  Orisha. BlS
  Phraseology. BlS
  So many feathers. BlS
  Under the edge of February. BlS
Cory (trans.), William Johnson
  The dead poet-friend. WBP1
Cosmopolite, sels. Georgia
  Douglas Johnson. BlS
Cosmos (universe)
  so? Alvin Greenberg. FroA
  Song of Yuan Tan-ch'iu. Li Po.
    GrAC
The cost of pretending. Peter
  Davison. TyW
The cost of worth. Josiah
  Gilbert Holland. WBP4
Costello (trans.), Louise S.
  Sonnet ("While yet these
    tears...") WBP3
  To Diane de Poitiers. WBP3
The cotter's Saturday night.
  Robert Burns. WBP1
Cotton, John
  Letters for the New England
    dead. Mary Baron. HoA
Countersong to Walt Whitman.
  Pedro Mir. NiR
Counting
  One old Oxford ox. Unknown
    IlTH
Counting the beats. Robert
  Graves. HaAP
Countries
  Birth of a country. Agnes
    Gergely. VoWA
Country Life
  Country girl. Kate Dodson. YoVA
  The country life. Richard Henry
    Stoddard. WBP1
  Dwelling in ease at Wang stream.
    Wang Wei. GrAC
  Gone. David McCord. ByM
  Hidden valley. E.G. Burrows.
    HoA
  Is it right to move to the
    country? Giovanni Giudici.
    NeIP
  Life in the boondocks. Archie
    Randolph Ammons. HaAP
  Old countryside. Louise Bogan.
    HaAP
  White blossoms. Robert Mezey.

VoWA
  Written after long rains at my
    villa.. Wang Wei . GrAC
Country girl. Kate Dodson. YoVA
The country life. Richard Henry
    Stoddard. WBP1
The country mouse and the city
    mouse. Richard Scrafton
    Sharpe. MiRN
Country night. Rocco Scotellaro.
    NeIP
County fair images. Dave Etter.
    PrVo
Couple at home. Florence
    Trefethen. StPo
The couple overhead. William
    Meredith. TyW
Courage
  The brave man. Wallace Stevens.
    SlW
  The song of the Savoyards.
    Henry Ames Blood. WBP3
Court, Wesli
  Academic curse: an epitaph. TyW
Courtesy
  Never again will I say. Moyshe
    Leyb Halpern. OnCP
The courtin'. James Russell
    Lowell. WBP2
Courtship
  Among the heather. William
    Allingham. WBP2
  An answer to another persuading
    a lady... Katherine Philips.
    HaAP
  Aux Italiens. Owen Meredith
    (Earl Lytton). WBP2
  The bailiff's daughter of
    Islingto. Unknown . WBP2
  The brookside. R.M. Milnes
    (Lord Houghton). WBP2
  Ca' the yowes. Isabel Pagan.
    WBP2
  Cooking and courtin. Unknown .
    WBP2
  The courtin'. James Russell
    Lowell. WBP2
  Doris: a pastoral. Arthur
    Joseph Munby. WBP2
  Duncan Gray cam' here to woo.
    Robert Burns. WBP2
  The earl o' quarterdeck. George
    MacDonald. WBP2
  The exchange. Samuel Taylor
    Coleridge. WBP2
  The friar of orders gray.
    Thomas Percy. WBP2
  Golden eyes. Rufinus Domesticus.
    WBP2
  How to ask and have. Samuel

Lover. WBP2
I prithee send me back my
  heart. Sir John Suckling.
  WBP2
I'm not myself at all. Samuel
  Lover. WBP2
The laird o' Cockpen. C.
  Oliphant, Baroness Nairne.
  WBP2
The little red lark. Alfred
  Percival Graves. WBP2
Live in my heart and pay no
  rent. Samuel Lover. WBP2
"Love me little, love me long."
  Unknown . WBP2
Love. Samuel Taylor Coleridge.
  WBP2
My eyes! how I love you. John
  Godfrey Saxe. WBP2
The night piece. Robert
  Herrick. WBP2
Othello, sels. William
  Shakespeare. WBP2
The passionate shepherd to his
  love. Christopher Marlowe.
  HaAP--LiHE
Phillida and Corydon. Nicholas
  Breton. WBP2
Popping cor. Unknown . WBP2
Rory O'More. Samuel Lover. WBP2
The siller croun. Susanna
  Blamire. WBP2
Somebod. Unknown . WBP2
Songs exchanged...Prince
  Okuninushi.. Unknown . FroC
Story of the gate. T. H.
  Robertson. WBP2
A subaltern's love-song. John
  Betjeman. HaAP
Sweet meeting of desires.
  Coventry Patmore. WBP2
The Vicar of Wakefield, sels.
  Oliver Goldsmith. WBP2
"Where are you going, my pretty
  maid?" Unknown . WBP2
Widow Machree. Samuel Lover.
  WBP2
Widow Malone. Charles Lever.
  WBP2
You. Jack Metropol. YoVA
Cousins
  How my cousin was killed.
    Gladys Cardiff. ReE
Covenant. Paul Auster. VoWA
The Coventry carol. Unknown.
    EeBC
Coventry carol. Robert Croo.
    PoCh
The cow. Knute Skinner. TeMP
Cowdery, Mae V.

I sit and wait for beauty. BlS

Cowley, Abraham
The chronicle. WBP2
The spring. HaAP

Cowper, William
The castaway. MTS
Epigram ("False, cruel, disappointed"). TyW
Epigram on the refusal of the university. TyW
Epitaph on a hare. HaAP
Friendship, sels. WBP1
Hatred and vengeance, my eternal portion. TyW
Light shining out of darkness. WBP4
Lines written during a period...insanity. HaAP
My mother's picture. WBP1
Oh! for a closer walk with God. EeBC
The poplar field. HaAP
The present good. WBP3
Sweet stream, that winds. WBP1
The task, sels. WBP3
To seek a friend. WBP1
To the immortal memory of the halibut... MTS

Cows
About the cows. Roger Pfingston. FroA
The cow. Knute Skinner. TeMP
Pretty cow. Jane Taylor. WBP1

Cows are coming home in Maine. Robert P. Tristram Coffin. DuD

Cox, Darryl
I am an actor. YoVA
Sunset. YoVA

Cox, Palmer
The brownies' joke book. TrWB

Cox, Robert
"My hands are cupped together." HoWM

Cox, Sherry S.
Things of the earth. YoVA

Coxe, Arthur Cleveland
The chimes of England. WBP4

Coyle, Carol
Dream. YoVA
off in the distance. YoVA

Coyotes
The boy and coyote. Simon J. Ortiz. ReE

Cozzens, Frederick Swartwout
An experience and a moral. WBP2

Crabbe, George
The approach of age. WBP3
Tales of the hall, sels. WBP3

The cracked bell. Charles

Baudelaire. FoFS

A cradle hymn. Isaac Watts. EeBC--ShBa

A cradle hymn, sels. Isaac Watts. WBP1

Cradle song. Yona Wallach. BuAC--VoWA

Cradle song. Yona Wallach. VoWA

A cradle song. William Blake. ShBa

Cradle song ("Sleep, little baby"). Unknown. WBP1

Cradle song without music. Carlos Martinez Rivas. NiR

Craik, Dinah Maria Mulock
Her likeness. WBP2
A Lancashire doxology. WBP4
Now and afterwards. WBP3
Only a woman. WBP3
Philip, my king. WBP1
Saint Christopher. WBP4
Sunday morning bells. WBP4
Too late. WBP3

Cranch, Christopher Pearse
Compensation. WBP3

Crandall, Patricia
Missing you. YoVA
Please leave. YoVA

Crane. Maruyama Kaoru. FroC

Crane in the pines. Tai Shu-lun. GrAC

Crane, Hart
At Melville's tomb. HaAP--MTS
The bridge, sels. HaAP
Praise for an urn. HaAP
Voyages, sels. HaAP
Voyages. MTS

Crane, Hart
Fish food. John Wheelwright. MTS

Crane, Stephen
God fashioned the ship of the world... MTS
The heart. TyW
A man adrift on a slim spar. MTS
The ocean said to me once. MTS

Cranes (birds)
Crane. Maruyama Kaoru . FroC
Crane in the pine. Tai Shu-lun. GrAC
Yellow crane towe. Ts'ui Hao . GrAC

Crashaw, Richard
The flaming heart, sels. HaAP
Hymn of the Nativity. HaAP
A hymn to...St. Teresa, sels. HaAP
In memory of...Lady Madre de Teresa. TyW

In the holy nativity of our
   lord God. ShBa
On the blessed Virgin's
   bashfulness. HaAP
Two went up into the temple to
   pray. HaAP--WBP4
Water turned into wine. WBP4
The widow's mites. WBP4
Wishes for the supposed
   mistress. WBP2
Crawford (L.Macartney), Julia
   Kathleen Mavourneen. WBP3
   We parted in silence. WBP3
Crazy Jane on the day of
   judgment. William Butler
   Yeats. SlW
Crazy quilt. Jane Yolen. BrBD
Creation
   The animals. Edwin Muir. EeBC
   A beginning and an end. Edouard
      Roditi. VoWA
   Ducks, sels. Frederick William
      Harvey. EeBC
   Examples of created systems.
      William Meredith. TeMP
   From the head. Louis Zukovsky.
      VoWA
   Gathering the sparks. Howard
      Schwartz. VoWA
   Genesis. Lotte Kramer. VoWA
   God's determinations, sels.
      Edward Taylor. HaAP
   Kashrut. Edouard Roditi. VoWA
   Lamentations. Louise Gluck.
      TeMP
   A new genesis. Avraham
      Shlonsky. VoWA
   Prologue ("In your words").
      Lazer Eichenrand. VoWA
   The pulley. George Herbert.
      EeBC--HaAP
   The rose. G.A. Studdert
      Kennedy. EeBC
   To a snowflake. Francis
      Thompson. EeBC
   When God first said. Natan
      Zach. VoWA
Creation of the child. Susan
   Litwack. VoWA
The **creature** of today. Jamie
   Howell. YoVA
Creeley, Robert
   The act of love. HaAP
   The crow. TyW
   A wicker basket. HaAP
Cricket. Unknown. FroC
Crickets
   Cricket. Unknown . FroC
   Haiku: 39 haiku. Masaoka Shiki.
      FroC

The **crickets** sang. Emily
   Dickinson. SlW
Crimen amoris. Paul Verlaine.
   FoFS
Cripples. Nina Cassian. VoWA
The **critic** on the hearth. L.E.
   Sissman. TyW
Criticism and Critics
   The critic on the hearth. L.E.
      Sissman. TyW
   The curse. John Millington
      Synge. TyW
   Eminent critic. John Frederick
      Nims. TyW
   An essay on criticism, sels.
      Alexander Pope. HaAP
   Pipling. Theodore Roethke. TyW
   To my least favorite reviewer.
      Howard Nemerov. TyW
   To the reviewers. Thomas Hood.
      TyW
   Valentine. Ernest Hemingway.
      TyW
The **crocodile.** Lewis Carroll
   (C.L. Dodgson). IlTH
The **crocodile.** Oliver Herford.
   IlTH
Crocodiles
   The crocodile. Lewis Carroll
      (C.L. Dodgson). IlTH
   "Oh, she sailed away on a
      lovely...day." Unknown . IlTH
The **crocuses.** Frances E.W.
   Harper. BlS
Crocuses
   The crocuses. Frances E.W.
      Harper. BlS
Cromwell, Oliver
   An Horatian ode...Cromwell's
      return... Andrew Marvell.
      HaAP
Cromwell, Richard
   The bleached ruffled leaves.
      YoVA
Croo, Robert
   Coventry carol. PoCh
Crookston, Grant
   Who is she? YoVA
Cross (see Eliot,G.),Marian E.

Cross, Kent
   Rodeo and fans. YoVA
Crossen, Stacy Jo
   Wings. ByM
Crossing. Anthony Barnett. VoWA
Crossing the Atlantic. Anne
   Sexton. MTS
Crossing the Yellow River to
   Ch'ing-ho. Wang Wei. GrAC
Crossing the bar. Alfred, Lord

Tennyson. MTS--WBP4
Crosson, Patrick
Cold air, numb fingers. YoVA
David. YoVA
Croston, Julie
Poled. YoVA
Crouch, Stanley
After the rain. LiHE
The **crow**. Robert Creeley. TyW
Crow, straight flier, but dark.
Laya Firestone. VoWA
A **crowne** of sonnets, sels. Lady
Mary (Sidney) Wroth. PaW
The **crowning** of Madeline. Marty
Bogan. YoVA
The **crows**. Arthur Rimbaud. FoFS
Crows
Crow, straight flier, but dark.
Laya Firestone. VoWA
The crow. Robert Creeley. TyW
The crows. Arthur Rimbaud. FoFS
The twa corbie. Unknown . HaAP
Crucial stew. Colette Inez. FroA
Crucifixion
Death on a crossing. Evangeline
Paterson. EeBC
Golgotha. Saint-Pol (Paul)
Roux. FreS
The happy man. Gilbert Keith
Chesterton. EeBC
Indifference. G.A. Studdert
Kennedy. EeBC
On the Crucifixion. Giles
Fletcher. EeBC
Still falls the rain. Edith
Sitwell. EeBC--ShBa
Cruel Frederick. Unknown. IlTH
Cruts, Cheryl
For Tammy & David. YoVA
Runners/journey into. YoVA
The **cry**. Deb Thomas. YoVA
A **cry**. Annette L. Roy. YoVA
Cry for a disused synagogue in
Booysens. Mannie Hirsch. VoWA
The **cry** of generations.
Mordechai Husid. VoWA
Cry of nature. Geraldine Keams.
ReE
The **cry** of the human. Elizabeth
Barrett Browning. WBP4
Crying
The bonnie broukit bairn.
Christopher Murray Grieve.
HaAP
The child who cried. Felice
Holman. ByM
The cry. Deb Thomas. YoVA
I heard her cry last night.
Sabrina Snyder. YoVA
A life-lesson. James Whitcomb

Riley. WBP1
The sad story of a little boy
who crie. Unknown . IlTH
A tear. Robyn Fischer. YoVA
A valediction: of weeping. John
Donne. HaAP
Crystal. Kristy MacKay. HoWM
Crystal
Crystal. Kristy MacKay. HoWM
"I'm a shining crystal." Kevin
Rock. HoWM
Crystal dawn. Alice A. Robbins.
StPo
Crystal pieces. Ron Simon. YoVA
Crystals like blood. Christopher
Murray Grieve. HaAP
Cuadra, Manolo
The warning: shout on the
corners. NiR
Cuadra, Pablo Antonio
Litany of the planes. NiR
The older brother. NiR
Poems in pieces. NiR
The secret of the burning
stars. NiR
Third class country. NiR
Tomasito. NiR
Urn with a political profile.
NiR
Written on a stone in the
road... NiR
Cuadra, Roberto
When? NiR
Cuba
Song of black Cubans. Federico
Garcia Lorca. SlW
The **cuckoo**. Takahashi Mushimaro.
FroC
Cuckoos
The cuckoo. Takahashi Mushimaro.
FroC
Thirty tanka. Fujiwara no
Shunzei. FroC
Cucumbers to pickles. Tammy A.
Osburn. YoVA
Cuddle doon. Alexander Anderson.
WBP1
Cullen, Countee
Incident. LiHE
Mary, Mother of Christ. PoCh
Simon the Cyrenian speaks. HaAP
Under the mistletoe. PoCh
Cumae, Italy
The ruins of Cumae, an ancient
city. Jacopo Sannazaro. ReLP
Cumberland, Julie
The child's marvel. YoVA
Cumberland,M.Clifford,Countess
Salve deux rex judaeorum...,
sels. Aemilia (Bassano)

Shakespeare. TyW
The **curtain** of the native land.
    Unknown. NiR
Curtains
    "A lace annuls itself totally."
        Stephane Mallarme. FoFS--FreS
Cushing, Kirsten
    Early spring. YoVA
Custer (1). Alison Baker. FroA
Custer (2). Alison Baker. FroA
Custer, George Armstrong
    Custer (1). Alison Baker. FroA
    Custer (2). Alison Baker. FroA
Customs. Juan Gelman. VoWA
A **cut** flower. Karl Shapiro. HaAP
Cut the grass. Archie Randolph
    Ammons. HaAP
Cutler, Bruce
    Results of a scientific survey.
        FroA
Cutting out a dress. Dennis
    Schmitz. TeMP
Cymbeline, sels. William
    Shakespeare. DoNG
Cymbeline, sels. William
    Shakespeare. WBP3
Cynewulf
    Christ, sels. MTS
Cynicism
    Child of Europe, sels. Czeslaw
        Milosz. CoP
Cypress Trees
    Sick cypres. Tu Fu . GrAC
The **Czech** master Teodoryk, sels.
    Jerzy Harasymowicz. CoP

D'Avalos prayer. John Masefield.
    MTS
DNA (molecule)
    Andy-Diana DNA letter. Andrew
        Weiman. HaAP
Dacey, Philip
    Form rejection letter. TeMP
    The ring poem... FroA
Dad. Elaine Feinstein. VoWA
Dad, I'm scared. Barbara Wilde.
    YoVA
Daddy. Sylvia Plath. LiHE--TyW
Daddy fell into the pond. Alfred
    Noyes. IlTH
The **daemon** lover. Unknown. MTS
Dafydd ap Gwilym
    The rattle bag, sels. TyW
A **dairy** of the sailors of the
    north. David Shulman. VoWA
Dairyman blues. Mike Rempel.
    YoVA

Daisies. Sheila Stauffer. YoVA
Daisies
    Daisies. Sheila Stauffer. YoVA
    For the candle light. Angelina
        Weld Grimke. BlS
Daisy. Francis Thompson. WBP3
Daisy Fraser. Edgar Lee Masters.
    HaAP--PrVo
Dake, Patti
    The old days. YoVA
Dallas, Texas
    Travels in the south. Simon J.
        Ortiz. ReE
The **dalliance** of the eagles.
    Walt Whitman. HaAP
Dallman, Elaine
    From the dust. VoWA
Dame, Kathie A.
    Leaf-line. StPo
    Merlin's Louisiana. StPo
    Pre-ponderance. StPo
Dameron, Tommy
    Blank reflections. HoWM
Damned fly. Gordon D. Leslie.
    StPo
Dan, the dust of Masada... Ruth
    Whitman. VoWA
Dana, Robert
    Mineral point. FroA
The **dance**. William Carlos
    Williams. HaAP
The **dancers**. Michael Field. WBP1
Dancing and Dancers
    Axioms. Gad Hollander. VoWA
    Bear. Peter Blue Cloud. ReE
    A circus dancer. Celia Dropkin.
        VoWA
    The dancers. Michael Field.
        WBP1
    Forest ballet. Krystal Siler.
        YoVA
    The gourd dancer. N. Scott
        Momaday. ReE
    Hasidim dance. Nelly Sachs.
        VoWA
    Hoop dancer. Paula Gunn Allen.
        ReE
    "In the music academy...", sel.
        Tu Fu . GrAC
    Indian dancer. Gladys Cardiff.
        ReE
    "Is it an oriental dancer?"
        Arthur Rimbaud. FreS
    Kitty Neil. John Francis
        Waller. WBP2
    Little Viennese waltz. Federico
        Garcia Lorca. SlW
    A pavane for the nursery.
        William Jay Smith. DuD
    Peg Leg Snelson. Melvin B.

Tolson. FroA
Ponca war dancers. Carter
    Revard. ReE
Skatetown boogie. Shari K.
    Wentz. YoVA
Some semblance of order.
    Charles David Wright. FroA
Song for a dance. Abraham
    Sutskever. VoWA
Streets. Paul Verlaine. FoFS
The villanelle. Donald
    Harington. FroA
Dandelions, raindrops. Lori
    Seiler. YoVA
Daniel, Debbie
    Today. YoVA
Daniel, Samuel
    Love is a sicknesss. WBP2
    Ulysses and the Siren. HaAP
Danner, Margaret
    At home in Dakar. BlS
    The elevator man adheres to
        form, sels. BlS
    A grandson is a a hoticeberg.
        BlS
    The rhetoric of Langston
        Hughes. BlS
Dante Alighieri
    Canto I, sels. DoNG
    Canto XXII, sels. DoNG
    Divine comedy, sels. WBP2
    The divine comedy, sels. WBP4
    Divine comedy, sels. WBP4
    My lady. WBP2
    Paradiso, sels. DoNG
Dante Alighieri (about)
    At Dante's grave. Ezra Zussman.
        VoWA
    If justice moved. Bettie M.
        Sellers. TyW
Danube (river)
    After an eclipse of the sun.
        Eugene Heimler. VoWA
Darby and Joan. Frederic Edward
    Wetherley. WBP2
Dario, Ruben
    The three kings. PoCh
    To Roosevelt, sels. NiR
The **dark**. Roy Fuller. DuD
The **dark** birds. Bert Meyers.
    VoWA
A **dark** hand. Itzik Manger. VoWA
The **dark** hills. Edwin Arlington
    Robinson. HaAP
Dark phrases. Ntozake Shange.
    BlS
The **dark** scent of prayer. Rose
    Drachler. VoWA
Dark sea. Maruyama Kaoru. FroC
Dark testament. Pauli Murray.

BlS
Dark thoughts are my companions.
    James Vincent Cunningham. TyW
Dark train. Jane Dulin. YoVA
The **darkling** thrush. Thomas
    Hardy. EvIm--HaAP
Darkness. Donna Skorczewski.
    YoVA
Darkness. Bartolo Cattafi. NeIP
Darkness. Heather Wiegand. YoVA
Darkness. John Goldhardt. YoVA
Darkness
    In this deep darkness. Natan
        Zach. VoWA
Darkness is thinning. Saint
    Gregory the Great. WBP4
Darkness is thinning. John Mason
    Neale (trans.). WBP4
Darkness/It drowns within
    itself. Karen Elizabeth
    Patterson. YoVA
Darley, George
    The gambols of children. WBP1
    The loveliness of love. WBP2
Darling, Marian J.
    Cartouche: the sign of the
        king. StPo
    Flowers on stone. StPo
Darr, Bryan
    Balloons. YoVA
Daufuskie. Mari Evans. BlS
Daufuskie: Jake. Mari Evans. BlS
The **daughters** of horseleech.
    Stanley Kunitz. TyW
Daughton, Gwen
    Wind poems. HoWM
Davenant, Sir William
    Daybreak. WBP2
    Wake all the dead! HaAP
Davening. Rochelle Ratner. VoWA
David. Patrick Crosson. YoVA
David
    Like David. Gabriel Preil. VoWA
    Translating. Ruth Whitman. VoWA
David, Megan A.
    The tower. YoVA
    Untitled. YoVA
Davidson (see Hoddis), Hans

Davidson, John
    A runnable stag. HaAP
Davies, W.H.
    One poet visits another. TyW
Davis II, Donald D.
    Destination Colorado. YoVA
Davis, Angela
    Angela Davis. Alice S. Cobb.
        BlS
Davis, Blind Gary
    Blow Gabriel. DoNG

De sheepfol'. Sarah Pratt M'Lean
    Greene. WBP4
DeFrees, Madeline
    First-class relics: letter to
    D. Finnell. TeMP
Deacon Morgan. Naomi Long
    Madgett. BlS
The **dead**. Mathilde Blind. WBP3
Dead. William Carlos Williams.
    DoNG
The **dead**. Jones Very. HaAP
The **Dead** Sea. Henryk Grynberg.
    VoWA
The **dead** bride. Geoffrey Hill.
    TyW
The **dead** by the side of the
    road. Gary Snyder. HaAP
The **dead** cities speak...living
    cities. Edmond Fleg. VoWA
Dead city. Louis Le Cardonnel.
    FreS
The **dead** doll. Margaret
    Vandergrift. WBP1
The **dead** friend. Alfred, Lord
    Tennyson. WBP1
Dead girl. Anna Hajnal. VoWA
A **dead** man is thirsty. Hector de
    Saint-Denys-Garneau. MoVT
Dead man's dump. Isaac
    Rosenberg. VoWA
The **dead** poet-friend. William
    Johnson Cory (trans.). WBP1
The **dead** poet-friend.
    Callimachus. WBP1
Dead, they'll burn you up....
    Marcus Argentarios. DoNG
Dear country cousin. E.G.
    Burrows. HoA
The **dear** ladies of Cincinnati.
    Anne Stevenson. HoA
A **death**. Kevin Hansen. YoVA
Death. Laura Fauth. YoVA
Death. Carolyn Nall. YoVA
Death. Diedre Reusser. YoVA
Death
    Adam's death. Gabriel Levin.
        VoWA
    Adieu, farewell earth's bliss.
        Thomas Nashe. HaAP
    Aella: a tragical interlude,
        sels. Thomas Chatterton.
        HaAP--WBP2
    After a time. Catherine Davis.
        LiHE
    After her death. Anne
        Stevenson. HoA
    After summer. Philip Bourke
        Marston. WBP3
    After. Philip Levine. VoWA
    Among so many concerns, sels.

Tadeusz Rozewicz. CoP
Ample make this bed. Emily
    Dickinson. DoNG
Ancient murderess night. Anna
    Margolin (R. Lebensboim).
    VoWA
Ancient of days. Anthony
    Rudolf. VoWA
Ancient stirring, sel. Ch'ang
    Chien . GrAC
And death shall have no
    dominion. Dylan Thomas. DoNG
Anne Rutledge. Edgar Lee
    Masters. DoNG--HaAP
Antony and Cleopatra. William
    Haines Lytle. WBP3
Apart from oneself. Alejandra
    Pizarnik. VoWA
Asleep, asleep. Lucy A.
    Bennett. WBP3
Aspatia's song. Francis
    Beaumont. HaAP
The atmosphere of death. Jenny
    Schroeder. YoVA
Because I could not stop for
    death. Emily Dickinson.
    DoNG--SlW
Because I could not stop for
    death. Emily Dickinson.
    EeBC--HaAP
Before the anaesthetic. Sir
    John Betjeman. EeBC
Beginning to end. Mike Evans.
    YoVA
Bells for John Whiteside's
    daughter. John Crowe Ransom.
    HaAP--LiHE
Between life and death.
    Frantisek Gottlieb. VoWA
Beyond the smiling and the
    weeping. Horatius Bonar. WBP3
Black thread. Bartolo Cattafi.
    NeIP
Blind. Israel Zangwill. WBP3
Blue stones. Larry Lewis. TeMP
The book of revelation, sel.
    Bible-New Testament . DoNG
The boomerang. Adriano Spatola.
    NeIP
The bottom drawer. Amelia Edith
    Barr. WBP3
The braes were bonny. John
    Logan. WBP3
Break, break, break. Alfred,
    Lord Tennyson. WBP3
The bustle in a house. Emily
    Dickinson. HaAP
Call from the afterworld. Jozef
    Habib Gerez. VoWA
Candle. Jacob Isaac Segal. VoWA

From here to there. Rachel
    Korn. VoWA
Grandma, may she rest in peace,
    died. Moishe Kulbak. OnCP
Grandmother/before i learned to
    crawl. Joseph L. Concha. ReE
Grief for the dea. Unknown .
    WBP3
The groundhog. Richard
    Eberhart. DoNG
Habeas corpus. Helen Hunt
    Jackson. WBP3
Hamlet, sels. William
    Shakespeare. DoNG
Hamlet, sels. William
    Shakespeare. WBP3
Happy are the dead. Henry
    Vaughan. WBP3
Hark, now everything is still.
    John Webster. HaAP
Here lies a lady. John Crowe
    Ransom. HaAP
Highland Mary. Robert Burns.
    WBP3
Holy sonnets, sels. John Donne.
    DoNG
The hour of death. Felicia
    Dorothea Hemans. WBP3
The hour. Uri Zvi Greenberg.
    VoWA
The house of life, sels. Dante
    Gabriel Rossetti. HaAP
How the waters closed above
    him. Emily Dickinson. LiHE
Humbly I confess that I am
    mortal. Elio Pagliarani. NeIP
Hush! Julia C. R. Dorr. WBP3
I died for beauty. Emily
    Dickinson. DoNG
I felt a funeral in my brain.
    Emily Dickinson. DoNG--LiHE
I followed a path. Patricia
    Parker. BlS
I hear a voice. H. Leivick
    (Leivick Halpern). VoWA
I heard a fly buzz when I died.
    Emily Dickinson. DoNG--SlW
I see a primeval light in the
    darkness. Andrew Liano. YoVA
I thought about you. Ronald C.
    Rowe. YoVA
I want to die while you love
    me. Georgia Douglas Johnson.
    BlS
I wende to ded. Unknown . HaAP
I would not live alway. William
    Augustus Muhlenberg. WBP3
If I should die tonight. Belle
    E. Smith. WBP3
If we must die. Claude McKay.

LiHE
The iliad, sel. Homer . DoNG
The imag. Tamura Ryuichi . FroC
Immediately following. Dawn
    March. YoVA
In harbor. Paul Hamilton Hayne.
    WBP3
In memoriam F.A.S.. Robert
    Louis Stevenson. WBP3
Inheritance. Frank O'Connor.
    TyW
Intensive care. Jay Johnston.
    YoVA
The invisible Carme. Zelda .
    BuAC
Isaac Leybush Peretz. Moishe
    Leib Halpern. VoWA
It was gentle. Chedva Harakavy.
    BuAC--VoWA
Jackie. Sherrie Booth. YoVA
Jeune fille et jeune fleur.
    Vis. Chateaubriand
    (F.Auguste). WBP3
Jim's kids. Eugene Fields. WBP3
John Knew-the-Crow, 1880.
    Marnie Walsh. ReE
Julius Caesar, sels. William
    Shakespeare. DoNG
Kaddish, sels. Allen Ginsberg.
    DoNG
The King of Denmark's ride.
    Caroline E. Sheridan Norton.
    WBP3
Kiowa song, sel. Unknown . ReE
The lady of the lake, sels. Sir
    Walter Scott. WBP3
Lament for Helodore. Meleager.
    WBP3
Lament for the makirs. William
    Dunbar. DoNG
Lament. Yonathan Ratosh. VoWA
The last farewell. Miyazawa
    Kenji. FroC
The last fire. Moishe
    Steingart. VoWA
The last night that she lived.
    Emily Dickinson. SlW
A latter purification. Haim
    Guri. VoWA
Lavender. Unknown. WBP3
Life-Death. Ronda Camerlinck.
    YoVA
Lines. Harriet Beecher Stowe.
    WBP3
Longing for his son, Furuchi.
    Yamanque no Okura. FroC
Love and death. Margaret Wade
    Deland. WBP3
Love song ("You had the
    legs...") Elio Pagliarani.

Prospice. Robert Browning.
  DoNG--WBP3
The psalms of David, sel.
  Bible-Old Testament . DoNG
Pshytik. Nahum Bomze. VoWA
The pulverized screen. Edmond
  Jabes. VoWA
The quick and the dead. Ilarie
  Voronca. VoWA
Rain. Haim Guri. VoWA
Raincoats for the dead. Albert
  Bellg. FroA
Rainy morning. Gail Greiner.
  YoVA
The reaper and the flowers.
  Henry Wadsworth Longfellow.
  WBP3
Reflections on the death of
  Scott Childs. Melody
  Prentiss. YoVA
A refusal the death, by fire,
  of a child. Dylan Thomas.
  DoNG
Requiescat. Matthew Arnold.
  WBP3
The resignation. Thomas
  Chatterton. WBP4
Rest. Jacob Isaac Segal. VoWA
Rest. Mary Woolsey Howland.
  WBP3
Resurrection of the dead. Aliza
  Shenhar. VoWA
Richard II, sels. William
  Shakespeare. DoNG
Sacco-Vanzetti. Moishe Leib
  Halpern. VoWA
Salvation. Aaron Zeitlin. OnCP
The secret of death. Sir Edwin
  Arnold. WBP3
Seeing a man lying dead..
  Kakinomoto no Hitomaro . FroC
She died in beauty. Charles
  Doyne Sillery. WBP3
The ship of death. David
  Herbert Lawrence. MTS
The shrouding of the Duchess of
  Malfi. John Webster. DoNG
Sic vita. Henry King. WBP3
Silence. Thomas Hood. DoNG
The sleep. Elizabeth Barrett
  Browning. WBP3
The sleeper of the valley.
  Arthur Rimbaud. FoFS
Softly woo away her breath.
  Barry Cornwall (B.W.
  Procter). WBP3
The soldier, sels. Zbigniew
  Herbert. CoP
The soldier. Rupert Brooke.
  DoNG

Someday I'll be dead. Leo
  Connellan. DoNG
A song for Simeon. Thomas
  Stearns Eliot. EeBC
The song of Hiawatha, sels.
  Henry Wadsworth Longfellow.
  WBP3
Song of a man...to die in a
  strange land. Mary Austin
  (trans.). ReE
Song of myself, sels. Walt
  Whitman. DoNG--SlW
Sonnet CXLVI. William
  Shakespeare. HaAP--WBP3
Sonnet LXVI. William
  Shakespeare. DonG--HaAP
Sonnet LXXI. William
  Shakespeare. DonG--HaAP
Sonnet LXXIII. William
  Shakespeare. HaAP--LiHE
Sonnets, sels. Frederick
  Goddard Tuckerman. HaAP
Streetcorner. Bill Knott. TeMP
Subjects and arguments
  for...desperation. Elio
  Pagliarani. NeIP
Sunken temple Tamura Ryuichi.
  FroC
Tabula rasa? Luciano Erba.
  NeIP
Tell us/what things die.
  William Packard. DoNG
The tempest, sels. William
  Shakespeare. DoNG
The term of death. Sarah Morgan
  Bryan Piatt. WBP3
Terminus. Ralph Waldo Emerson.
  DoNG
Thalatta! Thalatta! Joseph
  Brownlee Brown. WBP3
Thanatopsis. William Cullen
  Bryant. WBP3
There is no place. Aleksander
  Wat. VoWA
There's a certain slant of
  light. Emily Dickinson. HaAP
They are all gone. Henry
  Vaughan. DoNG--WBP3
Those betrayed at dawn.
  Stanislaw Wygodski. VoWA
Thou art gone to the grave.
  Reginald Heber. WBP3
Three tiny songs. Cid Corman.
  HoA
To Mary in heaven. Robert
  Burns. WBP3
To a gentleman and lady on the
  death... Phillis Wheatley.
  BlS
To death. Gluck (German poet).

Holden. FroA

December's eve, abroad. Anne
    Radcliffe. EvIm

December's eve, at home. Anne
    Radcliffe. EvIm

Deception. Nannie Eisenhardt.
    YoVA

Decker, Barbara
    Fairgrounds. YoVA

Decker, Mark
    Jazz music. HoWM

Decorations. Nishiwaki
    Junzaburo. FroC

A deed and a word. Charles
    Mackay. WBP4

Deep in the mountain. Unknown.
    FroC

The deer. Asya. VoWA

Deer
    The dee. Asya . VoWA
    Old miniatures. Leo Vroman.
        VoWA
    Tanka ("The stag that
        calls..."). Emperor Jomei
        (593-641). FroC
    A young deer/dust. Hemda Roth.
        BuAC--VoWA

Deer enclosure. Wang Wei. GrAC

Deer forest hermitage. Wang Wei.
    LuL

Deer hunting. Geary Hobson. ReE

The defeated. Linda Gregg. TeMP

Dekker, Thomas
    Art thou poor...? HaAP

del Monte, Crescenzo
    One thing to take, another to
        keep. VoWA
    A Roman Roman. VoWA
    Those Zionists. VoWA

Deland, Margaret Wade
    Affaire d'amour. WBP2
    Love and death. WBP3

Delicate the toad. Robert
    Francis. DuD

The delicate, plummeting bodies.
    Stephen Dobyns. TeMP

Delight in God. Francis Quarles.
    WBP4

Delight in disorder. Robert
    Herrick. HaAP

Delighted that Jippo has come...
    Rai San'yo. FroC

Demarest, Mary Lee
    My ain countree. WBP4

The demon lover. Unknown. HaAP

Denlinger, Steve
    Life dwells in the shadows.
        YoVA
    Portrait of a man. YoVA

Denniston, Helen

Anger of Cupid. YoVA

It. YoVA

Dentists
    The fantasy of imagination
        at..dentist's. Ginger Sandy.
        HoWM

Departmental. Robert Frost. LiHE

The departure. Jeremy Robson.
    VoWA

Deportation order. Franco
    Fortini. NeIP

Deppe, Errol
    God and man. YoVA

Depression. Pam Greenfield. YoVA

Depression. Joanne Louise
    Sullivan. YoVA

Depression before spring.
    Wallace Stevens. SlW

Derzhavin, Gavril Romanovich
    God. WBP4

The descent. William Carlos
    Williams. HaAP

Descent to Bohannon Lake. Jim
    Barnes. FroA

Description of virtue. Theodore
    de Beze. ReLP

A description of the morning.
    Jonathan Swift. HaAP

Desert. Agnes Gergely. VoWA

Desert march. Gerda Stein
    Norvig. VoWA

Desert song. Leslie Blackhurst.
    YoVA

Desert stone. Miriam Waddington.
    VoWA

Deserted cabin. John Haines.
    TeMP

Deserted shrine. Avner Treinin.
    VoWA

Desertion
    The light is my deligh. Zelda .
        BuAC

Deserts
    Afar in the desert. Thomas
        Pringle. WBP3
    Aji. Gary Bolick. YoVA
    Desert song. Leslie Blackhurst.
        YoVA
    Horizon without landscape. Tom
        Lowenstein. VoWA
    The quiet light of flies. Natan
        Zach. VoWA
    Treason of sand. Hemda Roth.
        VoWA

Design. Robert Frost. LiHE

Desire. Matthew Arnold. WBP4

Desire. Isaac de Botton. VoWA

Desnos reading the palms of
    men... Stephen Berg. VoWA

Desnos, Robert

I've dreamed of you so much.
  MoVT
There was a leaf. MoVT
Desnos, Robert (about)
  Desnos reading the palms of
    men... Stephen Berg. VoWA
Despair
  Bitter bread. Osip Mandelstam.
    VoWA
  Callous destruction. C. Edward
    Rogers. YoVA
  Depression. Joanne Louise
    Sullivan. YoVA
  Depression. Pam Greenfield.
    YoVA
  Fingers of war. Robin
    Brumbaugh. YoVA
  From good to bad. Robin Yard.
    YoVA
  Inquietude. Pauli Murray. BlS
  The leaden echo and the golden
    echo. Gerard Manley Hopkins.
    SlW
  The love song of J. Alfred
    Prufrock. Thomas Stearns
    Eliot. HaAP--SlW
  Muffled echoes brace my tomb.
    Barry T. Siford. YoVA
  Ode to a nightingale. John
    Keats. HaAP--LiHE
  On the west tower in Kuo-cho.
    Ts'en Shen . GrAC
  Rejection. Robyn Fischer. YoVA
  Self portrait. Terri Mayo. YoVA
  She was a half-turning whisper.
    Barry T. Siford. YoVA
  Stanzas written in dejection
    near Naples. Percy Bysshe
    Shelley. WBP3
  A taste of the blues. Judite E.
    Reis. YoVA
  Tears. Tina Smith. YoVA
  Worries. Beth Kroger. YoVA
Despondency rebuked. Arthur Hugh
  Clough. WBP3
Destination Colorado. Donald D.
  Davis II. YoVA
Destiny. Mona Cloys. YoVA
Destiny
  A ballad ("The night was
    clear"). Kelli McFarland.
    YoVA
  The careless gallant. Thomas
    Jordan. HaAP
  Changes. Sheila Stauffer. YoVA
  Destiny. Mona Cloys. YoVA
  The glories of our blood and
    state. James Shirley. HaAP
  Hap. Thomas Hardy. LiHE
  Invictus. William Ernest

Henley. WBP3
  Minus one. John Ciardi. HoA
  Night fades--the sun rises.
    Janice Sears. YoVA
  Race of doom. Angie Britt. YoVA
Destiny of the poet. Claude
  Vigee. VoWA
The **destroyed** whisper. Brenda L.
  Rittenhouse. YoVA
The **destruction** of Sennacherib.
  George Gordon,6th Baron
  Byron. HaAP
The **destruction** of Jerusalem...
  Isaac Rosenberg. VoWA
Detail from hell. Esther Fuller.
  YoVA
Devonshire, England
  Discontents in Devon, sels.
    Robert Herrick. TyW
Devotion. Philip Massinger. WBP4
Dew. Charles Reznikoff. VoWA
Dew
  A compendium of good tank.
    Furiwara no Teika . FroC
  Dew drops/Glide on threads of
    grass. Mindy McKitrick. YoVA
  Nature's gem. Geeta Pasi. YoVA
  On a drop of dew. Andrew
    Marvell. HaAP
  To Lady Ishikawa. Prince Otsu
    (663-686). FroC
Dew drops/Glide on threads of
  grass. Mindy McKitrick. YoVA
"Dew on it". Ryokan. FroC
Dewdrops of life. JoCarol Lacy.
  YoVA
Dewey, Colleen
  Life as a star. YoVA
Dewey, Joe
  Sports. YoVA
DiFilippo, Amy
  Sentiments. YoVA
diPasquale, Emanuel
  Incantation to...rid a sometime
    friend. TyW
Diagram. James F. King. StPo
A **dialogue** between body and
  soul. Andrew Marvell. HaAP
A **dialogue** betweene two
  shepheards, sels. Mary S.,
  Countess of Pembroke. PaW
Dialogue in a dream. Ryokan.
  FroC
Dialogue in the mountains. Li
  Po. GrAC
A **dialogue** on poverty. Yamanque
  no Okura. FroC
Dialogue with Herz. Antonio
  Porta. NeIP
Dialogue with the dead. Amelia

Rosselli. NeIP
Diamond. Jean Newton. HoWM
Diamond poem. Greg Poissant.
    YovA
Diamonds
    Diamond. Jean Newton. HoWM
Diana (goddess)
    Hymn to Diana. Ben Jonson. HaAP
Diarrhea. Yoshioka Minoru. FroC
Diaspora Jews. Rachel Boimwall.
    VoWA
Dibben, Dennis
    Some modern good turns. FroA
Dick, a maggot. Jonathan Swift.
    TyW
Dickey, James
    Cherrylog Road. HaAP
    Pursuit from under. HaAP
Dickey, Martha
    Studies from life. FroA
Dickey, William
    Face-Paintings of the Caduveo
        Indians. FroA
Dickinson, Charles M.
    The children. WBP1
Dickinson, Emily
    After great pain, a formal
        feeling comes. HaAP--LiHE
    Ample make this bed. DoNG
    Apparently with no surprise.
        LiHE
    Because I could not stop for
        death. DoNG--SlW
    Because I could not stop for
        death. EeBC--HaAP
    Bee! I'm expecting you. SlW
    The bustle in a house. HaAP
    The crickets sang. SlW
    Found wanting. WBP4
    Heaven. WBP4
    How many times these low feet
        staggered. HaAP
    How the waters closed above
        him. LiHE
    I died for beauty. DoNG
    I dreaded that first robin, so.
        HaAP
    I felt a funeral in my brain.
        DoNG--LiHE
    I heard a fly buzz when I died.
        DoNG--SlW
    I heard a fly buzz when I died.
        HaAP--LiHE
    I never saw a moor. EeBC
    I started early-I took my dog.
        HaAP--MTS
    I'm nobody! Who are you?   LiHE
    It dropped so slow-in my
        regard. HaAP
    The last night that she lived.

SlW
    Mine enemy is growing old.
        LiHE--TyW
    Much madness is divinest sense.
        LiHE
    My life closed twice before its
        close. DoNG
    My life had stood-a loaded gun.
        HaAP
    A narrow fellow in the grass.
        HaAP
    She dealt her pretty words like
        blades. HaAP
    There's a certain slant of
        light. HaAP
    We like March. SlW
    Went up a year this evening!
        HaAP
    What soft-cherubic creatures.
        HaAP--LiHE
    The wind begun to knead the
        grass. HaAP
    The wind took up the northern
        things. SlW
Dickinson, Emily (about)
    Letters for the New England
        dead. Mary Baron. HoA
Dickinson, Mary Lowe
    If we had but a day. WBP4
Dickson, Jerlene
    Do you see God. YoVA
    If. YoVA
The **dictator**. Courtney Strang.
    YoVA
Dictators. See Tyrants
The **dictionary**. Andrea Long.
    YoVA
Did they help me at the state
    hospital... Mbembe Milton
    Smith. FroA
Dies Irae. Thomas of Celano.
    WBP4
Dies Irae. General John A. Dix
    (trans.). WBP4
Dietzen, David
    A souvenir from childhood. YoVA
A **difference**. Tom Clark. HoA
Different minds. Richard
    Chenevix Trench. WBP4
The **difficulty** of being. Roland
    Giguere. MoVT
Dime call. Albert Goldbarth.
    VoWA
Dinna ask me. John Dunlop. WBP2
Dirce. Walter Savage Landor.
    HaAP
Directions from Zulu. Daniel
    Halpern. FroA
Directive. Robert Frost. HaAP
Dirge. Madeline Mason. StPo

Dirge without music. Edna St.
    Vincent Millay. DoNG
The **dirty** old man. William
    Allingham. WBP3
The **disabled** debauchee. John
    Wilmot, Earl Rochester. HaAP
The **disciples** after the
    Ascension. Arthur Penrhyn
    Stanley. WBP4
Discipline
    What someone said when he was
    spanked.... John Ciardi. RoRF
Discontents in Devon, sels.
    Robert Herrick. TyW
Disdain returned. Thomas Carew.
    WBP2
Disguises
    Aka. Frederick Eckman. FroA
Disillusionment at ten o'clock.
    Wallace Stevens. SlW
Dislike of nature. Ono Tozaburo.
    FroC
The **dismantled** ship. Walt
    Whitman. MTS
Dison, Jennifer Leigh
    Spruce Pine Mountain. YoVA
Disorder
    Delight in disorder. Robert
    Herrick. HaAP
Disparagement
    To detraction I present my
    poesie. John Marston. TyW
    Words as sharp as daggers.
    Susan A. Klee. YoVA
Distance spills itself. Yocheved
    Bat-Miriam. VoWA
Distant hills. Mei Yao-chen. LuL
"**Distant** men have no eyes..."
    Wang Wei. LuL
The **ditchdigger's** tears, sels.
    Pier Paolo Pasolini. NeIP
The **diver**. Robert Hayden. MTS
Divided. Jean Ingelow. WBP3
Divina commedia, I, sels. Henry
    Wadsworth Longfellow. HaAP
Divination. Jerred Metz. VoWA
Divine comedy, sels. Dante
    Alighieri. WBP2
Divine comedy, sels (trans.).
    George Gordon,6th Baron
    Byron. WBP2
The **divine** comedy, sels. Dante
    Alighieri. WBP4
The **divine** comedy, sels. Henry
    Francis Cary (trans.). WBP4
Divine comedy, sels. Dante
    Alighieri. WBP4
The **divine** image. William Blake.
    EeBC
Divine love. Bernhard van

Bauhuysen. ReLP
Diving into the wreck. Adrienne
    Rich. MTS
Divorce
    The broken home. James Merrill.
    HaAP
Dix (trans.), General John A.
    Dies Irae. WBP4
"**Do** never think it straunge".
    Lady Jane (Grey) Dudler. PaW
Do not accompany me. Shimon
    Halkin. VoWA
Do not go gentle into that good
    night. Dylan Thomas.
    LiHE--TyW
Do not go gentle into that good
    night. Dylan Thomas.
    DoNG--HaAP
Do you see God. Jerlene Dickson.
    YoVA
Dobell, Sydney
    Home, wounded. WBP3
    The milkmaid's song. WBP2
Dobson, Austin
    A gage d'amour. WBP2
    The sun-dial. WBP3
Dobyns, Stephen
    The delicate, plummeting
    bodies. TeMP
Dobzynski, Charles
    The fable merchant. VoWA
    Memory air. VoWA
    The never again. VoWA
    Zealot without a face. VoWA
The **dock**. Ivan Uriarte. NiR
Docker. Seamus Heaney. TyW
Doctor's row. Conrad Aiken. HaAP
Document. Tuvia Ruebner. VoWA
Document d'osieaux: document of
    birds. Takiguchi Shuzo. FroC
Dodd, Lee Wilson
    Valentine. Ernest Hemingway.
    TyW
Doddridge, Philip
    Amazing, beauteous change!
    WBP4
Dodge, Mary Mapes
    Little Miss Limberkin. MiRN
    Oh, no! IlTH
    The two mysteries. WBP3
Dodgson (see Lewis Carroll),C.

Dodson, Kate
    Country girl. YoVA
    Lambs. YoVA
    When Mama plucks the chickens.
    YoVA
"**Does** every Pride of evening
    smoke". Stephane Mallarme.
    FoFS--FreS

"Does he love me?"   Terri B.
    Johnson. YoVA
Dogs
    Age. Tomioka Taeko . FroC
    The ambiguous dog. Arthur
        Guiterman. IlTH
    Bobby. Kevin Hansen. YoVA
    Cerberus. H.L. Van Brunt. FroA
    Common sight. Donna
        Skorczewski. YoVA
    Gone. David McCord. ByM
    In the garden of the Turkish
        Consulate. Pinhas Sadeh. VoWA
    Landscape: . Ono Tozaburo .
        FroC
    Let dogs delight to bark and
        bite. Isaac Watts. WBP1
    The lonely puppy. Howard Folmer
        III. YoVA
    A loyal image. Darlene Gates.
        YoVA
    Migration. Sandie Nelson. ReE
    My dog Jack. Hayden Carruth.
        FroA
    My puppy. Aileen Fisher. RoRF
    The pardon. Richard Wilbur.
        LiHE
    The tale of the mice. Lewis
        Carroll (C.L. Dodgson). MiRN
    Timon speaks to a dog. Philip
        Hobsbaum. TyW
    Un chien Andalou. Henry F.
        Beechhold. StPo
Dolben, Digby Mackworth
    I asked for peace. EeBC
Dolcino to Margaret. Charles
    Kingsley. WBP2
Dole (trans.), Nathan Haskell
    The princess. WBP3
The dolefull lay of Clorinda,
    sels. Mary S., Countess of
    Pembroke. PaW
Doll's boy's asleep. Edward
    Estlin Cummings. DuD
Dollie. Samuel Minturn Peck.
    WBP1
Dolliver, Clara G.
    No baby in the house. WBP1
Dolls
    China doll eyes. Andrea Long.
        YoVA
    The dead doll. Margaret
        Vandergrift. WBP1
    Holy girl. Yoshioka Minoru
        FroC
    Notes to Joanne, LXI. John F.
        Kerr. ReE
Dolor. Theodore Roethke. LiHE
Dome cave preview. Joel Newton.
    HoWM

Domestics. Kattie M. Cumbo. BlS
Domett, Alfred
    A Christmas hymn. WBP4
Domin, Hilde
    Catalogue. VoWA
    Cologne. VoWA
    Dreamwater. VoWA
Don Juan, sels. George
    Gordon,6th Baron Byron. MTS
Don Juan, sels. George
    Gordon,6th Baron Byron.
    HaAP--TyW
Don't cry; don't go. Kelli
    McFarland. YoVA
"Don't cut the bamboo grass..."
    Unknown. FroC
"Don't cut the shrub on Idemi
    Beach". Unknown. FroC
Don't let it end. Stacey
    Ashford. YoVA
Don't let me down, comrade.
    Carlos Mejia Godoy. NiR
Don't say. Moshe Yungman. VoWA
Don't show me. Ruth Beker. VoWA
Donahey, LeAnnette
    The conspiracy. YoVA
    The last mistake. YoVA
Donaldson, Lexie
    Circus connection. YoVA
"Done begging..."   Ryokan. FroC
Done ia a battell on the dragon
    blak. William Dunbar. HaAP
Doneraile, Ireland
    The curse of Doneraile, sels.
        Patrick O'Kelly. TyW
The donkey. Gilbert Keith
    Chesterton. EeBC
A donkey will carry you. Jakov
    Steinberg. VoWA
Donkeys
    The donkey. Gilbert Keith
        Chesterton. EeBC
    The little donkey. Francis
        Jammes. PoCh
    The prayer of the donkey.
        Carmen Bernos de Gasztold.
        PoCh
Donne, John
    The anatomie of the world,
        sels. ShBa
    The anniversary. HaAP
    The calme. MTS
    The canonization. HaAP
    The curse. TyW
    Death, be not proud. HaAP--LiHE
    The ecstasy. HaAP
    The fever, sels. TyW
    "Go, and catch a falling star."
        HaAP
    Holy sonnets, sels. DoNG

Holy sonnets, sels. HaAP
A hymn to God the father.
   EeBC--HaAP
La corona, sels. ShBa
On death. EeBC
The relic. HaAP
The storme. MTS
The sun rising. HaAP
"Teach me how to repent." EeBC
A valediction: forbidding
   mourning. HaAP--LiHE
A valediction: of weeping. HaAP
Donnelly, Dorothy
   Consider the lilies. HoA
   A prospect of swans. HoA
   Three-toed sloth. HoA
   Wheels. HoA
Doolittle (H.D.), Hilda
   Helen. TyW
   Sea gods, sels. MTS
The doomed city. E.L. Mayo. FroA
A door slams. Scott Morgan. YoVA
Dor, Moshe
   Among the pine trees. VoWA
   The dwelling. VoWA
   Nightingales are not singing.
      VoWA
   Small bone ache. VoWA
Dora Williams. Edgar Lee
   Masters. HaAP
Dorat, Jean
   Paean our chant triumphal...
      ReLP
   A woman's nature. ReLP
Doris Maria, comrade. Ricardo
   Morales Aviles. NiR
Doris: a pastoral. Arthur Joseph
   Munby. WBP2
Dormouse. Stacey MacDougall.
   YoVA
Dorothy in the garret. John
   Townsend Trowbridge. WBP3
Dorr, Julia C. R.
   Hush! WBP3
Dorset (see Sackville,C.),Earl

Doty, Allison
   Important. HoWM
A double standard. Frances E.W.
   Harper. BlS
Double take at Relais de
   l'Espadon. Thadious M. Davis.
   BlS
Double-barrelled ding-dong-bat.
   Dennis Lee. BrBD
Doubly employed. Giancarlo
   Majorino. NeIP
The doubt of future foes.
   Elizabeth I; Queen of
   England. PaW

A doubting heart. Adelaide Anne
   Procter. WBP3
Douglas(A.D.G.Robinson),Marian
   Two pictures. WBP1
Douglas, Elizabeth (E.D.)
   E.D. in prise of Mr. William
      Foular. PaW
Douglas, Rebecca
   Separation. YoVA
   Thoughts of winter. YoVA
Douglass, Frederick
   Frederick Douglass. Robert
      Hayden. HoA
Dove. Norma Farber. PoCh
The dove. Heidi Grable. HoWM
Dover Beach. Matthew Arnold.
   LiHE--MTS
The Dover bitch. Anthony Hecht.
   LiHE
Doves. Joachim Neugroschel. VoWA
Doves
   Again my fond circle of doves.
      Baxter Hathaway. HoA
   The dove. Heidi Grable. HoWM
   Dove. Norma Farber. PoCh
   Feather dreams. Melissa Heiple.
      YoVA
   Pentecost. John Bennett. EeBC
Down dip the branches. Mark Van
   Doren. DuD
Downing, Mary
   Were I but his own wife. WBP2
Dowson, Ernest
   Non sum qualis eram bonae
      sub...Cynarae. HaAP
   Vitae summa brevis spem nos
      vetat... HaAP
Drachler, Rose
   As I am my father's. VoWA
   The dark scent of prayer. VoWA
   Isaac and Esau. VoWA
   The letters of the book. VoWA
   Under the shawl. VoWA
   Zippora returns to Moses at
      Rephidim. VoWA
Dracula
   The kiss. Robert Pack. TeMP
Draft of a reparations
   agreement. Don Pagis. VoWA
A drag race. Dale Mayfield. YoVA
Dragons
   Done ia a battell on the dragon
      blak. William Dunbar. HaAP
   A Mei-p'i lake son. Tu Fu .
      GrAC
   Thousand league poo. Tu Fu .
      GrAC
Drake, Leah Bodine
   Mouse heaven. MiRN
Drassel (N. Lessard), Nicole

The beacon. MoVT
Drawing. Roy Fuller. MiRN
Drawing of a woman. Shlomit
     Cohen. BuAC
Drayton, Michael
     Come, let us kisse and parte.
          WBP3
     Idea, sels. HaAP--LiHE
     Like an adventurous sea-farer
          am I. MTS
     Poly-olbion, sels. ShBa
     Since there's no help, come let
          us kiss. HaAP--LiHE
     To the Virginian voyage. HaAP
Dream. David Ignatow. VoWA
Dream. John Rutter. YoVA
A **dream.** Robin Yard. YoVA
Dream. Carol Coyle. YoVA
Dream. Danielle T. Reinke. YoVA
The **dream.** George Gordon,6th
          Baron Byron. WBP3
Dream. Joseph Eliya. VoWA
A **dream** about an aged humorist.
          Aaron Zeitlin. VoWA
Dream girl. Karen Snow. HoA
Dream of Barcelona: my ancient
          world. Takahashi Mutsuo. FroC
The **dream** of a lake. Kim Parker.
          HoWM
The **dream** of a rose. Terri
          Painter. HoWM
Dream on. Roseann Penner. YoVA
Dream seeker. King Kuka. ReE
The **dream** songs, sels. John
          Berryman. HaAP
Dream variations. Langston
          Hughes. HaAP
Dream-love. Christina Georgina
          Rossetti. HaAP
Dream-pedlary. Thomas Lovell
          Beddoes. HaAP
A **dream?.** Carolyn Heide. YoVA
The **dreame,** sels. Rachel Speght.
          PaW
Dreaming. Sondra Moss. YoVA
Dreaming. Nancy Willard. BrBD
Dreaming of Amaro. Sugawara no
          Michizane. FroC
Dreams. Nikki Giovanni. LiHE
Dreams
     Adolescence. Dennis Schmitz.
          FroA
     Anecdote of the prince of
          peacocks. Wallace Stevens.
          SlW
     At dawn. Patrick Michael Hearn.
          BrBD
     An autumn morning in
          Shokoku-ji. Gary Snyder. HaAP
     Benedicte, what dreamed I this

night. Unknown . HaAP
A black ros. Zelda . BuAC
A cantor's dream before...High
     Holy Days. Martin Robbins.
     VoWA
The child who cried. Felice
     Holman. ByM
Creation of the child. Susan
     Litwack. VoWA
The destroyed whisper. Brenda
     L. Rittenhouse. YoVA
Dialogue in a drea. Ryokan .
     FroC
A dream about an aged humorist.
     Aaron Zeitlin. VoWA
The dream of a rose. Terri
     Painter. HoWM
Dream on. Roseann Penner. YoVA
Dream-pedlary. Thomas Lovell
     Beddoes. HaAP
Dream. Danielle T. Reinke. YoVA
Dream. David Ignatow. VoWA
Dream. John Rutter. YoVA
A dream? Carolyn Heide. YoVA
Dreaming. Nancy Willard. BrBD
Dreaming. Sondra Moss. YoVA
Dreams: "Here we are, all, by
     day." Robert Herrick. HaAP
The Eve of St. Agnes. John
     Keats. HaAP--WBP3
Fantasy. Gwendolyn B. Bennett.
     BlS
A faun's afternoon. Stephane
     Mallarme. FoFS
For a memory. Tachihara Michizo.
     FroC
Friday, you look blue. Alfredo
     Giuliani. NeIP
Harlem. Langston Hughes. LiHE
He wishes for the clothes of
     heaven. William Butler Yeats.
     SlW
Hothouse soul. Maurice
     Maeterlinck. FreS
I am a drifter. Susan Mae
     Anderson. YoVA
"I blink my eye." Dee Dee
     Harris. HoWM
"I fell in paradise." Jerome
     Coleman. HoWM
I'm a dreamer. Kattie M. Cumbo.
     BlS
I've dreamed of you so much.
     Robert Desnos. MoVT
"In my hands are dreams." Greg
     Ellis. HoWM
"Innocence returned." Rokwaho
     (Daniel Thompson) . ReE
Journey beyond. Terra Manasco.
     YoVA

Tanka: 44 tank. Wakayama
   Bokusui . FroC
Tear. Arthur Rimbaud. FreS
Three poems for the Indian
   steelworkers. Joseph Bruchac.
   ReE
Vickie Loans-Arrow, 1971.
   Marnie Walsh. ReE
A voice from under the table.
   Richard Wilbur. HaAP
Wine cup in stone hollo. Yuan
   Chieh . GrAC
A winter wish. Robert Hinckley
   Messinger. WBP1
Wreathe the bowl. Thomas Moore.
   WBP1
Drinkwater, John
   Snail. RoRF
Driving the rafts. Moishe
   Kulbak. OnCP
Driving to the beach. Joanna
   Cole. ByM
Driving wheel. Sherley Anne
   Williams. BlS
Dropkin, Celia
   A circus dancer. VoWA
Dropping petals. Jean Lorrain
   (Paul Deval). FreS
The drops of life. Cindy Solis.
   YoVA
Drops of love. Marty Bogan. YoVA
The drowned. Stephen Spender.
   MTS
Drowning
   Alec Yeaton's son. Thomas
      Bailey Aldrich. MTS
   The drowned. Stephen Spender.
      MTS
   Epitaph ("One whom I knew, a
      student..") Alec Comfort.
      MTS
   Fish food. John Wheelwright.
      MTS
   Not waving but drowning.
      Florence M. ("Stevie") Smith.
      HaAP
   The three children. Unknown.
      WBP1
Druck, Kitty
   The loner. StPo
   A misunderstanding. StPo
   The perfect couple. StPo
   "Perfect rainbow arc." StPo
Drug Addiction
   Dormouse. Stacey MacDougall.
      YoVA
   Revelation. Carole C. Gregory.
      BlS
   Summer words for a sister
      addict. Sonia Sanchez. BlS

This world is too much with us.
   Marti Huerta. YoVA
You are mine. J.R. Collins.
   YoVA
Drummer Hodge. Thomas Hardy.
   HaAP
Drummer boy. William Stafford.
   FroA
Drummond, William
   Alexis, here she stayed. WBP2
Drummond, William (about)
   To William Drummond of
      Hawthornden. Mary Oxlie. PaW
Drums
   Tambour. Istvan Vas. VoWA
The drunken boat. Arthur
   Rimbaud. FoFS--FreS
The drunken stones of Prague.
   David Scheinert. VoWA
Drunken streets. Malka Locker.
   VoWA
The drunkenness of pain. Aliza
   Shenhar. VoWA
Dry root in a wash. Simon J.
   Ortiz. ReE
Dry salvages, sels. Thomas
   Stearns Eliot. ShBa
Dryden (trans.), John
   Veni creator spiritus. WBP4
Dryden, John
   Absalom and Achitopel, sels.
      HaAP
   Annus mirabilis, sels. MTS
   Farewell, ungrateful traitor.
      HaAP
   Mac Flecknoe, sels. HaAP
   Now stop your noses, reader....
      TyW
   The secular masque, sels.
      HaAP--ShBa
   A song for St. Cecilia's Day.
      HaAP
   To the memory of Mr. Oldham.
      HaAP
   Tyrannic love, sels. WBP2
Dschellaleddin. See J. Rumi

Du Bellay, Joachim
   Epitaph of a dog. ReLP
   Faustina...more suitably named
      Pandora. ReLP
Du Fu. See Tu Fu

Dubie, Norman
   The Pennacesse Leper Colony for
      Women... TeMP
Dubrovnik poem (Emilio
   Tolentino). Anthony Rudolf.
   VoWA
Duchesne, Venise

Dyer, Sir Edward
　　The lowest trees have tops.
　　　　HaAP
Dying. Alfred Alvarez. VoWA
The **dying** Christian to his soul.
　　　　Alexander Pope. WBP4
The **dying** gladiator. George
　　　　Gordon,6th Baron Byron. DoNG
The **dying** thief. Itzik Manger.
　　　　VoWA
Dying under a fall of stars.
　　　　Mark Elliott Shapiro. VoWA
Dykes, Rebecca G.
　　June. YoVA
Dynamo, sels. Julian Przybos.
　　　　CoP
The **dynasts,** sels. Thomas Hardy.
　　　　MTS

E.D. in prise of Mr. William
　　　　Foular. Elizabeth (E.D.)
　　　　Douglas. PaW
Eagle feather I. Phil George.
　　　　ReE
Eagle feather II. Phil George.
　　　　ReE
Eagle feather III. Phil George.
　　　　ReE
Eagle feather IV. Phil George.
　　　　ReE
Eagles
　　The dalliance of the eagles.
　　　　Walt Whitman. HaAP
　　The osprey suicides. Laurence
　　　　Lieberman. HoA
　　The story of a well-made
　　　　shield. N. Scott Momaday. ReE
wwohali. Carroll
　　　　Arnett/Gogisgi. ReE
The **earl** o' quarterdeck. George
　　　　MacDonald. WBP2
Early friendship. Aubrey Thomas
　　　　De Vere. WBP1
Early loses: a requiem. Alice
　　　　Walker. BlS
Early song. Carroll
　　　　Arnett/Gogisgi. ReE
Early spring. Kirsten Cushing.
　　　　YoVA
Early spring, writing my
　　　　feelings. Ch'ing-chiang. GrAC
Early supper. Barbara Howes. DuD
The **early** supper. Barbara Howes.
　　　　DuD
Ears
　　Ode on a plastic stapes. Chad
　　　　Walsh. HoA

Zara's ear-rings. John Gibson
　　　　Lockhart. WBP2
Earth. Mark Mitchell. YoVA
Earth
　　Assaulted earth VI. Jean
　　　　Orizet. MoVT
　　Assaulted earth III. Jean
　　　　Orizet. MoVT
　　The chestnut casts his
　　　　flambeaux, sels. Alfred
　　　　Edward Housman. TyW
　　Earth took of eart. Unknown .
　　　　HaAP
　　Earth, wind, & fire. Christine
　　　　Lynn Marshall. YoVA
　　End of the world. Jakov van
　　　　Hoddis (H.Davidson). VoWA
　　Genesis. Geoffrey Hill. HaAP
　　The geyser. Joseph Bruchac. ReE
　　Holy sonnets, sels. John Donne.
　　　　HaAP
　　It's a porcelain world. Lori
　　　　Seiler. YoVA
　　The malcontent, sels. John
　　　　Marston. TyW
　　Miriam Tazewell. John Crowe
　　　　Ransome. TyW
　　"My hands are cupped together."
　　　　Robert Cox. HoWM
　　off in the distance. Carol
　　　　Coyle. YoVA
　　On the world. Francis Quarles.
　　　　HaAP
　　Open earth. Clarisse Nicoidski.
　　　　VoWA
　　Our world. Teresa Evans. YoVA
　　Tanka ("To what shall I
　　　　compare..world?") Sami Mansei
　　　　FroC
　　Things of the earth. Sherry S.
　　　　Cox. YoVA
　　To the world. Andrea Zanzotto.
　　　　NeIP
　　The vanity of the world.
　　　　Francis Quarles. WBP3
　　We wait. Robert J. Conley. ReE
　　The world. Frederick William
　　　　Faber. WBP4
　　The world. Henry Vaughan. HaAP
　　The world. Sir Francis Bacon.
　　　　WBP3
The **earth** is a satellite of the
　　　　moon. Leonel Rugama. NiR
Earth took of earth. Unknown.
　　　　HaAP
Earth, wind, & fire. Christine
　　　　Lynn Marshall. YoVA
The **earthly** paradise, sels.
　　　　William Morris. PoCh
The **earthly** paradise, sels.

William Morris. WBP2
Earthquake. Kokan Shiren. FroC
Earthquakes
Earthquak. Kokan Shiren . FroC
Journey to New York, sels.
Ernesto Cardenal. NiR
Litany of the planes. Pablo
Antonio Cuadra. NiR
Nicaraguan riddle. Rogelio
Sinan. NiR
The older brother. Pablo
Antonio Cuadra. NiR
Oracle on Managua. Ernesto
Cardenal. NiR
Panchito rubble. Carlos Mejia
Godoy. NiR
Eason, Donald
If only they cared. YoVA
East Coker. Thomas Stearns
Eliot. HaAP
Easter
Christmas is really for the
children. Steve Turner. EeBC
Easter hymn. Henry Vaughan.
EeBC
Easter-wings. George Herbert.
HaAP
Lamentations. Louise Gluck.
TeMP
Light's glittering morn. John
Mason Neale. EeBC
Seven stanzas at Easter. John
Updike. EeBC
Two songs from a play. William
Butler Yeats. HaAP
Easter 1916. William Butler
Yeats. HaAP
Easter hymn. Henry Vaughan. EeBC
Easter-wings. George Herbert.
HaAP
Eastman, Charles Gamage
A picture. WBP1
Eastman, Elaine Goodale
Ashes of roses. WBP3
Easy does it. Henry Chapin. FroA
Easy to drift. Oliver Huckel.
WBP4
Eaton's boatyard. Philip Booth.
TeMP
Ebergart, Richard
Sea-ruck. MTS
Eberhart, Richard
The cancer cells. HaAP
The groundhog. DoNG
On a squirrel crossing the
road... LiHE
On shooting particles beyond
the world. TyW
Passage. FroA
To Alpha Dryden Eberhart...

TeMP
Echo from beyond. Joe S. Sando.
ReE
Echoes. Thomas Moore. WBP2
Eckman, Frederick
Aka. FroA
Lullaby ("What if, every
time...") FroA
Eclipse. Tomaz Salamun. VoWA
Eclogue IV. Andrea Zanzotto.
NeIP
Eclogue VII: Pollux. Giovanni
Spagnuoli (Mantuan). ReLP
Eclogue: Alcon. Baldassaro
Castliglione. ReLP
Ecologue II: Argus. Francesco
Petrarch. ReLP
Ecology
Al Capone in Alaska. Ishmael
Reed. TyW
The creature of today. Jamie
Howell. YoVA
Darkness. John Goldhardt. YoVA
Ironic rescue. Gina North. YoVA
Malediction. Barry Spacks. TyW
Oil. Linda Hogan. ReE
Pollution. Chris Patterson.
YoVA
Pollution. Susan Klopenstine.
YoVA
The ecstasy. John Donne. HaAP
Eczema. Donald Slavitt. TyW
Eczema
Eczema. Donald Slavitt. TyW
Eden. Lev Mak. VoWA
Eden revisited. Vassar Miller.
FroA
Eden's courtesy. Clive Staples
Lewis. EeBC
Eden, Garden of
Eden. Lev Mak. VoWA
The glory of the garden.
Rudyard Kipling. EeBC
The struggle with the angel.
Claude Vigee. VoWA
Edson, Russell
Pigeons. TeMP
Education
Against education. Charles
Churchill. TyW
Edward. Unknown. LiHE--TyW
Edward. Unknown. HaAP
Edwards, Amelia Blandford
Give me three grains of corn,
mother. WBP3
Edwards, Harry
How to change the U.S.A.. TyW
Edwards, Thomas
On the edition of Mr. Pope's
works.... TyW

Elegy: the poet
    mourns...Francis... Nicolas
    Bourbon. ReLP
The **elephant**. Unknown. IlTH
Elephants
    The elephant. Unknown . IlTH
    To the elephants. Nathan
        Alterman. VoWA
The **elevator** man adheres to
    form, sels. Margaret Danner.
    BlS
Elevators
    The ups and downs of the
        elevator car. Caroline D.
        Emerson. IlTH
Eleven. Archibald MacLeish. HaAP
Eleven tanka. Lady Ise. FroC
The **elf** and the dormouse. Oliver
    Herford. WBP1
Elf poem. Tracey Kenney. YoVA
Elifritz, Bonny
    Autumn. YoVA
Elijah
    Elijah in the house of the
        study. Mani Leib. OnCP
Elijah in the house of the
    study. Mani Leib. OnCP
Eliot (M.E.L. Cross), George
    O, may I join the choir
        invisible? WBP4
    Two lovers. WBP2
Eliot, Thomas Stearns
    Dry salvages, sels. ShBa
    East Coker. HaAP
    Gerontion. HaAP--ShBa
    Journey of the Magi. EeBC--PoCh
    Journey of the Magi. HaAP--ShBa
    Lines for an old man. TyW
    The love song of J. Alfred
        Prufrock. HaAP--SlW
    The love song of J. Alfred
        Prufrock. LiHE
    Marina. MTS
    Preludes. SlW
    The Rock, sels. EeBC
    A song for Simeon. EeBC
    Sweeney among the nightingales.
        HaAP
    The waste land. HaAP
Eliot, Thomas Stearns (about)
    To T.S. Eliot. Emanuel
        Litvinoff. VoWA
Elisha, Gavriela
    Where do these steps lead?
        BuAC
Eliya, Joseph
    Dream. VoWA
    Epilogue ("I too was a little
        child"). VoWA
    Rebecca. VoWA

    Slender maid. VoWA
    Your passing, fleet passing.
        VoWA
Elizabeth I, Qn of Eng (about)
    A chaine of pearle, sels. Diana
        Primrose. PaW
    Sonnet to Elizabet. Mary Queen
        of Scots . PaW
Elizabeth I; Queen of England
    The doubt of future foes. PaW
    On monsieur's departure. PaW
    When I was young and fair. PaW
    Written on a wall at Woodstock.
        PaW
Elizabeth, Queen of Bohemia
    On his mistress, the Queen of
        Bohemia. Sir Henry Wotton.
        HaAP--WBP2
Eller, David
    To a God unknown. VoWA
Elliot, Lady Charlotte
    The wife of Loki. WBP2
Elliott, Ebenezer
    The fox-hunters. TyW
Elliott, George P.
    Sayer. FroA
Elliott, Harley
    For the man who stole a rose.
        FroA
Ellis Island. Joseph Bruchac.
    ReE
Ellis, Greg
    "In my hands are dreams." HoWM
Ellis, Roger
    Girl in the cafeteria. YoVA
Elsewhere. Linda Pastan. VoWA
Elskamp, Max
    "And it is Christ, like a
        sailor." FreS
    "I have the sadness of a
        town..." FreS
    Reykjavik. FreS
Eluard (Eugene Grindel), Paul
    First, sels. MoVT
    To live here. MoVT
The **embrace**. Jack McGaha. YoVA
Emerson, Caroline D.
    The ups and downs of the
        elevator car. IlTH
Emerson, Ralph Waldo
    Brahma. HaAP--WBP4
    Concord hymn. HaAP
    Days. HaAP
    Friendship. WBP1
    Good-bye. WBP4
    Ode ("Though loath to grieve").
        HaAP
    The problem. WBP4
    Sea-shore. MTS
    Terminus. DoNG

Eminent critic. John Frederick
    Nims. TyW
Emmanuel (N. Mathieu), Pierre
    O grant. MoVT
    Only madmen understand. MoVT
The emmigrant lassie. John
    Stuart Blackie. WBP3
Emotion bay. Sandra Hilton. YoVA
The emotional painting. Sherlene
    Merritt. HoWM
Empedocles on Etna, sels.
    Matthew Arnold. TyW
The emperor. Tamura Ryuichi.
    FroC
Emperor Ojin's song. Unknown.
    FroC
The emperor of ice-cream.
    Wallace Stevens. HaAP
The empress brand trim: Ruby
    reminisces. Sherley Anne
    Williams. BlS
Empson, William
    Missing dates. HaAP
    Sea voyage. MTS
The empty apartment. Aaron
    Zeitlin. VoWA
Empty thoughts. Dennis Vass.
    YoVA
Emus
    "At the zoo remarked to an emu."
    Unknown . IlTH
En route. Theodore Weiss. TeMP
Enamel work on gold and silver.
    Pierre Louys. FreS
Encounter in Jerusalem. Fay
    Lipschitz. VoWA
Encounter in Safed. Moshe
    Yungman. VoWA
End of summer. Berl Pomerantz.
    VoWA
End of the line. John Taylor.
    FroA
The end of the play. William
    Makepeace Thackeray. WBP4
End of the war in Merida.
    Anthony Ostroff. FroA
The end of the weekend. Anthony
    Hecht. HaAP
End of the world. Jakov van
    Hoddis (H.Davidson). VoWA
An endless chain. Abraham
    Reisen. VoWA
The endless scroll. Don Hornsby.
    YoVA
The endless wall. Lisa Dunn.
    YoVA
The endless/Journey begins. Ryan
    Schroeder. YoVA
Endurance. Elissa Behle. YoVA
Enemies

The last enem. Ishihara Yoshiro
    . FroC
The enemy's portrait. Thomas
    Hardy. TyW
Engel, Julie A.
    It's a time for sad songs. YoVA
    What am I now. YoVA
England and the English
    Adlestrop. Edward Thomas. HaAP
    The anatomie of the world,
    sels. John Donne. ShBa
    England in 1819. Percy Bysshe
    Shelley. TyW
    London, 1802. William
    Wordsworth. HaAP
    The rebel Scot. John Cleveland.
    TyW
England in 1819. Percy Bysshe
    Shelley. TyW
The English cemetery. Franco
    Fortini. NeIP
The English struwwelpeter, sels.
    Heinrich Hoffmann. WBP1
English, Thomas Dunn
    Ben Bolt. WBP1
Enoch. Jones Very. HaAP
Enoch (Bible)
    Enoch. Jones Very. HaAP
Ensz, Joni
    Summer is wrapped with warmth.
    YoVA
    There was a smell of love in
    the air. YoVA
Envoi. E.L. Mayo. FroA
Envoi (1919). Ezra Pound. HaAP
The envoy of Mr. Cogito, sels.
    Zbigniew Herbert. CoP
Envy
    The faerie queene, sels. Edmund
    Spenser. TyW
Envying sculptors. Florence
    Trefethen. StPo
Epic. Pablo Neruda. NiR
"An epicure dining at Crew".
    Unknown. MiRN
Epidermal macabre. Theodore
    Roethke. TyW
Epigram ("A National Guard
    captain...") Fernando Silva.
    NiR
Epigram ("False, cruel,
    disappointed.") William
    Cowper. TyW
Epigram ("Haven't you read...")
    Ernesto Cardenal. NiR
Epigram ("The National
    Guard...") Ernesto Cardenal.
    NiR
Epigram XIX. Ernesto Cardenal.
    NiR

Epigram XXXII. Ernesto Cardenal.
    NiR
Epigram on Elphinstone's
    translation.... Robert Burns.
    TyW
Epigram on the refusal of the
    university. William Cowper.
    TyW
An epigram to the queen, then
    lying in. Ben Jonson. ShBa
Epigram: "How rightly you
    circle..." Angelo Poliziano.
    ReLP
Epigram: "You have as many
    qualities..." Bernhard van
    Bauhuysen. ReLP
Epigram: Of Secaurus, a riche
    man.... Tito Strozzi. ReLP
Epigram: The grave of
    Giovanni...Pontano. Giovanni
    Giovano Pontano. ReLP
Epigram: To the muses. Giovanni
    Giovano Pontano. ReLP
Epigram: an almond tree. Andrea
    Alciat. ReLP
Epigram: on doctors. Euricius
    Cordus. ReLP
Epigram: to Hans Holbein
    painter... Nicolas Bourbon.
    ReLP
Epigram: tobacco. Joannes
    Posthius. ReLP
Epilogue. Robert Browning. WBP4
Epilogue ("I too was a little
    child.") Joseph Eliya. VoWA
Epilogue ("My bibliography has
    grown.") Dallas Wiebe. TyW
Epiphany. Reginald Heber. WBP4
Epistle to a desponding sea-man.
    Philip Freneau. MTS
Epistle to be left in the earth.
    Archibald MacLeish. DoNG
The epistle to the reader. Mary
    Tattlewell (pseud.). PaW
Epitaph ("He killed himself with
    ardor.") Tristan Corbiere.
    FreS
Epitaph ("One whom I knew, a
    student..") Alec Comfort.
    MTS
Epitaph ("Posterity will ne'er
    survey.") George Gordon,6th
    Baron Byron. TyW
Epitaph ("because words fall
    short.") Anna L. Walters. ReE
Epitaph for Joaquin Pasos.
    Ernesto Cardenal. NiR
Epitaph for...Adolfo Baez Bone.
    Ernesto Cardenal. NiR
Epitaph of a dog. Joachim Du

Bellay. ReLP
Epitaph on Elizabeth, L.H.. Ben
    Jonson. HaAP
Epitaph on Galla, a childless
    woman. Giovanni Giovano
    Pontano. ReLP
Epitaph on Grace a young girl.
    Baldassare Castiglione. ReLP
Epitaph on James Grieve,Laird of
    Boghead. Robert Burns. TyW
Epitaph on a hare. William
    Cowper. HaAP
Epitaphs
    The grave. Shaul
    Tchernichovsky. VoWA
    Inscription on Melrose Abbe.
    Unknown . WBP3
    Requiem. Robert Louis
    Stevenson. DoNG
Epithalamion, sels. Edmund
    Spenser. WBP2
Epithalamium. Ioannes Secundus
    (Everaerts). ReLP
Epithalamium...Mary Queen of
    Scots... George Buchanan.
    ReLP
Epithalamium..marriage Mary
    Queen Scots. George Buchanan.
    ReLP
Epithalmion. Grace Schulman.
    FroA
The Epte Woods. Rene Char. MoVT
Equality, father!. Edith Bruck.
    VoWA
Equation of the heart, sels.
    Julian Przybos. CoP
The equilibrists. John Crowe
    Ransom. HaAP
Erasers. Cynthia R. Wolfe. YoVA
Erasmus, Desiderius
    De casa natalitia Jesu. ShBa
Erba, Luciano
    A first-rate equation. NeIP
    Incompatibility. NeIP
    La Grande Jeanne. NeIP
    Land and sea. NeIP
    Lombard-Venetian. NeIP
    Tabula rasa? NeIP
Erev Shabbos. Marc Kaminsky.
    VoWA
Ernsting, Marty
    Haiku ("The storm approaches.")
    YoVA
    Limerick:"There was once a
    hippo..." YoVA
Eros is missing. Charles Whibley
    (trans.). WBP2
Eros is missing. Meleager. WBP2
Eros turannos. Edwin Arlington
    Robinson. HaAP

Erotic Love
   again you slept with mr no man.
      Yona Wallach. BuAC
   Azuma uta & Sakimori no uta: 25
      sel. Unknown . FroC
   Blank verse for a fat demanding
      wife. Jim Lindsey. TyW
   Censorship. John Ciardi. TyW
   Cherrylog Road. James Dickey.
      HaAP
   A childless witch. Raquel
      Chalfi. VoWA
   A classic idyll. Avraham Huss.
      VoWA
   Eleven tanka. Lady Ise. FroC
   Epithalamium. Ioannes Secundus
      (Everaerts). ReLP
   Firday night after bathing.
      Stephen Levy. VoWA
   The first. Marya Mannes. FroA
   Gift hour. Maria Banus. VoWA
   God and nature. Musa Moris
      Farni. VoWA
   In adoration of lov. Takamura
      Kotaro . FroC
   Incident. Harvey Shapiro. FroA
   It fell on a summer's day.
      Thomas Campion. HaAP
   The jewels. Charles Baudelaire.
      FoFS
   Lethe. Charles Baudelaire. FoFS
   The minotaur. Robert Gibb. FroA
   Myself in an anatomical chart..
      Takahashi Mutsuo . FroC
   Other faces. Linda Kozusko.
      StPo
   Regret. Vassar Miller. LiHE
   Rowing in turns. David Swanger.
      TeMP
   Sea-monster. Gertrud Kolmar.
      VoWA
   Songs: 32 songs from the Ryojin
      Hish. Unknown . FroC
   The subverted flower. Robert
      Frost. HaAP
   That ac. Tanikawa Shuntaro .
      FroC
   Thirst. Musa Moris Farni. VoWA
   Twilight room. Hagiwara Sakutaro.
      FroC
   Two gardens. Yona Wallach. BuAC
   Winging it. Jack Myers. TeMP
   You fit into me. Margaret
      Atwood. TyW
   A young deer/dust. Hemda Roth.
      BuAC--VoWA
Erotopaegnia, sels. Edoardo
   Sanguineti. NeIP
Errandi, Diana
   Friends. YoVA

Erskine (Earl of Rosslyn),F.R.
   Bedtime. WBP1
Esau. Leib Kwitko. VoWA
Esau
   Esau. Leib Kwitko. VoWA
   Isaac and Esau. Rose Drachler.
      VoWA
"Esaw Wood sawed wood". Unknown.
   IlTH
Escape. Elissa Behle. YoVA
Escape. Ilya Rubin. VoWA
Escorting my mother home. Rai
   San'yo. FroC
An essay on criticism, sels.
   Alexander Pope. HaAP
An essay on man, sels. Alexander
   Pope. WBP4
An essay on man, sels. Alexander
   Pope. LiHE
The essence of winning. Jane
   Roberson. YoVA
Essex, Robert D., 2d Earl of
   On monsieur's departure.
      Elizabeth I; Queen of England.
      PaW
Estienne. Peter Klappert. TeMP
Estuary. Maruyama Kaoru. FroC
Et Cetera
   My sweet old etcetera. Edward
      Estlin Cummings. SlW
Etamines narratives. Takiguchi
   Shuzo. FroC
Etching. Tamura Ryuichi. FroC
Eternal Father, strong to save.
   William Whiting. MTS
Eternal emancipation. Mark
   Schaefer. YoVA
The eternal goodness. John
   Greenleaf Whittier. WBP4
Eternity. Arthur Rimbaud.
   FoFS--FreS
Eternity
   After the rain. Stanley Crouch.
      LiHE
   Eternity. Arthur Rimbaud.
      FoFS--FreS
   Home alone these last hours...
      Stephen Levy. VoWA
   Meditation (after Moses Ibn
      Ezra). Carl Rakosi. VoWA
Eternity/With the newly born.
   Kathy Hamm. YoVA
Ethics. Linda Pastan. TeMP
Etter, Dave
   County fair images. PrVo
Etter, Jan
   The sparkling water. YoVA
Etude. Joseph Brodsky. VoWA
Etude for voice and hand.
   Gabriel Levin. VoWA

Etude realiste. Algernon Charles
    Swinburne. WBP1
Eubanks, Donna
    Why? YoVA
Eulogies
    Short eulogy. Zali Gurevitch.
        VoWA
Europa rides a black bull.
    Antonio Porta. NeIP
Europe
    Farewell to Europe. William
        Pillen. VoWA
Europe, sels. William Blake.
    ShBa
The European night. Stanislav
    Vinaver. VoWA
Eurydice. Phyllis Thompson. TeMP
Euthanasia. Clark William
    Gaylor. WBP4
Evans, Mari
    ...And the old women gathered.
        BlS
    Daufuskie. BlS
    Daufuskie: Jake. BlS
    How will you call me, brother.
        BlS
Evans, Mike
    Beginning to end. YoVA
Evans, Teresa
    Our world. YoVA
Eve. Jakov Fichman. VoWA
The eve. Howard Schwartz. VoWA
The Eve of St. Agnes. John
    Keats. HaAP--WBP3
Eve's advice to the children of
    Israel. Joachim Neugroschel.
    VoWA
Eve's birth. Kim Chernin. VoWA
Eve's song in the garden. Lynn
    Gottlieb. VoWA
Eve. See Adam and Eve
Evelyn Hope. Robert Browning.
    WBP3
Even if. Rachel Fishman. VoWA
Even such is time. Sir Walter
    Ralegh. HaAP
Evening. Tristan Tzara. VoWA
Evening. Itzik Manger. VoWA
Evening
    And the silver turns into
        night. Nathan Yonathan. VoWA
    "The black goat moves..."
        Albert Samain. FreS
    A compendium of good tank.
        Furiwara no Teika . FroC
    December sunset. Jonathan
        Holden. FroA
    The evening darkens over.
        Robert Bridges. HaAP
    Evening harmony. Charles

    Baudelaire. FoFS
    An evening of fantasy. Linda
        Castliglione. YoVA
    Evening. Tristan Tzara. VoWA
    Idyl: sunset. Henrietta
        Cordelia Ray. BlS
    Lake Merritt sunset. Laurence
        Lieberman. PrVo
    Lament to Our Lady of the
        Evenings. Jules Laforgue.
        FreS
    Ode to evening. William
        Collins. HaAP
    A peaceful song. Natan Zach.
        VoWA
    To the divine neighbor. Judah
        Leib Teller. VoWA
    When Emperor Mommu visited...
        Prince Shiki (668-716). FroC
    The windmill of evening. Shlomo
        Reich. VoWA
Evening bread. Jacob Glatstein.
    VoWA
The evening darkens over. Robert
    Bridges. HaAP
Evening harmony. Charles
    Baudelaire. FoFS
Evening in the windowpanes XI.
    Georges Rodenbach. FreS
Evening in the walls. Jean Wahl.
    VoWA
An evening of fantasy. Linda
    Castliglione. YoVA
Evening of the rose. Anthony
    Rudolf. VoWA
Evening prayer. Arthur Rimbaud.
    FoFS
Evening rain. Gregoire Le Roy.
    FreS
Evening songs, sels. Unknown.
    FroC
An evening under newly cleared
    skies. Wang Wei. GrAC
Evening view from a boat. Meng
    Hao-jan. GrAC
Evening walk. David Einhorn.
    OnCP
Everaerts (see Secundus), Jan

Evermore. Sandra Payne. YoVA
Every land is exile. Claude
    Vigee. VoWA
Everybody but me. Margaret Goss
    Burroughs. BlS
Everything. James Paul. HoA
Everywhere. A. Almi. OnCP
Evil
    Christabel. Samuel Taylor
        Coleridge. EvIm
    Crimen amoris. Paul Verlaine.

FoFS

The seven old men. Charles
Baudelaire. FoFS

The snow-fiend. Anne Radcliffe.
EvIm

To the reader. Charles
Baudelaire. FoFS

Evil prayers. Remy de Gourmont.
FreS

Evolution
Genealogy. Donald Finkel. VoWA

Evolution of travel. Tim Miller.
YoVA

Ex-voto. Algernon Charles
Swinburne. MTS

Examen miscellaneum, sels.
Charles,Earl Dorset
Sackville. WBP2

Example. John Keble. WBP4

Examples of created systems.
William Meredith. TeMP

The exchange. Samuel Taylor
Coleridge. WBP2

Excretion
Evening prayer. Arthur Rimbaud.
FoFS

Executions
Billy in the darbies. Herman
Melville. HaAP

Last lines-1916. Padraic
Pearse. LiHE

Lines. Chediock Ticheborne.
WBP3

A London fete. Coventry
Patmore. HaAP

Tichborne's elegy. Chidiock
Tichborne. HaAP

An exequy. Henry King. HaAP

Exhortation to prayer. Margaret
Mercer. WBP4

The exile. Ernesto Gutierrez.
NiR

Exile
Climbing a tall building..
Chang Chiu-ling . GrAC

Every land is exile. Claude
Vigee. VoWA

The exile. Ernesto Gutierrez.
NiR

"Far, still farther, far..."
Gustave Kahn. FreS

Lament for the European exile.
A.L. Strauss. VoWA

National song. Ernesto
Cardenal. NiR

Rainy nigh. Sugawara no
Michizane . FroC

Second song...worship of the
goddess.. Wang Wei . GrAC

Sposob, sels. Czeslaw Milosz.

CoP

The time I haven't seen the
blue sky. Gioconda Belli. NiR

Written on a stone in the
road... Pablo Antonio Cuadra.
NiR

Exiled. Edna St. Vincent Millay.
MTS

Exits and entrances. Naomi Long
Madgett. BlS

Exodus. Harvey Shapiro. VoWA

Exodus 1940. Alfred Wolfenstein.
VoWA

Exodus from Egypt
The departure. Jeremy Robson.
VoWA

Desert stone. Miriam
Waddington. VoWA

Exodus. Harvey Shapiro. VoWA

Exotic perfume. Charles
Baudelaire. FoFS

Expectation. Aliza Shenhar. VoWA

An experience and a moral.
Frederick Swartwout Cozzens.
WBP2

Explanations. Jane St. John.
YoVA

Exploding gravy. X.J. Kennedy.
IlTH

The exploration of inner space.
Reginald Shephead. YoVA

The explosion. Philip Larkin.
HaAP

Expounding the Torah. Louis
Zukovsky. VoWA

Expressing my humble thoughts.
Otomo no Yakamochi. FroC

The extermination of the Jews.
Marvin Bell. VoWA

Extinction of plankton. Ono
Tozaburo. FroC

Extreme unction in Pa.. David
Ray. FroA

The eye. Sid Rowland. StPo

Eye of God. Jim Tollerud. ReE

Eyes. Clarisse Nicoidski. VoWA

Eyes
Black and blue eyes. Thomas
Moore. WBP2

Blue eyes. John Keats. WBP2

Explanations. Jane St. John.
YoVA

The eye. Sid Rowland. StPo

Eyes. Clarisse Nicoidski. VoWA

For a lost nigh. Tachihara
Michizo . FroC

O, do not wanton with those
eyes. Ben Jonson. WBP2

O, saw ye the lass? Richard
Ryan. WBP2

Cox. TrWB

The elf and the dormouse. Oliver Herford. WBP1

Elf poem. Tracey Kenney. YoVA

The fairies of the Caldon Low. Mary Howitt. WBP1

Fairy days. William Makepeace Thackeray. WBP1

Glen uig. Richard Hugo. TeMP

Goblin market. Christina Georgina Rossetti. EvIm

The golem. Shlomo Reich. VoWA

"Ol Erie McGreer." Elizabeth Garza. YoVA

The rape of the lock. Alexander Pope. HaAP

The stolen child. William Butler Yeats. EvIm

The fairies of the Caldon Low. Mary Howitt. WBP1

Fairs

After the fair. Thomas Hardy. HaAP

County fair images. Dave Etter. PrVo

Fairgrounds. Barbara Decker. YoVA

Fairy days. William Makepeace Thackeray. WBP1

Fairy tales. Itzik Manger. VoWA

Faith. George Santayana. WBP4

Faith. Frances Anne Kemble. WBP3

Faith

Aunt Phillis's guest. William Channing Gannett. WBP3

The balade...made & sange in Newgate. Anne (Kyme) Askew. PaW

The envoy of Mr. Cogito, sels. Zbigniew Herbert. CoP

The faith came first. Sydney Carter. EeBC

Faith. Frances Anne Kemble. WBP3

Faith. George Santayana. WBP4

The fight of faith. Anne (Kyme) Askew. WBP4

Franz Jagesttater's epistemology. Mark Halperin. TeMP

A god and yet a man. Unknown. HaAP

I am the way. Alice Meynell. EeBC

I asked for peace. Digby Mackworth Dolben. EeBC

I hold still. Julius Sturm. WBP3

I never saw a moor. Emily Dickinson. EeBC

If I could trust mine own self. Christina Georgina Rossetti. EeBC

Ilka blade o' grass keps its ain...dew. James Ballantine. WBP3

In memoriam, sels. Alfred, Lord Tennyson. WBP4

In no strange land. Francis Thompson. EeBC--HaAP

Meditation in verse, sel. Mary Queen of Scots . PaW

My peace I give unto you. G.A. Studdert Kennedy. EeBC

My times are in thy hand. Christopher Newman Hall. WBP4

No coward soul is mine. Emily Bronte. EvIm

The pilgrim's song. John Bunyan. EeBC

Poem on resignatio. Mary Queen of Scots . PaW

Prayer ("When I was just a little mite"). Guillaume Apollinaire. MoVT

The problem. Ralph Waldo Emerson. WBP4

Rabbi Ben Ezra. Robert Browning. WBP4

Religion and doctrine. John Hay. WBP4

The Rock, sels. Thomas Stearns Eliot. EeBC

The shepherd boy's song. John Bunyan. EeBC

A testimony. James Morton. YoVA

When my ship comes in. Robert Jones Burdette. WBP3

Faith and hope. Rembrandt Peale. WBP2

The **faith** came first. Sydney Carter. EeBC

The **faithful** lovers. Unknown. WBP2

Falconer, William

The midshipman. MTS

The shipwreck, sels. MTS

Falk, Marcia

Modern Kabbalist. VoWA

Shulamit in her dreams. VoWA

Woman through the window. VoWA

Fall. Chris Patterson. YoVA

Fall letter. Dave Kelly. FroA

The **fall** of Jerusalem, sels. Henry Hart Milman. WBP2

The **fall** of summer. Danny Callen. YoVA

The **fallen** tree. Robert Bly. TeMP

Fallen years. Sharon Ann

The worm. Willis Barnstone.
    FroA--VoWA
You're still my dad. Wendy
    Holubiczko. YoVA
Fatigue
    So we'll go more a-roving.
    George Gordon,6th Baron
    Byron. HaAP
    The weary dancers. Gloria Boyd.
    YoVA
The **faun**. Paul Verlaine. FoFS
A **faun's** afternoon. Stephane
    Mallarme. FoFS
Faun's head. Arthur Rimbaud.
    FoFS
Fauns
    A faun's afternoon. Stephane
    Mallarme. FoFS
    Faun's head. Arthur Rimbaud.
    FoFS
    The faun. Paul Verlaine. FoFS
Fauset, Jessie Redmon
    Oriflamme. BlS
    Touche. BlS
Faustina...more suitably named
    Pandora. Joachim Du Bellay.
    ReLP
Fauth, Laura
    Death. YoVA
    I need not suffer now. YoVA
Fear. Aldo Camerino. VoWA
Fear
    Chills. Mark Mitchell. YoVA
    Fear. Aldo Camerino. VoWA
    The feeling of fear... Ryan
    Schroeder. YoVA
    The intruder. Belinda J.
    Braley. YoVA
    "It is when the tribe is gone."
    Duff Bigger. FroA
    New thought. Jackie Pierce.
    YoVA
    When I have fears that I may
    cease to be. John Keats. HaAP
Fear no more the heat o' the
    sun. William Shakespeare.
    HaAP--LiHE
The **fear** of the innocent. Susan
    Lueders. YoVA
Fearer, Mark
    Chattahoochee trip. YoVA
    Summertime blues. YoVA
Fearing, Kenneth
    Love, 20c the first quarter
    mile. HaAP
The **feast** of Stephen. Anthony
    Hecht. HaAP
Feather dreams. Melissa Heiple.
    YoVA
Feather-stitching. Aileen

Fisher. MiRN
Feathers
    Eagle feather II. Phil George.
    ReE
    Eagle feather I. Phil George.
    ReE
    Eagle feather III. Phil George.
    ReE
February. Pier Paolo Pasolini.
    NeIP
Feeding the fire. Donald Finkel.
    VoWA
Feeling. Arthur Rimbaud. FoFS
The **feeling** of fear... Ryan
    Schroeder. YoVA
Feelings. Jennifer Haws. YoVA
Feelings. Deserie Fluck. YoVA
Feelings. Sara O'Brien. YoVA
Feelings at the end of Spring
    II. Tai Shu-lun. GrAC
Feet
    Feet, a sermon. James Paul. HoA
    How many times these low feet
    staggered. Emily Dickinson.
    HaAP
    "My feet thay haul me round the
    house" Gelett Burgess. IlTH
    Parts. Zishe Landau. VoWA
Feet, a sermon. James Paul. HoA
Fein, Cheri
    The obscene caller. TyW
Feinstein, Elaine
    Against winter. VoWA
    Dad. VoWA
    Survivors. VoWA
    Under stone. VoWA
Feldman, Alan
    The personals. TeMP
Feldman, Irving
    A curse. TyW
    The Pripet Marshes. VoWA
Feldman, Ruth
    Lilith. VoWA
Felix Randal. Gerard Manley
    Hopkins. HaAP--SlW
Fellow traveler. Patricia Celley
    Groth. StPo
The **female** convict. Letitia
    Elizabeth Landon. WBP3
Ferguson, Michelle Dawn
    Another day. YoVA
    Come back. YoVA
Ferguson, Samuel
    The pretty girl of Loch Dan.
    WBP1
Ferid ed-Din Attar
    The welcome. WBP1
Ferlinghetti, Lawrence
    Christ climbed down. ShBa
    In Goya's greatest scenes. LiHE

Fern hill. Dylan Thomas. LiHE
Fernandez, Francisco de Asis
    In cold blood. NiR
    In one's own and foreign land.
        NiR
    To Thomas Borge: dawn
        ceased..dream. NiR
    We lost our fear. NiR
Fernando, El Indio
    Indian lament. NiR
Ferns
    Today's ferns. Ono Tozaburo.
        FroC
    "The young fiddlehead ferns."
        Yomon Akara.   FroC
Fertility
    To hell with your fertility
        cult. Gary Snyder. TyW
Festival of the blind. Ishigaki
    Rin. FroC
Festivals
    After the Ch'ing-ming
        Festival... Liu-Ch'ang-ch'ing
        GrAC
    Autumn ("On the morning that a
        typhoon.") Nishiwaki Junzaburo
        FroC
    Cold Food Festiva. Han Hung.
        GrAC
    Written when I climbed the
        peak... Takahashi Mushimaro.
        FroC
Festivals of patience. Arthur
    Rimbaud. FoFS--FreS
Festus, sels. Philip James
    Bailey. WBP3
Festus, sels. Philip James
    Bailey. WBP4
Fetching water from the well.
    Unknown. WBP2
The fever, sels. John Donne. TyW
Fichman, Jakov
    Abishag. VoWA
    Eve. VoWA
A fiction. A. W. WBP2
Fiddler. Tarah Ting-pei Chang.
    YoVA
The fiddler. Martin Buber. VoWA
Fidelity
    Penelope. Lois Marie Harrod.
        StPo
Fidelty in doubt. Guiraud
    Leroux. WBP3
Fidelty in doubt. Harriet W.
    Preston (trans.). WBP3
The field mouse. William Sharp.
    MiRN
The field of night. Miriam
    Waddington. VoWA
Field, Edward

For Arthur Gregor. FroA
Field, Eugene
    A Dutch lullaby. WBP1
    Japanese lullaby. WBP1
    Jim's kids. WBP3
    The little peach. IlTH
    Seeing things. WBP1
Field, Greg
    Home cooking cafe. FroA
Field, Michael
    The dancers. WBP1
Field, Teena
    I am me. YoVA
Fields
    "I came to this spring
        field..." Yamabe no Akahito.
        FroC
    Ina field. Unknown. FroC
    June the twenty-second. Marnie
        Walsh. ReE
    Life in a field waiting. Raquel
        Chalfi. BuAC--VoWA
    Looking toward Peoria. G.E.
        Murray. PrVo
    "The wheat field." Nora
        Coggins. YoVA

Fifteen hokku. Shiba Sonome.
    FroC
Fifteen hokku. Naito Joso. FroC
Fifty-one tanka. Lady Izumi.
    FroC
The fight of faith. Anne (Kyme)
    Askew. WBP4
A figment of your imagination.
    Judy Ellen Mills. YoVA
The figure in the carpet. James
    Camp. TyW
"a figure...contemplating the
    mountain." Jie Zi Yuan Hua
    Zhuan. LuL
Figures of speech. Ellen De
    Haan. YoVA
Files, Lolita
    Why does poetry exist? YoVA
Filling station. Elizabeth
    Bishop. HaAP
Filth. Jean Lorrain (Paul
    Deval). FreS
Final soliloquy of the interior
    paramour. Wallace Stevens.
    HaAP
Finches
    Mechanism. Archie Randolph
        Ammons. HaAP
Finders keepers. Donald Finkel.
    VoWA
Finding self. Deborah Jowers.
    YoVA
Fine body. Josephine Clare. FroA

A **first-rate** equation. Luciano
    Erba. NeIP
Fischer, Otakar
  From the depths. VoWA
Fischer, Robyn
    Rejection. YoVA
    Summer storm. YoVA
    A tear. YoVA
The **fish**. Rupert Brooke. MTS
The **fish**. Marianne Moore. MTS
Fish. Mario Satz. VoWA
The **fish**. Elizabeth Bishop.
    HaAP--MTS
Fish
    After fish. Linda Hogan. ReE
    Cold creek. Maurice Kenny. ReE
    The fish. Elizabeth Bishop.
     HaAP--MTS
    The fish. Marianne Moore. MTS
    Fish. Mario Satz. VoWA
    The fish. Rupert Brooke. MTS
    Little fish. David Herbert
     Lawrence. SlW
    The song ("The song! the
     song!"). Hemda Roth. VoWA
    Thanksgiving. Linda Hogan. ReE
    To a fish. Leigh Hunt. MTS
    To the immortal memory of the
     halibut... William Cowper.
     MTS
Fish dock-Port Townsend. Gladys
    Cardiff. ReE
Fish food. John Wheelwright. MTS
A **fish** replies. Leigh Hunt. MTS
The **fish** turns into a man...
    Leigh Hunt. MTS
The **fish**, the man, and the
    spirit, sels. Leigh Hunt. MTS
The **fish**, the man, and the
    spirit. Leigh Hunt. HaAP
Fisher folk on the river. Fan
    Zhong-yan. LuL
The **fisher's** boy. Henry David
    Thoreau. MTS
Fisher, Aileen
    Birthday cake. MiRN
    Feather-stitching. MiRN
    My puppy. RoRF
    Winter mouse. MiRN
Fisher, Morgan
    The house within me. HoWM
    "Like a mountain/With rainbows
     of" HoWM
Fisher, Suzanne
    The letter. YoVA
    Report. YoVA
The **fisherman**. Ch'u Kuang-hsi.
    GrAC
Fisherman. Ouyang Xiu. LuL
The **fisherman**. William Butler

    Yeats. HaAP
Fishermen. Gabriel Preil. VoWA
Fishing and Fishermen
    At the fishhouses. Elizabeth
     Bishop. HaAP
    Fish dock-Port Townsend. Gladys
     Cardiff. ReE
    Fisher folk on the rive. Fan
     Zhong-yan. LuL
    The fisherma. Ch'u Kuang-hsi.
     GrAC
    Fisherma. Ouyang Xiu. LuL
    The fisherman. William Butler
     Yeats. HaAP
    Fishermen. Gabriel Preil. VoWA
    The perspective and limits of
     snapshots. Dave Smith. TeMP
    The purse-seine. Robinson
     Jeffers. HaAP
    River sno. Liu Tsung-yuan.
     GrAC
    The song of the fisherma. Ch'u
     Kuang-hsi. GrAC
    Two fishermen. Stanley Moss.
     VoWA
Fishman, Rachel
    Even if. VoWA
    In the beginning. VoWA
Fitzgerald (trans.), Edward
    The welcome. WBP1
Fitzgerald, Edward
    On Anne Allen. WBP3
    The Rubaiyat of Omar Khayyam,
     sels, tr. HaAP
Fitzgerald, Edward (about)
    To Edward Fitzgerald. Robert
     Browning. TyW
Fitzgerald, Robert
    Cobb would have caught it. HaAP
Fitzharris, James
    Skin the Goat's curse on Care.
     Unknown . TyW
Five little owls. Unknown. RoRF
Five songs, sels. Wystan Hugh
    Auden. LiHE
Five ways to kill a man. Edwin
    Brock. LiHE
Five years in jail. Carlos Jose
    Guadamuz. NiR
Flags
    Black flags are fluttering.
     David Vogel. VoWA
The **flaming** heart, sels. Richard
    Crashaw. HaAP
Flamingo. Fiona Mellor. YoVA
Flamingos
    Flamingo. Fiona Mellor. YoVA
Flaminio, Marcantonio
    Hymn to the dawn. ReLP
    Pastoral Lusus. ReLP

The poet compares his soul to a
  flower. ReLP
Psalm paraphrase CXXVIII. ReLP
Flannery, Patricia
  Pain. YoVA
Flantz, Richard
  Shir Ma'alot/a song of degrees.
    VoWA
Flatman, Thomas
  An appeal to cats...business of
    love. HaAP
The **flattered** flying fish. Emile
  Victor Rieu. IlTH
A **flayed** ox. Eugene Guillevic.
  MoVT
"A **flea** and a fly in a flue."
  Unknown. IlTH
The **flea** circus at Tivoli. Nancy
  Willard. HoA
Fleas
  The flea circus at Tivoli.
    Nancy Willard. HoA
  "A horse and a flea & three
    blind mice." Unknown . IlTH
Flecker, James Elroy
  The old ships. MTS
Fleg, Edmond
  The dead cities speak...living
    cities. VoWA
Fleming, Paul
  To myself. WBP3
Fletcher, Giles
  On the Crucifixion. EeBC
Fletcher, John
  Bloody brother, sels. WBP3
  The nice valour, sels. WBP3
Flies
  Damned fly. Gordon D. Leslie.
    StPo
  The fly. Karl Shapiro. TyW
  The fly. Raymond Queneau. MoVT
  I heard a fly buzz when I died.
    Emily Dickinson. DoNG--SlW
  The spider and the fly. Mary
    Howitt. WBP1
Flight 539. John Malcolm
  Brinnin. HoA
The **flight** into Egypt. Francis
  Mahony (Father Prout). WBP4
The **flight** of youth. Richard
  Henry Stoddard. WBP1
Flippin, Jan
  Me. YoVA
  Success. YoVA
Floating through life. Beth
  Hall. YoVA
The **flood**. Ewa Lipska. VoWA
The **flood**. Lev Mak. VoWA
Floods
  After the flood. Arthur

Rimbaud. SlW
The **flood**. Ewa Lipska. VoWA
The **fugitive's** apologue. Nanni
  Balestrini. NeIP
The **letter**. Charles Reznikoff.
  VoWA
Official iconography. Roberto
  Roversi. NeIP
"Wind of ruin, lurking rain." Tu
  Fu. GrAC
Floors
  "I wish my room had a floor."
    Gelett Burgess. IlTH
Florence, Italy
  Bat. David Herbert Lawrence.
    HaAP
Flores, Sharon
  Nine whacks. YoVA
Florida
  Pursuit. Robert Penn Warren.
    HaAP
Florimond. Ephraim Mikhael. FreS
The **flower**. George Herbert. WBP3
The **flower**. Connie Smallwood.
  HoWM
The **flower** opens to meet the
  dawn. Alison Tranbarger. YoVA
Flowers
  Apparently with no surprise.
    Emily Dickinson. LiHE
  Black flowers. Pierre Quillard.
    FreS
  By the water. Emile Verhaeren.
    FreS
  A compendium of good tank.
    Furiwara no Teika. FroC
  A cut flower. Karl Shapiro.
    HaAP
  The flower. Connie Smallwood.
    HoWM
  The ill-starred flower. Tristan
    Corbiere. FreS
  Lavender flowers. Susan West.
    YoVA
  The life of rooms IV. Georges
    Rodenbach. FreS
  Out of place. Jolene Nickell.
    YoVA
  Sonnet XCIX. William
    Shakespeare. WBP2
  "Spring" variation. Miyazawa
    Kenji. FroC
  Two flowers. Carrie Town. YoVA
  Why flowers change colors.
    Robert Herrick. HaAP
  The yellow flower. William
    Carlos Williams. HaAP
Flowers and moonlight
  on...Spring River. Yang-di.
    LuL

Flowers of winter: four songs.
  Duane BigEagle. ReE
Flowers on stone. Marian J.
  Darling. StPo
Flowers without fruit. John
  Henry, Cardinal Newman. WBP4
Fluck, Deserie
  December. YoVA
  Feelings. YoVA
Flute. Rivka Miriam. BuAC
Flutes
  Hearing a flute on the river
    Wang Ch'ang-ling. GrAC
  The hollow flute. Avner
    Strauss. VoWA
  Tree to flute. Anna Hajnal.
    VoWA
The **fly.** Karl Shapiro. TyW
The **fly.** Raymond Queneau. MoVT
A **fly** on the water. Paul Zweig.
  TeMP
"**Fly** to the desert, fly with
  me". Thomas Moore. WBP2
Flying
  The story of flying Robert.
    Heinrich Hoffmann. IlTH
The **flying** Dutchman. Edwin
  Arlington Robinson. MTS
Flying letters. Zerubavel
  Gilead. VoWA
Flyting of Dunbar and Kennedy,
  sels. William Dunbar. TyW
Fog. Elizabeth Pauketat. YoVA
Fog
  Boats in a fog. Robinson
    Jeffers. MTS
  Fog and town. Ishihara Yoshiro.
    FroC
  Fog. Elizabeth Pauketat. YoVA
  Potwor pan Cogito, sels.
    Zbigniew Herbert. CoP
Fog and town. Ishihara Yoshiro.
  FroC
Folk tune. Esther Raab.
  BuAC--VoWA
Follain, Jean
  The notice. MoVT
  Talking to oneself. MoVT
Follen, Eliza Lee
  The three little kittens. WBP1
Follow your saint, follow with
  accents... Thomas Campion.
  HaAP
Folmer III, Howard
  The lonely puppy. YoVA
Fondane (Fundoianu), Benjamin
  By the waters of Babylon. VoWA
  Hertza. VoWA
  Lullaby for an emigrant. VoWA
  Plain song. VoWA

The wandering Jew. VoWA
Fonesca Amador, Carlos
  Bitter days. NiR
Food and Eating
  The ambitious mouse. John
    Farrar. MiRN
  The ballad of bouillabaisse.
    William Makepeace Thackeray.
    WBP1
  The boy stood in the
    supper-roo. Unknown . IlTH
  Cherries. Lucien Stryk. TeMP
  The country mouse and the city
    mouse. Richard Scrafton
    Sharpe. MiRN
  The crocodile. Oliver Herford.
    IlTH
  Egg thoughts. Russell Hoban.
    BrBD
  "An epicure dining at Crew."
    Unknown. MiRN
  Exploding gravy. X.J. Kennedy.
    IlTH
  The flattered flying fish.
    Emile Victor Rieu. IlTH
  Glum-day sundae. Melanie D.
    Holiway. YoVA
  Henry King, who chewed bits of
    string... Hilaire Belloc.
    IlTH
  The invention of cuisine. Carol
    Muske. TeMP
  Little Miss Tucket. Unknown.
    RoRF
  "Me, myself and I." Unknown.
    IlTH
  My wise old grandpapa. Wilbur
    Howcroft. IlTH
  Sea food thought. John W.
    Moser. FroA
  Sneaky Bill. William Cole. IlTH
  The story of Augustus...
    Heinrich Hoffmann. IlTH
  Table manners-I. Gelett
    Burgess. IlTH
  Table manners-II. Gelett
    Burgess. IlTH
  Tohub. Jakov van Hoddis
    (H.Davidson). VoWA
  Who among you knows the
    essence..garlic? Garrett
    Hongo. HoA
  You must never bath in an Irish
    stew. Spike Milligan. IlTH
Football. Jack McDaniel. YoVA
Football
  Football. Jack McDaniel. YoVA
  Funky footbal. Fareedah Allah
    (Ruby Saunders) . BlS
Footnotes to "The

autobiography...") Mona Van Duyn. HaAP

Footsteps of angels. Henry Wadsworth Longfellow. WBP3

Footsteps of spring. Hayim Nachman Bialik. VoWA

For Adolf Eichmann. Primo Levi. VoWA

For Allan. Robert Frost. PoCh

For Anne Gregory. William Butler Yeats. SlW

For Annie. Edgar Allan Poe. WBP3

For Arthur Gregor. Edward Field. FroA

For Charlie's sake. John Williamson Palmer. WBP3

For Gabriel. Laya Firestone. VoWA

For Jukka: on indecision. Jean Shields. YoVA

For K.M. Scott Morgan. YoVA

(For K.M.E. & G.B.C.). Wendy S. Neidlinger. YoVA

For Lori Tazbah. Luci Tapahonso. ReE

For Murasaki. Josephine Jacobsen. FroA

For Peter. Lee Gerlach. HoA

For Tammy & David. Cheryl Cruts. YoVA

For Venice, sinking. Geraldine Clinton Little. StPo

For a certain night. Tachihara Michizo. FroC

For a friend. David Steingass. TyW

For a lost night. Tachihara Michizo. FroC

For a man who learned to swim when sixty. Diane Wakoski. FroA

For a memory. Tachihara Michizo. FroC

For a plague on the door... William Stafford. FroA

For a religious service to God. Lady Otomo no Sakanoue. FroC

For a voice that is singing. Aldo Camerino. VoWA

For an Egyptian boy, died c. 700 B.C.. Mary Baron. HoA

For an art of poetry 3. Raymond Queneau. MoVT

For an early retirement. Donald Hall. TyW

For an obligate parasite. Alan Dugan. TyW

For memories. Nishiwaki Junzaburo. FroC

For our soldiers who fell in Russia. Franco Fortini. VoWA

For rattlesnake. Peter Blue Cloud. ReE

For the Union dead. Robert Lowell. HaAP

For the Yiddish singers... Harvey Shapiro. VoWA

For the candle light. Angelina Weld Grimke. BlS

For the children who died..smallpox... Ryokan. FroC

For the man who stole a rose. Harley Elliott. FroA

For the parents of a dead child. Ryokan. FroC

For the rain in March... Roy A. Young Bear. ReE

For the time being, sels. Wystan Hugh Auden. PoCh--ShBa

For the white poets who would be Indian. Wendy Rose. ReE

For them. Hope Kienenberger. YoVA

For three days I traveled...mountains. Yuan Zong-dao. LuL

For you. Sherrie Booth. YoVA

Forbes, Jack
  Marilyn from a two-bit town. YoVA
  Scared. YoVA

Forced march. Miklos Radnoti. VoWA

Forche, Carolyn
  Reunion. TeMP

Foreign children. Robert Louis Stevenson. WBP1

A **foreign** country. Natan Zach. VoWA

Foreign lands. Robert Louis Stevenson. WBP1

Forest ballet. Krystal Siler. YoVA

A **forest** lane covered with moss. Mei Yao-chen. LuL

The **forest**, sels. Philostratus. WBP2

The **forest**, sels. Ben Jonson (trans.). WBP2

Forests
  A ballad of trees and the

Basho. FroC

Foster, Deborah Ann
The house is a shack. YoVA
There ain't nothing more
important.... YoVA

Foster, Stephen Collins
My old Kentucky home. WBP3
Old folks at home. WBP3

Foul water. Mordecai Temkin.
VoWA

Found wanting. Emily Dickinson.
WBP4

Fountains
Nichols Fountain. Virginia
Scott Miner. FroA

Four. Chaya Shenhav. BuAC

Four Christmas carols, sels.
Cheli Duran (trans.). PoCh

The four Zoas, sels. William
Blake. TyW

The four of them. Yehuda Karni.
VoWA

Four poems for Robin. Gary
Snyder. SlW

Four songs of life. Roy A. Young
Bear. ReE

Four songs: II. Andre Gide. MoVT

Four ways of writing one poem.
Hemda Roth. BuAC

Four# (4#). William Oandasan.
ReE

The fourth act. Chris Smith.
HoWM

Fowler (Foular), William
E.D. in prise of Mr. William
Foular. Elizabeth (E.D.)
Douglas. PaW

Fox (trans.), W. J.
The martyrs' hymn. WBP4

Fox, Henry (Baron Holland)
On Lord Holland's seat near
Margate.... Thomas Gray. TyW

The fox-hunters. Ebenezer
Elliott. TyW

Foxes
The fox-hunters. Ebenezer
Elliott. TyW
The red fox. Marnie Walsh. ReE

Fragment. Miklos Radnoti. VoWA

Fragment. Bruce Berlind. FroA

Fragments. Takiguchi Shuzo. FroC

Fragments ("In the gun muzzle").
Maruyama Kaoru. FroC

France and the French
Epigram ("False, cruel,
disappointed"). William
Cowper. TyW
The French historie, sels. Anne
(Edgcumbe) Trefusis. PaW
Wildfire. Judit Toth. VoWA

Francestown suite. Carole Oles.
TeMP

Francestown, New Hampshire
Francestown suite. Carole Oles.
TeMP

Francis I, King of France
On the death of her brother,
Francis . Marguerite de
Valois . WBP3

Francis II, King of France
Verses on the death of Francis
II, sel. Mary Queen of Scots.
PaW

Francis Xavier, Saint
My God, I love thee. WBP4

Francis, Robert
The buzz plane. TyW
The curse. TyW
Delicate the toad. DuD
Night train. DuD

Francisco, Nia
i have sat through sunlight.
ReE
men tell and talk. ReE

Francois the Dauphin
Elegy: the poet
mourns...Francis... Nicolas
Bourbon. ReLP

Frank Albert & Viola Benzena
Owens. Ntozake Shange. BlS

Frankenberg, Lloyd
The sea. MTS

Franz Jagesttater's
epistemology. Mark Halperin.
TeMP

Franz, Kim
Letters/tied up with a blue
ribbon. YoVA

"Frater ave atque vale." Alfred,
Lord Tennyson. HaAP

Fraternal exhortation. Raul
Javier Garcia. NiR

Freddy. Dennis Lee. BrBD

Frederick Douglass. Robert
Hayden. HoA

Free gift. Tony Mancuso. HoWM

"Free" style. Lisa McCormick.
YoVA

Freedman, William
Benediction. VoWA
Formations. VoWA

Freedom
Captured. Courtney Strang. YoVA
A chattel to freedom. Janet G.
Rice. YoVA
Dark testament. Pauli Murray.
BlS
Eagle feather IV. Phil George.
ReE
Liberty and peace, sels.

Phillis Wheatley. BlS
Midway. Naomi Long Madgett. BlS
Ode to freedom. Aaron Zeitlin.
    VoWA
Poems in pieces. Pablo Antonio
    Cuadra. NiR
Prayers to liberty. Anwar
    Shaul. VoWA
Rainier. Jim Tollerud. ReE
A special moment. Frank Lamont
    Phillips. FroA
Twilight of freedom. Osip
    Mandelstam. VoWA
Untitled ("Earth, wind, nor
    fire.") Aubrey W. Love. YoVA
A **freedom** song for the black
    woman. Carole C. Gregory. BlS
Freely, from a song sung by
    Jewish women. Stephen Levy.
    VoWA
Freeman, Carol
    Christmas morning I. PoCh
Freemon Hawthorne. Melvin B.
    Tolson. FroA
Freethinkers. Deborah Eibel.
    VoWA
The **French** historie, sels. Anne
    (Edgecumbe) Trefusis. PaW
The **French** mood. Abraham Abo
    Stolzenberg. VoWA
Freneau, Philip
    Captain Jones' invitation. MTS
    Epistle to a desponding sea-
    man. MTS
    The hurricane. MTS
    The Indian burying ground. HaAP

Freud, Sigmund
    In memory of Sigmund Freud.
    Wystan Hugh Auden. HaAP
The **friar** of orders gray. Thomas
    Percy. WBP2
Friar, Kimon
    Greek transfiguration. HoA
Friction. Lori Susan Avant. YoVA
Friday lunchbreak. Gregory Orr.
    TeMP
Friday, you look blue. Alfredo
    Giuliani. NeIP
Fried, Rivka
    Sabbath. VoWA
Fried, Susannah
    Scraps. VoWA
    To my father. VoWA
    Winter day. VoWA
Friedmann, Pavel
    The butterfly. VoWA
The **friend**. Nicholas Grimoald.
    WBP1
A **friend**. Douglas Parker. YoVA

Friend. Dianne Smith. YoVA
Friend and lover. Madeline
    Bridges(M.A.De Vere). WBP1
Friend who never came. William
    Stafford. FroA
Friend, Robert
    Identity. VoWA
    The practice of absence. VoWA
A **friend**/The person who calls.
    Carla Lower. YoVA
The **friendly** beasts. Unknown.
    PoCh
Friends. Diana Errandi. YoVA
Friendship. Ralph Waldo Emerson.
    WBP1
Friendship. Terri B. Johnson.
    YoVA
Friendship. Edward Young. WBP1
Friendship. Ken Wilson. YoVA
Friendship. Lori Frisk. YoVA
Friendship
    And doth not a meeting like
    this. Thomas Moore. WBP1
    Auld lang syne. Robert Burns.
    WBP1
    Benedicite. John Greenleaf
    Whittier. WBP1
    Bill and Joe. Oliver Wendell
    Holmes. WBP1
    Bonds. Kathy Johnson. YoVA
    The dead friend. Alfred, Lord
    Tennyson. WBP1
    Early friendship. Aubrey Thomas
    De Vere. WBP1
    Elegy on Captain Matthew
    Henderson. Robert Burns. WBP1
    For Peter. Lee Gerlach. HoA
    For you. Sherrie Booth. YoVA
    Friend and lover. Madeline
    Bridges(M.A.De Vere). WBP1
    Friend. Dianne Smith. YoVA
    A friend. Douglas Parker. YoVA
    The friend. Nicholas Grimoald.
    WBP1
    A friend/The person who calls.
    Carla Lower. YoVA
    Friends. Diana Errandi. YoVA
    Friendship. Edward Young. WBP1
    Friendship. Ken Wilson. YoVA
    Friendship. Lori Frisk. YoVA
    Friendship. Ralph Waldo
    Emerson. WBP1
    Friendship. Terri B. Johnson.
    YoVA
    Furtively. Nurit Zarchi. BuAC
    The garret. Thomas Moore. WBP1
    George. Steve Leifson. YoVA
    Greg. Jami Wald. YoVA
    Hamlet, sels. William
    Shakespeare. WBP1

I need not suffer now. Laura
    Fauth. YoVA
Incantation to...rid a sometime
    friend. Emanuel diPasquale.
    TyW
Jaffar. Leigh Hunt. WBP1
Jenny kissed me. Leigh Hunt.
    WBP1
John Smith. Lois-Long Anders.
    StPo
Lost. Shirley Johnson. YoVA
Love poem (for M.). Cary
    Waterman. TeMP
The mahogany-tree. William
    Makepeace Thackeray. WBP1
The memory of the heart. Daniel
    Webster. WBP1
A midsummer night's dream,
    sels. William Shakespeare.
    WBP1
Mors et vita. Samuel
    Waddington. WBP1
My friend. Brenda Bradley. YoVA
A newly found friend is like
    the sea. Keith Jost. YoVA
No more. Sally Ann Miemietz.
    YoVA
Parted friends. James
    Montgomery. WBP1
Platonic. William B. Terrett.
    WBP1
Sonnet LV. William Shakespeare.
    WBP1
Sonnet LVII. William
    Shakespeare. HaAP
Sonnet XXIX. William
    Shakespeare. HaAP--LiHE
Sonnet XXX. William
    Shakespeare. HaAP--WBP1
Sonnet XXXIII. William
    Shakespeare. HaAP--WBP2
Stars. Howard Moss. HoA
A temple to friendship. Thomas
    Moore. WBP1
To friends. Franco Fortini.
    NeIP
To seek a friend. William
    Cowper. WBP1
Understanding. Debbie Bolin.
    YoVA
The vale of Avoca. Thomas
    Moore. WBP1
Village hairdresser Anzai
    Hitoshi. FroC
A wayfaring song. Henry Van
    Dyke. WBP1
We are brethren a'. Robert
    Nicoll. WBP1
We have been friends together.
    Caroline Elizabeth S. Norton.

WBP1
We love but few. Unknown . WBP1
We met/and we were friends.
    Carolyn Barbor. YoVA
The welcome. Ferid ed-Din Attar.
    WBP1
Wife, children, and friends.
    Robert Nicoll. WBP1
Friendship, sels. William
    Cowper. WBP1
Friesen, Shelley
    Ghost town. YoVA
The **fringes**. Harris Lenowitz.
    VoWA
Frisk, Lori
    Friendship. YoVA
A **frog** he would a-wooing go.
    Mother Goose. MiRN
The **frog** prince. Florence M.
    ("Stevie") Smith. HaAP
Frogs
    Death of a naturalist. Seamus
        Heaney. HaAP
    Forty-one hokku on frogs. Matsuo
        Basho   FroC
    A frog he would a-wooing go.
        Mother Goose.   MiRN
    The frog prince. Florence M.
        ("Stevie") Smith. HaAP
    Powerless frog. Unknown.   FroC
from Janie. Faye Kicknosway.
    TeMP
From Jerusalem: a first poem.
    Gabriel Preil. VoWA
From Mount Nebo. Karl Wolfskehl.
    VoWA
From a correct address in a
    suburb... Helen Sorrells.
    LiHE
From a new height. Andrea
    Zanzotto. NeIP
From a window. Terri Wright.
    YoVA
"From all that dwell below the
    skies." Isaac Watts. EeBC
From an expedition to the
    Himalayas,sels. Wislawa
    Szymborska. CoP
From far, from even and morning.
    Alfred Edward Housman. HaAP
From good to bad. Robin Yard.
    YoVA
From heaven high I come to you.
    Martin Luther. PoCh
From here to there. Rachel Korn.
    VoWA
From life. Lazer Eichenrand.
    VoWA
From my mother's home. Leah
    Goldberg. BuAC--VoWA

From my mouth a song. William
  Oandasan. ReE
From the French by Ronsard.
  Paulus Melissus (Schede).
  ReLP
From the cavities of bones.
  Patricia Parker. BlS
From the crag. Mani Leib. VoWA
From the depths. Otakar Fischer.
  VoWA
From the dust. Elaine Dallman.
  VoWA
From the head. Louis Zukovsky.
  VoWA
From the provinces. Norman
  Rosten. HoA
From the recesses of a lowly
  spirit. Sir John Bowring.
  WBP4
Frontier and Pioneer Life
  An account of a visit... Ts'en
    Shen. GrAC
  Arriving at the frontier on a
    mission. Wang Wei. GrAC
  Big grave creek. Cid Corman.
    HoA
  Liang-chou songs, sel. Wang Han.
    GrAC
  Meeting an envoy on his way
    back.. Ts'en Shen. GrAC
  The north tower of Golden Fort.
    Kao Shih. GrAC
  Song of the white snow. Ts'en
    Shen. GrAC
  Traveling by river...Dragon
    Roar Rapid. Ts'en Shen. GrAC
  Unclassified poems of
    Ch'in-chou, sel. Tu Fu. GrAC
Frontier poems, sels. Lu Lun.
  GrAC
The frost. Hannah Flagg Gould.
  WBP1
Frost
  The frost. Hannah Flagg Gould.
    WBP1
Frost at midnight. Samuel Taylor
  Coleridge. HaAP
Frost, Robert
  Acquainted with the night. HaAP
  After apple-picking. LiHE
  Beyond words. TyW
  Birches. LiHE
  Departmental. LiHE
  Design. LiHE
  Directive. HaAP
  Fire and ice. LiHE--TyW
  For Allan. PoCh
  The hill wife. HaAP
  In hardwood groves. HaAP
  Mending wall. HaAP

The most of it. HaAP
Neither out far nor in deep.
  HaAP--MTS
Never again would birds' song
  be...same. HaAP
An old man's winter night. HaAP
Once by the Pacific. HaAP--MTS
"Out, out-" HaAP--LiHE
The pasture. RoRF
Provide, provide. HaAP--LiHE
The road not taken. HaAP
The silken tent. LiHE
Stopping by woods on a snowy
  evening. HaAP
The subverted flower. HaAP
Frost, Robert (about)
  A note to Mr. Frost. Henry F.
    Beechhold. StPo
  Thanks, Robert Frost. David
    Ray. TeMP
Fruit
  Still life. Yoshioka Minoru .
    FroC
The fruits. Daniel Ortega. NiR
Frustration. Cheryl Knaak. YoVA
Fuest, Milan
  Moses' account. VoWA
Fugato (coda). Gad Hollander.
  VoWA
Fugitive. Stephen Updegraff.
  YoVA
The fugitive's apologue. Nanni
  Balestrini. NeIP
The Fuhrer bunker, sels. William
  DeWitt Snodgrass. TyW
Fujiwara no Kamatari
  Upon marrying Yasumiko... FroC
Fujiwara no Shunzei
  Thirty tanka. FroC
Fulkerson, Mary
  On this day so full of gloom.
    YoVA
  Reflections in a daydream. YoVA
Full fathom five thy father
  lies. William Shakespeare.
  HaAP
Full fathom five. Sylvia Plath.
  MTS
The full moon. Rocco Scotellaro.
  NeIP
Fuller, Esther
  Detail from hell. YoVA
Fuller, Roy
  The dark. DuD
  Drawing. MiRN
Funeral oration for a mouse.
  Alan Dugan. HaAP
Funeral song. Maruyama Kaoru.
  FroC
Funeral train. Ishihara Yoshiro.

FroA
The game. Bonnie Waynick. YoVA
Gangemi, Kenneth
Classroom. BrBD
Ganging to and ganging frae.
Eliza Cook. WBP2
Gannett, William Channing
Aunt Phillis's guest. WBP3
The hills of the Lord. WBP4
In twos. WBP2
Garbage
The man on the dump. Wallace
Stevens. HaAP
Garcia, Alfred
I am what I am. YoVA
Garcia, Kirk
Trail of straw. ReE
Garcia, Raul Javier
Fraternal exhortation. NiR
The **garden.** Ezra Pound. SlW
The **garden.** Andrew Marvell. HaAP
The **garden** of Prosperine.
Algernon Charles Swinburne.
HaAP
The **garden** of love. William
Blake. HaAP--LiHE
The **garden** seat. Thomas Hardy.
HaAP
Gardens
Back into the garden. Sarah
Webster Fabio. BlS
The child in the garden. Henry
Van Dyke. WBP1
Come into the garden, Maud.
Alfred, Lord Tennyson. WBP2
Eighty-four tank. Furiwara no
Teika.   FroC
The garden. Andrew Marvell.
HaAP
In an abandoned garden.
Nishiwaki Junzaburo. FroC
In the garden of the Turkish
Consulate. Pinhas Sadeh. VoWA
Lilac garde. Yoshioka Minoru.
FroC
A little Dutch garden. Harriet
Whitney Durbin. WBP1
The mad gardener's song. Lewis
Carroll (C.L. Dodgson). IlTH
My garden. Thomas Edward Brown.
EeBC
Our hands in the garden. Anne
Hebert. MoVT
There is a garden in her face.
Unknown.   WBP2
Two gardens. Yona Wallach. BuAC
Gardner, Isabella
That was then. FroA
Gardner, Marla
The secret room. YoVA

The **garlic.** Bert Meyers. VoWA
Garmany, Michelle
One lonely leaf. YoVA
The universe. YoVA
The **garret.** Ezra Pound. SlW
The **garret.** Thomas Moore. WBP1
Garrison, Theodosia
The shepherd who stayed. PoCh
Garza, Elizabeth
"Ol Erie McGreer." YoVA
Gas from a burner. James Joyce.
TyW
Gas lamp. Willis Barnstone. VoWA
Gascoigne, George
And if I did, what then? HaAP
The lullaby of a lover. HaAP
Gasoline Stations
Filling station. Elizabeth
Bishop. HaAP
Working at a service station...
Dennis Finnell. FroA
Gastil, Denise L.
Another day, another time. YoVA
Gates of paradise, sels. William
Blake. HaAP
Gates, Darlene
A loyal image. YoVA
Memory lane. YoVA
Gathering firewood. Meng
Hao-jan. GrAC
Gathering the sparks. Howard
Schwartz. VoWA
Gatineau River, Canada
Water and worship: an open-air
service... Margaret Avison.
HaAP
Gatrel, Craig
Reflections of me. YoVA
Gaudeamus Igitur. John Aldington
Symonds (tr.). WBP1
Gay, John
Black-eyed Susan. MTS--WBP3
'Twas when the seas were
roaring. HaAP
Gay, Shelley
Two halves, when they/collide.
YoVA
Geese
A compendium of good tanka.
Furiwara no Teika. FroC
Sixty-four tanka. Saigyo   FroC
Snowgoose. Paula Gunn Allen.
ReE
Gelman, Juan
Customs. VoWA
The knife. VoWA
The stranger. VoWA
Genealogy. Donald Finkel. VoWA
The **general.** Siegfried Sassoon.
TyW

General strike 1969. Amelia
    Rosselli. NeIP
The generation gap. Fareedah
    Allah (Ruby Saunders). BlS
Generational. David Macfield.
    NiR
Generations. Moishe Steingart.
    VoWA
Genesis. Lotte Kramer. VoWA
Genesis. Geoffrey Hill. HaAP
Genitori. David Ray. TyW
Gentians
    Bavarian gentians. David
        Herbert Lawrence. HaAP--SlW
Geometry
    Figures of speech. Ellen De
        Haan. YoVA
    Joyce Kilmer, watch out! Ellen
        De Haan. YoVA
    Two hundred five/math. Maria
        Cardenas. YoVA
George. Steve Leifson. YoVA
George III, King of England
    In the first year of freedom's
        second.... George Gordon,6th
        Baron Byron. TyW
George, Emery
    Homage to Edward Hopper. HoA
    Solstice. HoA
George, Phil
    Eagle feather IV. ReE
    Eagle feather I. ReE
    Eagle feather III. ReE
    Eagle feather II. ReE
Gerber, Dan
    Love for instance. FroA
Gerez, Jozef Habib
    Call from the afterworld. VoWA
    We are acrobats. VoWA
    We fooled ourselves. VoWA
Gergely, Agnes
    Birth of a country. VoWA
    Conjuration. VoWA
    Desert. VoWA
Gerlach, Lee
    For Peter. HoA
    The pilot's day of rest. HoA
    The pilot's walk. HoA
Gerling, Donnelle
    Anonymous tragedy. YoVA
Germany and the Germans
    On a Rhine steamer. James
        Kenneth Stephen. TyW
    Wreathmakertraining. Karl
        Patten. FroA
Germination. Arlene Stone. VoWA
Gerock, Karl
    The children's church. WBPl
Gerontion. Thomas Stearns Eliot.
    HaAP--ShBa

Gestures
    Arriving at a new poem... David
        Curry. PrVo
Get you to the hell.... Caius
    Valerius Catullus. TyW
Getting lost in Nazi Germany.
    Marvin Bell. VoWA
The geyser. Joseph Bruchac. ReE
Ghetto song. Jacob Glatstein.
    OnCP
Ghetto twilight. Alter Brody.
    VoWA
Ghettos
    Elegy ("No more, no more...")
        Antoni Slonimski. VoWA
    Ghetto song. Jacob Glatstein.
        OnCP
    Ghetto twilight. Alter Brody.
        VoWA
    In a ghetto. Jacob Glatstein.
        VoWA
    In the ghetto. Hugo
        Sonnenschein. VoWA
    Jewish main street. Irving
        Layton. VoWA
    The stone &...grass in the
        Warsaw Ghetto. David
        Scheinert. VoWA
    To the Jews in Poland. Jozef
        Wittlin. VoWA
    Vilna. Moishe Kulbak. VoWA
Ghil, Rene
    Day of wrath. FreS
Ghiselin, Brewster
    The catch. HaAP
    Rattler, alert. HaAP
Ghitelman, David
    Grand Street & the Bowery. FroA
Ghost Towns
    Ghost town. Shelley Friesen.
        YoVA
Ghost town. Shelley Friesen.
    YoVA
Ghostly gladness. Richard Rolle.
    HaAP
Ghosts
    Alonzo the Monk and Fair
        Imogine. Matthew Gregory
        Lewis. EvIm
    Apparition. Stephane Mallarme.
        FoFS
    Giles Jollup the Grave...
        Matthew Gregory Lewis. EvIm
    The haunted palace. Edgar Allan
        Poe. EvIm
    Old house on the hill. Sherri
        Basinger. YoVA
Giant thunder. James Reeves. DuD
The giaour, sels. George
    Gordon,6th Baron Byron. WBP3

Gibb, Robert
    The minotaur. FroA
Gibbons, Gina
    Time. YoVA
Gide, Andre
    Four songs: II. MoVT
Gierut, Suzy
    Shell roses. YoVA
    Thought waves. YoVA
Gift from Kenya. May Miller. BlS
Gift hour. Maria Banus. VoWA
The gift of oneself. Valery
        Larbaud (C-M.Bonsignor). MoVT
Gift of the poem. Stephane
        Mallarme. FoFS
The gift, sels. Czeslaw Milosz.
        CoP
Gifts and Giving
    My gift to the world. Karen
        Tollett. YoVA
The gifts of God. George
        Herbert. WBP4
Giguere, Roland
    The difficulty of being. MoVT
    Night mastered. MoVT
Gilbert, Chris
    philonous' paradox. FroA
Gilbert, Sir William S.
    A most delightful day. IlTH
    The yarn of the Nancy Bell. MTS
Gilboa, Amir
    Birth. VoWA
    Isaac. VoWA
    Joshua's face. VoWA
    Moses. VoWA
    My brother was silent. VoWA
    Samson. VoWA
    Saul. VoWA
    Seeds of lead. VoWA
Gildner, Gary
    First practice. TyW
    Johann Gaertner (1793-1887).
        FroA
    Today they are roasting Rocky
        Norse. TeMP
    Tongue River psalm. FroA
Gilead, Zerubavel
    Absalom. VoWA
    Flying letters. VoWA
    Pomegranate tree in Jerusalem.
        VoWA
Giles Jollup the Grave...
        Matthew Gregory Lewis. EvIm
Gillespie, Robert
    When both my fathers die. FroA
The gillyflower of gold. William
        Morris. WBP2
Gilson, Pamela J.
    Love of yesterday. YoVA
Gimel. Stuart Z. Perkoff. VoWA

Gin the goodwife stint. Basil
        Bunting. TyW
Gingras, Carl
    An American thought. YoVA
Ginsberg, Allen
    Cafe in Warsaw. HaAP
    Howl, sels. SlW
    Kaddish. VoWA
    Kaddish, sels. DoNG
    A supermarket in California.
        HaAW--SlW
    Uptown. TyW

Gioseffi, Daniela
    Buildings. FroA
Giovanni, Nikki
    Dreams. LiHE
    Knoxville, Tennessee. BlS
    Mother's habits. BlS
    Nikki-Rosa. BlS
    Woman poem. BlS
The giraffe. Oliver Herford.
        IlTH
Giraffes
    The giraffe. Oliver Herford.
        IlTH
    Limerick:"... a stately
        giraffe." Margaret
        Vandergrift. IlTH
Giraud, Albert
    Autumn. FreS
    Red and white. FreS
    Sunset. FreS
Girl in the cafeteria. Roger
        Ellis. YoVA
The girl in the foreign movie.
        Patricia Goedicke. FroA
The girl of Cadiz. George
        Gordon,6th Baron Byron. WBP2
A girl of Pompeii. Edward
        Sanford Martin. WBP1
The girl of all periods.
        Coventry Patmore. WBP1
"A girl on a stream." Ts'ui Hao.
        GrAC
Girl with the green skirt. Dana
        Naone. ReE
Girls. Dan Andres. YoVA
Girls from home. Abraham Reisen.
        VoWA
The girls of Yueh. Li Po. GrAC
Girls plowing the fields. Tai
        Shu-lun. GrAC
Girls. See Youth
Giudici, Giovanni
    Is it right to move to the
        country? NeIP
    Roman epigram. NeIP
    You ask me what it means. NeIP
Giuliani, Alfredo

Animal song. NeIP
The days clinging to the city.
  NeIP
Friday, you look blue. NeIP
Letter from the mountain
  sanitarium. NeIP
The old man. NeIP
Predilictions. NeIP
Resurrection after the rain.
  NeIP
Who would have said it. NeIP
Give me more love or more
  disdain. Thomas Carew. WBP2
Give me the splendid silent sun.
  Walt Whitman. HaAP
Give me three grains of corn,
  mother. Amelia Blandford
  Edwards. WBP3
Give me thy heart. Adelaide Anne
  Procter. WBP4
Give place, ye lovers. Earl of
  Surrey (Henry Howard). WBP2
Given to Li Po. Tu Fu. GrAC
Giving up on the shore. Gabriel
  Preil. VoWA
Glad and blithe might ye be.
  Unknown. ShBa
Gladden, Washington
  Awakening. WBP3
  O Master, let me walk with
    thee. WBP4
  The pastor's reverie. WBP4
  Ultima veritas. WBP4
Glanz-Leyeles, A.
  Castles. VoWA
  Madison Square. VoWA
  White swan. VoWA
A glass of beer. James Stephens.
  TyW
Glass, Malcolm
  Staying ahead. FroA
Glatstein, Jacob
  Ballad ("He did not kill.")
    OnCP
  Biography. OnCP
  Evening bread. VoWA
  Ghetto song. OnCP
  I have never been here before.
    OnCP
  I'll find my self-belief. VoWA
  In a ghetto. VoWA
  Jewishness. OnCP
  Like weary trees. VoWA
  Loyal sins. VoWA
  Memorial poem. VoWA
  The messenger. OnCP
  Move on, Yiddish poet. VoWA
  Mozart. VoWA
  The poet lives. VoWA
  The shining fool. OnCP

Glazer (Schotz), Myra
  The first love poem. VoWA
  Recognition. BuAC
  Santa Caterina. BuAC--VoWA
  Thespian in Jerusalem. VoWA
Glazer, Joseph
  A visit home. VoWA
Glen uig. Richard Hugo. TeMP
The glories of our blood and
    state. James Shirley. HaAP
The glory of the garden. Rudyard
    Kipling. EeBC
Glover, Missy
  Whisper. YoVA
Gluck (German poet)
  To death. WBP3
Gluck, Louise
  Lamentations. TeMP
Glum-day sundae. Melanie D.
    Holiway. YoVA
The glutton. Robert Graves. TyW
Gluttonous talk. Yen
    Chen-ch'ing. GrAC
Glycon [or Glykon]
  Nothing but laughter, nothing.
    DoNG
Gnus
  "One day I went out to the zoo."
    G.T. Johnson. IlTH
Go down, Moses. Unknown. EeBC
Go sleep, ma honey. Edward D.
    Barker. WBP1
Go tell. Unknown. EeBC
Go throw them out. Moishe Leib
    Halpern. VoWA
"Go, and catch a falling star".
    John Donne. HaAP
Go, lovely rose!. Edmund Waller.
    WBP2
Go, lovely rose. Henry Kirke
    White. WBP2
Go, lovely rose!. Edmund Waller.
    HaAP--LiHE
The goat. Umberto Saba. VoWA
Goats
  The goat. Umberto Saba. VoWA
  Old Hogan's goat. Ogden Nash.
    IlTH
  Tracks. Joseph Torain. FroA
Goblin market. Christina
    Georgina Rossetti. EvIm
God. Sir John Bowring (trans.).
    WBP4
God. Isaac Rosenberg. VoWA
God. Gavril Romanovich
    Derzhavin. WBP4
God. Boris Slutsky. VoWA
God
  Abide with me. Henry Francis
    Lyte. WBP4

Abou Ben Adhem. Leigh Hunt.
  WBP4
The aim. Charles G. D. Roberts.
  WBP4
All is God's. Jakov de Haan.
  VoWA
Amoretti: LXVIII. Edmund
  Spenser. EeBC--HaAP
Argument against metaphor. Gad
  Hollander. VoWA
Art thou weary? Saint Stephen
  the Sabaite. WBP4
As sand. Natan Zach. VoWA
As spring the winter. Anne
  Dudley Bradstreet. EeBC
Ascription. Charles G. D.
  Roberts. WBP4
At God's command. Joseph
  Rolnik. VoWA
Before the anaesthetic. Sir
  John Betjeman. EeBC
Brahma. Ralph Waldo Emerson.
  HaAP--WBP4
"By cool Siloam's shady rill."
  Reginald Heber. WBP1
Caedmon's hym. Caedmon . EeBC
The call. George Herbert. WBP4
The celestial surgeon. Robert
  Louis Stevenson. EeBC
The cry of the human. Elizabeth
  Barrett Browning. WBP4
A dark hand. Itzik Manger. VoWA
De Profundis. Elizabeth Barrett
  Browning. WBP3
Delight in God. Francis
  Quarles. WBP4
Deserted shrine. Avner Treinin.
  VoWA
Different minds. Richard
  Chenevix Trench. WBP4
The divine image. William
  Blake. EeBC
Do you see God. Jerlene
  Dickson. YoVA
Dream seeker. King Kuka. ReE
An essay on man, sels.
  Alexander Pope. WBP4
Eternal Father, strong to save.
  William Whiting. MTS
The eternal goodness. John
  Greenleaf Whittier. WBP4
Father, thy will be done!
  Sarah Flower Adams. WBP4
The first love poem. Myra
  Glazer (Schotz). VoWA
The first one drew me. Rav
  Abraham Isaac Kook. VoWA
The flower. George Herbert.
  WBP3
A fly on the water. Paul Zweig.

TeMP
Forever friend. Patty Packwood.
  YoVA
Formations. William Freedman.
  VoWA
Foul water. Mordecai Temkin.
  VoWA
"From all that dwell below the
  skies." Isaac Watts. EeBC
From the depths. Otakar
  Fischer. VoWA
Ghostly gladness. Richard
  Rolle. HaAP
The gifts of God. George
  Herbert. WBP4
Give me thy heart. Adelaide
  Anne Procter. WBP4
God is everywhere. Robert
  Nicoll. WBP4
A god once commanded us. Leah
  Goldberg. VoWA
God our refuge. Richard
  Chenevix Trench. EeBC
God poem. Stanley Moss. VoWA
God's child. Carolyn D. Pierce.
  YoVA
God's gifts. Jakov de Haan.
  VoWA
God's grandeur. Gerard Manley
  Hopkins. EeBC--HaAP
God's sure help in sorrow.
  Anton Ulrich (Duke
  Brunswick). WBP3
God. Boris Slutsky. VoWA
God. Gavril Romanovich
  Derzhavin. WBP4
God. Isaac Rosenberg. VoWA
The great sad one. Uri Zvi
  Greenberg. VoWA
Hidden bow. Mordecai Temkin.
  VoWA
The hills of the Lord. William
  Channing Gannett. WBP4
Holy sonnets, sels. John Donne.
  HaAP
The holy spirit. Robert
  Herrick. WBP4
Hope of the human heart. R.M.
  Milnes (Lord Houghton). WBP4
Huswifery, sels. Edward Taylor.
  EeBC
A hymn to God the father. Ben
  Jonson. EeBC
Hymn, before sunrise... Samuel
  Taylor Coleridge. WBP4
I am my Beloved's... Hermann
  Hugo. ReLP
I say. Malka Heifetz Tussman.
  VoWA
I wonder. Jana Powell. YoVA

If God exists. Ewa Lipska. VoWA
If. Jerlene Dickson. YoVA
In memoriam, sels. Alfred, Lord Tennyson. WBP4
In no strange land. Francis Thompson. EeBC--HaAP
In the cabinet. Shlomo Vinner. VoWA
Inspiration. Henry David Thoreau. EeBC
"It is finished." Christina Georgina Rossetti. WBP1
Jewish hymn in Babylon. Henry Hart Milman. WBP4
Knocking, ever knocking. Harriet Beecher Stowe. WBP4
Last lines. Emily Bronte. EeBC
Lauds. John Berryman. HaAP
Lead, kindly light. John Henry, Cardinal Newman. WBP4
Let us learn. Melech Ravitch (Z.K. Bergner). VoWA
Light shining out of darkness. William Cowper. WBP4
Like a woman. Uri Zvi Greenberg. VoWA
Lines for the ancient scribes. Harvey Shapiro. VoWA
The living temple. Oliver Wendell Holmes. WBP4
Living waters. Caroline Spencer. WBP4
"Lord! when those glorious lights I see." George Wither. WBP4
The love of God supreme. Gerhard Tersteegen. WBP4
The love of God. Eliza Scudder. WBP4
Love the ruins. Malka Heifetz Tussman. VoWA
Love. Charles Francis Richardson. WBP4
Love. George Herbert. EeBC
Low spirits. Frederick William Faber. WBP4
Magnificat, sels. Paul Claudel. MoVT
A man adrift on a slim spar. Stephen Crane. MTS
Maranatha. Kristin Person. YoVA
The master's touch. Horatus Bonar. WBP4
May 20: very early morning. Luci Shaw. EeBC
Meditation (after Solomon Ibn Gabirol). Carl Rakosi. VoWA
Meditations of a Hindu prince. Sir Alfred Comyns Lyall. WBP4
A mighty fortress is our God.

Martin Luther. WBP4
Moral ode. David Rosenmann-Taub. VoWA
"My God said to me: My son...") Paul Verlaine. FoFS
My garden. Thomas Edward Brown. EeBC
My spirit longeth for thee. John Byrom. EeBC
The mystic's vision. Mathilde Blind. WBP4
A mystical ecstasy. Francis Quarles. WBP4
Nature's hymn to the deity. John Clare. EeBC
Non nobis domine. Rudyard Kipling. EeBC
O Lord, seek us. Christina Georgina Rossetti. EeBC
O Master, let me walk with thee. Washington Gladden. WBP4
O fire of God, the comforter. Saint Hildegarde. WBP4
Of hym that togyder wyll serve... Sebastian Brandt. WBP4
Oh! for a closer walk with God. William Cowper. EeBC
On the path. A.L. Strauss. VoWA
Our God, our help in ages past. Isaac Watts. WBP4
Over to God. Stephen Harrigan. FroA
Paths to God. Musa Moris Farni. VoWA
A peaceful song. Natan Zach. VoWA
Pied beauty. Gerard Manley Hopkins. LiHE--SlW
Pied beauty. Gerard Manley Hopkins. EeBC--HaAP
Pippa passes, sels. Robert Browning. WBP4
The practice of absence. Robert Friend. VoWA
Praise to God. Anna Letitia Barbauld. WBP4
Prayer and answer. Oliver Huckel. WBP4
Prayer of little hope. Jean Wahl. VoWA
Preparatory meditations, sels. Edward Taylor. HaAP
The presence. Jones Very. HaAP
Psalm ("Father/You are the trunk.") Howard Schwartz. VoWA
Psalm ("Oh Lord, I have been staring..") Eugene Heimler.

VoWA
Psalm paraphrase CXXVIII.
Marcantonio Flaminio. ReLP
A quer. Unknown . WBP4
Radiant is the world soul. Rav
Abraham Isaac Kook. VoWA
The right must win. Frederick
William Faber. WBP4
"Rock of ages." Edward H. Rice.
WBP4
Rocked in the cradle of the
deep. Emma Hart Willard.
MTS--WBP4
Scorn not the least. Robert
Southwell. WBP4
Seal of fire. Mordecai Temkin.
VoWA
Searching. Sherry Curry. YoVA
Slow oxen. Ilya Rubin. VoWA
Slowly meeting God. Theresa
Cantrell. YoVA
Small song. Luci Shaw. EeBC
Sometime. May Riley Smith. WBP4
A song to David, sels.
Christopher Smart. HaAP
Songs of the priestess. Malka
Heifetz Tussman. VoWA
Sonnet 56. William Alabaster.
ShBa
Sonnet 62. William Alabaster.
ShBa
Sonnet 66. William Alabaster.
ShBa
Speak. James Wright. HaAP
The spectator, sels. Joseph
Addison. WBP4
Sunrise. Charles Tennyson
Turner. WBP4
Te Deum Laudamu. Unknown . WBP4
Tenebrae. Paul Celan. VoWA
Thank you. Mary E. Israel. YoVA
There. Mary Elizabeth
Coleridge. EeBC
Thou art indeed just, Lord.
Gerard Manley Hopkins.
HaAP--LiHE
To a God unknown. David Eller.
VoWA
To a waterfowl. William Cullen
Bryant. EeBC
To heaven. Ben Jonson. HaAP
To-morrow. Lope de Vega. WBP4
The Trial. Gershom Scholem.
VoWA
The Twenty-third psalm. George
Herbert. EeBC
Van Elsen. Frederick George
Scott. WBP3
Veni creator spiritus. Saint
Gregory the Great. WBP4

Veni sancte spiritu. Robert II;
King of France . WBP4
The violin tree. Joel
Rosenberg. VoWA
Water turned into wine. Richard
Crashaw. WBP4
The way, the truth, and the
life. Theodore Parker. WBP4
When I was growing up. David
Vogel. VoWA
When gathering clouds around I
view. Sir Robert Grant. WBP4
When through the whirl of
wheels. G.A. Studdert
Kennedy. EeBC
Who? Dan Jaffe. FroA
The will of God. Frederick
William Faber. WBP4
With my God, the Smith. Uri Zvi
Greenberg. VoWA
Written on a wall at Woodstoc.
Elizabeth I; Queen of England
. PaW
Years. Anna Margolin (R.
Lebensboim). VoWA
Your presence. Mordecai Temkin.
VoWA
The zodiac of life. Pier
Manzoli (M.Palingenius). ReLP
Zurich, zum Storchen. Paul
Celan. VoWA
God and man. Errol Deppe. YoVA
God and nature. Musa Moris
Farni. VoWA
A god and yet a man?. Unknown.
HaAP
God fashioned the ship of the
world... Stephen Crane. MTS
God has pity on kindergarten
children. Yehuda Amichai.
VoWA
God is everywhere. Robert
Nicoll. WBP4
God made little kittens. Michael
Stanfield. YoVA
A god once commanded us. Leah
Goldberg. VoWA
God our refuge. Richard Chenevix
Trench. EeBC
God poem. Stanley Moss. VoWA
God said. Gioconda Belli. NiR
God's child. Carolyn D. Pierce.
YoVA
God's determinations, sels.
Edward Taylor. HaAP
God's gifts. Jakov de Haan. VoWA
God's grandeur. Gerard Manley
Hopkins. SlW
God's grandeur. Gerard Manley
Hopkins. EeBC--HaAP

God's language. Ruth Fainlight.
    VoWA
God's measurements. Laurence
    Lieberman. TeMP
God's sure help in sorrow.
    Catherine Winkworth (trans.).
    WBP3
God's sure help in sorrow. Anton
    Ulrich (Duke Brunswick). WBP3
God's-acre. Henry Wadsworth
    Longfellow. WBP3
Godolphin, Sidney
    Lord, when the wise men came
    from far. HaAP
The gods of copybook headings.
    Rudyard Kipling. TyW
Goebbels, Joseph
    The Fuhrer bunker, sels.
    William DeWitt Snodgrass. TyW
Goedicke, Patricia
    At the center of everything
    which..dying. FroA
    At the party. FroA
    The death balloon. FroA
    The girl in the foreign movie.
    FroA
Goethe, Johann Wolfgang von
    The comet. Paolo Volponi. NeIP
    Roman epigram. Giovanni
    Giudici. NeIP
Gogarty, Oliver St. John
    Leda and the swan. HaAP
Going and coming. Edward A.
    Jenks. WBP3
Going from the capital, sels. Tu
    Fu. GrAC
Going to school. Karla Kuskin.
    BrBD
Going to the north. Stanislaw
    Wygodski. VoWA
Going to town. Linda Hogan. ReE
Going to visit the Taoist...,
    sels. Li Po. GrAC
Gold and red leaves. Mary
    McMurtray. YoVA
Gold, Jiri
    In the cellars. VoWA
    An inhabited emptiness. VoWA
Goldbarth, Albert
    Dime call. VoWA
    Recipe. VoWA
Goldberg, Leah
    Answer. VoWA
    The eighth part (at least) of
    everything. BuAC
    From my mother's home.
    BuAC--VoWA
    A god once commanded us. VoWA
    Heavenly Jerusalem, Jerusalem
    of...Earth. BuAC--VoWA

Hill excursion. BuAC
In the Jerusalem hills, sels.
    BuAC
A look at a bee. BuAC
That poem that I didn't write.
    BuAC
Toward myself. VoWA
Goldemberg, Isaac
    Bar Mitzvah. VoWA
    The Jews in hell. VoWA
Golden age. Arthur Rimbaud.
    FoFS--FreS
Golden eyes. Andrew Lang
    (trans.). WBP2
Golden eyes. Rufinus Domesticus.
    WBP2
Golden fantasy. Tamura Ryuichi.
    FroC
The golden wedding. David Gray.
    WBP2
The golden wedding. David Gray.
    WBP2
Goldenmouthed. Stuart Merrill.
    FreS
Goldhardt, John
    Darkness. YoVA
Goldsmith, Oliver
    The Swiss peasant. WBP1
    The traveller, sels. WBP1
    The Vicar of Wakefield, sels.
    WBP2
    The wanderer's home. WBP1
    When lovely woman stoops to
    folly. HaAP
The golem. Shlomo Reich. VoWA
Golf
    Golf as a medicine. Greg
    Poissant. YoVA
Golf as a medicine. Greg
    Poissant. YoVA
Golgotha. Saint-Pol (Paul) Roux.
    FreS
Goll, Yvan
    Clandestine work. VoWA
    Lilith. VoWA
    Neila. VoWA
    Raziel. VoWA
Gomorrah
    Of the beloved caravan. Conny
    Hannes Meyer. VoWA
Gone. David McCord. ByM
Gonzales, Beth
    Love. YoVA
Good Friday. John Frederick
    Nims. TyW
Good Friday
    Good Friday. John Frederick
    Nims. TyW
Good King Arthur. Unknown. WBP1
The good beasts. Willis

Barnstone. VoWA
Good creatures, do you love your
    lives. Alfred Edward Housman.
    TyW
The good great man. Samuel
    Taylor Coleridge. WBP3
The good man in hell. Edwin
    Muir. TyW
Good morning. Mark Van Doren.
    DuD
Good neighbors. May Justus. MiRN
Good night and good morning.
    R.M. Milnes (Lord Houghton).
    WBP1
Good ol' days. Karen Simmons.
    YoVA
Good old rebel. Innes Randolph.
    TyW
A good play. Robert Louis
    Stevenson. WBP1
Good riddance to bad rubbish.
    Paul Goodman. TyW
The good shepherd with the kid.
    Matthew Arnold. WBP4
The good woman. Crystal MacLean.
    FroA
Good-bye. Unknown. WBP3
Good-bye. Ralph Waldo Emerson.
    WBP4
Goodman, Paul
    Good riddance to bad rubbish.
    TyW
    The Messiah-blower. FroA
Goodnight Richard Rabbit. Robert
    Kraus. TrWB
Gordillo, Fernando
    Andres. NiR
    The circumstance and the word.
    NiR
    The price of a country. NiR
The gorilla. Baxter Hathaway.
    HoA
Gorillas
    The gorilla. Baxter Hathaway.
    HoA
Gospels and Gospelers
    ...And the old women gathered.
    Mari Evans. BlS
    The meaning of Solentiname.
    Ernesto Cardenal. NiR
    Mourning poem for the queen of
    Sunday. Robert Hayden. HoA
Gosse, Edmund William
    Lying in the grass. WBP1
    Perfume. WBP2
Gottlieb, Frantisek
    Between life and death. VoWA
    Just a while. VoWA
Gottlieb, Lynn
    Eve's song in the garden. VoWA

Gottlieb, Phyllis
    The morning prayers of...Rabbi
    L.Yitzhok. VoWA
Gould, Hannah Flagg
    The frost. WBP1
The gourd dancer. N. Scott
    Momaday. ReE
Gourmont, Remy de
    Agatha. FreS
    Evil prayers. FreS
    Ursula. FreS
Government
    Cooperative counci. Takamura
    Kotaro . FroC
Goweitduweetza(Veronica Riley)
    Untitled journey. ReE
Goya, Jose de
    In Goya's greatest scenes.
    Lawrence Ferlinghetti. LiHE
Grable, Heidi
    The dove. HoWM
Grace
    The pangolin. Marianne Moore.
    HaAP
Grace for children. Robert
    Herrick. EeBC
Grace-At Meals
    Another grace for a child.
    Robert Herrick. EeBC
    Grace for children. Robert
    Herrick. EeBC
Gracious goodness. Marge Piercy.
    HoA
Grade, Chaim
    In wolfen teeth. OnCP
    The miracle. VoWA
    Refugees. VoWA
    The road of suffering. OnCP
    Without me you won't...see
    yourself. VoWA
Graham(Marquis Montrose),James
    My dear and only love. WBP2
Graham, Robert Cunningham
    If doughty deeds my lady
    please. WBP2
Grahame, James
    The poor man's day. WBP4
    The Sabbath, sels. WBP4
Grahame, Kenneth
    Wind in the willow, sels. PoCh
Grahn, Judy
    I have come to claim. LiHE
A grain of moonlight. Asya. VoWA
Grammar
    Ode to grammer. David Payne.
    YoVA
Gramsci's ashes. Pier Paolo
    Pasolini. NeIP
Gramsci, Antonio
    Gramsci's ashes. Pier Paolo

VoWA
    Living with gavity. Arthur B.
        Shenefelt. StPo
Gray eminences of rapture, sels.
    Miron Bialoszewski. CoP
Gray, David
    The golden wedding. WBP2
Gray, Thomas
    The bard, sels. TyW
    Elegy written in a country
        churchyard. WBP3
    Elegy written in a country
        churchyard. HaAP--LiHE
    On Lord Holland's seat near
        Margate.... TyW
    On a distant prospect of Eton
        College. WBP1
Gray,, David
    The golden wedding. WBP2
Grazing on the Great Peak. Tu
    Fu. GrAC
Greacen, Robert
    Curse. TyW
"The great bird flies." Li Po.
    GrAC
"A great dark drowsiness," Paul
    Verlaine. FoFS--FreS
The great glue mess. Scott Van
    Klaveren. YoVA
A great mosquito dance. Norman
    H. Russell. ReE
The great sad one. Uri Zvi
    Greenberg. VoWA
The great silke of Sule Skerrie.
    Unknown. MTS
The Greater Friendship Baptist
    Church. Carole C. Gregory.
    BlS
The greatest wisdom. Mark
    Childers. YoVA
Greece and the Greeks
    Byron in Greece. Norman Rosten.
        HoA
    Greek transfiguration. Kimon
        Friar. HoA
    A quality of air. Henry Chapin.
        FroA
Greek War of Independence
    Hellas, sels. Percy Bysshe
        Shelley. HaAP
Greek transfiguration. Kimon
    Friar. HoA
Green. Paul Verlaine. FoFS
The green grass under the snow.
    Annie A. Preston. WBP3
Green grow the rashes O. Robert
    Burns. WBP2
Green grow'th the holly. Henry
    VIII; King of England.
    PoCh--ShBa

The green of the summer rests in
    my hand. Ellen Ryan. YoVA
A green refrain. Avraham Huss.
    VoWA
"Green spring..." Ryokan. FroC
Greenberg, Alvin
    so? FroA
    sungrazer. FroA
Greenberg, Uri Zvi
    The great sad one. VoWA
    The hour. VoWA
    How it is. VoWA
    Like a woman. VoWA
    On the Pole. VoWA
    Song at the skirts of heaven.
        VoWA
    There is a box. VoWA
    The valley of men. VoWA
    With my God, the Smith. VoWA
Greene, Homer
    What my lover said. WBP2
Greene, Robert
    Philomela's ode. WBP2
    The shepherd and the king. WBP2
    The shepherd's wife's song.
        HaAP
Greene, Sarah Pratt M'Lean
    De sheepfol'. WBP4
Greenfield, Pam
    Depression. YoVA
Greenfield, Paul
    The widow. YoVA
Greenhouse. Phyllis Janik. PrVo
Greenwell, Randy
    The rain of life. YoVA
Greenwood cemetery. Crammond
    Kennedy. WBP3
Greer, Troya
    Thoughtful storm. YoVA
Greeting descendants. A.G.
    Sobin. FroA
Greeting from a distance. Hans
    Sahl. VoWA
Greetings
    Salutation. Stephane Mallarme.
        FoFS
Greg. Jami Wald. YoVA
Gregg, Linda
    The defeated. TeMP
Gregor (Goldenberg), Arthur
    At the trough. FroA
    Spirit-like before light. VoWA
Gregory the Great, Saint
    Darkness is thinning. WBP4
    Veni creator spiritus. WBP4
Gregory, Carole C.
    A freedom song for the black
        woman. BlS
    The Greater Friendship Baptist
        Church. BlS

Love letter. BlS
Revelation. BlS
Gregory, Horace
Siege at Stony Point. FroA
Greiner, Gail
Rainy morning. YoVA
Reminiscence. YoVA
Greville (Lord Brooke), Fulke
Caelica, sels. HaAP
O wearisome condition of
humanity. HaAP
Grey days. Jeff Isaacs. YoVA
Grey uncles. Ephraim Auerbach.
OnCP
A Greyport legend. Bret Harte.
MTS
Grief for the dead. Unknown.
WBP3
Grief. See Sorrow
Grieve, Christopher Murray
The bonnie broukit bairn. HaAP
Cattle show. HaAP
Crystals like blood. HaAP
The octopus. TyW
On the ocean floor. HaAP
Wheesht, wheesht. HaAP
Grieving over the times, sels.
Meng Yun-ch'ing. GrAC
Grieving over the death of the
nun Rigan. Lady Otomo no
Sakanoue. FroC
Griffen, Gerald Joseph
The sister of charity. WBP4
Griffin, Bartholomew
To Fidessa. WBP2
Grimke, Angelina Weld
At April. BlS
For the candle light. BlS
A Mona Lisa. BlS
To keep the memory of
C...Forten Grimke. BlS
Grimoald, Nicholas
The friend. WBP1
On friendship. WBP1
Grindel (see P.Eluard), Eugene

Grinding vibrato. Jayne Cortez.
BlS
Grochowiak, Stanislaw
The breasts of the queen...,
sels. CoP
Chimneys. CoP
A Christmas carol, sels. CoP
Skylark. CoP
Vengefulness. CoP
When nothing remains any
longer, sels. CoP
The widower. CoP
Zen. CoP
Grogan, Cathy

Shooting star. YoVA
Trespassing. YoVA
Grose, Merri
Fantasy of the mind. YoVA
Grossbardt, Andrew
A river in Asia. FroA
Grosskruetz, Bonnie
A stone. YoVA
Grossman, Allen
Lilith. VoWA
Grossman, Martin
The bread of our affliction.
VoWA
Into the book. VoWA
Groth, Patricia Celley
Fellow traveler. StPo
Penelope, unweaving. StPo
To the boy studying in Palmer
Square. StPo
The groundhog. Richard Eberhart.
DoNG
Groundhogs
The groundhog. Richard
Eberhart. DoNG
Growing Up
Caterpillar. Gleena Scholer.
YoVA
Dad, I'm scared. Barbara Wilde.
YoVA
A door slams. Scott Morgan.
YoVA
Eighteen. Maria Banus. VoWA
Friction. Lori Susan Avant.
YoVA
Growing is.... Melanie D.
Holiway. YoVA
Growing-up. Marjorie Nyland.
YoVA
I am sixteen. Penny Ward. YoVA
In little hands. Mani Leib.
VoWA
It hurts! Lori Susan Avant.
YoVA
Leo the late bloomer. Robert
Kraus. TrWB
Meditation (after Jehudah
Halevi). Carl Rakosi. VoWA
Moments of initiation. Kama
Kerpi. VooI
Native colours, sel.
Karoniaktatie (Alex Jacobs).
ReE
Seven times two. Jean Ingelow.
WBP1
Special people. Donna Izzo.
YoVA
That country road. Danny
Callen. YoVA
Tomorrow. Myra Cohn Livingston.
DuD

The tower. Don Pagis. VoWA
Untitled. Debbie Bolin. YoVA
What is it like? Cindy Loop.
    YoVA
When I am me. Felice Holman.
    ByM
When I was growing up. David
    Vogel. VoWA
Where do I go? Geeta Pasi.
    YoVA
You can't stop now. Etta Marie
    Beasley. YoVA
You talked and pleaded... Beth
    Lewis. YoVA
Growing is.... Melanie D.
    Holiway. YoVA
Growing old. Matthew Arnold.
    LiHE
Growing-up. Marjorie Nyland.
    YoVA
Grunewald, Alfred
    The lamp now flickers.
Grup, Peggy
    Clouds. YoVA
    Heaven on earth. YoVA
Grynberg, Henryk
    Anti-nostalgia. VoWA
    The Dead Sea. VoWA
    Listening to Confucius. VoWA
    Poplars. VoWA
Guadalajara, Mexico
    The instruction manual. John
        Ashbery. HaAP--SlW
Guadamuz, Carlos Jose
    Commander Julio. NiR
    Five years in jail. NiR
Guarino, Paula
    The clown. YoVA
    Forgotten. YoVA
Guatamala
    A letter from the hotel. Aliki
        Barnstone. FroA
Gubbinal. Wallace Stevens. SlW
Gucci fruit. E.B. Shaw (Jr.).
    YoVA
Gucci, Emilio
    Gucci fruit. E.B. Shaw (Jr.).
        YoVA
Guerica, Victoria
    In this room it is cold. YoVA
The guerrilla fighters. Horacio
    Bermudez. NiR
The guerrilla's tomb. Carlos
    Mejia Godoy. NiR
The guest. Unknown. EeBC
A guest comes. Tu Fu. GrAC
The guests. Franco Fortini. NeIP
Guests
    A guest come. Tu Fu. GrAC
Guevara, Che

The book of "Che." Leonel
    Rugama. NiR
In Rivas, Nicaragua. Jorge
    Eduardo Arellano. NiR
Guggenheim Fellowships
    Lines on being refused a
        Guggenheim.... Reed
        Whittemore. TyW
    No foundation. John Hollander.
        TyW
Guide to Jerusalem. Dennis Silk.
    VoWA
Guillen, Nicolas
    American rhymes. NiR
Guillevic, Eugene
    A flayed ox. MoVT
    Karnac I. MoVT
    Karnac II. MoVT
    "The saw enters the wood" MoVT
Guilt
    Grey uncles. Ephraim Auerbach.
        OnCP
    Innocence. Laura Purdy. YoVA
    The poem on the guilt. Avot
        Yeshurun. VoWA
Guilty, or not guilty?. Unknown.
    WBP3
Guiney, Louise Imogen
    Tryste Noel. WBP4
Guitars
    Her guitar. Frank Dempster
        Sherman. WBP2
    Poem 25. Norma Edith Egea. StPo
"Guitars, cellos and/women.."
    James F. King. StPo
Guiterman, Arthur
    The ambiguous dog. IlTH
    Sea-chill. MTS
Gulliver
    Like Gulliver. Nina Cassian.
        VoWA
Gulls
    Gulls over paradise. Madeline
        Mason. StPo
    Handicapped. Daniel Berrigan.
        FroA
    Sad partin. Maruyama Kaoru.
        FroC
    The sea-gull. Ogden Nash. MTS
    Song of the gul. Maruyama Kaoru
        . FroC
Gulls over paradise. Madeline
    Mason. StPo
Gun base. Maruyama Kaoru. FroC
Gunn, Thomson
    Moly. HaAP
    On the move. HaAP
Guns
    Fragments ("In the gun muzzle.")
        Maruyama Kaoru. FroC

Gun bas. Maruyama Kaoru . FroC

Gurevitch, Zali
    Not going with it. VoWA
    Short eulogy. VoWA

Guri, Haim
    Anath. VoWA
    And on my return. VoWA
    Isaac. VoWA
    A latter purification. VoWA
    My Samsons. VoWA
    Nine men out of a minyan. VoWA
    Rain. VoWA

Gurley, Rick
    How to write a poem. YoVA
    The shah of Iran. YoVA

Gusai, Monk
    Highly renowned, sels. FroC

Gutierrez, Alvaro
    Arms and letters. NiR

Gutierrez, Ernesto
    The exile. NiR
    The mosquitia. NiR
    My country is so tiny. NiR
    Oh country, my country. NiR

The **gutter**. Franco Fortini. VoWA

Gwynne, Fred
    The king who rained. TrWB
    The sixteen hand horse. TrWB

Gypsies
    The gypsy bible. Julian Tuwim.
      VoWA
    The gypsy laddi. Unknown . HaAP
    The scholar-gypsy. Matthew
      Arnold. HaAP

The **gypsy** bible. Julian Tuwim.
    VoWA

The **gypsy** laddie. Unknown. HaAP

The **gyres**. William Butler Yeats.
    HaAP

H.D. See Doolittle, Hilda

Haan, Jakov de
    All is God's. VoWA
    God's gifts. VoWA
    Hanukah. VoWA
    Sabbath. VoWA
    Unity. VoWA

Habakkuk. Edouard Roditi. VoWA

Habakkuk
    Habakkuk. Edouard Roditi. VoWA

Habeas corpus. Helen Hunt
    Jackson. WBP3

Habington, William
    To roses in the bosom of
      Castara. WBP2

Hacker, Marilyn

La Fontaine du Vaucluse for
    Marie Ponsot. TeMP

Hadsell, Kerry
    Together. YoVA

Hagar
    Hagar and Ishmael. Else
      Lasker-Schuler. VoWA
    Hagar's last night at
      Abraham's. Itzik Manger. OnCP
    The story of Abraham and Hagar.
      Edna Aphek. VoWA

Hagar and Ishmael. Else
    Lasker-Schuler. VoWA

Hagar to Ishmael. Deborah Eibel.
    VoWA

Hagar's last night at Abraham's.
    Itzik Manger. OnCP

Hagiwara Sakutaro
    The army. FroC
    Bamboo. FroC
    A barren area. FroC
    Cherry. FroC
    The corpse of a cat. FroC
    The hand is a cake. FroC
    An impression of early summer.
      FroC
    In the horse carriage. FroC
    Lover of love. FroC
    Night train. FroC
    The octopus that does not die.
      FroC
    On a trip. FroC
    Out of the inner shell of
      a...landscape. FroC
    Pinks and a blue cat. FroC
    Sickly face at the bottom of
      the ground. FroC
    Spring night. FroC
    Sunny spring. FroC
    Twilight room. FroC
    White public benches. FroC
    Yoshiwara. FroC

Hai. Stuart Z. Perkoff. VoWA

Haifa. David Knut. VoWA

Haifa, Israel
    Haifa. David Knut. VoWA

Haiku. Terri Reeves. YoVA

Haiku ("Colored leaves
    trickle.") Rosalie Williams.
    YoVA

Haiku ("The storm approaches.")
    Marty Ernsting. YoVA

Haiku: 100 haiku in free form.
    Ozaki Hosai. FroC

Haiku: 39 haiku. Masaoka Shiki.
    FroC

Hail, Raven
    Cherokee invocation. ReE
    Ritual to insure long life. ReE
    The tiger. ReE

Hail, captain of the continent.
    Pablo Neruda. NiR
Haines, John
    Deserted cabin. TeMP
Haining, James
    Riding the blinds. PrVo
Hair. Maxine Silverman. VoWA
Hair
    Bamboo & Oa. Miyazawa Kenji.
        FroC
    Combing. Gladys Cardiff. ReE
    Hair poem. Dana Naone. ReE
    Head of hair. Charles
        Baudelaire. FoFS
    Kissing her hair. Algernon
        Charles Swinburne. WBP2
    My strawlike hai. Asya . VoWA
    Nudities. Andre Spire. VoWA
    The rape of the lock. Alexander
        Pope. HaAP
    Sonnets from the Portuguese,
        sels. Elizabeth Barrett
        Browning. HaAP
    Tanka: 39 tanka. Yosano Akiko.
        FroC
    To his wife, when he fell ill.
        Mikata no Sami. FroC
    A tragic story. William
        Makepeace Thackeray. IlTH
    Zen poems, after Shinkichi
        Takahasi. Lucien Stryk. FroA
"The hair flight of a flame..."
    Stephane Mallarme. FoFS
Hair poem. Dana Naone. ReE
Hajnal, Anna
    Dead girl. VoWA
    Tree to flute. VoWA
Hales, Kristy
    My house of knowledge. HoWM
Half-tide ledge. Richard P.
    Blackmur. MTS
Half-waking. William Allingham.
    WBP1
Halfway. Maxine Kumin. TeMP
Halkin, Shimon
    Do not accompany me. VoWA
Hall, Beth
    Floating through life. YoVA
Hall, Carol
    He sacred me so. YoVA
Hall, Christopher Newman
    My times are in thy hand. WBP4
Hall, Donald
    For an early retirement. TyW
    Names of horses. HaAP
    Ox cart man. TeMP
Hall, John
    Saw. HoWM
Hall, Kathy
    Lunch. BrBD

Hall, Sam
    Sam Hal. Unknown. TyW
Hall-Evans, Jo Ann
    Cape Coast castle revisited.
        BlS
    Seduction. BlS
Hallam, Arthur Henry
    In memoriam, sels. Alfred, Lord
        Tennyson. HaAP
A halo. Ralph Salisbury. FroA
Halperin, Mark
    Concerning the dead. FroA
    Franz Jagesttater's
        epistemology. TeMP
Halpern (see H. Leivick), L.

Halpern, Daniel
    Directions from Zulu. FroA
    Return. TeMP
Halpern, Moishe Leib
    Considering the bleakness. VoWA
    Go throw them out. VoWA
    Isaac Leybush Peretz. VoWA
    Just because. VoWA
    Memento mori. VoWA
    Never again will I say. OnCP
    Sacco-Vanzetti. VoWA
    That's our lot. VoWA
    Zlotchev, my home. VoWA
Halpern, Moyshe Leyb
    Never again will I say. OnCP
Hamburger, Michael
    At Staufen. VoWA
    The search. VoWA
Hamer, Fannie Lou
    Remembering Fannie Lou Hamer.
        Thadious M. Davis. BlS
Hamilton, Alfred Starr
    Wheat metropolis. FroA
Hamilton, Elizabeth
    My ain fireside. WBP1
Hamlet (about)
    "Black northwind, howling
        downpur." Jules Laforgue.
        FreS
    Elegy of Fortinbras, sels.
        Zbigniew Herbert. CoP
    Midrash on Hamlet. Francis
        Landy. VoWA
Hamlet, sels. William
    Shakespeare. PoCh
Hamlet, sels. William
    Shakespeare. WBP4
Hamlet, sels. William
    Shakespeare. WBP1
Hamlet, sels. William
    Shakespeare. DoNG
Hamlet, sels. William
    Shakespeare. WBP3
Hamm, Kathy

Hardinge (trans.), William M.
    The grave of Sophocles. WBP3
Hardy, Thomas
    After the fair. HaAP
    Channel firing. HaAP
    The convergence of the twain.
        MTS
    The darkling thrush. EvIm--HaAP
    Drummer Hodge. HaAP
    During wind and rain. HaAP
    The dynasts, sels. MTS
    The enemy's portrait. TyW
    The garden seat. HaAP
    Hap. LiHE
    "I look into my glass." HaAP
    In time of "The breaking of
        nations." HaAP
    The man he killed. HaAP
    Neutral tones. HaAP
    The oxen. HaAP--PoCh
    The ruined maid. LiHE
    The self-unseeing. HaAP
    The voice. HaAP
    A wasted illness. EvIm
Hardy, Thomas (about)
    The heart of Thomas Hardy. Sir
        John Betjeman. TyW
Hares
    Epitaph on a hare. William
        Cowper. HaAP
Harington, Donald
    The villanelle. FroA
Harington, Sir John
    Hate and debate Rome.... TyW
Harjo, Joy
    Someone talking. ReE
    Three AM. ReE
    Too far into Arizona. ReE
Harjo, Susan Shown
    i breathe as the night
        breathes. ReE
    Waking-up thoughts. ReE
Hark! the herald angels sing.
    Charles Wesley. ShBa
Hark, now everything is still.
    John Webster. HaAP
Harkavi, H. See Harakavy, C.

Harlem. Langston Hughes. LiHE
Harnick, Sheldon
    The merry little minuet. TyW
Harp song of the Dane women.
    Rudyard Kipling. HaAP
Harper, Frances E.W.
    An appeal to my countrywomen.
        BlS
    The crocuses. BlS
    A double standard. BlS
    Learning to read. BlS
    She's free! BlS

Vashti. BlS
Harper, Michael S.
    Cannon arrested. FroA
    Mahalia. FroA
Harriet. Lorde Audre. BlS
Harrigan, Stephen
    Over to God. FroA
Harris, Dee Dee
    "I blink my eye." HoWM
Harrison, Jean S.
    Blue-jay January. StPo
    The jogger. StPo
Harrod, Lois Marie
    Canto 17. StPo
    Elegy for Jan. StPo
    Penelope. StPo
    "Tidedrops on seashelf." StPo
Harte, Bret
    A Greyport legend. MTS
    Her letter. WBP2
Hartley, Colleen
    People rush/push. YoVA
    "Raindrops; drown in tears."
        YoVA
Hartley, Douglas
    A car can be a toy. YoVA
Harvests and Harvesting
    The fruits. Daniel Ortega. NiR
    Hay mowing. Moishe Kulbak. OnCP
    Hurrahing in harvest. Gerard
        Manley Hopkins. EeBC
    Reapers. Jean Toomer. HaAP
    The solitary reaper. William
        Wordsworth. HaAP
    The wind on leave. Rene Char.
        MoVT
Harvey, Frederick William
    Ducks, sels. EeBC
Harvey, Ken
    Life in the rain. YoVA
    Little bunny. YoVA
    A portrait of Judy. YoVA
Has summer come without the
    rose?. Arthur O'Shaughnessy.
    WBP3
Hasidic Jew from Sadagora. Rose
    Auslander. VoWA
Hasidim dance. Nelly Sachs. VoWA
Hasidim. See Chassidim
Hass, Robert
    The origin of cities. TeMP
Hate
    The bastard from the bush.
        Henry Lawson. TyW
    The beginnings, sels. Rudyard
        Kipling. TyW
    Better to spit on the whip....
        Colette Inez. TyW
    Beyond words. Robert Frost. TyW
    Black Bull of Aldgate. Alfred,

FroA

The **haunted** palace. Edgar Allan Poe. EvIm

Havana, Cuba
The store in Havana. Jose Kozer. VoWA

Havdolah. Susan Litwack. VoWA

Havdolah wine. Miriam Ulinover. VoWA

"**Have** you seen the elephant." Unknown. IlTH

Havergal, Frances Ridley
I gave my life for thee. WBP4
Peace. WBP4

Hawk roosting. Ted Hughes. HaAP

Hawkins, Linda D.
Loneliness. YoVA

Hawks
Hawk roosting. Ted Hughes. HaAP
Hurt hawks. Robinson Jeffers. LiHE
Longing for my stray hawk.. Otomo no Yakamochi, FroC
Waiting for nighthawks in Illinois. Roger Pfingston. FroA

Haws, Jennifer
Feelings. YoVA

Hawtrey (trans.), Edward C.
The iliad, sels. WBP3

Hay
Haymaking song: Miyazaki perfectur. Unknown. FroC

Hay mowing. Moishe Kulbak. OnCP

Hay, John
Religion and doctrine. WBP4
A woman's love. WBP3

Hay, ay, hay, ay. Unknown. ShBa

Hayden, Robert
The diver. MTS
Frederick Douglass. HoA
Mourning poem for the queen of Sunday. HoA
The night-blooming cereus. HoA
O Daedalus, fly away home. HaAP
A plague of starlings. HoA
Those winter Sundays. HaAP--HoA
The whipping. TyW

Hayes, Ednah Procter Clarke
An opal. WBP2

Haymaking song: Miyazaki perfecture. Unknown. FroC

Hayne, Paul Hamilton
In harbor. WBP3
The mountain of the lovers, sels. WBP2
Patience. WBP4

The **haystack** in the floods. William Morris. HaAP

Hazo, Samuel

The next time you were there. FroA

He. John Ashbery. SlW

He and his family. Laura E. Richards. IlTH

He sacred me so. Carol Hall. YoVA

He said to. Marvin Bell. TeMP

He understands. Susan Brown. YoVA

He who was always nursing..human wound... Giancarlo Marmori. NeIP

He wishes for the clothes of heaven. William Butler Yeats. SlW

Head (human)
"I love to go to lectures." Gelett Burgess. IlTH
"If people's heads were not so dense." Gelett Burgess. IlTH
Thoughts on one's head. William Meredith. HaAP

Head of hair. Charles Baudelaire. FoFS

Headlines. Michele Morgan. YoVA

Headwaters. N. Scott Momaday. ReE

A **health.** Edward Coate Pinkney. WBP2

Health Resorts
Atam. Chugan Engetsu . FroC
The last resort. Robert Willson. FroA
Letter from the mountain sanitarium. Alfredo Giuliani. NeIP

Heaney, Seamus
The barn. HaAP
Death of a naturalist. HaAP
Docker. TyW

"**Hear** how in April near the acacias." Arthur Rimbaud. FoFS--FreS

Hear, O Israel! Andre Spire. VoWA

Hearing Tung T'ing play nomad pipe songs. Li Ch'i. GrAC

Hearing a flute on the river. Wang Ch'ang-ling. GrAC

Hearken to this heart forlorn. Holly Sadeghian. YoVA

Hearn, Patrick Michael
At dawn. BrBD
In the library. BrBD
Rhinos purple, hippos green. BrBD

The **heart.** Stephen Crane. TyW

The **heart.** David Ignatow. VoWA

Heart (human)

Heaven on earth. Peggy Grup.
      YoVA
Heaven-haven. Gerard Manley
      Hopkins. MTS--SlW
Heavenly Jerusalem, Jerusalem
      of...Earth. Leah Goldberg.
      BuAC--VoWA
Heber, Reginald
   "By cool Siloam's shady rill."
      WBP1
   Epiphany. WBP4
   If thou wert by my side, my
      love. WBP2
   Thou art gone to the grave.
      WBP3
Hebert, Anne
   Our hands in the garden. MoVT
   Presence. MoVT
   Seascape. MoVT
   There is certainly someone.
      MoVT
Hebrew (language)
   Buying a shop on Dizengoff.
      Erez Biton. VoWA
   The Hebrew of your poets, Zion.
      Charles Reznikoff. VoWA
   Language of ancients. Hayim
      Lenski. VoWA
Hebrew letters in the trees. J.
      Rutherford Willems. VoWA
Hebrew melodies, sels. George
      Gordon,6th Baron Byron. WBP2
The Hebrew of your poets, Zion.
      Charles Reznikoff. VoWA
Hebrew script. Tali Loewenthal.
      VoWA
The Hebrew sibyl. Ruth
      Fainlight. VoWA
Hebrew wedding. Henry Hart
      Milman. WBP2
Hecht, Anthony
   The Dover bitch. LiHE
   The end of the weekend. HaAP
   The feast of Stephen. HaAP
   A little cemetery, sels. TyW
   "More light! More light!"
      HaAP--VoWA
   An old malediction. TyW
Hedge, Frederic Henry
   A mighty fortress is our God.
      WBP4
Heide, Carolyn
   A dream? YoVA
   People. YoVA
   Toes. YoVA
Heide, Florence Parry
   Rocks. ByM
Heide, Jerold
   These be/Three final things.
      YoVA

Heimler, Eugene
   After an eclipse of the sun.
      VoWA
   Psalm ("Oh Lord, I have been
      staring..") VoWA
Heine, Heinrich
   The palm and the pine. WBP3
   Three holy kings from
      Morgenland. PoCh
Heiple, Melissa
   Feather dreams. YoVA
   Live. YoVA
   Soliloquy to a crowd. YoVA
Helen. Hilda Doolittle (H.D.).
      TyW
Helen of Troy
   Helen. Hilda Doolittle (H.D.).
      TyW
   Past ruined Ilion Helen lives.
      Walter Savage Landor. HaAP
   To Helen. Edgar Allan Poe. HaAP
Hell
   Alcestis. Maura Stanton. TeMP
   The curse. Robert Francis. TyW
   Detail from hell. Esther
      Fuller. YoVA
   Divine comedy, sel. Dante
      Alighieri . WBP4
   Eurydice. Phyllis Thompson.
      TeMP
   The Jews in hell. Isaac
      Goldemberg. VoWA
   Paradise lost, sels. John
      Milton. LiHE--TyW
   Revelations. Ryan Synovec. YoVA
   Sixty-four tank. Saigyo . FroC
   Specters, sels. Tadeusz Gajcy.
      CoP
Hellas, sels. Percy Bysshe
      Shelley. HaAP
Hellman, George Sidney
   The Hudson. WBP1
Helpmate. Henry Chapin. FroA
Hemans, Felicia Dorothea
   The hour of death. WBP3
Hemans, Felicia
   The homes of England. WBP1
Hemingway, Ernest
   Valentine. TyW
Hemmingson, Deb
   The first day. YoVA
   A light in the darkness. YoVA
Henderson, Misty
   "I have a secret nobody knows."
      HoWM
Henderson, Susan
   Childhood memory. YoVA
   Not that I really care. YoVA
Hendon, Saundra Lyn
   Behind the smoke stained glass.

YoVA
Heng-chiang lyrics, sels. Li Po.
    GrAC
Henley, William Ernest
    Falmouth. MTS
    Invictus. WBP3
Hennen, Tom
    Unusual things. FroA
    Usually an older female is the
        leader. FroA
    Working near Lake Traverse.
        FroA
Henning, Ruth
    i sing a song. YoVA
Henry IV, sels. William
        Shakespeare. MTS
Henry King, who chewed bits of
        string... Hilaire Belloc.
    IlTH
Henry V, sels. William
        Shakespeare. MTS
Henry VI, sels. William
        Shakespeare. WBP1
Henry VI, sels. William
        Shakespeare. MTS
Henry VIII; King of England
    Green grow'th the holly.
        PoCh--ShBa
Henry the Navigator
    The portrait of Prince Henry.
        Sydney Clouts. VoWA
Henry, Carla
    Our society. YoVA
Henson, Lance
    Anniversary poem...Cheyennes
        who died... ReE
    Impression...Cheyenne dog
        soldier. ReE
    The leaving. ReE
    Love poem ("the earth grows
        darker"). ReE
    Old country. ReE
    Portrait in February. ReE
    Seeing. ReE
    Snow song. ReE
Her creed. Sarah Knowles Bolton.
    WBP4
Her guitar. Frank Dempster
    Sherman. WBP2
Her letter. Bret Harte. WBP2
Her likeness. Dinah Maria Mulock
    Craik. WBP2
Her true body. Jerred Metz. VoWA
Herbers, Jodie
    A man whose life is his work.
        YoVA
Herbert, George
    The call. WBP4
    Christmas. ShBa
    The church porch, sels. WBP4

Church-monuments. HaAP
The collar. HaAP
Easter-wings. HaAP
The flower. WBP3
The gifts of God. WBP4
Jesu. EeBC
Jordan (I). HaAP
Love. EeBC
Peace. WBP4
The pearl. HaAP
Praise. WBP4
The pulley. EeBC--HaAP
Redemption. EeBC--HaAP
Said I not so? WBP4
The Twenty-third psalm. EeBC
Virtue immortal. WBP3
Virtue. HaAP
Herbert, Mary S. See Pembroke
Herbert, Zbigniew
    Elegy of Fortinbras, sels. CoP
    The envoy of Mr. Cogito, sels.
        CoP
    Napis, sels. CoP
    Pebble, sels. CoP
    Potwor pan Cogito, sels. CoP
    Rady, sels. CoP
    The soldier, sels. CoP
    A study of the object, sels.
        CoP
    To Apollo, sels. CoP
    To Marcus Aurelius, sels. CoP
Herbs
    Rose bay willow herb. Judy Ray.
        FroA
Here and now. Philip Levine.
    VoWA
Here lies Sir Tact. Timothy
    Steele. TyW
Here lies a lady. John Crowe
    Ransom. HaAP
Here we come a-wassailing.
    Unknown. PoCh
Heresy and Heretics
    The dwelling. Moshe Dor. VoWA
Herford, Oliver
    A belated violet. WBP1
    The crocodile. IlTH
    The elf and the dormouse. WBP1
    The first rose of summer. WBP1
    The giraffe. IlTH
    A love story. IlTH
    An ostrich. IlTH
    A seal. IlTH
Heritage. Linda Hogan. ReE
Heritage. Carol Lee Sanchez. ReE
Heritage. Gwendolyn B. Bennett.
    BlS
The heritage. James Russell
    Lowell. WBP1
Heritage

The ancestors. Anita Barrows.
  VoWA
Asante sana, te te. Thadious M.
  Davis. BlS
At home in Dakar. Margaret
  Danner. BlS
August. Joseph L. Concha. ReE
Beginnings. Erez Biton. VoWA
Ceremony. Kattie M. Cumbo. BlS
The child is the mother. Gloria
  C. Oden. BlS
(Conversations #2). Carol Lee
  Sanchez. ReE
Document. Tuvia Ruebner. VoWA
Dusty braces, sels. Gary
  Snyder. ReE
Early loses: a requiem. Alice
  Walker. BlS
Eye of God. Jim Tollerud. ReE
The eyes, the blood. David
  Meltzer. VoWA
A family album. Alter Brody.
  VoWA
The four of them. Yehuda Karni.
  VoWA
Four songs of life. Roy A.
  Young Bear. ReE
Four# (4#). William Oandasan.
  ReE
Gift from Kenya. May Miller.
  BlS
Grandfathers. Michael Castro.
  VoWA
The heritage. James Russell
  Lowell. WBP1
House in St. Petersburg.
  Stanley Burnshaw. VoWA
House of mirrors. Marjorie L.
  Turner. StPo
Ikce wichasha. Paula Gunn
  Allen. ReE
Language of ancients. Hayim
  Lenski. VoWA
The last remarkable man.
  Elizabeth Cook-Lynn. ReE
Lineage. Margaret Walker. BlS
Meron. Shirley Kaufman. BuAC
Nomen. Naomi Long Madgett. BlS
Not that far. May Miller. BlS
Notes to Joanne, LXXIV. John F.
  Kerr. ReE
Orisha. Jayne Cortez. BlS
Pass it on grandson. Ted
  Palmanteer. ReE
Phraseology. Jayne Cortez. BlS
Prophecy. Carol Lee Sanchez.
  ReE
Recipe. Albert Goldbarth. VoWA
Story from bear country. Leslie
  Marmon Silko. ReE

To some few Hopi ancestors.
  Wendy Rose. ReE
Travels in the south. Simon J.
  Ortiz. ReE
When sun came to riverwoman.
  Leslie Marmon Silko. ReE
Herman the helper. Robert Kraus.
  TrWB
Hermaphrodites
  Shekhina and the Kiddushim.
  Edouard Roditi. VoWA
The **hermit.** Guillaume
  Apollinaire. FreS
Hermits
  Deserted cabin. John Haines.
  TeMP
  For Jukka: on indecision. Jean
  Shields. YoVA
  The hermit. Guillaume
  Apollinaire. FreS
  The Vicar of Wakefield, sels.
  Oliver Goldsmith. WBP2
  With Wang Wei's "Stopping by
  recluse.... Lu Hsiang . GrAC
Hero and Leander, sels.
  Christopher Marlowe. WBP2
A **hero** in disguise. Frank
  Alexander Rossi. YoVA
Herod the Great
  The Coventry caro. Unknown .
  EeBC
  Mariam, fairie queene of Jewry,
  sels. Elizabeth (Tanfield)
  Cary. PaW
Herodias, sels. Stephane
  Mallarme. FreS
Heroes and Heroines
  Canto 17. Lois Marie Harrod.
  StPo
  I think continually of
  those...great. Stephen
  Spender. HaAP
  A poem for Anton Schmidt.
  William Pillen. VoWA
  Thomas A. Goodbody. Victor P.
  Rizzo. StPo
Herrick, Robert
  Another grace for a child. EeBC
  The argument of his book. HaAP
  Ceremonies for Christmas, sels.
  PoCh
  A Christmas carol. PoCh--ShBa
  Corinna's going a-Maying.
  HaAP--LiHE
  Delight in disorder. HaAP
  Discontents in Devon, sels. TyW
  Dreams: "Here we are, all, by
  day" HaAP
  Grace for children. EeBC
  The holy spirit. WBP4

The kiss. WBP2
My home. WBP4
The night piece. WBP2
No coming to God without
    Christ. EeBC
An ode on the birth of our
    Saviour. ShBa
The scare-fire. HaAP
A thanksgiving to God, for his
    house. HaAP
To Dianeme. WBP2
To the virgins, to make much of
    time. HaAP--WBP1
A true Lent. WBP4
Upon Julia's clothes. HaAP
Upon Scobble. TyW
Whenas in silks my Julia goes.
    WBP2
Why flowers change colors. HaAP
Herron, Angie
    The shell. YoVA
Herschberger, Ruth
    Mulberry Street. HoA
    Poem ("Love being what it
        is...") HoA
    Summer mansions. HoA
    Watergate. FroA
    Yaddo. FroA
Hertza. Benjamin Fondane
    (Fundoianu). VoWA
Herve Riel. Robert Browning. MTS
Hervey, Thomas Kibble
    Love ("There are who say the
        lover's..") WBP2
Herzberg, Judith
    Commentaries on the song of
        songs. VoWA
    Kinneret. VoWA
    Nearer. VoWA
    On the death of Sylvia Plath.
        VoWA
    The voice. VoWA
    Yiddish. VoWA
Herzl, Theodor
    Guide to Jerusalem. Dennis
        Silk. VoWA
Herzog, Megan
    The truth. YoVA
    Yesterday. YoVA
Hesperia. Algernon Charles
    Swinburne. WBP2
Hewitt, Geoff
    Ben plays hide & seek in the
        deep woods. FroA
    Chickens. FroA
Heyaashi guutah. Simon J. Ortiz.
    ReE
Heyen, William
    Redwings. TeMP
Heynen, Jim

Morning chores. TeMP
Heywood, Thomas
    The portrait. WBP2
    A woman killed with kindness,
        sels. WBP4
Hezutsu Tosaku
    "Affluence-define it as." FroC
    Dawn cherries. FroC
Hiatus. Margaret Avison. HaAP
Hickam, Mike
    Cupid's arrow. YoVA
Hickory, dickory, dock!. Mother
    Goose. MiRN
Hidden bow. Mordecai Temkin.
    VoWA
Hidden valley. E.G. Burrows. HoA
Hieroglyph. Paul Auster. VoWA
"The high hall and its funereal
    doors." Adolphe Rette. FreS
The higher good. Theodore
    Parker. WBP4
Highland Mary. Robert Burns.
    WBP3
Highly renowned, sels. Monk
    Gusai. FroC
Highschool. Cindy Chisum. YoVA
Hilarova, Dagmar
    Questions. VoWA
Hildegarde, Saint
    O fire of God, the comforter.
        WBP4
Hill excursion. Leah Goldberg.
    BuAC
The hill of Hua-Tzu. Pei. LuL
The hill of the hatchet-leaved
    bamboos. Pei. LuL
The hill wife. Robert Frost.
    HaAP
Hill, Geoffrey
    The dead bride. TyW
    Genesis. HaAP
    Mercian hymns, sels. HaAP
    The Pentecost castle, sels.
        HaAP
Hill, Jeanne
    Lines from a misplaced person.
        FroA
Hill, Joyce
    Time. YoVA
    The year 2000. YoVA
Hill, Pati
    "On the beach/a big dog lies."
        FroA
    "Time was/when all you had to
        do was." FroA
    "Two lovers sitting on a tomb."
        FroA
The hills of the Lord. William
    Channing Gannett. WBP4
Hills. See Mountains

The eve. Howard Schwartz. VoWA
Holiway, Melanie D.
  Glum-day sundae. YoVA
  Growing is.... YoVA
Holland and the Dutch
  The character of Holland, sels.
    Andrew Marvell. TyW
Holland, Josiah Gilbert
  Bitter sweet, sels. WBP1
  Bitter sweet, sels. WBP4
  The cost of worth. WBP4
  In the cellar. WBP1
Hollander, Gad
  Argument against metaphor. VoWA
  Axioms. VoWA
  Fugato (coda). VoWA
  In memoriam Paul Celan. VoWA
Hollander, John
  The lady's-maid's song. TyW
  No foundation. TyW
  The Ziz. VoWA
Hollenbeck, Dona Kay
  Thoughts. YoVA
Hollo, Anselm
  After Verlaine. FroA
  The caterpillar. FroA
  "vibrant mutants of the future."
    FroA
The **hollow** flute. Avner Strauss.
  VoWA
Holly
  A Christmas carol. Robert
    Herrick. PoCh--ShBa
  Green grow'th the holl. Henry
    VIII; King of England .
    PoCh--ShBa
  Holly and mistletoe. Eleanor
    Farjeon. PoCh
  The holly and the iv. Unknown .
    PoCh
Holly and mistletoe. Eleanor
    Farjeon. PoCh
The **holly** and the ivy. Unknown.
    PoCh
Hollywood, California
  Autobiography: Hollywood.
    Charles Reznikoff. VoWA
Holman, Felice
  The child who cried. ByM
  When I am me. ByM
Holmberg, Becky
  Ode to the traveler. YoVA
  Sonnet #1. YoVA
Holmes, Oliver Wendell
  The ballad of an oysterman. MTS
  Bill and Joe. WBP1
  The boys. WBP1
  The chambered Nautilus. MTS
  The last leaf. WBP3
  The living temple. WBP4

Old Ironsides. MTS
The old man dreams. WBP2
A sea dialogue. MTS
The voiceless. WBP3
Holocaust
  After an eclipse of the sun.
    Eugene Heimler. VoWA
  At Staufen. Michael Hamburger.
    VoWA
  Auschwitz from Columbo. Anne
    Ranasinghe. VoWA
  Burnt. Boris Slutsky. VoWA
  Chorus of the rescued. Nelly
    Sachs. VoWA
  Death fugue. Paul Celan. VoWA
  Don't show me. Ruth Beker. VoWA
  The extermination of the Jews.
    Marvin Bell. VoWA
  Forced march. Miklos Radnoti.
    VoWA
  Fragment. Miklos Radnoti. VoWA
  Getting lost in Nazi Germany.
    Marvin Bell. VoWA
  Holocaust 1944. Anne
    Ranasinghe. VoWA
  How they killed my grandmother.
    Boris Slutsky. VoWA
  An inhabited emptiness. Jiri
    Gold. VoWA
  The Jews. Mieczyslaw Jastrun.
    VoWA
  "More light! More light!"
    Anthony Hecht. HaAP--VoWA
  Mother. Julian Tuwim. VoWA
  Murder of a community. Daniel
    Weissbort. VoWA
  O night of the crying children.
    Nelly Sachs. VoWA
  O the chimneys. Nelly Sachs.
    VoWA
  One chord. Nelly Sachs. VoWA
  Picture postcards. Miklos
    Radnoti. VoWA
  Poplars. Henryk Grynberg. VoWA
  The Pripet Marshes. Irving
    Feldman. VoWA
  Shema. Primo Levi. VoWA
  Song ("Whipped by sorrow now.")
    Miklos Radnoti. VoWA
  Theresienstadt poem. Robert
    Mezey. VoWA
  The wall. Ludvik Askenazy. VoWA
  What secret desires of the
    blood. Nelly Sachs. VoWA
  Why would I have survived?
    Edith Bruck. VoWA
Holocaust 1944. Anne Ranasinghe.
    VoWA
Holtz, Barry
  Isaac. VoWA

Holubiczko, Wendy
You're still my dad. YoVA
The **holy** Balshemtov. Zishe
Landau. OnCP
Holy Communion
The child is the mother. Gloria
C. Oden. BlS
Holy Grail
Stretching forth the lance.
Pierre Louys. FreS
The waste land. Thomas Stearns
Eliot. HaAP
Holy Willie's prayer. Robert
Burns. TyW
Holy girl. Yoshioka Minoru. FroC
The **holy** innocents. Robert
Lowell. ShBa
Holy sonnets, sels. John Donne.
HaAP
Holy sonnets, sels. John Donne.
DoNG
The **holy** spirit. Robert Herrick.
WBP4
Holz, Arno
Phantasus: I, 8. PoCh
Homage to Andrew Jackson.
Carroll Arnett/Gogisgi. ReE
Homage to Edward Hopper. Emery
George. HoA
Homage to Sextus Propertius,
sels. Ezra Pound. HaAP
Homage to the third march on
Delano. Roberto Vargas. NiR
Home. Robert Bland (trans.).
WBP1
Home. Leonidas of Alexandria.
WBP1
Home. Maurice Kenny. ReE
Home alone these last hours...
Stephen Levy. VoWA
Home and Family Life
The admiral's daughter. E.G.
Burrows. HoA
The auld house. C. Oliphant,
Baroness Nairne. WBP1
Cleaning day. Jose Kozer. VoWA
The conspiracy. LeAnnette
Donahey. YoVA
The cotter's Saturday night.
Robert Burns. WBP1
Dress me, dear mother. Avraham
Shlonsky. VoWA
The eyes, the blood. David
Meltzer. VoWA
A family album. Alter Brody.
VoWA
The family of eight. Abraham
Reisen. VoWA
Halfway. Maxine Kumin. TeMP
The happy mother. Alexander

Laing. WBP1
He and his family. Laura E.
Richards. IlTH
Here and now. Philip Levine.
VoWA
Home. Leonidas of Alexandria.
WBP1
Home, sweet home. John Howard
Payne. WBP1
The homes of England. Felicia
Hemans. WBP1
The house beautiful. Robert
Louis Stevenson. WBP1
Houses, past and present. Eli
Bachar. VoWA
I knew by the smoke that so
gracefully... Thomas Moore.
WBP1
I remember, I remember. Thomas
Hood. WBP1
Important. Allison Doty. HoWM
The Ingle-side. Hew Ainslee.
WBP1
The little father... Gelett
Burgess. IlTH
Long Island springs. Howard
Moss. HoA
Mornings. Suzanne E. Berger.
TeMP
My home. Robert Herrick. WBP4
My song. Hayim Nachman Bialik.
VoWA
My wife and child. Henry R.
Jackson. WBP3
A New England home in winter,
sels. John Greenleaf
Whittier. WBP1
North. Maurice Kenny. ReE
Not one to spar. Unknown . WBP1
Out of the old house, Nancy.
Will Carleton. WBP1
A picture. Charles Gamage
Eastman. WBP1
Quiet house. Yoshioka Minoru.
FroC
Room poems. Eli Bachar. VoWA
The soldier's dream. Thomas
Campbell. WBP1
The things. Conrad Aiken. HaAP
Turning back. Michael Sheridan.
PrVo
Two pictures. Marian
Douglas(A.D.G.Robinson). WBP1
The walls of Urbino. Paolo
Volponi. NeIP
The wanderer's home. Oliver
Goldsmith. WBP1
When the cows come home. Agnes
E. Mitchell. WBP1
Zlotchev, my home. Moishe Leib

Ode in 1,000 lines, sel.
Takahashi Mutsuo.   FroC
The playboy of the demi-world:
1938. William Plomer. TyW
Sleeping wrestle. Takahashi
Mutsuo.   FroC
Winter: 1955. Takahashi Mutsuo.
FroC
Honest John's seven idols pawn
shop. Luci Abeita. ReE
Honey dripping from the comb.
James Whitcomb Riley. WBP1
The **honeymoon** of the muse.
Michael Van Walleghen. PrVo
Honeysuckle. James Paul. HoA
"Honeysuckle was the saddest
odor..." Thadious M. Davis.
BlS
Hongo, Garrett
On the road to paradise. HoA
Who among you knows the
essence..garlic? HoA
Yellow light. HoA
Honn, Cindy
Pumpkin. YoVA
Hood, Thomas
The bridge of sighs. WBP3
The death-bed. WBP3
Fair Ines. WBP3
Farewell, life. WBP3
I remember, I remember. WBP1
The lost heir. WBP1
Ruth. WBP1
A sailor's apology for
bow-legs. MTS
Sally Simpkin's lament. MTS
Silence. DoNG
The song of the shirt. WBP3
To my infant son. WBP1
To the reviewers. TyW
"What can an old man do but
die?" WBP3
Hooded crane tower. Wang
Chih-huan. GrAC
Hoop dancer. Paula Gunn Allen.
ReE
Hooper, Ellen Sturgis
Duty. WBP4
Hooper, Lucy H.
Three loves. WBP2
Hooper, Patricia
Nine o'clock (9:00). HoA
Other lives. HoA
Psalm ("It's not the sun.") HoA
Hope. William Dean Howells. MTS
Hope
Endurance. Elissa Behle. YoVA
Escape. Elissa Behle. YoVA
Flowers of winter: four songs.
Duane BigEagle. ReE

From an expedition to the
Himalayas,sels. Wislawa
Szymborska. CoP
"Hope shines like a blade of
straw..." Paul Verlaine.
FoFS--FreS
Imponderables. Alicia Callanan.
YoVA
Never despair. William Smith
O'Brien. WBP3
On this day so full of gloom.
Mary Fulkerson. YoVA
The pleasures of hope, sels.
Thomas Campbell. WBP4
The saddest fat. Unknown . WBP3
Spirit flowers. Della Burt. BlS
Thanks, Robert Frost. David
Ray. TeMP
Viewpoint on life. Aileen
Needleman. YoVA
Waking. Douglas Shearer. YoVA
The waste land. Thomas Stearns
Eliot. HaAP
Wondering. Donna Dunagan. YoVA
Hope and fear. Algernon Charles
Swinburne. WBP1
Hope deferred. Unknown. WBP2
Hope of the human heart. R.M.
Milnes (Lord Houghton). WBP4
"Hope shines like a blade of
straw..." Paul Verlaine.
FoFS--FreS
Hope, A.D.
Meditation on a bone. TyW
Hope, Alec Derwent
The brides. HaAP
Imperial Adam. HaAP
Meditation on a bone. TyW
Hopefully waiting. Anson D. F.
Randolph. WBP4
Hopeless grief. Elizabeth
Barrett Browning. WBP3
Hopkins, Gerard Manley
Felix Randal. HaAP--SlW
God's grandeur. SlW
God's grandeur. EeBC--HaAP
Heaven-haven. MTS--SlW
Hurrahing in harvest. EeBC
I wake and feel the fell of
dark,not day. HaAP--TyW
The leaden echo and the golden
echo. SlW
No worst, there is none. EeBC
Peace. EeBC
Pied beauty. EeBC--HaAP
Pied beauty. LiHE--SlW
Spring and fall. HaAP
Spring and fall. LiHE--SlW
Spring. EeBC--HaAP
Thou art indeed just, Lord.

HaAP--LiHE
The windhover. EeBC--HaAP
The windhover. LiHE
Hopkins, John H.
We three kings of Orient are.
PoCh
Hopkins, Lee Bennett
Boy on the bus. ByM
In the pitch of the night. ByM
Hopper, Edward
Homage to Edward Hopper. Emery
George. HoA
Hoppin, William J.
Charlie Machree. WBP2
Horace
To Thaliarchus. WBP1
An Horatian ode...Cromwell's
return... Andrew Marvell.
HaAP
Horizon without landscape. Tom
Lowenstein. VoWA
Horne, Frank
Kid stuff. PoCh
Horne, Lewis B.
Moving day. HoA
Muscae volitantes. HoA
Horner, Thomas "Jack"
Little Jack Horne. Unknown.
ShBa
Hornsby, Don
The endless scroll. YoVA
A quest. YoVA
"A **horse** and a flea & three
blind mice". Unknown. IlTH
Horse and riot. Ishihara
Yoshiro. FroC
The **horse** and the whip. Eliezer
Steinbarg. VoWA
The **horse** that died of shame. N.
Scott Momaday. ReE
The **horses**. Edwin Muir. HaAP
The **horses**. Maxine Kumin. DuD
Horses
"As I was standing in the
street." Unknown. IlTH
At grass. Philip Larkin. HaAP
Away with the old. David
Newton. YoVA
Black pony eating grass. Robert
Bly. FroA
Cooli. Yoshioka Minoru. FroC
Dawn horse. Valerie Zandoli.
YoVA
The day the Beatles lost one...
Dave Kelly. FroA
The gourd dancer. N. Scott
Momaday. ReE
The horses. Maxine Kumin. DuD
Names of horses. Donald Hall.
HaAP

Poem ("There I could never be a
boy.") Frank O'Hara. HoA
The sixteen hand horse. Fred
Gwynne. TrWB
The white horse. Chia Chih.
GrAC
The white horse. David Herbert
Lawrence. SlW
Horses at valley store. Leslie
Marmon Silko. ReE
Horvitz, Allan Kolski
King Saul. VoWA
The radiance of extinct stars.
VoWA
Hospital. Maurice Maeterlinck.
FreS
Hospitals
Between walls. William Carlos
Williams. SlW
Haiku: 39 haiku. Masaoka Shiki.
FroC
Hospital. Maurice Maeterlinck.
FreS
A study in terror. Tamura
Ryuichi. FroC
Hotel. Adam Wazyk. VoWA
Hotel paradiso e commerciale.
John Malcolm Brinnin. HoA
Hotels
Black Bull of Aldgate. Alfred,
Lord Tennyson. TyW
Hotel. Adam Wazyk. VoWA
Lombard-Venetian. Luciano Erba.
NeIP
Registered at the Bordello
Hotel(Vienna). Larry Rubin.
FroA
Hothouse ennui. Maurice
Maeterlinck. FreS
Hothouse soul. Maurice
Maeterlinck. FreS
Houghton (see Milnes,R.), Lord

The **hour.** Uri Zvi Greenberg.
VoWA
The **hour** of death. Felicia
Dorothea Hemans. WBP3
An **houre's** recreation in
musicke, sels. Unknown. WBP2
House (saibara). Unknown. FroC
The **house** beautiful. Robert
Louis Stevenson. WBP1
House in Meudon. Margarita
Aliger. VoWA
House in St. Petersburg. Stanley
Burnshaw. VoWA
The **house** is a shack. Deborah
Ann Foster. YoVA
The **house** of desire. Sherley
Anne Williams. BlS

The **house** of life, sels. Dante
Gabriel Rossetti. WBP2
The **house** of life, sels. Dante
Gabriel Rossetti. HaAP
House of mirrors. Marjorie L.
Turner. StPo
House of the living. Claude
Vigee. VoWA
The **house** of the mouse. Lucy
Sprague Mitchell. MiRN
The **house** was quiet and the
world...calm. Wallace
Stevens. HaAP
The **house** within me. Morgan
Fisher. HoWM
Household. Laura Jensen. TeMP
Houser, Kristi
May I see your I.D., please?
YoVA
Open to public, but don't
enter. YoVA
Houses
Directive. Robert Frost. HaAP
Etude. Joseph Brodsky. VoWA
The gutter. Franco Fortini.
VoWA
House (saibara), Unknown. FroC
The house is a shack. Deborah
Ann Foster. YoVA
House of the living. Claude
Vigee. VoWA
Hut on a ridge. Kama Kerpi.
VooI
"My house is made of graham
bread." Gelett Burgess. IlTH
New house. Rai San'yo. FroC
Sea of land. Guillaume
Apollinaire. MoVT
The Su family villa. Tsu Yung.
GrAC
A thanksgiving to God, for his
house. Robert Herrick. HaAP
To you building the new house.
Nelly Sachs. VoWA
Twenty-four tank. Minamoto no
Sanetomo. FroC
The **houses** were filled with
smoke. Leonel Rugama. NiR
Houses, past and present. Eli
Bachar. VoWA
Housman, Alfred Edward
Along the field as we came by.
HaAP
The chestnut casts his
flambeaux, sels. TyW
From far, from even and
morning. HaAP
Good creatures, do you love
your lives. TyW
Loveliest of trees, the cherry

now. HaAP
The oracles. HaAP
Terence, this is stupid stuff.
LiHE
To an athlete dying young.
HaAP--LiHE
When I was one-and-twenty. LiHE
With rue my heart is laden.
HaAP
Hovell-Thurlow, Edward, Baron
Beauty. WBP2
Hovey, Richard
Love in the winds. WBP2
How beastly the bourgeois is-.
D.H. Lawrence. TyW
How can I see you, love. David
Vogel. VoWA
How did he get here?. H. Leivick
(Leivick Halpern). VoWA
How did they fume, and stamp,and
roar.... Alexander Pope. TyW
How doth the little busy bee.
Isaac Watts. WBP1
How everything happens. May
Swenson. HaAP
How far is it to Bethlehem?.
Frances Chesterton. PoCh
How it goes on. Maxine Kumin.
FroA
How it is. Uri Zvi Greenberg.
VoWA
How many times these low feet
staggered. Emily Dickinson.
HaAP
How my cousin was killed. Gladys
Cardiff. ReE
How my father died. Nissim
Ezekiel. VoWA
How pleasant to know Mr. Lear!.
Edward Lear. HaAP
How spider saved Halloween.
Robert Kraus. TrWB
How the waters closed above him.
Emily Dickinson. LiHE
How they brought the good news
by sea. Norma Farber. PoCh
How they killed my grandmother.
Boris Slutsky. VoWA
How things fall. Donald Finkel.
VoWA
How through green-grassed
fields. Zishe Landau. OnCP
How to ask and have. Samuel
Lover. WBP2
How to change the U.S.A.. Harry
Edwards. TyW
How to hide Jesus. Steve Turner.
EeBC
How to reach the moon. Marsha
Pomerantz. VoWA

How to write a poem. Rick
    Gurley. YoVA
How will you call me, brother.
    Mari Evans. BlS
How, William Walshaw
    The word. WBP4
How? Abraham Sutskever.
    OnCp--VoWA
Howard, Jim
    Boy trash picker. FroA
    Newspaper hats. FroA
Howard, Mike
    My condolences. YoVA
    The sleeping man. YoVA
Howcroft, Wilbur
    My wise old grandpapa. IlTH
Howell, Jamie
    The creature of today. YoVA
Howells, William Dean
    Caprice. WBP2
    Hope. MTS
Howes, Barbara
    The early supper. DuD
    Early supper. DuD
Howitt, Mary
    The fairies of the Caldon Low.
        WBP1
    The spider and the fly. WBP1
Howitt, William
    The wind in a frolic. WBP1
Howl, sels. Allen Ginsberg. SlW
Howland, Mary Woolsey
    Rest. WBP3
Hoyt, Ralph
    Old. WBP3
Hsi Shih
    Ballad of peach blossom spring,
        sel. Wang Wei. GrAC
    Song of the roosting crow. Li
        Po. GrAC
Hsueh Chu
    Strong feelings, sels. GrAC
HuGos

    Nineteen twenty-seven (1927).
        NiR
    Wednesdays in Los Angeles. NiR
    Within me. NiR
Huang-fu Jan
    Mountain lodge. GrAC
    Wu Mountain high. GrAC
Hubbs, Deanna
    A memory. YoVA
Huckel, Oliver
    Easy to drift. WBP4
    Prayer and answer. WBP4
Hudibras, sels. Samuel Butler.
    WBP4
The Hudson. George Sidney
    Hellman. WBP1

Hudson River
    The Hudson. George Sidney
        Hellman. WBP1
    The Narrows. Joseph Bruchac.
        FroA
Hudson, Mary Clemmer Ames
    Something beyond. WBP3
Huerta, Marti
    This world is too much with us.
        YoVA
Hugh Selwyn Mauberley, sels.
    Ezra Pound. HaAP
Hughes, Langston
    Aunt Sue's stories. DuD
    Carol of the brown king.
        PoCh--ShBa
    Dream variations. HaAP
    Harlem. LiHE
    Long trip. MTS
    Moonlight night: Carmel. MTS
    The Negro speaks of rivers.
        HaAP
    Same in blues. LiHE
    Shepherd's song at Christmas.
        PoCh
    Winter moon. DuD
Hughes, Langston (about)
    The rhetoric of Langston
        Hughes. Margaret Danner. BlS
Hughes, Ted
    Hawk roosting. HaAP
    Law in the country of the cats.
        TyW
    Pike. HaAP
    Revenge fable. TyW
    Skylarks. HaAP
Hugo, Hermann
    I am my Beloved's... ReLP
Hugo, Richard
    Cataldo Mission. FroA
    Glen uig. TeMP
    With Kathy at Wisdom. FroA
Hui-Ming, Wang
    Why I carve these poems. FroA
Human relations, sels. Antonio
    Porta. NeIP
Human relations. C.H. Sisson.
    TyW
Humbly I confess that I am
    mortal. Elio Pagliarani. NeIP
Humility. James Montgomery. WBP4
Humorous Verse
    Sage counsel. Sir Arthur T.
        Quiller-Couch. WBP1
    Senryu: 47 senryu. Unknown.
        FroC
Humphries, Mike
    A hanging. YoVA
Humprhies, Mike
    The Castle of Dracul. YoVA

Hunger. Wendy S. Neidlinger.
    YoVA
Hunger
    The earth is a satellite of the
        moon. Leonel Rugama. NiR
    Freemon Hawthorne. Melvin B.
        Tolson. FroA
    Give me three grains of corn,
        mother. Amelia Blandford
        Edwards. WBP3
    Guilty, or not guilty. Unknown.
        WBP3
    Never again will I say. Moyshe
        Leyb Halpern. OnCP
    Pursuit from under. James
        Dickey. HaAP
    Song of the times. J. Adler.
        OnCP
    Two songs. Cecil Day Lewis.
        HaAP
Hunt (trans.), Leigh
    I dreamt I saw great Venus.
        WBP2
Hunt, Leigh
    Abou Ben Adhem. WBP4
    Cupid swallower. WBP2
    A fish replies. MTS
    The fish turns into a man...
        MTS
    The fish, the man, and the
        spirit. HaAP
    The fish, the man, and the
        spirit, sels. MTS
    Jaffar. WBP1
    Jenny kissed me. WBP1
    To J.H.. WBP1
    To a child during sickness.
        WBP1
    To a fish. MTS
Hunter, Kristen
    Sepia nightingale. BlS
Hunting and Hunters
    Beaver skin. Antonio Porta.
        NeIP
    Deer hunting. Geary Hobson. ReE
    First deer. Joseph Bruchac. ReE
    The great glue mess. Scott Van
        Klaveren. YoVA
    Natural law. William Oandasan.
        ReE
    Nine charms against the hunter.
        David Wagoner. TyW
    Returning from/scouting for
        meat. Minerva Allen. ReE
    A rough rhyme on a rough
        matter. Charles Kingsley.
        WBP3
    A runnable stag. John Davidson.
        HaAP
    Song by the wall. Wang

    Ch'ang-ling . GrAC
    Whoso list to hunt. Sir Thomas
        Wyatt. HaAP
    Wolf hunting near Nashoba. Jim
        Barnes. ReE
    The woman thin. Lorde Audre.
        BlS
"The hunting horn grieves..."
    Paul Verlaine. FoFS
The huntsmen. Walter De La Mare.
    DuD
Hurd, Peter
    A Miltonic sonnet for Mr.
        Johnson.... Richard Wilbur.
        TyW
Hurdy-gurdies
    Lament of the hurdy-gurdy.
        Jules Laforgue. FreS
Hurrahing in harvest. Gerard
    Manley Hopkins. EeBC
The hurricane. Philip Freneau.
    MTS
Hurricane. Patricia Viale Wuest.
    StPo
Hurricanes
    The hurricane. Philip Freneau
        MTS
The hurt. Heather Wiegand. YoVA
Hurt hawks. Robinson Jeffers.
    LiHE
Husbands. See Marriage
Hush! Julia C. R. Dorr. WBP3
Hush, honey. Fareedah Allah
    (Ruby Saunders). BlS
Husid, Mordechai
    The cry of generations. VoWA
    On the way. VoWA
    Windows. VoWA
Huss, Avraham
    A classic idyll. VoWA
    A green refrain. VoWA
    Nocturnal thoughts. VoWA
    Time. VoWA
Hustle. Tom Joyce. YoVA
The hustler. Unknown. TyW
Huston, Kelly
    If I could be. YoVA
Huswifery, sels. Edward Taylor.
    EeBC
Hut on a ridge. Kama Kerpi. VooI
Hut window. Paul Celan. VoWA
Hutton, Bobby
    Memorial. Sonia Sanchez. BlS
Hyacinths
    Water hyacinth. Kitahara Hakushu.
        FroC
Hyd, Absolon, thy gilte tresses
    clere. Geoffrey Chaucer. HaAP
Hyde, Lewis
    Ants. FroA

Hymn ("Some sort of fire
    leaped...") Otto Orban. VoWA
A hymn about a spoonful of soup.
    Jozef Wittlin. VoWA
A hymn for Christmas day. John
    Byrom. ShBa
Hymn of the Nativity. Richard
    Crashaw. HaAP
A hymn of the sea. William
    Cullen Bryant. MTS
A hymn on the nativity of my
    Saviour. Ben Jonson. ShBa
Hymn to Diana. Ben Jonson. HaAP
A hymn to God the father. Ben
    Jonson. EeBC
A hymn to God the father. John
    Donne. EeBC--HaAP
Hymn to Zeus. Cleanthes. WBP4
Hymn to dispell hatred at
    midnight. Yvor Winters. TyW
Hymn to intellectual beauty.
    Percy Bysshe Shelley. HaAP
Hymn to joy. Julia Cunningham.
    PoCh
Hymn to the dawn. Marcantonio
    Flaminio. ReLP
A hymn to...St. Teresa, sels.
    Richard Crashaw. HaAP
Hymn, before sunrise... Samuel
    Taylor Coleridge. WBP4
A hymne in praise of Neptune.
    Thomas Campion. MTS
An hymne of heavenly love, sels.
    Edmund Spenser. WBP4
Hypocrisy
    Christ climbed down. Lawrence
        Ferlinghetti. ShBa
    Christians at war. John F.
        Kendrick. TyW
    More sonnets at Christmas.
        Allen Tate. ShBa
    Truth. Gleena Scholer. YoVA

I accompany my uncle Shumpo on
    an outing. Rai San'yo. FroC
I am. John Clare. EeBC--HaAP
I am a Jew. David Martin. VoWA
I am a brick. Patrick Tolliver.
    HoWM
"I am a cat I wish." Julius
    Weiss. HoWM
I am a drifter. Susan Mae
    Anderson. YoVA
I am a king. I.Z. Rimon. VoWA
I am a leaf. Yehuda Amichai.
    VoWA
I am a raindrop. Korey Brown.

HoWM
I am an actor. Darryl Cox. YoVA
"I am exploring through
    the...body." Laura Hite. HoWM
I am from Ireland. Unknown. HaAP
I am here. Robert Mezey. VoWA
I am like a book. David Rokeah.
    VoWA
I am me. Teena Field. YoVA
I am my Beloved's... Hermann
    Hugo. ReLP
I am sitting here. Yehuda
    Amichai. VoWA
I am sixteen. Penny Ward. YoVA
"I am snow." Scott Bowman. HoWM
I am the only being whose doom.
    Emily Bronte. TyW
I am the way. Alice Meynell.
    EeBC
I am too close, sels. Wislawa
    Szymborska. CoP
I am what I am. Alfred Garcia.
    YoVA
"I and Pangor Ban my cat".
    Unknown. MiRN
I and thou, sels. Martin Buber.
    VoWA
I ask. Simone Routier. MoVT
I asked for peace. Digby
    Mackworth Dolben. EeBC
I belong to the Sandinista
    Front. Judith Reyes. NiR
"I blink my eye." Dee Dee
    Harris. HoWM
i breathe as the night breathes.
    Susan Shown Harjo. ReE
"I came back to the dwelling."
    Gustave Kahn. FreS
"I came to this spring
    field..." Yamabe no Akahito.
    FroC
I can remember us. Melody
    Marshall. YoVA
I care not for these ladies.
    Thomas Campion. HaAP
"I climb the road to Cold
    Mountain." Han-shan. LuL
I dared. Peggy Chapman. YoVA
I didn't find light by accident.
    Hayim Nachman Bialik. VoWA
I didn't know my soul. Avraham
    Ben-Yitzhak. VoWA
I died for beauty. Emily
    Dickinson. DoNG
"I do not like thee, Doctor
    Fell." Thomas (Tom) Brown.
    TyW
I do not wish to be old. Norman
    H. Russell. ReE
I don't have no bunny tail on my

behind. Alta. TyW
I don't know. Terri Reeves. YoVA
I don't know if Mount Zion. Abba
     Kovner. VoWA
"I don't like foreign
     languages..." Chiao-jan.
     GrAC
I done got so thirsty...
     Patricia Jones. BlS
I dreaded that first robin, so.
     Emily Dickinson. HaAP
i dream. Rokwaho (Daniel
     Thompson). ReE
"I dream of gentle verse..."
     Albert Samain. FreS
I dreamt I saw great Venus.
     Bion. WBP2
I dreamt I saw great Venus.
     Leigh Hunt (trans.). WBP2
"I eat my food/but is has no
     flavor." Unknown. FroC
I emptied. Yona Wallach. BuAC
"I fear thy kisses, gentle
     maiden." Percy Bysshe
     Shelley. WBP2
"I fell in paradise." Jerome
     Coleman. HoWM
I felt a funeral in my brain.
     Emily Dickinson. DoNG--LiHE
I followed a path. Patricia
     Parker. BlS
I gave my life for thee. Frances
     Ridley Havergal. WBP4
I give up...the lute. Sugawara
     no Michizane. FroC
I had a hippopotamus. Patrick
     Barrington. IlTH
I hate that drum's discordant
     sound. John Scott. TyW
I have a big favor to ask you,
     brothers. Zishe Landau. VoWA
I have a gentil cock. Unknown.
     HaAP
"I have a secret nobody knows."
     Misty Henderson. HoWM
I have come to claim. Judy
     Grahn. LiHE
"I have cupped in my hands..."
     David Newcomb. HoWM
I have never been here before.
     Jacob Glatstein. OnCP
i have sat through sunlight. Nia
     Francisco. ReE
"I have the sadness of a
     town..." Max Elskamp. FreS
I hear America singing. Walt
     Whitman. HaAP
I hear a voice. H. Leivick
     (Leivick Halpern). VoWA
I heard Immanuel singing. Vachel

Lindsay. HaAP
I heard a fly buzz when I died.
     Emily Dickinson. DoNG--SlW
I heard a fly buzz when I died.
     Emily Dickinson. HaAP--LiHE
I heard a noise and wished for a
     sight. Unknown. HaAP
I heard her cry last night.
     Sabrina Snyder. YoVA
I hid you. Miklos Radnoti. VoWA
"I hide my heart and not my
     deeds." Chiao-jan. GrAC
I hold still. Julius Sturm. WBP3
I just walk around, around,
     around. Moishe Kulbak. VoWA
I knew a woman. Theodore
     Roethke. HaAP
I knew by the smoke that so
     gracefully... Thomas Moore.
     WBP1
"I know a little pussy."
     Unknown. IlTH
I know nothing of the sleep...
     Giancarlo Marmori. NeIP
I left. Tuvia Ruebner. VoWA
"I look into my glass." Thomas
     Hardy. HaAP
i lost the song. Karoniaktatie
     (Alex Jacobs). ReE
I love mellow words... Jenny
     Schroeder. YoVA
I love my Jean. Robert Burns.
     WBP3
I love the woods. Leib Neidus.
     VoWA
"I love to go to lectures."
     Gelett Burgess. IlTH
I love what is not. Manfred
     Winkler. VoWA
I married in my youth a wife.
     James Vincent Cunningham. TyW
I muse not.... Francis Davison.
     TyW
I need not suffer now. Laura
     Fauth. YoVA
I never saw a moor. Emily
     Dickinson. EeBC
I often want to let my lines go.
     Leib Neidus. VoWA
I point out a bird. Quinton
     Duval. FroA
I praise myself. Eleonor Sigal.
     YoVA
I prithee send me back my heart.
     Sir John Suckling. WBP2
I promessi sposi. Cid Corman.
     HoA
"I put good rice in water."
     Unknown. FroC
I remember, I remember. Thomas

Hood. WBP1
"I saw a pretty thing." Douglas
    Tyson. HoWM
I saw a stable. Mary Elizabeth
    Coleridge. EeBC--PoCh
I saw thee. Ray Palmer. WBP4
I saw three ships. Unknown. EeBC
I saw two clouds at morning.
    John Gardiner C. Brainard.
    WBP2
I say. Malka Heifetz Tussman.
    VoWA
I scattered my sighs to the
    wind. Hayim Nachman Bialik.
    VoWA
I see a primeval light in the
    darkness. Andrew Liano. YoVA
I serve a mistress whiter than
    snow. Anthony Munday. HaAP
i sing a song. Ruth Henning.
    YoVA
I sing of a maiden (mayden).
    Unknown. HaAP--ShBa
I sing with my heart. Negor Len.
    NiR
I sit and sew. Alice
    Dunbar-Nelson. BlS
I sit and wait for beauty. Mae
    V. Cowdery. BlS
I started early-I took my dog.
    Emily Dickinson. HaAP--MTS
I stood in Jerusalem. Zelda.
    VoWA
I that in heill was and
    glaidnes. William Dunbar.
    HaAP
I the woman. Sandra Cisneros.
    PrVo
I think continually of
    those...great. Stephen
    Spender. HaAP
I think of oblivion. Yehuda
    Amichai. VoWA
I thought about you. Ronald C.
    Rowe. YoVA
I tried to write a poem. Della
    Rose. YoVA
I waited. Ulla Jonsson. YoVA
I wake and feel the fell of
    dark,not day. Gerard Manley
    Hopkins. HaAP--TyW
I want him to, take my soul. A.
    Ozello. YoVA
I want to die while you love me.
    Georgia Douglas Johnson. BlS
I want to go away. Lisa
    Matthews. YoVA
I want to write a Jewish poem.
    Gary Pacernick. VoWA
I wanted to... Sara Nikirk. YoVA

I was born with a hole. Henri
    Michaux. MoVT
i was once told how. Ted Ardans.
    YoVA
I watch my daughter running.
    Carolyn Pintye. StPo
I wende to dede. Unknown. HaAP
I will go away. Zvi Shargel.
    VoWA
"I wish my room had a floor."
    Gelett Burgess. IlTH
I wish my tongue were a quiver.
    L.A. MacKay. TyW
I woke up. Revenge. A., Jr.
    Poulin. TyW
I wonder. Jana Powell. YoVA
I wonder as I wander. John Jacob
    Niles. PoCh
I wondered... Debbie Moffat.
    YoVA
I would I were an excellent
    divine. Nicholas Breton. WBP4
I would not live alway. William
    Augustus Muhlenberg. WBP3
"I'd never dare to walk across."
    Gelett Burgess. IlTH
I'll find my self-belief. Jacob
    Glatstein. VoWA
I'm a cloud. Dwana Thomas. HoWM
I'm a dreamer. Kattie M. Cumbo.
    BlS
I'm a flower, sels. Nishiyama
    Soin. FroC
I'm a monkey. Robert Kraus. TrWB
"I'm a shining crystal." Kevin
    Rock. HoWM
I'm confused. Dianne Smith. YoVA
I'm going to work in my daddy's
    shop. Jeff Isaacs. YoVA
I'm nobody! Who are you? Emily
    Dickinson. LiHE
I'm not myself at all. Samuel
    Lover. WBP2
I'm not rich. Joseph Rolnik.
    VoWA
I'm soaked through with you.
    Rachel Korn. VoWA
I've dreamed of you so much.
    Robert Desnos. MoVT
I, mouse. Robert Kraus. TrWB
"I, silence am always last."
    Pulin Patel. HoWM
I, woman. Irma McLaurin. BlS
Icarus
    The artificer. Patricia E.
    Fann. YoVA
Ice. Dorothy Aldis. RoRF
Iceland, Reuben
    Over all the roof tops. OnCP
The idea of order at Key West.

Wallace Stevens. HaAP--MTS
Idea, sels. Michael Drayton.
    HaAP--LiHE
Identity. Robert Friend. VoWA
Identity
    Epitaph on Elizabeth, L.H. Ben
        Jonson. HaAP
    I'm nobody! Who are you? Emily
        Dickinson. LiHE
    Identity. Robert Friend. VoWA
    In disguise. Joseph Rolnik.
        VoWA
    Lady Clare. Alfred, Lord
        Tennyson. WBP2
    Lament, sels. Tadeusz Rozewicz.
        CoP
    May I see your I.D., please?
        Kristi Houser. YoVA
    Over wine, sels. Wislawa
        Szymborska. CoP
    Questions. Dagmar Hilarova.
        VoWA
    Recognition. Myra Glazer
        (Schotz). BuAC
    Root. Miklos Radnoti. VoWA
    Touch me. Mike Bacsi. YoVA
Idleness
    Irritated. Gwen Perkins. YoVA
    Pooh! Walter De La Mare. HaAP
    "Rags and tatters.... Ryokan .
        FroC
    The sluggard. Isaac Watts. HaAP
Idyl: sunrise. Henrietta
    Cordelia Ray. BlS
Idyl: sunset. Henrietta Cordelia
    Ray. BlS
Idyls of the king, sels. Alfred,
    Lord Tennyson. WBP4
If. Jerlene Dickson. YoVA
If. Christy Mason. YoVA
If God exists. Ewa Lipska. VoWA
If I could be. Kelly Huston.
    YoVA
If I could trust mine own self.
    Christina Georgina Rossetti.
    EeBC
If I forget thee. Emanuel
    Litvinoff. VoWA
If I should die tonight. Belle
    E. Smith. WBP3
If a man could keep his love.
    Todd Warne. YoVA
"If all the world were apple
    pie." Unknown. IlTH
If all went up in smoke. George
    Oppen. VoWA
If doughty deeds my lady please.
    Robert Cunningham Graham.
    WBP2
if everything happens that can't

be done. Edward Estlin
    Cummings. LiHE
if i was born on this bed. Ted
    Ardans. YoVA
"If it be true that any
    beauteous thing." John Edward
    Taylor (trans.). WBP2
"If it be true that any
    beauteous thing."
    Michaelangelo Buonarotti.
    WBP2
If justice moved. Bettie M.
    Sellers. TyW
If my hands were mute. Manfred
    Winkler. VoWA
If only. Christina Georgina
    Rossetti. EeBC
If only they cared. Donald
    Eason. YoVA
If only you knew. Carole Waters.
    YoVA
"If people's heads were not so
    dense." Gelett Burgess. IlTH
"If the streets were filled with
    glue." Gelett Burgess. IlTH
If thou wert by my side, my
    love. Reginald Heber. WBP2
If we had but a day. Mary Lowe
    Dickinson. WBP4
If we knew. May Riley Smith.
    WBP1
If we must die. Claude McKay.
    LiHE
If you could only live forever.
    Marlo Maconi. YoVA
If you could wish. Marlo Maconi.
    YoVA
Ignatow, David
    The business life. TyW
    Dream. VoWA
    The heart. VoWA
    Kaddish. VoWA
    My own house. TeMP
    Nineteen hundred five (1905).
        VoWA
    Thoughts. FroA
    Threnody. FroA
    A time of night. FroA
    With the sun's fire. FroA
Ikce wichasha. Paula Gunn Allen.
    ReE
Ikkyu Sojun
    "Blind Mori..." FroC
    "Contemplating the law..."
        FroC
    "Ten years in the brothels..."
        FroC
    "Who is the true
        transmitter..." FroC
Ikusa, Prince

On the occasion of the imperial
visit... FroC
Il penseroso. John Milton. HaAP
The **iliad**, sels. Homer. DoNG
The **iliad**, sels. Edward C.
Hawtrey (trans.). WBP3
The **iliad**, sels. Alexander Pope
(trans.). WBP3
The **iliad**, sels. Homer. WBP3
Ilka blade o' grass keps its
ain...dew. James Ballantine.
WBP3
The **ill-starred** flower. Tristan
Corbiere. FreS
Illinois
The angel and the clown. Vachel
Lindsay. PrVo
The honeymoon of the muse.
Michael Van Walleghen. PrVo
Illinois coalscapes. James
Ballowe. PrVo
Illness
At the center of everything
which..dying. Patricia
Goedicke. FroA
Diarrhea. Yoshioka Minoru.   FroC
Fifteen hokku. Naito Joso.   FroC
For Annie. Edgar Allan Poe.
WBP3
Haiku: 39 haiku. Masaoka Shiki.
FroC
I that in heill was and
glaidnes. William Dunbar.
HaAP
Lord Randal. Unknown. HaAP
Pine resin, sel. Arakida
Moritake. FroC
A stroke of good luck. Theodore
Weiss. StPo
Tanka: 15 tanka. Masaoka Shiki.
FroC
A wasted illness. Thomas Hardy.
EvIm
The windows. Stephane Mallarme.
FreS
Illusion. Vickie Rogers. YoVA
Illusion. Laury Powers. YoVA

(**im**)c-a-t(mo). Edward Estlin
Cummings. HaAP

The **image**. Tamura Ryuichi. FroC
Imagination
On imagination. Phillis

Wheatley. BlS
Think of it. Bette Killion. ByM
Imitations of old poems, sels.
Wei Ying-wu. GrAC
Immediately following. Dawn
March. YoVA
Immigration and Emigration
The arrival. Ernesto Cardenal.
NiR
The burning trees were
limitless. Jane Dulin. YoVA
Ellis Island. Joseph Bruchac.
ReE
An endless chain. Abraham
Reisen. VoWA
Instructions for crossing the
border. Don Pagis. VoWA
Newcomers. Abraham Reisen. VoWA
Prayer ("From your high
bridge...") Lev Mak. VoWA
Immortality
"Before this high hall had
collapsed." Tu Fu. GrAC
Epilogue. Robert Browning. WBP4
If you could only live forever.
Marlo Maconi. YoVA
It kindles all my sou. Casimir
the Great; King-Poland . WBP4
The last man. Thomas Campbell.
WBP4
Lines. Sir Walter Ralegh. WBP4
Matter and man immortal. Edward
Young. WBP4
Miscellaneous songs of Han
Wu-ti, sel. Wei Ying-wu.
GrAC
My life closed twice before its
close. Emily Dickinson. DoNG
Ode ("Our birth is but a
sleep...") William
Wordsworth. DoNG--WBP4
Ode: Intimations of
immortality. William
Wordsworth. HaAp--WBP4
Sailing to Byzantium. William
Butler Yeats. HaAP--LiHE
Tithonus. Alfred, Lord
Tennyson. HaAP
Virtue immortal. George
Herbert. WBP3
Wandering immortal. Wu Yun.
GrAC
When nothing remains any
longer, sels. Stanislaw
Grochowiak. CoP
Impact. Gordon D. Leslie. StPo
Imperial Adam. Alec Derwent
Hope. HaAP
Imperialism
1927. HuGos.   NiR

In memoriam, sels. Alfred, Lord
    Tennyson. WBP4
In memoriam, sels. Alfred, Lord
    Tennyson. HaAP
In memoriam, sels. Alfred, Lord
    Tennyson. WBP1--WBP3
In memoriam: LXXVIII, sels.
    Alfred, Lord Tennyson. PoCh
In memoriam: XXVIII, sels.
    Alfred, Lord Tennyson. PoCh
In memory of Francois Rabelais.
    Yunna Moritz. VoWA
In memory of Sigmund Freud.
    Wystan Hugh Auden. HaAP
In memory of W.B. Yeats, sels.
    Wystan Hugh Auden. TyW
In memory of W.B. Yeats. Wystan
    Hugh Auden. LiHE
In memory of...Lady Madre de
    Teresa. Richard Crashaw. TyW
In mourning for the summer.
    Tachihara Michizo. FroC
In my craft or sullen art. Dylan
    Thomas. HaAP
"In my hands I have memories."
    Paul Peninger. HoWM
"In my hands are dreams." Greg
    Ellis. HoWM
"In my heart there is weeping."
    Paul Verlaine. FoFS
In no strange land. Francis
    Thompson. EeBC--HaAP
In one's own and foreign land.
    Francisco de Asis Fernandez.
    NiR
In place of a curse. John
    Ciardi. HoA
In praise of blur. G.S. Sharat
    Chandra. FroA
In praise of limestone. Wystan
    Hugh Auden. HaAP
In praise of sake. Otomo no
    Tabito. FroC
In praise of the spring Casi.
    Giovanni Giovano Pontano.
    ReLP
In prison. May Riley Smith. WBP4
In response to a rumor.... James
    Wright. TyW
In romance with the concrete,
    sels. Miron Bialoszewski. CoP
In school-days. John Greenleaf
    Whittier. WBP1
In soft moss, in muted steps.
    David Einhorn. OnCP
In that green field. Rivka
    Miriam. BuAC
In the Jerusalem hills, sels.
    Leah Goldberg. BuAC
In the beginning. Rachel

Fishman. VoWA
In the cabinet. Shlomo Vinner.
    VoWA
In the cellar. Josiah Gilbert
    Holland. WBP1
In the cellars. Jiri Gold. VoWA
In the chambers of Reverand
    Tsan... Tu Fu. GrAC
In the courtyard. Miriam
    Ulinover. VoWA
In the dark, cold days of
    December. Cynthia D.
    McMillan. YoVA
In the discreet splendor. A.L.
    Strauss. VoWA
In the distance. Fuzoku Uta.
    FroC
In the distance. H.L. Van Brunt.
    FroA
In the dry riverbed. Zelda.
    BuAC--VoWA
"In the endless ennui/Of the
    meadowland." Paul Verlaine.
    FoFS
"In the evening view, the
    mountains..." Wang Wei. LuL
In the evening I walk by the
    river. Ouyang Xiu. LuL
In the eyes of a screech owl.
    Ono Tozaburo. FroC
"In the field I've roped
    off..." Yamabe no Akahito.
    FroC
In the first cave. Seymour
    Mayne. VoWA
In the first year of freedom's
    second.... George Gordon,6th
    Baron Byron. TyW
In the forest. Pinhas Sadeh.
    VoWA
In the garden of the Turkish
    Consulate. Pinhas Sadeh. VoWA
In the ghetto. Hugo
    Sonnenschein. VoWA
In the hole. John Ciardi. HoA
In the holy natviity of our lord
    God. Richard Crashaw. ShBa
In the horse carriage. Hagiwara
    Sakutaro. FroC
In the last flicker of the
    sinking sun. Peretz Markish.
    VoWA
In the library. Patrick Michael
    Hearn. BrBD
In the local museum. Walter De
    La Mare. HaAP
In the lodge where no one lives.
    Minerva Allen. ReE
In the middle of life, sels.
    Tadeusz Rozewicz. CoP

In the morning all over. William
    Stafford. FroA
In the morning. Jayne Cortez.
    BlS
In the mountains. Wang An-shi.
    LuL
"In the mountain's shadow."
    Ryokan. FroC
"In the music academy...", sels.
    Tu Fu. GrAC
In the old city. Yehuda Amichai.
    VoWA
In the old guerilla war. Linda
    Pastan. TyW
In the open fields. Hugo
    Sonnenschein. VoWA
In the pitch of the night. Lee
    Bennett Hopkins. ByM
In the post of assistant in
    Lo-yang... Wei Ying-wu. GrAC
In the season. Robert Louis
    Stevenson. WBP1
In the town. Eleanor Farjeon
    (trans.). PoCh
In the trail of the wind, sels.
    Unknown. ReE
In the twentieth century of my
    trespass. Galway Kinnell. TyW
In the week when Christmas
    comes. Eleanor Farjeon. PoCh
In this deep darkness. Natan
    Zach. VoWA
In this manner. Nanni
    Balestrini. NeIP
In this room it is cold.
    Victoria Guerica. YoVA
In time of "The breaking of
    nations." Thomas Hardy. HaAP
In time we will grow apart. Leah
    Wall. YoVA
In twos. William Channing
    Gannett. WBP2
In vistas of stone. Abraham Abo
    Stoltzenberg. VoWA
In wolfen teeth. Chaim Grade.
    OnCP
In your arms. Miklos Radnoti.
    VoWA
Ina field. Unknown. FroC
Incantation to...rid a sometime
    friend. Emanuel diPasquale.
    TyW
Incident. Harvey Shapiro. FroA
Incident. Countee Cullen. LiHE
Incompatibility. Luciano Erba.
    NeIP
Indeed, indeed, I cannot tell.
    Henry David Thoreau. TyW
Indian anthropologist.... Wendy
    Rose. ReE

Indian blood. Mary Tallmountain.
    ReE
The Indian burying ground.
    Philip Freneau. HaAP
Indian dancer. Gladys Cardiff.
    ReE
Indian lament. El Indio
    Fernando. NiR
Indian summer. Jennifer Rogers.
    YoVA
Indiana
    Memo to the 21st century.
        Philip Appleman. TeMP
Indians of America
    Acoma. William Oandasan. ReE
    Akwesasne. Maurice Kenny. ReE
    Anniversary poem...Cheyennes
        who died... Lance Henson. ReE
    Barbara's land - May, 1974.
        Geary Hobson. ReE
    The bare facts. Elizabeth
        Cook-Lynn. ReE
    Bars fight, August 28, 1746.
        Lucy Terry. BlS
    Blessings. Linda Hogan. ReE
    Bronze tablets! John F. Kerr.
        ReE
    California poem. Sandie Nelson.
        ReE
    Catoni. Jean Natoni. ReE
    (Conversations #4). Carol Lee
        Sanchez. ReE
    (Conversations #2). Carol Lee
        Sanchez. ReE
    (Conversations #1). Carol Lee
        Sanchez. ReE
    Dark testament. Pauli Murray.
        BlS
    Echo from beyond. Joe S. Sando.
        ReE
    Epitaph ("because words fall
        short"). Anna L. Walters. ReE
    Fire/rain. Peter Blue Cloud.
        ReE
    For Lori Tazbah. Luci
        Tapahonso. ReE
    For rattlesnake. Peter Blue
        Cloud. ReE
    For the rain in March... Roy A.
        Young Bear. ReE
    For the white poets who would
        be Indian. Wendy Rose. ReE
    Four songs of life. Roy A.
        Young Bear. ReE
    Going to town. Linda Hogan. ReE
    The gourd dancer. N. Scott
        Momaday. ReE
    Heritage. Carol Lee Sanchez.
        ReE
    Heritage. Linda Hogan. ReE

Heyaashi guutah. Simon J. Ortiz. ReE

Honest John's seven idols pawn shop. Luci Abeita. ReE

How my cousin was killed. Gladys Cardiff. ReE

i breathe as the night breathes. Susan Shown Harjo. ReE

i drea. Rokwaho (Daniel Thompson) . ReE

Ikce wichasha. Paula Gunn Allen. ReE

Impression...Cheyenne dog soldier. Lance Henson. ReE

In the lodge where no one lives. Minerva Allen. ReE

In the trail of the wind, sel. Unknown . ReE

Indian anthropologist.... Wendy Rose. ReE

Indian blood. Mary Tallmountain. ReE

The Indian burying ground. Philip Freneau. HaAP

Inspiratio. Karoniaktatie (Alex Jacobs) . ReE

Inspiration. Alex. See Karoniaktati Jacobs. ReE

John Knew-the-Crow, 1880. Marnie Walsh. ReE

Juanita, wife of Manuelito. Simon J. Ortiz. ReE

La tienda. Carol Lee Sanchez. ReE

Lonely warriors. R.A. Swanson. ReE

Long person. Gladys Cardiff. ReE

Mickey. Bernadette Chato. ReE

More conversations from the nightmare. Carol Lee Sanchez. ReE

Mountain spirits. King Kuka. ReE

Moving camp too far. Gladys Cardiff. ReE

Muted war drums. Adrian C. Louis. ReE

My people. Duane BigEagle. ReE

The natives of America. Ann Plato. BlS

Nilla northStar. Gladys Cardiff. ReE

Notes for a love letter from mid-America. Jim Barnes. ReE

Notes to Joanne, LXVI. John F. Kerr. ReE

Old man for his people. Harold Littlebird. ReE

Pass it on grandson. Ted Palmanteer. ReE

"People from the stars." Carter Revard. ReE

Poem for nana. June Jordan. BlS

Poems from the wisdom of Swimmer Snell. Robert J. Conley. ReE

Ponca war dancers. Carter Revard. ReE

Powwow. Carroll Arnett/Gogisgi. ReE

Powwow/and I am in your. Barney Bush. ReE

Prophecy. Carol Lee Sanchez. ReE

The pseudo-shaman's cliche. Adrian C. Louis. ReE

The rattlesnake band. Robert J. Conley. ReE

Roadman. Carroll Arnett/Gogisgi. ReE

A San Diego poem: January-February 1973. Simon J. Ortiz. ReE

Self-portrait: microcosm... Robert J. Conley. ReE

The significance of Veteran's Day. Simon J. Ortiz. ReE

Slim man canyon. Leslie Marmon Silko. ReE

Soalt in tleeyaga. Mary Tallmountain. ReE

Solemn spirits. R.A. Swanson. ReE

Someone talking. Joy Harjo. ReE

Story from bear country. Leslie Marmon Silko. ReE

Thirsty island. Jim Tollerud. ReE

Three AM. Joy Harjo. ReE

Three poems for the Indian steelworkers. Joseph Bruchac. ReE

Three thousand dollar death song. Wendy Rose. ReE

Time to kill in Gallup. Simon J. Ortiz. ReE

Tlanuwa. Carroll Arnett/Gogisgi. ReE

To Nilinigii. Bernadette Chato. ReE

To some few Hopi ancestors. Wendy Rose. ReE

Tocito visions. Grey Cohoe. ReE

Too far into Arizona. Joy Harjo. ReE

Travels in the south. Simon J. Ortiz. ReE

Tucson: first night. Paula Gunn

151

Isaac

Inside the lab. Joanne Ryder.
    BrBD
Inside/the tall. Karen Simmons.
    YoVA
Inspiration. Alex. See
    Karoniaktati Jacobs. ReE
Inspiration. Henry David
    Thoreau. EeBC
Inspiration. Karoniaktatie (Alex
    Jacobs). ReE
Inspiration
    Arriving at a new poem... David
    Curry. PrVo
    Narowistosc piora, sels. Jerzy
    Harasymowicz. CoP
    That enchanted place. Gwen
    Perkins. YoVA
The instinct of
    self-preservation. Nanni
    Balestrini. NeIP
Instincts. Karen Olsen. YoVA
The instruction manual. John
    Ashbery. HaAP--SlW
Instructions for crossing the
    border. Don Pagis. VoWA
Instructions for the Messiah.
    Myra Sklarew. VoWA
Intellect
    Hymn to intellectual beauty.
    Percy Bysshe Shelley. HaAP
    The idea of order at Key West.
    Wallace Stevens. HaAP--MTS
Intemperance
    The disabled debauchee. John
    Wilmot, Earl Rochester. HaAP
    Life goes on. Laura Peterson.
    YoVA
    Report. Suzanne Fisher. YoVA
Intensive care. Jay Johnston.
    YoVA
Interior. Joseph Milbauer. VoWA
Interview with Doctor Drink.
    James Vincent Cunningham. TyW
Intimations. Alma Johanna
    Koenig. VoWA
Into the book. Martin Grossman.
    VoWA
Introducing a madman. Keith
    Waldrop. TyW
Introduction to poetics, sels.
    Julian Przybos. CoP
The intruder. Belinda J. Braley.
    YoVA
Invalids at the window II.
    Georges Rodenbach. FreS
Invalids at the window XII.
    Georges Rodenbach. FreS
The invention of New Jersey.
    Jack Anderson. TyW
The invention of cuisine. Carol

Muske. TeMP
The invention of zero. Constance
    Urdang. VoWA
Inventory. Jacques Prevert. MoVT
Invictus. William Ernest Henley.
    WBP3
The invisible Carmel. Zelda.
    BuAC
Invitation to the voyage.
    Charles Baudelaire. FoFS
Ion, sels. Sir Thomas Noon
    Talfourd. WBP4
Iowa
    Coralville, in Iowa. Marvin
    Bell. FroA
    Malcolm, Iowa. Charles Itzin.
    FroA
Ireland and the Irish
    Easter 1916. William Butler
    Yeats. HaAP
    I am from Irelan. Unknown.
    HaAP
    Paudeen. William Butler Yeats.
    HaAP
    September 1913. William Butler
    Yeats. HaAP
    Under Ben Bulben. William
    Butler Yeats. HaAP
Irish melodies, sels. Thomas
    Moore. WBP2
The Irish spinning-wheel. Alfred
    Percival Graves. WBP2
Ironic rescue. Gina North. YoVA
Ironies
    Tautology. Nelo Risi. NeIP
Irritated. Gwen Perkins. YoVA
Irwin, Wallace
    The cares of a caretaker. IlTH
    The rhyme of the chivalrous
    shark. IlTH
    Science for the young. IlTH
"Is it an oriental dancer?"
    Arthur Rimbaud. FreS
Is it really? Kelly Palmer.
    YoVA
Is it right to move to the
    country? Giovanni Giudici.
    NeIP
"is not water, whether
    trickling..." Jie Zi Yuan
    Hua Zhuan. LuL
Isaac. A.C. Jacobs. VoWA
Isaac. Stanley Burnshaw. VoWA
Isaac. Haim Guri. VoWA
Isaac. Barry Holtz. VoWA
Isaac. Amir Gilboa. VoWA
Isaac
    Abraham and Isaac. Else
    Lasker-Schuler. VoWA
    The binding of Isaac. Itzik

Manger. OnCP
Isaac. A.C. Jacobs. VoWA
Isaac. Amir Gilboa. VoWA
Isaac. Barry Holtz. VoWA
Isaac. Haim Guri. VoWA
Isaac. Stanley Burnshaw. VoWA
The sacrifice. Chana Bloch.
    VoWA
Story of Isaac. Leonard Cohen.
    VoWA
Isaac Leybush Peretz. Moishe
    Leib Halpern. VoWA
Isaac and Esau. Rose Drachler.
    VoWA
Isaacs, Jeff
Grey days. YoVA
I'm going to work in my daddy's
    shop. YoVA
Isaacson, Jose
Pre-positions. VoWA
Isabella; or, the pot of basil.
    John Keats. EvIm
Iscah. Howard Schwartz. VoWA
Ise, Lady
Eleven tanka. FroC
Ishigaki Rin
Clams. FroC
Festival of the blind. FroC
Island ("I stand in a looking
    glass.") FroC
Landscape ("If you wait...")
    FroC
The pan, the pot, the burning
    fire... FroC
Roof. FroC
Tsuetsuki Pass. FroC
Ishihara Yoshiro
Commerce in the Caucasus. FroC
Fog and town. FroC
Funeral train. FroC
Horse and riot. FroC
The last enemy. FroC
Night robbers. FroC
Night's invitation. FroC
Sancho Panza's homecoming. FroC
Song of the ringing in the ear.
    FroC
You heard him say lonely, now.
    FroC
Ishikawa Takuboku
Handful of sand, sels. FroC
Sad toys, sels. FroC
Ishmael. Gabriel Levin. VoWA
Ishmael
Hagar and Ishmael. Else
    Lasker-Schuler. VoWA
Hagar to Ishmael. Deborah
    Eibel. VoWA
Ishmael. Gabriel Levin. VoWA
Islam

Cinderell. Fareedah Allah (Ruby
    Saunders). BlS
Hush, hone. Fareedah Allah
    (Ruby Saunders). BlS
Island. Rina Lasnier. MoVT
Island ("I stand in a looking
    glass.") Ishigaki Rin. FroC
Islands
Examples of created systems.
    William Meredith. TeMP
Sea-distances. Alfred Noyes.
    MTS
Isn't it funny? Lindy Padilla.
    YoVA
Israel and the Israelis
About her & about him. Miriam
    Oren. BuAC
At the western wall. Barbara F.
    Lefcovitz. VoWA
Beginning. David Rokeah. VoWA
A big woman screams out her
    guts. Shulamit Apfel. BuAC
Children's song. Arye Sivan.
    VoWA
Desert march. Gerda Stein
    Norvig. VoWA
Freethinkers. Deborah Eibel.
    VoWA
The Israeli Navy. Marvin Bell.
    VoWA
The mirrors of Jerusalem.
    Barbara F. Lefcovitz. VoWA
Since then. Yehuda Amichai.
    VoWA
Snow in the city. Danny Siegel.
    VoWA
Song for Dov Shamir. Dannie
    Abse. VoWA
Tabernacle of peace. Hayim
    Be'er. VoWA
Training on the shore. Shlomo
    Vinner. VoWA
Walking along the Sea of
    Galilee. David Knut. VoWA
The western wall. Shirley
    Kaufman. BuAC
When I came to Israel. Bert
    Meyers. VoWA
Israel, Mary E.
Thank you. YoVA
The **Israeli** Navy. Marvin Bell.
    VoWA
It. Helen Denniston. YoVA
It doesn't really matter. Jill
    Wubben. YoVA
It dropped so slow-in my regard.
    Emily Dickinson. HaAP
It fell on a summer's day.
    Thomas Campion. HaAP
It has died. John Scott. YoVA

It hurts. Ken Liu. YoVA
It hurts! Lori Susan Avant.
    YoVA
It is. Reginald Shephead. YoVA
"It is finished." Christina
    Georgina Rossetti. WBP1
It is not death to die. George
    Washington Bethune. WBP3
"It is when the tribe is gone."
    Duff Bigger. FroA
It kindles all my soul. Casimir
    the Great; King-Poland. WBP4
It says. Jon Silkin. VoWA
It was gentle. Chedva Harakavy.
    BuAC--VoWA
It would be so very easy. Judy
    Ellen Mills. YoVA
It's a porcelain world. Lori
    Seiler. YoVA
It's a secret. Jean Bland. YoVA
It's a time for sad songs. Julie
    A. Engel. YoVA
It's all the same. Thadious M.
    Davis. BlS
It's been months, my daughter.
    Gioconda Belli. NiR
It's raining. Guillaume
    Apollinaire. SlW
It's spring returning, it'
    spring & love. Unknown. HaAP
It's the boys. Mario Santos. NiR
Italy and the Italians
    De cultu virginis. Nanni
        Balestrini. NeIP
    The ditchdigger's tears, sels.
        Pier Paolo Pasolini. NeIP
    Gramsci's ashes. Pier Paolo
        Pasolini. NeIP
    Hotel paradiso e commerciale.
        John Malcolm Brinnin. HoA
    I promessi sposi. Cid Corman.
        HoA
    Industrial landscape. Giancarlo
        Majorino. NeIP
    Official iconography. Roberto
        Roversi. NeIP
    Roman rooms. Paolo Volponi.
        NeIP
    The shovel man. Carl Sandburg.
        HaAP
    The sun, the sun. Pier Paolo
        Pasolini. NeIP
Ite. Ezra Pound. HaAP
Itzin, Charles
    Malcolm, Iowa. FroA
Ivanhoe, sels. Sir Walter Scott.
    WBP4
Ivy
    A Christmas carol. Robert
        Herrick. PoCh--ShBa

The holly and the ivy. Unknown.
    PoCh
Izumi, Lady
    Fifty-one tanka. FroC
Izzo, Donna
    Special people. YoVA

JC's tiger. Sam Hamod. StPo
Jabberwocky. Lewis Carroll (C.L.
    Dodgson). IlTH
Jabes, Edmond
    The book rises out of the fire.
        VoWA
    A circular cry. VoWA
    The condemned. VoWA
    The pulverized screen. VoWA
    Song ("On the side of the
        road.") VoWA
    Song of the last Jewish child.
        VoWA
    Song of the trees of the black
        forest. VoWA
    Water. VoWA
Jaccottet, Philippe
    At one time. MoVT
    Solitaire. MoVT
Jackie. Sherrie Booth. YoVA
Jackson, Andrew
    Homage to Andrew Jackson.
        Carroll Arnett/Gogisgi. ReE
Jackson, Angela
    Lovesong ("You must not.") PrVo
Jackson, Helen Hunt
    Habeas corpus. WBP3
Jackson, Henry R.
    My wife and child. WBP3
Jackson, Mahalia
    Mahalia. Michael S. Harper.
        FroA
Jackson, Peggi
    To be an artist. YoVA
Jacob. Else Lasker-Schuler. VoWA
Jacob. Charles Reznikoff. VoWA
Jacob. Delmore Schwartz. VoWA
Jacob
    Jacob's winning. Richard
        Sherwin. VoWA
    Jacob. Charles Reznikoff. VoWA
    Jacob. Delmore Schwartz. VoWA
    Jacob. Else Lasker-Schuler.
        VoWA
    Wrestling Jacob. Charles
        Wesley. WBP4
Jacob and the angel. Stephen
    Mitchell. VoWA
Jacob's winning. Richard
    Sherwin. VoWA

Jacobs, A.C.
  Isaac. VoWA
  Painting. VoWA
  Poem for my grandfather. VoWA
  Yiddish poet. VoWA
Jacobs, Alex. See Karoniaktati
  Inspiration. ReE
Jacobsen, Josephine
  For Murasaki. FroA
  Power failure. FroA
Jacoby, Russell Powell
  My love. WBP2
Jacopone da Todi
  Stabat Mater Dolorosa. WBP4
Jaffar. Leigh Hunt. WBP1
Jaffe, Dan
  The owl in the rabbi's barn.
    VoWA
  This one is about the others.
    FroA
  Who? FroA
  Yahrzeit. VoWA
Jahnke, Mary
  The air. YoVA
Jailbird back to Jenny. Peter D.
  McKenzie. StPo
James, William
  The Brockton murder:...out of
    Wm James. Knute Skinner. TyW
Jammes, Francis
  The little donkey. PoCh
Janik, Phyllis
  Greenhouse. PrVo
Janis, Donna Marie
  Time. YoVA
Jannke, Mary
  Confusion. YoVA
January. Nishiwaki Junzaburo.
  FroC
January morning. William Carlos
  Williams. SlW
Japan and the Japanese
  Hokkaido. Jim Trifilio. FroA
Japanese beetles. X.J. Kennedy.
  HoA
Japanese lullaby. Eugene Field.
  WBP1
Jaramillo, Armando
  Almost beyond the churches of
    men. YoVA
  A song for candles. YoVA
Jarrell, Randall
  The bird of night. DuD
  The death of the ball turret
    gunner. HaAP--LiHE
  The mockingbird. DuD
  Next day. HaAP
  The woman at the Washington
    Zoo. HaAP
Jars. Paul Raboff. VoWA

Jastrun, Mieczyslaw
  The Jews. VoWA
Jazz. Tim Parker. HoWM
Jazz music. Mark Decker. HoWM
Jealousy. Jeanna Shry. YoVA
Jealousy
  For Tammy & David. Cheryl
    Cruts. YoVA
  Jealousy. Jeanna Shry. YoVA
Jeanie Morrison. William
  Motherwell. WBP3
Jeffers, Robinson
  Boats in a fog. MTS
  Hurt hawks. LiHE
  Love the wild swan. TyW
  Nova. HaAP
  The purse-seine. HaAP
Jehovah's Witnesses
  Journal, sels. Gayl Jones. BlS
The jellyfish. Ogden Nash. IlTH
Jenks, Edward A.
  Going and coming. WBP3
Jenks, Tudor
  An accomodating lion. IlTH
  Small and early. WBP1
Jenny kissed me. Leigh Hunt.
  WBP1
Jenny the juvenile juggler.
  Dennis Lee. BrBD
Jensen, Keith
  A world of lies. YoVA
Jensen, Laura
  Household. TeMP
Jent, Jennie
  The wild and wooly willows.
    YoVA
Jerome, Judson
  Child's game. DuD
Jerusalem. Rose Auslander. VoWA
Jerusalem. Antoni Slonimski.
  VoWA
Jerusalem. Jon Silkin. VoWA
Jerusalem. Shlomo Vinner. VoWA
Jerusalem. Ruben Kanalenstein.
  VoWA
Jerusalem
  Chambers of Jerusalem. Yehuda
    Karni. VoWA
  The destruction of Jerusalem...
    Isaac Rosenberg. VoWA
  Encounter in Jerusalem. Fay
    Lipschitz. VoWA
  From Jerusalem: a first poem.
    Gabriel Preil. VoWA
  Guide to Jerusalem. Dennis
    Silk. VoWA
  Heavenly Jerusalem, Jerusalem
    of...Earth. Leah Goldberg.
    BuAC--VoWA
  I stood in Jerusale. Zelda.

Gardner. FroA
This night. Osip Mandelstam.
  VoWA
To T.S. Eliot. Emanuel
  Litvinoff. VoWA
To the Jews in Poland. Jozef
  Wittlin. VoWA
A tribe searching. Shlomo
  Reich. VoWA
The valley of men. Uri Zvi
  Greenberg. VoWA
Verses on accepting the world.
  Joseph Brodsky. VoWA
The vigil. Shlomo Reich. VoWA
The wandering Jew. Benjamin
  Fondane (Fundoianu). VoWA
The wandering Jew. Robert
  Mezey. VoWA
Wandering Jews. Nancy Keesing.
  VoWA
We are acrobats. Jozef Habib
  Gerez. VoWA
We carry eggshells. Hanny
  Michaelis. VoWA
We fooled ourselves. Jozef
  Habib Gerez. VoWA
We go. Karl Wolfskehl. VoWA
Where Babylon ends. Nathaniel
  Tarn. VoWA
Windows. Mordechai Husid. VoWA
A woman from the Book of
  Genesis. David Knut. VoWA
The worm. Willis Barnstone.
  FroA--VoWA
Zealot without a face. Charles
  Dobzynski. VoWA
The Ziz. John Hollander. VoWA
The **Jews** in hell. Isaac
  Goldemberg. VoWA
Jicarilla in August. Ronald
  Rogers. ReE
Jie Zi Yuan Hua Zhuan
  "Clouds are the ornaments of
  sky..." LuL
  "a figure...contemplating the
  mountain." LuL
  "is not water, whether
  trickling..." LuL
  "When the moon is reflected on
  water..." LuL
  "When the wind subsides,
  waves..." LuL
Jim's kids. Eugene Field. WBP3
Jimenez, Juan Ramon
  Village. PoCh
Jimmy Jet and his tv set. Shel
  Silverstein. IlTH
Jing Hao
  "there was one gigantic pine
  tree..." LuL

Jippensha Ikku
  Deathbed verse. FroC
Jito (645-702), Empress
  Tanka ("Spring has passed.")
  FroC
  To old Lady Shii. FroC
Jitrik, Noe
  Addio a la mamma. VoWA
Job, sels. Bible-Old Testament.
  MTS
The **jogger**. Jean S. Harrison.
  StPo
The **jogger**: Denver to Kansas
  City. David Ray. FroA
Jogging. See Running & Runners
Johann Gaertner (1793-1887).
  Gary Gildner. FroA
John. N.M. Bodecker. RoRF
John Anderson, my jo. Robert
  Burns. WBP2
John Carey's second song. Thomas
  McGrath. FroA
John Knew-the-Crow, 1880. Marnie
  Walsh. ReE
John Smith. Lois-Long Anders.
  StPo
John Winter. Laurence Binyon.
  MTS
John's song. Joan Aiken. DuD
Johnson, Don
  The children's hour. TeMP
Johnson, G.T.
  "One day I went out to the zoo."
  IlTH
Johnson, Georgia Douglas
  Aliens, sels. BlS
  Cosmopolite, sels. BlS
  The heart of a woman. BlS
  I want to die while you love
  me. BlS
  My little dreams. BlS
  A paradox, sels. BlS
  Smothered fires. BlS
Johnson, Helene
  Bottled. BlS
  Magalu. BlS
  The road. BlS
  Summer matures. BlS
  Trees at night. BlS
Johnson, Kathy
  Bonds. YoVA
Johnson, Lyndon Baines
  A Miltonic sonnet for Mr.
  Johnson.... Richard Wilbur.
  TyW
Johnson, Samuel
  A short song of congratulation.
  HaAP
Johnson, Shirley
  Lost. YoVA

Johnson, Siddie Joe
    Midnight in Bonnie's stall.
      PoCh
Johnson, Terri B.
    "Does he love me?" YoVA
    Friendship. YoVA
    The love that we miss. YoVA
Johnson, Thomas
    The best dance hall in Iuka,
      Mississippi. FroA
Johnston, Jay
    Intensive care. YoVA
The joining. Gerda Stein Norvig.
    VoWA
The jolly shepherd Wat. Unknown.
    ShBa
Jomei (593-641), Emperor
    Climbing Mount Kagu... FroC
    Tanka ("The stag that
      calls...") FroC
Jonas, Rosalie
    Ballade des belles
      milatraisses. BlS
    Brother Baptis' on woman
      suffrage. BlS
Jones (see Baraka, I.), LeRoi

Jones (tr.), Sir William
    The baby. WBP1
Jones, Becky
    Sharing. YoVA
    Spring. YoVA
Jones, Gayl
    Journal, sels. BlS
    Many die here. BlS
    Satori. BlS
    Tripart. BlS
Jones, Lamont
    The almighty Thor. HoWM
Jones, Maxine
    My favorite time of year. YoVA
Jones, Patricia
    I done got so thirsty... BlS
    Why I like movies. BlS
Jones, Richard
    Three car poems. FroA
Jonson (trans.), Ben
    The forest, sels. WBP2
Jonson, Ben
    Answer to Master Wither's
      song... WBP2
    "Drink to me only with thine
      eyes," WBP2
    An epigram to the queen, then
      lying in. ShBa
    Epitaph on Elizabeth, L.H..
      HaAP
    A hymn on the nativity of my
      Saviour. ShBa
    Hymn to Diana. HaAP

    A hymn to God the father. EeBC
    A little shrub growing by. TyW
    O, do not wanton with those
      eyes. WBP2
    An ode to himself, sels. ShBa
    An ode: to himself. HaAP
    On my first son. HaAP
    On my son. DoNG
    Still to be neat, still to be
      dressed. HaAP
    To heaven. HaAP
    To the memory...William
      Shakespeare. HaAP
    The triumph of Charis. WBP2
    A vision of beauty. WBP2
Jonsson, Ulla
    A child is born. YoVA
    I waited. YoVA
Jordan (I). George Herbert. HaAP
Jordan, John
    Spring. YoVA
Jordan, June
    Poem for nana. BlS
Jordan, Thomas
    The careless gallant. HaAP
Joseph
    Pharaoh and Joseph. Else
      Lasker-Schuler. VoWA
Joseph, Lawrence
    When you've been here long
      enough. HoA
Josephine. Alexander Resnikoff.
    IlTH
Joshua
    Joshua's face. Amir Gilboa.
      VoWA
    Moses and Joshua. Else
      Lasker-Schuler. VoWA
Joshua's face. Amir Gilboa. VoWA
Jost, Keith
    A newly found friend is like
      the sea. YoVA
    An old rustic school building.
      YoVA
Journal, sels. Gayl Jones. BlS
Journey. Rick Morris. YoVA
Journey beyond. Terra Manasco.
    YoVA
Journey of the Magi. Thomas
    Stearns Eliot. EeBC--PoCh
Journey of the Magi. Thomas
    Stearns Eliot. HaAP--ShBa
Journey to New York, sels.
    Ernesto Cardenal. NiR
The journey to the insane
    asylum. Alfred Lichtenstein.
    VoWA
The journey with hands and arms.
    Benjamin Saltman. VoWA
Jouve, Pierre Jean

Wallace Stevens. HaAP--MTS
Kherdian, David
Melkon. FroA
Uncle Jack. FroA
Kicknosway, Faye
from Janie. TeMP
Kid stuff. Frank Horne. PoCh
Kienenberger, Hope
For them. YoVA

(kill the flowers) put words....
Ted Ardans. YoVA

Killion, Bette
Think of it. ByM
Kimball, J. Horace
To the memory of J. Horace
Kimbal. Ada . BlS
King Lear, sels. William
Shakespeare. TyW
Kings and Queens
The bard, sels. Thomas Gray.
TyW
Kinnell, Galway
In the twentieth century of my
trespass. TyW
Kiowa song, sels. Unknown. ReE
Kipling, Rudyard
The beginnings, sels. TyW
The glory of the garden. EeBC
The gods of copybook headings.
TyW
Non nobis domine. EeBC
Kirkpatrick, David
Blue heaven. YoVA
A **kiss.** Dennis Vass. YoVA
The **kiss.** Robert Pack. TeMP
Kisses
First kiss. Cindy Loop. YoVA
A kiss. Dennis Vass. YoVA
Kissie Lee. Margaret Walker. BlS
Kites
Ride the wind. Allen Lord. YoVA
Klappert, Peter
Estienne. TeMP
Klee, Susan A.
Save. YoVA
Words as sharp as daggers. YoVA
Klein, A.M.
And in that drowning instant.
VoWA
Klopenstine, Susan
The lady and the bearded. YoVA
Pollution. YoVA

Sea breeze. YoVA
Klopstock, Friedrich Gottlieb
My recovery. WBP4
Klu Klux Klan
The best dance hall in Iuka,
Mississippi. Thomas Johnson.
FroA
Klubak, Moyshe
Grandma. OnCP
Knaak, Cheryl
Frustration. YoVA
Kneisel, Jan
Winter twosome. YoVA
The **knife.** Juan Gelman. VoWA
Knife whetter. Takamura Kotaro.
FroC
The **knight.** Ron Farnsworth. YoVA
Knight, Etheridge
We free singers be. FroA
Knights and Knighthood
The haystack in the floods.
William Morris. HaAP
The knight. Ron Farnsworth.
YoVA
Lament of the poor knight
errant. Jules Laforgue. FreS
Tale. Stuart Merrill. FreS
Knives
Knife whette. Takamura Kotaro .
FroC
The knife. Juan Gelman. VoWA
Whittling. John Pierpont. WBP1
Knocking, ever knocking. Harriet
Beecher Stowe. WBP4
Knoepfle, John
At the roadside. FroA
Those who come what will they
say of us. FroA
Vachel Lindsay. PrVo
The **knot.** Stanley Kunitz. HaAP
The **knot.** Tom Clark. HoA
A **knot** of blue. Samuel Minturn
Peck. WBP1
Knott, Bill
Streetcorner. TeMP
Knowledge
The dreame, sels. Rachel
Speght. PaW
My house of knowledge. Kristy
Hales. HoWM
Of course I know. Zishe Landau.
VoWA
Ourobouros. Jorge Plescoff.
VoWA
Red light. I. Amiri Baraka
(LeRoi Jones). SlW
Tree of knowledge. Edward
Lowbury. VoWA
Knox, William
Mortality. WBP3

Tonight. StPo
Will. LiHE
Kunde, Rainie
Death threat. YoVA
Kunitz, Stanley
The daughters of horseleech.
TyW
The knot. HaAP
The war against the trees. HaAP
Kunjufu, Johari M.
Ceremony. BlS
The promise. BlS
Return. BlS
Kurland, Joni
War. YoVA
Kuskin, Karla
Going to school. BrBD
Near the window, sels. ByM
Kuskner, Aleksandr
To Boris Pasternak. VoWA
Kwitko, Leib
Esau. VoWA
My fiddle. VoWA
Kyme. See Askew, Anne

Kynaston, Sir Francis
To Cynthia. HaAP
Kyogoku Tamekane
Twenty-three tanka. FroC

L'Engle, Madeleine
O simplicitas. EeBC
Three songs of Mary, sels. PoCh
L'allegro. John Milton. HaAP

La Fontaine du Vaucluse for
Marie Ponsot. Marilyn Hacker.
TeMP
La Grande Jeanne. Luciano Erba.
NeIP
La belle dame sans merci. John
Keats. HaAP
La corona, sels. John Donne.
ShBa
La tienda. Carol Lee Sanchez.
ReE
Labe, Louise
Sonnet ("While yet these
tears...") WBP3
Labor. Lucille Day. VoWA
Labor Unions
Talking union: 1964. L.E.
Sissman. TyW
Labor and Laborers
Blue collar. Robert Pregulman.

YoVA
I'm going to work in my daddy's
shop. Jeff Isaacs. YoVA
Labor song. Denis Florence
MacCarthy. WBP1
The laborer. William D.
Gallagher. WBP4
Rout. Philip Booth. FroA
When through the whirl of
wheels. G.A. Studdert
Kennedy. EeBC
Work. G.A. Studdert Kennedy.
EeBC
Labor song. Denis Florence
MacCarthy. WBP1
Laboratories
Inside the lab. Joanne Ryder.
BrBD
The laborer. William D.
Gallagher. WBP4
Laborintus, sels. Edoardo
Sanguineti. NeIP
Labyrinths
The tapestry. Howard Nemerov.
TeMP
"A lace annuls itself totally."
Stephane Mallarme. FoFS--FreS
Lachman, Sol
Sukkot. VoWA
Lacy, JoCarol
Bobo the clown. YoVA
Dewdrops of life. YoVA
The ladder has no steps. Jorge
Plescoff. VoWA
The ladder of Saint Augustine.
Henry Wadsworth Longfellow.
WBP4
Ladies' voices. Gertrude Stein.
SlW
Ladles
Gray eminences of rapture,
sels. Miron Bialoszewski. CoP
A lady. William DeWitt
Snodgrass. TyW
Lady Ann Bothwell's lament.
Unknown. WBP3
Lady Clara Vere de Vere. Alfred,
Lord Tennyson. WBP3
Lady Clare. Alfred, Lord
Tennyson. WBP2
The lady and the bearded. Susan
Klopenstine. YoVA
The lady in black. Emile
Verhaeren. FreS
The lady of the lake, sels. Sir
Walter Scott. WBP3
The lady's-maid's song. John
Hollander. TyW
Lady, lady. Anne Spencer. BlS
Ladybug's Christmas. Norma

A cry. Annette L. Roy. YoVA
Fifty-one tanka. Lady Izumi.
  FroC
"The hunting horn grieves..."
  Paul Verlaine. FoFS
Lady Ann Bothwell's lamen.
  Unknown. WBP3
A lament ("O world! O life! O
  Time!") Percy Bysshe
  Shelley. WBP3
My heid is like to rend,
  Willie. William Motherwell.
  WBP3
Prometheus, sel. Aeschylus .
  WBP3
Remembrance. Emily Bronte. HaAP
Song ("The linnet in the rocky
  dells.") Emily Bronte. HaAP
Thirty tank. Fujiwara no
  Shunzei . FroC
Twenty-seven hokk. Natsume
  Seibi . FroC
When lilacs last in the
  dooryard bloom'd. Walt
  Whitman. HaAP
With rue my heart is laden.
  Alfred Edward Housman. HaAP
The lamp goes out. Sugawara no
  Michizane. FroC
The lamp now flickers. Alfred
  Grunewald.
Lamplighter barn. Myra Cohn
  Livingston. RoRF
Lamps
  Song of the lam. Maruyama Kaoru.
  FroC
Lamumba, Patrice
  Anniversary. Giancarlo
  Majorino. NeIP
A Lancashire doxology. Dinah
  Maria Mulock Craik. WBP4
Lance, Angela
  Just one picture. YoVA
Land and sea. Luciano Erba. NeIP
The land o' the leal. C.
  Oliphant, Baroness Nairne.
  WBP3
The land of counterpane. Robert
  Louis Stevenson. WBP1
The land of poetry, sels.
  Czeslaw Milosz. CoP
The land of story-books. Robert
  Louis Stevenson. WBP1
Landau, Zishe
  The holy Balshemtov. OnCP
  How through green-grassed
  fields. OnCP
  I have a big favor to ask you,
  brothers. VoWA
  The little pig. VoWA

Of course I know. VoWA
Parts. VoWA
Softly let us all vanish. OnCP
Tuesday. VoWA
Landing. Rafael Alberti. NiR
The landlady's daughter. Ludwig
  Uhland. WBP2
The landlady's daughter. J.S.
  Dwight (trans.). WBP2
Landon, Letitia Elizabeth
  The female convict. WBP3
Landor, Walter Savage
  Alas! 'tis very sad to hear.
  TyW
  Children. WBP1
  Dirce. HaAP
  Farewell. WBP3
  Man. WBP3
  On seeing a hair of Lucretia
  Borgia. HaAP
  Past ruined Ilion Helen lives.
  HaAP
  Remain, ah not in youth alone.
  HaAP
  Rose Aylmer. HaAP--WBP2
  To youth. WBP1
  Well I remember how you smiled.
  HaAP
Landscape. Abraham Sutskever.
  VoWA
Landscape ("If you wait...")
  Ishigaki Rin. FroC
The landscape inspector.
  Miyazawa Kenji. FroC
Landscape: 6. Ono Tozaburo. FroC
Landscape: 7. Ono Tozaburo. FroC
Landy, Francis
  Lament for Azazel. VoWA
  Midrash on Hamlet. VoWA
  The princess who fled the
  castle. VoWA
  Selichos. VoWA
Lane, Pinkie Gordon
  Migration. BlS
  Nocturne. BlS
  On being head of the English
  department. BlS
  Sexual privacy of women on
  welfare. BlS
  When you read this poem. BlS
  Who is my brother? BlS
Lane, Randy
  Song ("Sometimes in the fast
  food...") FroA
Lang (trans.), Andrew
  Golden eyes. WBP2
  Lament for Helodore. WBP3
  Spring. WBP2
Langer, Jiri Mordecai
  On the margins of a poem. VoWA

Riddle of night. VoWA
Langour. Paul Verlaine. FreS
Language
"I don't like foreign
languages..." Chiao-jan .
GrAC
Nothingness. Aharon Amir. VoWA
Language of ancients. Hayim
Lenski. VoWA
Lanier, Sidney
A ballad of trees and the
Master. EeBC--WBP4
A ballad of trees and the
master. WBP4
The ship of earth. MTS
Lantz, Lauren
Your eyes. YoVA
Lanyer, Aemilia (Bassano)
Salve deux rex judaeorum...,
sels. PaW
Lapping waves/cooling rinsing
the sand. Doug Penner. YoVA
Larbaud (C-M.Bonsignor),Valery
The gift of oneself. MoVT
The sea. MoVT
Larch Trees
Larch tree. Kitahara Hakushu .
FroC
Larch trees. Kitahara Hakushu.
FroC
Larcom, Lucy
By the fireside. WBP1
Large order. Lois-Long Anders.
StPo
Large red man reading. Wallace
Stevens. HaAP
Larkin, Philip
At grass. HaAP
The explosion. HaAP
Lines on a young lady's
photograph album. HaAP
Poetry of departures. LiHE
Send no money. TyW
A study of reading habits. TyW
Larks
Blood and feathers. Jacques
Prevert. MoVT
Skylark. Stanislaw Grochowiak.
CoP
Skylarks. Ted Hughes. HaAP
To a skylark. Percy Bysshe
Shelley. HaAP
Larsen, Lori
Yellow. YoVA
Lasker-Schuler, Else
Abel. VoWA
Abraham and Isaac. VoWA
Hagar and Ishmael. VoWA
Homesickness. VoWA
Jacob. VoWA

Lord, listen. VoWA
Moses and Joshua. VoWA
Pharaoh and Joseph. VoWA
Saul. VoWA
Lasnier, Rina
Island. MoVT
Paths. MoVT
Song ("You told me: 'I have
need..'") MoVT
The last. Ezra Zussman. VoWA
Last came, and last did go. John
Milton. TyW
The last chance. Jim Barnes. ReE
The last chantey. Rudyard
Kipling. MTS
A last cry for truth. Bonnie
Bowers. YoVA
The last dream. Roy A. Young
Bear. ReE
The last enemy. Ishihara
Yoshiro. FroC
The last farewell. Miyazawa
Kenji. FroC
The last fire. Moishe Steingart.
VoWA
The last laugh. Wilfred Owen.
LiHE
The last leaf. Oliver Wendell
Holmes. WBP3
The last leaf. John Pollen
(trans.). WBP3
The last leaf. Aleksandr
Sergeyevich Puskin. WBP3
Last lines. Emily Bronte. EeBC
Last lines-1916. Padraic Pearse.
LiHE
The last man. Thomas Campbell.
WBP4
The last mistake. LeAnnette
Donahey. YoVA
Last month depression. Karen
Westerfield. YoVA
Last night. Theophile Marzials
(trans.). WBP2
The last night that she lived.
Emily Dickinson. SlW
The last ones. Don Pagis. VoWA
The last remarkable man.
Elizabeth Cook-Lynn. ReE
The last resort. Robert Willson.
FroA
Last will and testament.
Rigoberto Lopez Perez. NiR
The last wolf. Mary
Tallmountain. ReE
The last words of my English
grandmother. William Carlos
Williams. SlW
A late manuscript...Schocken
Institute. Gabriel Preil.

VoWA
A late movie. William Matthews.
    TeMP
The late passenger. Clive
    Staples Lewis. EeBC
Late-flowering lust. John
    Betjeman. TyW
The latest decalogue. Arthur
    Hugh Clough. HaAP
A latter purification. Haim
    Guri. VoWA
Lattimore, Richmond
    December fragments. PoCh
Lauds. John Berryman. HaAP
Laughing corn. Carl Sandburg.
    PrVo
Laughter
    Let us laugh. Zvi Shargel. VoWA
Lauriger Hoartius. John
    Aldington Symonds (tr.). WBP1
Laus infantium. William Canton.
    WBP1
Lavatories
    Lu. He.'s story, sels. Miron
    Bialoszewski. CoP
Lavender. Unknown. WBP3
Lavender flowers. Susan West.
    YoVA
Law
    The six hundred thousand
    letters. Harvey Shapiro. VoWA
Law in the country of the cats.
    Ted Hughes. TyW
Lawd, dese colored chillum.
    Fareedah Allah (Ruby
    Saunders). BlS
Lawn-mowers
    Beer drops. Melba Joyce Boyd.
    BlS
    It has died. John Scott. YoVA
Lawrence, D.H.
    How beastly the bourgeois is-.
    TyW
    Willy wet-leg. TyW
Lawrence, David Herbert
    Bat. HaAP
    Bavarian gentians. HaAP--SlW
    Butterfly. SlW
    Little fish. SlW
    Middle of the world. HaAP
    Nothing to save. SlW
    Piano. HaAP
    Sea-weed. MTS
    The sea. MTS
    The ship of death. MTS
    Snake. SlW
    They say the sea is loveless.
    MTS
    Whales weep not! MTS
    The white horse. SlW

Lawson, Henry
    The bastard from the bush. TyW
The lay of the last minstrel,
    sels. Sir Walter Scott. WBP2
Lay your head on my shoulder.
    Yehuda Amichai. VoWA
Layton, Irving
    Jewish main street. VoWA
    Letter to a librarian. TyW
Le Cardonnel, Louis
    Dead city. FreS
Le Gallienne, Richard
    Song ("She's somewhere in the
    sunlight.") WBP3
    What of the darkness? WBP3
Le Roy, Gregoire
    Death ("This evening the
    fatal...") FreS
    Evening rain. FreS
    The ride of the Valkyries. FreS
    Shadow music. FreS
LeBlanc, David
    Recipe for tranquillity. YoVA
Lea, Gayle
    Bore! bore! bore! YoVA
Lead, kindly light. John Henry,
    Cardinal Newman. WBP4
The leaden echo and the golden
    echo. Gerard Manley Hopkins.
    SlW
Leaf. Joseph L. Concha. ReE
The leaf of his stalk became a
    sword. Salomon de la Selva.
    NiR
Leaf-line. Kathie A. Dame. StPo
Leah. Shirley Kaufman. VoWA
Leah
    Leah. Shirley Kaufman. VoWA
A lean day in a convict's suit.
    Jean Wahl. VoWA
Lear, Edward
    The broom, the shovel, the
    poker... IlTH
    Calico pie. IlTH
    How pleasant to know Mr. Lear!
    HaAP
    The jumblies. MTS--WBP1
    Limerick:"...old person of
    Ware". IlTH--WBP1
    Limerick:"...old man with a
    nose". WBP1
    Limerick:"...old man, who when
    little". WBP1
    Limerick:"...old person of
    Philae". WBP1
    Limerick:"...old man of Aosta".
    WBP1
    Limerick:"...old person of
    Cromer." WBP1
    Limerick:"...old man of

Toulouse." WBPl

Limerick:"..old man who said,
  'Well'!" WBPl

Limerick:"..old man of
  Marseilles." WBPl

Limerick:"..old man of the
  Dee." WBPl

Limerick:"..old man on some
  rocks." WBPl

Limerick:"..old man with a
  beard." IlTH--WBPl

Limerick:"..old person whose
  habits." WBPl

Limerick:"..old person of
  Chili." WBPl

Limerick:"..old man of the
  Nile." WBPl

Limerick:"..old man of
  Kamschatka." WBPl

Limerick:"..old man who said,
  'Hush!'" IlTH--WBPl

Limerick:"..old man who said
  'How'" WBPl

Limerick:"..old person of
  Hurst." WBPl

Limerick:"..old person of
  Buda." WBPl

Limerick:"..old man in a boat."
  WBPl

Limerick:"..old man of the
  west." WBPl

Limerick:"..old man in a tree."
  WBPl

Limerick:"..young lady in
  blue." WBPl

Limerick:"..young lady of
  Clare." WBPl

Limerick:"..young lady of
  Norway." WBPl

Limerick:"..young lady of
  Greenwich." WBPl

Limerick:"..young person of
  Smyrna." WBPl

Mr. and Mrs. Spikky Sparrow.
  WBPl

The owl and the pussycat.
  IlTH--WBPl

The quangle wangle's hat. IlTH

The table and the chair. IlTH

Learning

April inventory. William DeWitt
  Snodgrass. LiHE

Fellow traveler. Patricia
  Celley Groth. StPo

Poetics. Andre Spire. VoWA

A summing up. Gabriel Preil.
  VoWA

Learning by doing. Howard
  Nemerov. HaAP

Learning to read. Frances E.W.

Harper. BlS

Leave us alone, sels. Tadeusz
  Rozewicz. CoP

Leaves

Autumn. Bonny Elifritz. YoVA

Beautiful dead leaᶠ. Takamura
  Kotaro. FroC

The bleached ruffled leaves.
  Richard Cromwell. YoVA

Choka ("When Emperor Tenji.")
  Princess Nukada. FroC

Gold and red leaves. Mary
  McMurtray. YoVA

I am a leaf. Yehuda Amichai.
  VoWA

In hardwood groves. Robert
  Frost. HaAP

Leaf-line. Kathie A. Dame. StPo

Leaf. Joseph L. Concha. ReE

My own house. David Ignatow.
  TeMP

One lonely leaf. Michelle
  Garmany. YoVA

Raking leaves. James F. King.
  StPo

Song of a lady from Mi. Unknown.
  FroC

Sweeping leave. Ryushu Shutaku.
  FroC

There was a leaf. Robert
  Desnos. MoVT

Leaves of grass, sels. Walt
  Whitman. HaAP

The **leaving**. Lance Henson. ReE

Leaving Wang-Chuan cottage. Wang
  Wei. LuL

Leda

Leda and the swan. Oliver St.
  John Gogarty. HaAP

Leda and the swan. William
  Butler Yeats. LiHE

Leda and the swan. Oliver St.
  John Gogarty. HaAP

Leda and the swan. William
  Butler Yeats. LiHE

Lee, Dennis

Double-barrelled ding-dong-bat.
  BrBD

Freddy. BrBD

Jenny the juvenile juggler.
  BrBD

Schoolyard rimes, sels. BrBD

Lee, Don L.

The self-hatred of Don L. Lee.
  TyW

Lee, Rena

An old story. VoWA

Lefcovitz, Barbara F.

At the western wall. VoWA

Driftwood dybbuk. VoWA

The mirrors of Jerusalem. VoWA
The leg. Karl Shapiro. HaAP
Legend. Jules Laforgue. FreS
Legendary and melancholic
    themes. Henri de Regnier.
    FreS
Leggett, William
    Meeting above. WBP4
Legs
    The leg. Karl Shapiro. HaAP
    A sailor's apology for
      bow-legs. Thomas Hood. MTS
Leib, Mani
    Be still. OnCP
    Elijah in the house of the
      study. OnCP
    From the crag. VoWA
    In little hands. VoWA
    A plum. VoWA
    Psalmodist. VoWA
    The pyre of my Indian summer.
      VoWA
    They. VoWA
    Winter. VoWA
Leifson, Steve
    George. YoVA
    Love is. YoVA
Leigh, Henry
    The twins. IlTH
Leiris, Michel
    Miser. MoVT
    The time of hearts. MoVT
Leivick (Leivick Halpern), H.
    Forever. OnCP
    How did he get here? VoWA
    I hear a voice. VoWA
    Through the whole long night.
      VoWA
    Two times two is four. VoWA
Lemly, Becky
    Words and nonsense! YoVA
Lemmons, Dwight
    The tree. HoWM
Lemon. Mario Satz. VoWA
Lemon elegy. Takamura Kotaro.
    FroC
Lemons
    Lemon elegy. Takamura Kotaro.
      FroC
    Lemon. Mario Satz. VoWA
Len, Negor
    I sing with my heart. NiR
Lenowitz, Harris
    The fringes. VoWA
    Panegyric. VoWA
Lenski, Hayim
    Language of ancients. VoWA
    Purity. VoWA
    Upon the lake. VoWA
Lenski, Lois

    Snack. BrBD
Lent
    A true Lent. Robert Herrick.
      WBP4
Leo Tolstoy. Carolyn Pintye.
    StPo
Leo the late bloomer. Robert
    Kraus. TrWB
Leonel Rugama. Francisco Santos.
    NiR
Leonidas of Alexandria
    Home. WBP1
    On the picture of an infant.
      WBP1
Lepanto. Gilbert Keith
    Chesterton. MTS
Lepers
    The Pennacesse Leper Colony for
      Women... Norman Dubie. TeMP
Ler to loven as I love thee.
    Unknown. ShBa
Lermontov, Mikhail Y.
    To a portrait of Lermontov.
      Margarita Aliger. VoWA
Leroux, Guiraud
    Fidelty in doubt. WBP3
Les silhouettes. Oscar Wilde.
    MTS
Lesbianism. See Homosexuality
Leslie, Gordon D.
    Damned fly. StPo
    Impact. StPo
    Nightcap. StPo
Lessard (see N.Drassel),Nicole

A **lesson** in hammocks. James
    Schevill. FroA
A **lesson** in translation. Gabriel
    Preil. VoWA
The **lesson** of a former
    visit..Jang Creek. Yuan
    Chieh. GrAC
Lester tells of Wanda and the
    big snow. Paul Zimmer. FroA
Let Spurus tremble. Alexander
    Pope. TyW
Let dogs delight to bark and
    bite. Isaac Watts. WBP1
Let her have it. William Cole.
    BrBD
Let it be. Jeanne Neal. YoVA
Let me tell you about myself.
    Tomioka Taeko. FroC
Let not woman e'er complain.
    Robert Burns. WBP2
Let us laugh. Zvi Shargel. VoWA
Let us learn. Melech Ravitch
    (Z.K. Bergner). VoWA
Let's talk, mother. Edith Bruck.
    VoWA

Life as a star. Colleen Dewey.
    YoVA
Life dwells in the shadows.
    Steve Denlinger. YoVA
Life goes on. Laura Peterson.
    YoVA
Life in a fairy tale. Susan
    Yielding. YoVA
Life in the boondocks. Archie
    Randolph Ammons. HaAP
Life in the rain. Ken Harvey.
    YoVA
Life is. Bert Spence. YoVA
Life is... Lori Wharton. YoVA
The life of hard times. Joshua
    Tan Pai. VoWA
The life of rooms IV. Georges
    Rodenbach. FreS
The life of rooms VII. Georges
    Rodenbach. FreS
The life of rooms XVII. Georges
    Rodenbach. FreS
Life of the letters. Emily
    Borenstein. VoWA
Life with you, love. Sandra
    Sanford. YoVA
Life-Death. Ronda Camerlinck.
    YoVA
A life-lesson. James Whitcomb
    Riley. WBP1
Lifelong. Rachel Boimwall. VoWA
Light. Francis W. Bourdillon.
    WBP2
Light
    City of light. Nahum Bomze.
        VoWA
    The fourth act. Chris Smith.
        HoWM
    The soft light/vanilla icing.
        Cindi Kennedy. YoVA
Light a candle. Zelda. VoWA
A light in the darkness. Deb
    Hemmingson. YoVA
The light is my delight. Zelda.
    BuAC
Light of Judea. Claude Vigee.
    VoWA
The light of the harem, sels.
    Thomas Moore. WBP3
The light of the harem, sels.
    Thomas Moore. WBP2
The light of the world. B.
    Alquit (Eliezer Blum). VoWA
Light shining out of darkness.
    William Cowper. WBP4
The light'ood fire. John Henry
    Boner. WBP1
Light's glittering morn. John
    Mason Neale. EeBC
Lights. Ernesto Cardenal. NiR

Like David. Gabriel Preil. VoWA
Like Gulliver. Nina Cassian.
    VoWA
Like a beach. Harvey Shapiro.
    VoWA
Like a laverock in the lift.
    Jean Ingelow. WBP2
"Like a mountain/With rainbows
    of". Morgan Fisher. HoWM
Like a pearl. Hayim Naggid. VoWA
Like a woman. Uri Zvi Greenberg.
    VoWA
Like a young Levite. Osip
    Mandelstam. VoWA
Like an adventurous sea-farer am
    I. Michael Drayton. MTS
Like weary trees. Jacob
    Glatstein. VoWA
Likes and Dislikes
    "I saw a pretty thing." Douglas
        Tyson. HoWM
    No. Natan Zach. VoWA
    Song of the ringing in the ea.
        Ishihara Yoshiro . FroC
    These I have loved. Michelle
        Thiessen. YoVA
    These are my favorite things.
        Donna Funk. YoVA
    Why I like movies. Patricia
        Jones. BlS
    Winter evenin. Anzai Hitoshi .
        FroC
Lilac garden. Yoshioka Minoru.
    FroC
Lilacs
    Moon flowers. Fiona Mellor.
        YoVA
Lilies
    Consider the lilies. Dorothy
        Donnelly. HoA
    Enamel work on gold and silver.
        Pierre Louys. FreS
    Tanka ("A bell lily
        blooming...") Lady Otomo no
        Sakanoue. FroC
Lilith. Primo Levi. VoWA
Lilith. Donald Finkel. VoWA
Lilith. Yvan Goll. VoWA
Lilith. Ruth Feldman. VoWA
Lilith. Allen Grossman. VoWA
Lilith. Ruth Fainlight. VoWA
Lilith
    Lilith. Allen Grossman. VoWA
    Lilith. Donald Finkel. VoWA
    Lilith. Primo Levi. VoWA
    Lilith. Ruth Fainlight. VoWA
    Lilith. Ruth Feldman. VoWA
    Lilith. Yvan Goll. VoWA
    Waiting for Lilith. Jascha
        Kessler. VoWA

Limerick:".. a stately giraffe."
    Margaret Vandergrift. IlTH
Limerick:"..a barber of Kew."
    Cosmo Monkhouse. IlTH
Limerick:"..a young man who was
    bitten." Unknown. IlTH
Limerick:"..an arch armadillo."
    Carolyn Wells. IlTH
Limerick:"..old person of
    Hurst." Edward Lear. WBP1
Limerick:"..old man of Aosta."
    Edward Lear. WBP1
Limerick:"..old man, who when
    little." Edward Lear. WBP1
Limerick:"..old man who said
    'How'" Edward Lear. WBP1
Limerick:"..old man of
    Kamschatka." Edward Lear.
    WBP1
Limerick:"..old man in a boat."
    Edward Lear. WBP1
Limerick:"..old man who said,
    'Hush!'" Edward Lear.
    IlTH--WBP1
Limerick:"..old man of the
    west." Edward Lear. WBP1
Limerick:"..old man who said,
    'Well'!" Edward Lear. WBP1
Limerick:"..old person of Buda."
    Edward Lear. WBP1
Limerick:"..old man of the Dee."
    Edward Lear. WBP1
Limerick:"..old man in a tree."
    Edward Lear. WBP1
Limerick:"..old man of
    Marseilles." Edward Lear.
    WBP1
Limerick:"..old person whose
    habits." Edward Lear. WBP1
Limerick:"..old person of
    Cromer." Edward Lear. WBP1
Limerick:"..old man with a
    beard." Edward Lear.
    IlTH--WBP1
Limerick:"..old man on some
    rocks." Edward Lear. WBP1
Limerick:"..old person of Ware."
    Edward Lear. IlTH--WBP1
Limerick:"..old person of
    Chili." Edward Lear. WBP1
Limerick:"..old man of the
    Nile." Edward Lear. WBP1
Limerick:"..old man with a
    nose." Edward Lear. WBP1
Limerick:"..old man of
    Toulouse." Edward Lear. WBP1
Limerick:"..old person of
    Philae." Edward Lear. WBP1
Limerick:"..small boy of
    Quebec." Rudyard Kipling.

WBP1
Limerick:"..young lady of
    Niger." Unknown. IlTH--WBP1
Limerick:"..young lady of
    Norway." Edward Lear. WBP1
Limerick:"..young lady in blue."
    Edward Lear. WBP1
Limerick:"..young lady of
    Greenwich." Edward Lear. WBP1
Limerick:"..young lady of
    Clare." Edward Lear. WBP1
Limerick:"..young person of
    Smyrna." Edward Lear. WBP1
Limerick:"There was once a
    hippo..." Marty Ernsting.
    YoVA
Limericks
    LIMERICKS HISTORICAL AND
    HYSTERICAL. Ray Allen
    Billington (ed.). LiHA
Limestone
    In praise of limestone. Wystan
    Hugh Auden. HaAP
Limited. Carl Sandburg. HaAP
Lin Bu
    Written while viewing the
    river...autumn. LuL
Lincoln, Abraham
    O captain! my captain! Walt
    Whitman. MTS
    When lilacs last in the
    dooryard bloom'd. Walt
    Whitman. HaAP--WBP3
Lindon, J.A.
    Trouble with dinner. BrBD
Lindsay, Blanche Fitzroy, Lady
    My heart is a lute. WBP2
    Sonnet (suggested by Mr. Watt's
    picture). WBP3
Lindsay, Vachel
    The angel and the clown. PrVo
    I heard Immanuel singing. HaAP
Lindsay, Vachel (about)
    Vachel Lindsay. John Knoepfle.
    PrVo
Lindsey, Jim
    Blank verse for a fat demanding
    wife. TyW
Lineage. Margaret Walker. BlS
Lines. Harriet Beecher Stowe.
    WBP3
Lines. Sir Walter Ralegh. WBP4
Lines. Chediock Ticheborne. WBP3
Lines ("From fair Jamaica's..")
    Ada. BlS
Lines ("My spirit leans...")
    Ada. BlS
Lines for a Christmas card.
    Hilaire Belloc. TyW
Lines for an old man. Thomas

Stearns Eliot. TyW
Lines for the ancient scribes.
   Harvey Shapiro. VoWA
Lines from a misplaced person.
   Jeanne Hill. FroA
Lines on a young lady's
   photograph album. Philip
   Larkin. HaAP
Lines on being refused a
   Guggenheim.... Reed
   Whittemore. TyW
Lines to a don. Hilaire Belloc.
   TyW
Lines to a tree. Judah Leib
   Teller. VoWA
Lines to an Indian air. Percy
   Bysshe Shelley. WBP2
Lines written during a
   period...insanity. William
   Cowper. HaAP
Lines written...above Tintern
   Abbey. William Wordsworth.
   HaAP
Ling-ch'e
   "Now old, my heart is at peace."
      GrAC
   Spending the night at East
      Forest Temple. GrAC
Ling-yi
   About to leave Yi-feng Temple.
      GrAC
   A new spring at Yi-feng. GrAC
Linze, Georges
   "A child/against the light."
      MoVT
   Poem of the city by night. MoVT
The lion and the mouse. Jeffreys
   Taylor. MiRN
Lions
   An accomodating lion. Tudor
      Jenks. IlTH
   "A handsome young noble of
      Spain." Unknown . IlTH
   The lion and the mouse.
      Jeffreys Taylor. MiRN
Lipkin, Jean
   Apocalpyse. VoWA
Lipschitz, Fay
   The aleph bet. VoWA
   Encounter in Jerusalem. VoWA
   Judean summer. VoWA
Lipska, Ewa
   The cock. VoWA
   The flood. VoWA
   If God exists. VoWA
   Wedding. VoWA
Listen to the bird. Laya
   Firestone. VoWA
"Listen to the gentle song..."
   Paul Verlaine. FreS

The listeners. Walter De La
   Mare. HaAP
Listening. Hanny Michaelis. VoWA
Listening to Confucius. Henryk
   Grynberg. VoWA
Listening to her. Natan Zach.
   VoWA
Litany. Sir Robert Grant. WBP4
A litany in time of plague.
   Thomas Nashe. LiHE
Litany of sleep. Tristan
   Corbiere. FreS
Litany of the planes. Pablo
   Antonio Cuadra. NiR
Little Bell. Thomas Westwood.
   WBP1
Little Billee. William Makepeace
   Thackeray. MTS
A little Dutch garden. Harriet
   Whitney Durbin. WBP1
Little Jack Horner. Unknown.
   ShBa
Little Miss Limberkin. Mary
   Mapes Dodge. MiRN
Little Miss Tuckett. Unknown.
   RoRF
Little Orphan Annie. James
   Whitcomb Riley. WBP1
"Little Poll Parrot." Mother
   Goose. MiRN
Little Viennese waltz. Federico
   Garcia Lorca. SlW
Little bunny. Ken Harvey. YoVA
The little car. Guillaume
   Apollinaire. SlW
A little carol of the Virgin.
   Lope de Vega. PoCh
A little cemetery, sels. Anthony
   Hecht. TyW
A little child's hymn. Francis
   Turner Palgrave. WBP1
The little donkey. Francis
   Jammes. PoCh
The little father... Gelett
   Burgess. IlTH
Little feet. Elizabeth Akers.
   WBP1
Little fish. David Herbert
   Lawrence. SlW
A little girl's dream world.
   Della Burt. BlS
Little goldenhair. Mrs. F. Burge
   Smith. WBP1
The little house in Lithuania.
   Samuel Marshak. VoWA
The little milliner. Robert
   Buchanan. WBP2
The little peach. Eugene Field.
   IlTH
The little pig. Zishe Landau.

VoWA
"The little priest of Felton."
   Mother Goose. MiRN
The little red lark. Alfred
   Percival Graves. WBP2
A little shrub growing by. Ben
   Jonson. TyW
A little something for William
   Whipple. Dave Oliphant. FroA
"Little tree." Edward Estlin
   Cummings. PoCh
Little tune: I ("Some place or
   other..") Stephane Mallarme.
   FoFS
Little, Geraldine Clinton
   For Venice, sinking. StPo
Little, Lizzie M.
   Life. WBP2
Littlebird, Harold
   December 22, 1977. ReE
   Old man for his people. ReE
Littledale (trans.), R. F.
   O fire of God, the comforter.
   WBP4
Litvinoff, Emanuel
   If I forget thee. VoWA
   To T.S. Eliot. VoWA
Litwack, Susan
   Creation of the child. VoWA
   Havdolah. VoWA
   Inscape. VoWA
   Tonight everyone in the
   world...dreaming. VoWA
Liu Ch'ang-ch'ing
   Facing the moon on the river.
   GrAC
   Seeing off his Reverence
   Ling-ch'e. GrAC
Liu Hsi-yi
   Song for the white hair. GrAC
Liu Tsung-yuan
   River snow. GrAC
Liu, Ken
   It hurts. YoVA
Liu-Ch'ang-ch'ing
   After the Ch'ing-ming
   Festival... GrAC
Live. Melissa Heiple. YoVA
Live in my heart and pay no
   rent. Samuel Lover. WBP2
Living in sin. Adrienne Rich.
   LiHE
Living on. Dianna Olsen. YoVA
The living temple. Oliver
   Wendell Holmes. WBP4
Living waters. Caroline Spencer.
   WBP4
Living with gavity. Arthur B.
   Shenefelt. StPo
Livingston, Myra Cohn

Buildings. RoRF
Lamplighter barn. RoRF
Tomorrow. DuD
Lloyd, Bubba
   Reflections. YoVA
Loadamia. William Wordsworth.
   WBP2
Lobdell, Mark
   A poor old man. YoVA
Lochaber no more. Allan Ramsay.
   WBP3
Lochinvar. Sir Walter Scott.
   WBP2
Locker, Malka
   Clocks. VoWA
   Drunken streets. VoWA
Locker-Lampson, Frederick
   To my grandmother. WBP1
   The widow's mite. WBP3
Lockhart, John Gibson
   Zara's ear-rings. WBP2
Locksley Hall. Alfred, Lord
   Tennyson. WBP3
Locust Trees
   The locust tree in flower.
   William Carlos Williams. SlW
The locust tree in flower.
   William Carlos Williams. SlW
Locusts of silence. Seymour
   Mayne. VoWA
Lodge, Thomas
   "Blessed is the land where
   Sons..." PaW
   Rosalynd's complaint. WBP2
   Rosalynd. WBP2
Lodgers. Julian Tuwim. VoWA
Loewenthal, Tali
   Hebrew script. VoWA
The log. Marjorie L. Turner.
   StPo
Logan, Danny
   Beautiful sleeper. YoVA
   True verdict. YoVA
Logan, John
   The braes were bonny. WBP3
Logan, Lori
   The moment you left. YoVA
Lola. Yona Wallach. BuAC
Lombard-Venetian. Luciano Erba.
   NeIP
Lombardozzi, Christy
   Children. YoVA
   The road of life. YoVA
London. Emile Verhaeren. FreS
London. William Blake. HaAP
London churches. R.M. Milnes
   (Lord Houghton). WBP3
A London fete. Coventry Patmore.
   HaAP
London, 1802. William

Wordsworth. HaAP

London, England

    The aucthour...maketh her wyll..., sels. Isabella Whitney. PaW

    Composed upon Westminster Bridge. William Wordsworth. HaAP

    Lame sonnet. Paul Verlaine. FreS

    London. Emile Verhaeren. FreS

    London. William Blake. HaAP

    The maner of her wyll..., sels. Isabella Whitney. PaW

    When I came to London. Rachael Castelete. VoWA

Loneliness. Linda D. Hawkins. YoVA

Loneliness. Michelle Thiessen. YoVA

Loneliness. Nancy Ross. YoVA

Loneliness

    Again. Daryl Lynn Stewart. YoA

    Alone. Itzik Manger. OnCP--VoWA

    Alone. Lisa Smith. YoVA

    An artistry of happiness. Judy Ellen Mills. YoVA

    Buildings. Daniela Gioseffi. FroA

    Conversations. Luci Tapahonso. ReE

    The dark. Roy Fuller. DuD

    The four of them. Yehuda Karni. VoWA

    In an alien place. Leib Neidus. VoWA

    John's song. Joan Aiken. DuD

    Loneliness. Linda D. Hawkins. YoVA

    Loneliness. Michelle Thiessen. YoVA

    Loneliness. Nancy Ross. YoVA

    The loner. Kitty Druck. StPo

    Motels, hotels, other people's houses. H.L. Van Brunt. FroA

    Mr. Flood's party. Edwin Arlington Robinson. HaAP--LiHE

    On my wander flute. Abraham Sutskever. OnCp--VoWA

    Only lonely. Terra Manasco. YoVA

    Relationships. Venise Duchesne. YoVA

    Remembering Emperor Tenji. Princess Nukada. FroC

    Ruins. Sandie Nelson. ReE

    So confused. Tammie Slaughter. YoVA

    Threats of the witness, sels.

Yves Bonnefoy. MoVT

    Together. Kerry Hadsell. YoVA

    Untitled. Claire Dugan. YoVA

    Who then extends his arms to me. David Einhorn. OnCP

    You heard him say lonely, no. Ishihara Yoshiro . FroC

The **lonely** crowd. Bob Carter. YoVA

Lonely dreams of love. Laura Shonkwiler. YoVA

The **lonely** puppy. Howard Folmer III. YoVA

Lonely warriors. R.A. Swanson. ReE

The **loner.** Kitty Druck. StPo

The **Long** Island night. Howard Moss. TeMP

Long Island springs. Howard Moss. HoA

Long Island, New York

    The Long Island night. Howard Moss. TeMP

    Long Island springs. Howard Moss. HoA

Long person. Gladys Cardiff. ReE

The **long** trail. Rudyard Kipling. MTS

Long trip. Langston Hughes. MTS

Long winter night. Ryokan. FroC

Long, Andrea

    China doll eyes. YoVA

    The dictionary. YoVA

Long, long ago. Unknown. PoCh

The **longest** tale about the longest tail. Alexander Resnikoff. IlTH

Longfellow (trans.), Henry W.

    Beware. WBP1

    Song of the silent land. WBP4

    To-morrow. WBP4

Longfellow, Henry Wadsworth

    The building of the ship, sels. MTS

    Christmas bells, sels. PoCh

    Christmas bells. EeBC

    The day is done. WBP1

    Divina commedia, I, sels. HaAP

    Footsteps of angels. WBP3

    God's-acre. WBP3

    The hanging of the crane, sels. WBP1

    The Jewish Cemetery at Newport. HaAP

    King Robert of Sicily. WBP4

    The ladder of Saint Augustine. WBP4

    Maidenhood. WBP1

    My lost youth. WBP1

    A psalm of life. WBP4

The rainy day. WBP3
The reaper and the flowers.
    WBP3
Resignation. WBP3
Sante Filomena. WBP4
Seaweed. MTS
Serenade ("Stars of the summer
    night!") WBP2
The sifting of Peter. WBP4
The song of Hiawatha, sels.
    WBP3
The sound of the sea. MTS
The Spanish student, sels. WBP2
There was a little girl. WBP1
The tide rises, the tide falls.
    MTS
Ultima Thule. MTS
The village blacksmith. WBP1
The wreck of the Hesperus. MTS
Longfellow, Samuel
    Vesper hymn. WBP4
Longing. Rachel Korn. VoWA
Longing for his son, Furuchi.
    Yamanque no Okura. FroC
Longing for my stray hawk...
    Otomo no Yakamochi. FroC
The lonliness of...long distance
    runner. Alden Nowlan. TyW
Look. William Stafford. FroA
A look at a bee. Leah Goldberg.
    BuAC
Look down from the high terrace.
    Wang Wei. GrAC
Looking at Mount Fuji in the
    distance. Yamabe no Akahito.
    FroC
Looking at Yue-Tai Mountain...
    Yang Wan-li. LuL
Looking for Maimonides:
    Tiberias. Shirley Kaufman.
    VoWA
Looking for a country...original
    name. Colleen J. McElroy. BlS
Looking for a home. Bert Stern.
    FroA
Looking toward Peoria. G.E.
    Murray. PrVo
Loop, Cindy
    First kiss. YoVA
    Portrait of love. YoVA
    What is it like? YoVA
Looting. Jascha Kessler. HoA
Lopez Perez, Rigoberto
    Anxiety. NiR
    Last will and testament. NiR
Lopez Perez, Rigoberto (about)
    Ramps and ramps and ramps...
    Leonel Rugama. NiR
Lopez, Rigoberto Perez
    Anxiety. NiR

Loquat. Nishiwaki Junzaburo.
    FroC
Lorca, Federico Garcia
    Ballad of luna, luna. SlW
    Dawn. SlW
    Little Viennese waltz. SlW
    The moon rises. SlW
    Song of black Cubans. SlW
Lord Randal. Unknown. HaAP
Lord Walter's wife. Elizabeth
    Barrett Browning. HaAP--WBP2
"Lord! when those glorious
    lights I see." George Wither.
    WBP4
Lord, Allen
    Ride the wind. YoVA
Lord, it belongs not to my care.
    Richard Baxter. EeBC
Lord, listen. Else
    Lasker-Schuler. VoWA
Lord, when the wise men came
    from far. Sidney Godolphin.
    HaAP
Lorde Audre
    Chain. BlS
    Coal. BlS
    Harriet. BlS
    Naturally. BlS
    Summer oracle. BlS
    The woman thing. BlS
Lorna slope. Andrea Zanzotto.
    NeIP
Lorrain (Paul Deval), Jean
    Dropping petals. FreS
    Filth. FreS
    "Modern times! Modern times!"
    FreS
    Narcissus. FreS
Los Angeles, California
    Yellow light. Garrett Hongo.
    HoA
"Los Pastores." Edith Agnew.
    PoCh
Loss
    Climbing Hsien Mountain with
    other. Meng Hao-jan . GrAC
    Isabella; or, the pot of basil.
    John Keats. EvIm
    Note in a sanitorium. Ray
    Amorosi. FroA
    Nothing to save. David Herbert
    Lawrence. SlW
    One art. Elizabeth Bishop. HaAP
    Only to lose. Carolyn Tilghman.
    YoVA
    Perished. Mary Louise Ritter.
    WBP3
    The song of wandering Aengus.
    William Butler Yeats. SlW
    There're no whistles from the

crowd. Sally Campbell. YoVA
The widower. Stanislaw
Grochowiak. CoP
Losse in delayes. Robert
Southwell. WBP4
Lost. Shirley Johnson. YoVA
The **lost** Pleiad. William Gilmore
Simms. WBP4
The **lost** baby poem. Lucille
Clifton. BlS
Lost contact. Sylvia Wheeler.
FroA
Lost dreams. Sheryl Chapman.
YoVA
"**Lost** face of summer." Vita C.
Ungaro. StPo
The **lost** heir. Thomas Hood. WBP1
Lost in Yucatan. Tom McKeown.
Lost in sulphur canyons. Jim
Barnes. ReE
Lost in time. Eddy Shipman. HoWM
The **lost** sheep. Elizabeth
Cecilia Clephane. WBP4
The **lost** son. Theodore Roethke.
HaAP
Lot (Bible)
His wife. Shirley Kaufman. BuAC
Lotichius, Petrus Secundus
Elegy II: to Melchior Zobel his
cousin. ReLP
Lotus pool. Mei Yao-chen. LuL
Louis, Adrian C.
Muted war drums. ReE
The pseudo-shaman's cliche. ReE
Louys, Pierre
Enamel work on gold and silver.
FreS
Stretching forth the lance.
FreS
Love. Kevin Beasely. YoVA
Love. George Buchanan. ReLP
Love. Itzik Manger. OnCP
Love. Beth Gonzales. YoVA
Love. Debbie Moffat. YoVA
Love. George Herbert. EeBC
Love. Jean Bland. YoVA
Love. Samuel Taylor Coleridge.
WBP2
Love. Charles Francis
Richardson. WBP4
Love
The act of love. Robert
Creeley. HaAP
Advice to a girl. Thomas
Campion. WBP2
Advice. Yehuda Amichai. VoWA
An affair. Paula Cordier. YoVA
Aliso. Unknown . HaAP
Amber child. John Lukas. YoVA
And I love you. Penny Ward.

YoVA
Art-flower. Tristan Corbiere.
FreS
As you came from the holy land.
Sir Walter Ralegh. HaAP
As you like it, sels. William
Shakespeare. WBP2
Athulf and Ethilda. Sir Henry
Taylor. WBP2
Bedouin love-song. Bayard
Taylor. WBP2
Beginning of lov. Tanikawa
Shuntaro . FroC
being to timelessness as it's
to time. Edward Estlin
Cummings. HaAP
Believe me, if all those
endearing... Thomas Moore.
WBP2
Bird-window-flying. Tess
Gallagher. TeMP
Blest as the immortal god.
Sappho . WBP2
"Blind Mori..." Ikkyu Sojun.
FroC
Bonny Barbara Alla. Unknown.
LiHE
Caelica, sels. Fulke Greville
(Lord Brooke). HaAP
A Christmas scene. Thomas
Osborne Davis. WBP2
The clod and the pebble.
William Blake. EeBC
Come inside me. John Lukas.
YoVA
Come, rest in this bosom.
Thomas Moore. WBP2
Constancy. Sir John Suckling.
WBP2
Crazy Jane on the day of
judgment. William Butler
Yeats. SlW
Crimen amoris. Paul Verlaine.
FoFS
A crowne of sonnets, sels. Lady
Mary (Sidney) Wroth. PaW
Dandelions, raindrops. Lori
Seiler. YoVA
Dinna ask me. John Dunlop. WBB2
"Does he love me?" Terri B.
Johnson. YoVA
Don't let it end. Stacey
Ashford. YoVA
Duellum. Charles Baudelaire.
FoFS
The dule's I' this bonnet o'
mine. Edwin Waugh. WBP2
Echoes. Thomas Moore. WBP2
Eighteen tankas...to Otomo no
Yakamochi. Lady Kasa. FroC

The fear of the innocent. Susan Lueders. YoVA

Feelings. Sara O'Brien. YoVA

Fifty-one tanka. Lady Izumi. FroC

A figment of your imagination. Judy Ellen Mills. YoVA

The fire of love. Charles,Earl Dorset Sackville. WBP2

First lov. Kitahara Hakushu . FroC

First love's goodbye. Melody Luretha Camm. YoVA

First love. John Clare. HaAP

"Fly to the desert, fly with me." Thomas Moore. WBP2

Follow your saint, follow with accents... Thomas Campion. HaAP

Forget thee? John Moultrie. WBP2

Four poems for Robin. Gary Snyder. SlW

Freely, from a song sung by Jewish women. Stephen Levy. VoWA

From the French by Ronsard. Paulus Melissus (Schede). ReLP

Ganging to and ganging frae. Eliza Cook. WBP2

The gillyflower of gold. William Morris. WBP2

Girl in the cafeteria. Roger Ellis. YoVA

He sacred me so. Carol Hall. YoVA

He understands. Susan Brown. YoVA

Her letter. Bret Harte. WBP2

Hesperia. Algernon Charles Swinburne. WBP2

His mother's love. Noah Stern. VoWA

Hope deferred.Unknown. WBP2

The house of desire. Sherley Anne Williams. BlS

The house of life, sels. Dante Gabriel Rossetti. WBP2

How can I see you, love. David Vogel. VoWA

I dreamt I saw great Venus. Bion. WBP2

I hid you. Miklos Radnoti. VoWA

I love what is not. Manfred Winkler. VoWA

I saw two clouds at morning. John Gardiner C. Brainard. WBP2

I want him to, take my soul. A.

Ozello. YoVA

I wondered... Debbie Moffat. YoVA

I'm a flower, sel. Nishiyama Soin . FroC

I'm soaked through with you. Rachel Korn. VoWA

If a man could keep his love. Todd Warne. YoVA

If doughty deeds my lady please. Robert Cunningham Graham. WBP2

If only you knew. Carole Waters. YoVA

In a gondola. Robert Browning. WBP2

In memory of...Lady Madre de Teresa. Richard Crashaw. TyW

Indeed, indeed, I cannot tell. Henry David Thoreau. TyW

It doesn't really matter. Jill Wubben. YoVA

Just one picture. Angela Lance. YoVA

Kate Temple's song. James Carnegie (Earl Southesk). WBP2

Lady Clare. Alfred, Lord Tennyson. WBP2

The lady and the bearded. Susan Klopenstine. YoVA

The landlady's daughter. Ludwig Uhland. WBP2

Last night. Theophile Marzials (trans.). WBP2

A letter catches up with me. Eric Chaet. VoWA

The letter. Suzanne Fisher. YoVA

A letter...to her constant lover, sels. Isabella Whitney. PaW

Life with you, love. Sandra Sanford. YoVA

A light in the darkness. Deb Hemmingson. YoVA

Lines to an Indian air. Percy Bysshe Shelley. WBP2

A little girl's dream world. Della Burt. BlS

The little milliner. Robert Buchanan. WBP2

Lochinvar. Sir Walter Scott. WBP2

Longing. Rachel Korn. VoWA

Look. William Stafford. FroA

Love ("Such a starved bank of moss.") Robert Browning. WBP2

Love ("There are who say the lover's..') Thomas Kibble

The common room. James Shirley.
   WBP2
Constance. Unknown.   WBP2
Cumnor Hall. William Julius
   Mickle. WBP3
Cupid's arrow. Mike Hickam.
   YoVA
Divine comedy, sel. Dante
   Alighieri . WBP2
Dorothy in the garret. John
   Townsend Trowbridge. WBP3
The dream. George Gordon,6th
   Baron Byron. WBP3
A dream. Robin Yard. YoVA
Fair Ines. Thomas Hood. WBP3
The faithful lover. Unknown .
   WBP2
Feelings. Jennifer Haws. YoVA
The fire-worshippers, sels.
   Thomas Moore. WBP3
For K.M.. Scott Morgan. YoVA
Forever uncontested. R.M.
   Milnes (Lord Houghton). WBP2
Forget. Denise Ridley. YoVA
Forget. Duane Bryant. YoVA
Give me more love or more
   disdain. Thomas Carew. WBP2
Has summer come without the
   rose? Arthur O'Shaughnessy.
   WBP3
Hearken to this heart forlorn.
   Holly Sadeghian. YoVA
I dared. Peggy Chapman. YoVA
I'm confused. Dianne Smith.
   YoVA
Isn't it funny? Lindy Padilla.
   YoVA
Let not woman e'er complain.
   Robert Burns. WBP2
The light of the harem, sels.
   Thomas Moore. WBP3
Lost dreams. Sheryl Chapman.
   YoVA
Love not. Caroline E. Sheridan
   Norton. WBP3
The love once shared by us....
   Devara Kolom. YoVA
Maud Muller. John Greenleaf
   Whittier. WBP3
Me n' you. Lisa Shorter. YoVA
Measure for measure, sels.
   William Shakespeare. WBP3
A midsummer night's dream,
   sels. William Shakespeare.
   WBP3
My dear and only love. James
   Graham(Marquis Montrose).
   WBP2
My dream. Paula Rotenberger.
   YoVA

Only a woman. Dinah Maria
   Mulock Craik. WBP3
Pass and regret. Annette L.
   Roy. YoVA
"Raindrops; drown in tears."
   Colleen Hartley. YoVA
A renunciation. Edward Vere
   (Earl of Oxford). WBP2
Rivalry in love. William Walsh.
   WBP2
Rosalynd's complaint. Thomas
   Lodge. WBP2
The sea wall. Jennifer Rogers.
   YoVA
Si jeunesse savait! Edmund
   Clarence Stedman. WBP2
Sonnet CXLVIII. William
   Shakespeare. WBP2
A stone. Bonnie Grosskruetz.
   YoVA
To Chloe. Peter Pindar (John
   Wolcott). WBP2
To a portrait. Arthur Symons.
   WBP3
Twelfth night, sels. William
   Shakespeare. WBP3
Waiting for the grapes. William
   Maginn. WBP2
Waly, waly. Unknown.   HaAP--WBP3
Why so pale and wan? Sir John
   Suckling. WBP2
A woman's answer. Adelaide Anne
   Procter. WBP2
A woman's complain. Unknown .
   WBP2
Woman's inconstancy. Sir Robert
   Ayton. WBP3
A woman's love. John Hay. WBP3
Love - Wedded. See Marriage
Love Affairs
   Kouta: 10 kouta from the
   Kanginsh. Unknown . FroC
   "Should you hide in the rock
   tomb." Unknown . FroC
   Teika, a No pla. Komparu
   Zenchiku . FroC
   Thinking of Prince Hozumi...
   Princess Tajima (?-708). FroC
   When her secret affair...was
   revealed. Princess Tajima
   (?-708). FroC
Love among the ruins. Robert
   Browning. HaAP
Love and death. Margaret Wade
   Deland. WBP3
Love and hate. Frank O'Connor.
   TyW
Love and life. John Wilmot, Earl
   Rochester. HaAP
Love asleep beneath a tree. Tito

Strozzi. ReLP

Love calls us to...things of this world. Richard Wilbur. HaAP

Love for instance. Dan Gerber. FroA

Love in the valley. George Meredith. WBP2

Love in the winds. Richard Hovey. WBP2

Love is. Steve Leifson. YoVA

Love is a sicknesss. Samuel Daniel. WBP2

Love letter. David Ray. TyW

Love letter. Carole C. Gregory. BlS

Love letter. Etta Marie Beasley. YoVA

Love lightens labor. Unknown. WBP2

"Love me little, love me long." Unknown. WBP2

Love not. Caroline E. Sheridan Norton. WBP3

"Love not me for comely grace." Unknown. WBP2

The love of God. Eliza Scudder. WBP4

The love of God supreme. John Wesley (trans.). WBP4

The love of God supreme. Gerhard Tersteegen. WBP4

Love of yesterday. Pamela J. Gilson. YoVA

The love once shared by us.... Devara Kolom. YoVA

Love poem. Linda Wagner. FroA

Love poem ("the earth grows darker.") Lance Henson. ReE

Love poem (for M.). Cary Waterman. TeMP

A love poem for all...women I have known. Charles Bukowski. TeMP

Love song ("In the light of the moon.") Hayim Be'er. VoWA

Love song ("You had the legs...") Elio Pagliarani. NeIP

The love song of J. Alfred Prufrock. Thomas Stearns Eliot. LiHE

The love song of J. Alfred Prufrock. Thomas Stearns Eliot. HaAP--SlW

Love song: I and thou. Alan Dugan. LiHE

A love story. Oliver Herford. IlTH

The love that we miss. Terri B.

Johnson. YoVA

Love the ruins. Malka Heifetz Tussman. VoWA

Love the wild swan. Robinson Jeffers. TyW

Love's complaint. Lady Otomo no Sakanoue. FroC

Love's enigma. Vickie Rogers. YoVA

Love's labor's lost, sels. William Shakespeare. WBP2

Love's logic. Unknown. WBP2

Love's pain. Lori Margheim. YoVA

Love's philosophy. Percy Bysshe Shelley. WBP2

Love's silence. Sir Philip Sidney. WBP2

Love's young dream. Thomas Moore. WBP2

Love's zealots. Judite E. Reis. YoVA

Love, 20c the first quarter mile. Kenneth Fearing. HaAP

Love, Aubrey W.
  Inflation. YoVA
  Untitled ("As the night creeps...") YoVA
  Untitled ("Earth, wind, nor fire.") YoVA

The love-knot. Nora Perry. WBP2

Love/Kissing, sharing... Dianne Smith. YoVA

Lovelace, Richard
  To Althea, from prison. HaAP
  To Lucasra: Going to the wars. HaAP--WBP3
  To Lucasta. WBP3
  To Lucasta: Going beyond the seas. MTS

Loveliest of trees, the cherry now. Alfred Edward Housman. HaAP

The loveliness of love. George Darley. WBP2

Lovell, Kenneth
  Pallbearer. YoVA

Lovely Mary Donnelly. William Allingham. WBP2

Lover of love. Hagiwara Sakutaro. FroC

Lover, Samuel
  The angel's whisper. WBP1
  How to ask and have. WBP2
  I'm not myself at all. WBP2
  Live in my heart and pay no rent. WBP2
  The low-backed car. WBP2
  Rory O'More. WBP2
  Widow Machree. WBP2

Lovers' wine. Charles

Baudelaire. FoFS
Lovesong ("You must not.")
    Angela Jackson. PrVo
Loving. Shirley Kaufman. VoWA
Loving Mad Tom. Unknown. HaAP
Low spirits. Frederick William
    Faber. WBP4
The low-backed car. Samuel
    Lover. WBP2
Lowbury, Edward
    In an old Jewish cemetery,
       Prague, 1970. VoWA
    Tree of knowledge. VoWA
Lowell, James Russell
    Auf wiedersehen. WBP3
    The courtin'. WBP2
    The first snow-fall. WBP3
    The heritage. WBP1
    My love. WBP2
    On board the '76. MTS
    Palinode. WBP3
    She came and went. WBP1
    Sonnet ("I thought our love at
       full...") WBP2
    Sonnet ("My love, I have no
       fear...") WBP2
    Sonnet ("Our love is not a
       fading...") WBP2
    Tempora mutantur. HaAP
    The vision of Sir Launfal. WBP4
    A winter-evening hymn to my
       fire, sels. WBP1
Lowell, Maria White
    The morning-glory. WBP3
Lowell, Robert
    After the surprising
       conversions. HaAP
    For the Union dead. HaAP
    The holy innocents. ShBa
    The Quaker graveyard in
       Nantucket. HaAP--MTS
    Skunk hour. HaAP
Lowenstein, Tom
    Horizon without landscape. VoWA
    Nausicaa with some attendants.
       VoWA
    Noah in New England. VoWA
Lower, Carla
    A friend/The person who calls.
       YoVA
The lowest trees have tops. Sir
    Edward Dyer. HaAP
A loyal image. Darlene Gates.
    YoVA
Loyal sins. Jacob Glatstein.
    VoWA
Lu Hsiang
    With Wang Wei's "Stopping by
       recluse..." GrAC
Lu Lun

Frontier poems, sels. GrAC
Meeting a sick soldier. GrAC
Parting from Li Tuan. GrAC
Lu. He.'s story, sels. Miron
    Bialoszewski. CoP
Lucas, Charlotte
    Shadows are forever. YoVA
Lucas, Kansas
    In Lucas, Kansas. Jonathan
       Williams. FroA
Lucifer in starlight. George
    Meredith. HaAP
Lucinda Matlock. Edgar Lee
    Masters. DoNG--HaAP
Luck. Raymond Carver. TeMP
Lueders, Susan
    The fear of the innocent. YoVA
    Forever is a long time. YoVA
Lukas, John
    Amber child. YoVA
    Come inside me. YoVA
Lulla la, lulla lulla lullaby.
    William Byrd. ShBa
Lullabies
    Cradle song. Yona Wallach. VoWA
    The lullaby of a lover. George
       Gascoigne. HaAP
Lullaby. Edith Sitwell. ShBa
Lullaby ("Lay your sleeping
    head...") Wystan Hugh Auden.
    HaAP
Lullaby ("Sleep now.") Shlomo
    Vinner. VoWA
Lullaby ("The long canoe.")
    Robert Hillyer. DuD
Lullaby ("What if, every
    time...") Frederick Eckman.
    FroA
Lullaby for Miriam. Richard
    Beer-Hofmann. VoWA
Lullaby for an emigrant.
    Benjamin Fondane (Fundoianu).
    VoWA
Lullaby in Auschwitz. Pierre
    Morhange. VoWA
The lullaby of a lover. George
    Gascoigne. HaAP
Lully, lulley, lully, lulley.
    Unknown. HaAP
Lumbering and Lumbermen
    Why log truck drivers rise
       earlier... Gary Snyder. SlW
Lunatics. Raquel Chalfi. BuAC
Lunch. Kathy Hall. BrBD
Lunch. Kenneth Koch. SlW
Lust
    Blue blaze trail. James F.
      King. StPo
    The breasts of the queen...,
      sels. Stanislaw Grochowiak.

CoP
Lust ("Flesh, sole fruit
   tasted...") Paul Verlaine.
   FreS
Lust ("Lust, fruit of
   death...") Albert Samain.
   FreS
Sonnet CXXIX. William
   Shakespeare. HaAP--LiHE
Lust ("Flesh, sole fruit
   tasted...") Paul Verlaine.
   FreS
Lust ("Lust, fruit of
   death...") Albert Samain.
   FreS
Lusus IV: Damis' vow to
   Bacchus... Andrea Navagero.
   ReLP
Lusus XXI: Cupid and Hyella.
   Andrea Navagero. ReLP
Lusus XXII: prayer to night.
   Andrea Navagero. ReLP
Lusus XXXVII. Andrea Navagero.
   ReLP
The lute in the attic. Kenneth
   Patchen. DoNG
Lutes
   I give up...the lute. Sugawara
      no Michizane. FroC
   My heart is a lute. Blanche
      Fitzroy, Lady Lindsay. WBP2
   My lute, awake. Sir Thomas
      Wyatt. HaAP
   Of my lady Isabella playing on
      the lute. Edmund Waller. HaAP
Luther, Martin
   From heaven high I come to you.
      PoCh
   The martyrs' hymn. WBP4
   A mighty fortress is our God.
      WBP4
Luulay mine liking. Unknown.
   ShBa
Lux, Thomas
   Graveyard by the sea. TeMP
Luzzato. Charles Reznikoff. VoWA
Lyall, Sir Alfred Comyns
   Meditations of a Hindu prince.
      WBP4
Lycidas. John Milton. HaAP--WBP3
Lying in a hammock at William
   Duffy's... James Wright. HaAP
Lying in the grass. Edmund
   William Gosse. WBP1
A lyke-wake dirge. Unknown. HaAP
Lyly, John
   Alexander and Campaspe, sels.
      WBP2
Lynn (E.E. Beers), Ethel
   Weighing the baby. WBP1

Lyte, Henry Francis
   Abide with me. WBP4
Lytle, William Haines
   Antony and Cleopatra. WBP3
Lyttelton (Baron...), George
   Tell me, my heart, if this be
      love. WBP2
Lytton, Baron (see Bulwer-L)

Lytton, Earl (see O. Meredith)

Mac Flecknoe, sels. John Dryden.
   HaAP
MacAndrew, Barbara Miller
   Coming. WBP4
MacCarthy, Denis Florence
   The bell-founder, sels. WBP1
   Labor song. WBP1
MacDiarmid(pseud),H.See Grieve

MacDonald, George
   The baby. WBP1
   A Christmas prayer. PoCh
   The earl o' quarterdeck. WBP2
MacDougall, Stacey
   Dormouse. YoVA
MacKay, Kristy
   Crystal. HoWM
MacKay, L.A.
   I wish my tongue were a quiver.
      TyW
MacLean, Crystal
   The good woman. FroA
MacLeish, Archibald
   Ars Poetica. HaAP--LiHE
   Eleven. HaAP
   Epistle to be left in the
      earth. DoNG
   Where the hayfields where. DuD
   You, Andrew Marvell. HaAP
MacManus (see Carbery), Anna

MacNeice, Louis
   Passage steamer. MTS
   The sunlight on the garden.
      HaAP
Macartney (see J.Crawford), L.

Macbeth, sels. William
   Shakespeare. DoNG
Mace, Frances Laughton
   'Only waiting.' WBP4
Macfield, David
   Generational. NiR
   There is nothing in the city.
      NiR

To David Tejada Peralta. NiR
Unite. NiR
Zoologies for today. NiR
Machinery
  Something precise. Bartolo
    Cattafi. NeIP
Machinum analyticus. Glenn
    Reitz. YoVA
Mackay, Charles
  Day breaks. WBP4
  A deed and a word. WBP4
  Small beginnings. WBP4
  Tell me, ye winged winds. WBP4
Maconi, Marlo
  If you could only live forever.
    YoVA
  If you could wish. YoVA
Macrin, Jean Salmon
  To the nymph Brissa. ReLP
Mad Rosalinde. Shulamit Apfel.
    BuAC
The **mad** gardener's song. Lewis
    Carroll (C.L. Dodgson). IlTH
Mad like a bull when hit
    unexpectedly. Mark W. Unruh.
    YoVA
Mad song. Emile Verhaeren. FreS
Madame mouse. Edith Sitwell.
    MiRN
Madge Wildfire's death song. Sir
    Walter Scott. HaAP
Madgett, Naomi Long
  Black woman. BlS
  Deacon Morgan. BlS
  Exits and entrances. BlS
  Midway. BlS
  New day. BlS
  Nomen. BlS
Madison Square. A.
    Glanz-Leyeles. VoWA
Madonna near Barbice, sels.
    Jerzy Harasymowicz. CoP
Maeterlinck, Maurice
  Hospital. FreS
  Hothouse ennui. FreS
  Hothouse soul. FreS
  My soul. FreS
Magalu. Helene Johnson. BlS
The **Magdalene** with perfumes.
    Saint-Pol (Paul) Roux. FreS
The **Magi.** William Butler Yeats.
    PoCh--ShBa
The **Magi.** William Butler Yeats.
    HaAP
Magi
  Carol of the brown king.
    Langston Hughes. PoCh--ShBa
  Carol of the three kings.
    William Stanley Merwin. PoCh
  Journey of the Magi. Thomas

  Stearns Eliot. EeBC--PoCh
  Lord, when the wise men came
    from far. Sidney Godolphin.
    HaAP
  The three kings. Ruben Dario.
    PoCh
  We three kings of Orient are.
    John H. Hopkins. PoCh
Magic
  In the trail of the wind, sel.
    Unknown . ReE
  Penny pictures. Paul Verlaine.
    FreS
  Thrice toss these oaken ashes
    in the air. Thomas Campion.
    HaAP
Magic lantern. William Stafford.
    FroA
The **magic** wood. Henry Treece.
    DuD
Maginn, William
  Waiting for the grapes. WBP2
Magna est veritas. Coventry
    Patmore. HaAP
Magnificat, sels. Paul Claudel.
    MoVT
Magnolias
  My wife and . Unknown . FroC
Mahalia. Michael S. Harper. FroA
The **mahogany-tree.** William
    Makepeace Thackeray. WBP1
Mahony (Father Prout), Francis
  The flight into Egypt. WBP4
Maid of Athens, ere we part.
    George Gordon,6th Baron
    Byron. WBP3
A **maiden's** ideal of a husband.
    Henry Carey. WBP2
Maidenhood. Henry Wadsworth
    Longfellow. WBP1
Maimonides, Moses
  Looking for Maimonides:
    Tiberias. Shirley Kaufman.
    VoWA
The **main-deep.** James Stephens.
    MTS
Maine
  Cows are coming home in Maine.
    Robert P. Tristram Coffin.
    DuD
  Skunk hour. Robert Lowell. HaAP
Mainstream. John Reinke. YoVA
Maiorana, Lynn
  In a spin. YoVA
  They're lost/So many times.
    YoVA
Majia Godoy, Carlos
  The watchword. NiR
Majia Godoy, Luis
  The inheritance. NiR

Majorino, Giancarlo
  Anniversary. NeIP
  Doubly employed. NeIP
  Industrial landscape. NeIP
  Myopia. NeIP
  Rip. NeIP
Mak, Lev
  Eden. VoWA
  The flood. VoWA
  Prayer ("From your high
    bridge...") VoWA
Makai, Emil
  The comet. VoWA
Make we merry. Unknown. ShBa
Make-up. Mike Bacsi. YoVA
Malanga, Gerard
  What I have done. FroA
Malcolm X (Malcolm Little)
  A poem for black hearts. I.
    Amiri Baraka (LeRoi Jones).
    SlW
Malcolm, Iowa. Charles Itzin.
    FroA
The **malcontent,** sels. John
    Marston. TyW
The **Maldive** shark. Herman
    Melville. TyW--MTS
Malediction. Barry Spacks. TyW
Mallarme, Stephane
  Another fan. FoFS
  Apparition. FoFS
  Charles Baudelaire's tomb. FoFS
  The chastened clown. FoFS
  "Concealed from the
    overwhelming cloud."
    FoFS--FreS
  "Does every Pride of evening
    smoke." FoFS--FreS
  Fan. FoFS
  A faun's afternoon. FoFS
  Gift of the poem. FoFS
  "The hair flight of a flame..."
    FoFS
  Herodias, sels. FreS
  "A lace annuls itself totally."
    FoFS--FreS
  Little tune: I ("Some place or
    other..") FoFS
  "Of the soul all things" FoFS
  Prose for de Esseintes.
    FoFS--FreS
  "Risen from the rump..."
    FoFS--FreS
  Saint. FoFS
  Salutation. FoFS
  Sea breeze. FoFS
  Sigh. FreS
  Sonnet ("Her pure nails
    consecrating..") FoFS--FreS
  Sonnet ("Victoriously the

    beautiful...") FoFS--FreS
  Sonnet ("When the shadow
    menaced...") FoFS--FreS
  Sonnet ("Will the virgin...")
    FoFS--FreS
  The tomb of Edgar Allan Poe.
    FoFS--FreS
  Tomb. FoFS
  The windows. FreS
  "With my books closed again..."
    FoFS
Maloney, J.J.
  Poems from prison. FroA
Man. Walter Savage Landor. WBP3
Man
  The closed system. Larry
    Eigner. VoWA
  A fish replies. Leigh Hunt. MTS
  The fish, the man, and the
    spirit. Leigh Hunt. HaAP
  If only they cared. Donald
    Eason. YoVA
  A lamentation (after Solomon Ib
    Gabirol). Carl Rakosi. VoWA
  Man is nothing but. Shaul
    Tchernichovsky. VoWA
  Manfred. George Gordon,6th
    Baron Byron. EvIm
  Maps to nowhere. David
    Rosenberg. VoWA
  The rise of man. John White
    Chadwick. WBP4
  Vessels. Howard Schwartz. VoWA
A **man** adrift on a slim spar.
    Stephen Crane. MTS
The **man** he killed. Thomas Hardy.
    HaAP
The **man** in the moon. James
    Whitcomb Riley. WBP1
Man is nothing but. Shaul
    Tchernichovsky. VoWA
Man of my life. Ronda
    Camerlinck. YoVA
The **man** on the dump. Wallace
    Stevens. HaAP
Man sails the deep a while.
    Robert Louis Stevenson. MTS
a **man** who had fallen among
    thieves. Edward Estlin
    Cummings. HaAP
A **man** whose life is his work.
    Jodie Herbers. YoVA
Man's mortality. Simon Wastell.
    WBP3
Man's thoughts. Richard V.H.
    Sceiford. YoVA
Manasco, Terra
  Journey beyond. YoVA
  Only lonely. YoVA
Mancuso, Tony

Your totem is the opulent
serpent. NeIP

Marot, Clement
To Diane de Poitiers. WBP3

Marquis, Don
Prudence. I1TH

Marrakesh, Morocco
Crystal dawn. Alice A. Robbins.
StPo

A **marriage**. Anthony Barnett.
VoWA

Marriage
The ache of marriage. Denise
Levertov. LiHE
Along the field as we came by.
Alfred Edward Housman. HaAP
Azuma uta & Sakimori no uta: 25
sel. Unknown . FroC
A ballad upon a wedding, sels.
Sir John Suckling. WBP2
Blank verse for a fat demanding
wife. Jim Lindsey. TyW
The brides. Alec Derwent Hope.
HaAP
Connubial life. James Thomson.
WBP2
Couple at home. Florence
Trefethen. StPo
The couple overhead. William
Meredith. TyW
Darby and Joan. Frederic Edward
Wetherley. WBP2
The day returns, my bosom
burns. Robert Burns. WBP2
Dolcino to Margaret. Charles
Kingsley. WBP2
The eggs and the horse. Unknown.
WBP2
Emperor Ojin's son. Unknown.
FroC
Epithalamion, sels. Edmund
Spenser. WBP2
Epithalamium..marriage Mary
Queen Scots. George Buchanan.
ReLP
Erev Shabbos. Marc Kaminsky.
VoWA
Eros turannos. Edwin Arlington
Robinson. HaAP
The fairest thing in mortal
eyes. Charles, Duc d'
Orleans. WBP3
Faith and hope. Rembrandt
Peale. WBP2
The farmer's wife. Anne Sexton.
LiHE
The golden wedding. David Gray.
WBP2
Hebrew wedding. Henry Hart
Milman. WBP2

The hill wife. Robert Frost.
HaAP
I don't have no bunny tail on
my behin. Alta . TyW
I married in my youth a wife.
James Vincent Cunningham. TyW
If thou wert by my side, my
love. Reginald Heber. WBP2
In 728, longing for his
deceased wif. Otomo no Tabito.
FroC
In grief after his wife's deat.
Kakinomoto no Hitomaro.   FroC
In twos. William Channing
Gannett. WBP2
A juggle of myrtle twigs.
Edward Codish. VoWA
Julius Caesar, sels. William
Shakespeare. WBP2
June. Rebecca G. Dykes. YoVA
Just the two of u. Tomioka
Taeko . FroC
Letter to my wife. Miklos
Radnoti. VoWA
Like a laverock in the lift.
Jean Ingelow. WBP2
Loadamia. William Wordsworth.
WBP2
The lonliness of...long
distance runner. Alden
Nowlan. TyW
Lord Walter's wife. Elizabeth
Barrett Browning. HaAP--WBP2
Love lightens labo. Unknown .
WBP2
Love song: I and thou. Alan
Dugan. LiHE
The milkmaid's song. Sydney
Dobell. WBP2
Minstrel's marriage song.
Thomas Chatterton. WBP2
Modern love, sels. George
Meredith. HaAP--LiHE
More conversations from the
nightmare. Carol Lee Sanchez.
ReE
My ain wife. Alexander Laing.
WBP2
My love. James Russell Lowell.
WBP2
My wife's a winsome wee thing.
Robert Burns. WBP2
Nervous prostration. Anna
Wickham. TyW
The newly-wedded. Winthrop
Mackworth Praed. WBP2
Newlyweds. Arthur Rimbaud. FreS
Night fight. Marge Piercy. TeMP
Nilla northStar. Gladys
Cardiff. ReE

Not ours the vows. Bernard
  Barton. WBP2
O lay thy hand in mine, dear!
  Gerald Massey. WBP2
On his dead wife. John Milton.
  HaAP
Paradise lost, sels. John
  Milton. WBP2
The personals. Alan Feldman.
  TeMP
The poet's bridal-day song.
  Allan Cunningham. WBP2
The poet's song to his wife.
  Barry Cornwall (B.W.
  Procter). WBP2
Polyeucte, sels. Pierre
  Corneille. WBP2
Possession. Bayard Taylor. WBP2
Possession. Owen Meredith (Earl
  Lytton). WBP2
The retort. George Pope Morris.
  WBP2
Rhyme-prose on the marriage...
  Oe no Asatsuna . FroC
The rime of the ancient
  mariner. Samuel Taylor
  Coleridge. HaAP
The ring poem... Philip Dacey.
  FroA
The ring. Robert Pack. FroA
The river merchant's wife: a
  letter. Ezra Pound. HaAP--SlW
Rochester's song to Jane Eyre.
  Charlotte Bronte. EvIm
Sabbatical. Linda Zisquit. VoWA
Serenade. Alan Britt. FroA
She was a phantom of delight.
  William Wordsworth. WBP2
The silly old ma. Unknown . TyW
Song ("The bride she is
  winsome...") Joanna Baillie.
  WBP2
Song of the bride. Susan
  Mernit. VoWA
Sonnet ("I thought our love at
  full...") James Russell
  Lowell. WBP2
Sonnet ("My love, I have no
  fear...") James Russell
  Lowell. WBP2
Sonnet ("Our love is not a
  fading...") James Russell
  Lowell. WBP2
Sonnet CXVI. William
  Shakespeare. HaAP--LiHE
Sonnets from the Portuguese,
  sels. Elizabeth Barrett
  Browning. WBP2
There's nae luck about the
  house. Jean Adam. WBP2

These two. Howard Schwartz.
  VoWA
Thou hast sworn by thy God, my
  Jeanie. Allan Cunningham.
  WBP2
"Till death us part." Arthur
  Penrhyn Stanley. WBP2
To my dear and loving husband.
  Anne Dudley Bradstreet. HaAP
Tree poem on my wife's
  birthday. Tom Hanna. FroA
Two lovers. George Eliot
  (M.E.L. Cross). WBP2
Upon Scobble. Robert Herrick.
  TyW
Upon marrying Yasumiko...
  Fujiwara no Kamatari. FroC
A Vilna puzzle. Sasha Chorny.
  VoWA
The voice. Thomas Hardy. HaAP
The vow. Carl Rakosi. FroA
The waste land. Thomas Stearns
  Eliot. HaAP
Wedding. Alain Grandbois. MoVT
Wedding. Ewa Lipska. VoWA
The wedding. Leilani Strong.
  YoVA
Were I but his own wife. Mary
  Downing. WBP2
Widow. Felix Pollak. FroA
The wife a-lost. William
  Barnes. HaAP
The wife of Loki. Lady
  Charlotte Elliot. WBP2
Wife, children, and friends.
  Robert Nicoll. WBP1
Woman's will. John Godfrey
  Saxe. WBP2
The worn wedding-ring. William
  Cox Bennett. WBP2
Marryat, Frederick
  The captain stood on the
    carronade. MTS
  Port admiral. MTS
Marsh in early morning. Marjorie
  L. Turner. StPo
Marshak, Samuel
  The little house in Lithuania.
    VoWA
Marshall, Christine Lynn
  Earth, wind, & fire. YoVA
Marshall, Melody
  I can remember us. YoVA
Marston, John
  The malcontent, sels. TyW
  To detraction I present my
    poesie. TyW
Marston, Philip Bourke
  After summer. WBP3
Martial

Epigram on Elphinstone's
    translation.... Robert Burns.
    TyW
Martial variations, sels. Amelia
    Rosselli. NeIP
Martin (trans.), Sir Theodore
    Homeward bound. WBP1
Martin, David
    I am a Jew. VoWA
Martin, Edward Sanford
    A girl of Pompeii. WBP1
Martinez Rivas, Carlos
    Cradle song without music. NiR
Martinez, Maggie
    Storm. YoVA
Martley, John
    A budget of paradoxes. WBP2
The martyrs' hymn. Martin
    Luther. WBP4
The martyrs' hymn. W. J. Fox
    (trans.). WBP4
Marullo (see Marullus), M.

Marullus, Michael Tarchaniota
    To Nearera: "Every time you
        turn..." ReLP
    To Nearera: "My sweete..."
        ReLP
Maruyama Kaoru
    Anchor. FroC
    Crane. FroC
    Dark sea. FroC
    Dusk ("The river is black").
        FroC
    Estuary. FroC
    Fragments ("In the gun
        muzzle"). FroC
    Funeral song. FroC
    Gun base. FroC
    Sad parting. FroC
    Song of the gull. FroC
    Song of the lamp. FroC
    Song of the sail. FroC
Marvell, Andrew
    Bermudas. MTS
    The character of Holland, sels.
        TyW
    A dialogue between body and
        soul. HaAP
    The garden. HaAP
    An Horatian ode...Cromwell's
        return... HaAP
    On a drop of dew. HaAP
    To his coy mistress. HaAP--LiHE
    Tom May's death, sels. HaAP
    The vows. TyW
Mary Magdalene
    The blessed Magdalene
        weeping... Jacob Bidermann.
        ReLP

The Magdalene with perfumes.
    Saint-Pol (Paul) Roux. FreS
Mary Queen of Scots
    Meditation in verse, sels. PaW
    Poem on life. PaW
    Poem on resignation. PaW
    Poem on sacrifice. PaW
    Poem...on the morning of her
        execution. PaW
    Sonnet to Elizabeth. PaW
    Sonnet to Ronsard. PaW
    Sonnets to Bothwell. PaW
    Verses on the death of Francis
        II, sels. PaW
Mary Queen of Scots (about)
    And though I liked not the
        religion. Sir Nicholas
        Throckmorton. ShBa
    The doubt of future foe.
        Elizabeth I; Queen of England.
        PaW
    Epithalamium...Mary Queen of
        Scots... George Buchanan.
        ReLP
Mary, Mother of Christ. Countee
    Cullen. PoCh
Mary, Virgin
    At dawn the Virgin is born.
        Lope de Vega. PoCh
    At the manger Mary sings.
        Wystan Hugh Auden. EeBC
    The Blessed Virgin offers
        violets... Marius Bettinus.
        ReLP
    An epigram to the queen, then
        lying in. Ben Jonson. ShBa
    Epigram: "You have as many
        qualities..." Bernhard van
        Bauhuysen. ReLP
    I sing of a maiden (mayden).
        Unknown . HaAP--ShBa
    La corona, sels. John Donne.
        ShBa
    The Mother of God. William
        Butler Yeats. ShBa
    On the blessed Virgin's
        bashfulness. Richard Crashaw.
        HaAP
    Our friend, the Virgin Mary.
        Janet Campbell. ReE
    A penitent considers...coming
        of Mary. Gwendolyn Brooks.
        PoCh
    Stabat Mater Dolorosa. Jacopone
        da Todi . WBP4
    Verbum caro factum est. Unknown.
        ShBa
Mary, pondering. James F. King.
    StPo
Mary; Queen of Hungary

Reflections. YoVA
Self portrait. YoVA
Mbembe Milton Smith
Did they help me at the state
hospital... FroA
McAdams, Julie
My brother. YoVA
The rose. YoVA
McBride, Mekeel
The will to live. TeMP
McCartney, Scott
To be an American. YoVA
The years. YoVA
McCord, David
A Christmas package: no. 7.
PoCh
A Christmas package: no. 8.
PoCh
Come Christmas. PoCh
Gone. ByM
The star in the pail. ByM
This is my rock. RoRF
Write me a verse. MiRN
McCormick, Lisa
"Free" style. YoVA
McCreery, James Luckey
There is no death. WBP3
McDaniel, Jack
Football. YoVA
McElroy, Colleen J.
Caledonia. BlS
Looking for a
country...original name. BlS
Ruth. BlS
A woman's song. BlS
McFarland, Kelli
A ballad ("The night was
clear"). YoVA
Don't cry; don't go. YoVA
McGaha, Jack
The embrace. YoVA
McGrath, Thomas
John Carey's second song. FroA
Travelling song. FroA
McHugh, Heather
Retired school-teacher. TeMP
McKay, Claude
If we must die. LiHE
The white city. TyW
McKenzie, Martha W.
"Clenched against winter." StPo
The clouded pounce. StPo
Pregeometry. StPo
Ski flyers. StPo
McKenzie, Peter D.
Jailbird back to Jenny. StPo
Morning. StPo
McKeown, Tom
The graveyard road. HoA
Lost in Yucatan.

Night clouds. HoA
McKitrick, Mindy
Dew drops/Glide on threads of
grass. YoVA
Grandma's place. YoVA
McLaughlin, Joe-Ann
Another mother and child. FroA
McLaurin, Irma
I, woman. BlS
The mask. BlS
To a gone era. BlS
McMillan, Cynthia D.
In the dark, cold days of
December. YoVA
McMurtray, Mary
Gold and red leaves. YoVA
McNall, Sally
Metaphors. FroA
McPherson, Sandra
His body. TeMP
Me. Jan Flippin. YoVA
Me n' you. Lisa Shorter. YoVA
"Me, myself and I." Unknown.
IlTH
Meals
Early supper. Barbara Howes.
DuD
"An epicure dining at Crew."
Unknown.   MiRN
Lunch. Kathy Hall. BrBD
Lunch. Kenneth Koch. SlW
Snack. Lois Lenski. BrBD
Trouble with dinner. J.A.
Lindon. BrBD
The **meaning** of Solentiname.
Ernesto Cardenal. NiR
The **means** to attain happy life.
Earl of Surrey (Henry
Howard). WBP1
Measure for measure, sels.
William Shakespeare. WBP3
Measure for measure, sels.
William Shakespeare. DoNG
Mechanism. Archie Randolph
Ammons. HaAP
Medici, Lorenzo de'
Epigram: "How rightly you
circle..." Angelo Poliziano.
ReLP
Meditation. Charles Baudelaire.
FoFS
Meditation. Beyle
Schaechter-Gottesman. VoWA
Meditation (after Jehudah
Halevi). Carl Rakosi. VoWA
Meditation (after Moses Ibn
Ezra). Carl Rakosi. VoWA
Meditation (after Solomon Ibn
Gabirol). Carl Rakosi. VoWA
The **meditation** hut at Shan-fu

Temple. Wei Ying-wu. GrAC
Meditation in verse, sels. Mary
  Queen of Scots. PaW
Meditation on a bone. Alec
  Derwent Hope. TyW
Meditation on a bone. A.D. Hope.
  TyW
Meditations of a Hindu prince.
  Sir Alfred Comyns Lyall. WBP4
Mediterranean. Ruth Whitman.
  VoWA
The **Mediterranean.** Allen Tate.
  HaAP--MTS
Mediterranean. Israel Pincas.
  VoWA
Mediterranean Sea
  The Mediterranean. Allen Tate.
    HaAP--MTS
  Mediterranean. Ruth Whitman.
    VoWA
  Mediterranean. Israel Pincas.
    VoWA
  Middle of the world. David
    Herbert Lawrence. HaAP
The **meeting.** John Greenleaf
  Whittier. WBP4
The **meeting.** Howard Moss. HoA
Meeting a bear. David Wagoner.
  HaAP
Meeting a sick soldier. Lu Lun.
  GrAC
Meeting above. William Leggett.
  WBP4
Meeting an envoy on his way
  back... Ts'en Shen. GrAC
Megged, Matti
  The Akedah. VoWA
  The phoenix. VoWA
  White bird. VoWA
Mei Yao-chen
  Clouds on the mountain. LuL
  Distant hills. LuL
  A forest lane covered with
    moss. LuL
  Lotus pool. LuL
A **Mei-p'i** lake song. Tu Fu. GrAC
Meinke, J. Peter
  Advice to my son. LiHE
Mejia Godoy, Carlos
  Don't let me down, comrade. NiR
  The guerrilla's tomb. NiR
  Panchito rubble. NiR
  Peasant mass. NiR
  The watchword. NiR
Mejia Sanchez, Ernesto
  Caesar and the flesh. NiR
Melancholy
  The nice valour, sels. John
    Fletcher. WBP3
  Ode on melancholy. John Keats.

HaAP
Meleager
  Eros is missing. WBP2
  Lament for Helodore. WBP3
  Spring. WBP2
Melissus (Schede), Paulus
  From the French by Ronsard.
    ReLP
Melkon. David Kherdian. FroA
Mellor, Fiona
  Flamingo. YoVA
  Moon flowers. YoVA
Melody. Shmuel Moreh. VoWA
Melons. Moshe Yungman. VoWA
Melons
  Planting melon. Wei Ying-wu.
    GrAC
  Yamashir. Unknown. FroC
Meltzer, David
  Coda. VoWA
  The eyes, the blood. VoWA
  Tell them I'm struggling to
    sing... VoWA
Melville, Herman
  Billy in the darbies. HaAP
  Commemorative of a naval
    victory. HaAP--MTS
  The Maldive shark. TyW--MTS
  The march into Virginia. HaAP
  To Ned. MTS
  The tuft of kelp. MTS
Melville, Herman (about)
  At Melville's tomb. Hart Crane.
    HaAP--MTS
A **memento** for mortality. William
  Basse. HaAP
Memento mori. Moishe Leib
  Halpern. VoWA
Memento vivendi. Eva Brudne.
  VoWA
Memo. Hans Sahl. VoWA
Memo to the 21st century. Philip
  Appleman. TeMP
Memorial. Sonia Sanchez. BlS
Memorial poem. Jacob Glatstein.
  VoWA
Memoriam II. Franco Fortini.
  VoWA
Memories. Suzanne Tanner. YoVA
Memories. Pennie M. Paulson.
  YoVA
Memories. Kathie Bryant. YoVA
Memories
  Behind the smoke stained glass.
    Saundra Lyn Hendon. YoVA
  Biography. Jacob Glatstein.
    OnCP
  Childhood memory. Susan
    Henderson. YoVA
  The cold heaven. William Butler

Yeats. HaAP

Coming back home. Roy A. Young Bear. ReE

Conjuration. Agnes Gergely. VoWA

Crystals like blood. Christopher Murray Grieve. HaAP

During wind and rain. Thomas Hardy. HaAP

For memorie. Nishiwaki Junzaburo. FroC

Forget not yet. Sir Thomas Wyatt. HaAP

A gage d'amour. Austin Dobson. WBP2

Good ol' days. Karen Simmons. YoVA

Haiku. Terri Reeves. YoVA

Handful of sand, sel. Ishikawa Takuboku . FroC

"I came back to the dwelling." Gustave Kahn. FreS

I can remember us. Melody Marshall. YoVA

"In my hands I have memories." Paul Peninger. HoWM

Long winter nigh. Ryokan . FroC

The Magi. William Butler Yeats. HaAP

Memories. Kathie Bryant. YoVA

Memories. Pennie M. Paulson. YoVA

Memories. Suzanne Tanner. YoVA

Memory (Proem. Kitahara Hakushu. FroC

Memory lane. Darlene Gates. YoVA

Memory of Pink. Kitahara Hakushu . FroC

Memory. Dahlia Ravikovich. BuAC

The monasteries lift gold domes. Yocheved Bat-Miriam. VoWA

My true memor. Asya . VoWA

The old days. Patti Dake. YoVA

"On peaks before...' Ryokan. FroC

Photograph. Cindy Niemi. YoVA

Rain for ke-waik bu-ne-ya. Paula Gunn Allen. ReE

Remembering earth. Jules Supervielle. MoVT

Remembering. Clarisse Nicoidski. VoWA

Remembering. Judit Toth. VoWA

Reminiscence. Gail Greiner. YoVA

Reunion. Carolyn Forche. TeMP

Scraps. Susannah Fried. VoWA

Second ballad. Jean Cassou. MoVT

Sentimental colloquy. Paul Verlaine. FoFS

The simple joys of life. Kama Kerpi. VooI

The snow has melted,...memories remain. Scott May. YoVA

So will I. Charlotte Zolotow. ByM

Spleen ("I have more memories..."). Charles Baudelaire. FoFS

Still your footprint delicate... Giancarlo Marmori. NeIP

The swan. Charles Baudelaire. FoFS

Tanka ("Plovers over the evening waves.") Kakinomoto no Hitomaro . FroC

There ain't nothing more important.... Deborah Ann Foster. YoVA

Thinking about the past. Donald Justice. TeMP

Thought waves. Suzy Gierut. YoVA

To Alpha Dryden Eberhart... Richard Eberhart. TeMP

To a gone era. Irma McLaurin. BlS

Tucson: first night. Paula Gunn Allen. ReE

When I was old and weary. Gail Gallone. YoVA

Wingspan. Bartolo Cattafi. NeIP

Memory. Dahlia Ravikovich. BuAC

A **memory.** Deanna Hubbs. YoVA

Memory ("Clear water, like the salt...") Arthur Rimbaud. FoFS--FreS

Memory (Proem). Kitahara Hakushu. FroC

Memory air. Charles Dobzynski. VoWA

Memory lane. Darlene Gates. YoVA

Memory of Pinks. Kitahara Hakushu. FroC

Memory of another climate. Gabriel Preil. VoWA

The **memory** of the heart. Daniel Webster. WBP1

Memory's epitaph to Sir Philip Sidney. George Benedicti. ReLP

Men

(For K.M.E. & G.B.C.) Wendy S. Neidlinger. YoVA

men tell   and talk. Nia

Francisco. ReE
Portrait of a man. Steve
    Denlinger. YoVA
Unpainted. Joyce Quindipan.
    YoVA
men tell   and talk. Nia
    Francisco. ReE
The men's room in the college
    chapel. William DeWitt
    Snodgrass. TyW
Mendelssohn, Asher
    Cordoba. VoWA
Mending wall. Robert Frost. HaAP
Meng Chiao
    Sending Lu Ch'ang off on his
        way.., sels. GrAC
    To Governor Wei of Su-chou.
        GrAC
Meng Hao-jan
    Boating on Yeh Creek. GrAC
    Climbing Hsien Mountain with
        others. GrAC
    Climbing to Camphor Pavilion...
        GrAC
    Evening view from a boat. GrAC
    Gathering firewood. GrAC
    On a visit to T'ien-t'ai
        Mountain. GrAC
    Parting from Wang Wei. GrAC
    Seeking the monk Chan... GrAC
    Setting out early from Yu-p'u
        Pool. GrAC
    Spending the night on the
        Chien-te River. GrAC
    Spring dawn. GrAC
    Year's end, returning to my
        southern... GrAC
Meng Hao-jan (about)
    "Close your gate fast..." Wang
        Wei. GrAC
    To Meng Hao-ja. Li Po. GrAC
Meng Yun-ch'ing
    Blocked by winds on the Pien
        River. GrAC
    Grieving over the times, sels.
        GrAC
    Sadness. GrAC
Mental acquarium V. Georges
    Rodenbach. FreS
Mercer, Margaret
    Exhortation to prayer. WBP4
The merchant of Venice, sels.
    William Shakespeare. WBP2
Merchants
    The fable merchant. Charles
        Dobzynski. VoWA
Mercian hymns, sels. Geoffrey
    Hill. HaAP
Merciles beautee. Geoffrey
    Chaucer. HaAP

Mercury (element)
    Crystals like blood.
        Christopher Murray Grieve.
        HaAP
Mercy
    God has pity on kindergarten
        children. Yehuda Amichai.
        VoWA
    Poem...on the morning of her
        executio. Mary Queen of Scots.
        PaW
Meredith (Earl Lytton), Owen
    Aux Italiens. WBP2
    The chess-board. WBP2
    The portrait. WBP3
    Possession. WBP2
Meredith, George
    Love in the valley. WBP2
    Lucifer in starlight. HaAP
    Modern love, sels. HaAP--LiHE
Meredith, William
    The couple overhead. TyW
    Examples of created systems.
        TeMP
    The open sea. MTS
    Thoughts on one's head. HaAP
Merlin and Vivien, sels. Alfred,
    Lord Tennyson. WBP2
Merlin's Louisiana. Kathie A.
    Dame. StPo
Mernit, Susan
    The scholar's wife. VoWA
    Song of the bride. VoWA
Meron. Shirley Kaufman. BuAC
Merrill, James
    The broken home. HaAP
    Page from the Koran. TeMP
Merrill, Stuart
    Goldenmouthed. FreS
    The mysterious song. FreS
    Nocturne. FreS
    The red city. FreS
    Tale. FreS
Merritt, Sherlene
    The emotional painting. HoWM
Merry Christmas!. Elder Olson.
    FroA
A merry game. Unknown. IlTH
Merry it is. Unknown. HaAP
The merry little minuet. Sheldon
    Harnick. TyW
Merwin, William Stanley
    Carol of the three kings. PoCh
    Letter. HaAP
    Separation. HaAP
    Things. HaAP
    To Dana for her birthday. TeMP
The message. Leilani Strong.
    YoVA
Message. Gyorgy Raba. VoWA

The **messenger**. Jacob Glatstein.
  OnCP
The **Messiah**. Moshe Yungman. VoWA
Messiah. Alexander Pope. WBP4
Messiah
  Encounter in Safed. Moshe
    Yungman. VoWA
  Evening walk. David Einhorn.
    OnCP
  The field of night. Miriam
    Waddington. VoWA
  Instructions for the Messiah.
    Myra Sklarew. VoWA
  The messenger. Jacob Glatstein.
    OnCP
  The Messiah-blower. Paul
    Goodman. FroA
  Messiah. Alexander Pope. WBP4
  The Messiah. Moshe Yungman.
    VoWA
  The shining fool. Jacob
    Glatstein. OnCP
  When the days grow long. Hayim
    Nachman Bialik. VoWA
The **Messiah-blower**. Paul
  Goodman. FroA
Messinger, Robert Hinckley
  A winter wish. WBP1
Metaphors. Sally McNall. FroA
Metaphors. Miklos Radnoti. VoWA
Metaphors of a magnifico.
  Wallace Stevens. SlW
Metaphors. See Similes
Metropol, Jack
  You. YoVA
Metz, Jerred
  Angels in the house. VoWA
  Divination. VoWA
  Her true body. VoWA
  Speak like rain. VoWA
A **Mexican** scrapbook. Dave
  Oliphant. FroA
Meyer, Conny Hannes
  The beast that rode the
    unicorn. VoWA
  Of the beloved caravan. VoWA
Meyers, Bert
  The dark birds. VoWA
  The garlic. VoWA
  When I came to Israel. VoWA
Meyers, Ronald
  Winter. YoVA
Meynell, Alice
  I am the way. EeBC
  Renouncement. WBP2
  Unto us a son is given. EeBC
Mezey, Robert
  The celebration. FroA
  I am here. VoWA
  New Year's Eve in solitude.

VoWA
Theresienstadt poem. VoWA
The wandering Jew. VoWA
White blossoms. VoWA
Mice. Rose Fyleman. MiRN
Mice
  A-apple pie. Walter De La Mare.
    MiRN
  The ambitious mouse. John
    Farrar. MiRN
  Anne and the field mouse. Ian
    Serraillier. MiRN
  Birds of a feathe. Mother Goose.
    MiRN
  Birthday cake. Aileen Fisher.
    MiRN
  A cat came fiddlin. Mother
    Goose . MiRN
  Celebration. Menke Katz. MiRN
  The city mouse and the garden
    mouse. Christina Georgina
    Rossetti. MiRN
  Conversation. Rose Fyleman.
    MiRN
  The country mouse and the city
    mouse. Richard Scrafton
    Sharpe. MiRN
  Drawing. Roy Fuller. MiRN
  Eiptaph on a dormouse. Johm
    Huddlestone Wynne. MiRN
  "An epicure dining at Crew."
    Unknown   MiRN
  Feather-stitching. Aileen
    Fisher. MiRN
  The field mouse. William Sharp.
    MiRN
  A frog he would a-wooing g.
    Mother Goose . MiRN
  Funeral oration for a mouse.
    Alan Dugan. HaAP
  Good neighbors. May Justus.
    MiRN
  Hickory, dickory, dock. Mother
    Goose . MiRN
  The house of the mouse. Lucy
    Sprague Mitchell. MiRN
  "I and Pangor Ban my cat."
    Unknown . MiRN
  I, mouse. Robert Kraus. TrWB
  The lion and the mouse.
    Jeffreys Taylor. MiRN
  Little Miss Limberkin. Mary
    Mapes Dodge. MiRN
  "Little Poll Parrot." Mother
    Goose . MiRN
  "The little priest of Felton."
    Mother Goose . MiRN
  Madame mouse. Edith Sitwell.
    MiRN
  The mice celebrate Christmas.

Alf Proysen. MiRN
Mice in the hay. Leslie Norris.
  PoCh
Mice. Rose Fyleman. MiRN
Miller and mouse. Mother Goose.
  MiRN
The miser and the mouse.
  Christopher Smart. MiRN
Miss Jan. Unknown . MiRN
Missing. A.A. Milne. MiRN
Mouse heaven. Leah Bodine
  Drake. MiRN
The mouse in the wainscot. Ian
  Serraillier. MiRN
Mouse night: one of our games.
  William Stafford. MiRN
Mouse's nest. John Clare. MiRN
The mouse's petition. Anna
  Laetitia Barbauld. MiRN
Mouse's tail. Lewis Carroll
  (C.L. Dodgson). MiRN
The mouse. Elizabeth
  Coatsworth. MiRN
Mouse. Mary Ann Hoberman. MiRN
The prayer of the mouse. Carmen
  Bernos de Gasztold. MiRN
Santa Claus and the mouse.
  Emilie Poulsson. MiRN
The tale of the mice. Lewis
  Carroll (C.L. Dodgson). MiRN
There was a wee bit mouski.
  Unknown . MiRN
Three blind mic. Mother Goose .
  MiRN
"Three little mice ran up the
  stairs."Unknown . MiRN
Three little mice (or Six...)
  Mother Goose . MiRN
To a mouse. Robert Burns.
  MiRN--LiHE
Winter mouse. Aileen Fisher.
  MiRN
Write me a verse. David McCord.
  MiRN
The mice celebrate Christmas.
  Alf Proysen. MiRN
Mice in the hay. Leslie Norris.
  PoCh
Michael, The Archangel
  The angel Michael. Anath
    Bental. VoWA
Michaelangelo Buonarotti
  "If it be true that any
    beauteous thing." WBP2
  The might of one fair face.
    WBP2
Michaelis, Hanny
  Listening. VoWA
  Under restless clouds. VoWA
  We carry eggshells. VoWA

Michaux, Henri
  Carry me off. MoVT
  I was born with a hole. MoVT
Michlin, Sonya M.
  The secret. HoWM
Mickey. Bernadette Chato. ReE
Mickle, William Julius
  Cumnor Hall. WBP3
Mid-August at Sourdough
  Mountain... Gary Snyder. HaAP
Mid-current song. Ts'ui Kuo-fu.
  GrAC
Mid-ocean in war-time. Joyce
  Kilmer. MTS
Middle Age
  Catching up. David Walker. FroA
  Feelings at the end of Spring
    II. Tai Shu-lun . GrAC
  The middle-aged. Adrienne Rich.
    LiHE
  Sad is our youth, for it is
    ever going. Aubrey Thomas De
    Vere. WBP3
Middle East
  Saul, afterward, riding east.
    John Malcolm Brinnin. HoA
Middle of the world. David
  Herbert Lawrence. HaAP
The middle-aged. Adrienne Rich.
  LiHE
Middle-class autumn. Douglas
  Shearer. YoVA
Midnight. Rosalie Williams. YoVA
Midnight and ten minutes. Shlomo
  Vinner. VoWA
Midnight in Bonnie's stall.
  Siddie Joe Johnson. PoCh
Midrash on Hamlet. Francis
  Landy. VoWA
The midshipman. William
  Falconer. MTS
A midsummer night's dream, sels.
  William Shakespeare. WBP1
A midsummer night's dream, sels.
  William Shakespeare. WBP3
Midway. Naomi Long Madgett. BlS
Miemietz, Sally Ann
  No more. YoVA
  Pain. YoVA
The might of one fair face. John
  Edward Taylor (trans.). WBP2
The might of one fair face.
  Michaelangelo Buonarotti.
  WBP2
A mighty fortress is our God.
  Frederic Henry Hedge. WBP4
A mighty fortress is our God.
  Martin Luther. WBP4
Migration. Sandie Nelson. ReE
Migration. Pinkie Gordon Lane.

BlS
Mikata no Sami
To his wife, when he fell
ill... FroC
Mikhael, Ephraim
Florimond. FreS
The priest. FreS
Miklos Radnoti. Willis
Barnstone. VoWA
Milbauer, Joseph
Interior. VoWA
Paris by night. VoWA
Milk and Milking
Kitty of Coleraine. Charles
Dawson Shanly. WBP2
The milking-maid. Christina
Georgina Rossetti. WBP2
The milkmaid's song. Sydney
Dobell. WBP2
Queen Mary, sels. Alfred, Lord
Tennyson. WBP2
The **milking-maid.** Christina
Georgina Rossetti. WBP2
The **milkmaid's** song. Sydney
Dobell. WBP2
Milkmen
Dairyman blues. Mike Rempel.
YoVA
My mother's milkman. Diane
Wakoski. TeMP
Milkweed
Open. Joseph Bruchac. FroA
The **mill.** John Taylor. FroA
The **mill.** Edwin Arlington
Robinson. HaAP
Millay, Edna St. Vincent
Dirge without music. DoNG
Exiled. MTS
Fatal interview, sels. HaAP
Passer mortus est. DoNG
Miller and mouse. Mother Goose.
MiRN
The **miller's** daughter, sels.
Alfred, Lord Tennyson. WBP2
Miller, Joaquin
Columbus. MTS
Miller, Lisa Jastrab
The subway. YoVA
Untitled. YoVA
Miller, May
Gift from Kenya. BlS
Not that far. BlS
Miller, Michael L.
Victory. YoVA
Miller, Tim
Evolution of travel. YoVA
Ode to Faber College. YouVA
Ode to Three Mile Island. YoVA
Miller, Vassar
A clash with cliches. FroA

Eden revisited. FroA
Regret. LiHE
Miller, William
Willie Winkie. WBP1
Millers
The mill. Edwin Arlington
Robinson. HaAP
Miller and mous. Mother Goose .
MiRN
Milligan, Spike
You must never bath in an Irish
stew. IlTH
Mills (Jr.), Ralph J.
Brief thaw. PrVo
Chelsea churchyard. FroA
Grasses. FroA
Mills, Judy Ellen
An artistry of happiness. YoVA
A figment of your imagination.
YoVA
It would be so very easy. YoVA
Milman, Henry Hart
The fall of Jerusalem, sels.
WBP2
Hebrew wedding. WBP2
Jewish hymn in Babylon. WBP4
Milne, A.A.
Missing. MiRN
Milnes (Lord Houghton), R.M.
Anima mundi, sels. WBP4
The brookside. WBP2
Forever uncontested. WBP2
Good night and good morning.
WBP1
Hope of the human heart. WBP4
London churches. WBP3
Milnes (Lord Houghton) [trans], R.M.
The palm and the pine. WBP3
WBP1
Milosz, Czeslaw
Child of Europe, sels. CoP
The gift, sels. CoP
The land of poetry, sels. CoP
A moral treatise, sels. CoP
The poor poet, sels. CoP
Rivers grow small, sels. CoP
A song on the end of the world,
sels. CoP
Sposob, sels. CoP
Throughout our lands, sels. CoP
To Father Ch., sels. CoP
To Raja Rao, sels. CoP
Warsaw, sels. CoP
Milosz, Oscar-Venceslas de
Salome. FreS
Milton. Henrietta Cordelia Ray.
BlS
Milton the early riser. Robert
Kraus. TrWB
Milton, John

Il penseroso. HaAP
L'allegro. HaAP
Last came, and last did go. TyW
Lycidas. HaAP--WBP3
Ode: on the morning of Christ's
    nativity. ShBa
On his blindness. EeBC--HaAP
On his blindness. WBP4
On his dead wife. HaAP
On the late massacre in
    Piedmont. HaAP
On the morning of Christ's
    nativity. WBP4
Paradise lost, sels. MTS
Paradise lost, sels. LiHE--TyW
Paradise lost, sels. WBP4
Paradise lost, sels. WBP2
Paradise regained, sels. PoCh
Samson Agonistes, sels. WBP3
Sonnet XVII. LiHE
Sonnet XVIII. TyW
Sonnet to Cyriack Skinner. WBP3
Milton, John (about)
    Milton. Henrietta Cordelia Ray.
        BlS
A Miltonic sonnet for Mr.
    Johnson.... Richard Wilbur.
    TyW
Milwaukee, Wisconsin
    Walking Milwaukee. Harold Witt.
        HoA
Minamoto no Sanetomo
    Twenty-four tanka. FroC
Minamoto no Shitago
    Song of the tailess ox. FroC
Mind
    Fantasy of the mind. Merri
        Grose. YoVA
    Self-delusion. Mark Childers.
        YoVA
    Thoughts. Dona Kay Hollenbeck.
        YoVA
Mine enemy is growing old. Emily
    Dickinson. LiHE--TyW
Miner, Virginia Scott
    Nichols Fountain. FroA
Mineral point. Robert Dana. FroA
"Mingling with the wind."
    Ryokan. FroC
Mining and Miners
    A curse on mine-owner. Unknown.
        TyW
    The explosion. Philip Larkin.
        HaAP
    Illinois coalscapes. James
        Ballowe. PrVo
    Mineral point. Robert Dana.
        FroA
    Thirty tanka. Tachibana Akemi.
        FroC

The ministry of angels. Edmund
    Spenser. WBP4
Miniver Cheevy. Edwin Arlington
    Robinson. LiHE
Minor key. Judah Leib Teller.
    VoWA
The minotaur. Robert Gibb. FroA
Minstrel's marriage song. Thomas
    Chatterton. WBP2
Minstrel's song. Thomas
    Chatterton. WBP3
Minus one. John Ciardi. HoA
The Minyan. Jack Myers. VoWA
Mir, Pedro
    Countersong to Walt Whitman.
        NiR
The miracle. Chaim Grade. VoWA
Mirages
    Autobiography, sels. Jim
        Barnes. ReE
Miriam Tazewell. John Crowe
    Ransome. TyW
Miriam Tazewell. John Crowe
    Ransom. TyW
Miriam, Rivka
    Flute. BuAC
    In that green field. BuAC
Miroir de miroir: mirror of a
    mirror. Takiguchi Shuzo. FroC
Mirror. Sylvia Plath. HaAP
Mirror farming. Robert Morgan.
    TeMP
Mirrors
    From my mother's home. Leah
        Goldberg. BuAC--VoWA
    Miroir de miroir: mirror of a
        mirro. Takiguchi Shuzo . FroC
    Mirror. Sylvia Plath. HaAP
    Results of a scientific survey.
        Bruce Cutler. FroA
    Sonnets to Orpheus, sels.
        Rainer Maria Rilke. SlW
    To a lady admiring herself...
        Thomas Randolph. WBP2
The mirrors of Jerusalem.
    Barbara F. Lefcovitz. VoWA
Misanthropy and Misanthropes
    Animals are passing from our
        lives. Philip Levine. TyW
    The complete misanthropist.
        Morris Bishop. TyW
    The day of judgment. Jonathan
        Swift. TyW
    Good creatures, do you love
        your lives. Alfred Edward
        Housman. TyW
    The hustle. Unknown . TyW
    Paradise lost, sels. John
        Milton. LiHE--TyW
    Sam Hall. Unknown. TyW

A satire against reason &
    mankind, sels. John Wilmot,
    Earl Rochester. TyW
Shitty. Kingsley Amis. TyW
Timon speaks to a dog. Philip
    Hobsbaum. TyW
Timons of Athens, sels. William
    Shakespeare. TyW
Miscellaneous poems at three
    lakes. Yuan Zhong-dao. LuL
Miscellaneous songs of Han
    Wu-ti, sels. Wei Ying-wu.
    GrAC
Miser. Michel Leiris. MoVT
The miser and the mouse.
    Christopher Smart. MiRN
Misers
    The miser and the mouse.
    Christopher Smart. MiRN
Miss Jane. Unknown. MiRN
Miss Rosie. Lucille Clifton. BlS
Missing. A.A. Milne. MiRN
Missing dates. William Empson.
    HaAP
Missing you. Patricia Crandall.
    YoVA
Missionaries
    Magalu. Helene Johnson. BlS
    Two families. Charles G. Bell.
    FroA
Missionaries in the jungle.
    Linda Piper. BlS
Mist on the water. Patricia E.
    Fann. YoVA
Mistletoe
    Holly and mistletoe. Eleanor
    Farjeon. PoCh
    Under the mistletoe. Countee
    Cullen. PoCh
Mistral, Gabriela
    To Noel. PoCh
Misty dawn. Luci Tapahonso. ReE
Misty lady. Debby Buckley. YoVA
A misunderstanding. Kitty Druck.
    StPo
Mitchell, Agnes E.
    When the cows come home. WBP1
Mitchell, Lucy Sprague
    The house of the mouse. MiRN
Mitchell, Mark
    Chills. YoVA
    Earth. YoVA
Mitchell, Silas Weir
    The Quaker graveyard. WBP3
Mitchell, Stephen
    Abraham. VoWA
    Adam in love. VoWA
    Jacob and the angel. VoWA
Miura Chora
    Seventeen hokku. FroC

Mixed feelings. John Ashbery.
    HaAP
Miyazawa Kenji
    Bamboo & Oak. FroC
    The breeze comes filling the
    valley. FroC
    The landscape inspector. FroC
    The last farewell. FroC
    Night. FroC
    November 3rd. FroC
    Okhotsk elegy. FroC
    The prefectural engineer's
    statement... FroC
    Rest. FroC
    Spring & Asura. FroC
    "Spring" variation." FroC
    Traveler. FroC
Mizer, Ray
    To a loudmouth pontificator.
    TyW
Moan, moan, ye dying gales.
    Henry Neele. WBP3
Mock on, mock on, Voltaire,
    Rousseau. William Blake. HaAP
The mockingbird. Randall
    Jarrell. DuD
Mockingbirds
    The mockingbird. Randall
    Jarrell. DuD
Modde, Michelle J.
    Parting. YoVA
    Seeing you. YoVA
Model. Archie Randolph Ammons.
    FroA
Modern Kabbalist. Marcia Falk.
    VoWA
The modern fable. Nishiwaki
    Junzaburo. FroC
Modern love, sels. George
    Meredith. HaAP--LiHE
"Modern times! Modern times!"
    Jean Lorrain (Paul Deval).
    FreS
Modesty
    Today I am modest. Esther Raab.
    BuAC
Moffat, Debbie
    I wondered... YoVA
    Love. YoVA
Moir, David Macbeth
    The rustic lad's lament in the
    town. WBP3
Molly Means. Margaret Walker.
    BlS
Molodovsky, Kadya
    And yet. VoWA
    In life's stable. VoWA
    The mother. OnCP
    My "fatherlands." OnCP
    Night visitors. VoWA

The singer. OnCP
When my eye loses its hue. OnCP
Moly. Thomson Gunn. HaAP
Momaday, N. Scott
The gourd dancer. ReE
Headwaters. ReE
The horse that died of shame.
ReE
Krasnopresneskaya station. ReE
Rainy Mountain Cemetery. ReE
The story of a well-made
shield. ReE
Mombert, Alfred
The Chimera. VoWA
The moment you left. Lori Logan.
YoVA
Moments of initiation. Kama
Kerpi. VooI
Momma's song. Ginger D. Barker.
YoVA
A Mona Lisa. Angelina Weld
Grimke. BlS
Mona Lisa
At the Louvre. E.L. Mayo. FroA
The monasteries lift gold domes.
Yocheved Bat-Miriam. VoWA
Moncada, Jose Santos
Zero hour. Ernesto Cardenal.
NiR
Moncrief, Rhonda
We together. YoVA
Money
Summer celestial. Stanley
Plumly. TeMP
Money in the bank. W.D. Ehrhart.
FroA
Monimbo. Octavio Robleto. NiR
Monkeys
I'm a monkey. Robert Kraus.
TrWB
Monkhouse, Cosmo
Limerick:"..a barber of Kew."
IlTH
"There was once an old man of
Brest." IlTH
Monks
Seeking the monk Chan.. Meng
Hao-jan . GrAC
Monnier, Mathilde-Anna
Forgetting. MoVT
Monologue for Cassandra, sels.
Wislawa Szymborska. CoP
Monroe, Marilyn
I have come to claim. Judy
Grahn. LiHE
Montezuma. D.F. Alderson. IlTH
Montgomery, James
Forever with the Lord. WBP4
Humility. WBP4
Parted friends. WBP1

What is prayer? WBP4
Montgomery, Michele
World gone mad. YoVA
Montrose(see J.Graham),Marquis

Monument to Pushkin. Joseph
Brodsky. VoWA
Monuments
Life dwells in the shadows.
Steve Denlinger. YoVA
Moon
Ballad of luna, luna. Federico
Garcia Lorca. SlW
The dawn of love. Henrietta
Cordelia Ray. BlS
The earth is a satellite of the
moon. Leonel Rugama. NiR
Eighteen tank. Ariwara no
Narihira. FroC
Facing the moon on the river.
Liu Ch'ang-ch'ing. GrAC
The full moon. Rocco
Scotellaro. NeIP
Grieving over the times, sel.
Meng Yun-ch'ing . GrAC
How to reach the moon. Marsha
Pomerantz. VoWA
Lunatics. Raquel Chalfi. BuAC
The man in the moon. James
Whitcomb Riley. WBP1
The moon is round. John Carper.
HoWM
Moon light. Patti Buskirk. YoVA
The moon rises. Federico Garcia
Lorca. SlW
"The moon shines white..."
Paul Verlaine. FoFS--FreS
Moonlight. Paul Verlaine. FoFS
The rabbit in the moon. Ryokan.
FroC
Room conditioner. Archie
Randolph Ammons. TeMP
September 13, 1959 (Variation).
Andrea Zanzotto. NeIP
Shining like paned glass.
Janice A. Carpenter. YoVA
Ten tanka. Myoe. FroC
This lunar beauty. Wystan Hugh
Auden. SlW
Visions for breakfast. Jane
Dulin. YoVA
Winter moon. Langston Hughes.
DuD
Moon flowers. Fiona Mellor. YoVA
The moon is round. John Carper.
HoWM
The moon is teaching Bible.
Zelda. BuAC--VoWA
Moon light. Patti Buskirk. YoVA
The moon rises. Federico Garcia

Lorca. SlW
"The **moon** shines white..." Paul
   Verlaine. FoFS--FreS
Moonlight. Paul Verlaine. FoFS
Moonlight night: Carmel.
   Langston Hughes. MTS
Moonlit night. Tu Fu. GrAC
Moore, Clement Clarke
   A visit from St. Nicholas.
      PoCh--WBP1
Moore, Clement C.
   A visit from St. Nicholas. PoCh
Moore, David
   The parade. YoVA
Moore, John
   A gaggle of geese, a pride of
      lions. DuD

Moore, Lilian
   Until I saw the sea. ByM
Moore, Marianne
   A carriage from Sweden. HaAP
   The fish. MTS
   A grave. HaAP--MTS
   The pangolin. HaAP
   Poetry ("I too, dislike it...)
      HaAP
   The steeple-jack. HaAP
Moore, Richard
   Busby, whose verse no piercing
      beams... TyW
Moore, Scott
   Twenty-eight to twenty (28 to
      20). YoVA
   Year after year. YoVA
Moore, Thomas
   And doth not a meeting like
      this. WBP1
   As slow our ship. WBP3
   Believe me, if all those
      endearing... WBP2
   Black and blue eyes. WBP2
   Come, rest in this bosom. WBP2
   The duke is the lad to frighten
      a lass. TyW
   Echoes. WBP2
   Farewell!-but whenever. WBP3
   The fire-worshippers, sels.
      WBP3
   "Fly to the desert, fly with
      me." WBP2
   The garret. WBP1
   I knew by the smoke that so
      gracefully... WBP1
   Irish melodies, sels. WBP2
   The light of the harem, sels.
      WBP3
   The light of the harem, sels.
      WBP2

Love's young dream. WBP2
A temple to friendship. WBP1
The vale of Avoca. WBP1
Verses written in an album.
   WBP2
Wreathe the bowl. WBP1
Moral ode. David Rosenmann-Taub.
   VoWA
A moral treatise, sels. Czeslaw
   Milosz. CoP
Morales Avila, Ricardo
   Casimoro three times over. NiR
Morales Aviles, Ricardo
   Brief letter to my wife. NiR
   Doris Maria, comrade. NiR
   Pancasan. NiR
   Santa Barbara. NiR
   We-others. NiR
Morales, Beltran
   Breakfast. NiR
   The unbearable presence. NiR
Morality
   The equilibrists. John Crowe
      Ransom. HaAP
   The lamed-vov. Rose Auslander.
      VoWA
More conversations from the
   nightmare. Carol Lee Sanchez.
   ReE
"More light! More light!"
   Anthony Hecht. HaAP--VoWA
More sonnets at Christmas. Allen
   Tate. ShBa
Moreas, Jean
   Agnes. FreS
   Chimaera. FreS
   Song ("Feet have stepped
      on...flowers.") FreS
Moreh, Shmuel
   Melody. VoWA
   The return. VoWA
   The tree of hatred. VoWA
Morgan, Edwin
   The computer's first Christmas
      card. PoCh
Morgan, Frederick
   Bones. FroA
Morgan, Michele
   Headlines. YoVA
Morgan, Robert
   Mirror farming. TeMP
Morgan, Scott
   A door slams. YoVA
   For K.M.. YoVA
Morgan, Tracy Lynn
   Mother. YoVA
Morhange, Pierre
   Jew. VoWA
   Lullaby in Auschwitz. VoWA
   Salomon. VoWA

Crucial stew. Colette Inez. FroA

Dream girl. Karen Snow. HoA

For an obligate parasite. Alan Dugan. TyW

From a new height. Andrea Zanzotto. NeIP

The full moon. Rocco Scotellaro. NeIP

In memoriam I. Franco Fortini. VoWA

Kaddish, sels. Allen Ginsberg. DoNG--VoWA

Kaddish. David Ignatow. VoWA

Let's talk, mother. Edith Bruck. VoWA

Love. Itzik Manger. OnCP

Momma's song. Ginger D. Barker. YoVA

Mother die. Saito Mokichi . FroC

Mother's habits. Nikki Giovanni. BlS

The mother's hope. Laman Blanchard. WBP1

Mother. Aldo Camerino. VoWA

Mother. Anwar Shaul. VoWA

The mother. Kadya Molodovsky. OnCP

Mother. Tracy Lynn Morgan. YoVA

Mouse's nest. John Clare. MiRN

My mama moved among the days. Lucille Clifton. BlS

My mother as a young woman. Wendy S. Neidlinger. YoVA

My mother's picture. William Cowper. WBP1

My mother. Hayim Naggid. VoWA

My nightingale. Rose Auslander. VoWA

Ode to mother. Susan Zielke. YoVA

Paedotrophia. Scevole (G.) de Sainte-Marthe. ReLP

Revelation. Carole C. Gregory. BlS

Rock me to sleep. Elizabeth Akers. WBP1

Ruth. Colleen J. McElroy. BlS

Seven times six. Jean Ingelow. WBP1

A someday song for Sophia. Rochelle Ratner. TeMP

The song of the old mother. William Butler Yeats. WBP1

Threnody. David Ignatow. FroA

Tired mothers. May Riley Smith. WBP1

Trembling. Aliza Shenhar. VoWA

Whiteness. Yunna Moritz. VoWA

Worming of a madde dogge, sels. Constantia Munda (pseud.). PaW

Motherwell, William

Jeanie Morrison. WBP3

My heid is like to rend, Willie. WBP3

Moths

Under the sign of the moth. David Wagoner. TeMP

Motion Pictures

To the film industry in crisis. Frank O'Hara. SlW

Watching the out-door movie show. Ann Struthers. FroA

Why I like movies. Patricia Jones. BlS

You take my hand and. Margaret Atwood. HaAP

Motto-death is like a mask... Jacobus Catsius (Kats). ReLP

Moultrie, John

Forget thee? WBP2

Mount Fuji

Looking at Mount Fuji in the distance. Yamabe no Akahito. FroC

Mount Zion

I don't know if Mount Zion. Abba Kovner. VoWA

The **mountain**. Hengenike Riyong. VooI

Mountain lodge. Huang-fu Jan. GrAC

The **mountain** of the lovers, sels. Paul Hamilton Hayne. WBP2

Mountain spirits. King Kuka. ReE

The **mountain** that got little. William Stafford. FroA

Mountains

Climbing Kasuga Field. Yamabe no Akahito. FroC

Climbing Mount Kagu... Emperor Jomei (593-641). FroC

Clouds on the mountain. Mei Yao-chen. LuL

Cold mountain. Chiao-jan. GrAC

A compendium of good tanka. Furiwara no Teika. FroC

Composed on the 5th of the 10th month... Yamabe no Akahito FroC

Deer enclosure. Wang Wei. GrAC

Dialogue in the mountain. Li Po. GrAC

Distant hills. Mei Yao-chen. LuL

Drifting on East Creek of Mao Mountain. Ch'u Kuang-hsi,

GrAC
"a figure...contemplating the
mountain." Jie Zi Yuan Hua
Zhuan . LuL
For three days I
traveled...mountains. Yuan
Zong-dao . LuL
Grazing on the Great Peak. Tu Fu.
GrAC
Headwaters. N. Scott Momaday.
ReE
Hill excursion. Leah Goldberg.
BuAC
The hill of Hua-Tz. Pei. . LuL
The hill of the hatchet-leaved
bamboo. Pei . LuL
"I climb the road to Cold
Mountain." Han-shan. LuL
"In the evening view, the
mountains..." Wang Wei. LuL
In the mountain. Wang An-shi .
LuL
Inscribed on a painting. Shen
Zhou. LuL
Leaving Wang-Chuan cottage. Wang
Wei. LuL
Looking at Yue-Tai Mountain...
Yang Wan-li. LuL
Mid-August at Sourdough
Mountain... Gary Snyder. HaAP
Mountain lodge. Huang-fu Jan.
GrAC
The mountain that got little.
William Stafford. FroA
The mountain. Hengenike Riyong.
VooI
Navajo chant, sel. Unknown.
ReE
On a visit to T'ien-t'ai
Mountain. Meng Hao-jan   GrAC
On the occasion of the imperial
visit... Prince Ikusa. FroC
Reaching the foot of Pei-ku
Mountain. Wang Wan . GrAC
Sitting alone in Jing-ting
Mountain. Li Bo . LuL
Spruce Pine Mountain. Jennifer
Leigh Dison. YoVA
"Ten years in the brothels..."
Ikkyu Sojun . FroC
To Wei Tzu-ch'u. Wang Chi-yu.
GrAC
Tsuetsuki Pass. Ishigaki Rin.
FroC
With Kao Shih and Hsueh Chu,
climbing.. Ts'en Shen. GrAC
Written at mauve garden...Zhu
Yi-zun. LuL
Wu Mountain high. Huang-fu Jan
GrAC

Mourning and melancholia. Alfred
Alvarez. VoWA
Mourning for my teacher Hokuju.
Yosa Buson. FroC
Mourning poem for the queen of
Sunday. Robert Hayden. HoA
Mourningsong for Anne. David
Posner. FroA
The mouse. Elizabeth Coatsworth.
MiRN
Mouse. Mary Ann Hoberman. MiRN
Mouse heaven. Leah Bodine Drake.
MiRN
The mouse in the wainscot. Ian
Serraillier. MiRN
Mouse night: one of our games.
William Stafford. MiRN
Mouse's nest. John Clare. MiRN
The mouse's petition. Anna
Laetitia Barbauld. MiRN
Mouse's tail. Lewis Carroll
(C.L. Dodgson). MiRN
Mouth. Clarisse Nicoidski. VoWA
Mouths
    Mouth. Clarisse Nicoidski. VoWA
Move on, Yiddish poet. Jacob
Glatstein. VoWA
Moving
    Moving day. Lewis B. Horne. HoA
    On the move. Thomson Gunn. HaAP
Moving camp too far. Gladys
Cardiff. ReE
Moving day. Lewis B. Horne. HoA
Mozart. Jacob Glatstein. VoWA
Mozart, Wolfgang Amadeus
    Mozart. Jacob Glatstein. VoWA
    The phoenix of Mozart. Claude
Vigee. VoWA
Mr. Finney's turnip. Unknown.
IlTH
Mr. Flood's party. Edwin
Arlington Robinson.
HaAP--LiHE
Mr. Nobody. Unknown. IlTH
Mr. and Mrs. Spikky Sparrow.
Edward Lear. WBP1
Mrs. Johnson objects. Clara Ann
Thompson. BlS
Mrs. Peck-Pigeon. Eleanor
Farjeon. RoRF
Ms. L. Robin Collins. YoVA
Much madness is divinest sense.
Emily Dickinson. LiHE
The mudtower. Anne Stevenson.
HoA
Mueller, Lisel
    The blind leading the blind.
TeMP
    First snow in Lake County. PrVo
Muffled echoes brace my tomb.

Barry T. Siford. YoVA
Muhlenberg, William Augustus
I would not live alway. WBP3
Muir, Edwin
Abraham. EeBC
The animals. EeBC
The good man in hell. TyW
The horses. HaAP
Mukai Kyorai
Twenty hokku. FroC
Mulattos
Aliens, sels. Georgia Douglas
Johnson. BlS
Cosmopolite, sels. Georgia
Douglas Johnson. BlS
Mulberry Street. Ruth
Herschberger. HoA
Munby, Arthur Joseph
Apres. WBP3
Doris: a pastoral. WBP2
Munda (pseud.), Constantia
Worming of a madde dogge, sels.
PaW
Munday, Anthony
I serve a mistress whiter than
snow. HaAP
Murder
The Brockton murder:...out of
Wm James. Knute Skinner. TyW
Five ways to kill a man. Edwin
Brock. LiHE
How my cousin was killed.
Gladys Cardiff. ReE
Porphyria's lover. Robert
Browning. HaAP
Sea lullaby. Elinor Wylie. MTS
Sweeney among the nightingales.
Thomas Stearns Eliot. HaAP
What the animals said. Peter
Serchuk. HoA
Murder of a community. Daniel
Weissbort. VoWA
Muret, Marc-Antoine de
To Margaris. ReLP
Murray, G.E.
Looking toward Peoria. PrVo
Shelby County, Ohio, November
1974. FroA
Murray, Les A.
Bagman O'Reilly's curse. TyW
Murray, Pauli
Dark testament. BlS
Inquietude. BlS
Song ("Because I know
deep..."). BlS
Muscae volitantes. Lewis B.
Horne. HoA
Musee des Beaux Arts. Wystan
Hugh Auden. HaAP--LiHE
Museums

After spending all day at
the..Museum... Alan Britt.
FroA
At the Jewish Museum. Linda
Pastan. VoWA
At the museum. Andrea Siegel.
YoVA
(Conversations #1). Carol Lee
Sanchez. ReE
Ethics. Linda Pastan. TeMP
In the local museum. Walter De
La Mare. HaAP
Music. Alice Dunbar-Nelson. BlS
Music. Nan Smith. HoWM
Music. Elizbeth Scott. YoVA
Music. Charles Baudelaire. FoFS
Music. Margaret Cameron. YoVA
Music
Autumn ("The bandaged rain...")
Tamura Ryuichi . FroC
Autumn music. Gabriel Preil.
VoWA
Cantata. Marlys Weber. YoVA
Everything. James Paul. HoA
Hearing Tung T'ing play nomad
pipe song. Li Ch'i . GrAC
Honeysuckle. James Paul. HoA
Hunger. Wendy S. Neidlinger.
YoVA
Jazz music. Mark Decker. HoWM
Jazz. Tim Parker. HoWM
Listening. Hanny Michaelis.
VoWA
Melody. Shmuel Moreh. VoWA
"The music is a dancer." George
Hinson. HoWM
Music. Alice Dunbar-Nelson. BlS
Music. Charles Baudelaire. FoFS
Music. Elizbeth Scott. YoVA
Music. Margaret Cameron. YoVA
Music. Nan Smith. HoWM
Night poem in an abandoned
music room. William Pillen.
VoWA
The orchestra. William Carlos
Williams. HaAP
Perhaps its only music. Natan
Zach. VoWA
Player. Stephen Dunning. FroA
Shadow music. Gregoire Le Roy.
FreS
"Soft melodic tunes." Cathy
Cameron. HoWM
Splendor. Shin Shalom. VoWA
A study in terror. Tamura
Ryuichi. FroC
Winter music. Tamura Ryuichi.
FroC
"The music is a dancer." George
Hinson. HoWM

Musical shuttle. Harvey Shapiro.
      VoWA
Musings. William Barnes. HaAP
Muske, Carol
      The invention of cuisine. TeMP
The **mute** city. Lazer Eichenrand.
      VoWA
Muted war drums. Adrian C.
      Louis. ReE
My "fatherlands." Kadya
      Molodovsky. OnCP
My Arkansas. Maya Angelou. BlS
My Bohemian life. Arthur
      Rimbaud. FoFS
"**My** God said to me: My son...")
      Paul Verlaine. FoFS
My God, I love thee. Edward
      Caswall (trans.). WBP4
My God, I love thee. Saint
      Francis Xavier. WBP4
My Mr. Politician. Jane St.
      John. YoVA
My Samsons. Haim Guri. VoWA
My ain countree. Mary Lee
      Demarest. WBP4
My ain fireside. Elizabeth
      Hamilton. WBP1
My ain wife. Alexander Laing.
      WBP2
My beautiful lady. Thomas
      Woolner. WBP2
My body. Rachel Korn. VoWA
My brigantine. James Fenimore
      Cooper. MTS
My brother. Julie McAdams. YoVA
My brother was silent. Amir
      Gilboa. VoWA
My child. John Pierpont. WBP3
My choice. William Browne. WBP2
My condolences. Mike Howard.
      YoVA
My country is so tiny. Ernesto
      Gutierrez. NiR
My creed. Alice Carey. WBP4
My darling dear, my daisy
      flower. John Skelton. HaAP
My days among the dead. Robert
      Southey. WBP4
My dead. Rachel Blaustein
      (Bluwstein). VoWA
My dear and only love. James
      Graham(Marquis Montrose).
      WBP2
My dog Jack. Hayden Carruth.
      FroA
My dream. Paula Rotenberger.
      YoVA
My eyes! how I love you. John
      Godfrey Saxe. WBP2
My familiar dream. Paul

Verlaine. FoFS
My father. Abraham Chalfi. VoWA
My father and I have always been
      close. Paula Sullivan. YoVA
my father moved through dooms of
      love. Edward Estlin Cummings.
      HaAP
My father's country. Duane
      BigEagle. ReE
My father's song. Simon J.
      Ortiz. ReE
My father, who's still alive.
      Jose Kozer. VoWA
My favorite time of year. Maxine
      Jones. YoVA
My feelings. Li Po. GrAC
"**My** feet thay haul me round the
      house." Gelett Burgess. IlTH
My fiddle. Leib Kwitko. VoWA
My friend. Brenda Bradley. YoVA
My galley charged with
      forgetfulness. Sir Thomas
      Wyatt. HaAP--MTS
My garden. Thomas Edward Brown.
      EeBC
My gift to the world. Karen
      Tollett. YoVA
My grandparents' house. Sara
      Tollefson. YoVA
My great, great grandfather.
      Mark Weiss. HoWM
"**My** hands are cupped together".
      Robert Cox. HoWM
My heart is a lute. Blanche
      Fitzroy, Lady Lindsay. WBP2
My heid is like to rend, Willie.
      William Motherwell. WBP3
My home. Robert Herrick. WBP4
"**My** house is made of graham
      bread." Gelett Burgess. IlTH
My house of knowledge. Kristy
      Hales. HoWM
My kin talk. Anna Margolin (R.
      Lebensboim). VoWA
My lady. Charles Eliot Norton
      (trans.). WBP2
My lady. Dante Alighieri. WBP2
My land. Brenda Bradley. YoVA
My last breath. Jeanne Neal.
      YoVA
My last duchess. Robert
      Browning. HaAP--LiHE
My life closed twice before its
      close. Emily Dickinson. DoNG
My life had stood-a loaded gun.
      Emily Dickinson. HaAP
My little dreams. Georgia
      Douglas Johnson. BlS
My little girl. Samuel Minturn
      Peck. WBP1

My lost youth. Henry Wadsworth
    Longfellow. WBP1
My love. Klaudette Kelsey. YoVA
My love. Russell Powell Jacoby.
    WBP2
My love. James Russell Lowell.
    WBP2
My lute, awake. Sir Thomas
    Wyatt. HaAP
My mama moved among the days.
    Lucille Clifton. BlS
My mother. Hayim Naggid. VoWA
My mother as a young woman.
    Wendy S. Neidlinger. YoVA
My mother's bible. George Pope
    Morris. WBP1
My mother's milkman. Diane
    Wakoski. TeMP
My mother's picture. William
    Cowper. WBP1
My mother's shoes. Rayzel
    Zychlinska. VoWA
My name is.... Pauline Clarke.
    RoRF
My nightingale. Rose Auslander.
    VoWA
My old Kentucky home. Stephen
    Collins Foster. WBP3
My own house. David Ignatow.
    TeMP
My papa's waltz. Theodore
    Roethke. HaAP
My peace I give unto you. G.A.
    Studdert Kennedy. EeBC
My people. Duane BigEagle. ReE
My poor raging sisters. Esther
    Raab. BuAC
My puppy. Aileen Fisher. RoRF
My recovery. W. Taylor (trans.).
    WBP4
My recovery. Friedrich Gottlieb
    Klopstock. WBP4
My secret with the clown.
    Krystal Siler. YoVA
My shadow. Robert Louis
    Stevenson. WBP1
My son and I. Philip Levine.
    FroA
My song. Hayim Nachman Bialik.
    VoWA
My soul. Maurice Maeterlinck.
    FreS
My soul hovers over me. Joshua
    Tan Pai. VoWA
My spirit longeth for thee. John
    Byrom. EeBC
My strawlike hair. Asya. VoWA
My sweet old etcetera. Edward
    Estlin Cummings. SlW
My sweet sweeting. Unknown. WBP2

My sweetest Lesbia, let us live
    and love. Thomas Campion.
    HaAP
My sweetheart's face. John Allan
    Wyeth. WBP2
My thatched roof is
    ruined...autumn wind. Tu Fu.
    GrAC
My tiger. Sam Hamod. StPo
My times are in thy hand.
    Christopher Newman Hall. WBP4
My true memory. Asya. VoWA
My true-love hath my heart. Sir
    Philip Sidney. WBP2
My white book of poems. Rachel
    Blaustein (Bluwstein). VoWA
"My whole soul by now spent."
    Henri Thomas. MoVT
My wife and I. Unknown. FroC
My wife and child. Henry R.
    Jackson. WBP3
My wife's a winsome wee thing.
    Robert Burns. WBP2
My wise old grandpapa. Wilbur
    Howcroft. IlTH
Myers, Frederic William Henry
    On a grave at Grindelwald. WBP3
Myers, Jack
    Day of Atonement. VoWA
    The Minyan. VoWA
    Winging it. TeMP
Myers, Kelly J.
    That's life. YoVA
Myoe
    Ten tanka. FroC
Myopia. Giancarlo Majorino. NeIP
Myrrh-bearers. Margaret Junkin
    Preston. WBP4
Myself departing. Takahashi
    Mutsuo. FroC
Myself in an anatomical chart...
    Takahashi Mutsuo. FroC
Myself in the guise...ancient
    goddess. Takahashi Mutsuo.
    FroC
Myself of the Onan legend.
    Takahashi Mutsuo. FroC
Myself with a glory hole.
    Takahashi Mutsuo. FroC
The mysterious song. Stuart
    Merrill. FreS
The mystic's vision. Mathilde
    Blind. WBP4
A mystical ecstasy. Francis
    Quarles. WBP4
Myth on Mediterranean Beach:
    Aphrodite... Robert Penn
    Warren. HaAP
Mythology, Greek & Roman
    Atlanta in Calydon, sels.

Algernon Charles Swinburne.
HaAP
Canto II. Ezra Pound. HaAP
The garden of Prosperine.
Algernon Charles Swinburne.
HaAP

NHR. Jack Hirschman. VoWA
Naggid, Hayim
After the war. VoWA
Like a pearl. VoWA
My mother. VoWA
A snow in Jerusalem. VoWA
Naigreshel, Mendel
Nation. VoWA
What will remain after me?
VoWA
Nairne, C. Oliphant, Baroness
The auld house. WBP1
The laird o' Cockpen. WBP2
The land o' the leal. WBP3
Naito Joso
Fifteen hokku. FroC
Najlis, Michele
Now as you walk along the
roads... NiR
They pursued us in the night.
NiR
To Leonel Rugama. NiR
Naked thoughts, sels. Russell
Soaba. VooI
Nall, Carolyn
Death. YoVA
Names. Grace Schulman. StPo
Names
Choosing a name. Mary Lamb.
WBP1
My name is.... Pauline Clarke.
RoRF
Names. Grace Schulman. StPo
Naming of parts. Henry Reed.
LiHE
Privilege. Alejandra Pizarnik.
VoWA
The ultimate question. Penny
Lynn Turbeville. YoVA
Names of horses. Donald Hall.
HaAP
Naming of parts. Henry Reed.
LiHE
Nantucket. William Carlos
Williams. HaAP--SlW
Nantucket, Massachusetts
The Quaker graveyard in
Nantucket. Robert Lowell.
HaAP--MTS
Naomi

At the crossroad. Itzik Manger.
OnCP
Naone, Dana
Girl with the green skirt. ReE
Hair poem. ReE
Thought of going home. ReE
Untitled ("I make...poetic
pauses"). ReE
Napis, sels. Zbigniew Herbert.
CoP
Nappy edges. Ntozake Shange. BlS
Narcissus. Jean Lorrain (Paul
Deval). FreS
Narcissus
Narcissus. Jean Lorrain (Paul
Deval). FreS
Narcissus pseudonarcissus. Elio
Pagliarani. NeIP
Narowistosc piora, sels. Jerzy
Harasymowicz. CoP
A narrow fellow in the grass.
Emily Dickinson. HaAP
The narrow sea. Robert Graves.
MTS
The Narrows. Joseph Bruchac.
FroA
Nash, Ogden
The jellyfish. IlTH
The kitten. IlTH
The new Nutcracker Suite, sels.
PoCh
The octopus. MTS
Old Hogan's goat. IlTH
The parent. IlTH
The pig. IlTH
The sea-gull. MTS
The shark. IlTH
The termite. IlTH
Very like a whale. HaAP
Nashe, Thomas
Adieu, farewell earth's bliss.
HaAP
A litany in time of plague.
LiHE
Nation. Mendel Naigreshel. VoWA
National song. Ernesto Cardenal.
NiR
Native colours, sels.
Karoniaktatie (Alex Jacobs).
ReE
The natives of America. Ann
Plato. BlS
The nativity. Henry Vaughan.
ShBa
The Nativity. Clive Staples
Lewis. EeBC
The Nativity of Christ. Robert
Southwell. EeBC
The Nativity of our Lord.
Christopher Smart. HaAP--ShBa

Natoni, Jean
    Catoni. ReE
Natsume Seibi
    Twenty-seven hokku. FroC
Natura naturans. Arthur Hugh
    Clough. HaAP
Natural law. William Oandasan.
    ReE
Naturally. Lorde Audre. BlS
Nature. Kathy Hamm. YoVA
Nature. Mary Voss. YoVA
Nature
    The air. Mary Jahnke. YoVA
    At a fragrance of plums. Matsuo
        Basho. FroC
    At the trough. Arthur Gregor
        (Goldenberg). FroA
    The battle of Zion Canyon.
        Shelly Qualls. YoVA
    Broad bea. Matsuo Basho . FroC
    Correspondences. Charles
        Baudelaire. FoFS
    Cry of nature. Geraldine Keams.
        ReE
    Cut the grass. Archie Randolph
        Ammons. HaAP
    Dislike of nature. Ono Tozaburo.
        FroC
    Fern hill. Dylan Thomas. LiHE
    Fifteen hokku. Shiba Sonome.
        FroC
    Lines written...above Tintern
        Abbey. William Wordsworth.
        HaAP
    Mainstream. John Reinke. YoVA
    Misty lady. Debby Buckley. YoVA
    The moon is teaching Bible.
        Zelda . BuAC--VoWA
    The most of it. Robert Frost.
        HaAP
    Natura naturans. Arthur Hugh
        Clough. HaAP
    Nature's conversation. David
        Nelson. YoVA
    Nature. Mary Voss. YoVA
    Ode to the traveler. Becky
        Holmberg. YoVA
    Outdoors. Gene Davis. YoVA
    Pastoral Lusus. Marcantonio
        Flaminio. ReLP
    Prayer for the great family.
        Gary Snyder. HaAP
    Sensation. Arthur Rimbaud. SlW
    The sense of the sleigh-of-hand
        man. Wallace Stevens. HaAP
    Seventy-six hokku. Matsuo Basho.
        FroC
    Thirty-three hokku. Takarai
        Kikaku. FroC
    Three poets at Yuyam. Botange

    Shohaku. FroC
    Twenty-nine hokku. Tan Taigi.
        FroC
    Twenty-one hokku. Nozawa Boncho.
        FroC
    Twenty-three hokku. Uejima
        Onitsura. FroC
Nature of success. Gary Norris.
    YoVA
Nature's conversation. David
    Nelson. YoVA
Nature's gem. Geeta Pasi. YoVA
Nature's hymn to the deity. John
    Clare. EeBC
Nature's mercy. Todd Warne. YoVA
Nausicaa with some attendants.
    Tom Lowenstein. VoWA
Nautilus
    The chambered Nautilus. Oliver
        Wendell Holmes. MTS
Navagero, Andrea
    Lusus IV: Damis' vow to
        Bacchus... ReLP
    Lusus XXI: Cupid and Hyella.
        ReLP
    Lusus XXII: prayer to night.
        ReLP
    Lusus XXXVII. ReLP
Navajo chant, sels. Unknown. ReE
Naval Battles
    Captain Jones' invitation.
        Philip Freneau. MTS
    The captain stood on the
        carronade. Frederick Marryat.
        MTS
    The captain. Alfred, Lord
        Tennyson. MTS
    The dynasts, sels. Thomas
        Hardy. MTS
    Herve Riel. Robert Browning.
        MTS
    Lepanto. Gilbert Keith
        Chesterton. MTS
    On board the '76. James Russell
        Lowell. MTS
    Song of myself, sels. Walt
        Whitman. MTS
Navy, Great Britain
    Admirals all. Henry Newbolt.
        MTS
    Henry V, sels. William
        Shakespeare. MTS
Nazis
    A Christmas carol, sels.
        Stanislaw Grochowiak. CoP
    Today the Nazis forces marched.
        Melech Ravitch (Z.K.
        Bergner). OnCP
Neal, Jeanne
    Let it be. YoVA

My last breath. YoVA
To be me. YoVA
Neale (trans.), John Mason
Art thou weary? WBP4
Darkness is thinning. WBP4
Praise of the celestiral
country. WBP4
Neale, John Mason
Light's glittering morn. EeBC
Near. Abba Kovner. VoWA
Near the window, sels. Karla
Kuskin. ByM
Nearer. Judith Herzberg. VoWA
Nearer home. Phoebe Cary. WBP4
Nearing home. Unknown. MTS
Neb, Sheri
What is color? YoVA
The **necessity** of rejection.
James Schevill. FroA
NeeSmith, D.H.
Winter's the best. YoVA
The **need** to love. Shlomo Vinner.
VoWA
Needleman, Aileen
Viewpoint on life. YoVA
Neele, Henry
Moan, moan, ye dying gales.
WBP3
Negative. Yoshioka Minoru. FroC
Negev Desert
The joining. Gerda Stein
Norvig. VoWA
Neglected child. Anthony
Pressley. YoVA
The **Negro** speaks of rivers.
Langston Hughes. HaAP
Negroes
Answer to Voznesensky &
Evtushenko. Frank O'Hara. HoA
Aunt Sue's stories. Langston
Hughes. DuD
Black pride. Margaret Goss
Burroughs. BlS
Bottled. Helene Johnson. BlS
Carol of the brown king.
Langston Hughes. PoCh--ShBa
Cold term. I. Amiri Baraka
(LeRoi Jones). SlW
Domestics. Kattie M. Cumbo. BlS
Dream variations. Langston
Hughes. HaAP
The elevator man adheres to
form, sels. Margaret Danner.
BlS
Exits and entrances. Naomi Long
Madgett. BlS
Frederick Douglass. Robert
Hayden. HoA
A grandson is a a hoticeberg.
Margaret Danner. BlS

Heritage. Gwendolyn B. Bennett.
BlS
How will you call me, brother.
Mari Evans. BlS
The hustle. Unknown . TyW
Incident. Countee Cullen. LiHE
It hurts. Ken Liu. YoVA
Lawd, dese colored chillu.
Fareedah Allah (Ruby
Saunders) . BlS
Learning to read. Frances E.W.
Harper. BlS
Many die here. Gayl Jones. BlS
Mourning poem for the queen of
Sunday. Robert Hayden. HoA
Mrs. Johnson objects. Clara Ann
Thompson. BlS
Nappy edges. Ntozake Shange.
BlS
New day. Naomi Long Madgett.
BlS
Nikki-Rosa. Nikki Giovanni. BlS
Nortboun'. Lucy Ariel Williams.
BlS
Only in this way. Margaret Goss
Burroughs. BlS
Oriflamme. Jessie Redmon
Fauset. BlS
Postcard from London, 23. 10.
1972. Andrew Salkey. FroA
The road. Helene Johnson. BlS
Satori. Gayl Jones. BlS
Song ("I am weaving a song of
waters"). Gwendolyn B.
Bennett. BlS
Still I rise. Maya Angelou. BlS
The sundays of Satin-Legs
Smith. Gwendolyn Brooks. LiHE
To soulfolk. Margaret Goss
Burroughs. BlS
To usward. Gwendolyn B.
Bennett. BlS
Tripart. Gayl Jones. BlS
U name this one. Carolyn M.
Rodgers. BlS
Under the edge of February.
Jayne Cortez. BlS
Who is my brother? Pinkie
Gordon Lane. BlS
Neidlinger, Wendy S.
(For K.M.E. & G.B.C.). YoVA
Hunger. YoVA
My mother as a young woman.
YoVA
Neidus, Leib
I love the woods. VoWA
I often want to let my lines
go. VoWA
In an alien place. VoWA
Neighbors. Mary Ann Hoberman.

Mulberry Street. Ruth
    Herschberger. HoA
There's nothing to do in New
    York. Tomioka Taeko . FroC
West Fifty-Seventh Street.
    Byron Vazakas. FroA
New day. Naomi Long Madgett. BlS
A new dress. Rachel Korn. VoWA
A new genesis. Avraham Shlonsky.
    VoWA
New graveyard, Jerusalem.
    Shirley Kaufman. VoWA
New heaven, new war. Robert
    Southwell. ShBa
New house. Rai San'yo. FroC
New prince, new pomp. Robert
    Southwell. ShBa
A new spring at Yi-feng.
    Ling-yi. GrAC
New thought. Jackie Pierce. YoVA
The new year for trees. Howard
    Schwartz. VoWA
Newbolt, Henry
    Admirals all. MTS
Newcomb, David
    "I have cupped in my hands..."
    HoWM
Newcomers. Abraham Reisen. VoWA
A newly found friend is like the
    sea. Keith Jost. YoVA
The newly-wedded. Winthrop
    Mackworth Praed. WBP2
Newlyweds. Arthur Rimbaud. FreS
Newman, John Henry, Cardinal
    Flowers without fruit. WBP4
    Lead, kindly light. WBP4
    Zeal and love. TyW
Newspaper hats. Jim Howard. FroA
Newspapers
    All the dirt that's fit to pot.
    Vita C. Ungaro. StPo
    Headlines. Michele Morgan. YoVA
Newton, David
    Adrift. YoVA
    Away with the old. YoVA
Newton, Jean
    Diamond. HoWM
Newton, Joel
    Dome cave preview. HoWM
Next day. Randall Jarrell. HaAP
The next time you were there.
    Samuel Hazo. FroA
next to of course god america i.
    Edward Estlin Cummings. LiHE
Next year, in Jerusalem. Shirley
    Kaufman. VoWA
Niagara Falls. Philip Parisi.
    FroA
Niagara Falls
    Niagara Falls. Philip Parisi.

FroA
Nicaragua
    The arrival. Ernesto Cardenal.
    NiR
    As long as.. Unknown . NiR
    Cradle song without music.
    Carlos Martinez Rivas. NiR
    The curtain of the native land.
    Unknown . NiR
    The dock. Ivan Uriarte. NiR
    Epigram XIX. Ernesto Cardenal.
    NiR
    God said. Gioconda Belli. NiR
    I sing with my heart. Negor
    Len. NiR
    My country is so tiny. Ernesto
    Gutierrez. NiR
    National song. Ernesto
    Cardenal. NiR
    Oh country, my country. Ernesto
    Gutierrez. NiR
    The price of a country.
    Fernando Gordillo. NiR
    There is nothing in the city.
    David Macfield. NiR
    Third class country. Pablo
    Antonio Cuadra. NiR
    Three corpses. Unknown . NiR
    Tomorrow, my son, all will be
    different. Edwin Castro. NiR
    Wasteland collage. Hector
    Vargas. NiR
    We'll be new. Gioconda Belli.
    NiR
    What are you Nicaragua?
    Gioconda Belli. NiR
    Within me. HuGos   NiR
Nicaraguan Revolutions
    The secret of the burning
    stars. Pablo Antonio Cuadra.
    NiR
    Tomasito. Pablo Antonio Cuadra.
    NiR
    The warning: shout on the
    corners. Manolo Cuadra. NiR
Nicaraguan Revolutions
    American rhymes. Nicolas
    Guillen. NiR
    Andres. Fernando Gordillo. NiR
    Anxiety. Rigoberto Lopez Perez.
    NiR
    Arms and letters. Alvaro
    Gutierrez. NiR
    Ay patria. Otto Rene Castillo.
    NiR
    Biography. Leonel Rugama. NiR
    The boys. Roberto Uriarte. NiR
    Brief letter to my wife.
    Ricardo Morales Aviles. NiR
    Casimoro three times over.

Acquainted with the night. Robert Frost. HaAP

All day we've longed for night. Sarah Webster Fabio. BlS

All night long. Nina Cassian. VoWA

"All through the night." Ryokan. FroC

Andrew's bedtime story. Ian Serraillier. DuD

At arm's length. Shirley Bossert. FroA

At night. Rachel Boimwall. VoWA

Aunt Sue's stories. Langston Hughes. DuD

The bird of night. Randall Jarrell. DuD

Called back. Charles Wright. TeMP

Child's game. Judson Jerome. DuD

A clear midnight. Walt Whitman. HaAP

Country night. Rocco Scotellaro. NeIP

Cows are coming home in Maine. Robert P. Tristram Coffin. DuD

The crickets sang. Emily Dickinson. SlW

The dark. Roy Fuller. DuD

Darkness. Heather Wiegand. YoVA

The day is done. Henry Wadsworth Longfellow. WBPl

Delicate the toad. Robert Francis. DuD

Disillusionment at ten o'clock. Wallace Stevens. SlW

The ditchdigger's tears, sels. Pier Paolo Pasolini. NeIP

Down dip the branches. Mark Van Doren. DuD

Dunce song 6. Mark Van Doren. DuD

The early supper. Barbara Howes. DuD

The European night. Stanislav Vinaver. VoWA

Fatal interview, sels. Edna St. Vincent Millay. HaAP

Forgetting. Mathilde-Anna Monnier. MoVT

Fragment. Takiguchi Shuzo . FroC

A gaggle of geese, a pride of lions. John Moore. DuD

Giant thunder. James Reeves. DuD

Good night and good morning. R.M. Milnes (Lord Houghton). WBPl

The happy family. John Ciardi. DuD

The horses. Maxine Kumin. DuD

The huntsmen. Walter De La Mare. DuD

Impressions of night. Jami Wald. YoVA

In the discreet splendor. A.L. Strauss. VoWA

In the pitch of the night. Lee Bennett Hopkins. ByM

John Carey's second song. Thomas McGrath. FroA

John's song. Joan Aiken. DuD

The lamp goes ou. Sugawara no Michizane . FroC

The leaving. Lance Henson. ReE

The Long Island night. Howard Moss. TeMP

Lullaby ("The long canoe.") Robert Hillyer. DuD

Lusus XXII: prayer to night. Andrea Navagero. ReLP

The magic wood. Henry Treece. DuD

Meditation. Charles Baudelaire. FoFS

Midnight and ten minutes. Shlomo Vinner. VoWA

Midnight. Rosalie Williams. YoVA

Minor key. Judah Leib Teller. VoWA

The mockingbird. Randall Jarrell. DuD

New Year's Eve in solitude. Robert Mezey. VoWA

Nigh. Tu Fu . LuL

Night ("No matter how fast I run.") Tanikawa Shuntaro . FroC

Night clouds. Tom McKeown. HoA

Night landscape. Joan Aiken. DuD

Night mastered. Roland Giguere. MoVT

Night train. Robert Francis. DuD

Night visitors. Kadya Molodovsky. VoWA

Night's invitation. Ishihara Yoshiro. FroC

Night. Aldo Camerino. VoWA

Nightcap. Gordon D. Leslie. StPo

Nocturn cabbage. Carl Sandburg. DuD

Nocturnal thoughts. Avraham Huss. VoWA

Here lies Sir Tact. Timothy
Steele. TyW
A little shrub growing by. Ben
Jonson. TyW
Song of the young noble. Ku
K'uang . GrAC
The toad-eater. Robert Burns.
TyW
Nobles, Robin
Breakin' up. YoVA
nobody loses all the time.
Edward Estlin Cummings. LiHE
Nobody's business. James Tate.
TeMP
Nocturn cabbage. Carl Sandburg.
DuD
Nocturnal sounds. Kattie M.
Cumbo. BlS
Nocturnal thoughts. Avraham
Huss. VoWA
Nocturne. Stuart Merrill. FreS
Nocturne. Pinkie Gordon Lane.
BlS
Noel, Thomas
The pauper's drive. WBP3
The noise of the waters. Dahlia
Ravikovich. BuAC
A noiseless patient spider. Walt
Whitman. HaAP
Nokes (trans.), W.F.
Polyeucte, sels. WBP2
Nokondi (the helpless creature).
Hengenike Riyong. VooI
Nomad's utopia. Antonio Porta.
NeIP
Nomen. Naomi Long Madgett. BlS
Non nobis domine. Rudyard
Kipling. EeBC
Non sum qualis eram bonae
sub...Cynarae. Ernest Dowson.
HaAP
Non-stop-shows, sels. Tadeusz
Rozewicz. CoP
Noon songs, sels. Unknown. FroC
Norris, Gary
Nature of success. YoVA
Norris, Leslie
The camels, the kings' camels.
PoCh
Mice in the hay. PoCh
The park at evening. DuD
The quiet-eyed cattle. PoCh
The stable cat. PoCh
Nortboun'. Lucy Ariel Williams.
BlS
North. Maurice Kenny. ReE
North Atlantic. Carl Sandburg.
MTS
The north tower of Golden Fort.
Kao Shih. GrAC

North, Gina
Ironic rescue. YoVA
Norton (trans.), Charles Eliot
My lady. WBP2
Norton, Caroline Elizabeth S.
We have been friends together.
WBP1
Norton, Caroline E. Sheridan
The King of Denmark's ride.
WBP3
Love not. WBP3
Norvig, Gerda Stein
Desert march. VoWA
The joining. VoWA
The tree of life is also a tree
of fire. VoWA
Not at all, or all in all.
Alfred, Lord Tennyson. WBP2
Not going with it. Zali
Gurevitch. VoWA
Not ideas about the thing but...
Wallace Stevens. HaAP
Not like a cypress. Yehuda
Amichai. VoWA
Not one to spare. Unknown. WBP1
Not ours the vows. Bernard
Barton. WBP2
Not that I really care. Susan
Henderson. YoVA
Not that far. May Miller. BlS
Not waving but drowning.
Florence M. ("Stevie") Smith.
HaAP
Note in a sanitorium. Ray
Amorosi. FroA
A note to Mr. Frost. Henry F.
Beechhold. StPo
Notes for a love letter from
mid-America. Jim Barnes. ReE
Notes on the post-Industrial
Revolution. Edward Morin.
FroA
Notes to Joanne, LXI. John F.
Kerr. ReE
Notes to Joanne, LXIII. John F.
Kerr. ReE
Notes to Joanne, LXXIV. John F.
Kerr. ReE
Notes to Joanne, LXVI. John F.
Kerr. ReE
Nothing but laughter, nothing.
Glycon [or Glykon]. DoNG
Nothing but leaves. Lucy E.
Akerman. WBP4
Nothing to save. David Herbert
Lawrence. SlW
Nothingness. Aharon Amir. VoWA
The notice. Jean Follain. MoVT
Notre Dame de Paris
Cathedral in the thrashing rain.

Takamura Kotaro . FroC
Notre Dame perfected by
    reflection. Harold Witt. HoA
Notre Dame perfected by
    reflection. Harold Witt. HoA
Nova. Robinson Jeffers. HaAP
November
    Parable: November. Stephen
        Tapscott. FroA
November 3rd. Miyazawa Kenji.
    FroC
"Now Christmas is come."
    Unknown. PoCh
Now I have forgotten all. David
    Vogel. VoWA
Now and afterwards. Dinah Maria
    Mulock Craik. WBP3
Now as you walk along the
    roads... Michele Najlis. NiR
Now it can be told. Philip
    Levine. VoWA
"Now old, my heart is at peace."
    Ling-ch'e. GrAC
Now stop your noses, reader...
    John Dryden. TyW
Now the summer's come. Unknown.
    HaAP
Now welcom, somer. Geoffrey
    Chaucer. HaAP
Nowlan, Alden
    The lonliness of...long
        distance runner. TyW
Noyes, Alfred
    Daddy fell into the pond. IlTH
    Sea-distances. MTS
    Sunlight and sea. MTS
Noyle, Ken
    The sea. MTS
Nozawa Boncho
    Twenty-one hokku. FroC
Nuclear Power
    Ode to Three Mile Island. Tim
        Miller. YoVA
    Psalm-people power at the
        die-in. Denise Levertov. FroA
    To a victim of radiation.
        Arturo Vivante. FroA
Nude descending a staircase.
    X.J. Kennedy. HoA
Nudities. Andre Spire. VoWA
Nukada, Princess
    Choka ("When Emperor Tenji").
        FroC
    Remembering Emperor Tenji. FroC
    Tanka ("At Nikitatsu...") FroC
The **nun** and harp. Harriet
    Prescott Spofford. WBP3
Nuns
    Grieving over the death of the
        nun Rigan. Lady Otomo no

Sakanoue. FroC
Halfway. Maxine Kumin. TeMP
Heaven-haven. Gerard Manley
    Hopkins. MTS--SlW
Missionaries in the jungle.
    Linda Piper. BlS
Nurses
    Herodias, sels. Stephane
        Mallarme. FreS
    Terro. Kitahara Hakushu . FroC
Nursing Homes
    At the nursing home. David
        Payne. YoVA
    At the nursing home. John Cain.
        FroA
Nyland, Marjorie
    Growing-up. YoVA
The **nymph's** reply to the
    shepherd. Sir Walter Ralegh.
    WBP2
The **nymph's** reply to the
    shepherd. Sir Walter Ralegh.
    HaAP--LiHE
Nymphs
    Epigram: To the muses. Giovanni
        Giovano Pontano. ReLP
    A faun's afternoon. Stephane
        Mallarme. FoFS
    The poet speaks to the
        nymphs... Giovanni Giovano
        Pontano. ReLP
    Slender maid. Joseph Eliya.
        VoWA
    To the nymph Brissa. Jean
        Salmon Macrin. ReLP

O Daedalus, fly away home.
    Robert Hayden. HaAP
O God! have mercy in this
    dreadful hour. Robert
    Southey. MTS
O Lord, seek us. Christina
    Georgina Rossetti. EeBC
O Master, let me walk with thee.
    Washington Gladden. WBP4
O all down within the pretty
    meadow. Kenneth Patchen. HaAP
O captain! my captain!. Walt
    Whitman. MTS
"O diaphanous geraniums, magic
    warriors." Jules Laforgue.
    FreS
O fire of God, the comforter.
    Saint Hildegarde. WBP4
O fire of God, the comforter. R.
    F. Littledale (trans.). WBP4
O grant. Pierre Emmanuel (N.

Mathieu). MoVT

O lay thy hand in mine, dear!
Gerald Massey. WBP2

O little town of Bethlehem.
Phillips Brooks. WBP4

O mistress mine, where are you
roaming? William
Shakespeare. HaAP

O night of the crying children.
Nelly Sachs. VoWA

"O seasons, O castles," Arthur
Rimbaud. FoFS--FreS

O simplicitas. Madeleine
L'Engle. EeBC

O the chimneys. Nelly Sachs.
VoWA

O wearisome condition of
humanity. Fulke Greville
(Lord Brooke). HaAP

O'Brien, Sara
Feelings. YoVA
Short love. YoVA

O'Brien, William Smith
Never despair. WBP3

O'Connor, Frank
Inheritance. TyW
Love and hate. TyW

O'Grady, Tom
Aubade after the party. FroA

O'Hara, Frank
Answer to Voznesensky &
Evtushenko. HoA
The day Lady died. HoA--SlW
Poem ("Hate is only one of
many...") SlW
Poem ("There I could never be a
boy.") HoA
Poem ("think of filth...),
sels. TyW
Sleeping on the wind. SlW
A step away from them. HoA
A terrestrial cuckoo. SlW
To the film industry in crisis.
SlW
To the harbormaster. MTS
A true account of talking to
the sun... SlW
Why I am not a painter. HoA

O'Kelly, Patrick
The curse of Doneraile, sels.
TyW

O'Shaughnessy, Arthur
Has summer come without the
rose? WBP3

O, beautiful they move. William
Pillen. VoWA

O, do not wanton with those
eyes. Ben Jonson. WBP2

O, fairest of rural maids.
William Cullen Bryant. WBP2

O, may I join the choir
invisible? George Eliot
(M.E.L. Cross). WBP4

O, my luve's like a red, red
rose. Robert Burns. WBP3

O, saw ye bonnie Leslie? Robert
Burns. WBP3

O, saw ye the lass?. Richard
Ryan. WBP2

Oak Trees
Sylvan glory. William Ardell
Gamble (Jr.). YoVA

Oandasan, William
Acoma. ReE
Four# (4#). ReE
From my mouth a song. ReE
Natural law. ReE
Silent afternoon. ReE
Summer night and her/scent. ReE
Who am I? ReE

The obscene caller. Cheri Fein.
TyW

Obscenity
On obscenity. Tanikawa Shuntaro
FroC

Observation at dawn. Abba
Kovner. VoWA

Observing the past at Yueh. Li
Po. GrAC

Observing the past on Chi Hill,
sels. Ch'en Tzu-ang. GrAC

Obstacles
"The wall." Nora Coggins. YoVA

Occidente (see Brooks), Maria

The ocean said to me once.
Stephen Crane. MTS

Ocean. See Sea

October snow. Mary Trimble. PrVo

The octopus. Christopher Murray
Grieve. TyW

The octopus. Ogden Nash. MTS

The octopus that does not die.
Hagiwara Sakutaro. FroC

Octopuses
The octopus that does not die.
Hagiwara Sakutaro. FroC
The octopus. Christopher Murray
Grieve. TyW
The octopus. Ogden Nash. MTS

Octoroons
Ballade des belles
milatraisses. Rosalie Jonas.
BlS

Ode ("Old tumbril rolling with
me...") X.J. Kennedy. TeMP

Ode ("Our birth is but a
sleep...") William
Wordsworth. DoNG--WBP4

Ode ("Though loath to grieve")

Ralph Waldo Emerson. HaAP
Ode in 1,000 lines, sels.
   Takahashi Mutsuo. FroC
Ode on a Grecian urn. John
   Keats. HaAP--LiHE
Ode on a decision to settle for
   less. William Pillen. VoWA
Ode on a plastic stapes. Chad
   Walsh. HoA
Ode on melancholy. John Keats.
   HaAP
An ode on the birth of our
   Saviour. Robert Herrick. ShBa
Ode to Faber College. Tim
   Miller. YouVA
Ode to Terminus. Wystan Hugh
   Auden. HaAP
Ode to Three Mile Island. Tim
   Miller. YoVA
Ode to a nightingale. John
   Keats. HaAP--LiHE
Ode to a nightingale. John
   Keats. WBP3
Ode to an old man. Yoshioka
   Minoru. FroC
Ode to duty. William Wordsworth.
   WBP4
Ode to evening. William Collins.
   HaAP
Ode to freedom. Aaron Zeitlin.
   VoWA
Ode to grammer. David Payne.
   YoVA
An ode to himself, sels. Ben
   Jonson. ShBa
Ode to mother. Susan Zielke.
   YoVA
Ode to solitude. Alexander Pope.
   WBP1
Ode to the Finnish dead. Chad
   Walsh. HoA
Ode to the traveler. Becky
   Holmberg. YoVA
Ode to the west wind. Percy
   Bysshe Shelley. HaAP--MTS
Ode, written in...1746. William
   Collins. HaAP
Ode: Intimations of immortality.
   William Wordsworth.
   HaAp--WBP4
Ode: Intimations of immortality,
   sels. William Wordsworth.
   DoNG
Ode: on the morning of Christ's
   nativity. John Milton. ShBa
An ode: to himself. Ben Jonson.
   HaAP
Oden, Gloria C.
   The child is the mother. BlS
Odors

Exotic perfume. Charles
   Baudelaire. FoFS
"The petals of your face."
   James F. King. StPo
A phantom. Charles Baudelaire.
   FoFS
Summer night and her/scent.
   William Oandasan. ReE
The odyssey, sels. Homer. DoNG
The odyssey, sels. Homer. MTS
Oe no Asatsuna
   Rhyme-prose on the marriage...
   FroC
Oedipus
   Antigone and Oedipus. Henrietta
   Cordelia Ray. BlS
Of Thomas Traherne & the pebble
   outside. Sydney Clouts. VoWA
Of a painter and a baker.
   Theodore de Beze. ReLP
Of angels. E.L. Mayo. FroA
Of autumn. Veronica Porumbacu.
   VoWA
Of course I know. Zishe Landau.
   VoWA
Of his love Caelia. Girolamo
   Angeriano. ReLP
Of hym that togyder wyll
   serve... Alexander Barclay
   (trans.). WBP4
Of hym that togyder wyll
   serve... Sebastian Brandt.
   WBP4
Of my lady Isabella playing on
   the lute. Edmund Waller. HaAP
Of one that is so fair and
   bright. Unknown. HaAP
Of the admirable city Venice.
   Jacopo Sannazaro. ReLP
Of the beloved caravan. Conny
   Hannes Meyer. VoWA
Of the infelicitie of lovers.
   Giovanni Giovano Pontano.
   ReLP
Of the last verses in the book.
   Edmund Waller. HaAP
"Of the soul all things".
   Stephane Mallarme. FoFS
Of three or four in a room.
   Yehuda Amichai. VoWA
off in the distance. Carol
   Coyle. YoVA
Offa, King of England
   Mercian hymns, sels. Geoffrey
   Hill. HaAP
Offhand composition III. Wang
   Wei. GrAC
Official iconography. Roberto
   Roversi. NeIP
Oh breeze. Rae Cline. YoVA

Oh country, my country. Ernesto
    Gutierrez. NiR
Oh wert thou in the cauld blast.
    Robert Burns. HaAP
Oh! for a closer walk with God.
    William Cowper. EeBC
Oh, no!. Mary Mapes Dodge. IlTH
"Oh, she sailed away on a
    lovely...day." Unknown. IlTH
Ohio
    Shelby County, Ohio, November
    1974. G.E. Murray. FroA
Ohlenkamp, Terry
    The temptation. YoVA
Oil. Linda Hogan. ReE
Okaru and Kampei. Kitahara
    Hakushu. FroC
Okhotsk elegy. Miyazawa Kenji.
    FroC
Oklahoma
    Lost in sulphur canyons. Jim
    Barnes. ReE
Oklahoma boyhood. Duane
    BigEagle. ReE
"Ol Erie McGreer". Elizabeth
    Garza. YoVA
Old. Ralph Hoyt. WBP3
Old Age
    Advice from old age. Ryan
    Synovec. YoVA
    Aging. Ingrid Schulz. YoVA
    The auld folks. Andrew Park.
    WBP1
    The bean eaters. Gwendolyn
    Brooks. BlS--HaAP
    Darby and Joan. Frederic Edward
    Wetherley. WBP2
    Dirge. Madeline Mason. StPo
    Eleven tanka. Lady Ise. FroC
    Faith and hope. Rembrandt
    Peale. WBP2
    Father William. Lewis Carroll
    (C.L. Dodgson). IlTH
    From the crag. Mani Leib. VoWA
    The golden wedding. David
    Gray. WBP2
    Growing old. Matthew Arnold.
    LiHE
    I do not wish to be old. Norman
    H. Russell. ReE
    John Anderson, my jo. Robert
    Burns. WBP2
    The last dream. Roy A. Young
    Bear. ReE
    The last leaf. Aleksandr
    Sergeyevich Puskin. WBP3
    The last leaf. Oliver Wendell
    Holmes. WBP3
    My tiger. Sam Hamod. StPo
    "Now old, my heart is at peace."

Ling-ch'e . GrAC
    Ode to an old ma. Yoshioka
    Minoru . FroC
    Of the last verses in the book.
    Edmund Waller. HaAP
    Old age. Stephen G. Widner.
    YoVA
    The old man dreams. Oliver
    Wendell Holmes. WBP2
    The old man rocks in the wind.
    Betsy Wray. YoVA
    An old man's winter night.
    Robert Frost. HaAP
    The old man. Beth Kroger. YoVA
    Old man. Reginald Shephead.
    YoVA
    The old vagabond. Pierre-Jean
    de Beranger. WBP3
    Old. Ralph Hoyt. WBP3
    On the road to Chorrera. Arlo
    Bates. WBP2
    A poor old man. Mark Lobdell.
    YoVA
    Resolution and independence.
    William Wordsworth. HaAP
    Retired school-teacher. Heather
    McHugh. TeMP
    The seated ones. Arthur
    Rimbaud. FoFS
    Sick, sending away a concubine.
    Ssu-k'ung Shu. GrAC
    Sixty-four tanka. Saigyo. FroC
    Spontaneous poem I. Chiao-jan
    GrAC
    Thirteen hokku. Kaai Chigetsu.
    FroC
    To waken an old lady. William
    Carlos Williams. HaAP
    Untitled ("As the night
    creeps..."). Aubrey W. Love.
    YoVA
    "What can an old man do but
    die?" Thomas Hood. WBP3
    The white knight's ballad.
    Lewis Carroll (C.L. Dodgson).
    HaAP
    A woman who's arrived at a ripe
    old age. Zelda. BuAC
    The world is not a fenced-off
    garden. Jakov Steinberg. VoWA
    Yuusthiwa. Simon J. Ortiz. ReE
Old Hogan's goat. Ogden Nash.
    IlTH
Old Ironsides. Oliver Wendell
    Holmes. MTS
Old Jewish cemetery in Worms.
    Alfred Kittner. VoWA
Old Noah's ark. Unknown. IlTH
Old Witherington. Dudley
    Randall. TyW

Old age. Stephen G. Widner. YoVA
The **old** arm-chair. Eliza Cook.
    WBP1
Old cigar store wooden Indian.
    James Cliftonne Morris. StPo
Old country. Lance Henson. ReE
Old countryside. Louise Bogan.
    HaAP
The **old** days. Patti Dake. YoVA
The **old** familiar faces. Charles
    Lamb. WBP3
Old folks at home. Stephen
    Collins Foster. WBP3
Old house on the hill. Sherri
    Basinger. YoVA
The **old** maid. George Barlow.
    WBP2
An **old** malediction. Anthony
    Hecht. TyW
The **old** man. Beth Kroger. YoVA
The **old** man. Alfredo Giuliani.
    NeIP
Old man. Reginald Shephead. YoVA
The **old** man dreams. Oliver
    Wendell Holmes. WBP2
Old man for his people. Harold
    Littlebird. ReE
The **old** man rocks in the wind.
    Betsy Wray. YoVA
The **old** man said: two. Carroll
    Arnett/Gogisgi. ReE
An **old** man's winter night.
    Robert Frost. HaAP
Old men climbing. Norman H.
    Russell. ReE
Old miniatures. Leo Vroman. VoWA
The **old** oaken bucket. Samuel
    Woodworth. WBP1
An **old** rustic school building.
    Keith Jost. YoVA
The **old** sexton. Park Benjamin.
    WBP3
The **old** ships. James Elroy
    Flecker. MTS
Old soldiers home at
    Marshalltown, Iowa. Jim
    Barnes. FroA
An **old** story. Rena Lee. VoWA
An **old** sweetheart of mine. James
    Whitcomb Riley. WBP2
The **old** trip by dream train.
    Brendan Galvin. TeMP
The **old** vagabond. Pierre-Jean de
    Beranger. WBP3
The **old** village choir. Benjamin
    F. Taylor. WBP4
Old-school punishment. Unknown.
    WBP1
Oldenburg, E.W.
    In Canterbury Cathedral. EeBC

The **older** brother. Pablo Antonio
    Cuadra. NiR
Oldham, John
    Upon the author of a play
    called Sodom. TyW
Oldham, John (about)
    To the memory of Mr. Oldham.
    John Dryden. HaAP
Oles, Carole
    Francestown suite. TeMP
Oliphant, Dave
    A little something for William
    Whipple. FroA
    A Mexican scrapbook. FroA
"Oliver Oglethorpe ogled an
    owl..." Unknown. IlTH
Olsen, Dianna
    Living on. YoVA
Olsen, Karen
    Instincts. YoVA
Olsen, Michelle
    With love. YoVA
Olson, Elder
    Merry Christmas! FroA
Ombres, Rossana
    Bella and the golem. VoWA
Omi, Japan
    Passing by the wasted capital
    in Omi. Kakinomoto no Hitomaro.
    FroC
On Anne Allen. Edward
    Fitzgerald. WBP3
On Hitomaro's death. Yosami.
    FroC
On Lord Holland's seat near
    Margate.... Thomas Gray. TyW
On Queen Caroline's deathbed.
    Alexander Pope.
On Tanabata. Yamanque no Okura.
    FroC
On Zacchaeus. Francis Quarles.
    HaAP
On a Rhine steamer. James
    Kenneth Stephen. TyW
On a child who lived one minute.
    X.J. Kennedy. HoA
On a cock at Rochester. Sir
    Charles Sedley. TyW
On a day off going to meet
    Censor Wang... Wei Ying-wu.
    GrAC
On a distant prospect of Eton
    College. Thomas Gray. WBP1
On a drawing by Flavio. Philip
    Levine. VoWA
On a drop of dew. Andrew
    Marvell. HaAP
On a girdle. Edmund Waller. WBP2
On a grave at Grindelwald.
    Frederic William Henry Myers.

On the death of Sylvia Plath.
    Judith Herzberg. VoWA
On the death of an infant. Dirk
    Smits. WBP1
On the death of her brother,
    Francis I. Marguerite de
    Valois. WBP3
On the death of an infant. H.S.
    Van Dyk (trans.). WBP1
On the edition of Mr. Pope's
    works.... Thomas Edwards. TyW
On the industrial highway.
    Daniel Hoffman. TeMP
On the late massacre in
    Piedmont. John Milton. HaAP
On the margins of a poem. Jiri
    Mordecai Langer. VoWA
On the morning of Christ's
    nativity. John Milton. WBP4
On the move. Thomson Gunn. HaAP
On the night train from Oxford.
    E.L. Mayo. FroA
On the occasion of the imperial
    visit... Prince Ikusa. FroC
On the ocean floor. Christopher
    Murray Grieve. HaAP
On the path. A.L. Strauss. VoWA
On the photograph of a man I
    never saw. Hyam Pultzik. VoWA
On the picture of an infant.
    Samuel Rogers (trans). WBP1
On the picture of an infant.
    Leonidas of Alexandria. WBP1
On the porch of the antique
    dealer. Paul Ramsey. FroA
On the road. Paul Laurence
    Dunbar. WBP2
On the road there stands a tree.
    Itzik Manger. VoWA
On the road to Chorrera. Arlo
    Bates. WBP2
On the road to paradise. Garrett
    Hongo. HoA
On the roads of Yamashio.
    Unknown. FroC
On the sea. John Keats. MTS
On the site of a mulberry
    tree.... Dante Gabriel
    Rossetti. TyW
On the sixth floor. Bartolo
    Cattafi. NeIP
On the tombs in Westminster
    Abbey. Francis Beaumont. WBP3
On the topic "Stone bridge
    stream." Chiao-jan. GrAC
On the way. Mordechai Husid.
    VoWA
On the west tower in Kuo-chou.
    Ts'en Shen. GrAC
On the wide stairs. Yehuda

Amichai. VoWA
On the world. Francis Quarles.
    HaAP
On this day so full of gloom.
    Mary Fulkerson. YoVA
On travel. Unknown. FroC
On traveling. Takechino
    Kurohito. FroC
On vacation:a poem to record my
    thoughts. Sugawara no
    Michizane. FroC
Once. Alice Walker. BlS
Once by the Pacific. Robert
    Frost. HaAP--MTS
One art. Elizabeth Bishop. HaAP
One chord. Nelly Sachs. VoWA
One day. Stuart Wahlstrom. YoVA
"One day I went out to the zoo."
    G.T. Johnson. IlTH
The one from the horizon. Emile
    Verhaeren. FreS
One goes with me along the
    shore. Manfred Winkler. VoWA
The One hundred fifty-first
    psalm (151). Karl Shapiro.
    VoWA
One lonely leaf. Michelle
    Garmany. YoVA
One of many. Marcie L. Burleson.
    YoVA
One old Oxford ox. Unknown. IlTH
One plant for man-made oil. Ono
    Tozaburo. FroC
One poet visits another. W.H.
    Davies. TyW
One thing to take, another to
    keep. Crescenzo del Monte.
    VoWA
The one who is missing. Abraham
    Chalfi. VoWA
One writing against his prick.
    Unknown. TyW
One-sided love. Kitahara
    Hakushu. FroC
Only a "me". Eileen Kampman.
    YoVA
Only a woman. Dinah Maria Mulock
    Craik. WBP3
"Only a year ago, - a ringing
    voice." Harriet Beecher
    Stowe. WBP3
Only in this way. Margaret Goss
    Burroughs. BlS
Only joy, now here you are. Sir
    Philip Sidney. HaAP
Only lonely. Terra Manasco. YoVA
Only madmen understand. Pierre
    Emmanuel (N. Mathieu). MoVT
Only to lose. Carolyn Tilghman.
    YoVA

Szymborska. CoP
Overcast. Pierre Reverdy. MoVT
Owen, Wilfred
   Anthem for doomed youth. HaAP
   Arms and the boy. HaAP
   Dulce et decorum est. LiHE--TyW
   The last laugh. LiHE
The owl and the pussycat. Edward
   Lear. IlTH--WBPl
The owl in the rabbi's barn. Dan
   Jaffe. VoWA
Owls
   The bird of night. Randall
      Jarrell. DuD
   Blue owl song. Alfred Kittner.
      VoWA
   Five little owls. Unknown. RoRF
   In the eyes of a screech owl.
      Ono Tozaburo. FroC
   Nightowl. Lisa Thoms. YoVA
   The owl and the pussycat.
      Edward Lear. IlTH--WBPl
Ox cart man. Donald Hall. TeMP
The oxen. Thomas Hardy.
   HaAP--PoCh
Oxen
   A flayed ox. Eugene Guillevic.
      MoVT
   Song of praise for an ox.
      Abraham Sutskever. VoWA
   Song of the tailess ox. Minamoto
      no Shitago. FroC
Oxford, England
   Epigram on the refusal of the
      university. William Cowper.
      TyW
   On the night train from Oxford.
      E.L. Mayo. FroA
Oxlie, Mary
   To William Drummond of
      Hawthornden. PaW
Oysters
   The ballad of an oysterman.
      Oliver Wendell Holmes. MTS
Ozaki Hosai
   Haiku: 100 haiku in free form.
      FroC
Ozello, A.
   I want him to, take my soul.
      YoVA
Ozerov, Lev
   Babi Yar. VoWA
Ozick, Cynthia
   A riddle. VoWA
   The wonder-teacher. VoWA
Ozymandias. Percy Bysshe
   Shelley. DoNG--LiHE

P'an Shu
   The ancient temple of Hsiang
      Yu. GrAC
P'ei Ti
   Striped apricot lodge. GrAC
Pacernick, Gary
   I want to write a Jewish poem.
      VoWA
Pacific Ocean
   Once by the Pacific. Robert
      Frost. HaAP--MTS
   The slow Pacific swell. Yvor
      Winters. MTS
Pacific sonnets, sels. George
   Barker. MTS
Pack, Robert
   The kiss. TeMP
   The ring. FroA
Packard, William
   On the anniversary of my dying.
      DoNG
   Peaceable kingdom, sels. DoNG
   Tell us/what things die. DoNG
Packwood, Patty
   Forever friend. YoVA
Padilla, Lindy
   Isn't it funny? YoVA
Paean our chant triumphal...
   Jean Dorat. ReLP
Paedotrophia. Scevole (G.) de
   Sainte-Marthe. ReLP
Pagan, Isabel
   Ca' the yowes. WBP2
Page from the Koran. James
   Merrill. TeMP
Pagis, Don
   Autobiography. VoWA
   Brothers. VoWA
   Draft of a reparations
      agreement. VoWA
   The grand duke of New York.
      VoWA
   Instructions for crossing the
      border. VoWA
   The last ones. VoWA
   Scrawled in pencil... VoWA
   The tower. VoWA
Pagliarani, Elio
   Humbly I confess that I am
      mortal. NeIP
   Love song ("You had the
      legs...") NeIP
   Narcissus pseudonarcissus. NeIP
   Poeme antipoeme. NeIP
   Subjects and arguments
      for...desperation. NeIP
Pahlevi, M.Reza (shah of Iran)
   The shah of Iran. Rick Gurley.
      YoVA

A **pail/Against** a fence. Doug
   Penner. YoVA
Pain. Sally Ann Miemietz. YoVA
Pain. Patricia Flannery. YoVA
Pain
   After great pain, a formal
     feeling comes. Emily
     Dickinson. HaAP--LiHE
   The drunkenness of pain. Aliza
     Shenhar. VoWA
   Farewell, ungrateful traitor.
     John Dryden. HaAP
   How it is. Uri Zvi Greenberg.
     VoWA
   The hurt. Heather Wiegand. YoVA
   Pain. Sally Ann Miemietz. YoVA
   Preludes. Thomas Stearns Eliot.
     SlW
   Shechem. David Shevin. VoWA
   Small bone ache. Moshe Dor.
     VoWA
   Soul tattoos. Wendy Rose. ReE
Painted men. Stanford K. Acomb.
   YoVA
The **painter**. John Ashbery. SlW
Painter, Terri
   The dream of a rose. HoWM
The **painting**. Mark Dunnagan.
   HoWM
Painting. A.C. Jacobs. VoWA
Painting and Painters
   Approaching the canvas.
     Kathleen Spivack. TeMP
   The beacons. Charles
     Baudelaire. FoFS
   The Czech master Teodoryk,
     sels. Jerzy Harasymowicz. CoP
   The emotional painting.
     Sherlene Merritt. HoWM
   The enemy's portrait. Thomas
     Hardy. TyW
   Homage to Edward Hopper. Emery
     George. HoA
   Musee des Beaux Arts. Wystan
     Hugh Auden. HaAP--LiHE
   My last duchess. Robert
     Browning. HaAP--LiHE
   Nikos painting. Kenneth O.
     Hanson. FroA
   Of a painter and a baker.
     Theodore de Beze. ReLP
   The painter. John Ashbery. SlW
   The painting. Mark Dunnagan.
     HoWM
   Pictures on the wall. Zvi
     Shargel. VoWA
   Pisanello's studies of men
     hanging... John Wheatcroft.
     FroA
   Seeing Grand Secretary

     Yu's...mural. Wang Chi-yu.
     GrAC
   To S.M.a young African
     painter... Phillis Wheatley.
     BlS
   To be an artist. Peggi Jackson.
     YoVA
   What is left? Istvan Vas. VoWA
   Why I am not a painter. Frank
     O'Hara. HoA
Painting of an underground
   river. Mark Bobbitt. HoWM
Palabras carinosas. Thomas
   Bailey Aldrich. WBP2
Palaces
   Song ("The palace of
     Yoshino...") Yamabe no
     Akahito . FroC
   Strong feelings, sel. Hsueh Chu.
     GrAC
   Yu-hua Palace. Tu Fu. GrAC
The **Palatine**. John Greenleaf
   Whittier. MTS
Palgrave, Francis Turner
   A little child's hymn. WBP1
Palinode. James Russell Lowell.
   WBP3
Pallais, Azarias H.
   Granada and Leon. NiR
Pallbearer. Kenneth Lovell. YoVA
The **pallid** thunderstricken sigh
   for gain. Alfred, Lord
   Tennyson. TyW
The **palm** and the pine. Heinrich
   Heine. WBP3
The **palm** and the pine. R. Milnes
   (Lord Houghton)(tr). WBP3
Palmanteer, Ted
   Pass it on grandson. ReE
Palmer, John Williamson
   For Charlie's sake. WBP3
   Thread and song. WBP1
Palmer, Kelly
   Is it really? YoVA
   The poets know it. YoVA
Palmer, Ray
   I saw thee. WBP4
Palmer, William Pitt
   The smack in school. WBP1
The **pan**, the pot, the burning
   fire... Ishigaki Rin. FroC
Pancasan. Ricardo Morales
   Aviles. NiR
Pancharis: I. Jean Bonefons.
   ReLP
Pancharis: XVI. Jean Bonefons.
   ReLP
Pancharis: XXIV. Jean Bonefons.
   ReLP
Panchito rubble. Carlos Mejia

Godoy. NiR
Pandora
  Faustina...more suitably named
    Pandora. Joachim Du Bellay.
    ReLP
Panegyric. Harris Lenowitz. VoWA
The **pangolin.** Marianne Moore.
    HaAP
Pankovich, Cary
  Teenage crush. YoVA
Pao Chao
  Hard traveling, sels. GrAC
Papuan folk songs, sels.
    Unknown. VooI
Paque, Mary Jo
  Selfish beauty. YoVA
A **parable.** Mathilde Blind. WBP1
Parable: November. Stephen
    Tapscott. FroA
Parables
  The bayonet and the needle.
    Eliezer Steinbarg. VoWA
  The horse and the whip. Eliezer
    Steinbarg. VoWA
  Shatnes or uncleanliness.
    Eliezer Steinbarg. VoWA
  The umbrella, the cane, and the
    broom. Eliezer Steinbarg.
    VoWA
The **parade.** David Moore. YoVA
Parades
  The parade. David Moore. YoVA
Paradise. Willis Barnstone. VoWA
Paradise. Frederick William
    Faber. WBP4
Paradise. Chana Bloch. VoWA
Paradise
  On the road to paradise.
    Garrett Hongo. HoA
Paradise lost, sels. John
    Milton. WBP4
Paradise lost, sels. John
    Milton. LiHE--TyW
Paradise lost, sels. John
    Milton. WBP2
Paradise lost, sels. John
    Milton. MTS
Paradise regained, sels. John
    Milton. PoCh
Paradiso, sels. Dante Alighieri.
    DoNG
A **paradox,** sels. Georgia Douglas
    Johnson. BlS
A **paragraph.** Hayden Carruth.
    FroA
The **pardon.** Richard Wilbur. LiHE
The **pardoner's** tale. Geoffrey
    Chaucer. HaAP
The **parent.** Ogden Nash. IlTH
Parenthood

Advice to my son. J. Peter
    Meinke. LiHE
Changing the children. Maxine
    Kumin. StPo
A farewell. Charles Kingsley.
    WBP1
Father and sons. Harvey
    Shapiro. FroA
For the parents of a dead chil.
    Ryokan . FroC
Frost at midnight. Samuel
    Taylor Coleridge. HaAP
Genitori. David Ray. TyW
I am here. Robert Mezey. VoWA
On my first son. Ben Jonson.
    HaAP
The parent. Ogden Nash. IlTH
The spring of my life, sel.
    Kobayashi Issa . FroC
Suprised by joy-impatient as
    the wind. William Wordsworth.
    HaAP
To comfort my little son and
    daughter. Sugawara no
    Michizane. FroC
The **parents-without-partners**
    picnic. Ted Schaefer. FroA
Pariah. Tristan Corbiere. FreS
Paris by night. Joseph Milbauer.
    VoWA
Paris, France
  The next time you were there.
    Samuel Hazo. FroA
  Paris by night. Joseph
    Milbauer. VoWA
  Paris; this April sunset...
    Edward Estlin Cummings. SlW
  The southeast ramparts of the
    Seine. Judit Toth. VoWA
  Zone. Guillaume Apollinaire.
    SlW
Paris; this April sunset...
    Edward Estlin Cummings. SlW
Parisi, Philip
  Niagara Falls. FroA
Parisian dream. Charles
    Baudelaire. FoFS
The **park** at evening. Leslie
    Norris. DuD
"**Park** of silence, fatal
    opacity." Gustave Kahn. FreS
Park, Andrew
  The auld folks. WBP1
Parker, Douglas
  A friend. YoVA
Parker, Kim
  The dream of a lake. HoWM
Parker, Patricia
  From the cavities of bones. BlS
  I followed a path. BlS

There is a woman in this town.
  BlS
Parker, Theodore
  The higher good. WBP4
  The way, the truth, and the
    life. WBP4
Parker, Tim
  Jazz. HoWM
Parks
  The park at evening. Leslie
    Norris. DuD
Parnell, Thomas
  When your beauty appears. WBP2
Parrots
  "Little Poll Parrot." Mother
    Goose . MiRN
Parsifal. Paul Verlaine. FreS
Parted friends. James
    Montgomery. WBP1
Parties
  At the party. Patricia
    Goedicke. FroA
  Aubade after the party. Tom
    O'Grady. FroA
Parting. Coventry Patmore. WBP3
Parting. Wang Chih-huan. GrAC
Parting. Wang Wei. GrAC
Parting. Shlomo Vinner. VoWA
Parting. Gabriel Preil. VoWA
Parting. Michelle J. Modde. YoVA
Parting at morning. Robert
    Browning. MTS
Parting from Li Tuan. Lu Lun.
    GrAC
Parting from Wang Wei. Meng
    Hao-jan. GrAC
A **parting** hymn. Charlotte Forten
    (Grimke). BlS
The **parting** lovers. William R.
    Alger (trans.). WBP3
A **parting** talk with Seigan. Rai
    San'yo. FroC
Parting. See Separation
Parts. Zishe Landau. VoWA
Pasa thalassa thalassa. Edwin
    Arlington Robinson. MTS
Pasi, Geeta
  Nature's gem. YoVA
  Where do I go? YoVA
Pasolini, Pier Paolo
  The day of my death. NeIP
  The ditchdigger's tears, sels.
    NeIP
  February. NeIP
  Gramsci's ashes. NeIP
  The ring. NeIP
  A sea promenade. NeIP
  The sun, the sun. NeIP
Pasos, Joaquin
  Kick them out with violence, if

need be. NiR
Pasos, Joaquin
  Epitaph for Joaquin Pasos.
    Ernesto Cardenal. NiR
Pass and regret. Annette L. Roy.
    YoVA
Pass it on grandson. Ted
    Palmanteer. ReE
Passage. Richard Eberhart. FroA
The **passage.** Sarah Taylor Austin
    (trans.). WBP3
The **passage.** Ludwig Uhland. WBP3
A **passage** in the life of Saint
    Augustine. Unknown. WBP4
Passage steamer. Louis MacNeice.
    MTS
Passages. Maria Kohr. YoVA
Passer mortus est. Edna St.
    Vincent Millay. DoNG
A **passer-by.** Robert Bridges. MTS
Passing away. John Pierpont.
    WBP4
Passing by the wasted capital in
    Omi. Kakinomoto no Hitomaro.
    FroC
The **passionate** shepherd to his
    love. Christopher Marlowe.
    WBP2
The **passionate** shepherd to his
    love. Christopher Marlowe.
    HaAP--LiHE
Passover. Rose Auslander. VoWA
Passover
  Passover. Rose Auslander. VoWA
  Seder, 1944. Friedrich Torberg.
    VoWA
  to an ancient sanctuary during
    holy-week. Muriel Fath. StPo
The **past.** Yoshioka Minoru. FroC
The **past.** Sherry Carman. YoVA
Past ruined Ilion Helen lives.
    Walter Savage Landor. HaAP
Pastan, Linda
  After reading Nelly Sachs. VoWA
  At the Jewish Museum. VoWA
  Elsewhere. VoWA
  Ethics. TeMP
  In the old guerilla war. TyW
  Pears. VoWA
  Why not? FroA
  Yom Kippur. VoWA
Pasternak, Boris L.
  To Boris Pasternak. Aleksandr
    Kuskner. VoWA
The **pastor's** reverie. Washington
    Gladden. WBP4
Pastoral Lusus. Marcantonio
    Flaminio. ReLP
Pastorale. Yoshioka Minoru. FroC
The **pasture.** Robert Frost. RoRF

Patapan. Bernard De la Monnoye.
    PoCh
Patchen, Kenneth
    The lute in the attic. DoNG
    O all down within the pretty
        meadow. HaAP
Patel, Pulin
    "I, silence am always last."
        HoWM
Paterson, Evangeline
    And that will be heaven. EeBC
    Death on a crossing. EeBC
Paths. Rina Lasnier. MoVT
The paths of prayer. Edouard
    Roditi. VoWA
Paths to God. Musa Moris Farni.
    VoWA
Patience. Paul Hamilton Hayne.
    WBP4
Patience
    The angel of patience. John
        Greenleaf Whittier. WBP3
    i have sat through sunlight.
        Nia Francisco. ReE
    On his blindness. John Milton.
        EeBC--HaAP
    Patience taught by nature.
        Elizabeth Barrett Browning.
        EeBC
    Patience. Paul Hamilton Hayne.
        WBP4
    Sonnet XVII. John Milton. LiHE
Patience taught by nature.
        Elizabeth Barrett Browning.
        EeBC
Patmore, Coventry
    The angel in the house, sels.
        WBP2
    The girl of all periods. WBP1
    A London fete. HaAP
    Magna est veritas. HaAP
    Parting. WBP3
    The revelation. HaAP
    Sly thoughts. WBP2
    Sweet meeting of desires. WBP2
Patricide
    Edward. Unknown . HaAP
    Edward. Unknown . LiHE--TyW
    Etchin. Tamura Ryuichi . FroC
Patriotism
    Pariah. Tristan Corbiere. FreS
    Poly-olbion, sels. Michael
        Drayton. ShBa
    To be an American. Scott
        McCartney. YoVA
Patroling Barnegat. Walt
    Whitman. MTS
Patten, Karl
    Wreathmakertraining. FroA
Patterson, Chris

Fall. YoVA
Pollution. YoVA
Patterson, Karen Elizabeth
    Darkness/It drowns within
        itself. YoVA
    A song of fall. YoVA
Paudeen. William Butler Yeats.
    HaAP
Pauketat, Elizabeth
    Fog. YoVA
Paul, James
    Everything. HoA
    Feet, a sermon. HoA
    Honeysuckle. HoA
    This town. HoA
Paul, Saint
    The conversion of Saint Paul.
        John Keble. WBP4
Paulson, Pennie M.
    Memories. YoVA
The pauper's drive. Thomas Noel.
    WBP3
Pause a moment. Asya. VoWA
A pavane for the nursery.
    William Jay Smith. DuD
Payne, David
    At the nursing home. YoVA
    Ode to grammer. YoVA
Payne, John Howard
    Clari, the maid of Milan, sels.
        WBP1
    Home, sweet home. WBP1
Payne, Sandra
    Evermore. YoVA
    Wind bends. YoVA
Peace. George Herbert. WBP4
Peace. Gerard Manley Hopkins.
    EeBC
Peace. Frances Ridley Havergal.
    WBP4
Peace. Unknown. WBP3
Peace. Michelle Yancy. YoVA
Peace. Henry Vaughan. HaAP--WBP4
Peace
    After the raiders have gone.
        Yuan Chieh . GrAC
    Aspects of the sea. Sharon
        Watson. YoVA
    Forty years peace. Arye Sivan.
        VoWA
    A grasshopper. Richard Wilbur.
        HaAP
    Peace Unknown . WBP3
    Peace. Frances Ridley Havergal.
        WBP4
    Peace. George Herbert. WBP4
    Peace. Gerard Manley Hopkins.
        EeBC
    Peace. Michelle Yancy. YoVA
    Pleading voices. Shalom Katav.

VoWA

Peace Corps
Breakfast. Beltran Morales. NiR
Peaceable kingdom, sels. William
Packard. DoNG
A peaceful song. Natan Zach.
VoWA
Peaches
The little peach. Eugene Field.
IlTH
Peacock, Thomas Love
The war-song of Dinas Vawr.
HaAP
Peale, Rembrandt
Faith and hope. WBP2
Pear Trees
Pears. Linda Pastan. VoWA
To a blossoming pear tree.
James Wright. HaAP
The pearl. George Herbert. HaAP
Pearls
Sixty-four tanka. Saigyo.   FroC
Pearls of the faith, sels. Sir
Edwin Arnold. WBP3
Pears. Linda Pastan. VoWA
Pearse, Padraic
Last lines-1916. LiHE
Peasant mass. Carlos Mejia
Godoy. NiR
The peasant women of Cua.
Ernesto Cardenal. NiR
Peasants
Market day. Roberto Roversi.
NeIP
The Swiss peasant. Oliver
Goldsmith. WBP1
To the waggoner's daughter.
Rocco Scotellaro. NeIP
Pebble, sels. Zbigniew Herbert.
CoP
Peck, Samuel Minturn
Dollie. WBP1
A knot of blue. WBP1
My little girl. WBP1
Peddlers and Peddling
Fine knacks for ladies. Unknown.
HaAP
Pedlar. Sharon Nelson. VoWA
Pedlar. Sharon Nelson. VoWA
Peg Leg Snelson. Melvin B.
Tolson. FroA
Peg of Limavaddy. William
Makepeace Thackeray. WBP1
Pei
The hill of Hua-Tzu. LuL
The hill of the hatchet-leaved
bamboos. LuL
Pelicans
"A wonderful bird is the
pelican." Unknown . IlTH

Pembroke, Countess (about)
On the Countess Dowager of
Pembroke. William Browne.
HaAP
Pembroke, Mary S., Countess of
A dialogue betweene two
shepheards, sels. PaW
The dolefull lay of Clorinda,
sels. PaW
Pencils
Personified pencil. Lisa Thoms.
YoVA
Penelope. Lois Marie Harrod.
StPo
Penelope, unweaving. Patricia
Celley Groth. StPo
Peninger, Paul
"In my hands I have memories."
HoWM
A penitent considers...coming of
Mary. Gwendolyn Brooks. PoCh
The Pennacesse Leper Colony for
Women... Norman Dubie. TeMP
Penner, Doug
Castles/Just waiting. YoVA
Lapping waves/cooling rinsing
the sand. YoVA
A pail/Against a fence. YoVA
Penner, Roseann
Dream on. YoVA
Penny pictures. Paul Verlaine.
FreS
Pensacola, Florida
Travels in the south. Simon J.
Ortiz. ReE
Pentecost. Ai. TeMP
Pentecost. John Bennett. EeBC
Pentecost
Pentecost. John Bennett. EeBC
The Pentecost castle, sels.
Geoffrey Hill. HaAP
Peony fallen. Yosa Buson. FroC
People. Carolyn Heide. YoVA
People
People. Carolyn Heide. YoVA
"People from the stars." Carter
Revard. ReE
People rush/push. Colleen
Hartley. YoVA
Per pacem ad lucem. Adelaide
Anne Procter. WBP4
Perceptions
Illusion. Laury Powers. YoVA
A realitic point of view. Tammy
Scheid. YoVA
Percolating highway. Michael
Castro. VoWA
Percy, Thomas
The friar of orders gray. WBP2
The perfect couple. Kitty Druck.

StPo

The **perfect** gift. Edmund Vance
Cooke. PoCh

"**Perfect** rainbow arc." Kitty
Druck. StPo

The **perfection** of snow. Andrea
Zanzotto. NeIP

Perfume. Edmund William Gosse.
WBP2

Perhaps. Rachel Blaustein
(Bluwstein). BuAC--VoWA

Perhaps its only music. Natan
Zach. VoWA

Pericles, sels. William
Shakespeare. MTS

Period piece. Bruce Berlind.
FroA

A **periphrastic** insult, not a
banal. James Vincent
Cunningham. TyW

Perished. Mary Louise Ritter.
WBP3

Perkins, Gwen
Irritated. YoVA
That enchanted place. YoVA

Perkoff, Stuart Z.
Aleph. VoWA
Gimel. VoWA
Hai. VoWA

Perry, Nora
The love-knot. WBP2
Riding down. WBP1

Perserverance
Try agai. Unknown . WBP1

Persian miniature. Jane Shore.
TeMP

Person, Kristin
Maranatha. YoVA

The **personals**. Alan Feldman.
TeMP

Personified pencil. Lisa Thoms.
YoVA

The **perspective** and limits of
snapshots. Dave Smith. TeMP

Peseroff, Joyce
Approaching absolute zero. TeMP

Pessimism
Of three or four in a room.
Yehuda Amichai. VoWA
To Raja Rao, sels. Czeslaw
Milosz. CoP

"The **petals** of your face." James
F. King. StPo

Peter Pan
Who am I. Edward Williams. HoWM

Peters, Tiffany
Picture 4. HoWM

Peterson, Laura
A false face in a bottle. YoVA
Life goes on. YoVA

Peterson, Robert
Robert's Rules of Order. FroA

A **petition** to time. Barry
Cornwall (B.W. Procter). WBP1

Petrarch, Francesco
Ecologue II: Argus. ReLP

Peyser, Shoshana
Sunrise. YoVA

Pfingston, Roger
About the cows. FroA
Waiting for nighthawks in
Illinois. FroA

Phantasus: I, 8. Arno Holz. PoCh

A **phantom**. Charles Baudelaire.
FoFS

Pharaoh and Joseph. Else
Lasker-Schuler. VoWA

Pheasant. Nishiwaki Junzaburo.
FroC

Pheasants
Pheasan. Nishiwaki Junzaburo .
FroC

Philip Van Artevelde, sels. Sir
Henry Taylor. WBP1

Philip, Sir Sidney
The dolefull lay of Clorinda,
sels. Mary S., Countess of
Pembroke. PaW

Philip, my king. Dinah Maria
Mulock Craik. WBP1

Philips, Katherine
An answer to another persuading
a lady... HaAP

Phillida and Corydon. Nicholas
Breton. WBP2

Phillips (trans.), Ambrose
Blest as the immortal gods.
WBP2

Phillips, Frank Lamont
A special moment. FroA

Phillips, Nancy
A solitary tear. YoVA

Phillis is my only love. Sir
Charles Sedley. WBP2

Philomela's ode. Robert Greene.
WBP2

philonous' paradox. Chris
Gilbert. FroA

The **philosopher** toad. Rebecca S.
Nichols. WBP4

Philosophy and Philosophers
In a lecture-room. Arthur Hugh
Clough. WBP4
On philosopher. Unknown . TyW

Philostratus
The forest, sels. WBP2

The **phoenix**. Matti Megged. VoWA

Phoenix. Rose Auslander. VoWA

Phoenix
The phoenix. Matti Megged. VoWA

The **phoenix** of Mozart. Claude
    Vigee. VoWA
Photograph. Cindy Niemi. YoVA
Photography and Photographers
    Lines on a young lady's
        photograph album. Philip
        Larkin. HaAP
    The opposite field. Dabney
        Stuart. TeMP
    The perspective and limits of
        snapshots. Dave Smith. TeMP
The **photos** from summer camp.
    Izora Corpman. FroA
Phraseology. Jayne Cortez. BlS
Physicians
    Delighted that Jippo has come..
        Rai San'yo . FroC
    Doctor's row. Conrad Aiken.
        HaAP
    Epigram: on doctors. Euricius
        Cordus. ReLP
Physiologus, sels. Unknown. MTS
Piano. David Herbert Lawrence.
    HaAP
"The **piano** that a frail hand
    kisses..." Paul Verlaine.
    FoFS
Pianos
    Lament of the pianos..rich
        neighborhoods. Jules
        Laforgue. FreS
    "The piano that a frail hand
        kisses..." Paul Verlaine.
        FoFS
    Piano. David Herbert Lawrence.
        HaAP
Piatt, John James
    To a lady. WBP2
Piatt, Sarah Morgan Bryan
    The term of death. WBP3
    The witch in the glass. WBP1
Picasso. Robbie Whitfield. HoWM
Picasso, Pablo
    Picasso. Robbie Whitfield. HoWM
Pickles
    Cucumbers to pickles. Tammy A.
        Osburn. YoVA
A **picture.** Charles Gamage
    Eastman. WBP1
Picture 4. Tiffany Peters. HoWM
A **picture** of death. George
    Gordon,6th Baron Byron. WBP3
Picture postcards. Miklos
    Radnoti. VoWA
Pictures of memory. Alice Cary.
    WBP1
Pictures on the wall. Zvi
    Shargel. VoWA
Pied beauty. Gerard Manley
    Hopkins. EeBC--HaAP

Pied beauty. Gerard Manley
    Hopkins. LiHE--SlW
Piedmont, Italy
    On the late massacre in
        Piedmont. John Milton. HaAP
Pierce, Carolyn D.
    God's child. YoVA
Pierce, Jackie
    The clown. YoVA
    New thought. YoVA
Pierce, Loretta
    Balloons. YoVA
Piercy, Marge
    Gracious goodness. HoA
    Night fight. TeMP
    The root canal. HoA
    To be of use. HoA
Pierpont, John
    My child. WBP3
    Passing away. WBP4
    Whittling. WBP1
Pies
    A-apple pie. Walter De La Mare.
        MiRN
    "Baby and I/Were baked in a
        pie." Unknown . IlTH
    "If all the world were apple
        pie." Unknown . IlTH
    Punch and Jud. Unknown . RoRF
The **pig.** Ogden Nash. IlTH
Pigeons. Russell Edson. TeMP
Pigeons
    A dawn of Jaffa pigeons. Eli
        Bachar. VoWA
    from Janie. Faye Kicknosway.
        TeMP
    Mrs. Peck-Pigeon. Eleanor
        Farjeon. RoRF
    Pigeons. Russell Edson. TeMP
Pignotti, Lamberto
    Poetry and politics. NeIP
    Reductions, sels. NeIP
    Zero life, sels. NeIP
Pigs
    Birds of a feathe. Mother Goose.
        MiRN
    Hog at the manger. Norma
        Farber. PoCh
    The little pig. Zishe Landau. .
        VoWA
    Moly. Thomson Gunn. HaAP
    The pig. Ogden Nash. IlTH
    Roland the minstrel pig.
        William Steig. TrWB
    This one is about the others.
        Dan Jaffe. FroA
    Today they are roasting Rocky
        Norse. Gary Gildner. TeMP
Pike. Ted Hughes. HaAP
Pike

Pike. Ted Hughes. HaAP

The pilgrim's song. John Bunyan.
EeBC

The pilgrimage. Sir Walter
Ralegh. EeBC--WBP4

The pilgrimage to Testour. Ryvel
(Raphael Levy). VoWA

Pilgrimages and Pilgrims
Pilgrims. Joseph Brodsky. VoWA

Pilgrims. Joseph Brodsky. VoWA

The pill. Austin Clarke. TyW

Pillen, William
Farewell to Europe. VoWA
Night poem in an abandoned
music room. VoWA
O, beautiful they move. VoWA
Ode on a decision to settle for
less. VoWA
Poem ("To be sad in the
morning.") VoWA
A poem for Anton Schmidt. VoWA

Pilon, Jean-Guy
Shades. MoVT
Trees. MoVT

The pilot's day of rest. Lee
Gerlach. HoA

The pilot's walk. Lee Gerlach.
HoA

Pilpul. Rodger Kamenetz. VoWA

Pincas, Israel
Mediterranean. VoWA

Pindar (John Wolcott), Peter
To Chloe. WBP2

Pine Trees
Among the pine trees. Moshe
Dor. VoWA
Pine resin, sel. Arakida
Moritake . FroC
"there was one gigantic pine
tree..." Jing Hao . LuL
Trees at night. Helene Johnson.
BlS

Pine resin, sels. Arakida
Moritake. FroC

Pinkney, Edward Coate
A health. WBP2

Pinks and a blue cat. Hagiwara
Sakutaro. FroC

Pinsky, Robert
Tennis. TeMP

Pintye, Carolyn
Albert Einstein. StPo
I watch my daughter running.
StPo
Leo Tolstoy. StPo

Pioneers. See Frontier

The piper. William Blake. WBP1

Piper, Linda
Missionaries in the jungle. BlS
Sweet Ethel. BlS

Pipers
The piper. William Blake. WBP1

Pipling. Theodore Roethke. TyW

Pippa passes, sels. Robert
Browning. WBP4

Pippa's song. Robert Browning.
EeBC

Pisanello's studies of men
hanging... John Wheatcroft.
FroA

Piscatory eclogue II: Galatea.
Jacopo Sannazaro. ReLP

Pittman, Al
Roger was a razor fish. RoRF

Pity for dissolution, sels. Yuan
Chieh. GrAC

Pitying himself...the execution
place. Prince Arima
(640-658). FroC

Pius IX, Pope
To Pius IX. John Greenleaf
Whittier. TyW

Pizarnik, Alejandra
Apart from oneself. VoWA
Dawn. VoWA
The mask and the poem. VoWA
Privilege. VoWA
The tree of Diana. VoWA
Vertigos or contemplation of
something... VoWA
Who will stop his hand... VoWA

Placard. Mario Cajina Vega. NiR

Place me under your wing. Hayim
Nachman Bialik. VoWA

Places
Where do these steps lead?
Gavriela Elisha. BuAC

Plague
A litany in time of plague.
Thomas Nashe. LiHE

A plague of starlings. Robert
Hayden. HoA

The plaidie. Charles Sibley.
WBP2

Plain song. Benjamin Fondane
(Fundoianu). VoWA

Plain, humble letters. David
Vogel. VoWA

The planet on the table. Wallace
Stevens. HaAP

Plankton
Extinction of plankton. Ono
Tozaburo. FroC

Plant Life
"Clenched against winter."
Martha W. McKenzie. StPo
Seventy-six hokku. Matsuo Basho.
FroC

Planting melons. Wei Ying-wu.
GrAC

Plants and Planting
    And the silver turns into
        night. Nathan Yonathan. VoWA
    Cattails. Debbie Farrar. YoVA
    Greenhouse. Phyllis Janik. PrVo
    Nocturn cabbage. Carl Sandburg.
        DuD
    The toadstool wood. James
        Reeves. DuD
Plants-Artifical
    Six small songs for a silver
        flute. Barry Spacks. TeMP
    Squash blossom shit and heishi
        horrors. Luci Abeita. ReE
Plath, Sylvia
    Blackberrying. HaAP
    Daddy. LiHE--TyW
    Full fathom five. MTS
    Mirror. HaAP
    Tulips. HaAP
Plath, Sylvia (about)
    On the death of Sylvia Plath.
        Judith Herzberg. VoWA
Plato, Ann
    The natives of America. BlS
    Reflections on visiting the
        grave... BlS
    To the first of August. BlS
Platonic. William B. Terrett.
    WBP1
The **playboy** of the demi-world:
    1938. William Plomer. TyW
Player. Stephen Dunning. FroA
Playful poem. Chiao-jan. GrAC
Playful quatrains, sels. Tu Fu.
    GrAC
Playing Cards
    The rape of the lock. Alexander
        Pope. HaAP
Plea for the future. Kelli
    Stevens. YoVA
Pleading voices. Shalom Katav.
    VoWA
Please leave. Patricia Crandall.
    YoVA
Please say something. Tomioka
    Taeko. FroC
The **pleasures** of hope, sels.
    Thomas Campbell. WBP4
Pledge. Avraham Shlonsky. VoWA
Plescoff, Jorge
    The ladder has no steps. VoWA
    Ourobouros. VoWA
    Tongues of fire. VoWA
    Violins in repose. VoWA
Plomer, William
    The playboy of the demi-world:
        1938. TyW
Ploughing on Sunday. Wallace
    Stevens. SlW

Plowing
    Ploughing on Sunday. Wallace
        Stevens. SlW
A **plum.** Mani Leib. VoWA
The **plumber** arrives at Three
    Mile Island. Robert Stewart.
    FroA
Plumly, Stanley
    Summer celestial. TeMP
Plums
    A plum. Mani Leib. VoWA
    Thirty-five Tanka. Ki no
        Tsurayuki.   FroC
    This is just to say. William
        Carlos Williams. SlW
    To a poor old woman. William
        Carlos Williams. SlW
The **plundered** heart. Arthur
    Rimbaud. FoFS
Poe, Edgar Allan
    The city in the sea. MTS
    For Annie. WBP3
    The haunted palace. EvIm
    Sonnet - to science. TyW
    To Helen. HaAP--WBP2
    To one in paradise.

Poe, Edgar Allan (about)
    The tomb of Edgar Allan Poe.
        Stephane Mallarme. FoFS--FreS
Poem ("Hate is only one of
    many...") Frank O'Hara. SlW
A **poem** ("High and lofty, tiers
    of rock.") Su Shi. LuL
Poem ("In the earnest path of
    duty.") Charlotte Forten
    (Grimke). BlS
Poem ("Love being what it
    is...") Ruth Herschberger.
    HoA
Poem ("There I could never be a
    boy") Frank O'Hara. HoA
Poem ("To be sad in the
    morning") William Pillen.
    VoWA
Poem ("think of filth...), sels.
    Frank O'Hara. TyW
Poem 25. Norma Edith Egea. StPo
Poem 25. Edith R. Kaltovich
    (trans.). StPo
Poem about your face. Nathan
    Alterman. VoWA
Poem at thirty. Sonia Sanchez.
    BlS
A **poem** for Anton Schmidt.
    William Pillen. VoWA
Poem for a stone. Rokwaho
    (Daniel Thompson). ReE
A **poem** for black hearts. I.
    Amiri Baraka (LeRoi Jones).

TyW
Epigram on the refusal of the
   university. William Cowper.
   TyW
Estienne. Peter Klappert. TeMP
Etamines narrative. Takiguchi
   Shuzo . FroC
Face on the daguerreotype.
   Norman Rosten. HoA
Finders keepers. Donald Finkel.
   VoWA
For an art of poetry 3. Raymond
   Queneau. MoVT
For the white poets who would
   be Indian. Wendy Rose. ReE
Four ways of writing one poem.
   Hemda Roth. BuAC
Get you to the hell.... Caius
   Valerius Catullus. TyW
Goldenmouthed. Stuart Merrill.
   FreS
"Honeysuckle was the saddest
   odor..." Thadious M. Davis.
   BlS
How did they fume, and
   stamp,and roar... Alexander
   Pope. TyW
How pleasant to know Mr. Lear!
   Edward Lear. HaAP
How to write a poem. Rick
   Gurley. YoVA
Hugh Selwyn Mauberley, sels.
   Ezra Pound. HaAP
I am like a book. David Rokeah.
   VoWA
I didn't find light by
   accident. Hayim Nachman
   Bialik. VoWA
"I dream of gentle verse..."
   Albert Samain. FreS
I often want to let my lines
   go. Leib Neidus. VoWA
I tried to write a poem. Della
   Rose. YoVA
If all went up in smoke. George
   Oppen. VoWA
In a spring still not written
   of. Robert Wallace. LiHE
In my craft or sullen art.
   Dylan Thomas. HaAP
Ite. Ezra Pound. HaAP
January morning. William Carlos
   Williams. SlW
Jordan (I). George Herbert.
   HaAP
A Judezmo writer in Turkey
   angry. Stephen Levy. VoWA
The land of poetry, sels.
   Czeslaw Milosz. CoP
Large red man reading. Wallace

Stevens. HaAP
Memo. Hans Sahl. VoWA
Miklos Radnoti. Willis
   Barnstone. VoWA
Money in the bank. W.D.
   Ehrhart. FroA
Move on, Yiddish poet. Jacob
   Glatstein. VoWA
My white book of poems. Rachel
   Blaustein (Bluwstein). VoWA
Myopia. Giancarlo Majorino.
   NeIP
Napis, sels. Zbigniew Herbert.
   CoP
Ode ("Though loath to grieve.")
   Ralph Waldo Emerson. HaAP
An ode to himself, sels. Ben
   Jonson. ShBa
On a day off going to meet
   Censor Wang.. Wei Ying-wu .
   GrAC
On being head of the English
   department. Pinkie Gordon
   Lane. BlS
On burning a dull poem.
   Jonathan Swift. TyW
On first looking into Chapman's
   Homer. John Keats. HaAP--LiHE
On poetry: a rhapsody, sels.
   Jonathan Swift. HaAP
On the margins of a poem. Jiri
   Mordecai Langer. VoWA
One poet visits another. W.H.
   Davies. TyW
Only joy, now here you are. Sir
   Philip Sidney. HaAP
The planet on the table.
   Wallace Stevens. HaAP
A poem-good or bad-a
   thing...-flat. Melech Ravitch
   (Z.K. Bergner). VoWA
Poem? Joan Gable. YoVA
Poeme antipoeme. Elio
   Pagliarani. NeIP
The poet lives. Jacob
   Glatstein. VoWA
Poetastery. David Bedell. YoVA
Poetry ("I too, dislike it...")
   Marianne Moore. HaAP
Poetry and politics. Lambert6
   Pignotti. NeIP
The poets know it. Kelly
   Palmer. YoVA
The poor poet, sels. Czeslaw
   Milosz. CoP
Powdered stars. Vita C. Ungaro.
   StPo
Psalmodist. Mani Leib. VoWA
Raisins and nuts. Charles
   Reznikoff. VoWA

The poppy. Cid Corman. HoA
Popping corn. Unknown. WBP2
The poppy. Cid Corman. HoA
Porphyria's lover. Robert
    Browning. HaAP
Port admiral. Frederick Marryat.
    MTS
Port of many ships. John
    Masefield. MTS
Porta, Antonio
    Beaver skin. NeIP
    Dialogue with Herz. NeIP
    Europa rides a black bull. NeIP
    Human relations, sels. NeIP
    Nomad's utopia. NeIP
    To open. NeIP
    The wind blows on the border.
        NeIP
    Zero, sels. NeIP
Portait of a widow. Avner
    Strauss. VoWA
Porter, Roy Arlington
    The quagmire of thought. YoVA
Porter, Susan
    The sun. YoVA
The portrait. Thomas Heywood.
    WBP2
A portrait. Elizabeth Barrett
    Browning. WBP1
Portrait. Madeline Mason. StPo
The portrait. Owen Meredith
    (Earl Lytton). WBP3
Portrait. John Unterecker. TeMP
Portrait in February. Lance
    Henson. ReE
A portrait of Judy. Ken Harvey.
    YoVA
The portrait of Prince Henry.
    Sydney Clouts. VoWA
Portrait of a man. Steve
    Denlinger. YoVA
Portrait of love. Cindy Loop.
    YoVA
The portrait's all feet. Rocco
    Scotellaro. NeIP
Ports
    Port of many ships. John
        Masefield. MTS
Porumbacu, Veronica
    Of autumn. VoWA
Poseidon's law. Rudyard Kipling.
    MTS
Posner, David
    Mourningsong for Anne. FroA
Possession. Owen Meredith (Earl
    Lytton). WBP2
Possession. Bayard Taylor. WBP2
Possessions. See Wealth
Postcard from London, 23. 10.
    1972. Andrew Salkey. FroA

A postcard from the volcano.
    Wallace Stevens. HaAP
Postcards. Mark Vinz. FroA
Posthius, Joannes
    Epigram: tobacco. ReLP
Pottery
    Anecdote of a jar. Wallace
        Stevens. SlW
    Jars. Paul Raboff. VoWA
    Pottery maker. Laura
        Watchempino. ReE
Pottery maker. Laura
    Watchempino. ReE
Potwor pan Cogito, sels.
    Zbigniew Herbert. CoP
Poulin, A., Jr.
    I woke up. Revenge. TyW
Poulsson, Emilie
    Santa Claus and the mouse. MiRN
Pound, Ezra
    Alba. HaAP--SlW
    Ancient music. TyW
    Canto II. HaAP
    Canto LXXXI, sels. HaAP
    Canto XLV. TyW
    Envoi (1919). HaAP
    The garden. SlW
    The garret. SlW
    Homage to Sextus Propertius,
        sels. HaAP
    Hugh Selwyn Mauberley, sels.
        HaAP
    In a station of the Metro. HaAP
    Ite. HaAP
    The return. HaAP
    The river merchant's wife: a
        letter. HaAP--SlW
    Separation on the river Kiang.
        SlW
    Sestina: Altaforte. SlW
    Taking leave of a friend. SlW
    A virginal. LiHE
Poverty
    Boy trash picker. Jim Howard.
        FroA
    Building a person. Stephen
        Dunn. FroA
    A dialogue on poverty. Yamanque
        no Okura. FroC
    Hard traveling, sel. Pao Chao.
        GrAC
    Over the hill to the
        poor-house. Will Carleton.
        WBP3
    The pauper's drive. Thomas
        Noel. WBP3
    The song of the shirt. Thomas
        Hood. WBP3
    "They are dear fish to me."
        Unknown. WBP3

Powdered stars. Vita C. Ungaro.
    StPo
Powell, Jana
    I wonder. YoVA
Powell, Todd
    The sun and its friends. HoWM
Power failure. Josephine
    Jacobsen. FroA
Powerless frog. Unknown. FroC
Powers, Laury
    Illusion. YoVA
Powwow. Carroll Arnett/Gogisgi.
    ReE
Powwow/and I am in your. Barney
    Bush. ReE
Practical Jokes
    A most delightful day. Sir
        William S. Gilbert. IlTH
The practice of absence. Robert
    Friend. VoWA
Praed, Winthrop Mackworth
    The newly-wedded. WBP2
Prague, Czechoslovakia
    In Prague. Paul Celan. VoWA
Praise. George Herbert. WBP4
Praise for an urn. Hart Crane.
    HaAP
Praise of the celestiral
    country. Bernard of Cluny
    (Morlaix). WBP4
Praise of the celestiral
    country. John Mason Neale
    (trans.). WBP4
Praise to God. Anna Letitia
    Barbauld. WBP4
Pratt, Anna Maria
    A mortifying mistake. WBP1
The prayer. Jones Very. EeBC
Prayer ("Forgive me, you...in a
    name.") Avraham Shlonsky.
    VoWA
Prayer ("From your high
    bridge...") Lev Mak. VoWA
Prayer ("When I was just a
    little mite.") Guillaume
    Apollinaire. MoVT
Prayer and answer. Oliver
    Huckel. WBP4
Prayer for Kafka and ourselves.
    Anthony Rudolf. VoWA
A prayer for a perfect day.
    Margaret Cameron. YoVA
A prayer for my daughter.
    William Butler Yeats.
    HaAP--TyW
Prayer for the great family.
    Gary Snyder. HaAP
A prayer for tomorrow's
    children. Karen Lidman. YoVA
Prayer of little hope. Jean

Wahl. VoWA
The prayer of the donkey. Carmen
    Bernos de Gasztold. PoCh
The prayer of the mouse. Carmen
    Bernos de Gasztold. MiRN
Prayer: "O God!though sorrow be
    my fate." Mary; Queen of
    Hungary. WBP4
The prayers. Howard Schwartz.
    VoWA
Prayers
    answering a late call. Muriel
        Fath. StPo
    The caliph and satan. James
        Freeman Clarke. WBP4
    Cherokee invocation. Raven
        Hail. ReE
    D'Avalos prayer. John
        Masefield. MTS
    The dark scent of prayer. Rose
        Drachler. VoWA
    Darkness is thinning. Saint
        Gregory the Great. WBP4
    Davening. Rochelle Ratner. VoWA
    Desire. Matthew Arnold. WBP4
    Divina commedia, I, sels. Henry
        Wadsworth Longfellow. HaAP
    Early song. Carroll
        Arnett/Gogisgi. ReE
    Evil prayers. Remy de Gourmont.
        FreS
    Exhortation to prayer. Margaret
        Mercer. WBP4
    For a religious service to God.
        Lady Otomo no Sakanoue. FroC
    From the recesses of a lowly
        spirit. Sir John Bowring.
        WBP4
    Hamlet, sels. William
        Shakespeare. WBP4
    The higher good. Theodore
        Parker. WBP4
    His answer. Clara Ann Thompson.
        BlS
    The journey with hands and
        arms. Benjamin Saltman. VoWA
    Kaddish. Allen Ginsberg. VoWA
    The ladder has no steps. Jorge
        Plescoff. VoWA
    Lord, listen. Else
        Lasker-Schuler. VoWA
    The morning prayers of...Rabbi
        L.Yitzhok. Phyllis Gottlieb.
        VoWA
    The paths of prayer. Edouard
        Roditi. VoWA
    A prayer for a perfect day.
        Margaret Cameron. YoVA
    A prayer for tomorrow's
        children. Karen Lidman. YoVA

The prayer of the mouse. Carmen
  Bernos de Gasztold. MiRN
The prayer. Jones Very. EeBC
Prayer: "O God!though sorrow be
  my fate." Mary; Queen of
  Hungary . WBP4
The prayers. Howard Schwartz.
  VoWA
Ritual to insure long life.
  Raven Hail. ReE
Scroll. Stanley Moss. VoWA
Seasons of prayer. Henry Ware
  (Jr.). WBP4
Selichos. Francis Landy. VoWA
Song of the closing service.
  Aliza Shenhar. VoWA
The time for prayer. G.
  Bennett. WBP4
Two went up into the temple to
  pray. Richard Crashaw.
  HaAP--WBP4
The unfinished prayer. Unknown.
  WBP1
The universal prayer. Alexander
  Pope. WBP4
What is prayer? James
  Montgomery. WBP4
The words. Norman H. Russell.
  ReE
Prayers to liberty. Anwar Shaul.
  VoWA
Pre-ponderance. Kathie A. Dame.
  StPo
Pre-positions. Jose Isaacson.
  VoWA
Predilictions. Alfredo Giuliani.
  NeIP
The prefectural engineer's
  statement... Miyazawa Kenji.
  FroC
Pregeometry. Martha W. McKenzie.
  StPo
Pregnancy
  men tell   and talk. Nia
    Francisco. ReE
  Misty dawn. Luci Tapahonso. ReE
Pregulman, Robert
  Blue collar. YoVA
Preil, Gabriel
  Arriving. VoWA
  Autumn music. VoWA
  Biographical note. VoWA
  Fishermen. VoWA
  From Jerusalem: a first poem.
    VoWA
  Giving up on the shore. VoWA
  A late manuscript...Schocken
    Institute. VoWA
  A lesson in translation. VoWA
  Letter out of the gray. VoWA

  Like David. VoWA
  Memory of another climate. VoWA
  Parting. VoWA
  Rains on the islands. VoWA
  A summing up. VoWA
  Words of oblivion and peace.
    VoWA
Preil, Gabriel (about)
  The grand duke of New York. Don
    Pagis. VoWA
Prelude. David Rosenmann-Taub.
  VoWA
The prelude, sels. William
  Wordsworth. HaAP--TyW
Preludes. Thomas Stearns Eliot.
  SlW
Prelutsky, Jack
  The troll. IlTH
Premonition. Tamura Ryuichi.
  FroC
Prentiss, Melody
  Reflections on the death of
    Scott Childs. YoVA
Preparatory meditations, sels.
  Edward Taylor. HaAP
The presence. Jones Very. HaAP
Presence. Anne Hebert. MoVT
The present. Franco Fortini.
  NeIP
The present good. William
  Cowper. WBP3
The present's presence. Joyce
  Quindipan. YoVA
The preserver. Stephen
  Updegraff. YoVA
Pressley, Anthony
  Neglected child. YoVA
Preston (trans.), Harriet W.
  Fidelty in doubt. WBP3
Preston, Annie A.
  The green grass under the snow.
    WBP3
Preston, Margaret Junkin
  Myrrh-bearers. WBP4
Pretending to sleep. Judith
  Thurman. ByM
Pretty cow. Jane Taylor. WBP1
The pretty girl of Loch Dan.
  Samuel Ferguson. WBP1
Prevert, Jacques
  Blood and feathers. MoVT
  Inventory. MoVT
  So many forests. MoVT
The price of a country. Fernando
  Gordillo. NiR
Price, Sarah
  Swimmer's ear. YoVA
Pride. Dahlia Ravikovich. BuAC
Pride and Vanity
  Canto LXXXI, sels. Ezra Pound.

room." Gelett Burgess. IlTH

Propertius, Sextus
Homage to Sextus Propertius, sels. Ezra Pound. HaAP

Prophecy. Carol Lee Sanchez. ReE

Prophets and Prophecy
From the provinces. Norman Rosten. HoA
Monologue for Cassandra, sels. Wislawa Szymborska. CoP
To Apollo, sels. Zbigniew Herbert. CoP
The word. Gustave Kahn. VoWA

Prose for de Esseintes. Stephane Mallarme. FoFS--FreS

Prose of the Transsiberian, sels. Blaise Cendrars (F. Sauser). MoVT

The **prospect.** Elizabeth Barrett Browning. WBP4

A **prospect** of swans. Dorothy Donnelly. HoA

Prospice. Robert Browning. DoNG--WBP3

Prostitution and Prostitutes
Beautiful snow. James M. Watson. WBP3
Daisy Fraser. Edgar Lee Masters. HaAP--PrVo
La Grande Jeanne. Luciano Erba. NeIP
"Modern times! Modern times!" Jean Lorrain (Paul Deval). FreS
Songs: 32 songs from the Ryojin Hisho. Unknown . FroC
Sweet Ethel. Linda Piper. BlS
To the memory of Zulma. Tristan Corbiere. FreS
Unseen spirits. Nathaniel Parker Willis. WBP3
The white devil, sels. John Webster. TyW

Prostration. David Semah. VoWA

Protection
Place me under your wing. Hayim Nachman Bialik. VoWA
Seeds of lead. Amir Gilboa. VoWA
Who will give cover? Anadad Eldan. VoWA

Proud beggarman. Jane St. John. YoVA

Proust on Noah. Eisig Silberschlag. VoWA

Provide, provide. Robert Frost. HaAP--LiHE

Proysen, Alf
The mice celebrate Christmas. MiRN

Prudence. Don Marquis. IlTH

Przybos, Julian
Autumn 1942, sels. CoP
Dynamo, sels. CoP
Equation of the heart, sels. CoP
Introduction to poetics, sels. CoP
Letter, sels. CoP
Roofs, sels. CoP
Since last year, sels. CoP
Wiosna 1969, sels. CoP

Psalm ("Father/You are the trunk.") Howard Schwartz. VoWA

Psalm ("It's not the sun.") Patricia Hooper. HoA

Psalm ("No one kneads us again...") Paul Celan. VoWA

Psalm ("Oh Lord, I have been staring..") Eugene Heimler. VoWA

Psalm ("There are very few moments.") Avraham Ben-Yitzhak. VoWA

Psalm CIV, sels. Bible-Old Testament. MTS

Psalm CVII, sels. Bible-Old Testament. MTS

Psalm LXXVII, sels. Bible-Old Testament. MTS

A **psalm** of life. Henry Wadsworth Longfellow. WBP4

Psalm of the jealous god. Henry Abramovitch. VoWA

Psalm paraphrase CXXVIII. Marcantonio Flaminio. ReLP

Psalm-people power at the die-in. Denise Levertov. FroA

Psalmodist. Mani Leib. VoWA

The **psalms** of David, sels. Bible-Old Testament. DoNG

Pseudo gens. Lynn Scheurell. YoVA

The **pseudo-shaman's** cliche. Adrian C. Louis. ReE

Pshytik. Nahum Bomze. VoWA

Psychoanalysis
The private theater. Nelo Risi. NeIP

The **pulley.** George Herbert. EeBC--HaAP

Pultzik, Hyam
The begetting of Cain. VoWA
The King of Ai. VoWA
On the photograph of a man I never saw. VoWA

The **pulverized** screen. Edmond Jabes. VoWA

Pumpkin. Cindy Honn. YoVA

Pumpkins
Pumpkin. Cindy Honn. YoVA
Punch and Judy. Unknown. RoRF
Punishment
A hanging. Mike Humphries. YoVA
Songs: 32 songs from the Ryojin
Hisho. Unknown . FroC
Puppets
The marionette. Dahlia
Ravikovich. BuAC
Okaru and Kampe. Kitahara
Hakushu . FroC
Purdy, Laura
Innocence. YoVA
Summer. YoVA
Purgatory of hell, sels. Edoardo
Sanguineti. NeIP
Purity. Hayim Lenski. VoWA
Purpose
In the hole. John Ciardi. HoA
The **purpose** of life. Suzanne
Tanner. YoVA
The **purse-seine.** Robinson
Jeffers. HaAP
Pursuit. Robert Penn Warren.
HaAP
Pursuit. Vern Rutsala. FroA
Pursuit from under. James
Dickey. HaAP
Pushkin, Alexsandr S.
Monument to Pushkin. Joseph
Brodsky. VoWA
Puskin, Aleksandr Sergeyevich
The last leaf. WBP3
Put aside and forgotten. Frank
Alexander Rossi. YoVA
Put off thy bark from shore...
Frederick Goddard Tuckerman.
MTS
"Put on mourning, October..."
Adolphe Rette. FreS
Put your word to my lips. Rachel
Korn. VoWA
The **pyre** of my Indian summer.
Mani Leib. VoWA

Qua cursum Ventus. Arthur Hugh
Clough. MTS--WBP3
Qua cursum ventus. Arthur Hugh
Clough. MTS--WBP3
Qua song. Colette Inez. FroA
"Quack!" said the billy-goat.
Charles Causley. RoRF
The **quagmire** of thought. Roy
Arlington Porter. YoVA
The **Quaker** graveyard in
Nantucket. Robert Lowell.

HaAP--MTS
The **Quaker** graveyard. Silas Weir
Mitchell. WBP3
A **quality** of air. Henry Chapin.
FroA
Qualls, Shelly
The battle of Zion Canyon. YoVA
A bomb. YoVA
The **quangle** wangle's hat. Edward
Lear. IlTH
Quarles, Francis
Delight in God. WBP4
A mystical ecstasy. WBP4
On Zacchaeus. HaAP
On the world. HaAP
The vanity of the world. WBP3
Quatrain. Tu Fu. LuL
Queen Mary, sels. Alfred, Lord
Tennyson. WBP2
Queneau, Raymond
The fly. MoVT
For an art of poetry 3. MoVT
A **query.** Unknown. WBP4
A **quest.** Don Hornsby. YoVA
Questions. Dagmar Hilarova. VoWA
Questions
An alphabet of questions.
Charles Edward Carryl. IlTH
Ask me no more. Thomas Carew.
HaAP
The last. Ezra Zussman. VoWA
To inscribe on a picture of a
skull.. Ryokan . FroC
The **quick** and the dead. Ilarie
Voronca. VoWA
Quiet house. Yoshioka Minoru.
FroC
The **quiet** light of flies. Natan
Zach. VoWA
Quiet, dear quiet. Emily CoBabe.
YoVA
The **quiet-eyed** cattle. Leslie
Norris. PoCh
Quillard, Pierre
Black flowers. FreS
Quiller-Couch, Sir Arthur T.
Sage counsel. WBP1
Quilts
Crazy quilt. Jane Yolen. BrBD
Rodowod gory odosobnienia,
sels. Miron Bialoszewski. CoP
Quindipan, Joyce
The present's presence. YoVA
U.S. patented. YoVA
Unpainted. YoVA

R. Alcona to J. Brenzaida. Emily

Landscape: 6. Ono Tozaburo.
    FroC
Limited. Carl Sandburg. HaAP
Night landscape. Joan Aiken.
    DuD
Night train. Hagiwara Sakutaro.
    FroC
Night train. Robert Francis.
    DuD
The old trip by dream train.
    Brendan Galvin. TeMP
September. Cesare Vivaldi. NeIP
Words from the window of a
    railway car. Anatoly Steiger.
    VoWA
Rain. Haim Guri. VoWA
The rain. Bonnie Baer. YoVA
Rain
    After Verlaine. Anselm Hollo.
        FroA
    The boy of summer. Barney Bush.
        ReE
    Cathedral in the thrashing rai.
        Takamura Kotaro . FroC
    Dry root in a wash. Simon J.
        Ortiz. ReE
    Evening rain. Gregoire Le Roy.
        FreS
    I am a raindrop. Korey Brown.
        HoWM
    It's raining. Guillaume
        Apollinaire. SlW
    The king who rained. Fred
        Gwynne. TrWB
    Life in the rain. Ken Harvey.
        YoVA
    Martial variations, sels.
        Amelia Rosselli. NeIP
    Night rain at Guang-Ko. Yang
        Wan-li . LuL
    The night rain drips..., sel.
        Tai Shu-lun . GrAC
    The old man. Alfredo Giuliani.
        NeIP
    Poem for a stone. Rokwaho
        (Daniel Thompson) . ReE
    Predilictions. Alfredo
        Giuliani. NeIP
    Rain ("The south wind...")
        Nishiwaki Junzaburo . FroC
    Rain on the roof. Coates
        Kinney. WBP1
    The rain. Bonnie Baer. YoVA
    Rain/wet dreary. Wendy Taddio.
        YoVA
    The raindrop. Carla Smith. HoWM
    Rains on the islands. Gabriel
        Preil. VoWA
    The rainy day. Henry Wadsworth
        Longfellow. WBP3

    Rainy days. Joy West. YoVA
    Resurrection after the rain.
        Alfredo Giuliani. NeIP
    Rhapsody on rain. Gabriel
        Audisio. MoVT
    Silent afternoon. William
        Oandasan. ReE
    Summer storm. Robyn Fischer.
        YoVA
    Ten tanka. Myoe . FroC
    Thirty tanka. Fujiwara no
        Shunzei . FroC
    Visiting Wang Stream after a
        rain. Ssu-k'ung Shu . GrAC
    "Water to draw." Ryokan . FroC
    You made it rai. Fareedah Allah
        (Ruby Saunders) . BlS
Rain ("The south wind...")
    Nishiwaki Junzaburo. FroC
Rain for ke-waik bu-ne-ya. Paula
    Gunn Allen. ReE
Rain has fallen on the history
    books. David Rosenberg. VoWA
The rain of life. Randy
    Greenwell. YoVA
Rain on the roof. Coates Kinney.
    WBP1
Rain/wet dreary. Wendy Taddio.
    YoVA
Rainbow and you. Tachihara
    Michizo. FroC
Rainbows and sandcastles. Laurie
    Campbell. YoVA
Raincoats for the dead. Albert
    Bellg. FroA
The raindrop. Carla Smith. HoWM
"Raindrops; drown in tears."
    Colleen Hartley. YoVA
Rainier. Jim Tollerud. ReE
Rains on the islands. Gabriel
    Preil. VoWA
Rainy Mountain Cemetery. N.
    Scott Momaday. ReE
A rainy day. Trent Conrad. HoWM
The rainy day. Henry Wadsworth
    Longfellow. WBP3
Rainy days. Joy West. YoVA
Rainy morning. Gail Greiner.
    YoVA
Rainy night. Sugawara no
    Michizane. FroC
Raisins and nuts. Charles
    Reznikoff. VoWA
Raking leaves. James F. King.
    StPo
Rakosi, Carl
    The avocado pit. FroA
    The China policy. FroA
    A lamentation (after Solomon Ib
        Gabirol). VoWA

Meditation (after Jehudah
    Halevi). VoWA
Meditation (after Solomon Ibn
    Gabirol). VoWA
Meditation (after Moses Ibn
    Ezra). VoWA
The vow. FroA
Ralegh, Sir Walter
As you came from the holy land.
    HaAP
The conclusion. DoNG
Even such is time. HaAP
The lie. HaAP
Lines. WBP4
The nymph's reply to the
    shepherd. WBP2
The nymph's reply to the
    shepherd. HaAP--LiHE
The pilgrimage. EeBC--WBP4
Ramps and ramps and ramps...
    Leonel Rugama. NiR
Ramsay, Allan
Lochaber no more. WBP3
Ramsey, Paul
On the porch of the antique
    dealer. FroA
Ranasinghe, Anne
Auschwitz from Columbo. VoWA
Holocaust 1944. VoWA
Randall, Dudley
Blackberry sweet. HaAP
Old Witherington. TyW
Randolph, Anson D. F.
Hopefully waiting. WBP4
Randolph, Innes
Good old rebel. TyW
Randolph, Thomas
To a lady admiring herself...
    WBP2
Random thoughts on the
    Shinkokinshu... Anzai
    Hitoshi. FroC
Rands, William Brighty
Topsy-turvy world. IlTH
Rankin, Jeremiah Eames
The babie. WBP1
Rankin, Rush
The woman who combed. FroA
Ransom, John Crowe
Bells for John Whiteside's
    daughter. HaAP--LiHE
The equilibrists. HaAP
Here lies a lady. HaAP
Miriam Tazewell. TyW
Winter remembered. HaAP
Ransome, John Crowe
Miriam Tazewell. TyW
Rape
The raper from Passenack.
    William Carlos Williams. TyW

The **rape** of the lock. Alexander
    Pope. HaAP
The **rape** of the lock, sels.
    Alexander Pope. WBP2
The **raper** from Passenack.
    William Carlos Williams. TyW
Rapids by the luan trees. Wang
    Wei. GrAC
Ratner, Rochelle
Davening. VoWA
The poor shammes of Berditchev.
    VoWA
A someday song for Sophia. TeMP
Ratosh, Yonathan
Lament. VoWA
Rats
Birds of a feather. Mother Goose.
    MiRN
A frog he would a-wooing go.
    Mother Goose . MiRN
The tale of the mice. Lewis
    Carroll (C.L. Dodgson). MiRN
The **rattle** bag, sels. Dafydd ap
    Gwilym. TyW
Rattler, alert. Brewster
    Ghiselin. HaAP
The **rattlesnake** band. Robert J.
    Conley. ReE
Rattlesnakes
Rattler, alert. Brewster
    Ghiselin. HaAP
Raub, Deborah L.
Waiting... YoVA
Ravikovich, Dahlia
A dress of fire (or, The
    dress). BuAC--VoWA
Hard winter, sels. VoWA
The marionette. BuAC
Memory. BuAC
The noise of the waters. BuAC
Pride. BuAC
Requiem after seventeen years.
    VoWA
Surely you remember. VoWA
Time caught in a net. BuAC
Ravitch (Z.K. Bergner), Melech
Conscience. VoWA
Let us learn. VoWA
A poem-good or bad-a
    thing...-flat. VoWA
Today the Nazis forces marched.
    OnCP
Twelve lines about the burning
    bush. VoWA
Twilight thoughts in Israel.
    VoWA
Verses written on sand. VoWA
Ray. Otto Orban. VoWA
Ray, David
Extreme unction in Pa.. FroA

Genitori. TyW
The jogger: Denver to Kansas
   City. FroA
Love letter. TyW
Thanks, Robert Frost. TeMP
Ray, Henrietta Cordelia
   Antigone and Oedipus. BlS
   The dawn of love. BlS
   Idyl: sunrise. BlS
   Idyl: sunset. BlS
   Milton. BlS
   Robert G. Shaw. BlS
   To my father. BlS
Ray, Judy
   Rose bay willow herb. FroA
Raya Brenner. Pinhas Sadeh. VoWA
Rayford, Julian Lee
   Junkyards. FroA
Raymond (Anne Stillman), Grace
   Birth. WBP1
Raymond, Rossiter Worthington
   Blessed are they. WBP3
   Christus consolator. WBP3
Raziel. Yvan Goll. VoWA
Razor Fish
   Roger was a razor fish. Al
      Pittman. RoRF
Reaching out. Sam Hamod. StPo
Reaching the foot of Pei-ku
   Mountain. Wang Wan. GrAC
Reading a letter from home.
   Sugawara no Michizane. FroC
Reading books, sels. Rai San'yo.
   FroC
A realitic point of view. Tammy
   Scheid. YoVA
Reality
   Final soliloquy of the interior
      paramour. Wallace Stevens.
      HaAP
   Ode on a decision to settle for
      less. William Pillen. VoWA
   Perhaps. Rachel Blaustein
      (Bluwstein). BuAC--VoWA
   Sixty-four tanka. Saigyo . FroC
Reality brought to a student.
   Hope Campbell. YoVA
The reaper and the flowers.
   Henry Wadsworth Longfellow.
   WBP3
Reapers. Jean Toomer. HaAP
Reason for your suffering.
   Tanikawa Shuntaro. FroC
Reb Hanina. Paul Raboff. VoWA
Rebecca. Shirley Kaufman. BuAC
Rebecca. Joseph Eliya. VoWA
Rebecca
   Dream. Joseph Eliya. VoWA
   Rebecca. Joseph Eliya. VoWA
   Rebecca. Shirley Kaufman. BuAC

The rebel Scot. John Cleveland.
   TyW
Rebellion
   The collar. George Herbert.
      HaAP
   The lesson of a former
      visit..Jang Cree. Yuan Chieh.
      GrAC
   Pity for dissolution, sel. Yuan
      Chieh . GrAC
   To the young rebels. E.L. Mayo.
      FroA
Rebensboim (see A.Margolin),R.

A receipt for writing a novel.
   Mary Alcock. EvIm
Recipe. Albert Goldbarth. VoWA
Recipe for tranquillity. David
   LeBlanc. YoVA
Recluse. Aldo Camerino. VoWA
Recognition. Myra Glazer
   (Schotz). BuAC
Reconciliation. Walt Whitman.
   HaAP
Reconciliation. David
   Rosenmann-Taub. VoWA
Reconciliation
   Make-up. Mike Bacsi. YoVA
Red and white. Albert Giraud.
   FreS
The red city. Stuart Merrill.
   FreS
The red fox. Marnie Walsh. ReE
Red light. I. Amiri Baraka
   (LeRoi Jones). SlW
Red pine. Chiao-jan. GrAC
The red wheelbarrow. William
   Carlos Williams. SlW
A red, red rose. Robert Burns.
   LiHE
Redemption. George Herbert.
   EeBC--HaAP
Reductions, sels. Lamberto
   Pignotti. NeIP
Redwings. William Heyen. TeMP
A reed. Osip Mandelstam.
Reed, Henry
   Naming of parts. LiHE
   Sailor's harbour. MTS
Reed, Ishmael
   Al Capone in Alaska. TyW
Reeves, James
   The catipoce. IlTH
   Giant thunder. DuD
   The toadstool wood. DuD
Reeves, Terri
   Haiku. YoVA
   I don't know. YoVA
Reflections. Terri Mayo. YoVA
Reflections. Bubba Lloyd. YoVA

Reflections in a daydream. Mary
    Fulkerson. YoVA
Reflections of me. Craig Gatrel.
    YoVA
Reflections on visiting the
    grave... Ann Plato. BlS
Reflections on the death of
    Scott Childs. Melody
    Prentiss. YoVA
Refugees. Chaim Grade. VoWA
Refugees
    Beyond memory. Monny de Boully.
        VoWA
    Exodus 1940. Alfred
        Wolfenstein. VoWA
    Refugees. Chaim Grade. VoWA
    We go. Karl Wolfskehl. VoWA
A refusal the death, by fire, of
    a child. Dylan Thomas. DoNG
Regelson, Abraham
    Moses on Mount Nebo. VoWA
Regicide
    The King of Ai. Hyam Pultzik.
        VoWA
Registered at the Bordello
    Hotel(Vienna). Larry Rubin.
    FroA
Regnier, Henri de
    Legendary and melancholic
        themes. FreS
    Salute to the foreign one. FreS
Regret. Vassar Miller. LiHE
Reich, Shlomo
    The golem. VoWA
    A tribe searching. VoWA
    The vigil. VoWA
    The windmill of evening. VoWA
Reid, Alastair
    Curiosity. LiHE
Reincarnation
    Spring & Asur. Miyazawa Kenji .
        FroC
Reinke, Danielle T.
    Dream. YoVA
    Innervisions. YoVA
Reinke, John
    The baying yearning of the
        norse horn. YoVA
    Mainstream. YoVA
    Women within prison. YoVA
Reis, Judite E.
    Love's zealots. YoVA
    A taste of the blues. YoVA
Reisen, Abraham
    An endless chain. VoWA
    The family of eight. VoWA
    Girls from home. VoWA
    Newcomers. VoWA
    What is the case in point?
        VoWA

Reitz, Glenn
    Machinum analyticus. YoVA
    Rock and roll, till death do us
        part. YoVA
Rejection. Robyn Fischer. YoVA
Rejoice and be merry. Unknown.
    EeBC
Relationships. Venise Duchesne.
    YoVA
The relic. John Donne. HaAP
Relics. David Wagoner. FroA
Religion
    And did those feet in ancient
        time. William Blake. HaAP
    The burning bush. Norman
        Nicholson. EeBC
    Day breaks. Charles Mackay.
        WBP4
    The dead. Jones Very. HaAP
    From the provinces. Norman
        Rosten. HoA
    The garden of love. William
        Blake. HaAP--LiHE
    Her creed. Sarah Knowles
        Bolton. WBP4
    Impact. Gordon D. Leslie. StPo
    Madonna near Barbice, sels.
        Jerzy Harasymowicz. CoP
    Mock on, mock on, Voltaire,
        Rousseau. William Blake. HaAP
    My creed. Alice Carey. WBP4
    My recovery. Friedrich Gottlieb
        Klopstock. WBP4
    O, may I join the choir
        invisible? George Eliot
        (M.E.L. Cross). WBP4
    Rady, sels. Zbigniew Herbert.
        CoP
    Sunday morning. Wallace
        Stevens. LiHE
    Two fishermen. Stanley Moss.
        VoWA
    Upon a dead man's head. John
        Skelton. HaAP
    What was his creed. Unknown .
        WBP4
Religion and doctrine. John Hay.
    WBP4
Religious Intolerance
    The balade...made & sange in
        Newgate. Anne (Kyme) Askew.
        PaW
Remain, ah not in youth alone.
    Walter Savage Landor. HaAP
The remedies. Joseph Bruchac.
    ReE
Remember Sabbath days. Larry
    Eigner. VoWA
Remembering. Judit Toth. VoWA
Remembering. Clarisse Nicoidski.

VoWA

Remembering Emperor Tenji.
    Princess Nukada. FroC
Remembering Fannie Lou Hamer.
    Thadious M. Davis. BlS
Remembering Lutsky. Rayzel
    Zychlinska. VoWA
Remembering earth. Jules
    Supervielle. MoVT
Remembrance. Emily Bronte. HaAP
Remembrance of things past.
    Horace Coleman. FroA
Reminiscence. Gail Greiner. YoVA
Remnants
    Ashkelon. Anthony Rudolf. VoWA
Remond (Crashaw), Francois
    The third elegie. ReLP
Rempel, Mike
    Dairyman blues. YoVA
Renouncement. Alice Meynell.
    WBP2
A renunciation. Edward Vere
    (Earl of Oxford). WBP2
Reparations
    Draft of a reparations
        agreement. Don Pagis. VoWA
Repentance
    A hymn to God the father. John
        Donne. EeBC--HaAP
    "Teach me how to repent." John
        Donne. EeBC
    Twenty-four tanka. Minamoto no
        Sanetomo . FroC
Report. Suzanne Fisher. YoVA
Repose. Alfred Lichtenstein.
    VoWA
Repose
    Just a while. Frantisek
        Gottlieb. VoWA
    Repose. Alfred Lichtenstein.
        VoWA
Reprise of one of A.G.'s best
    poems! I. Amiri Baraka
    (LeRoi Jones). TeMP
Requiem. Robert Louis Stevenson.
    DoNG
Requiem after seventeen years.
    Dahlia Ravikovich. VoWA
Requier, Augustus Julian
    Baby Zulma's Christmas carol.
        WBP1
Requiescat. Matthew Arnold. WBP3
The resignation. Thomas
    Chatterton. WBP4
Resignation. Henry Wadsworth
    Longfellow. WBP3
Resmerski, John C.
    Sonship. FroA
Resnikoff, Alexander
    Josephine. IlTH

The longest tale about the
    longest tail. IlTH
Resolution. Edward Wilde. YoVA
Resolution and independence.
    William Wordsworth. HaAP
Resorts. See Health Resorts
Rest. Miyazawa Kenji. FroC
Rest. Mary Woolsey Howland. WBP3
Rest. Jacob Isaac Segal. VoWA
Restaurants
    Home cooking cafe. Greg Field.
        FroA
    Song ("Sometimes in the fast
        food...") Randy Lane. FroA
Resting place. Jon Silkin. VoWA
Results of a scientific survey.
    Bruce Cutler. FroA
Resurrection. David Nelson. YoVA
Resurrection after the rain.
    Alfredo Giuliani. NeIP
Resurrection of the dead. Aliza
    Shenhar. VoWA
Resurrection, The. See Easter
Retired school-teacher. Heather
    McHugh. TeMP
Retirement
    In the post of assistant in
        Lo-yang.. Wei Ying-wu . GrAC
    "To bow and accept the end."
        Sandra Hilton. YoVA
The retort. George Pope Morris.
    WBP2
The retreat. Henry Vaughan.
    HaAP--ShBa
Retrospection. Charlotte Bronte.
    EvIm
Rette, Adolphe
    "The high hall and its funereal
        doors" FreS
    "Put on mourning, October..."
        FreS
    Wakes. FreS
Return. Sheila Troutman. YoVA
The return. Shmuel Moreh. VoWA
The return. Ezra Pound. HaAP
Return. Daniel Halpern. TeMP
Return. Johari M. Kunjufu. BlS
The return, sels. Tadeusz
    Rozewicz. CoP
Returning from/scouting for
    meat. Minerva Allen. ReE
Returning to Mount Sung. Wang
    Wei. GrAC
Returning, we hear larks. Isaac
    Rosenberg. VoWA
Reunion. Jon Smith. YoVA
Reunion. Carolyn Forche. TeMP
Reunited love. Richard
    Doddtridge Blackmore. WBP2
Reusser, Diedre

Death. YoVA
Revard, Carter
    "People from the stars" ReE
    Ponca war dancers. ReE
    Wazhazhe grandmother. ReE
Revelation. Carole C. Gregory.
        BlS
The revelation. Coventry
        Patmore. HaAP
Revelations. Ryan Synovec. YoVA
Revelations
    I emptied. Yona Wallach. BuAC
Revenge
    I woke up. Revenge. A., Jr.
        Poulin. TyW
    Revolt. Rachel Blaustein
        (Bluwstein). VoWA
Revenge fable. Ted Hughes. TyW
Reverdy, Pierre
    Overcast. MoVT
    The sound of bells. MoVT
Reversibility. Charles
        Baudelaire. FoFS
Reviewing footsteps. Bonnie
        Berckes. YoVA
A revisit. Jon Smith. YoVA
Revolt. Rachel Blaustein
        (Bluwstein). VoWA
Revolution
    Bitter days. Carlos Fonesca
        Amador. NiR
    The book of "Che." Leonel
        Rugama. NiR
    Letter, sels. Julian Przybos.
        CoP
    Pentecos. Ai . TeMP
    Revolutions. Pablo Neruda. NiR
    Without tears for the roses.
        Nanni Balestrini. NeIP
Revolutionary petunias. Alice
        Walker. BlS
Revolutions. Pablo Neruda. NiR
Reyes, Judith
    I belong to the Sandinista
        Front. NiR
Reykjavik. Max Elskamp. FreS
Reykjavik, Iceland
    Reykjavik. Max Elskamp. FreS
Reynolds, Lloyd J.
    "Weathergrams are poems..."
        FroA
Reynolds, Sir Joshua
    When Sir Joshua Reynolds died.
        William Blake. TyW
Reynolds, Tim
    To a bad heart. TyW
Reznikoff, Charles
    Autobiography: Hollywood. VoWA
    The body is like roots
        stretching. VoWA

Dew. VoWA
The Hebrew of your poets, Zion.
        VoWA
Jacob. VoWA
Lament of the Jewish women for
        Tammuz. VoWA
The letter. VoWA
Luzzato. VoWA
Out of the strong, sweetness.
        VoWA
Raisins and nuts. VoWA
Te Deum. VoWA
Rhapsody on rain. Gabriel
        Audisio. MoVT
The rhetoric of Langston Hughes.
        Margaret Danner. BlS
Rhinoceros
    Rhinos purple, hippos green.
        Patrick Michael Hearn. BrBD
Rhinos purple, hippos green.
        Patrick Michael Hearn. BrBD
Rhyme for night. Joan Aiken. DuD
The rhyme of the chivalrous
        shark. Wallace Irwin. IlTH
Rhyme-prose on the marriage...
        Oe no Asatsuna. FroC
Ribh considers Christian
        love.... William Butler
        Yeats. TyW
Rice
    The breeze comes filling the
        valley. Miyazawa Kenji . FroC
    Evening songs, sel. Unknown .
        FroC
    Morning songs, sel. Unknown .
        FroC
    Noon songs, sel. Unknown . FroC
    Rest. Miyazawa Kenji . FroC
    Rice-planting song: Aomori
        prefecture. Unknown . FroC
    Ripples. Unknown . FroC
Rice, Edward H.
    "Rock of ages." WBP4
Rice, Janet G.
    Aquaintance. YoVA
    A chattel to freedom. YoVA
Rice-planting song: Aomori
        prefecture. Unknown. FroC
Rich, Adrienne
    Diving into the wreck. MTS
    Living in sin. LiHE
    The middle-aged. LiHE
Richard Cory. Edwin Arlington
        Robinson. HaAP--LiHE
Richard II, sels. William
        Shakespeare. DoNG
Richard III, sels. William
        Shakespeare. MTS
Richards, Laura E.
    He and his family. IlTH

The shark. IlTH
Richardson, Charles Francis
  Love. WBP4
A riddle. Cynthia Ozick. VoWA
Riddle of night. Jiri Mordecai
    Langer. VoWA
The ride of the Valkyries.
    Gregoire Le Roy. FreS
Ride the wind. Allen Lord. YoVA
The ride-by-nights. Walter De La
    Mare. DuD
Riding down. Nora Perry. WBP1
Riding the blinds. James
    Haining. PrVo
Riding westward. Harvey Shapiro.
    VoWA
Ridley, Denise
  Forget. YoVA
Rieu, Emile Victor
  The flattered flying fish. IlTH
  Sir Smasham Uppe. IlTH
The right must win. Frederick
    William Faber. WBP4
"A right-handed fellow named
    Wright." Unknown. IlTH
Riley, James Whitcomb
  At sea. MTS
  The days gone by. WBP1
  Honey dripping from the comb.
    WBP1
  A life-lesson. WBP1
  Little Orphan Annie. WBP1
  The man in the moon. WBP1
  An old sweetheart of mine. WBP2
Rilke, Rainer Maria
  Annunciation over the
    shepherds, sels. PoCh
  Childhood. SlW
  Sonnets to Orpheus, sels. SlW
Rimbaud, Arthur
  After the flood. SlW
  The bewildered ones. FoFS
  The black currant river. FoFS
  Brussels. FreS
  Comedy of thirst. FoFS
  The crows. FoFS
  Dawn. SlW
  The drunken boat. FoFS--FreS
  Eternity. FoFS--FreS
  Evening prayer. FoFS
  Faun's head. FoFS
  Feeling. FoFS
  Festivals of patience.
    FoFS--FreS
  Golden age. FoFS--FreS
  "Hear how in April near the
    acacias." FoFS--FreS
  "Is it an oriental dancer?"
    FreS
  Kindly morning thought.

  FoFS--FreS
  The lice seekers. SlW
  May banners. FoFS--FreS
  Memory ("Clear water, like the
    salt...") FoFS--FreS
  My Bohemian life. FoFS
  Newlyweds. FreS
  "O seasons, O castles."
    FoFS--FreS
  The plundered heart. FoFS
  Poets seven years old. SlW
  Royalty. SlW
  The seated ones. FoFS
  Sensation. SlW
  Shame. FoFS
  The sleeper of the valley. FoFS
  Song of the highest tower.
    FoFS--FreS
  "The star wept pink..." FoFS
  Tear. FreS
  Venus Anadyomene. FoFS
  Vowels. FoFS--SlW
  The women who seek for lice.
    FoFS
Rimbaud, Arthur (about)
  Crimen amoris. Paul Verlaine.
    FoFS
The rime of the ancient mariner.
    Samuel Taylor Coleridge.
    HaAP--MTS
The rime of the ancient mariner.
    Samuel Taylor Coleridge. HaAP
Rimon, I.Z.
  I am a king. VoWA
The ring. Pier Paolo Pasolini.
    NeIP
The ring. Robert Pack. FroA
The ring poem... Philip Dacey.
    FroA
Riots
  Horse and rio. Ishihara Yoshiro.
    FroC
Rip. Giancarlo Majorino. NeIP
Ripple/Folds of time. Barbara
    Smith. YoVA
Ripples. Unknown. FroC
The rise of man. John White
    Chadwick. WBP4
"Risen from the rump..."
    Stephane Mallarme. FoFS--FreS
Risi, Nelo
  Apple trees apple trees apple
    trees. NeIP
  Maneuvers. NeIP
  The other side. NeIP
  The private theater. NeIP
  Tautology. NeIP
  Trinita dei Monti..NeIP
  Variations on white, sels. NeIP
Risque. John Rutter. YoVA

The **rites** for cousin Vit.
  Gwendolyn Brooks. HaAP
Rittenhouse, Brenda L.
  The destroyed whisper. YoVA
  The morning wind of the mind.
  YoVA
Ritter, Mary Louise
  Perished. WBP3
  Why? WBP2
  Wings. WBP1
Ritual to insure long life.
  Raven Hail. ReE
Rivalry in love. William Walsh.
  WBP2
The **river**. Leo Vroman. VoWA
The **River** Duddon, sels. William
  Wordsworth. HaAP
A **river** in Asia. Andrew
  Grossbardt. FroA
"The **river** is white in itself."
  Yuan Zhong-dao. LuL
The **river** merchant's wife: a
  letter. Ezra Pound. HaAP--SlW
The **river** of rivers in
  Connecticut. Wallace Stevens.
  HaAP
River snow. Liu Tsung-yuan. GrAC
Rivers
  Adrift. David Newton. YoVA
  "Among a thousand clouds..."
  Han-shan . LuL
  The banks of a river. Abraham
  Sutskever. VoWA
  The black currant river. Arthur
  Rimbaud. FoFS
  Charlie Machree. William J.
  Hoppin. WBP2
  Chattahoochee trip. Mark
  Fearer. YoVA
  Dusk ("The river is black.")
  Maruyama Kaoru . FroC
  Flowers and moonlight
  on...Spring River. Yang-di.
  LuL
  Heng-chiang lyrics, sel. Li Po.
  GrAC
  In the evening I walk by the
  river. Ouyang Xiu . LuL
  Morning breaks over the Huai
  River. Su Shi . LuL
  The mudtower. Anne Stevenson.
  HoA
  The Negro speaks of rivers.
  Langston Hughes. HaAP
  On coming to the capital from
  Omi.. Kakinomoto no Hitomaro.
  FroC
  Painting of an underground
  river. Mark Bobbitt. HoWM
  A river in Asia. Andrew

  Grossbardt. FroA
  "The river is white in itself."
  Yuan Zhong-dao . LuL
  The river of rivers in
  Connecticut. Wallace Stevens.
  HaAP
  The river. Leo Vroman. VoWA
  Separation on the river Kiang.
  Ezra Pound. SlW
  Setting out early from Yu-p'u
  Poo. Meng Hao-jan . GrAC
  Sixty-four tanka. Saigyo . FroC
  Thirty tanka. Fujiwara no
  Shunzei. FroC
  Tongue River psalm. Gary
  Gildner. FroA
  Written while viewing the
  river...autumn. Lin Bu . LuL
Rivers grow small, sels. Czeslaw
  Milosz. CoP
Riyong, Hengenike
  Civilization. VooI
  Death ("My weak body rests.")
  VooI
  The death of my grandfather.
  VooI
  The mountain. VooI
  Nokondi (the helpless
  creature). VooI
Rizzo, Victor P.
  The race. StPo
  Thomas A. Goodbody. StPo
  Twice the thief. StPo
The **road**. Helene Johnson. BlS
The **road** not taken. Robert
  Frost. HaAP
The **road** of life. Christy
  Lombardozzi. YoVA
The **road** of suffering. Chaim
  Grade. OnCP
The **road** to hate. Patrick
  Kavanaugh. TyW
Roadman. Carroll Arnett/Gogisgi.
  ReE
Roads and Trails
  At the roadside. John Knoepfle.
  FroA
  The dead by the side of the
  road. Gary Snyder. HaAP
  Descent to Bohannon Lake. Jim
  Barnes. FroA
  On the industrial highway.
  Daniel Hoffman. TeMP
  Paths. Rina Lasnier. MoVT
  The road not taken. Robert
  Frost. HaAP
  Song ("Feet have stepped
  on...flowers.") Jean Moreas.
  FreS
The **roads** of Ch'ang-an, sels.

Ch'u Kuang-hsi. GrAC
Robbins, Alice A.
Crystal dawn. StPo
Untitled ("When I look/into
your eyes.") StPo
Robbins, Martin
A cantor's dream before...High
Holy Days. VoWA
Roberson, Jane
The essence of winning. YoVA
Robert G. Shaw. Henrietta
Cordelia Ray. BlS
Robert II; King of France
Veni sancte spiritus. WBP4
Robert of Angou (d. 1343)
Ecologue II: Argus. Francesco
Petrarch. ReLP
Robert's Rules of Order. Robert
Peterson. FroA
Roberts, Charles G. D.
The aim. WBP4
Ascription. WBP4
Roberts, Elizabeth Madox
Christmas morning. PoCh
Robertson, T. H.
Story of the gate. WBP2
Robin Adair. Lady Caroline
Keppel. WBP3
Robinson(see Douglas,M.),A.D.G

Robinson, Edwin Arlington
The dark hills. HaAP
Eros turannos. HaAP
The flying Dutchman. MTS
The mill. HaAP
Miniver Cheevy. LiHE
Mr. Flood's party. HaAP--LiHE
Pasa thalassa thalassa. MTS
Richard Cory. HaAP--LiHE
The sheaves. HaAP
Robleto, Octavio
Elegy for the guerrilla
fighter. NiR
Monimbo. NiR
Robson, Jeremy
The departure. VoWA
Rocha, Luis
The optimist's dream. NiR
Thirty times thirty. NiR
Roche, James J.
A sailor's yarn. MTS
Rochester's song to Jane Eyre.
Charlotte Bronte. EvIm
Rochester, John Wilmot, Earl
The disabled debauchee. HaAP
Love and life. HaAP
A satire against reason &
mankind, sels. TyW
Song ("Love a woman? You're an
ass!") TyW

Rock and Roll (music)
Fame. Ingrid Schulz. YoVA
Rock and roll, till death do us
part. Glenn Reitz. YoVA
Rock and roll, till death do us
part. Glenn Reitz. YoVA
Rock me to sleep. Elizabeth
Akers. WBP1
"Rock of ages." Edward H. Rice.
WBP4
Rock, Kevin
"I'm a shining crystal." HoWM
The Rock, sels. Thomas Stearns
Eliot. EeBC
Rocked in the cradle of the
deep. Emma Hart Willard.
MTS--WBP4
Rocks. Florence Parry Heide. ByM
Rocks
In the Jerusalem hills, sels.
Leah Goldberg. BuAC
Over the three nipple-stones.
Paul Celan. VoWA
Pebble, sels. Zbigniew Herbert.
CoP
Pride. Dahlia Ravikovich. BuAC
This is my rock. David McCord.
RoRF
Rodenbach, Georges
Evening in the windowpanes XI.
FreS
Invalids at the window XII.
FreS
Invalids at the window II. FreS
The life of rooms IV. FreS
The life of rooms VII. FreS
The life of rooms XVII. FreS
Mental acquarium V. FreS
Rodeo. Randy Ruml. YoVA
Rodeo and fans. Kent Cross. YoVA
Rodeos
Rodeo and fans. Kent Cross.
YoVA
Rodeo. Randy Ruml. YoVA
Rodger, Alexander
Behave yoursel' before folk.
WBP2
Rodgers, Carolyn M.
Jesus was crucified or: it must
be deep. BlS
Masquerade. BlS
Poem for some black women. BlS
U name this one. BlS
Roditi, Edouard
A beginning and an end. VoWA
Habakkuk. VoWA
Kashrut. VoWA
The paths of prayer. VoWA
Shekhina and the Kiddushim.
VoWA

Rodowod gory odosobnienia, sels.
Miron Bialoszewski. CoP
Roethke, Theodore
The ceiling. IlTH
Dolor. LiHE
Elegy for Jane. HaAP--LiHE
Epidermal macabre. TyW
I knew a woman. HaAP
In a dark time. HaAP
The lost son. HaAP
My papa's waltz. HaAP
Pipling. TyW
The waking. HaAP
Where knock is open wide. HaAP
Roger was a razor fish. Al
Pittman. RoRF
Rogers (trans), Samuel
On the picture of an infant.
WBP1
Rogers, C. Edward
At the bar. YoVA
Callous destruction. YoVA
Rogers, Jennifer
Indian summer. YoVA
The sea wall. YoVA
Spellbinder. YoVA
Rogers, Robert Cameron
The shadow rose. WBP3
Rogers, Ronald
Bus. ReE
Jicarilla in August. ReE
Sandia crest. ReE
Rogers, Vickie
Illusion. YoVA
Love's enigma. YoVA
Rokeah, David
Beginning. VoWA
I am like a book. VoWA
Rokwaho (Daniel Thompson)
i dream. ReE
"Innocence returned." ReE
Poem for a stone. ReE
Roland the minstrel pig. William
Steig. TrWB
Rolle, Richard
Ghostly gladness. HaAP
Rolnik, Joseph
At God's command. VoWA
I'm not rich. VoWA
In disguise. VoWA
A Roman Roman. Crescenzo del
Monte. VoWA
Roman epigram. Giovanni Giudici.
NeIP
Roman rooms. Paolo Volponi. NeIP
The romance of the swan's nest.
Elizabeth Barrett Browning.
WBP1
Romance? - Romance! Debby
Buckley. YoVA

Romano, Angela
A brother. YoVA
Rome. Ianus Vitalis. ReLP
Rome, Italy
Hate and debate Rome.... Sir
John Harington. TyW
Roman epigram. Giovanni
Giudici. NeIP
Rome. Ianus Vitalis. ReLP
Ronsard, Pierre de
Sonnet to Ronsar. Mary Queen of
Scots . PaW
Roof. Ishigaki Rin. FroC
"The roof it has a lazy time".
Gelett Burgess. IlTH
Roofs
My thatched roof is
ruined...autumn wind. Tu Fu .
GrAC
Roof. Ishigaki Rin . FroC
"The roof it has a lazy time"
Gelett Burgess. IlTH
Roofs, sels. Julian Przybos. CoP
Rooftop. Willis Barnstone. FroA
Room conditioner. Archie
Randolph Ammons. TeMP
Room poems. Eli Bachar. VoWA
Room service. John W. Moser.
FroA
Rooms
The life of rooms XVII. Georges
Rodenbach. FreS
Rooney, Anne
Scan. YoVA
Roosevelt, Franklin Delano
The visitor. George Bogin. FroA
Roosevelt, Theodore
To Roosevelt, sels. Ruben
Dario. NiR
Root. Miklos Radnoti. VoWA
The root canal. Marge Piercy.
HoA
Rorate celi desuper. William
Dunbar. ShBa
Rory O'More. Samuel Lover. WBP2
Rosalynd. Thomas Lodge. WBP2
Rosalynd's complaint. Thomas
Lodge. WBP2
The rose. Julie McAdams. YoVA
The rose. G.A. Studdert Kennedy.
EeBC
Rose Aylmer. Walter Savage
Landor. HaAP--WBP2
Rose bay willow herb. Judy Ray.
FroA
Rose, Della
I tried to write a poem. YoVA
Rose, Wendy
For the white poets who would
be Indian. ReE

Indian anthropologist.... ReE
Soul tattoos. ReE
Three thousand dollar death
  song. ReE
To some few Hopi ancestors. ReE
Trickster: 1977. ReE
Roseliep, Raymond
  When I was nine. FroA
Rosenberg, Betsy
  Bird song. VoWA
  Unearthing. VoWA
Rosenberg, David
  Maps to nowhere. VoWA
  Rain has fallen on the history
    books. VoWA
Rosenberg, Isaac
  Break of day in the trenches.
    VoWA
  Chagrin. VoWA
  Dead man's dump. VoWA
  The destruction of Jerusalem...
    VoWA
  God. VoWA
  The Jew. VoWA
  Returning, we hear larks. VoWA
  The unicorn, sels. VoWA
Rosenberg, Joel
  The first wedding in the world.
    VoWA
  The violin tree. VoWA
Rosenmann-Taub, David
  Elegy and Kaddish. VoWA
  Moral ode. VoWA
  Prelude. VoWA
  Reconciliation. VoWA
  Sabbath. VoWA
  To a young girl. VoWA
Rosenstiel, Sharon Ann
  Come. YoVA
  Fallen years. YoVA
Roses
  The act. William Carlos
    Williams. SlW
  Ashes of roses. Elaine Goodale
    Eastman. WBP3
  Dropping petals. Jean Lorrain
    (Paul Deval). FreS
  The first rose of summer.
    Oliver Herford. WBP1
  For the man who stole a rose.
    Harley Elliott. FroA
  Go, lovely rose. Henry Kirke
    White. WBP2
  Go, lovely rose! Edmund
    Waller. WBP2
  Go, lovely rose! Edmund
    Waller. HaAP--LiHE
  "My whole soul by now spent,"
    Henri Thomas. MoVT
  A red, red rose. Robert Burns.

  LiHE
  The rose. G.A. Studdert
    Kennedy. EeBC
  The rose. Julie McAdams. YoVA
  Selfish beauty. Mary Jo Paque.
    YoVA
  The shadow rose. Robert Cameron
    Rogers. WBP3
  Shell roses. Suzy Gierut. YoVA
  The white ros. Unknown . WBP2
Roses gone wild. John Taylor.
    FroA
Rosh Pina. David Knut. VoWA
Rosh Pina, Israel
  Rosh Pina. David Knut. VoWA
Roskolenko, Harry
  Come unto us who are...laden.
    FroA
  Symbols. FroA
  Waiting for God. FroA
Ross, Nancy
  Loneliness. YoVA
  The silhouette. YoVA
Rosselli, Amelia
  Dialogue with the dead. NeIP
  General strike 1969. NeIP
  Martial variations, sels. NeIP
  No one. NeIP
  Snow. NeIP
Rossetti, Christina Georgina
  A better resurrection. EeBC
  By the sea. MTS
  A Christmas carol, sels.
    PoCh--ShBa
  The city mouse and the garden
    mouse. MiRN
  Dream-love. HaAP
  Goblin market. EvIm
  If I could trust mine own self.
    EeBC
  If only. EeBC
  "It is finished." WBP1
  The milking-maid. WBP2
  O Lord, seek us. EeBC
  Sleep at sea. MTS
  The three enemies. WBP4
  Up-hill. HaAP--WBP4
Rossetti, Dante Gabriel
  The house of life, sels. HaAP·
  The house of life, sels. WBP2
  The nevermore. WBP3
  On the site of a mulberry
    tree.... TyW
  The sea-limits. MTS
  Sister Helen. EvIm
  The woodspurge. HaAP
Rossi, Frank Alexander
  A hero in disguise. YoVA
  Put aside and forgotten. YoVA
Rosslyn (see F.Erskine), Earl

Rosten, Norman
  Byron in Greece. HoA
  Face on the daguerreotype. HoA
  From the provinces. HoA
Rotenberger, Paula
  My dream. YoVA
Roth, Hemda
  Four ways of writing one poem.
    BuAC
  The song ("The song! the
    song!"). VoWA
  Treason of sand. VoWA
  A young deer/dust. BuAC--VoWA
Roth, Joseph
  Ahasuerus. VoWA
Rothenberg, Jerome
  The alphabet came to me. VoWA
  A letter to Paul Celan in
    memory. VoWA
A rough rhyme on a rough matter.
    Charles Kingsley. WBP3
Round. Rachel Boimwall. VoWA
"Rounds, grapes, roses!"
    Gustave Kahn. FreS
Rout. Philip Booth. FroA
Routier, Simone
  I ask. MoVT
  Snow and nostalgia. MoVT
Roux, Saint-Pol (Paul)
  Golgotha. FreS
  The Magdalene with perfumes.
    FreS
Roversi, Roberto
  The Hiroshima bomb. NeIP
  Market day. NeIP
  Official iconography. NeIP
  Political customs. NeIP
Rowe, Laurie
  What happened to the real me?
    YoVA
  Words. YoVA
Rowe, Ronald C.
  I thought about you. YoVA
  Smile Renee. YoVA
Rowing in turns. David Swanger.
    TeMP
Rowing songs, sels. Yuan Chieh.
    GrAC
Rowland, Sid
  Blackbird. StPo
  The eye. StPo
Roy, Annette L.
  A cry. YoVA
  Pass and regret. YoVA
Royalty. Arthur Rimbaud. SlW
Rozewicz, Tadeusz
  Among so many concerns, sels.
    CoP
  And I too was in Arcady, sels.

CoP
  Conversation with the prince,
    sels. CoP
  Falling, sels. CoP
  In the middle of life, sels.
    CoP
  Lament, sels. CoP
  Leave us alone, sels. CoP
  Non-stop-shows, sels. CoP
  The return, sels. CoP
  The survivor, sels. CoP
Ruan Ji
  The autumn is beginning. LuL
Ruark, Gibbons
  Nightmare inspection tour...
    TyW
The Rubaiyat of Omar Khayyam,
    sels, tr. Edward Fitzgerald.
    HaAP
Rubin, Ilya
  Escape. VoWA
  Handful of ashes. VoWA
  No sense grieving. VoWA
  Poem from 'The Revolution'.
    VoWA
  Slow oxen. VoWA
Rubin, Larry
  The brother-in-law. TyW
  Registered at the Bordello
    Hotel(Vienna). FroA
Rudnitsky, Leah
  Birds are drowsing on the
    branches. VoWA
Rudolf, Anthony
  Ancient of days. VoWA
  Ashkelon. VoWA
  Dubrovnik poem (Emilio
    Tolentino). VoWA
  Evening of the rose. VoWA
  Hands up. VoWA
  Prayer for Kafka and ourselves.
    VoWA
Rudolph, Lee
  Warming up for the real thing.
    TyW
Ruebner, Tuvia
  Among iron fragments. VoWA
  Document. VoWA
  First days. VoWA
  I left. VoWA
Rufinus Domesticus
  Golden eyes. WBP2
Rugama, Leonel
  Biography. NiR
  The book of "Che." NiR
  The bowls are empty. NiR
  The earth is a satellite of the
    moon. NiR
  The houses were filled with
    smoke. NiR

Safed and I. Molly Myerowitz
    Levine. BuAC--VoWA
Safed, Israel
    Safed and I. Molly Myerowitz
    Levine. BuAC--VoWA
    Safed. David Knut. VoWA
Sage counsel. Sir Arthur T.
    Quiller-Couch. WBP1
Sahl, Hans
    Greeting from a distance. VoWA
    Memo. VoWA
Said I not so?. George Herbert.
    WBP4
Saigon, Vietnam
    A black soldier remembers.
    Horace Coleman. FroA
Saigyo
    Sixty-four tanka. FroC
Sail and oar. Robert Graves. MTS
Sailing on Jo-yeh Creek in
    spring. Chi-wu Ch'ien. GrAC
Sailing to Byzantium. William
    Butler Yeats. HaAP--LiHE
The sailor boy. Alfred, Lord
    Tennyson. MTS
A sailor's apology for bow-legs.
    Thomas Hood. MTS
Sailor's harbour. Henry Reed.
    MTS
A sailor's yarn. James J. Roche.
    MTS
Sails
    Song of the sail. Maruyama Kaoru.
    FroC
Saint. Stephane Mallarme. FoFS
Saint Agnes. Alfred, Lord
    Tennyson. WBP4
Saint Balshemtov. Itzik Manger.
    OnCP
Saint Christopher. Dinah Maria
    Mulock Craik. WBP4
Sainte-Marthe, Scevole (G.) de
    Paedotrophia. ReLP
Saints lose back. Nancy Willard.
    HoA
Saito Mokichi
    Mother dies. FroC
Sakaki, or a sacred tree.
    Unknown. FroC
Salamun, Tomaz
    Air. VoWA
    Eclipse. VoWA
Sales, Alvin
    While walking along the
    seashore. HoWM
A salesman is an it that stinks
    excuse. Edward Estlin
    Cummings. TyW
Salis, Johann Gaudenz von
    Song of the silent land. WBP4

Salisbury, Ralph
    A halo. FroA
Salkey, Andrew
    Postcard from London, 23. 10.
    1972. FroA
Sally Simpkin's lament. Thomas
    Hood. MTS
Sally in our alley. Henry Carey.
    WBP2
Salmon
    Salmon cycle. Avner Treinin.
    VoWA
Salmon cycle. Avner Treinin.
    VoWA
Salome. Oscar-Venceslas de
    Milosz. FreS
Salome
    Mariam, fairie queene of Jewry,
    sels. Elizabeth (Tanfield)
    Cary. PaW
    "On eveings feverish and
    gamy..." Albert Samain. FreS
    Salome. Oscar-Venceslas de
    Milosz. FreS
Salomon. Pierre Morhange. VoWA
Saltman, Benjamin
    The fathers. VoWA
    The journey with hands and
    arms. VoWA
Salutation. Stephane Mallarme.
    FoFS
Salute to the foreign one. Henri
    de Regnier. FreS
Salvation. Aaron Zeitlin. OnCP
Salvation
    Redemption. George Herbert.
    EeBC--HaAP
Salve deux rex judaeorum...,
    sels. Aemilia (Bassano)
    Lanyer. PaW
Sam Hall. Unknown. TyW
Samain, Albert
    "The black goat moves..." FreS
    "I dream of gentle verse..."
    FreS
    Lust ("Lust, fruit of
    death...") FreS
    "On eveings feverish and
    gamy..." FreS
    Spiritual love. FreS
The same dream. Shlomit Cohen.
    VoWA
Same in blues. Langston Hughes.
    LiHE
The same voice, always. Yves
    Bonnefoy. MoVT
Sami Mansei
    Tanka ("To what shall I
    compare..world?) FroC
Samson. Amir Gilboa. VoWA

Samson
   Love letter. Carole C. Gregory.
      BlS
   My Samsons. Haim Guri. VoWA
   Samson rends his clothes.
      Anadad Eldan. VoWA
   Samson. Amir Gilboa. VoWA
Samson Agonistes, sels. John
      Milton. WBP3
Samson rends his clothes. Anadad
      Eldan. VoWA
A San Diego poem:
      January-February 1973. Simon
      J. Ortiz. ReE
San Francisco, California
   The house of desire. Sherley
      Anne Williams. BlS
Sanchez, Carol Lee
   (Conversations #2). ReE
   (Conversations #1). ReE
   (Conversations #4). ReE
   Heritage. ReE
   La tienda. ReE
   More conversations from the
      nightmare. ReE
   Prophecy. ReE
Sanchez, Mejia
   The death of Somoza. NiR
   The Somozas. NiR
Sanchez, Sonia
   Memorial. BlS
   Poem at thirty. BlS
   Summer words for a sister
      addict. BlS
Sancho Panza's homecoming.
      Ishihara Yoshiro. FroC
Sandburg, Carl
   Bones. MTS
   Cool tombs. HaAP
   Laughing corn. PrVo
   Limited. HaAP
   Nocturn cabbage. DuD
   North Atlantic. MTS
   The sea hold. MTS
   The shovel man. HaAP
   Young sea. MTS
Sanderson, Mike
   Stereo. YoVA
The Sandgate girl's lamentation.
      Unknown. TyW
Sandia crest. Ronald Rogers. ReE
Sandino. Pablo Neruda. NiR
Sandino, Augusto Cesar
   Anxiety. Rigoberto Perez Lopez.
      NiR
   Hail, captain of the continent.
      Pablo Neruda. NiR
   Nineteen twenty-seven (1927.
      HuGos . NiR
   Sandino. Pablo Neruda. NiR

   Zero hour. Ernesto Cardenal.
      NiR
Sando, Joe S.
   Echo from beyond. ReE
Sandy, Ginger
   The fantasy of imagination
      at..dentist's. HoWM
Sanford, Sandra
   The clown. YoVA
   Life with you, love. YoVA
Sangster, Margaret E. M.
   Are the children at home? WBP3
Sanguineti, Edoardo
   Erotopaegnia, sels. NeIP
   Laborintus, sels. NeIP
   Purgatory of hell, sels. NeIP
Sannazaro, Jacopo
   Of the admirable city Venice.
      ReLP
   Piscatory eclogue II: Galatea.
      ReLP
   The ruins of Cumae, an ancient
      city. ReLP
Sansom, Clive
   The witnesses, sels. PoCh
Santa Barbara. Ricardo Morales
      Aviles. NiR
Santa Caterina. Myra Glazer
      (Schotz). BuAC--VoWA
Santa Claus. Walter De La Mare.
      PoCh
Santa Claus. Howard Nemerov.
      HaAP
Santa Claus
   Merry Christmas! Elder Olson.
      FroA
   Santa Claus and the mouse.
      Emilie Poulsson. MiRN
   Santa Claus. Howard Nemerov.
      HaAP
   Santa Claus. Walter De La Mare.
      PoCh
   Santa does his thing. Lori Lynn
      Beard. YoVA
   A visit from St. Nicholas.
      Clement Clarke Moore.
      PoCh--WBP1
   A visit from St. Nicholas.
      Clement C. Moore. PoCh
Santa Claus and the mouse.
      Emilie Poulsson. MiRN
Santa Croce, Italy
   In Santa Croce. Franco Fortini.
      NeIP
Santa does his thing. Lori Lynn
      Beard. YoVA
Santayana, George
   Faith. WBP4
Sante Filomena. Henry Wadsworth
      Longfellow. WBP4

Santos des Praslin, Christian
    Barren the landscape, sels. NiR
Santos, Francisco
    Leonel Rugama. NiR
Santos, Mario
    It's the boys. NiR
Sappho
    Blest as the immortal gods.
        WBP2
Sarah. Edna Aphek. VoWA
Sarah. Delmore Schwartz. VoWA
Sarah
        Abraham and Sarah. Itzik
            Manger. VoWA
        Iscah. Howard Schwartz. VoWA
        Sarah. Delmore Schwartz. VoWA
        Sarah. Edna Aphek. VoWA
Sarai. Joseph Sherman. VoWA
Sassoon, Siegfried
    The general. TyW
Satan
        The caliph and satan. James
            Freeman Clarke. WBP4
        The demon love. Unknown . HaAP
        Gates of paradise, sels.
            William Blake. HaAP
        Lucifer in starlight. George
            Meredith. HaAP
Satellites. Ellen L. Kisthardt.
    StPo
Satire XIII, sels. Juvenal. WBP4
A **satire** against reason &
        mankind, sels. John Wilmot,
        Earl Rochester. TyW
Satiric Verse
        Ancient music. Ezra Pound. TyW
        Comic verse. Takamura Kotaro.
            FroC
        Japanese beetles. X.J. Kennedy.
            HoA
        The rape of the lock. Alexander
            Pope. HaAP
        To a suckling satirist. Tristan
            Corbiere. FreS
        Wynter ys icumen in. Frank
            Sidgwick. TyW
Satori. Gayl Jones. BlS
The **satraps.** Pablo Neruda. NiR
Sattler, Lisa
    The butterflies. YoVA
Satz, Mario
    Coconut. VoWA
    Fish. VoWA
    Lemon. VoWA
Saul. Else Lasker-Schuler. VoWA
Saul. Amir Gilboa. VoWA
Saul
        King Saul. Allan Kolski
            Horvitz. VoWA
        Saul's song of love. Shaul

    Tchernichovsky. VoWA
        Saul. Amir Gilboa. VoWA
        Saul. Else Lasker-Schuler. VoWA
        The unicorn, sels. Isaac
            Rosenberg. VoWA
Saul's song of love. Shaul
    Tchernichovsky. VoWA
Saul, afterward, riding east.
    John Malcolm Brinnin. HoA
Sauser(see Cendrars), Frederic

The **savage** beast. William Carlos
    Williams. TyW
Save. Susan A. Klee. YoVA
Saw. John Hall. HoWM
"The **saw** enters the wood".
    Eugene Guillevic. MoVT
Saws
        "The saw enters the wood"
            Eugene Guillevic. MoVT
        Saw. John Hall. HoWM
Sawyer, Ruth
    Words from an old Spanish
        carol. PoCh
Saxe, John Godfrey
    My eyes! how I love you. WBP2
    Woman's will. WBP2
Say hello to John. Sherley Anne
    Williams. BlS
Sayer. George P. Elliott. FroA
Scan. Anne Rooney. YoVA
Scandals
        Watergate. Ruth Herschberger.
            FroA
The **scare-fire.** Robert Herrick.
    HaAP
Scared. Jack Forbes. YoVA
Sceiford, Richard V.H.
    Man's thoughts. YoVA
Schaechter-Gottesman, Beyle
    Meditation. VoWA
Schaefer, Mark
    Eternal emancipation. YoVA
Schaefer, Ted
    Anxiety pastorale. FroA
    The parents-without-partners
        picnic. FroA
Schaeffer, Susan Fromberg
    Yahrzeit. VoWA
Schede (see Melissus), Paul

Scheid, Tammy
    A realitic point of view. YoVA
Scheinert, David
    The drunken stones of Prague.
        VoWA
    The stone &...grass in the
        Warsaw Ghetto. VoWA
Scheurell, Lynn
    Pseudo gens. YoVA

Music. YoVA

Scott, Frederick George
Van Elsen. WBP3

Scott, Gerald Wayne
The promise. YoVA

Scott, John
I hate that drum's discordant
sound. TyW
It has died. YoVA

Scott, Sir Walter
Ivanhoe, sels. WBP4
The lady of the lake, sels.
WBP3
The lay of the last minstrel,
sels. WBP2
Lochinvar. WBP2
Madge Wildfire's death song.
HaAP
Marmion, sels. WBP2
Marmion, sels. PoCh
Song ("A weary lot is thine,
fair maid.") WBP3
Verses in the style of the
Druids, sels. TyW

The scourge reddened...blood of
Jesus. Jacob Bidermann. ReLP

Scourges
The French mood. Abraham Abo
Stoltzenberg. VoWA
The scourge reddened...blood of
Jesus. Jacob Bidermann. ReLP

Scraps. Susannah Fried. VoWA

Scrawled in pencil... Don Pagis.
VoWA

Scribe. Paul Auster. VoWA

Scroll. Stanley Moss. VoWA

Scudder, Eliza
The love of God. WBP4
Vesper hymn. WBP4

Sculpting in the imperial
presence. Takamura Kotaro.
FroC

Sculpture and Sculptors
Envying sculptors. Florence
Trefethen. StPo
Sculpting in the imperial
presenc. Takamura Kotaro .
FroC
What I have done. Gerard
Malanga. FroA

The sea. David Herbert Lawrence.
MTS

The sea. Valery Larbaud
(C-M.Bonsignor). MoVT

The sea. Lloyd Frankenberg. MTS

The sea. Ken Noyle. MTS

Sea
as is the sea marvelous. Edward
Estlin Cummings. MTS
At sea. James Whitcomb Riley.

MTS

The ballad of Dead Men's Bay.
Algernon Charles Swinburne.
MTS

The baying yearning of the
norse horn. John Reinke. YoVA

Bones. Carl Sandburg. MTS

Break, break, break. Alfred,
Lord Tennyson. HaAP--MTS

Calm morning at sea. Sara
Teasdale. MTS

The calme. John Donne. MTS

The Canterbury tales, sels.
Geoffrey Chaucer. MTS

Childe Harold's pilgrimage,
sels. George Gordon,6th Baron
Byron. MTS

Christmas at sea. Robert Louis .
Stevenson. MTS

The city in the sea. Edgar
Allan Poe. MTS

The daemon love. Unknown . MTS

Dark sea. Maruyama Kaoru . FroC

Don Juan, sels. George
Gordon,6th Baron Byron. MTS

The dream of a lake. Kim
Parker. HoWM

Emotion bay. Sandra Hilton.
YoVA

Eternal Father, strong to save.
William Whiting. MTS

Ex-voto. Algernon Charles
Swinburne. MTS

Exiled. Edna St. Vincent
Millay. MTS

The faerie queene, sels. Edmund
Spenser. MTS

The flying Dutchman. Edwin
Arlington Robinson. MTS

The forsaken merman. Matthew
Arnold. MTS

Gift of the poem. Stephane
Mallarme. FoFS

A grave. Marianne Moore.
HaAP--MTS

A Greyport legend. Bret Harte.
MTS

Half-tide ledge. Richard P.
Blackmur. MTS

Henry VI, sels. William
Shakespeare. MTS

Home-thoughts, from the sea.
Robert Browning. MTS

Hope. William Dean Howells. MTS

A hymn of the sea. William
Cullen Bryant. MTS

I started early-I took my dog.
Emily Dickinson. HaAP--MTS

Job, sel. Bible-Old Testament .
MTS

To Ailsa Rock. John Keats. MTS
To Marguerite-continued.
  Matthew Arnold. MTS
"Toward the elusive open
  sky..." Gustave Kahn. FreS
'Twas when the seas were
  roaring. John Gay. HaAP
Twenty-four tanka. Minamoto no
  Sanetomo.   FroC
A vision of the sea. Percy
  Bysshe Shelley. MTS
A visit from the sea. Robert
  Louis Stevenson. MTS
Voyages, sels. Hart Crane. HaAP
Voyages. Hart Crane. MTS
Who has not walked upon the
  shore. Robert Bridges. MTS
Winter ocean. John Updike. MTS
Young sea. Carl Sandburg. MTS
Sea Shells. See Shells
Sea Voyages. See Travel
The sea and the hills. Rudyard
  Kipling. MTS
Sea breeze. Stephane Mallarme.
  FoFS
Sea breeze. Susan Klopenstine.
  YoVA
A sea dialogue. Oliver Wendell
  Holmes. MTS
A sea dirge. Lewis Carroll (C.L.
  Dodgson). MTS
Sea dreams, sels. Alfred, Lord
  Tennyson. WBP1
Sea food thought. John W. Moser.
  FroA
Sea gods, sels. Hilda Doolittle
  (H.D.). MTS
The sea hold. Carl Sandburg. MTS
Sea lullaby. Elinor Wylie. MTS
Sea of land. Guillaume
  Apollinaire. MoVT
The sea of silence exhales
  secrets. Hayim Nachman
  Bialik. VoWA
A sea promenade. Pier Paolo
  Pasolini. NeIP
Sea surface full of clouds.
  Wallace Stevens. MTS
Sea voyage. William Empson. MTS
The sea wall. Jennifer Rogers.
  YoVA
Sea-change. John Masefield. MTS
Sea-chill. Arthur Guiterman. MTS
Sea-distances. Alfred Noyes. MTS
Sea-fever. John Masefield. MTS
Sea-games. Aliza Shenhar. VoWA
The sea-gull. Ogden Nash. MTS
The sea-limits. Dante Gabriel
  Rossetti. MTS
Sea-monster. Gertrud Kolmar.

VoWA
Sea-ruck. Richard Ebergart. MTS
Sea-shore. Ralph Waldo Emerson.
  MTS
Sea-weed. David Herbert
  Lawrence. MTS
The seafarer. Unknown. MTS
A seal. Oliver Herford. IlTH
Seal of fire. Mordecai Temkin.
  VoWA
Seals
  The great silke of Sule Skerri.
    Unknown . MTS
  A seal. Oliver Herford. IlTH
Seamen
  Anchor. Maruyama Kaoru . FroC
  Bermudas. Andrew Marvell. MTS
  Black-eyed Susan. John Gay.
    MTS--WBP3
  The castaway. William Cowper.
    MTS
  Childe Harold's pilgrimage,
    sels. George Gordon,6th Baron
    Byron. MTS
  Commemorative of a naval
    victory. Herman Melville.
    HaAP--MTS
  D'Avalos prayer. John
    Masefield. MTS
  A dairy of the sailors of the
    north. David Shulman. VoWA
  Daufuskie: Jake. Mari Evans.
    BlS
  Epistle to a desponding
    sea-man. Philip Freneau. MTS
  Harp song of the Dane women.
    Rudyard Kipling. HaAP
  Henry IV, sels. William
    Shakespeare. MTS
  John Winter. Laurence Binyon.
    MTS
  Little Billee. William
    Makepeace Thackeray. MTS
  The midshipman. William
    Falconer. MTS
  Nearing hom. Unknown . MTS
  Never more, sailor. Walter De
    La Mare. MTS
  O God! have mercy in this
    dreadful hour. Robert
    Southey. MTS
  Pacific sonnets, sels. George
    Barker. MTS
  Pericles, sels. William
    Shakespeare. MTS .
  Port admiral. Frederick
    Marryat. MTS
  Psalm CVII, sel. Bible-Old
    Testament . MTS
  The Quaker graveyard in

Nantucket. Robert Lowell.
  HaAP--MTS
The rime of the ancient
  mariner. Samuel Taylor
  Coleridge. HaAP--MTS
The sailor boy. Alfred, Lord
  Tennyson. MTS
The seafarer. Unknown . MTS
Sir Patrick Spens. Unknown . MTS
Sir Patrick Spens. Unknown .
  HaAP
Song of the galley-slaves.
  Rudyard Kipling. HaAP
Song of the master and
  boatswain. Wystan Hugh Auden.
  MTS
The tempest, sels. William
  Shakespeare. MTS
To Ned. Herman Melville. MTS
The yarn of the Nancy Bell. Sir
  William S. Gilbert. MTS
The **search**. Michael Hamburger.
  VoWA
The **search**. Henry Vaughan. ShBa
The **searching**. Alice S. Cobb.
  BlS
Searching. Sherry Curry. YoVA
Searching. Greg Stricklin. YoVA
Sears, Edward Hamilton
  The angels' song. WBP4
Sears, Janice
  Night fades--the sun rises.
  YoVA
Sears, Kathy
  The confetti thrown by many a
  hands. YoVA
Seascape. Elizabeth Bishop. MTS
Seascape. Anne Hebert. MoVT
Seascape. Stephen Spender. MTS
Seashore
  Another day. Michelle Dawn
  Ferguson. YoVA
  At the slackening of the tide.
  James Wright. MTS
  The beacon. Nicole Drassel (N.
  Lessard). MoVT
  Broke loose. Linda Kozusko.
  StPo
  By the sea. Christina Georgina
  Rossetti. MTS
  The cares of a caretaker.
  Wallace Irwin. IlTH
  Castles/Just waiting. Doug
  Penner. YoVA
  The constant. Archie Randolph
  Ammons. HaAP
  A day at the beach. Betsy Wray.
  YoVA
  "Don't cut the shrub on Idemi
  Beach." Unknown . FroC

Dover Beach. Matthew Arnold.
  LiHE--MTS
Driving to the beach. Joanna
  Cole. ByM
Expressing my humble thought.
  Otomo no Yakamochi . FroC
The fisher's boy. Henry David
  Thoreau. MTS
Graveyard by the sea. Thomas
  Lux. TeMP
Haiku: 39 haiku. Masaoka Shiki.
  FroC
Handful of sand, sel. Ishikawa
  Takuboku . FroC
Heaven on earth. Peggy Grup.
  YoVA
Impressions of a beach. Tracey
  Gallagher. YoVA
Koyorogi. Fuzoku Uta . FroC
Lapping waves/cooling rinsing
  the sand. Doug Penner. YoVA
Okhotsk elegy. Miyazawa Kenji.
  FroC
"On the beach/a big dog lies."
  Pati Hill. FroA
One goes with me along the
  shore. Manfred Winkler. VoWA
A parable. Mathilde Blind. WBP1
Rocks. Florence Parry Heide.
  ByM
A sea promenade. Pier Paolo
  Pasolini. NeIP
Sea-shore. Ralph Waldo Emerson.
  MTS
The shell. Angie Herron. YoVA
Song ("Our sovereign
  familiar...") Yamabe no
  Akahito . FroC
The steeple-jack. Marianne
  Moore. HaAP
Sunny. Robert Vander Molen.
  FroA
Tanka: 44 tanka. Wakayama
  Bokusui   FroC
To Giovanni. Cesare Vivaldi.
  NeIP
To open. Antonio Porta. NeIP
Until I saw the sea. Lilian
  Moore. ByM
While walking along the
  seashore I saw... Michael
  White. HoWM
While walking along the
  seashore. Alvin Sales. HoWM
Seasickness
  A channel crossing. Rupert
  Brooke. MTS
  Sea-chill. Arthur Guiterman.
  MTS
The **seaside** well. Unknown. WBP4

"The **season** greeter". Yomon
    Akara. FroC
The **seasons**. Janet Brack. YoVA
Seasons
    A difference. Tom Clark. HoA
    Eighty-seven hokku. Yosa Buson.
        FroC
    Fifty-one tanka. Lady Izumi.
        FroC
    A green refrain. Avraham Huss.
        VoWA
    Imitations of old poems, sel.
        Wei Ying-wu . GrAC
    A pail/Against a fence. Doug
        Penner. YoVA
    Peony fallen. Yosa Buson . FroC
    The poet's wedding, sels.
        Krzysztof Kamil Baczynski.
        CoP
    The promise. Gerald Wayne
        Scott. YoVA
    The seasons. Janet Brack. YoVA
    Seventeen hokku. Chiyojo. FroC
    A short winter tale. Natan
        Zach. VoWA
    Sixteen hokku. Kato Kyotai.
        FroC
    Solstice. Emery George. HoA
    Tanka: 21 tanka from the
        Kokinsh. Unknown . FroC
    Twenty-one hokku. Kaya Shirao.
        FroC
    Year after year. Scott Moore.
        YoVA
Seasons of prayer. Henry Ware
    (Jr.). WBP4
The **seated** ones. Arthur Rimbaud.
    FoFS
Seaweed. Henry Wadsworth
    Longfellow. MTS
Seaweed
    Sea-weed. David Herbert
        Lawrence. MTS
    Seaweed. Henry Wadsworth
        Longfellow. MTS
Secaucus, New Jersey
    In a prominent bar in Secaucus
        one day. X.J. Kennedy. HoA
Second ballad. Jean Cassou. MoVT
The **second** coming. William
    Butler Yeats. LiHE--ShBa
The **second** coming. William
    Butler Yeats. HaAP
Second song...worship of the
    goddess... Wang Wei. GrAC
Secret. Gwendolyn B. Bennett.
    BlS
The **secret**. Sonya M. Michlin.
    HoWM
The **secret** of death. Sir Edwin

Arnold. WBP3
The **secret** of the burning stars.
    Pablo Antonio Cuadra. NiR
The **secret** room. Marla Gardner.
    YoVA
The **secret** sea. Jules
    Supervielle. MoVT
The **secret** self, sels. Moishe
    Kulbak. OnCP
Secrets
    "I have a secret nobody knows."
        Misty Henderson. HoWM
    Place me under your wing. Hayim
        Nachman Bialik. VoWA
The **secular** masque, sels. John
    Dryden. HaAP--ShBa
Secundus (Everaerts), Ioannes
    Basia: I. ReLP
    Basia: VII. ReLP
    Basia: XIII. ReLP
    Epithalamium. ReLP
Seder, 1944. Friedrich Torberg.
    VoWA
Sedley, Sir Charles
    On a cock at Rochester. TyW
    Phillis is my only love. WBP2
    Song ("Love still has
        something...sea.") WBP2
Sedoka: 13 sedoka. Unknown. FroC
Seduction. Jo Ann Hall-Evans.
    BlS
see you soon. Tomioka Taeko.
    FroC
The **seed** growing secretly. Henry
    Vaughan. WBP4
Seeds of lead. Amir Gilboa. VoWA
Seeing. Lance Henson. ReE
Seeing Grand Secretary
    Yu's...mural. Wang Chi-yu.
    GrAC
Seeing a man lying dead...
    Kakinomoto no Hitomaro. FroC
Seeing off his Reverence
    Ling-ch'e. Liu Ch'ang-ch'ing.
    GrAC
Seeing things. Eugene Field.
    WBP1
Seeing you. Michelle J. Modde.
    YoVA
Seeking the monk Chan... Meng
    Hao-jan. GrAC
Segal, Jacob Isaac
    Candle. VoWA
    Rest. VoWA
Seiler, Lori
    Dandelions, raindrops. YoVA
    It's a porcelain world. YoVA
    When you hurt. YoVA
Seismograph. Ephraim Auerbach.
    VoWA

To a Taoist on Ch'uan-chiao Mountai. Wei Ying-wu . GrAC

To her absent sailor. John Greenleaf Whittier. WBP3

To say 'good-bye'. Paul White. YoVA

To someone. Takamura Kotaro . FroC

Torn. Connie Sue Young. YoVA

Twenty hokku. Mukai Kyorai . FroC

Twenty-four hokku. Takai Kito . FroC

Untitled ("I make...poetic pauses.") Dana Naone. ReE

Upon excusing himself from a banque. Yamanque no Okura . FroC

We parted in silence. Julia Crawford (L.Macartney). WBP3

We together. Rhonda Moncrief. YoVA

West stream at Ch'u-cho. Wei Ying-wu . GrAC

What ails this heart of mine? Susanna Blamire. WBP3

The wife to her husband. Unknown. WBP3

Ye goathered gods. Sir Philip Sidney. HaAP

Yesterday. Megan Herzog. YoVA

You never understood. Penny Walck. YoVA

Your passing, fleet passing. Joseph Eliya. VoWA

Separation on the river Kiang. Ezra Pound. SlW

Sepia fashion show. Maya Angelou. BlS

Sepia nightingale. Kristen Hunter. BlS

September. Cesare Vivaldi. NeIP

September 13, 1959 (Variation). Andrea Zanzotto. NeIP

September 1913. William Butler Yeats. HaAP

The **sequence** of generations. Hayim Be'er. VoWA

Serchuk, Peter
What the animals said. HoA

Serenade. Alan Britt. FroA

Serenade ("Stars of the summer night!"). Henry Wadsworth Longfellow. WBP2

A **serenade** for two poplars. Esther Raab. BuAC--VoWA

Serraillier, Ian
Andrew's bedtime story. DuD
Anne and the field mouse. MiRN
Falling asleep. DuD

The mouse in the wainscot. MiRN
The tickler rhyme. RoRF

Servants
Domestics. Kattie M. Cumbo. BlS

Service
A deed and a word. Charles Mackay. WBP4
Duty. Ellen Sturgis Hooper. WBP4
Flowers without fruit. John Henry, Cardinal Newman. WBP4
If we had but a day. Mary Lowe Dickinson. WBP4
Ion, sels. Sir Thomas Noon Talfourd. WBP4
Ode to duty. William Wordsworth. WBP4
Offhand composition II. Wang Wei . GrAC
Pippa passes, sels. Robert Browning. WBP4
The sister of charity. Gerald Joseph Griffen. WBP4
The vision of Sir Launfal. James Russell Lowell. WBP4
What I live for. George Linnaeus Banks. WBP4

Sessler, Thomas
Burnt debris. VoWA
When the day. VoWA
You move forward. VoWA

Sesson Yubai
"In heaven and earth, no ground..." FroC

Sestina: Altaforte. Ezra Pound. SlW

Set me whereas the sun doth parch..green. Earl of Surrey (Henry Howard). HaAP

Setting out early from Hsia-chou. Ch'ing-chiang. GrAC

Setting out early from Yu-p'u Pool. Meng Hao-jan. GrAC

Setting out from Hiroshima... Rai San'yo. FroC

The **seven** old men. Charles Baudelaire. FoFS

Seven stanzas at Easter. John Updike. EeBC

Seven tankas written in early 753. Otomo no Yakamochi. FroC

Seven times four. Jean Ingelow. WBP1

Seven times one. Jean Ingelow. WBP1

Seven times six. Jean Ingelow. WBP1

Seven times three. Jean Ingelow. WBP2

Sonnet XXIX. WBP1
Sonnet XXX. HaAP--WBP1
Sonnet XXXIII. HaAP--WBP2
Spring. HaAP
The tempest, sels. DoNG
The tempest, sels. MTS
Timons of Athens, sels. TyW
Twelfth night, sels. DoNG
Twelfth night, sels. WBP2
Twelfth night, sels. WBP3
Winter. HaAP
Shakespeare, William (about)
    On the site of a mulberry
        tree.... Dante Gabriel
        Rossetti. TyW
    To the memory...William
        Shakespeare. Ben Jonson. HaAP
Shall I come, sweet love, to
    thee. Thomas Campion. HaAP
Shalom, Shin
    Splendor. VoWA
Shame. Arthur Rimbaud. FoFS
Shame
    The horse that died of shame.
        N. Scott Momaday. ReE
Shange, Ntozake
    Dark phrases. BlS
    Frank Albert & Viola Benzena
        Owens. BlS
    Nappy edges. BlS
    No more love poems #1. BlS
Shanly, Charles Dawson
    Kitty of Coleraine. WBP2
Shapiro, Harvey
    Exodus. VoWA
    Father and sons. FroA
    For the Yiddish singers... VoWA
    Incident. FroA
    Like a beach. VoWA
    Lines for the ancient scribes.
        VoWA
    Musical shuttle. VoWA
    Nineteen seventy-six (1976).
        FroA
    Riding westward. VoWA
    The six hundred thousand
        letters. VoWA
Shapiro, Karl
    The alphabet. VoWA
    A cut flower. HaAP
    Elegy for a dead soldier. HaAP
    The fly. TyW
    Jew. VoWA
    The leg. HaAP
    The One hundred fifty-first
        psalm (151). VoWA
    Waiting in front of the
        columnar..school. HaAP
Shapiro, Mark Elliott
    Dying under a fall of stars.

VoWA
Shargel, Zvi
    I will go away. VoWA
    Let us laugh. VoWA
    Pictures on the wall. VoWA
Sharing. Becky Jones. YoVA
The shark. Laura E. Richards.
    IlTH
The shark. Ogden Nash. IlTH
Sharks. Kaneko Mitsuharu. FroC
Sharks
    The Maldive shark. Herman
        Melville. TyW--MTS
    The rhyme of the chivalrous
        shark. Wallace Irwin. IlTH
    Sally Simpkin's lament. Thomas
        Hood. MTS
    Shark. Kaneko Mitsuharu . FroC
    The shark. Laura E. Richards.
        IlTH
    The shark. Ogden Nash. IlTH
Sharp, William
    The field mouse. MiRN
Sharpe, Richard Scrafton
    The country mouse and the city
        mouse. MiRN
Shatnes or uncleanliness.
    Eliezer Steinbarg. VoWA
Shaul, Anwar
    Mother. VoWA
    Prayers to liberty. VoWA
    To a cactus seller. VoWA
Shaw (Jr.), E.B.
    Gucci fruit. YoVA
Shaw, Luci
    May 20: very early morning.
        EeBC
    Small song. EeBC
Shaw, Robert Gould
    Robert G. Shaw. Henrietta
        Cordelia Ray. BlS
She. Manfred Winkler. VoWA
She came and went. James Russell
    Lowell. WBP1
She comes majestic with
    her...sails. Robert Southey.
    MTS
She dealt her pretty words like
    blades. Emily Dickinson. HaAP
She died in beauty. Charles
    Doyne Sillery. WBP3
She dwelt among the untrodden
    ways. William Wordsworth.
    HaAP
"She is not fair to outward
    view." Hartley Coleridge.
    WBP2
She sang, dear song, lullay.
    Unknown. ShBa
She tied up her few things. John

Clare. HaAP
"She walks in beauty, like the
night." George Gordon,6th
Baron Byron. WBP2
She was a half-turning whisper.
Barry T. Siford. YoVA
She was a phantom of delight.
William Wordsworth. WBP2
She's free!. Frances E.W.
Harper. BlS
Shearer, Douglas
Middle-class autumn. YoVA
Waking. YoVA
The sheaves. Edwin Arlington
Robinson. HaAP
Shechem. David Shevin. VoWA
Sheep
De sheepfol'. Sarah Pratt
M'Lean Greene. WBP4
The lost sheep. Elizabeth
Cecilia Clephane. WBP4
Sheep and lambs. Katharine Tynan
Hinkson. WBPl
Shekhina. Karl Wolfskehl. VoWA
Shekhina and the Kiddushim.
Edouard Roditi. VoWA
Shekhina. See Shekinah
Shekinah
Matronita. Dennis Silk. VoWA
NHR. Jack Hirschman. VoWA
Shekhina and the Kiddushim.
Edouard Roditi. VoWA
Shekhina. Karl Wolfskehl. VoWA
Zohara. Jack Hirschman. VoWA
Shelby County, Ohio, November
1974. G.E. Murray. FroA
The shell. James Stephens. MTS
The shell. Angie Herron. YoVA
Shell roses. Suzy Gierut. YoVA
Shelley, Percy Bysshe
The Cenci, sels. TyW
England in 1819. TyW
Hellas, sels. HaAP
Hymn to intellectual beauty.
HaAP
"I fear thy kisses, gentle
maiden." WBP2
A lament ("O world! O life! O
Time!") WBP3
Lines to an Indian air. WBP2
Love's philosophy. WBP2
Ode to the west wind. HaAP--MTS
Ozymandias. DoNG--LiHE
Similes for two political
characters.... TyW
Stanzas written in dejection
near Naples. WBP3
Time. MTS
To a skylark. HaAP
A vision of the sea. MTS

Shells
The shell. James Stephens. MTS
Shelton, Richard
Face. TeMP
Shema. Primo Levi. VoWA
Shen Zhou
Inscribed on a painting. LuL
Shenefelt, Arthur B.
Living with gavity. StPo
Shenhar, Aliza
The Akedah. VoWA
The drunkenness of pain. VoWA
Expectation. VoWA
Resurrection of the dead. VoWA
Sea-games. VoWA
Song of the closing service.
VoWA
Trembling. VoWA
Shenhav, Chaya
Four. BuAC
Shephead, Reginald
The exploration of inner space.
YoVA
It is. YoVA
Old man. YoVA
The shepherd and the king.
Robert Greene. WBP2
The shepherd boy's song. John
Bunyan. EeBC
Shepherd in Capri. Nishiwaki
Junzaburo. FroC
The shepherd who stayed.
Theodosia Garrison. PoCh
Shepherd's song at Christmas.
Langston Hughes. PoCh
The shepherd's wife's song.
Robert Greene. HaAP
The shepherds. Henry Vaughan.
ShBa
Shepherds and Shepherdesses
The good shepherd with the kid.
Matthew Arnold. WBP4
Shepherds and Sheperdesses
Henry VI, sels. William
Shakespeare. WBPl
Shepherds and Shepherdesses
The shepherd's wife's song.
Robert Greene. HaAP
Sheridan (Lady Gifford), Helen
Lament of the Irish emigrant.
WBP3
Sheridan (see Norton),Caroline

Sheridan, Michael
Turning back. PrVo
Sherman, Frank Dempster
Her guitar. WBP2
On some buttercups. WBP2
The shadows. WBPl
Sherman, Joseph

Sarai. VoWA
Sherwin, Richard
  Jacob's winning. VoWA
Shevin, David
  Dawn. VoWA
  Shechem. VoWA
Shiba Sonome
  Fifteen hokku. FroC
The **shield** of Achilles. Wystan
  Hugh Auden. HaAP
Shields, Jean
  Coming of age. YoVA
  For Jukka: on indecision. YoVA
  Water spots. YoVA
Shighan-the Navajo way.
  Bernadette Chato. ReE
Shiki (668-716), Prince
  In joy. FroC
  When Emperor Mommu visited...
    FroC
Shikishi, Princess
  Seventy-eight tanka. FroC
Shimazaki Toson
  Birdless country. FroC
  The coconut. FroC
  Song for the burial of my
    mother. FroC
  Song: thoughts of a traveler.
    FroC
The **shining** fool. Jacob
  Glatstein. OnCP
Shining like paned glass. Janice
  A. Carpenter. YoVA
The **ship** of Rio. Walter De La
  Mare. MTS
The **ship** of death. David Herbert
  Lawrence. MTS
The **ship** of earth. Sidney
  Lanier. MTS
Shipman, Eddy
  Lost in time. HoWM
Ships
  After the sea-ship. Walt
    Whitman. MTS
  Annus mirabilis, sels. John
    Dryden. MTS
  The beauty of the ship. Walt
    Whitman. MTS
  The building of the ship, sels.
    Henry Wadsworth Longfellow.
    MTS
  Cargoes. John Masefield. MTS
  The dismantled ship. Walt
    Whitman. MTS
  Estuar. Maruyama Kaoru . FroC
  God fashioned the ship of the
    world... Stephen Crane. MTS
  In cabin'd ships at sea. Walt
    Whitman. MTS
  Joy, shipmate, joy! Walt

  Whitman. MTS
  My brigantine. James Fenimore
    Cooper. MTS
  My galley charged with
    forgetfulness. Sir Thomas
    Wyatt. HaAP--MTS
  Old Ironsides. Oliver Wendell
    Holmes. MTS
  The old ships. James Elroy
    Flecker. MTS
  Passage steamer. Louis
    MacNeice. MTS
  A passer-by. Robert Bridges.
    MTS
  A sailor's yarn. James J.
    Roche. MTS
  She comes majestic with
    her...sails. Robert Southey.
    MTS
  The ship of Rio. Walter De La
    Mare. MTS
  Ships that pass in the night.
    Paul Laurence Dunbar. MTS
  Songs for all seas, all ships.
    Walt Whitman. MTS
  Though all the fates should
    prove unkind. Henry David
    Thoreau. HaAP
  Troopship for France, War II.
    George Bogin. FroA
  Where lies the land to which
    the ship..? Arthur Hugh
    Clough. MTS
  Where lies the land to which
    yon ship..? William
    Wordsworth. MTS
  With ships the sea was
    sprinkled far... William
    Wordsworth. MTS
  The wreck. Walter De La Mare.
    MTS
  The yachts. William Carlos
    Williams. MTS
Ships that pass in the night.
  Paul Laurence Dunbar. MTS
The **shipwreck**, sels. William
  Falconer. MTS
Shipwrecks
  Alec Yeaton's son. Thomas
    Bailey Aldrich. MTS
  "Concealed from the
    overwhelming cloud." Stephane
    Mallarme. FoFS--FreS
  Diving into the wreck. Adrienne
    Rich. MTS
  The Palatine. John Greenleaf
    Whittier. MTS
  The shipwreck, sels. William
    Falconer. MTS
  The wreck of the Hesperus.

She was a half-turning whisper.
YoVA
The **sifting** of Peter. Henry
Wadsworth Longfellow. WBP4
Sigal, Eleonor
I praise myself. YoVA
Sigh. Stephane Mallarme. FreS
Sightseeing on a winter day.
Wang Wei. GrAC
The **significance** of Veteran's
Day. Simon J. Ortiz. ReE
Signs over the house, sels.
Jerzy Harasymowicz. CoP
Silberschlag, Eisig
Abraham. VoWA
Proust on Noah. VoWA
Silence. Brian Stifel. HoWM
Silence. Thomas Hood. DoNG
Silence
Giving up on the shore. Gabriel
Preil. VoWA
"I, silence am always last"
Pulin Patel. HoWM
My brother was silent. Amir
Gilboa. VoWA
On soun. Wei Ying-wu . LuL
The sea of silence exhales
secrets. Hayim Nachman
Bialik. VoWA
Silence. Brian Stifel. HoWM
Silent afternoon. William
Oandasan. ReE
Silent baby. Ellen Bartlett
Currier. WBP1
Siler, Krystal
Forest ballet. YoVA
My secret with the clown. YoVA
The **silhouette.** Nancy Ross. YoVA
Silk, Dennis
Guide to Jerusalem. VoWA
Matronita. VoWA
The **silken** tent. Robert Frost.
LiHE
Silkin, Jon
The coldness. VoWA
Death of a son. VoWA
It says. VoWA
Jerusalem. VoWA
Resting place. VoWA
A word about freedom & identity
Tel Aviv. VoWA
Silko, Leslie Marmon
Horses at valley store. ReE
Slim man canyon. ReE
Story from bear country. ReE
When sun came to riverwoman.
ReE
Sill, Edward Rowland
A morning thought. WBP3
The **siller** croun. Susanna

Blamire. WBP2
Sillery, Charles Doyne
She died in beauty. WBP3
The **silly** old man. Unknown. TyW
Silva II: Agrius. George
Buchanan. ReLP
Silva, Fernando
Epigram ("A National Guard
captain...") NiR
Silver flight. Douglas Morris.
YoVA
The **silver** swan. Unknown. HaAP
Silverman, Maxine
Hair. VoWA
Silverstein, Shel
Jimmy Jet and his tv set. IlTH
Jumping rope. BrBD
Tree house. RoRF
Simeon (Bible)
A song for Simeon. Thomas
Stearns Eliot. EeBC
Simic, Charles
Butcher shop. TeMP
Simile. Tracey Kenney. YoVA
Similes and Metaphors
As sand. Natan Zach. VoWA
Very like a whale. Ogden Nash.
HaAP
Similes for two political
characters... Percy Bysshe
Shelley. TyW
Simmias
The grave of Sophocles. WBP3
Simmons, Karen
Good ol' days. YoVA
Inside/the tall. YoVA
Simms, William Gilmore
The lost Pleiad. WBP4
Mother and child. WBP1
Night storm. MTS
Simon the Cyrenian speaks.
Countee Cullen. HaAP
Simon, Ron
Car. YoVA
Crystal pieces. YoVA
Simple Simon. Unknown. IlTH
The **simple** joys of life. Kama
Kerpi. VooI
A **simple** pleasure. Scott Van
Klaveren. YoVA
Simplicity. Louis Simpson. LiHE
Simplicity
The happiest heart. John Vance
Cheney. WBP1
Song ("Wandering winds whip.")
Courtney Strang. YoVA
Still to be neat, still to be
dressed. Ben Jonson. HaAP
Thinking on high antiquity. Yuan
Chieh . GrAC

Simpson, Louis
   Simplicity. LiHE
Sin. Emile Verhaeren. FreS
Sin
   Easy to drift. Oliver Huckel.
     WBP4
   First confession. X.J. Kennedy.
     LiHE
   A hymn to God the father. John
     Donne. EeBC--HaAP
   Loyal sins. Jacob Glatstein.
     VoWA
   Nothing but leaves. Lucy E.
     Akerman. WBP4
   Poled. Julie Croston. YoVA
   Preparatory meditations, sels.
     Edward Taylor. HaAP
   Said I not so? George Herbert.
     WBP4
   The sifting of Peter. Henry
     Wadsworth Longfellow. WBP4
   Sin. Emile Verhaeren. FreS
   Stone the woman, let the man go
     fre. Unknown . WBP4
   To Father Ch., sels. Czeslaw
     Milosz. CoP
   Unity. Jakov de Haan. VoWA
   Wallenstein, sels. Samuel
     Taylor Coleridge. WBP4
Sinai
   Burning sand of Sinai. Nelly
     Sachs. VoWA
Sinan, Rogelio
   Nicaraguan riddle. NiR
Since last year, sels. Julian
   Przybos. CoP
Since then. Yehuda Amichai. VoWA
Since there's no help, come let
   us kiss. Michael Drayton.
   HaAP--LiHE
"Sing hey! Sing hey!" Unknown.
   PoCh
The singer. Kadya Molodovsky.
   OnCP
Singing and Singers
   Animal song. Alfredo Giuliani.
     NeIP
   The argument of his book.
     Robert Herrick. HaAP
   The condition. T. Carmi. VoWA
   Envoi (1919). Ezra Pound. HaAP
   For a voice that is singing.
     Aldo Camerino. VoWA
   From my mouth a song. William
     Oandasan. ReE
   Fugato (coda). Gad Hollander.
     VoWA
   Grinding vibrato. Jayne Cortez.
     BlS
   i lost the son. Karoniaktatie

   (Alex Jacobs) . ReE
   The idea of order at Key West.
     Wallace Stevens. HaAP--MTS
   Jesus saves or Don't ask me to
     join AA... Elizabeth
     Cook-Lynn. ReE
   Lovesong ("You must not").
     Angela Jackson. PrVo
   Mandolin. Paul Verlaine. FoFS
   Memorial. Sonia Sanchez. BlS
   Musical shuttle. Harvey
     Shapiro. VoWA
   My song. Hayim Nachman Bialik.
     VoWA
   The mysterious song. Stuart
     Merrill. FreS
   Naked thoughts, sels. Russell
     Soaba. VooI
   The old village choir. Benjamin
     F. Taylor. WBP4
   A paragraph. Hayden Carruth.
     FroA
   Secret. Gwendolyn B. Bennett.
     BlS
   Sepia nightingale. Kristen
     Hunter. BlS
   Shir Ma'alot/a song of degrees.
     Richard Flantz. VoWA
   The singer. Kadya Molodovsky.
     OnCP
   Siren song. Margaret Atwood.
     HaAP
   There once was a girl named
     Jill. Susie Tacoronte. YoVA
   We free singers be. Etheridge
     Knight. FroA
Sinking into virgin snow. Sara
   Tollefson. YoVA
Sir Galahad. Alfred, Lord
   Tennyson. WBP4
Sir Launcelot and Queen
   Guinevere. Alfred, Lord
   Tennyson. WBP2
Sir Patrick Spens. Unknown. MTS
Sir Patrick Spens. Unknown. HaAP
Sir Smasham Uppe. Emile Victor
   Rieu. IlTH
Siren song. Margaret Atwood.
   HaAP
Sirens. Elliott Coleman. FroA
Sissman, L.E.
   The critic on the hearth. TyW
   Talking union: 1964. TyW
Sisson, C.H.
   Human relations. TyW
Sister Bernardo. Heather Wilde.
   FroA
Sister Helen. Dante Gabriel
   Rossetti. EvIm
Sister Zahava. Edith Bruck. VoWA

The **sister** of charity. Gerald
    Joseph Griffen. WBP4
Sisters. Patty Corbett. YoVA
Sit down, sad soul. Barry
    Cornwall (B.W. Proctor). WBP4
Sitek, Lisa
    "Drift out to sea." HoWM
Sitting alone by Ching-t'ing
    Mountain. Li Po. GrAC
Sitting alone in Jing-ting
    Mountain. Li Bo. LuL
Sitwell, Edith
    Lullaby. ShBa
    Madame mouse. MiRN
    Still falls the rain.
        EeBC--ShBa
Sivan, Arye
    Children's song. VoWA
    Forty years peace. VoWA
    In Jerusalem are women. VoWA
    To Xanadu, which is Beth Shaul.
        VoWA
The **six** hundred thousand
    letters. Harvey Shapiro. VoWA
Six playful quatrains, sels. Tu
    Fu. GrAC
Six small songs for a silver
    flute. Barry Spacks. TeMP
The **sixteen** hand horse. Fred
    Gwynne. TrWB
Sixteen hokku. Kato Kyotai. FroC
Sixth (6th) state. Mary C.
    Colver. StPo
Sixty-four tanka. Saigyo. FroC
Skatetown boogie. Shari K.
    Wentz. YoVA
Skating
    "Free" style. Lisa McCormick.
        YoVA
Skelton laureate, defender....
    John Skelton. TyW
Skelton, John
    My darling dear, my daisy
        flower. HaAP
    Skelton laureate, defender....
        TyW
    Upon a dead man's head. HaAP
Skepticism
    philonous' paradox. Chris
        Gilbert. FroA
Ski flyers. Martha W. McKenzie.
    StPo
Skiing
    Ski flyers. Martha W. McKenzie.
        StPo
Skin the Goat's curse on Carey.
    Unknown. TyW
Skinner, Knute
    The Brockton murder:...out of
        Wm James. TyW

The cow. TeMP
Sklar, Morty
    Poem to the sun. FroA
Sklarew, Myra
    Benediction. VoWA
    Instructions for the Messiah.
        VoWA
    What is a Jewish poem? VoWA
Skorczewski, Donna
    Common sight. YoVA
    Darkness. YoVA
Skunk hour. Robert Lowell. HaAP
"A **skunk** sat on a stump."
    Unknown. IlTH
Sky
    "The sky is, above the roof."
        Paul Verlaine. FoFS
"The **sky** is, above the roof."
    Paul Verlaine. FoFS
Skylark. Stanislaw Grochowiak.
    CoP
Skylarks. Ted Hughes. HaAP
Slater, Robert
    Survival kit. FroA
    The survivors. FroA
Slaughter
    The pas. Yoshioka Minoru . FroC
Slaughter, Tammy
    Baby. YoVA
Slaughter, Tammie
    So confused. YoVA
Slavery
    Dark testament. Pauli Murray.
        BlS
    Daufuskie. Mari Evans. BlS
    Double take at Relais de
        l'Espadon. Thadious M. Davis.
        BlS
    Early loses: a requiem. Alice
        Walker. BlS
    Go down, Mose. Unknown . EeBC
    Lines ("From fair Jamaica's..")
        Ada . BlS
    The mask. Irma McLaurin. BlS
    The promise. Johari M. Kunjufu.
        BlS
    She's free! Frances E.W.
        Harper. BlS
    To the first of August. Ann
        Plato. BlS
    To the king's most excellent
        majesty. Phillis Wheatley.
        BlS
Slavitt, Donald
    Eczema. TyW
The **sleep.** Elizabeth Barrett
    Browning. WBP3
Sleep
    After Sunday dinner we uncles
        snooze. John Ciardi. HoA

Autumn night: to Ch'iu Ta. Wei
Ying-wu . GrAC
Beautiful sleeper. Danny Logan.
YoVA
Briar Rose. Anne Sexton. EvIm
Child's evening hymn. Sabine
Baring-Gould. WBP1
Cuddle doon. Alexander
Anderson. WBP1
Doll's boy's asleep. Edward
Estlin Cummings. DuD
A Dutch lullaby. Eugene Field.
WBP1
Falling asleep. Ian
Serraillier. DuD
Flying letters. Zerubavel
Gilead. VoWA
Go sleep, ma honey. Edward D.
Barker. WBP1
"A great dark drowsiness." Paul
Verlaine. FoFS--FreS
Green. Paul Verlaine. FoFS
Half-waking. William Allingham.
WBP1
I am too close, sels. Wislawa
Szymborska. CoP
I know nothing of the sleep...
Giancarlo Marmori. NeIP
In bed. Charlotte Zolotow. BrBD
In the horse carriag. Hagiwara
Sakutaro . FroC
In your arms. Miklos Radnoti.
VoWA
Japanese lullaby. Eugene Field.
WBP1
Kehi shrine. Unknown. FroC
Litany of sleep. Tristan
Corbiere. FreS
Lullaby ("Sleep now.") Shlomo
Vinner. VoWA
Lullaby ("What if, every
time...") Frederick Eckman.
FroA
Lullaby for Miriam. Richard
Beer-Hofmann. VoWA
Mary, pondering. James F. King.
StPo
Milton the early riser. Robert
Kraus. TrWB
Nigh. Miyazawa Kenji . FroC
Portrait. John Unterecker. TeMP
Pretending to sleep. Judith
Thurman. ByM
Serenade ("Stars of the summer
night!"). Henry Wadsworth
Longfellow. WBP2
Six small songs for a silver
flute. Barry Spacks. TeMP
The sleeper. Sydney Clouts.
VoWA

Sleeping on the wind. Frank
O'Hara. SlW
Spending the night in a tower..
Tu Fu . GrAC
The stones of sleep. E.L. Mayo.
FroA
Two kid. Unknown . FroC
Under the sign of the moth.
David Wagoner. TeMP
Verses to be slandered. Paul
Verlaine. FreS
Voice in the dark. A.L.
Strauss. VoWA
Waiting... Deborah L. Raub.
YoVA
Weep you no more, sad fountain.
Unknown . HaAP
Sleep at sea. Christina Georgina
Rossetti. MTS
The **sleeper.** Sydney Clouts. VoWA
The **sleeper** of the valley.
Arthur Rimbaud. FoFS
Sleeping beauty. Alfred, Lord
Tennyson. WBP2
The **sleeping man.** Mike Howard.
YoVA
Sleeping on the wind. Frank
O'Hara. SlW
Sleeping wrestler. Takahashi
Mutsuo. FroC
Sleepless on a summer night.
Umberto Saba. VoWA
Sleepy hollow. William Ellery
Channing. WBP3
Slender maid. Joseph Eliya. VoWA
Slenderness
Poking fun at a lean ma. Otomo
no Yakamochi . FroC
Slim man canyon. Leslie Marmon
Silko. ReE
Slonimski, Antoni
Conrad. VoWA
Conversation with a countryman.
VoWA
Elegy ("No more, no more...")
VoWA
Jerusalem. VoWA
Slope. Nishiwaki Junzaburo. FroC
Sloths
Three-toed sloth. Dorothy
Donnelly. HoA
The **slow** Pacific swell. Yvor
Winters. MTS
Slow oxen. Ilya Rubin. VoWA
Slowly meeting God. Theresa
Cantrell. YoVA
The **sluggard.** Isaac Watts. HaAP
A **slumber** did my spirit seal.
William Wordsworth. HaAP
Slums

Missionaries in the jungle.
  Linda Piper. BlS
Slutsky, Boris
  Burnt. VoWA
  Dreams of Auschwitz. VoWA
  God. VoWA
  How they killed my grandmother.
    VoWA
Sly thoughts. Coventry Patmore.
  WBP2
The smack in school. William
  Pitt Palmer. WBP1
Small and early. Tudor Jenks.
  WBP1
Small beginnings. Charles
  Mackay. WBP4
Small bone ache. Moshe Dor. VoWA
Small song. Luci Shaw. EeBC
Small town. William Joyce. FroA
Smallwood, Connie
  The flower. HoWM
Smart, Christopher
  Jubilate agno, sels. HaAP
  The miser and the mouse. MiRN
  The Nativity of our Lord.
    HaAP--ShBa
  A song to David, sels. HaAP
Smile Renee. Ronald C. Rowe.
  YoVA
Smile and never heed me. Charles
  Swain. WBP2
Smile at me. Musa Moris Farni.
  VoWA
Smiles
  Intimations. Alma Johanna
    Koenig. VoWA
  Smile at me. Musa Moris Farni.
    VoWA
The smiling mouth and laughing
  eyen grey. Charles, Duc d'
  Orleans. HaAP
Smith, Barbara
  Ripple/Folds of time. YoVA
Smith, Belle E.
  If I should die tonight. WBP3
Smith, Carla
  The raindrop. HoWM
Smith, Chris
  The fourth act. HoWM
Smith, Dave
  The perspective and limits of
    snapshots. TeMP
Smith, Dianne
  Friend. YoVA
  I'm confused. YoVA
  Love/Kissing, sharing... YoVA
Smith, Florence M. ("Stevie")
  Bye baby bother. TyW
  The frog prince. HaAP
  Not waving but drowning. HaAP

Smith, Jon
  Reunion. YoVA
  A revisit. YoVA
Smith, Lisa
  Alone. YoVA
Smith, May Riley
  If we knew. WBP1
  In prison. WBP4
  Sometime. WBP4
  Tired mothers. WBP1
Smith, Mrs. F. Burge
  Little goldenhair. WBP1
Smith, Nan
  Music. HoWM
Smith, Seba
  The mother's sacrifice. WBP1
Smith, Tina
  Tears. YoVA
Smith, Walter C.
  The self-exiled. WBP4
Smith, William Jay
  A pavane for the nursery. DuD
Smits, Dirk
  On the death of an infant. WBP1
Smothered fires. Georgia Douglas
  Johnson. BlS
Snack. Lois Lenski. BrBD
Snail. John Drinkwater. RoRF
Snails
  Snail. John Drinkwater. RoRF
Snake. David Herbert Lawrence.
  SlW
Snakes
  A narrow fellow in the grass.
    Emily Dickinson. HaAP
  Returning from/scouting for
    meat. Minerva Allen. ReE
  Snake. David Herbert Lawrence.
    SlW
  To a fine young woman. William
    Wycherley. TyW
  Yetzer ha Ra. Edward Codish.
    VoWA
  Your totem is the opulent
    serpent. Giancarlo Marmori.
    NeIP
Sneaky Bill. William Cole. IlTH
Snodgrass, William DeWitt
  April inventory. LiHE
  The Fuhrer bunker, sels. TyW
  A lady. TyW
  The men's room in the college
    chapel. TyW
  A teen-ager. TyW
Snow. Amelia Rosselli. NeIP
Snow
  As snow fell. Matt Braunstein.
    YoVA
  Cold air, numb fingers. Patrick
    Crosson. YoVA

Falling snow. Allen T. Stekl. YoVA

First snow in Lake County. Lisel Mueller. PrVo

The first snow-fall. James Russell Lowell. WBP3

From a window. Terri Wright. YoVA

"I am snow." Scott Bowman. HoWM

I waited. Ulla Jonsson. YoVA

"In the field I've roped off..." Yamabe no Akahito . FroC

Lester tells of Wanda and the big snow. Paul Zimmer. FroA

Morning. Peter D. McKenzie. StPo

October snow. Mary Trimble. PrVo

The perfection of snow. Andrea Zanzotto. NeIP

Seven tankas written in early 75. Otomo no Yakamochi . FroC

Sinking into virgin snow. Sara Tollefson. YoVA

Snow and nostalgia. Simone Routier. MoVT

Snow in October. Alice Dunbar-Nelson. BlS

Snow. Amelia Rosselli. NeIP

Snowflake ballerina. Lisabeth White. YoVA

To Lady Fujiwara. Emperor Temmu (645-686). FroC

To a snowflake. Francis Thompson. EeBC

Village in a snowstorm. Norbert Krapf. FroA

Snow and nostalgia. Simone Routier. MoVT

The **snow** has melted,...memories remain. Scott May. YoVA

A **snow** in Jerusalem. Hayim Naggid. VoWA

Snow in October. Alice Dunbar-Nelson. BlS

Snow in the city. Danny Siegel. VoWA

The **snow** man. Wallace Stevens. HaAP

Snow song. Lance Henson. ReE

Snow, Karen
   Dream girl. HoA

The **snow-fiend**. Anne Radcliffe. EvIm

Snow-girl. Yunna Moritz. VoWA

Snowflake ballerina. Lisabeth White. YoVA

Snowgoose. Paula Gunn Allen. ReE

Snyder, Carl

School. YoVA

Snyder, Gary

August on sourdough, a visit... SlW

An autumn morning in Shokoku-ji. HaAP

The dead by the side of the road. HaAP

Dusty braces, sels. ReE

Four poems for Robin. SlW

Mid-August at Sourdough Mountain... HaAP

Prayer for the great family. HaAP

To hell with your fertility cult. TyW

Turtle island, sels. ReE

Why log truck drivers rise earlier... SlW

Snyder, Sabrina

I heard her cry last night. YoVA

So abruptly. Shlomit Cohen. BuAC

So confused. Tammie Slaughter. YoVA

So cruel prison. Earl of Surrey (Henry Howard). HaAP

So many feathers. Jayne Cortez. BlS

So many forests. Jacques Prevert. MoVT

So misunderstood. Richard Calam. YoVA

So sweet love seemed. Robert Seymour Bridges. WBP2

So we'll go more a-roving. George Gordon,6th Baron Byron. HaAP

So will I. Charlotte Zolotow. ByM

so? Alvin Greenberg. FroA

Soaba, Russell

Naked thoughts, sels. VooI

Soalt in tleeyaga. Mary Tallmountain. ReE

Sobin, A.G.

Greeting descendants. FroA

Soccer

The sun, the sun. Pier Paolo Pasolini. NeIP

Sodom

The red city. Stuart Merrill. FreS

Sodom's sister city. Yehuda Amichai. VoWA

The **soft** light/vanilla icing. Cindi Kennedy. YoVA

"**Soft** melodic tunes." Cathy Cameron. HoWM

Softly let us all vanish. Zishe

Landau. OnCP
Softly woo away her breath.
    Barry Cornwall (B.W.
    Procter). WBP3
Soggarth aroon. John Banim. WBP4
Solar systems. Aaron Carr. ReE
The **soldier**. Rupert Brooke. DoNG
"Soldier an' sailor too."
    Rudyard Kipling. MTS
The **soldier's** dream. Thomas
    Campbell. WBP1
The **soldier**, sels. Zbigniew
    Herbert. CoP
Soldiers
    The Anniad. Gwendolyn Brooks.
      BlS
    The black draftee from Dixie.
      Carrie Williams Clifford. BlS
    David. Patrick Crosson. YoVA
    Elegy for a dead soldier. Karl
      Shapiro. HaAP
    For our soldiers who fell in
      Russia. Franco Fortini. VoWA
    The general. Siegfried Sassoon.
      TyW
    He said to. Marvin Bell. TeMP
    Home, wounded. Sydney Dobell.
      WBP3
    Lonely warriors. R.A. Swanson.
      ReE
    Meeting a sick soldie. Lu Lun.
      GrAC
    Nightmare inspection tour...
      Gibbons Ruark. TyW
    Old soldiers home at
      Marshalltown, Iowa. Jim
      Barnes. FroA
    The soldier. Rupert Brooke.
      DoNG
    War. Joni Kurland. YoVA
    We are the warrior/spirits.
      R.A. Swanson. ReE
    We begin by loving and
      compromise, sels. Gioconda
      Belli. NiR
Solemn spirits. R.A. Swanson.
    ReE
Soliloquy of the Spanish
    cloister. Robert Browning.
    TyW
Soliloquy to a crowd. Melissa
    Heiple. YoVA
Solis, Cindy
    The drops of life. YoVA
Solitaire. Philippe Jaccottet.
    MoVT
The **solitary**. Mary Barnard. FroA
The **solitary** reaper. William
    Wordsworth. HaAP
A **solitary** tear. Nancy Phillips.

YoVA
Solitude
    En route. Theodore Weiss. TeMP
    The game of glass. Judith Mary
      Spacek. YoVA
    Innervisions. Danielle T.
      Reinke. YoVA
    Near the window, sels. Karla
      Kuskin. ByM
    Ode to solitude. Alexander
      Pope. WBP1
    Oklahoma boyhood. Duane
      BigEagle. ReE
    Out of the inner shell of
      a...landscap. Hagiwara
      Sakutaro . FroC
    Sitting alone by Ching-t'ing
      Mountain. Li Po. GrAC
    Today. Debbie Daniel. YoVA
    Up in the pine. Nancy Dingman
      Watson. ByM
    What happened to the real me?
      Laurie Rowe. YoVA
Solomon
    Solomon & Morolph: their last
      encounter. Oscar Levertin.
      VoWA
Solomon & Morolph: their last
    encounter. Oscar Levertin.
    VoWA
Solstice. Emery George. HoA
Some modern good turns. Dennis
    Dibben. FroA
Some semblance of order. Charles
    David Wright. FroA
Somebody. Unknown. WBP2
Somebody said that it couldn't
    be done. Unknown. IlTH
Someday I'll be dead. Leo
    Connellan. DoNG
A **someday** song for Sophia.
    Rochelle Ratner. TeMP
Someone talking. Joy Harjo. ReE
Something beyond. Mary Clemmer
    Ames Hudson. WBP3
Something precise. Bartolo
    Cattafi. NeIP
Sometime. May Riley Smith. WBP4
Sometimes I want to go up.
    Rachel Korn. VoWA
Somewhere I have never
    travelled... Edward Estlin
    Cummings. SlW
Somewhere you exist. Manfred
    Winkler. VoWA
Sommerer, Sabrina
    A matter of time. YoVA
Somoza (Jr.), Anastasio
    The optimist's dream. Luis
    Rocha. NiR

To David Tejada Peralta. David
   Macfield. NiR
Zoologies for today. David
   Macfield. NiR
Somoza (Sr.), Anastasio
   The death of Somoza. Mejia
      Sanchez. NiR
   Epigram XXXII. Ernesto
      Cardenal. NiR
   Somoza unveils the statute of
      Somoza... Ernesto Cardenal.
      NiR
   Zero hour. Ernesto Cardenal.
      NiR
Somoza unveils the statute of
   Somoza... Ernesto Cardenal.
   NiR
Somoza, Luis
   When? Roberto Cuadra. NiR
The Somozas. Mejia Sanchez. NiR
A song (".../That seemed so
   brief...') Howard Schwartz.
   VoWA
Song ("A weary lot is thine,
   fair maid.") Sir Walter
   Scott. WBP3
A song ("Ask me no more where
   Jove...") Thomas Carew. WBP2
Song ("Because I know deep...")
   Pauli Murray. BlS
Song ("Feet have stepped
   on...flowers.") Jean Moreas.
   FreS
A song ("Good neighbour, why do
   you...") Unknown. TyW
Song ("I am weaving a song of
   waters.") Gwendolyn B.
   Bennett. BlS
Song ("Love a woman? You're an
   ass!) John Wilmot, Earl
   Rochester. TyW
Song ("Love still has
   something...sea.") Sir
   Charles Sedley. WBP2
Song ("Make this night
   loveable.") Wystan Hugh
   Auden. TyW
Song ("My wife is far away.")
   Prince Aki. FroC
Song ("On the side of the
   road.") Edmond Jabes. VoWA
Song ("Our sovereign
   familiar...") Yamabe no
   Akahito. FroC
Song ("She's somewhere in the
   sunlight.") Richard Le
   Gallienne. WBP3
Song ("Sometimes in the fast
   food...") Randy Lane. FroA
Song ("The bride she is

winsome...") Joanna Baillie.
   WBP2
Song ("The linnet in the rocky
   dells.") Emily Bronte. HaAP
Song ("The palace of
   Yoshino...") Yamabe no
   Akahito. FroC
Song ("The shape alone let
   others prize.") Mark Akenside.
   WBP2
The song ("The song! the
   song!") Hemda Roth. VoWA
Song ("The sparrow that was
   beautiful.") Nicolas
   Bourbon. ReLP
Song ("Wandering winds whip.")
   Courtney Strang. YoVA
Song ("When from the sod the
   flowerets.") Walther von der
   Vogelweide. WBP2
Song ("When from the sod the
   flowerets.") Edgar Taylor
   (trans.). WBP2
Song ("Whipped by sorrow now.")
   Miklos Radnoti. VoWA
Song ("With a basket, a lovely
   basket.") Emperor Yuryaku
   (418-479). FroC
Song ("You told me: 'I have
   need..'") Rina Lasnier. MoVT
Song at the skirts of heaven.
   Uri Zvi Greenberg. VoWA
Song by the walls. Wang
   Ch'ang-ling. GrAC
Song for Dov Shamir. Dannie
   Abse. VoWA
Song for General Chao. Ts'en
   Shen. GrAC
A song for Pedro J. Chamorro,
   sels. Jose Arauz Mairena. NiR
A song for Simeon. Thomas
   Stearns Eliot. EeBC
A song for St. Cecilia's Day.
   John Dryden. HaAP
Song for a dance. Abraham
   Sutskever. VoWA
A song for candles. Armando
   Jaramillo. YoVA
Song for the burial of my
   mother. Shimazaki Toson. FroC
Song for the south of the lake.
   Ts'ui Kuo-fu. GrAC
Song for the white hair. Liu
   Hsi-yi. GrAC
Song form. I. Amiri Baraka
   (LeRoi Jones). SlW
Song of Egla. Maria Brooks
   (M.del Occidente). WBP3
The song of Hiawatha, sels.
   Henry Wadsworth Longfellow.

WBP3
Song of P'eng-ya. Tu Fu. GrAC
Song of Yuan Tan-ch'iu. Li Po.
    GrAC
Song of a lady from Mie.
    Unknown. FroC
Song of a man...to die in a
    strange land. Mary Austin
    (trans.). ReE
Song of black Cubans. Federico
    Garcia Lorca. SlW
Song of degrees. Paul Auster.
    VoWA
A song of fall. Karen Elizabeth
    Patterson. YoVA
Song of myself, sels. Walt
    Whitman. DoNG--SlW
Song of myself, sels. Walt
    Whitman. MTS
Song of occident. Claude Vigee.
    VoWA
Song of praise for an ox.
    Abraham Sutskever. VoWA
Song of thanksgiving (variant).
    Pierre Jean Jouve. MoVT
The song of the Savoyards. Henry
    Ames Blood. WBP3
Song of the bride. Susan Mernit.
    VoWA
The song of the camp. Bayard
    Taylor. WBP2
Song of the closing service.
    Aliza Shenhar. VoWA
The song of the fisherman. Ch'u
    Kuang-hsi. GrAC
Song of the galley-slaves.
    Rudyard Kipling. HaAP
Song of the gull. Maruyama
    Kaoru. FroC
Song of the highest tower.
    Arthur Rimbaud. FoFS--FreS
Song of the lamp. Maruyama
    Kaoru. FroC
Song of the last Jewish child.
    Edmond Jabes. VoWA
Song of the master and
    boatswain. Wystan Hugh Auden.
    MTS
The song of the old mother.
    William Butler Yeats. WBP1
Song of the ringing in the ear.
    Ishihara Yoshiro. FroC
Song of the roosting crows. Li
    Po. GrAC
Song of the sail. Maruyama
    Kaoru. FroC
The song of the shirt. Thomas
    Hood. WBP3
Song of the silent land. Johann
    Gaudenz von Salis. WBP4

Song of the silent land. Henry
    W. Longfellow (trans.). WBP4
Song of the soaring hawk.
    Chiao-jan. GrAC
Song of the tailess ox. Minamoto
    no Shitago. FroC
Song of the times. J. Adler.
    OnCP
Song of the trees of the black
    forest. Edmond Jabes. VoWA
Song of the white snow. Ts'en
    Shen. GrAC
Song of the wineshop. Wei
    Ying-wu. GrAC
Song of the young nobles. Ku
    K'uang. GrAC
The song of wandering Aengus.
    William Butler Yeats. SlW
Song of yen. Kao Shih. GrAC
A song on gazing at Chung-nan
    Mountain. Wang Wei. GrAC
A song on the end of the world,
    sels. Czeslaw Milosz. CoP
A song to David, sels.
    Christopher Smart. HaAP
A song to your blood. Molly
    Myerowitz Levine. BuAC
Song: thoughts of a traveler.
    Shimazaki Toson. FroC
Songs exchanged...Prince
    Okuninushi... Unknown. FroC
Songs for all seas, all ships.
    Walt Whitman. MTS
Songs of experience, sels.
    William Blake. HaAP
Songs of the priestess. Malka
    Heifetz Tussman. VoWA
Songs to a lady moonwalker.
    Abraham Sutskever. VoWA
Songs: 32 songs from the Ryojin
    Hisho. Unknown. FroC
Sonnenschein, Hugo
    In the ghetto. VoWA
    In the open fields. VoWA
Sonnet #1. Becky Holmberg. YoVA
Sonnet ("Her pure nails
    consecrating..."). Stephane
    Mallarme. FoFS--FreS
Sonnet ("I had no thought of
    violets..") Alice
    Dunbar-Nelson. BlS
Sonnet ("I thought our love at
    full...") James Russell
    Lowell. WBP2
Sonnet ("Muses, that sing
    Love's...") George Chapman.
    WBP2
Sonnet ("My love, I have no
    fear...") James Russell
    Lowell. WBP2

Blessed are they that mourn.
William Cullen Bryant. WBP3
The defeated. Linda Gregg. TeMP
The dirty old man. William
Allingham. WBP3
Distance spills itself.
Yocheved Bat-Miriam. VoWA
Dolor. Theodore Roethke. LiHE
Facing the sno. Tu Fu . GrAC
"A girl on a stream." Ts'ui Hao.
GrAC
Gubbinal. Wallace Stevens. SlW
Hard winter, sels. Dahlia
Ravikovich. VoWA
Hopeless grief. Elizabeth
Barrett Browning. WBP3
"I have the sadness of a
town..." Max Elskamp. FreS
I scattered my sighs to the
wind. Hayim Nachman Bialik.
VoWA
In memoriam, sels. Alfred, Lord
Tennyson. WBP1--WBP3
In wolfen teeth. Chaim Grade.
OnCP
Lady Clara Vere de Vere.
Alfred, Lord Tennyson. WBP3
Lay your head on my shoulder.
Yehuda Amichai. VoWA
Locksley Hall. Alfred, Lord
Tennyson. WBP3
Man. Walter Savage Landor. WBP3
Merry it i. Unknown . HaAP
Moan, moan, ye dying gales.
Henry Neele. WBP3
My song. Hayim Nachman Bialik.
VoWA
The nevermore. Dante Gabriel
Rossetti. WBP3
No worst, there is none. Gerard
Manley Hopkins. EeBC
The nun and harp. Harriet
Prescott Spofford. WBP3
On another's sorrow. William
Blake. EeBC
The princess. Bjornstjerne
Bjornson. WBP3
Put your word to my lips.
Rachel Korn. VoWA
Reason for your sufferin.
Tanikawa Shuntaro . FroC
Resignation. Henry Wadsworth
Longfellow. WBP3
Sad toys, sel. Ishikawa
Takuboku . FroC
Sadness. Meng Yun-ch'ing. GrAC
Sixty-four tanka. Saigyo, FroC
Sorrowing on the death of his
mistress. Otomo no Yakamochi.
FroC

Spleen ("When the low, heavy
sky...") Charles Baudelaire.
FoFS
Spring and fall. Gerard Manley
Hopkins. LiHE--SlW
Stanzas for music. George
Gordon,6th Baron Byron. HaAP
Still sorrowing. Otomo no
Yakamochi . FroC
Strange plan. Zelda . BuAC
"Such a great sorrow came..."
Gustave Kahn. FreS
The sun-dial. Austin Dobson.
WBP3
Tears, idle tears. Alfred, Lord
Tennyson. HaAP
Tears. Elizabeth Barrett
Browning. WBP3
Though I've a clever head.
Unknown . HaAP
Venus and Cupid. Mark Alexander
Boyd. HaAP
Waly, waly. Unknown. HaAP--WBP3
The widow's lament in
springtime. William Carlos
Williams. HaAP
The woodspurge. Dante Gabriel
Rossetti. HaAP
Sorrow ("Over the granite.")
Nishiwaki Junzaburo. FroC
Sorrowing on the death of his
mistress. Otomo no Yakamochi.
FroC
A **sort** of song. William Carlos
Williams. FroA
Soul
The blossoming of a soul.
Dalynne Bunting. YoVA
The body is like roots
stretching. Charles
Reznikoff. VoWA
A dialogue between body and
soul. Andrew Marvell. HaAP
The ecstasy. John Donne. HaAP
The fine sand, the terrible
sand. Zelda. BuAC
I didn't know my soul. Avraham
Ben-Yitzhak. VoWA
Judge not. Adelaide Anne
Procter. WBP4
Mental acquarium V. Georges
Rodenbach. FreS
My soul hovers over me. Joshua
Tan Pai. VoWA
My soul. Maurice Maeterlinck.
FreS
"Of the soul all things."
Stephane Mallarme. FoFS
On the wide stairs. Yehuda
Amichai. VoWA

The poet compares his soul to a
   flower. Marcantonio Flaminio.
   ReLP
Soul tattoos. Wendy Rose. ReE
Sound Reproduction (systems)
   Stereo. Mike Sanderson. YoVA
The sound of bells. Pierre
   Reverdy. MoVT
The sound of the sea. Henry
   Wadsworth Longfellow. MTS
Sound out your voices, morning
   prayers. Zelda. BuAC
Sounds
   Absence of noise Presence of
      sound. Olga Broumas. TeMP
   Day of wrath. Rene Ghil. FreS
   Nocturnal sounds. Kattie M.
      Cumbo. BlS
   Sounds ("The sounds flow.")
      Tanikawa Shuntaro . FroC
   Spring dawn. Meng Hao-jan. GrAC
   They walk on cats' paws. Rocco
      Scotellaro. NeIP
Sounds ("The sounds flow.")
   Tanikawa Shuntaro. FroC
South cottage. Wang Wei. GrAC
South wind. Nathan Yonathan.
   VoWA
The southeast ramparts of the
   Seine. Judit Toth. VoWA
Southey, Robert
   My days among the dead. WBP4
   O God! have mercy in this
      dreadful hour. MTS
   She comes majestic with
      her...sails. MTS
Southwell, Robert
   The burning Babe. HaAP--ShBa
   A child of my choice. EeBC
   Losse in delayes. WBP4
   The Nativity of Christ. EeBC
   New heaven, new war. ShBa
   New prince, new pomp. ShBa
   Scorn not the least. WBP4
   Times go by turns. WBP3
A souvenir from childhood. David
   Dietzen. YoVA
Space and Space Travel
   The bowls are empty. Leonel
      Rugama. NiR
   Dome cave preview. Joel Newton.
      HoWM
   The earth is a satellite of the
      moon. Leonel Rugama. NiR
   Journey. Rick Morris. YoVA
   On shooting particles beyond
      the world. Richard Eberhart.
      TyW
   Solar systems. Aaron Carr. ReE
Spacek, Judith Mary

The game of glass. YoVA
Tears. YoVA
Spacks, Barry
   Malediction. TyW
   Six small songs for a silver
      flute. TeMP
Spagnuoli (Mantuan), Giovanni
   Eclogue VII: Pollux. ReLP
The Spanish student, sels. Henry
   Wadsworth Longfellow. WBP2
Sparkling and bright. Charles
   Fenno Hoffman. WBP1
The sparkling water. Jan Etter.
   YoVA
Sparrow bathing. Ono Tozaburo.
   FroC
Sparrow flock. Ono Tozaburo.
   FroC
Sparrows
   In the morning all over.
      William Stafford. FroA
   Mr. and Mrs. Spikky Sparrow.
      Edward Lear. WBP1
   Song ("The sparrow that was
      beautiful.") Nicolas
      Bourbon. ReLP
   Sparrow bathing. Ono Tozaburo.
      FroC
   Sparrow flock. Ono Tozaburo.
      FroC
Spatola, Adriano
   The boomerang. NeIP
   Sterility in metamorphosis.
      NeIP
Speak. James Wright. HaAP
Speak like rain. Jerred Metz.
   VoWA
Speaking of poetry. John Peale
   Bishop. LiHE
A special moment. Frank Lamont
   Phillips. FroA
Special people. Donna Izzo. YoVA
A speck of sand. Paul Celan.
   VoWA
The spectator, sels. Joseph
   Addison. WBP4
Specters, sels. Tadeusz Gajcy.
   CoP
Speght, Rachel
   The dreame, sels. PaW
   Mortalities memorandum, sels.
      PaW
Spellbinder. Jennifer Rogers.
   YoVA
Spence, Bert
   Life is. YoVA
Spencer, Anne
   At the carnival. BlS
   Before the feast of Shushan.
      BlS

Lady, lady. BlS
Letter to my sister. BlS
Substitution. BlS
Spencer, Caroline
Living waters. WBP4
Spencer, Theodore
The Californians. TyW
Spencer, William Robert
Too late I stayed. WBP1
Spender, Stephen
The drowned. MTS
I think continually of
those...great. HaAP
Seascape. MTS
Spending the night in Yung-yang.
Wei Ying-wu. GrAC
Spending the night on the
Chien-te River. Meng Hao-jan.
GrAC
Spending the night at East
Forest Temple. Ling-ch'e.
GrAC
Spending the night in a tower...
Tu Fu. GrAC
Spending the night...Fragrance
Mt Temple. Li Ch'i. GrAC
Spenser, Edmund
Amoretti: LXVIII. EeBC--HaAP
Epithalamion, sels. WBP2
The faerie queene, sels. TyW
The faerie queene, sels. WBP4
The faerie queene, sels. MTS
An hymne of heavenly love,
sels. WBP4
The ministry of angels. WBP4
Spider. Norma Farber. PoCh
The spider and the fly. Mary
Howitt. WBP1
Spiders
Darkness/It drowns within
itself. Karen Elizabeth
Patterson. YoVA
Design. Robert Frost. LiHE
How spider saved Halloween.
Robert Kraus. TrWB
A noiseless patient spider.
Walt Whitman. HaAP
One of many. Marcie L.
Burleson. YoVA
The spider and the fly. Mary
Howitt. WBP1
Spider. Norma Farber. PoCh
The spinner. Madeline Bridges
(M.A.De Vere). WBP3
Spinning
Dorothy in the garret. John
Townsend Trowbridge. WBP3
The Irish spinning-wheel.
Alfred Percival Graves. WBP2
The spinner. Madeline Bridges

(M.A.De Vere). WBP3
The spinning girl. Nathan
Alterman. VoWA
The spinning-wheel song. John
Francis Waller. WBP2
A spinster's tale. Alice Cary.
WBP2
Summer spinning. Unknown. FroC
The spinning girl. Nathan
Alterman. VoWA
The spinning-wheel song. John
Francis Waller. WBP2
A spinster's tale. Alice Cary.
WBP2
Spire, Andre
The ancient law. VoWA
Hear, O Israel! VoWA
Nudities. VoWA
Poetics. VoWA
Pogroms. VoWA
Spirit flowers. Della Burt. BlS
The spirit land. Jones Very.
HaAP
The spirit-land. Jones Very.
WBP4
Spirit-like before light. Arthur
Gregor (Goldenberg). VoWA
Spiritual love. Albert Samain.
FreS
Spit. Charles Kenneth Williams.
VoWA
Spit, cat, spit!. Mother Goose.
TyW
Spivack, Kathleen
Approaching the canvas. TeMP
Spleen ("I am like the
king...") Charles
Baudelaire. FoFS
Spleen ("I have more
memories...") Charles
Baudelaire. FoFS
Spleen ("When the low, heavy
sky...") Charles Baudelaire.
FoFS
Splendor. Shin Shalom. VoWA
Spofford, Harriet Prescott
The nun and harp. WBP3
Spoils. Robert Graves. HaAP
Spontaneous poem I. Chiao-jan.
GrAC
Sports. Joe Dewey. YoVA
Sports
Sports. Joe Dewey. YoVA
Sposob, sels. Czeslaw Milosz.
CoP
Spouting whale. Takamura Kotaro.
FroC
Spring. Gerard Manley Hopkins.
EeBC--HaAP
The spring. Abraham Cowley. HaAP

Spring. Meleager. WBP2
Spring. Moishe Kulbak. VoWA
Spring. Becky Jones. YoVA
Spring. Andrew Lang (trans.).
    WBP2
Spring. William Shakespeare.
    HaAP
Spring. John Jordan. YoVA
Spring
    "Breath of spring..." Ryokan .
        FroC
    Desire. Isaac de Botton. VoWA
    Early spring. Kirsten Cushing.
        YoVA
    Eclogue IV. Andrea Zanzotto.
        NeIP
    Eleven tanka. Lady Ise. FroC
    Footsteps of spring. Hayim
        Nachman Bialik. VoWA
    "Green spring..." Ryokan . FroC
    I dreaded that first robin, so.
        Emily Dickinson. HaAP
    In joy. Prince Shiki (668-716).
        FroC
    It's spring returning, it'
        spring & love. Unknown. HaAP
    Lament of the springtime. Jules
        Laforgue. FreS
    Not ideas about the thing
        but... Wallace Stevens. HaAP
    Now welcom, somer. Geoffrey
        Chaucer. HaAP
    Our love is like spring. Laura
        Brinkman. YoVA
    Quatrai. Tu Fu . LuL
    Seventeen hokk. Miura Chora .
        FroC
    Seventy-eight tanka. Princess
        Shikishi. FroC
    Spring and all, sels. William
        Carlos Williams. HaAP
    Spring fever. Richard Calam.
        YoVA
    Spring is like perhaps a hand.
        Edward Estlin Cummings. SlW
    The spring snow trickled.
        Charles E. Boetsch. YoVA
    Spring. Becky Jones. YoVA
    Spring. Gerard Manley Hopkins.
        EeBC--HaAP
    Spring. John Jordan. YoVA
    Spring. Moishe Kulbak. VoWA
    Spring. William Shakespeare.
        HaAP
    Su Creek Pavilion. Tai Shu-lun.
        GrAC
    The sun, the sun. Pier Paolo
        Pasolini. NeIP
    Sunny sprin. Hagiwara Sakutaro.
        FroC

Thirteen hokku. Konishi Raizan.
    FroC
Twelve Tankas witten in early
    75. Otomo no Yakamochi . FroC
Twenty-three tank. Kyogoku
    Tamekane . FroC
Spring & Asura. Miyazawa Kenji.
    FroC
Spring and all, sels. William
    Carlos Williams. HaAP
Spring and fall. Gerard Manley
    Hopkins. LiHE--SlW
Spring and fall. Gerard Manley
    Hopkins. HaAP
Spring dawn. Meng Hao-jan. GrAC
Spring fever. Richard Calam.
    YoVA
Spring in the old world. Philip
    Levine. FroA
Spring is like perhaps a hand.
    Edward Estlin Cummings. SlW
Spring night. Hagiwara Sakutaro.
    FroC
The spring of my life, sels.
    Kobayashi Issa. FroC
The spring snow trickled.
    Charles E. Boetsch. YoVA
Spring song. Bliss Carman. WBP1
Spring sunday on Quaker Street.
    Tom Bass. FroA
"Spring" variation. Miyazawa
    Kenji. FroC
Springs
    In praise of the spring Casi.
        Giovanni Giovano Pontano.
        ReLP
Spruce Pine Mountain. Jennifer
    Leigh Dison. YoVA
Squash blossom shit and heishi
    horrors. Luci Abeita. ReE
Squirrels
    On a squirrel crossing the
        road... Richard Eberhart.
        LiHE
    Unusual. Larry Eigner. FroA
Ssu-k'ung Shu
    Sick, sending away a
        concumbine. GrAC
    Visiting Wang Stream after a
        rain. GrAC
    Visiting the recluse Hu... GrAC
St. Francis of Assisi &
    the...Jews. Jozef Wittlin.
    VoWA
St. Ives. Unknown. IlTH
St. John, Jane
    Explanations. YoVA
    My Mr. Politician. YoVA
    Proud beggarman. YoVA
St. Luke, sels. Bible-New

Testament. PoCh
Stabat Mater Dolorosa. Jacopone
  da Todi. WBP4
Stabat Mater Dolorosa. Abraham
  Coles (trans.). WBP4
The **stable** cat. Leslie Norris.
  PoCh
Stafford, William
  Answerers. TeMP
  At the un-national monument...
    HaAP
  Drummer boy. FroA
  The farm on the great plains.
    HaAP
  For a plague on the door...
    FroA
  Friend who never came. FroA
  In the morning all over. FroA
  Look. FroA
  Magic lantern. FroA
  The mountain that got little.
    FroA
  Mouse night: one of our games.
    MiRN
  Surviving a poetry circuit.
    FroA
  Traveling through the dark.
    HaAP
Staley, Deb
  Toes. YoVA
Stanfield, Michael
  God made little kittens. YoVA
Stanley, Arthur Penrhyn
  The disciples after the
    Ascension. WBP4
  "Till death us part." WBP2
Stanton, Maura
  Alcestis. TeMP
Stanzas for music. George
  Gordon,6th Baron Byron. HaAP
Stanzas written on the road...
  George Gordon,6th Baron
  Byron. WBP2
Stanzas written in dejection
  near Naples. Percy Bysshe
  Shelley. WBP3
The **star** in the pail. David
  McCord. ByM
The **star** of Bethlehem. Henry
  Kirke White. WBP4
"The **star** wept pink..." Arthur
  Rimbaud. FoFS
Star-mist. John Keble. WBP4
Star/Starlight. Karen Tollett.
  YoVA
Starlings
  A plague of starlings. Robert
    Hayden. HoA
Stars. Howard Moss. HoA
The **stars.** Gabriel Audisio. MoVT

Stars
  "Before you depart/Pale morning
    star." Paul Verlaine. FoFS
  Bright star! Would I were
    steadfast... John Keats.
    HaAP--WBP3
  Examples of created systems.
    William Meredith. TeMP
  Life as a star. Colleen Dewey.
    YoVA
  The lost Pleiad. William
    Gilmore Simms. WBP4
  Shooting star. Cathy Grogan.
    YoVA
  "Shooting star/Shooting star."
    Donna Williams. HoWM
  Sonnet ("Her pure nails
    consecrating..") Stephane
    Mallarme. FoFS--FreS
  The star in the pail. David
    McCord. ByM
  The star of Bethlehem. Henry
    Kirke White. WBP4
  Star/Starlight. Karen Tollett.
    YoVA
  The stars on the shabbat.
    Avraham Shlonsky. VoWA
  The stars. Gabriel Audisio.
    MoVT
  "Twinkle, twinkle, little star."
    Unknown . WBP1
  The universe. Michelle Garmany.
    YoVA
The **stars** on the shabbat.
  Avraham Shlonsky. VoWA
Stars, sels. John Keble. WBP4
Starting from scratch. Carolyn
  Tilghman. YoVA
Starting over. Shirley Kaufman.
  VoWA
Statues
  JC's tiger. Sam Hamod. StPo
  Old cigar store wooden Indian.
    James Cliftonne Morris. StPo
Stauffer, Sheila
  Changes. YoVA
  Daisies. YoVA
Staying ahead. Malcolm Glass.
  FroA
Stealing. Ono Tozaburo. FroC
Stearns, Tommy
  The tallest tree. YoVA
Stedman, Edmund Clarence
  Si jeunesse savait! WBP2
  The undiscovered country. WBP4
Steele, Timothy
  Here lies Sir Tact. TyW
The **steeple-jack.** Marianne
  Moore. HaAP
Steig, William

The dictator. YoVA
Song ("Wandering winds whip.")
   YoVA
The **strange** guest. Itzik Manger.
   VoWA
Strange plant. Zelda. BuAC
The **stranger.** Juan Gelman. VoWA
The **stranger** cat. N.P. Babcock.
   IlTH
Strangford (trans.), Lord
   Blighted love. WBP3
Strauss, A.L.
   In the discreet splendor. VoWA
   Lament for the European exile.
      VoWA
   On the path. VoWA
   Voice in the dark. VoWA
Strauss, Avner
   The hollow flute. VoWA
   Portait of a widow. VoWA
Streetcorner. Bill Knott. TeMP
Streets. Paul Verlaine. FoFS
Streets
   Drunken streets. Malka Locker.
      VoWA
Strength
   Yesterday's tomorrow. Alicia
      Callanan. YoVA
Stretching forth the lance.
   Pierre Louys. FreS
Stricklin, Greg
   Searching. YoVA
   Time sea. YoVA
Strike. Gioconda Belli. NiR
Strikes and Strikers
   General strike 1969. Amelia
      Rosselli. NeIP
   Strike. Gioconda Belli. NiR
Striped apricot lodge. P'ei Ti.
   GrAC
Strode, William
   Kisses. WBP2
A **stroke** of good luck. Theodore
   Weiss. StPo
Strong feelings, sels. Hsueh
   Chu. GrAC
Strong, Leilani
   The message. YoVA
   The wedding. YoVA
Strozzi, Tito
   Epigram: Of Secaurus, a riche
      man.... ReLP
   Love asleep beneath a tree.
      ReLP
The **struggle** with the angel.
   Claude Vigee. VoWA
Struggles. Venise Duchesne. YoVA
Struggling at the kill. Shlomit
   Cohen. BuAC
Struthers, Ann

Watching the out-door movie
   show. FroA
Stryk, Lucien
   Cherries. TeMP
   Farmer. FroA
   Zen poems, after Shinkichi
      Takahasi. FroA
Stuart, Dabney
   The opposite field. TeMP
Studebaker, Tammy
   Time. YoVA
Students
   Elegy for Jane. Theodore
      Roethke. HaAP--LiHE
   To the boy studying in Palmer
      Square. Patricia Celley
      Groth. StPo
   Waiting in front of the
      columnar..school. Karl
      Shapiro. HaAP
Studies from life. Martha
   Dickey. FroA
A **study** in terror. Tamura
   Ryuichi. FroC
A **study** of reading habits.
   Philip Larkin. TyW
A **study** of the object, sels.
   Zbigniew Herbert. CoP
Sturm, Julius
   I hold still. WBP3
Su Creek Pavilion. Tai Shu-lun.
   GrAC
Su Shi
   Morning breaks over the Huai
      River. LuL
   A poem ("High and lofty, tiers
      of rock.") LuL
The **Su** family villa. Tsu Yung.
   GrAC
A **subaltern's** love-song. John
   Betjeman. HaAP
Subjects and arguments
   for...desperation. Elio
   Pagliarani. NeIP
Subnarcosis. Andrea Zanzotto.
   NeIP
Substitution. Anne Spencer. BlS
Suburbs
   Morning chores. Jim Heynen.
   TeMP
The **subverted** flower. Robert
   Frost. HaAP
The **subway.** Lisa Jastrab Miller.
   YoVA
Subways
   In a station of the Metro. Ezra
      Pound. HaAP
   The subway. Lisa Jastrab
      Miller. YoVA
Success. Kevin Beasely. YoVA

FroC
That act. FroC
Two portraits. FroC
Tanka ("A bell lily
    blooming...") Lady Otomo no
    Sakanoue. FroC
Tanka ("At Nikitatsu...")
    Princess Nukada. FroC
Tanka ("I saw the sun set...")
    Emperor Tenji (?-671). FroC
Tanka ("Plovers over the evening
    waves.") Kakinomoto no
    Hitomaro. FroC
Tanka ("Spring has passed.")
    Empress Jito (645-702). FroC
Tanka ("The city of Nara...")
    Ono no Oyu. FroC
Tanka ("The stag that
    calls...") Emperor Jomei
    (593-641). FroC
Tanka ("To what shall I
    compare..world?) Sami
    Mansei. FroC
Tanka: 15 tanka. Masaoka Shiki.
    FroC
Tanka: 21 tanka from the
    Kokinshu. Unknown. FroC
Tanka: 23 tanka on love.
    Unknown. FroC
Tanka: 39 tanka. Yosano Akiko.
    FroC
Tanka: 44 tanka. Wakayama
    Bokusui. FroC
Tanner, Suzanne
    Memories. YoVA
    The purpose of life. YoVA
Tapahonso, Luci
    Conversations. ReE
    For Lori Tazbah. ReE
    Misty dawn. ReE
Tape mark. Nanni Balestrini.
    NeIP
The tapestry. Howard Nemerov.
    TeMP
Tapscott, Stephen
    Parable: November. FroA
Tarn, Nathaniel
    Where Babylon ends. VoWA
Tarred and Feathered
    Between the world and me.
    Richard Wright. LiHE
The task, sels. William Cowper.
    WBP3
Tasso, Torquato
    To the Princess Lucretia. WBP2
A taste of the blues. Judite E.
    Reis. YoVA
Tate, Allen
    The Mediterranean. HaAP--MTS
    More sonnets at Christmas. ShBa

Sonnets at Christmas. HaAP
Tate, James
    Nobody's business. TeMP
Tattlewell (pseud.), Mary
    The epistle to the reader. PaW
Tautology. Nelo Risi. NeIP
Taylor (trans.), Edgar
    Song ("When from the sod the
    flowerets.") WBP2
Taylor (trans.), W.
    My recovery. WBP4
Taylor (trans.), John Edward
    "If it be true that any
    beauteous thing." WBP2
    The might of one fair face.
    WBP2
Taylor, Bayard
    Bedouin love-song. WBP2
    Possession. WBP2
    The song of the camp. WBP2
Taylor, Benjamin F.
    The old village choir. WBP4
Taylor, Edward
    God's determinations, sels.
    HaAP
    Huswifery, sels. EeBC
    Preparatory meditations, sels.
    HaAP
Taylor, Henry
    Campaign promise. TyW
Taylor, Jane
    Pretty cow. WBP1
Taylor, Jeffreys
    The lion and the mouse. MiRN
Taylor, Jeremy
    Heaven. WBP4
Taylor, John
    End of the line. FroA
    The mill. FroA
    Roses gone wild. FroA
Taylor, Sir Henry
    Athulf and Ethilda. WBP2
    Heart-rest. WBP1
    Philip Van Artevelde, sels.
    WBP1
Tchernichovsky, Shaul
    The death of Tammuz. VoWA
    The grave. VoWA
    Man is nothing but. VoWA
    Saul's song of love. VoWA
Te Deum. Charles Reznikoff. VoWA
Te Deum Laudamus. Unknown. WBP4
"Teach me how to repent." John
    Donne. EeBC
Teaching and Teachers
    Academic curse: an epitaph.
    Wesli Court. TyW
    Epilogue ("My bibliography has
    grown.") Dallas Wiebe. TyW
    For an early retirement. Donald

Te Deum. Charles Reznikoff. VoWA

A thanksgiving to God, for his house. Robert Herrick. HaAP

That act. Tanikawa Shuntaro. FroC

That country road. Danny Callen. YoVA

That enchanted place. Gwen Perkins. YoVA

"That one feels fleeing from a soul..." Paul Verlaine. FoFS

That poem that I didn't write. Leah Goldberg. BuAC

That was then. Isabella Gardner. FroA

That's life. Kelly J. Myers. YoVA

That's our lot. Moishe Leib Halpern. VoWA

the Cambridge ladies... Edward Estlin Cummings. LiHE

the anthologist. Muriel Fath. StPo

There. Mary Elizabeth Coleridge. EeBC

There ain't nothing more important... Deborah Ann Foster. YoVA

There is a box. Uri Zvi Greenberg. VoWA

There is a garden in her face. Unknown. WBP2

There is a woman in this town. Patricia Parker. BlS

There is certainly someone. Anne Hebert. MoVT

There is no death. James Luckey McCreery. WBP3

There is no holding back...victory, sels. Gioconda Belli. NiR

There is no place. Aleksander Wat. VoWA

There is nothing in the city. David Macfield. NiR

There once was a girl named Jill. Susie Tacoronte. YoVA

There once was a boy named Timmy. Susan Bueno. YoVA

There was a leaf. Robert Desnos. MoVT

There was a little girl. Henry Wadsworth Longfellow. WBP1

There was a smell of love in the air. Joni Ensz. YoVA

There was a wee bit mousikie. Unknown. MiRN

There was a wee bit mouskie. Unknown. MiRN

"There was an old woman called nothing." Unknown. IlTH

"There was once an old man of Brest." Cosmo Monkhouse. IlTH

There was once a lady who swalled a fly. Unknown. IlTH

"there was one gigantic pine tree..." Jing Hao. LuL

There're no whistles from the crowd. Sally Campbell. YoVA

There's a certain slant of light. Emily Dickinson. HaAP

There's nae luck about the house. Jean Adam. WBP2

"There's no need to light a night light." Unknown. IlTH

There's nothing to do in New York. Tomioka Taeko. FroC

Theresa, Saint, of Avila
The flaming heart, sels. Richard Crashaw. HaAP
A hymn to...St. Teresa, sels. Richard Crashaw. HaAP

Theresienstadt poem. Robert Mezey. VoWA

These I have loved. Michelle Thiessen. YoVA

These are my favorite things. Donna Funk. YoVA

These be/Three final things. Jerold Heide. YoVA

These two. Howard Schwartz. VoWA

Theseus and Ariadne. Robert Graves. HaAP

Thespian in Jerusalem. Myra Glazer (Schotz). VoWA

They. Mani Leib. VoWA

They are all gone. Henry Vaughan. DoNG--WBP3

"They are dear fish to me." Unknown. WBP3

They flee from me. Sir Thomas Wyatt. HaAP--LiHE

They followed me. Gioconda Belli. NiR

They pursued us in the night. Michele Najlis. NiR

They say the sea is loveless. David Herbert Lawrence. MTS

They walk on cats' paws. Rocco Scotellaro. NeIP

They're lost/So many times. Lynn Maiorana. YoVA

Thiessen, Michelle
Loneliness. YoVA
These I have loved. YoVA

Thieves
Night robber. Ishihara Yoshiro. FroC
Stealing. Ono Tozaburo.   FroC

The **things**. Conrad Aiken. HaAP
Things. William Stanley Merwin.
  HaAP
Things of the earth. Sherry S.
  Cox. YoVA
Think of it. Bette Killion. ByM
Thinkin' long. Ethna Carbery
  (Anna MacManus). WBP3
Thinking about the past. Donald
  Justice. TeMP
Thinking of Prince Hozumi...
  Princess Tajima (?-708). FroC
Thinking on high antiquity. Yuan
  Chieh. GrAC
Third class country. Pablo
  Antonio Cuadra. NiR
The **third** elegie. Francois
  Remond (Crashaw). ReLP
Thirst. Musa Moris Farni. VoWA
Thirsty island. Jim Tollerud.
  ReE
Thirteen hokku. Konishi Raizan.
  FroC
Thirteen hokku. Kaai Chigetsu.
  FroC
Thirteen ways of looking at a
  blackbird. Wallace Stevens.
  SlW
Thirty tanka. Fujiwara no
  Shunzei. FroC
Thirty tanka. Tachibana Akemi.
  FroC
Thirty times thirty. Luis Rocha.
  NiR
Thirty-five Tanka. Ki no
  Tsurayuki. FroC
The **thirty-one** camels. Rachel
  Korn. VoWA
Thirty-three hokku. Takarai
  Kikaku. FroC
This is just to say. William
  Carlos Williams. SlW
This is my rock. David McCord.
  RoRF
This living hand. John Keats.
  HaAP
This lunar beauty. Wystan Hugh
  Auden. SlW
"**This** morning while waiting for
  the bus." Chris Matekovich.
  HoWM
This night. Osip Mandelstam.
  VoWA
This night. Nathan Alterman.
  VoWA
This one is about the others.
  Dan Jaffe. FroA
This town. James Paul. HoA
This world is too much with us.
  Marti Huerta. YoVA

Thom, William
  The motherless bairn. WBP1
Thomas A. Goodbody. Victor P.
  Rizzo. StPo
Thomas Rymer. Unknown. HaAP
Thomas of Celano
  Dies Irae. WBP4
Thomas, Deb
  The cry. YoVA
  Winter elements. YoVA
Thomas, Dwana
  I'm a cloud. HoWM
Thomas, Dylan
  And death shall have no
    dominion. DoNG
  Do not go gentle into that good
    night. DoNG--HaAP
  Do not go gentle into that good
    night. LiHE--TyW
  Fern hill. LiHE
  In my craft or sullen art. HaAP
  A refusal the death, by fire,
    of a child. DoNG
Thomas, Edward
  Adlestrop. HaAP
Thomas, Evan
  To the noble women of Llanarth
    Hall,sels. TyW
Thomas, Henri
  "My whole soul by now spent."
    MoVT
  Yesterday and tomorrow. MoVT
Thompson (see Rokwaho), Daniel

Thompson, Clara Ann
  His answer. BlS
  Mrs. Johnson objects. BlS
Thompson, Francis
  Daisy. WBP3
  In no strange land. EeBC--HaAP
  To a snowflake. EeBC
Thompson, Phyllis
  Eurydice. TeMP
  The wind of the cliff Ka Hea.
    FroA
Thoms, Lisa
  Nightowl. YoVA
  Personified pencil. YoVA
Thomson, James
  Connubial life. WBP2
Thor (Norse mythology)
  The almighty Thor. Lamont
    Jones. HoWM
Thoreau, Henry David
  The fisher's boy. MTS
  Indeed, indeed, I cannot tell.
    TyW
  Inspiration. EeBC
  Though all the fates should
    prove unkind. HaAP

Thorn, Lisa M.
    Being a teenager. YoVA
    Waves of time. YoVA
Thorpe, Rose Hartwick
    Curfew must not ring to-night.
        WBP2
Those Zionists. Crescenzo del
    Monte. VoWA
Those betrayed at dawn.
    Stanislaw Wygodski. VoWA
Those days of depression. Susan
    Mae Anderson. YoVA
Those high school years!. Donya
    L. Tutle. YoVA
Those last, late hours of
    Christmas Eve. Lou Anne
    Welte. PoCh
Those who come what will they
    say of us. John Knoepfle.
    FroA
Those winter Sundays. Robert
    Hayden. HaAP--HoA
Thou art gone to the grave.
    Reginald Heber. WBP3
Thou art indeed just, Lord.
    Gerard Manley Hopkins.
    HaAP--LiHE
Thou hast sworn by thy God, my
    Jeanie. Allan Cunningham.
    WBP2
Thou shalt not. Malka Heifetz
    Tussman. VoWA
"Though I lie here." Ryokan.
    FroC
Though I've a clever head.
    Unknown. HaAP
Though all the fates should
    prove unkind. Henry David
    Thoreau. HaAP
Thought
    Conceptions. Lang Zimmerman.
        YoVA
    Empty thoughts. Dennis Vass.
        YoVA
    Golden fantasy. Tamura Ryuichi.
        FroC
    It's a time for sad songs.
        Julie A. Engel. YoVA
    Just because. Moishe Leib
        Halpern. VoWA
    Just think. Paul Celan. VoWA
    Man's thoughts. Richard V.H.
        Sceiford. YoVA
    Meditation. Beyle
        Schaechter-Gottesman. VoWA
    The modern fable. Nishiwaki
        Junzaburo. FroC
    Nineteen twenty-nine (1929).
        Wystan Hugh Auden. SlW
    The quagmire of thought. Roy

    Arlington Porter. YoVA
    The secret room. Marla Gardner.
        YoVA
    Soliloquy to a crowd. Melissa
        Heiple. YoVA
    Substitution. Anne Spencer. BlS
    Twilight thoughts in Israel.
        Melech Ravitch (Z.K.
        Bergner). VoWA
    An unraveled thought. Shlomit
        Cohen. VoWA
Thought of going home. Dana
    Naone. ReE
"Thought this body, I know."
    Kino Sadamaru. FroC
Thought waves. Suzy Gierut. YoVA
Thoughtful storm. Troya Greer.
    YoVA
Thoughts. Dona Kay Hollenbeck.
    YoVA
Thoughts. David Ignatow. FroA
Thoughts for my grandmother.
    Laya Firestone. VoWA
Thoughts of heaven. Robert
    Nicoll. WBP4
Thoughts of life. James Heaton.
    YoVA
Thoughts of winter. Rebecca
    Douglas. YoVA
Thoughts on one's head. William
    Meredith. HaAP
Thoughts on the commandments.
    George Augustus Baker. WBP2
Thoughts while reading. Zhu Xi.
    LuL
Thousand league pool. Tu Fu.
    GrAC
Thread and song. John Williamson
    Palmer. WBP1
Threats of the witness, sels.
    Yves Bonnefoy. MoVT
Three AM. Joy Harjo. ReE
Three Mile Island,Pennsylvania
    Accident at Three Mile Island.
        Jim Barnes. FroA
    Ode to Three Mile Island. Tim
        Miller. YoVA
    The plumber arrives at Three
        Mile Island. Robert Stewart.
        FroA
Three blind mice. Mother Goose.
    MiRN
Three car poems. Richard Jones.
    FroA
The three children. Unknown.
    WBP1
Three corpses. Unknown. NiR
The three enemies. Christina
    Georgina Rossetti. WBP4
Three holy kings from

Morgenland. Heinrich Heine.
PoCh
The three kings. Ruben Dario.
PoCh
The three little kittens. Eliza
Lee Follen. WBP1
Three little mice (or Six...).
Mother Goose. MiRN
"Three little mice ran up the
stairs." Unknown. MiRN
Three loves. Lucy H. Hooper.
WBP2
Three poems for the Indian
steelworkers. Joseph Bruchac.
ReE
Three poets at Yuyama. Botange
Shohaku. FroC
Three songs of Mary, sels.
Madeleine L'Engle. PoCh
Three streets. Umberto Saba.
VoWA
Three thousand dollar death
song. Wendy Rose. ReE
Three tiny songs. Cid Corman.
HoA
Three years she grew in sun and
shower. William Wordsworth.
HaAP--WBP1
Three-toed sloth. Dorothy
Donnelly. HoA
Threes. Henry Chapin. FroA
Threnody. David Ignatow. FroA
Thrice toss these oaken ashes in
the air. Thomas Campion. HaAP
Throckmorton, Sir Nicholas
And though I liked not the
religion. ShBa
Through problems do we see.
Susan West. YoVA
Through the whole long night. H.
Leivick (Leivick Halpern).
VoWA
Throughout our lands, sels.
Czeslaw Milosz. CoP
Thrushes
The darkling thrush. Thomas
Hardy. EvIm--HaAP
Thule
Ultima Thule. Henry Wadsworth
Longfellow. MTS
Thule, the period of
cosmography. Unknown. HaAP
Thunder. Debbie Farrar. YoVA
Thunder
Thunder. Debbie Farrar. YoVA
The waste land. Thomas Stearns
Eliot. HaAP
Thurlow (see Hovell-Thurlow),E

Thurman, Judith

Pretending to sleep. ByM
Tiberias, Israel
Looking for Maimonides:
Tiberias. Shirley Kaufman.
VoWA
Tichborne's elegy. Chidiock
Tichborne. HaAP
Tichborne, Chidiock
Tichborne's elegy. HaAP
Ticheborne, Chediock
Lines. WBP3
The tickler rhyme. Ian
Serraillier. RoRF
The tidbit and the clodder baw.
Ellen De Haan. YoVA
Tide
At the slackening of the tide.
James Wright. MTS
Climbing to Camphor Pavilion..
Meng Hao-jan . GrAC
The tide rises, the tide falls.
Henry Wadsworth Longfellow.
MTS
The tide rises, the tide falls.
Henry Wadsworth Longfellow.
MTS
"Tidedrops on seashelf." Lois
Marie Harrod. StPo
Tiempo (Israel Zeitlin), Cesar
The Jewish cemetery. VoWA
Ties. Guillaume Apollinaire.
MoVT
The tiger. Raven Hail. ReE
Tiger. Mary Ann Hoberman. RoRF
Tiger-lily. Raquel Chalfi. BuAC
Tigers
Folk tune. Esther Raab.
BuAC--VoWA
Jungle incident. Russell Gordon
Carter. IlTH
Limerick:" .young lady of
Niger. Unknown . IlTH--WBP1
Nature's mercy. Todd Warne.
YoVA
Tiger. Mary Ann Hoberman. RoRF
The tiger. Raven Hail. ReE
The tyger. William Blake.
HaAP--LiHE
Tilghman, Carolyn
Only to lose. YoVA
Starting from scratch. YoVA
"Till death us part." Arthur
Penrhyn Stanley. WBP2
Time. Donna Marie Janis. YoVA
Time. Tammy Studebaker. YoVA
Time. Gina Gibbons. YoVA
Time. Lori Margheim. YoVA
Time. Joyce Hill. YoVA
Time. Donya L. Tutle. YoVA
Time. Hiram Amerson. YoVA

Time. Avraham Huss. VoWA
Time. Percy Bysshe Shelley. MTS
Time. Pamela Maxwell. YoVA
Time
  The anniversary. John Donne.
    HaAP
  Another day, another time.
    Denise L. Gastil. YoVA
  As yesterday was washed away.
    Laurie Campbell. YoVA
  Axioms. Gad Hollander. VoWA
  The boy Urashima of Mizuno.
    Takahashi Mushimaro . FroC
  Break, break, break. Alfred,
    Lord Tennyson. HaAP--MTS
  Climbing to the heights of
    Pao-yi Templ. Wei Ying-wu .
    GrAC
  The clock. Charles Baudelaire.
    FoFS
  Come unto us who are...laden.
    Harry Roskolenko. FroA
  Corona. Paul Celan. VoWA
  Counting the beats. Robert
    Graves. HaAP
  The day after the day before.
    Lang Zimmerman. YoVA
  Days. Ralph Waldo Emerson. HaAP
  Dry salvages, sels. Thomas
    Stearns Eliot. ShBa
  East Coker. Thomas Stearns
    Eliot. HaAP
  Eternity/With the newly born.
    Kathy Hamm. YoVA
  Even such is time. Sir Walter
    Ralegh. HaAP
  Evermore. Sandra Payne. YoVA
  February. Pier Paolo Pasolini.
    NeIP
  The garden seat. Thomas Hardy.
    HaAP
  Haiku ("Colored leaves
    trickle.") Rosalie Williams.
    YoVA
  In Sung, sel. Kao Shih . GrAC
  In a spin. Lynn Maiorana. YoVA
  In mourning for the summe.
    Tachihara Michizo . FroC
  Lifelong. Rachel Boimwall. VoWA
  Lines from a misplaced person.
    Jeanne Hill. FroA
  Losse in delayes. Robert
    Southwell. WBP4
  Lost in time. Eddy Shipman.
    HoWM
  Love and life. John Wilmot,
    Earl Rochester. HaAP
  "Mingling with the wind." Ryokan.
    FroC
  Observing the past on Chi Hill,

    sel. Ch'en Tzu-ang . GrAC
  Ode: Intimations of
    immortality. William
    Wordsworth. HaAp--WBP4
  Painted men. Stanford K. Acomb.
    YoVA
  Passage. Richard Eberhart. FroA
  Passages. Maria Kohr. YoVA
  The past. Sherry Carman. YoVA
  A petition to time. Barry
    Cornwall (B.W. Procter). WBP1
  Pre-positions. Jose Isaacson.
    VoWA
  The present. Franco Fortini.
    NeIP
  Ripple/Folds of time. Barbara
    Smith. YoVA
  "Rounds, grapes, roses!"
    Gustave Kahn. FreS
  Save. Susan A. Klee. YoVA
  Solitaire. Philippe Jaccottet.
    MoVT
  Sonnet LXV. William
    Shakespeare. HaAP
  Stone. E.L. Mayo. FroA
  Sunset. Darryl Cox. YoVA
  The time of hearts. Michel
    Leiris. MoVT
  Time passe. Kitahara Hakushu .
    FroC
  Time. Avraham Huss. VoWA
  Time. Donna Marie Janis. YoVA
  Time. Donya L. Tutle. YoVA
  Time. Gina Gibbons. YoVA
  Time. Hiram Amerson. YoVA
  Time. Joyce Hill. YoVA
  Time. Lori Margheim. YoVA
  Time. Pamela Maxwell. YoVA
  Time. Tammy Studebaker. YoVA
  To the virgins, to make much of
    time. Robert Herrick.
    HaAP--WBP1
  Today's one helluva day!
    Edward Wilde. YoVA
  Tomorrow. Bob Carter. YoVA
  Too late I stayed. William
    Robert Spencer. WBP1
  Too late. Rachel Korn. VoWA
  Villa on Chung-nan Mountai.
    Wang Wei . GrAC
  The wall. Cesare Vivaldi. NeIP
  Waves of time. Lisa M. Thorn.
    YoVA
  The years. Scott McCartney.
    YoVA
  Yesterday and tomorrow. Henri
    Thomas. MoVT
  Zero life, sels. Lamberto
    Pignotti. NeIP
Time ("Alms for the hunting

turn..." Michael Tarchaniota Marullus. ReLP

To Nearera: "My sweete..." Michael Tarchaniota Marullus. ReLP

To Ned. Herman Melville. MTS

To Nilinigii. Bernadette Chato. ReE

To Noel. Gabriela Mistral. PoCh

To P'ei Ti. Wang Wei. GrAC

To Pius IX. John Greenleaf Whittier. TyW

To Raja Rao, sels. Czeslaw Milosz. CoP

To Roosevelt, sels. Ruben Dario. NiR

To S.M.a young African painter... Phillis Wheatley. BlS

To Secretary Ling-hu. Li Shang-yin. GrAC

To Stella. Giovanni Giovano Pontano. ReLP

To T.S. Eliot. Emanuel Litvinoff. VoWA

To Thaliarchus. Sir Stephen Vere (trans.). WBP1

To Thaliarchus. Horace. WBP1

To Thomas Borge: dawn ceased..dream. Francisco de Asis Fernandez. NiR

To W.L.G. on reading his 'Chosen queen'. Charlotte Forten (Grimke). BlS

To Wei Tzu-ch'un. Wang Chi-yu. GrAC

To William Drummond of Hawthornden. Mary Oxlie. PaW

To Xanadu, which is Beth Shaul. Arye Sivan. VoWA

To a God unknown. David Eller. VoWA

To a Highland girl. William Wordsworth. WBP1

To a Taoist on Ch'uan-chiao Mountain. Wei Ying-wu. GrAC

To a bad heart. Tim Reynolds. TyW

To a blossoming pear tree. James Wright. HaAP

To a cactus seller. Anwar Shaul. VoWA

To a child born in time of small war. Helen Sorrells. LiHE

To a child during sickness. Leigh Hunt. WBP1

To a dark girl. Gwendolyn B. Bennett. BlS

To a fine young woman. William Wycherley. TyW

To a fish. Leigh Hunt. MTS

To a gentleman and lady on the death... Phillis Wheatley. BlS

To a gone era. Irma McLaurin. BlS

To a lady. John James Piatt. WBP2

To a lady admiring herself... Thomas Randolph. WBP2

To a loudmouth pontificator. Ray Mizer. TyW

To a mouse. Robert Burns. MiRN--LiHE

To a mouse. Robert Burns. HaAP

To a poor old woman. William Carlos Williams. SlW

To a portrait. Arthur Symons. WBP3

To a portrait of Lermontov. Margarita Aliger. VoWA

To a skylark. Percy Bysshe Shelley. HaAP

To a snowflake. Francis Thompson. EeBC

To a suckling satirist. Tristan Corbiere. FreS

To a tyrant. Joseph Brodsky. VoWA

To a victim of radiation. Arturo Vivante. FroA

To a waterfowl. William Cullen Bryant. EeBC

To a young girl. David Rosenmann-Taub. VoWA

to an ancient sanctuary during holy-week. Muriel Fath. StPo

To an athlete dying young. Alfred Edward Housman. HaAP--LiHE

To autumn. John Keats. HaAP

To be a master in your house. Natan Zach. VoWA

To be an American. Scott McCartney. YoVA

To be an artist. Peggi Jackson. YoVA

To be me. Jeanne Neal. YoVA

To be of use. Marge Piercy. HoA

"To bow and accept the end." Sandra Hilton. YoVA

To comfort my little son and daughter. Sugawara no Michizane. FroC

To death. Gluck (German poet). WBP3

To detraction I present my poesie. John Marston. TyW

To friends. Franco Fortini. NeIP

To heaven. Ben Jonson. HaAP

To heaven approached a Sufi saint. Jalal ed-Din Rumi. WBP4

To hell with your fertility cult. Gary Snyder. TyW

To her absent sailor. John Greenleaf Whittier. WBP3

To her sister misteris A.B., sels. Isabella Whitney. PaW

To him. Judy Comstock. YoVA

To his coy mistress. Andrew Marvell. HaAP--LiHE

To his ladie beloved. Angelo Poliziano. ReLP

To his mistress. Nicolas Bourbon. ReLP

To his wife, when he fell ill... Mikata no Sami. FroC

To inscribe on a picture of a skull... Ryokan. FroC

To insure survival. Simon J. Ortiz. ReE

To keep the memory of C...Forten Grimke. Angelina Weld Grimke. BlS

To live here. Paul Eluard (Eugene Grindel). MoVT

To my child. Abraham Sutskever. VoWA

To my dear and loving husband. Anne Dudley Bradstreet. HaAP

To my descendant, sels. Tadeusz Gajcy. CoP

To my father. Henrietta Cordelia Ray. BlS

To my father. Susannah Fried. VoWA

To my grandmother. Frederick Locker-Lampson. WBP1

To my infant son. Thomas Hood. WBP1

To my least favorite reviewer. Howard Nemerov. TyW

To my neighbors on Jank Creek. Yuan Chieh. GrAC

To my parents, sels. Krzysztof Kamil Baczynski. CoP

To myself. Catherine Winkworth (trans.). WBP3

To myself. Paul Fleming. WBP3

To old Lady Shii. Empress Jito (645-702). FroC

To one in paradise. Edgar Allan Poe. WBP2

To open. Antonio Porta. NeIP

To roses in the bosom of Castara. William Habington. WBP2

To say 'good-bye'. Paul White. YoVA

To seek a friend. William Cowper. WBP1

To some few Hopi ancestors. Wendy Rose. ReE

To someone. Takamura Kotaro. FroC

To soulfolk. Margaret Goss Burroughs. BlS

To the Jews in Poland. Jozef Wittlin. VoWA

To the Princess Lucretia. Torquato Tasso. WBP2

To the Rt Hon William..., sels. Phillis Wheatley. BlS

To the Virginian voyage. Michael Drayton. HaAP

To the boy studying in Palmer Square. Patricia Celley Groth. StPo

To the death of...Orlando Narvaez. Unknown. NiR

To the divine neighbor. Judah Leib Teller. VoWA

To the elephants. Nathan Alterman. VoWA

To the eternal madame. Tristan Corbiere. FreS

To the film industry in crisis. Frank O'Hara. SlW

To the first of August. Ann Plato. BlS

To the harbormaster. Frank O'Hara. MTS

To the immortal memory of the halibut... William Cowper. MTS

To the king's most excellent majesty. Phillis Wheatley. BlS

To the memory of Zulma. Tristan Corbiere. FreS

To the memory of J. Horace Kimball. Ada. BlS

To the memory of Mr. Oldham. John Dryden. HaAP

To the memory...William Shakespeare. Ben Jonson. HaAP

To the muses. William Blake. HaAP

To the noble women of Llanarth Hall,sels. Evan Thomas. TyW

To the nymph Brissa. Jean Salmon Macrin. ReLP

To the reader. Charles Baudelaire. FoFS

To the reader...friendly to poetrie. Anne (Edgcumbe) Trefusis. PaW

To the reviewers. Thomas Hood. TyW

To the unco guid. Robert Burns. WBP4

To the virgins, to make much of time. Robert Herrick. HaAP--WBP1

To the waggoner's daughter. Rocco Scotellaro. NeIP

To the world. Andrea Zanzotto. NeIP

To the young rebels. E.L. Mayo. FroA

To turn from love. Sarah Webster Fabio. BlS

To usward. Gwendolyn B. Bennett. BlS

To waken an old lady. William Carlos Williams. HaAP

To whoever finds this. Barbara Clark. YoVA

To you building the new house. Nelly Sachs. VoWA

To youth. Walter Savage Landor. WBP1

To-morrow. Lope de Vega. WBP4

To-morrow. Henry W. Longfellow (trans.). WBP4

To: my boyfriend. Vicki Blowe. YoVA

The toad-eater. Robert Burns. TyW

Toads
   Delicate the toad. Robert Francis. DuD
   The philosopher toad. Rebecca S. Nichols. WBP4

The toadstool wood. James Reeves. DuD

Tobacco
   Epigram: tobacco. Joannes Posthius. ReLP

A toccata at Galuppi's. Robert Browning. HaAP

Tocito visions. Grey Cohoe. ReE

Todaiji Temple, Japan
   God's measurements. Laurence Lieberman. TeMP

Today. Debbie Daniel. YoVA

Today I am modest. Esther Raab. BuAC

Today the Nazis forces marched. Melech Ravitch (Z.K. Bergner). OnCP

Today they are roasting Rocky Norse. Gary Gildner. TeMP

Today was different. Peggi Wilson. YoVA

Today's communique. Leonel Rugama. NiR

Today's ferns. Ono Tozaburo. FroC

Today's one helluva day!. Edward Wilde. YoVA

Toes. Deb Staley. YoVA

Toes. Carolyn Heide. YoVA

Toes
   Toes. Carolyn Heide. YoVA
   Toes. Deb Staley. YoVA

Together. Becky Cairel. YoVA

Together. Kerry Hadsell. YoVA

Together forever. Jackie Bowman. YoVA

Tohub. Jakov van Hoddis (H.Davidson). VoWA

Tollefson, Sara
   Bold white face. YoVA
   My grandparents' house. YoVA
   Sinking into virgin snow. YoVA

Tollerud, Jim
   Eye of God. ReE
   Rainier. ReE
   Thirsty island. ReE
   Twentieth century. ReE

Tollett, Karen
   My gift to the world. YoVA
   Star/Starlight. YoVA

Tolliver, Patrick
   I am a brick. HoWM

Tolson, Melvin B.
   Freemon Hawthorne. FroA
   Peg Leg Snelson. FroA
   Sootie Joe. FroA

Tolstoy, Leo
   Leo Tolstoy. Carolyn Pintye. StPo

Tom May's death, sels. Andrew Marvell. HaAP

Tomasito. Pablo Antonio Cuadra. NiR

Tomb. Stephane Mallarme. FoFS

Tomb. David Semah. VoWA

The tomb of Edgar Allan Poe. Stephane Mallarme. FoFS--FreS

Tomboys
   Me. Jan Flippin. YoVA

Tombs. See Cemeteries

Tomioka Taeko
   Age. FroC
   Between-. FroC
   Just the two of us. FroC
   Let me tell you about myself. FroC
   Please say something. FroC
   see you soon. FroC
   There's nothing to do in New York. FroC

Tomorrow, my son, all will be different. Edwin Castro. NiR

Tomorrow. Bob Carter. YoVA

Tomorrow. Myra Cohn Livingston.

tower... GrAC
Suffering the early autumn
   heat. GrAC
Thousand league pool. GrAC
Unclassified poems of
   Ch'in-chou, sels. GrAC
View of the winds. GrAC
Walking alone by the
   riverbank..., sels. GrAC
"Wind of ruin, lurking rain"
   GrAC
Yangtze and Han. GrAC
Yu-hua Palace. GrAC
Tu Fu (about)
On the day of mankind: to Tu Fu.
   Kao Shih . GrAC
On the road to paradise.
   Garrett Hongo. HoA
Tuckerman, Frederick Goddard
Put off thy bark from shore...
   MTS
Sonnets, sels. HaAP
Tucson: first night. Paula Gunn
   Allen. ReE
Tuesday. Zishe Landau. VoWA
The **tuft** of kelp. Herman
   Melville. MTS
Tulips. Sylvia Plath. HaAP
Tulips
Tulips. Sylvia Plath. HaAP
Turbeville, Penny Lynn
The ultimate question. YoVA
Turn blind. Paul Celan. VoWA
Turner, Charles Tennyson
Letty's globe. WBP1
Sunrise. WBP4
Turner, Marjorie L.
House of mirrors. StPo
The log. StPo
Marsh in early morning. StPo
Turner, Steve
Christmas is really for the
   children. EeBC
How to hide Jesus. EeBC
Turning back. Michael Sheridan.
   PrVo
Turnips
Mr. Finney's turnip. Unknown.
   IlTH
Turtle island, sels. Gary
   Snyder. ReE
Tussman, Malka Heifetz
At the well. VoWA
I say. VoWA
Love the ruins. VoWA
Songs of the priestess. VoWA
Thou shalt not. VoWA
Water without sound. VoWA
Tutankhamen
Cartouche: the sign of the

king. Marian J. Darling. StPo
Tutle, Donya L.
Those high school years! YoVA
Time. YoVA
"A **tutor** who tooted a flute,"
   Carolyn Wells. IlTH
Tuwim, Julian
The gypsy bible. VoWA
Jewboy. VoWA
Lodgers. VoWA
Mother. VoWA
The **twa** corbies. Unknown. HaAP

'**Twas when** the seas were
   roaring. John Gay. HaAP

Twelfth night, sels. William
   Shakespeare. DoNG
Twelfth night, sels. William
   Shakespeare. WBP2
Twelfth night, sels. William
   Shakespeare. WBP3
Twelve Tankas witten in early
   750. Otomo no Yakamochi. FroC
The **twelve** days of Christmas.
   Unknown. PoCh
Twelve lines about the burning
   bush. Melech Ravitch (Z.K.
   Bergner). VoWA
Twentieth century. Jim Tollerud.
   ReE
Twenty hokku. Mukai Kyorai. FroC
Twenty-eight to twenty (28 to
   20). Scott Moore. YoVA
Twenty-four hokku. Takai Kito.
   FroC
Twenty-four tanka. Minamoto no
   Sanetomo. FroC
Twenty-nine hokku. Tan Taigi.
   FroC
Twenty-one hokku. Kaya Shirao.
   FroC
Twenty-one hokku. Nozawa Boncho.
   FroC
Twenty-seven hokku. Natsume
   Seibi. FroC
The **Twenty-third** psalm. George
   Herbert. EeBC
Twenty-three hokku. Uejima
   Onitsura. FroC
Twenty-three tanka. Kyogoku
   Tamekane. FroC
Twice the thief. Victor P.
   Rizzo. StPo

Twilight of freedom. Osip
    Mandelstam. VoWA
Twilight room. Hagiwara
    Sakutaro. FroC
Twilight thoughts in Israel.
    Melech Ravitch (Z.K.
    Bergner). VoWA
"Twinkle, twinkle, little star."
    Unknown. WBP1
The twins. Henry Leigh. IlTH
Two. Margarita Aliger. VoWA
Two. Moishe Kulbak. VoWA
The two angels. John Greenleaf
    Whittier. WBP4
Two circles. Norman H. Russell.
    ReE
Two families. Charles G. Bell.
    FroA
Two fishermen. Stanley Moss.
    VoWA
Two flowers. Carrie Town. YoVA
Two gardens. Yona Wallach. BuAC
Two halves, when they/collide.
    Shelley Gay. YoVA
Two hundred five/math. Maria
    Cardenas. YoVA
Two kids. Unknown. FroC
Two lovers. George Eliot (M.E.L.
    Cross). WBP2
"Two lovers sitting on a tomb."
    Pati Hill. FroA
Two monkeys by Bruegel, sels.
    Wislawa Szymborska. CoP
The two mysteries. Mary Mapes
    Dodge. WBP3
Two pictures. Marian
    Douglas(A.D.G.Robinson). WBP1
Two portraits. Tanikawa
    Shuntaro. FroC
The two rabbis. John Greenleaf
    Whittier. WBP4
Two refugees. Mordecai Marcus.
    VoWA
Two sayings. Elizabeth Barrett
    Browning. WBP4
Two songs. Cecil Day Lewis. HaAP
Two songs from a play. William
    Butler Yeats. HaAP
Two times two is four. H.
    Leivick (Leivick Halpern).
    VoWA
The two waitings. John White
    Chadwick. WBP3
Two went up into the temple to
    pray. Richard Crashaw.
    HaAP--WBP4
The two worlds. Mortimer
    Collins. WBP4
The tyger. William Blake.
    HaAP--LiHE

Tyrannic love, sels. John
    Dryden. WBP2
Tyrants and Tyranny
    Caesar and the flesh. Ernesto
        Mejia Sanchez. NiR
    The dictator. Courtney Strang.
        YoVA
    Epigram ("Haven't you
        read...") Ernesto Cardenal.
        NiR
    Poems in pieces. Pablo Antonio
        Cuadra. NiR
    The satraps. Pablo Neruda. NiR
    The Somozas. Mejia Sanchez. NiR
    To a tyrant. Joseph Brodsky.
        VoWA
    The unbearable presence.
        Beltran Morales. NiR
    Urn with a political profile.
        Pablo Antonio Cuadra. NiR
    You wake up to cannon fire.
        Ernesto Cardenal. NiR
Tyson, Douglas
    "I saw a pretty thing." HoWM
Tzara, Tristan
    Evening. VoWA
    Mothers. VoWA

U name this one. Carolyn M.
    Rodgers. BlS
U.S. patented. Joyce Quindipan.
    YoVA
Uejima Onitsura
    Twenty-three hokku. FroC
Ugliness
    Ugly chile. Clarence Williams.
        TyW
Ugly chile. Clarence Williams.
    TyW
Uhland, Ludwig
    The landlady's daughter. WBP2
    The passage. WBP3
Ulinover, Miriam
    Havdolah wine. VoWA
    In the courtyard. VoWA
Ullman, Leslie
    Proof. FroA
Ulrich (Duke Brunswick), Anton
    God's sure help in sorrow. WBP3
Ultima Thule. Henry Wadsworth
    Longfellow. MTS
Ultima veritas. Washington
    Gladden. WBP4
The ultimate question. Penny
    Lynn Turbeville. YoVA
Ulysses. Alfred, Lord Tennyson.
    LiHE--MTS

Ulysses and the Siren. Samuel
    Daniel. HaAP
The **umbrella**, the cane, and the
    broom. Eliezer Steinbarg.
    VoWA
Un chien Andalou. Henry F.
    Beechhold. StPo
The **unbearable** presence. Beltran
    Morales. NiR
Unchanging. Frederich M. von
    Bodenstedt. WBP3
Unclassified poems of
    Ch'in-chou, sels. Tu Fu. GrAC
Uncle Jack. David Kherdian. FroA
Uncles
    Grey uncles. Ephraim Auerbach.
        OnCP
    Uncle Jack. David Kherdian.
        FroA
Under Ben Bulben. William Butler
    Yeats. HaAP
Under a single star, sels.
    Wislawa Szymborska. CoP
Under a tree. Matsuo Basho. FroC
Under my window. Thomas
    Westwood. WBP1
Under restless clouds. Hanny
    Michaelis. VoWA
Under stone. Elaine Feinstein.
    VoWA
Under the earth. Abraham
    Sutskever. VoWA
Under the edge of February.
    Jayne Cortez. BlS
Under the mistletoe. Countee
    Cullen. PoCh
Under the ruins of Poland. Itzik
    Manger. VoWA
Under the shawl. Rose Drachler.
    VoWA
Under the sign of the moth.
    David Wagoner. TeMP
Under the wood. Unknown. HaAP
Understanding. Debbie Bolin.
    YoVA
The **undiscovered** country. Edmund
    Clarence Stedman. WBP4
Unearthing. Betsy Rosenberg.
    VoWA
The **unfinished** prayer. Unknown.
    WBP1
Ungaro, Vita C.
    All the dirt that's fit to pot.
        StPo
    "Lost face of summer." StPo
    Powdered stars. StPo
    Sunflowers in a storm. StPo
The **unicorn**, sels. Isaac
    Rosenberg. VoWA
'The **unillumined** verge.' Robert

Bridges. WBP3
Unite. David Macfield. NiR
The **United** Fruit Co.. Pablo
    Neruda. NiR
United States
    An American thought. Carl
        Gingras. YoVA
    Art in America. Theodore Weiss.
        StPo
    Dark testament. Pauli Murray.
        BlS
    I hear America singing. Walt
        Whitman. HaAP
    In Goya's greatest scenes.
        Lawrence Ferlinghetti. LiHE
    next to of course god america
        i. Edward Estlin Cummings.
        LiHE
    Reprise of one of A.G.'s best
        poems! I. Amiri Baraka
        (LeRoi Jones). TeMP
    U.S. patented. Joyce Quindipan.
        YoVA
    We wait. Robert J. Conley. ReE
Unity. Jakov de Haan. VoWA
Unity
    Ties. Guillaume Apollinaire.
        MoVT
The **universal** prayer. Alexander
    Pope. WBP4
The **universe**. Michelle Garmany.
    YoVA
The **unknown** citizen. Wystan Hugh
    Auden. LiHE
The **unliberated** woman. Rusty
    Breshears. YoVA
Unpainted. Joyce Quindipan. YoVA
The **unquiet** grave. Unknown. HaAP
An **unraveled** thought. Shlomit
    Cohen. VoWA
Unruh, Mark W.
    Mad like a bull when hit
        unexpectedly. YoVA
The **unseen** playmate. Robert
    Louis Stevenson. WBP1
Unseen spirits. Nathaniel Parker
    Willis. WBP3
An **unsuspected** fact. Edward
    Cannon. IlTH
Unterecker, John
    Portrait. TeMP
Until I saw the sea. Lilian
    Moore. ByM
Until we're free. Gioconda
    Belli. NiR
Untitled. Debbie Bolin. YoVA
Untitled. Lisa Jastrab Miller.
    YoVA
Untitled. Megan A. David. YoVA
Untitled. Claire Dugan. YoVA

autobiogrpahy..."). HaAP

Van Dyk (trans.), H.S.
   On the death of an infant. WBP1
Van Dyke, Henry
   The child in the garden. WBP1
   A wayfaring song. WBP1
Van Elsen. Frederick George
      Scott. WBP3
Van Gemert, Angela
   Autumn. YoVA
   No rose colored glasses. YoVA
   Wide eyed love. YoVA
Van Klaveren, Scott
   The great glue mess. YoVA
   Kristen Diane. YoVA
   A simple pleasure. YoVA
Van Lerberghe, Charles
   Autumn-strewn ground. FreS
Van Overschelde, Mark
   Baseball. YoVA
Van Sice, Cathy
   We. YoVA
Van Walleghen, Michael
   The honeymoon of the muse. PrVo
Vander Molen, Robert
   Sunny. FroA
Vandergrift, Margaret
   The dead doll. WBP1
   Limerick:"... a stately
      giraffe." IlTH
Vanitas vanitatum. John Webster.
      DoNG
Vanity. Unknown. WBP4
The vanity of the world. Francis
      Quarles. WBP3
Vanity. See Pride and Vanity
Vargas, Hector
   Wasteland collage. NiR
Vargas, Roberto
   Homage to the third march on
      Delano. NiR
Variations on white, sels. Nelo
      Risi. NeIP
Vas, Istvan
   Catacombs. VoWA
   Just this. VoWA
   Tambour. VoWA
   What is left? VoWA
Vases
   "Risen from the rump..."
      Stephane Mallarme. FoFS--FreS
Vashti. Frances E.W. Harper. BlS
Vass, Dennis
   Empty thoughts. YoVA
   A kiss. YoVA
Vaughan, Henry
   Christ's nativity. ShBa
   Easter hymn. EeBC
   Happy are the dead. WBP3
   The nativity. ShBa

Peace. HaAP--WBP4
The retreat. HaAP--ShBa
The search. ShBa
The seed growing secretly. WBP4
The shepherds. ShBa
They are all gone. DoNG--WBP3
The true Christmas. ShBa
The world. HaAP
Vaughn, Angela
   Yesterday and today. YoVA
Vazakas, Byron
   West Fifty-Seventh Street. FroA
Vega, Lope de
   At dawn the Virgin is born.
      PoCh
   A little carol of the Virgin.
      PoCh
   To-morrow. WBP4
Venable, William Henry
   The school girl. WBP1
Vengefulness. Stanislaw
      Grochowiak. CoP
Veni creator spiritus. Saint
      Gregory the Great. WBP4
Veni creator spiritus. John
      Dryden (trans.). WBP4
Veni sancte spiritus. Catharine
      Winkworth (trans.). WBP4
Veni sancte spiritus. Robert II;
      King of France. WBP4
Venice, Italy
   For Venice, sinking. Geraldine
      Clinton Little. StPo
   Of the admirable city Venice.
      Jacopo Sannazaro. ReLP
Venus (goddess)
   Venus Anadyomene. Arthur
      Rimbaud. FoFS
Venus Anadyomene. Arthur
      Rimbaud. FoFS
Venus and Cupid. Mark Alexander
      Boyd. HaAP
Verbum caro factum est. Unknown.
      ShBa
Vere (Earl of Oxford), Edward
   A renunciation. WBP2
Vere (trans.), Sir Stephen
   To Thaliarchus. WBP1
Verhaeren, Emile
   By the water. FreS
   The lady in black. FreS
   London. FreS
   Mad song. FreS
   The one from the horizon. FreS
   Sin. FreS
Verlaine, Paul
   Allegory. FoFS
   Art of poetry. FoFS--FreS
   Autumn song. FoFS--FreS
   "Before you depart/Pale morning

star." FoFS
Brussels: merry-go-round.
    FoFS--FreS
Brussels: simple frescoes. FreS
Crimen amoris. FoFS
The faun. FoFS
"A great dark drowsiness."
    FoFS--FreS
Green. FoFS
"Hope shines like a blade of
    straw..." FoFS--FreS
"The hunting horn grieves..."
    FoFS
"In my heart there is weeping."
    FoFS
"In the endless ennui/Of the
    meadowland." FoFS
Kaleidoscope. FoFS--FreS
Lame sonnet. FreS
Langour. FreS
"Listen to the gentle song..."
    FreS
Lust ("Flesh, sole fruit
    tasted...") FreS
Mandolin. FoFS
"The moon shines white..."
    FoFS--FreS
Moonlight. FoFS
"My God said to me: My
    son...") FoFS
My familiar dream. FoFS
Nevermore. FoFS
Parsifal. FreS
Penny pictures. FreS
"The piano that a frail hand
    kisses..." FoFS
Sentimental colloquy. FoFS
"The sky is, above the roof"
    FoFS
Streets. FoFS
"That one feels fleeing from a
    soul..." FoFS
The time for lovers. FoFS
Verses to be slandered. FreS
With muted strings. FoFS
Verlaine, Paul (about)
Tomb. Stephane Mallarme. FoFS
Vermeer recalled. Henry F.
    Beechhold. StPo
Vermeer, Jan
Vermeer recalled. Henry F.
    Beechhold. StPo
Verses in the style of the
    Druids, sels. Sir Walter
    Scott. TyW
Verses on accepting the world.
    Joseph Brodsky. VoWA
Verses on the death of Francis
    II, sels. Mary Queen of
    Scots. PaW

Verses to be slandered. Paul
    Verlaine. FreS
Verses written on sand. Melech
    Ravitch (Z.K. Bergner). VoWA
Verses written in an album.
    Thomas Moore. WBP2
A version of a song of failure.
    Larry Eigner. FroA
Vertigos or contemplation of
    something... Alejandra
    Pizarnik. VoWA
Very like a whale. Ogden Nash.
    HaAP
Very, Jones
    The dead. HaAP
    Enoch. HaAP
    Life. WBP4
    The prayer. EeBC
    The presence. HaAP
    The spirit land. HaAP
    The spirit-land. WBP4
Vesper hymn. Eliza Scudder. WBP4
Vesper hymn. Samuel Longfellow.
    WBP4
Vessels. Howard Schwartz. VoWA
Veteran's Day
    The significance of Veteran's
    Day. Simon J. Ortiz. ReE
"vibrant mutants of the future."
    Anselm Hollo. FroA
The Vicar of Wakefield, sels.
    Oliver Goldsmith. WBP2
Vickie Loans-Arrow, 1971. Marnie
    Walsh. ReE
Victory. Michael L. Miller. YoVA
Victory
    The essence of winning. Jane
    Roberson. YoVA
    Hustle. Tom Joyce. YoVA
    Lights. Ernesto Cardenal. NiR
    There is no holding
    back...victory, sels.
    Gioconda Belli. NiR
    Victory. Michael L. Miller.
    YoVA
    The watchword. Carlos Majia
    Godoy. NiR
Vida, Marcus Hieronymus
    The art of poetry. ReLP
    The game of chess. ReLP
View of the winds. Tu Fu. GrAC
Viewpoint on life. Aileen
    Needleman. YoVA
Vigee, Claude
    Destiny of the poet. VoWA
    Every land is exile. VoWA
    House of the living. VoWA
    Light of Judea. VoWA
    The phoenix of Mozart. VoWA
    Poetry ("What then is poetry?)

VoWA
Song of occident. VoWA
The struggle with the angel.
  VoWA
The tree of death. VoWA
The wanderer. VoWA
The vigil. Shlomo Reich. VoWA
Vilbert, Thomas P.
  Christmas nonsense. YoVA
  Sonnet to woodland peace. YoVA
Villa on Chung-nan Mountain.
  Wang Wei. GrAC
Village. Juan Ramon Jimenez.
  PoCh
Village Life
  Broadax. Nishiwaki Junzaburo.
    FroC
  Highly renowned, sels. Monk
    Gusai. FroC
  Naked thoughts, sels. Russell
    Soaba. VooI
  Villages. Henry Bataille. FreS
The village blacksmith. Henry
  Wadsworth Longfellow. WBP1
Village hairdresser. Anzai
  Hitoshi. FroC
Village in a snowstorm. Norbert
  Krapf. FroA
Villages. Henry Bataille. FreS
The villanelle. Donald
  Harington. FroA
Vilna. Moishe Kulbak. VoWA
A Vilna puzzle. Sasha Chorny.
  VoWA
Vinaver, Stanislav
  A cathedral. VoWA
  The European night. VoWA
  An inscription. VoWA
Vineyards
  Lorna slope. Andrea Zanzotto.
    NeIP
  Lusus IV: Damis' vow to
    Bacchus... Andrea Navagero.
    ReLP
Vinner, Shlomo
  In the cabinet. VoWA
  Jerusalem. VoWA
  Lullaby ("Sleep now.") VoWA
  Midnight and ten minutes. VoWA
  The need to love. VoWA
  Parting. VoWA
  Training on the shore. VoWA
Vinz, Mark
  Postcards. FroA
A violet in her hair. Charles
  Swain. WBP2
Violets
  A belated violet. Oliver
    Herford. WBP1
  Sonnet ("I had no thought of

violets..") Alice
  Dunbar-Nelson. BlS
The violin tree. Joel Rosenberg.
  VoWA
Violins and Violinists
  A cat came fiddling. Mother
    Goose. MiRN
  The fiddler. Martin Buber. VoWA
  Fiddler. Tarah Ting-pei Chang.
    YoVA
  My fiddle. Leib Kwitko. VoWA
Violins in repose. Jorge
  Plescoff. VoWA
A virginal. Ezra Pound. LiHE
Virtue. George Herbert. HaAP
Virtue
  Blessed are those who sow
    and...not reap. Avraham
    Ben-Yitzhak. VoWA
  A chaine of pearle, sels. Diana
    Primrose. PaW
  Christabel. Samuel Taylor
    Coleridge. EvIm
  The cost of worth. Josiah
    Gilbert Holland. WBP4
  Description of virtue. Theodore
    de Beze. ReLP
  Example. John Keble. WBP4
  Gracious goodness. Marge
    Piercy. HoA
  I would I were an excellent
    divine. Nicholas Breton. WBP4
  A love story. Oliver Herford.
    IlTH
  An order...to two younger
    sisters, sels. Isabella
    Whitney. PaW
  Small beginnings. Charles
    Mackay. WBP4
  Virtue. George Herbert. HaAP
Virtue immortal. George Herbert.
  WBP3
The vision. Cynthia R. Wolfe.
  YoVA
Vision
  Muscae volitantes. Lewis B.
    Horne. HoA
The vision of Sir Launfal. James
  Russell Lowell. WBP4
Vision of a fair woman. Unknown.
  WBP2
A vision of beauty. Ben Jonson.
  WBP2
A vision of the sea. Percy
  Bysshe Shelley. MTS
Visions for breakfast. Jane
  Dulin. YoVA
A visit from St. Nicholas.
  Clement C. Moore. PoCh
A visit from St. Nicholas.

Clement Clarke Moore.
PoCh--WBP1
A **visit** from the sea. Robert
Louis Stevenson. MTS
A **visit** home. Joseph Glazer.
VoWA
Visiting Wang Stream after a
rain. Ssu-k'ung Shu. GrAC
Visiting the recluse Hu...
Ssu-k'ung Shu. GrAC
The **visitor**. Lisa Dunn. YoVA
The **visitor**. George Bogin. FroA
Vitae summa brevis spem nos
vetat... Ernest Dowson. HaAP
Vitalis, Ianus
Rome. ReLP
Vivaldi, Cesare
Mother, I won't forget. NeIP
September. NeIP
To Giovanni. NeIP
Voyage. NeIP
The wall. NeIP
Vivante, Arturo
To a victim of radiation. FroA
Vogel, David
Black flags are fluttering.
VoWA
Days were great as lakes. VoWA
How can I see you, love. VoWA
In fine transparent words. VoWA
Now I have forgotten all. VoWA
Our childhood spilled into our
hearts. VoWA
Plain, humble letters. VoWA
When I was growing up. VoWA
Vogelwiede. See Walther..

The **voice**. Thomas Hardy. HaAP
Voice. Tamura Ryuichi. FroC
The **voice**. Judith Herzberg. VoWA
The **voice**. Philip Levine. TeMP
A **voice** from under the table.
Richard Wilbur. HaAP
Voice in the dark. A.L. Strauss.
VoWA
A **voice** out of the tabernacle.
Louis Zukovsky. VoWA
The **voiceless**. Oliver Wendell
Holmes. WBP3
Voices
Another voice. Paolo Volponi.
NeIP
Ladies' voices. Gertrude Stein.
SlW
"Listen to the gentle song..."
Paul Verlaine. FreS
Voice in the dark. A.L.
Strauss. VoWA
The voice. Judith Herzberg.
VoWA

Volcano clouds: parting. Ts'en
Shen. GrAC
Volponi, Paolo
Another voice. NeIP
The comet. NeIP
Roman rooms. NeIP
Summer's end. NeIP
Tomorrow is March already...
NeIP
The walls of Urbino. NeIP
Voronca, Ilarie
The quick and the dead. VoWA
The seven-league boots. VoWA
Voss, Mary
Bizarre. YoVA
Nature. YoVA
The **vow**. Carl Rakosi. FroA
Vowels. Arthur Rimbaud.
FoFS--SlW
Vowels
Vowels. Arthur Rimbaud.
FoFS--SlW
The **vows**. Andrew Marvell. TyW
The **voyage**. Caroline Atherton
Mason. WBP4
Voyage. Cesare Vivaldi. NeIP
Voyage. Stanislaw Wygodski. VoWA
The **voyage**. Charles Baudelaire.
FoFS
Voyages. Hart Crane. MTS
Voyages, sels. Hart Crane. HaAP
Vroman, Leo
Old miniatures. VoWA
The river. VoWA
Vulnerability. Bartolo Cattafi.
NeIP

W., A.
A fiction. WBP2
Waddington, Miriam
Desert stone. VoWA
The field of night. VoWA
The survivors. VoWA
Waddington, Samuel
Mors et vita. WBP1
Wagner, Linda
Love poem. FroA
Wagoner, David
Meeting a bear. HaAP
Nine charms against the hunter.
TyW
Relics. FroA
Under the sign of the moth.
TeMP
Walking in a swamp. HaAP
Wahl, Jean
Decayed time. VoWA

Evening in the walls. VoWA
A lean day in a convict's suit.
    VoWA
Prayer of little hope. VoWA
Wahlstrom, Stuart
One day. YoVA
"Wait for moonlight." Ryokan.
    FroC
Waiting. John Burroughs. WBP3
Waiting
Breaking off from waiting.
    Clarisse Nicoidski. VoWA
The green grass under the snow.
    Annie A. Preston. WBP3
Hopefully waiting. Anson D. F.
    Randolph. WBP4
"I put good rice in water."
    Unknown . FroC
Kouta: 10 kouta from the
    Kanginshu. Unknown   FroC
Landscape ("If you wait...")
    Ishigaki Rin . FroC
'Only waiting'. Frances
    Laughton Mace. WBP4
Song ("She's somewhere in the
    sunlight.") Richard Le
    Gallienne. WBP3
The two waitings. John White
    Chadwick. WBP3
Waiting. John Burroughs. WBP3
The wind of the cliff Ka Hea.
    Phyllis Thompson. FroA
Waiting for God. Harry
    Roskolenko. FroA
Waiting for Lilith. Jascha
    Kessler. VoWA
Waiting for nighthawks in
    Illinois. Roger Pfingston.
    FroA
Waiting for the grapes. William
    Maginn. WBP2
Waiting in front of the
    columnar..school. Karl
    Shapiro. HaAP
Waiting to be born. R.M.
    Bantista. ReE
Waiting... Deborah L. Raub. YoVA
Wakayama Bokusui
Tanka: 44 tanka. FroC
Wake all the dead!. Sir William
    Davenant. HaAP
Wakes. Adolphe Rette. FreS
The **waking.** Theodore Roethke.
    HaAP
Waking. Douglas Shearer. YoVA
Waking-up thoughts. Susan Shown
    Harjo. ReE
Wakoski, Diane
For a man who learned to swim
    when sixty. FroA

My mother's milkman. TeMP
Walck, Penny
You never understood. YoVA
Wald, Jami
Greg. YoVA
Impressions of night. YoVA
Winter night. YoVA
Waldrop, Keith
Introducing a madman. TyW
Waldrop, Rosmarie
Confession to settle a curse.
    TyW
Wales
Carmarthen bar. John Malcolm
    Brinnin. HoA
Lines written...above Tintern
    Abbey. William Wordsworth.
    HaAP
Walker, Alice
Early loses: a requiem. BlS
Once. BlS
Revolutionary petunias. BlS
Walker, David
Catching up. FroA
Walker, Margaret
Ballad of the hoppy-toad. BlS
Kissie Lee. BlS
Lineage. BlS
Molly Means. BlS
Walking
1929. Wystan Hugh Auden. SlW
Autobiography: Hollywood.
    Charles Reznikoff. VoWA
Elegy ("While walking at
    dusk..."). Pinhas Sadeh. VoWA
Evening walk. David Einhorn.
    OnCP
Feeling. Arthur Rimbaud. FoFS
Human relations, sels. Antonio
    Porta. NeIP
I just walk around, around,
    around. Moishe Kulbak. VoWA
"If the streets were filled
    with glue." Gelett Burgess.
    IlTH
Lost contact. Sylvia Wheeler.
    FroA
The morning after...love.
    Kattie M. Cumbo. BlS
Sad toys, sel. Ishikawa
    Takuboku . FroC
Travelogue. Nishiwaki Junzaburo
    FroC
The way to the lighthouse.
    Nishiwaki Junzaburo. . FroC
Walking Milwaukee. Harold Witt.
    HoA
Walking alone by the
    riverbank..., sels. Tu Fu.
    GrAC

Walking along the Sea of
    Galilee. David Knut. VoWA
Walking home at night. Daniel
    Weissbort. VoWA
Walking in a swamp. David
    Wagoner. HaAP
The **wall**. Cesare Vivaldi. NeIP
The **wall**. Ludvik Askenazy. VoWA
"The **wall**." Nora Coggins. YoVA
Wall, Leah
    In time we will grow apart.
        YoVA
Wallace, Robert
    In a spring still not written
        of. LiHE
Wallach, Yona
    again you slept with mr no man.
        BuAC
    All this so tasteless and
        threatening. BuAC
    Cradle song. BuAC--VoWA
    Cradle song. VoWA
    Death; she was always here.
        VoWA
    I emptied. BuAC
    Lola. BuAC
    A terrible heart. BuAC
    Two gardens. BuAC
    When the angels are exhausted.
        VoWA
Wallenstein, sels. Samuel Taylor
    Coleridge. WBP4
Waller, Edmund
    Go, lovely rose! WBP2
    Go, lovely rose! HaAP--LiHE
    Of my lady Isabella playing on
        the lute. HaAP
    Of the last verses in the book.
        HaAP
    On a girdle. WBP2
Waller, John Francis
    Kitty Neil. WBP2
    The spinning-wheel song. WBP2
Walls
    Mending wall. Robert Frost.
        HaAP
    Susano-o's son. Unknown . FroC
    The wall. Cesare Vivaldi. NeIP
The **walls** of Urbino. Paolo
    Volponi. NeIP
The **walrus** and the carpenter.
    Lewis Carroll (C.L. Dodgson).
    IlTH--WBP1
Walruses
    The walrus and the carpenter.
    Lewis Carroll (C.L. Dodgson).
    IlTH--WBP1
Walsh, Chad
    Ode on a plastic stapes. HoA
    Ode to the Finnish dead. HoA

Walsh, Marnie
    Angelina Runs-Against. ReE
    Bessie Dreaming Bear, 1960. ReE
    John Knew-the-Crow, 1880. ReE
    June the twenty-second. ReE
    The red fox. ReE
    Vickie Loans-Arrow, 1971. ReE
Walsh, William
    Rivalry in love. WBP2
Walters, Anna L.
    Epitaph ("because words fall
        short.") ReE
    On the banks of black bear
        creek. ReE
Walther von der Vogelweide
    Song ("When from the sod the
        flowerets"). WBP2
Waly, waly. Unknown. HaAP--WBP3
The **wanderer**. Claude Vigee. VoWA
The **wanderer**. Wystan Hugh Auden.
    SlW
The **wanderer's** home. Oliver
    Goldsmith. WBP1
The **wandering** Jew. Robert Mezey.
    VoWA
The **wandering** Jew. Benjamin
    Fondane (Fundoianu). VoWA
Wandering Jews. Nancy Keesing.
    VoWA
Wandering chorus. B. Alquit
    (Eliezer Blum). VoWA
Wandering immortals. Wu Yun.
    GrAC
Wanderlust
    The joys of the road. Bliss
        Carman. WBP1
    Travelling song. Thomas
        McGrath. FroA
    The wanderer. Wystan Hugh
        Auden. SlW
Wang An-shi
    In the mountains. LuL
Wang Ch'ang-ling
    Autumn evening on the great
        lake. GrAC
    An autumn song for Ch'ang-hsin
        Palace. GrAC
    Campaign song. GrAC
    Dawn song. GrAC
    Hearing a flute on the river.
        GrAC
    Song by the walls. GrAC
    Written to serve as..reply..my
        most,sels. GrAC
Wang Chao-chun. Ch'u Kuang-hsi.
    GrAC
Wang Chi-yu
    Seeing Grand Secretary
     Yu's...mural. GrAC
    To Wei Tzu-ch'un. GrAC

Wang Chih-huan
    Hooded crane tower. GrAC
    Parting. GrAC
Wang Han
    Liang-chou songs, sels. GrAC
Wang Wan
    Reaching the foot of Pei-ku
        Mountain. GrAC
Wang Wei
    Arriving at the frontier on a
        mission. GrAC
    At the rapids of the Luan
        family. LuL
    Ballad of peach blossom spring,
        sels. GrAC
    Climbing Pien-chuen Temple.
        GrAC
    "Close your gate fast..." GrAC
    Crossing the Yellow River to
        Ch'ing-ho. GrAC
    Deer enclosure. GrAC
    Deer forest hermitage. LuL
    "Distant men have no eyes..."
        LuL
    Duckweed pond. LuL
    Dwelling in ease at Wang
        stream. GrAC
    Egret dyke. LuL
    An evening under newly cleared
        skies. GrAC
    His Majesty leads the Prince of
        Ch'i... GrAC
    "In the evening view, the
        mountains..." LuL
    Leaving Wang-Chuan cottage. LuL
    Look down from the high
        terrace. GrAC
    Offhand composition III. GrAC
    On the Double Ninth:
        remembering... GrAC
    Parting. GrAC
    Rapids by the luan trees. GrAC
    Returning to Mount Sung. GrAC
    Second song...worship of the
        goddess... GrAC
    Sightseeing on a winter day.
        GrAC
    A song on gazing at Chung-nan
        Mountain. GrAC
    South cottage. GrAC
    To P'ei Ti. GrAC
    Villa on Chung-nan Mountain.
        GrAC
    Written after long rains at my
        villa... GrAC
Wang Wei (about)
    Parting from Wang Wei. Meng
        Hao-jan . GrAC
    Visiting the recluse Hu..
        Ssu-k'ung Shu.   GrAC

War. Joni Kurland. YoVA
War. Anthony Ostroff. FroA
War
    After our war. John Balaban.
        FroA
    After the raiders have gon.
        Yuan Chieh . GrAC
    After the war. Hayim Naggid.
        VoWA
    The Akedah. Matti Megged. VoWA
    Anonymous tragedy. Donnelle
        Gerling. YoVA
    Anthem for doomed youth.
        Wilfred Owen. HaAP
    Appendix to the Anniad.
        Gwendolyn Brooks. BlS
    Arms and the boy. Wilfred Owen.
        HaAP
    The author's apology. T. Carmi.
        VoWA
    Break of day in the trenches.
        Isaac Rosenberg. VoWA
    Campaign song. Wang Ch'ang-ling.
        GrAC
    Channel firing. Thomas Hardy.
        HaAP
    Chi gate, sel. Kao Shih . GrAC
    Christians at war. John F.
        Kendrick. TyW
    The dark hills. Edwin Arlington
        Robinson. HaAP
    Dead man's dump. Isaac
        Rosenberg. VoWA
    Dulce et decorum est. Wilfred
        Owen. LiHE--TyW
    End of the war in Merida.
        Anthony Ostroff. FroA
    First practice. Gary Gildner.
        TyW
    Franz Jagesttater's
        epistemology. Mark Halperin.
        TeMP
    The horses. Edwin Muir. HaAP
    I hate that drum's discordant
        sound. John Scott. TyW
    I have never been here before.
        Jacob Glatstein. OnCP
    Improvised while living
        in...the capital. Taikyoku
        Zosu   FroC
    In Sung. Keng Wei . GrAC
    In the old guerilla war. Linda
        Pastan. TyW
    In time of "The breaking of
        nations." Thomas Hardy. HaAP
    The last laugh. Wilfred Owen.
        LiHE
    The last mistake. LeAnnette
        Donahey. YoVA
    Lullaby. Edith Sitwell. ShBa

A matter of time. Sabrina
Sommerer. YoVA
Naming of parts. Henry Reed.
LiHE
Observing the past at Yueh. Li
Po. GrAC
Ode, written in...1746. William
Collins. HaAP
Page from the Koran. James
Merrill. TeMP
The parents-without-partners
picnic. Ted Schaefer. FroA
Picture postcards. Miklos
Radnoti. VoWA
The pilot's day of rest. Lee
Gerlach. HoA
The pilot's walk. Lee Gerlach.
HoA
Remembrance of things past.
Horace Coleman. FroA
Sestina: Altaforte. Ezra Pound.
SlW
Smothered fires. Georgia
Douglas Johnson. BlS
Song of ye. Kao Shih . GrAC
Sonnet #1. Becky Holmberg. YoVA
Time sea. Greg Stricklin. YoVA
To Lucasra: Going to the wars.
Richard Lovelace. HaAP--WBP3
To my parents, sels. Krzysztof
Kamil Baczynski. CoP
To whoever finds this. Barbara
Clark. YoVA
The unknown citizen. Wystan
Hugh Auden. LiHE
The war-song of Dinas Vawr.
Thomas Love Peacock. HaAP
War. Anthony Ostroff. FroA
Waste. G.A. Studdert Kennedy.
EeBC
The wheel. James Cole. FroA
When I came back to dancing
misery. George Hitchcock.
TeMP
Written in Chi. Kao Shih. GrAC
Written on the road while
returning... Li Chia-yu. GrAC
The war against the trees.
Stanley Kunitz. HaAP
War walking near. Roy A. Young
Bear. ReE
The war-song of Dinas Vawr.
Thomas Love Peacock. HaAP
Warbler. Anzai Hitoshi. FroC
Ward, Penny
And I love you. YoVA
I am sixteen. YoVA
Ware (Jr.), Henry
Sèasons of prayer. WBP4
Warming up for the real thing.

Lee Rudolph. TyW
Warne, Todd
If a man could keep his love.
YoVA
Nature's mercy. YoVA
The warning: shout on the
corners. Manolo Cuadra. NiR
Warren, Robert Penn
Myth on Mediterranean Beach:
Aphrodite... HaAP
Pursuit. HaAP
Warsaw, Poland
Willows in Alma-Ata. Aleksander
Wat. VoWA
Warsaw, sels. Czeslaw Milosz.
CoP
Wassail, wassail, wassail, sing
we. Unknown. ShBa
Waste. G.A. Studdert Kennedy.
EeBC
The waste land. Thomas Stearns
Eliot. HaAP
A wasted illness. Thomas Hardy.
EvIm
Wasteland collage. Hector
Vargas. NiR
Wastell, Simon
Man's mortality. WBP3
Wat, Aleksander
There is no place. VoWA
Willows in Alma-Ata. VoWA
The watch. May Swenson. HaAP
Watchempino, Laura
Pottery maker. ReE
Watches. See Clocks
Watching a young girl going
alone... Takahashi Mushimaro.
FroC
Watching for Papa. Unknown. WBP3
Watching the fieldhands. Wei
Ying-wu. GrAC
Watching the out-door movie
show. Ann Struthers. FroA
Watching the sun rise over Mount
Zion. Ruth Whitman. VoWA
The watchword. Carlos Majia
Godoy. NiR
The watchword. Carlos Mejia
Godoy. NiR
Water. Edmond Jabes. VoWA
Water
At the rapids of the Luan
family. Wang Wei. LuL
"Distant men have no eyes..."
Wang Wei . LuL
Eighteen tanka. Ariwara no
Narihira. FroC
Fifteen hokku. Naito Joso. FroC
Horses at valley store. Leslie
Marmon Silko. ReE

We go. Karl Wolfskehl. VoWA
We have been friends together.
    Caroline Elizabeth S. Norton.
    WBP1
We like March. Emily Dickinson.
    S1W
We lost our fear. Francisco de
    Asis Fernandez. NiR
We love but few. Unknown. WBP1
We met/and we were friends.
    Carolyn Barbor. YoVA
We parted in silence. Julia
    Crawford (L.Macartney). WBP3
We real cool. Gwendolyn Brooks.
    HaAP
We three kings of Orient are.
    John H. Hopkins. PoCh
We together. Rhonda Moncrief.
    YoVA
We tried to tell you at
    different times. Beth Lewis.
    YoVA
We wait. Robert J. Conley. ReE
We wear the mask. Paul Laurence
    Dunbar. LiHE
We'll be new. Gioconda Belli.
    NiR
We-others. Ricardo Morales
    Aviles. NiR
Wealth
    "Affluence-define it as."
    Hezutsu Tosaku . FroC
    A short song of congratulation.
    Samuel Johnson. HaAP
    The suicides of the rich.
    Victor Contoski. FroA
    Things. William Stanley Merwin.
    HaAP
The weary dancers. Gloria Boyd.
    YoVA
"Weathergrams are poems..."
    Lloyd J. Reynolds. FroA
Weber, Marlys
    Cantata. YoVA
Webster, Daniel
    The memory of the heart. WBP1
Webster, John
    Call for the robin-redbreast &
    the wren. HaAP
    Hark, now everything is still.
    HaAP
    The shrouding of the Duchess of
    Malfi. DoNG
    Vanitas vanitatum. DoNG
    The white devil, sels. TyW
Wedding. Ewa Lipska. VoWA
The wedding. Leilani Strong.
    YoVA
Wedding. Alain Grandbois. MoVT
Wednesdays in Los Angeles.

HuGos. NiR
Weep you no more, sad fountains.
    Unknown. HaAP
Wei Ying-wu
    At the prefectural library in
    the rain. GrAC
    Autumn night: to Ch'iu Tan.
    GrAC
    Climbing the tower. GrAC
    Climbing to the heights of
    Pao-yi Temple. GrAC
    Imitations of old poems, sels.
    GrAC
    In the post of assistant in
    Lo-yang... GrAC
    The meditation hut at Shan-fu
    Temple. GrAC
    Miscellaneous songs of Han
    Wu-ti, sels. GrAC
    On a day off going to meet
    Censor Wang... GrAC
    On sound. LuL
    Planting melons. GrAC
    Song of the wineshop. GrAC
    Spending the night in
    Yung-yang. GrAC
    To a Taoist on Ch'uan-chiao
    Mountain. GrAC
    Watching the fieldhands. GrAC
    West stream at Ch'u-chou. GrAC
Weighing the baby. Ethel Lynn
    (E.E. Beers). WBP1
Weightlifting
    The temptation. Terry
    Ohlenkamp. YoVA
Weiman, Andrew
    Andy-Diana DNA letter. HaAP
Weiss, Julius
    "I am a cat I wish." HoWM
Weiss, Mark
    My great, great grandfather.
    HoWM
Weiss, Theodore
    Art in America. StPo
    En route. TeMP
    A stroke of good luck. StPo
Weissbort, Daniel
    Anniversary. VoWA
    Murder of a community. VoWA
    Walking home at night. VoWA
The welcome. Ferid ed-Din Attar.
    WBP1
The welcome. Thomas Osborne
    Davis. WBP2
The welcome. Edward Fitzgerald
    (trans.). WBP1
Welcome, welcome, do I sing.
    William Browne. WBP2
Weldon Kees. Larry Levis. FroA
Welfare line. R.A. Swanson. ReE

Well I remember how you smiled.
    Walter Savage Landor. HaAP
Well, wanton eye. Charles, Duc
    d' Orleans. HaAP
Wells
    Fetching water from the well.
        Unknown. WBP2
    Naked thoughts, sels. Russell
        Soaba. VooI
    The old oaken bucket. Samuel
        Woodworth. WBP1
    The seaside well. Unknown. WBP4
Wells, Carolyn
    Advice to children. IlTH
    "A canner, exceedingly canny."
        IlTH
    Limerick:" .an arch armadillo."
        IlTH
    "A tutor who tooted a flute."
        IlTH
Welte, Lou Anne
    Those last, late hours of
        Christmas Eve. PoCh
Went up a year this evening!
    Emily Dickinson. HaAP
Wentz, Shari K.
    Skatetown boogie. YoVA
Were I as base as is the lowly
    plain. Joshua Sylvester. WBP2
Were I but his own wife. Mary
    Downing. WBP2
Wesley (trans.), John
    The love of God supreme. WBP4
Wesley, Charles
    Hark! the herald angels sing.
        ShBa
    Wrestling Jacob. WBP4
West Fifty-Seventh Street. Byron
    Vazakas. FroA
West lake. Yuan Hong-dao. LuL
West stream at Ch'u-chou. Wei
    Ying-wu. GrAC
West, Joy
    Rainy days. YoVA
West, Susan
    Lavender flowers. YoVA
    Through problems do we see.
        YoVA
Westerfield, Karen
    Ballad of Aeradrel. YoVA
    Last month depression. YoVA
The western wall. Shirley
    Kaufman. BuAC
Western wind. Unknown. HaAP
Westwood, Thomas
    Little Bell. WBP1
    Under my window. WBP1
The wet month. Henry Bataille.
    FreS
Wetherley, Frederic Edward

Darby and Joan. WBP2
Whales and Whaling
    Al Capone in Alaska. Ishmael
        Reed. TyW
    Beaver skin. Antonio Porta.
        NeIP
    Physiologus, sel. Unknown. MTS
    Spouting whale. Takamura Kotaro
        FroC
    Whales weep not! David Herbert
        Lawrence. MTS
Whales weep not!. David Herbert
    Lawrence. MTS
Wharton, Lori
    Life is... YoVA
What I have done. Gerard
    Malanga. FroA
What I live for. George Linnaeus
    Banks. WBP4
What I see. Kathy Wootton. HoWM
What a strange place this is!
    Janet Brack. YoVA
What ails this heart of mine?
    Susanna Blamire. WBP3
What am I now. Julie A. Engel.
    YoVA
What am I? Abraham Abo
    Stoltzenberg. VoWA
What are you Nicaragua?
    Gioconda Belli. NiR
What can I do? Unknown. FroC
"What can an old man do but
    die?" Thomas Hood. WBP3
What cheer?. Unknown. ShBa
What did I dream?. Robert
    Graves. DuD
What eagle saw in the west.
    Duane BigEagle. ReE
What happened to the real me?
    Laurie Rowe. YoVA
What if you had dared. Stephen
    G. Widner. YoVA
what is. Edward Estlin Cummings.
    MTS
What is a Jewish poem? Myra
    Sklarew. VoWA
What is color? Sheri Neb. YoVA
What is it like? Cindy Loop.
    YoVA
What is left? Istvan Vas. VoWA
What is poetry? Eileen Kampman.
    YoVA
What is prayer? James
    Montgomery. WBP4
What is the case in point?
    Abraham Reisen. VoWA
What is to be. Terri Bloomfield.
    YoVA
What my lover said. Homer
    Greene. WBP2

What of the darkness? Richard
   Le Gallienne. WBP3

What secret desires of the
   blood. Nelly Sachs. VoWA

What soft-cherubic creatures.
   Emily Dickinson. HaAP--LiHE

What someone said when he was
   spanked.... John Ciardi. RoRF

What the animals said. Peter
   Serchuk. HoA

What was his creed?. Unknown.
   WBP4

What will remain after me?.
   Mendel Naigreshel. VoWA

"The wheat field". Nora Coggins.
   YoVA

Wheat metropolis. Alfred Starr
   Hamilton. FroA

Wheatcroft, John
   Pisanello's studies of men
   hanging... FroA

Wheatley, Phillis
   Liberty and peace, sels. BlS
   On imagination. BlS
   To S.M.a young African
   painter... BlS
   To a gentleman and lady on the
   death... BlS
   To the Rt Hon William..., sels.
   BlS
   To the king's most excellent
   majesty. BlS

The wheel. James Cole. FroA

Wheelbarrows
   The red wheelbarrow. William
   Carlos Williams. SlW
   Spring and all, sels. William
   Carlos Williams. HaAP

Wheeler, Sylvia
   Lost contact. FroA

Wheeling, West Virginia
   In response to a rumor....
   James Wright. TyW

Wheels. Dorothy Donnelly. HoA

Wheels
   Contra mortem. Hayden Carruth.
   TeMP
   Wheels. Dorothy Donnelly. HoA

Wheelwright, John
   Fish food. MTS

Wheesht, wheesht. Christopher
   Murray Grieve. HaAP

When. Susan Coolidge (Sarah
   Woolsey). WBP4

When Emperor Mommu visited...
   Prince Shiki (668-716). FroC

When Empress Jito
   visited...Yoshino. Kakinomoto
   no Hitomaro. FroC

When God first said. Natan Zach.

   VoWA

When I am me. Felice Holman. ByM

When I came back to dancing
   misery. George Hitchcock.
   TeMP

When I came to Israel. Bert
   Meyers. VoWA

When I came to London. Rachael
   Castelete. VoWA

When I have fears that I may
   cease to be. John Keats. HaAP

When I have fears that I may
   cease to be. John Keats.
   DoNG--LiHE

When I heard the learn'd
   astronomer,sels. Walt
   Whitman. HaAP-LiHE

When I want to speak. Rav
   Abraham Isaac Kook. VoWA

When I was growing up. David
   Vogel. VoWA

When I was nine. Raymond
   Roseliep. FroA

When I was old and weary. Gail
   Gallone. YoVA

When I was one-and-twenty.
   Alfred Edward Housman. LiHE

When I was young and fair.
   Elizabeth I; Queen of
   England. PaW

When Mama plucks the chickens.
   Kate Dodson. YoVA

When Prince Karu camped
   in...Aki. Kakinomoto no
   Hitomaro. FroC

When Sir Joshua Reynolds died.
   William Blake. TyW

"When a doctor doctors another
   doctor." Unknown. IlTH

When both my fathers die. Robert
   Gillespie. FroA

When gathering clouds around I
   view. Sir Robert Grant. WBP4

When he was in Iwami province...
   Kakinomoto no Hitomaro. FroC

When her secret affair...was
   revealed. Princess Tajima
   (?-708). FroC

"When it comes to poets."
   Yadoyano Meshimoro. FroC

When lilacs last in the dooryard
   bloom'd. Walt Whitman. HaAP

When lilacs last in the dooryard
   bloom'd. Walt Whitman.
   HaAP--WBP3

When lovely woman stoops to
   folly. Oliver Goldsmith. HaAP

When my eye loses its hue. Kadya
   Molodovsky. OnCP

"When my eyes are misted."

White swan. A. Glanz-Leyeles. VoWA

White, Henry Kirke
  Go, lovely rose. WBP2
  The star of Bethlehem. WBP4

White, Lisabeth
  Snowflake ballerina. YoVA

White, Michael
  While walking along the seashore I saw... HoWM

White, Paul
  To say 'good-bye'. YoVA

Whiteness. Yunna Moritz. VoWA

Whitfield, Robbie
  Picasso. HoWM

Whiting, William
  Eternal Father, strong to save. MTS

Whitman, Ruth
  Dan, the dust of Masada... VoWA
  Mediterranean. VoWA
  Translating. VoWA
  Watching the sun rise over Mount Zion. VoWA

Whitman, Walt
  After the sea-ship. MTS
  The beauty of the ship. MTS
  A clear midnight. HaAP
  The dalliance of the eagles. HaAP
  The dismantled ship. MTS
  Give me the splendid silent sun. HaAP
  A hand-mirror. TyW
  I hear America singing. HaAP
  In cabin'd ships at sea. MTS
  Joy, shipmate, joy! MTS
  Leaves of grass, sels. HaAP
  A noiseless patient spider. HaAP
  O captain! my captain! MTS
  Out of the cradle endlessly rocking. DoNG--HaAP
  Patroling Barnegat. MTS
  Reconciliation. HaAP
  Song of myself, sels. DoNG--SlW
  Song of myself, sels. MTS
  Songs for all seas, all ships. MTS
  When I heard the learn'd astronomer,sels. HaAP-LiHE
  When lilacs last in the dooryard bloom'd. HaAP--WBP3
  When lilacs last in the dooryard bloom'd. HaAP

Whitman, Walt (about)
  Face on the daguerreotype. Norman Rosten. HoA

Whitney, Isabella
  The aucthour...maketh her wyll..., sels. PaW
  A letter...to her constant lover, sels. PaW
  The maner of her wyll..., sels. PaW
  An order...to two younger sisters, sels. PaW
  A sweet nosegay, sels. PaW
  To her sister misteris A.B., sels. PaW

Whittemore, Reed
  Lines on being refused a Guggenheim.... TyW

Whittier, John Greenleaf
  The angel of patience. WBP3
  The barefoot boy. WBP1
  Benedicite. WBP1
  Burning drift-wood. MTS
  The eternal goodness. WBP4
  In school-days. WBP1
  Maud Muller. WBP3
  The meeting. WBP4
  A New England home in winter, sels. WBP1
  The Palatine. MTS
  The tent on the beach, sels. WBP3
  To Pius IX. TyW
  To her absent sailor. WBP3
  The two angels. WBP4
  The two rabbis. WBP4

Whittling. John Pierpont. WBP1

Who am I. Edward Williams. HoWM

Who am I? William Oandasan. ReE

Who among you knows the essence..garlic? Garrett Hongo. HoA

Who has not walked upon the shore. Robert Bridges. MTS

Who is my brother? Pinkie Gordon Lane. BlS

Who is she? Grant Crookston. YoVA

"Who is the true transmitter..." Ikkyu Sojun. FroC

Who killed John Keats? George Gordon,6th Baron Byron. TyW

Who says. Musa Moris Farni. VoWA

Who so pale and wan, fond lover? Sir John Suckling. HaAP--LiHE

Who then extends his arms to me. David Einhorn. OnCP

Who will give cover? Anadad Eldan. VoWA

Who will stop his hand... Alejandra Pizarnik. VoWA

Who would have said it. Alfredo Giuliani. NeIP

Who? Dan Jaffe. FroA
Whodunit. Florence Trefethen.
     StPo
Whoso list to hunt. Sir Thomas
     Wyatt. HaAP
Why I am not a painter. Frank
     O'Hara. HoA
Why I can't write my
     autobiography. Rodger
     Kamenetz. VoWA
Why I carve these poems. Wang
     Hui-Ming. FroA
Why I like movies. Patricia
     Jones. BlS
Why does poetry exist? Lolita
     Files. YoVA
Why flowers change colors.
     Robert Herrick. HaAP
Why log truck drivers rise
     earlier... Gary Snyder. SlW
Why not? Linda Pastan. FroA
Why so pale and wan? Sir John
     Suckling. WBP2
Why thus longing? Samuel
     Winslow Sewall. WBP4
Why would I have survived?
     Edith Bruck. VoWA
Why? Donna Eubanks. YoVA
Why? Melba Joyce Boyd. BlS
Why? Mary Louise Ritter. WBP2
A wicker basket. Robert Creeley.
     HaAP
Wickham, Anna
     Nervous prostration. TyW
Wide eyed love. Angela Van
     Gemert. YoVA
Widner, Stephen G.
     Old age. YoVA
     What if you had dared. YoVA
Widow. Felix Pollak. FroA
The widow. Paul Greenfield. YoVA
Widow Machree. Samuel Lover.
     WBP2
Widow Malone. Charles Lever.
     WBP2
The widow's lament in
     springtime. William Carlos
     Williams. HaAP
The widow's mite. Frederick
     Locker-Lampson. WBP3
The widow's mites. Richard
     Crashaw. WBP4
The widower. Stanislaw
     Grochowiak. CoP
Widows
     Portait of a widow. Avner
     Strauss. VoWA
     The widow's mite. Frederick
     Locker-Lampson. WBP3
     The widow. Paul Greenfield.

     YoVA
Wiebe, Dallas
     Epilogue ("My bibliography has
     grown.") TyW
Wiegand, Heather
     Darkness. YoVA
     The hurt. YoVA
     Oriental wonder. YoVA
The wife a-lost. William Barnes.
     HaAP
Wife of Kohelet. Shlomit Cohen.
     BuAC--VoWA
The wife of Loki. Lady Charlotte
     Elliot. WBP2
The wife to her husband.
     Unknown. WBP3
Wife, children, and friends.
     Robert Nicoll. WBP1
Wilbur, Richard
     A Christmas hymn. PoCh
     A grasshopper. HaAP
     Junk. HaAP
     Love calls us to...things of
     this world. HaAP
     A Miltonic sonnet for Mr.
     Johnson... TyW
     The pardon. LiHE
     Transit. TeMP
     A voice from under the table.
     HaAP
The wild and wooly willows.
     Jennie Jent. YoVA
Wild orchards. Nurit Zarchi.
     BuAC
The wild swans at Coole. William
     Butler Yeats. SlW
Wilde, Barbara
     Dad, I'm scared. YoVA
Wilde, Edward
     Resolution. YoVA
     Today's one helluva day! YoVA
Wilde, Heather
     Sister Bernardo. FroA
Wilde, Oscar
     Les silhouettes. MTS
Wildfire. Judit Toth. VoWA
Wilhelmina Mergenthaler. Harry
     P. Taber. IlTH
Wilk, Melvin
     Blessing. VoWA
Will. Maxine Kumin. LiHE
The will of God. Frederick
     William Faber. WBP4
The will to live. Mekeel
     McBride. TeMP
Will, Frederic
     A fire a simple fire. FroA
Willard, Emma Hart
     Rocked in the cradle of the
     deep. MTS--WBP4

Willard, Nancy
    Bone poem. HoA
    Dreaming. BrBD
    The flea circus at Tivoli. HoA
    Moss. HoA
    Saints lose back. HoA
    When there were trees. HoA
Willems, J. Rutherford
    Hebrew letters in the trees.
        VoWA
Williams, Charles Kenneth
    Spit. VoWA
Williams, Clarence
    Ugly chile. TyW
Williams, Donna
    "Shooting star/Shooting star."
        HoWM
Williams, Edward
    Who am I. HoWM
Williams, Jonathan
    In Lucas, Kansas. FroA
Williams, Lucy Ariel
    Nortboun'. BlS
Williams, Rosalie
    Haiku ("Colored leaves
        trickle.") YoVA
    Midnight. YoVA
Williams, Sherley Anne
    Driving wheel. BlS
    The empress brand trim: Ruby
        reminisces. BlS
    The house of desire. BlS
    Say hello to John. BlS
Williams, William Carlos
    The act. SlW
    The aftermath. FroA
    Between walls. SlW
    The dance. HaAP
    Dead. DoNG
    The descent. HaAP
    January morning. SlW
    The last words of my English
        grandmother. SlW
    The locust tree in flower. SlW
    Nantucket. HaAP--SlW
    The orchestra. HaAP
    The raper from Passenack. TyW
    The red wheelbarrow. SlW
    The savage beast. TyW
    A sort of song. FroA
    Spring and all, sels. HaAP
    This is just to say. SlW
    To a poor old woman. SlW
    To waken an old lady. HaAP
    Tract. LiHE
    The widow's lament in
        springtime. HaAP
    The yachts. MTS
    The yellow flower. HaAP
Willie Winkie. William Miller.

WBP1
Willis, Nathaniel Parker
    The annoyer. WBP2
    Unseen spirits. WBP3
Willows
    The wild and wooly willows.
        Jennie Jent. YoVA
Willows in Alma-Ata. Aleksander
    Wat. VoWA
Willson, Robert
    The last resort. FroA
Willy wet-leg. D.H. Lawrence.
    TyW
Wilson, Ken
    Friendship. YoVA
    Winter. YoVA
Wilson, Peggi
    Today was different. YoVA
    Your hands. YoVA
The wind. Robert Louis
    Stevenson. WBP1
Wind
    As you like it, sels. William
        Shakespeare. WBP3
    Autumn wind. Akera Kanko,   FroC
    In the open fields. Hugo
        Sonnenschein. VoWA
    Ode to the west wind. Percy
        Bysshe Shelley. HaAP--MTS
    Oh breeze. Rae Cline. YoVA
    The ring. Pier Paolo Pasolini.
        NeIP
    Sea breeze. Susan Klopenstine.
        YoVA
    South wind. Nathan Yonathan.
        VoWA
    Western wind. Unknown   HaAP
    Where banshee wind is. Mary
        Tallmountain. ReE
    The wind begun to knead the
        grass. Emily Dickinson. HaAP
    Wind bends. Sandra Payne. YoVA
    The wind in a frolic. William
        Howitt. WBP1
    Wind poems. Gwen Daughton. HoWM
    The wind took up the northern
        things. Emily Dickinson. SlW
    The wind. Robert Louis
        Stevenson. WBP1
The wind begun to knead the
    grass. Emily Dickinson. HaAP
Wind bends. Sandra Payne. YoVA
The wind blows on the border.
    Antonio Porta. NeIP
The wind in a frolic. William
    Howitt. WBP1
Wind in the willow, sels.
    Kenneth Grahame. PoCh
"Wind of ruin, lurking rain." Tu
    Fu. GrAC

Winter moon. Langston Hughes.
    DuD
Winter mouse. Aileen Fisher.
    MiRN
Winter music. Tamura Ryuichi.
    FroC
Winter night. Jami Wald. YoVA
Winter ocean. John Updike. MTS
Winter over nothing. Elliott
    Coleman. FroA
Winter remembered. John Crowe
    Ransom. HaAP
Winter saint. Archie Randolph
    Ammons. TyW
Winter tree. Brian Dye. HoWM
Winter twosome. Jan Kneisel.
    YoVA
Winter wakens all my care.
    Unknown. HaAP
A winter wish. Robert Hinckley
    Messinger. WBP1
Winter's cold. Scott Hoenshel.
    YoVA
Winter's the best. D.H.
    NeeSmith. YoVA
A winter-evening hymn to my
    fire, sels. James Russell
    Lowell. WBP1
Winter: 1955. Takahashi Mutsuo.
    FroC
Winters, Yvor
    Hymn to dispell hatred at
        midnight. TyW
    The slow Pacific swell. MTS
Wiosna 1969, sels. Julian
    Przybos. CoP
Wisdom
    East Coker. Thomas Stearns
        Eliot. HaAP
    The greatest wisdom. Mark
        Childers. YoVA
    The old man said: two. Carroll
        Arnett/Gogisgi. ReE
Wishes
    "I am a cat I wish." Julius
        Weiss. HoWM
    If you could wish. Marlo
        Maconi. YoVA
    Seeing you. Michelle J. Modde.
        YoVA
Wishes for the supposed
    mistress. Richard Crashaw.
    WBP2
Wisteria
    Tanka: 15 tank. Masaoka Shiki .
        FroC
A witch cracking up. Raquel
    Chalfi. BuAC
A witch going down to Egypt.
    Raquel Chalfi. VoWA

The witch in the glass. Sarah
    Morgan Bryan Piatt. WBP1
A witch without a cover. Raquel
    Chalfi. BuAC
Witch, witch. Rose Fyleman. RoRF
Witchcraft
    A late movie. William Matthews.
        TeMP
    Molly Means. Margaret Walker.
        BlS
    The ride-by-nights. Walter De
        La Mare. DuD
    Sister Helen. Dante Gabriel
        Rossetti. EvIm
    A witch cracking up. Raquel
        Chalfi. BuAC
    A witch without a cover. Raquel
        Chalfi. BuAC
    Witch, witch. Rose Fyleman.
        RoRF
With Kao Shih and Hsueh Chu,
    climbing... Ts'en Shen. GrAC
With Kathy at Wisdom. Richard
    Hugo. FroA
With Wang Wei's "Stopping by
    recluse..." Lu Hsiang. GrAC
With a book at twilight. Jakov
    Steinberg. VoWA
With love. Michelle Olsen. YoVA
With muted strings. Paul
    Verlaine. FoFS
With my God, the Smith. Uri Zvi
    Greenberg. VoWA
"With my books closed again..."
    Stephane Mallarme. FoFS
With my grandfather. Zelda. VoWA
With poems already begun. Rachel
    Korn. VoWA
With rue my heart is laden.
    Alfred Edward Housman. HaAP
With ships the sea was sprinkled
    far... William Wordsworth.
    MTS
With the sun's fire. David
    Ignatow. FroA
Wither, George
    The author's resolution, in a
        sonnet. WBP2
    Christmas. WBP1
    Fair virtue, sels. WBP2
    "Lord! when those glorious
        lights I see." WBP4
    Sonnet upon a stolen kiss. WBP2
Within me. HuGos. NiR
Within myself. Ingrid Schulz.
    YoVA
Without me you won't...see
    yourself. Chaim Grade. VoWA
Without tears for the roses.
    Nanni Balestrini. NeIP

The **witnesses**. X.J. Kennedy.
  PoCh
The **witnesses**, sels. Clive
  Sansom. PoCh
Witt, Harold
  Notre Dame perfected by
    reflection. HoA
  Superbull. FroA
  Walking Milwaukee. HoA
Wittlin, Jozef
  A hymn about a spoonful of
    soup. VoWA
  On the Jewish day of
    judgment...1942. VoWA
  St. Francis of Assisi &
    the...Jews. VoWA
  To the Jews in Poland. VoWA
Wives. See Marriage
Wolcott (see Peter Pindar), J.

Wolf hunting near Nashoba. Jim
  Barnes. ReE
Wolfe, Cynthia R.
  Erasers. YoVA
  The vision. YoVA
Wolfenstein, Alfred
  Exodus 1940. VoWA
Wolfskehl, Karl
  From Mount Nebo. VoWA
  Shekhina. VoWA
  We go. VoWA
Wolsey, Thomas, Cardinal
  King Henry VIII, sels. William
    Shakespeare. WBP3
Wolves
  The last wolf. Mary
    Tallmountain. ReE
The **woman** at the Washington Zoo.
  Randall Jarrell. HaAP
A **woman** from the Book of
  Genesis. David Knut. VoWA
A **woman** killed with kindness,
  sels. Thomas Heywood. WBP4
Woman me. Maya Angelou. BlS
Woman poem. Nikki Giovanni. BlS
The **woman** poet. Gertrud Kolmar.
  VoWA
The **woman** thing. Lorde Audre.
  BlS
Woman through the window. Marcia
  Falk. VoWA
The **woman** who combed. Rush
  Rankin. FroA
A **woman** who's arrived at a ripe
  old age. Zelda. BuAC
A **woman's** answer. Adelaide Anne
  Procter. WBP2
A **woman's** complaint. Unknown.
  WBP2
Woman's inconstancy. Sir Robert

  Ayton. WBP3
A **woman's** love. John Hay. WBP3
A **woman's** nature. Jean Dorat.
  ReLP
A **woman's** question. Adelaide
  Anne Procter. WBP2
A **woman's** song. Colleen J.
  McElroy. BlS
Woman's will. John Godfrey Saxe.
  WBP2
Women. May Swenson. LiHE
Women
  Adam's curse. William Butler
    Yeats. SlW
  Agatha. Alfred Austin. WBP3
  Agatha. Remy de Gourmont. FreS
  Agnes. Jean Moreas. FreS
  All this so tasteless and
    threatening. Yona Wallach.
    BuAC
  At night, she sees voices.
    Chedva Harakavy. BuAC
  An autumn song for Ch'ang-hsin
    Palace. Wang Ch'ang-ling.
    GrAC
  Autumn-strewn ground. Charles
    Van Lerberghe. FreS
  Bedouin woman. Shulamit Apfel.
    BuAC
  Before the feast of Shushan.
    Anne Spencer. BlS
  Behind the shadow. Ellen L.
    Kisthardt. StPo
  Bel woman. Roman C. Adrian. ReE
  The cage. Avner Treinin. VoWA
  Combing. Gladys Cardiff. ReE
  "The comedian said it." Duff
    Bigger. FroA
  Condemned women. Charles
    Baudelaire. FoFS
  Cradle song. Yona Wallach.
    BuAC--VoWA
  The defeated. Linda Gregg. TeMP
  Dora Williams. Edgar Lee
    Masters. HaAP
  Doris Maria, comrade. Ricardo
    Morales Aviles. NiR
  Drawing of a woman. Shlomit
    Cohen. BuAC
  The dream songs, sels. John
    Berryman. HaAP
  Enamel work on gold and silver.
    Pierre Louys. FreS
  The epistle to the reader. Mary
    Tattlewell (pseud.). PaW
  Epitaph on Galla, a childless
    woman. Giovanni Giovano
    Pontano. ReLP
  Flute. Rivka Miriam. BuAC
  For Anne Gregory. William

Butler Yeats. SlW
From a correct address in a suburb... Helen Sorrells. LiHE
From the cavities of bones. Patricia Parker. BlS
The garden. Ezra Pound. SlW
Girls. Dan Andres. YoVA
The good woman. Crystal MacLean. FroA
"The hair flight of a flame..." Stephane Mallarme. FoFS
A health. Edward Coate Pinkney. WBP2
The heart of a woman. Georgia Douglas Johnson. BlS
Her likeness. Dinah Maria Mulock Craik. WBP2
Household. Laura Jensen. TeMP
Hyd, Absolon, thy gilte tresses clere. Geoffrey Chaucer. HaAP
I care not for these ladies. Thomas Campion. HaAP
I knew a woman. Theodore Roethke. HaAP
I serve a mistress whiter than snow. Anthony Munday. HaAP
I sing of a maiden (mayden. Unknown . HaAP--ShBa
I the woman. Sandra Cisneros. PrVo
In Egypt. Paul Celan. VoWA
In a prominent bar in Secaucus one day. X.J. Kennedy. HoA
In that green field. Rivka Miriam. BuAC
Inscape. Susan Litwack. VoWA
The Jewish woman. Gertrud Kolmar. VoWA
Juanita, wife of Manuelito. Simon J. Ortiz. ReE
Just this. Istvan Vas. VoWA
Kiss toward the absolut. Takiguchi Shuzo . FroC
Kissie Lee. Margaret Walker. BlS
La Fontaine du Vaucluse for Marie Ponsot. Marilyn Hacker. TeMP
The lady in black. Emile Verhaeren. FreS
The lady's-maid's song. John Hollander. TyW
Let me tell you about mysel. Tomioka Taeko . FroC
Letter to my sister. Anne Spencer. BlS
Lola. Yona Wallach. BuAC
Lombard-Venetian. Luciano Erba. NeIP

A look at a bee. Leah Goldberg. BuAC
Love poem (for M.). Cary Waterman. TeMP
A love poem for all...women I have known. Charles Bukowski. TeMP
Marilyn from a two-bit town. Jack Forbes. YoVA
The marionette. Dahlia Ravikovich. BuAC
Masquerade. Carolyn M. Rodgers. BlS
Mixed feelings. John Ashbery. HaAP
A Mona Lisa. Angelina Weld Grimke. BlS
My poor raging sisters. Esther Raab. BuAC
Nudities. Andre Spire. VoWA
Of his love Caelia. Girolamo Angeriano. ReLP
Orange chiffon. Jayne Cortez. BlS
Pancharis: I. Jean Bonefons. ReLP
Pancharis: XVI. Jean Bonefons. ReLP
Pancharis: XXIV. Jean Bonefons. ReLP
A paradox, sels. Georgia Douglas Johnson. BlS
The Pennacesse Leper Colony for Women... Norman Dubie. TeMP
A phantom. Charles Baudelaire. FoFS
Poeme antipoeme. Elio Pagliarani. NeIP
Provide, provide. Robert Frost. HaAP--LiHE
Revolutionary petunias. Alice Walker. BlS
Roman rooms. Paolo Volponi. NeIP
Rose Aylmer. Walter Savage Landor. HaAP--WBP2
The ruined maid. Thomas Hardy. LiHE
Salute to the foreign one. Henri de Regnier. FreS
Salve deux rex judaeorum..., sels. Aemilia (Bassano) Lanyer. PaW
The scholar's wife. Susan Mernit. VoWA
Sexual privacy of women on welfare. Pinkie Gordon Lane. BlS
Shades. Jean-Guy Pilon. MoVT
She dwelt among the untrodden

ways. William Wordsworth.
HaAP

Shulamit in her dreams. Marcia
Falk. VoWA

The silken tent. Robert Frost.
LiHE

The smiling mouth and laughing
eyen grey. Charles, Duc d'
Orleans. HaAP

Soalt in tleeyaga. Mary
Tallmountain. ReE

Song ("Love a woman? You're an
ass!) John Wilmot, Earl
Rochester. TyW

Songs to a lady moonwalker.
Abraham Sutskever. VoWA

Songs: 32 songs from the Ryojin
Hisho. Unknown . FroC

Sterility in metamorphosis.
Adriano Spatola. NeIP

Struggling at the kill. Shlomit
Cohen. BuAC

Susie Asado. Gertrude Stein.
SlW

Tegona of Mama. Takahashi
Mushimaro. FroC

A terrible heart. Yona Wallach.
BuAC

the Cambridge ladies... Edward
Estlin Cummings. LiHE

There is a woman in this town.
Patricia Parker. BlS

"There was an old woman called
nothing." Unknown . IlTH

Tiger-lily. Raquel Chalfi. BuAC

To Fannia. Giovanni Giovano
Pontano. ReLP

To Margaris. Marc-Antoine de
Muret. ReLP

To Nearera: "Every time you
turn..." Michael Tarchaniota
Marullus. ReLP

To Nearera: "My sweete..."
Michael Tarchaniota Marullus.
ReLP

To Stella. Giovanni Giovano
Pontano. ReLP

To a cactus seller. Anwar
Shaul. VoWA

To his mistress. Nicolas
Bourbon. ReLP

To the eternal madame. Tristan
Corbiere. FreS

Transit. Richard Wilbur. TeMP

Triolet ("All women born...")
Robert Bridges. TyW

Two portraits. Tanikawa Shuntaro.
FroC

Ursula. Remy de Gourmont. FreS

Usually an older female is the

leader. Tom Hennen. FroA

Vashti. Frances E.W. Harper.
BlS

A virginal. Ezra Pound. LiHE

Wang Chao-chun. Ch'u Kuang-hsi.
GrAC

What soft-cherubic creatures.
Emily Dickinson. HaAP--LiHE

White magic, sels. Krzysztof
Kamil Baczynski. CoP

Wife of Kohelet. Shlomit Cohen.
BuAC--VoWA

Woman me. Maya Angelou. BlS

Woman through the window.
Marcia Falk. VoWA

A woman's nature. Jean Dorat.
ReLP

Women. May Swenson. LiHE

Women - Black

The Anniad. Gwendolyn Brooks.
BlS

An appeal to my countrywomen.
Frances E.W. Harper. BlS

Black sister. Kattie M. Cumbo.
BlS

Black woman. Naomi Long
Madgett. BlS

Blackberry sweet. Dudley
Randall. HaAP

Caledonia. Colleen J. McElroy.
BlS

Ceremony. Johari M. Kunjufu.
BlS

Cinderella. Fareedah Allah. (Ruby
Saunders). BlS

Dark phrases. Ntozake Shange.
BlS

Dreams. Nikki Giovanni. LiHE

Driving wheel. Sherley Anne
Williams. BlS

The empress brand trim: Ruby
reminisces. Sherley Anne
Williams. BlS

Frank Albert & Viola Benzena
Owens. Ntozake Shange. BlS

A freedom song for the black
woman. Carole C. Gregory. BlS

The generation gap. Fareedah
Allah (Ruby Saunders). BlS

Grinding vibrato. Jayne Cortez.
BlS

Harriet. Lorde Audre. BlS

The house of desire. Sherley
Anne Williams. BlS

Hush, honey. Fareedah Allah
(Ruby Saunders). BlS

I done got so thirsty...
Patricia Jones. BlS

I, woman. Irma McLaurin. BlS

Jesus was crucified or: it must

Whittier. WBP4
The old village choir. Benjamin
  F. Taylor. WBP4
Ultima veritas. Washington
  Gladden. WBP4
Vesper hymn. Eliza Scudder.
  WBP4
Vesper hymn. Samuel Longfellow.
  WBP4
The word. William Walshaw How.
  WBP4
Worth, Valerie
Body. FroA
Christmas lights. PoCh
Christmas ornaments. PoCh
Wotton, Sir Henry
On his mistress, the Queen of
  Bohemia. HaAP--WBP2
Wray, Betsy
A day at the beach. YoVA
The old man rocks in the wind.
  YoVA
Wreathe the bowl. Thomas Moore.
  WBP1
Wreathmakertraining. Karl
  Patten. FroA
The **wreck.** Walter De La Mare.
  MTS
The **wreck** of the Hesperus. Henry
  Wadsworth Longfellow. MTS
Wrestlers
Sleeping wrestler. Takahashi
  Mutsuo. FroC
Wrestling Jacob. Charles Wesley.
  WBP4
Wright, Angie
A poor child's Christmas. YoVA
Wright, Charles David
Some semblance of order. FroA
Wright, Charles
Called back. TeMP
Wright, James
At the slackening of the tide.
  MTS
In response to a rumor.... TyW
Lying in a hammock at William
  Duffy's... HaAP
Speak. HaAP
To a blossoming pear tree. HaAP
Wright, Richard
Between the world and me. LiHE
Wright, Terri
From a window. YoVA
Sunrise. YoVA
Write me a verse. David McCord.
  MiRN
Writing and Writers
Form rejection letter. Philip
  Dacey. TeMP
I wanted to... Sara Nikirk.

YoVA
A receipt for writing a novel.
  Mary Alcock. EvIm
A sort of song. William Carlos
  Williams. FroA
Writing to Aaron. Denise
  Levertov. FroA
Written after long rains at my
  villa... Wang Wei. GrAC
Written after swimming..Sestos
  to Abydos. George Gordon,6th
  Baron Byron. MTS
Written at mauve garden... Zhu
  Yi-zun. LuL
Written at the Tung-ch'ing-yang
  lodge... Li Chia-yu. GrAC
Written in Chi. Kao Shih. GrAC
Written on a stone in the
  road... Pablo Antonio Cuadra.
  NiR
Written on a wall at Woodstock.
  Elizabeth I; Queen of
  England. PaW
Written on the road while
  returning... Li Chia-yu. GrAC
Written on the Meditation
  Garden... Ch'ang Chien. GrAC
Written on the cottage wall...
  Ch'ien Ch'i. GrAC
Written on the Tung-p'ing road.
  Kao Shih. GrAC
Written to serve as..reply..my
  most,sels. Wang Ch'ang-ling.
  GrAC
Written when I climbed the
  peak... Takahashi Mushimaro.
  FroC
Written while viewing the
  river...autumn. Lin Bu. LuL
Wroth, Lady Mary (Sidney)
A crowne of sonnets, sels. PaW
Wu Mountain high. Huang-fu Jan.
  GrAC
Wu Yun
Wandering immortals. GrAC
Wubben, Jill
It doesn't really matter. YoVA
Wuest, Patricia Viale
Alicia aardvark. StPo
Butter yellow kitchen. StPo
Hurricane. StPo
wwohali. Carroll Arnett/Gogisgi.
  ReE
Wyatt, Sir Thomas
Forget not yet. HaAP
My galley charged with
  forgetfulness. HaAP--MTS
My lute, awake. HaAP
They flee from me. HaAP--LiHE
Whoso list to hunt. HaAP

Wycherley, William
  To a fine young woman. TyW
Wyeth, John Allan
  My sweetheart's face. WBP2
Wygodski, Stanislaw
  Going to the north. VoWA
  Those betrayed at dawn. VoWA
  Voyage. VoWA
  Winter journey. VoWA
Wylie, Elinor
  Sea lullaby. MTS
Wynne, Johm Huddlestone
  Eiptaph on a dormouse. MiRN
Wynter ys icumen in. Frank
      Sidgwick. TyW

X-rays
  Bone poem. Nancy Willard. HoA

The **yachts.** William Carlos
      Williams. MTS
Yaddo. Ruth Herschberger. FroA
Yadoyano Meshimoro
  "When it comes to poets." FroC
Yahrzeit. Susan Fromberg
      Schaeffer. VoWA
Yahrzeit. Dan Jaffe. VoWA
Yamabe no Akahito
  Climbing Kasuga Field. FroC
  Composed on the 5th of the 10th
    month... FroC
  "I came to this spring
    field..." FroC
  "In the field I've roped
    off...") FroC
  Looking at Mount Fuji in the
    distance. FroC
  Song ("Our sovereign
    familiar...") FroC
  Song ("The palace of
    Yoshino...") FroC
Yamanque no Okura
  A dialogue on poverty. FroC
  Longing for his son, Furuchi.
    FroC
  On Tanabata. FroC
  Upon excusing himself from a
    banquet. FroC
Yamashiro. Unknown. FroC
Yancy, Michelle
  Peace. YoVA
Yang Wan-li
  Looking at Yue-Tai Mountain...
    LuL

  Night rain at Guang-Kou. LuL
Yang-di
  Flowers and moonlight
    on...Spring River. LuL
Yangtze and Han. Tu Fu. GrAC
Yard, Robin
  A dream. YoVA
  From good to bad. YoVA
The **yarn of the Nancy Bell.** Sir
      William S. Gilbert. MTS
Yaulabuta: the passion of
      Kailaga. Unknown. VooI
Ye goathered gods. Sir Philip
      Sidney. HaAP
The **year 2000.** Joyce Hill. YoVA
Year after year. Scott Moore.
      YoVA
Year end. Akera Kanko. FroC
Year's end, returning to my
      southern... Meng Hao-jan.
      GrAC
Yearning. Li Po. GrAC
Years. Anna Margolin (R.
      Lebensboim). VoWA
The **years.** Scott McCartney. YoVA
Yeats, William Butler
  Adam's curse. SlW
  Among school children. HaAP
  Byzantium. HaAP
  The cold heaven. HaAP
  Crazy Jane on the day of
    judgment. SlW
  Easter 1916. HaAP
  The fisherman. HaAP
  For Anne Gregory. SlW
  The gyres. HaAP
  He wishes for the clothes of
    heaven. SlW
  The lamentation of an old
    pensioner. HaAP--TyW
  Leda and the swan. LiHE
  The Magi. HaAP
  The Magi. PoCh--ShBa
  The Mother of God. ShBa
  Paudeen. HaAP
  A prayer for my daughter.
    HaAP--TyW
  Ribh considers Christian
    love.... TyW
  The sad shepherd. MTS
  Sailing to Byzantium.
    HaAP--LiHE
  The second coming. LiHE--ShBa
  The second coming. HaAP
  September 1913. HaAP
  The song of the old mother.
    WBP1
  The song of wandering Aengus.
    SlW
  The stolen child. EvIm

Ravikovich. BuAC
To Thaliarchu. Horace . WBP1
To a Highland girl. William
  Wordsworth. WBP1
To a young girl. David
  Rosenmann-Taub. VoWA
To the virgins, to make much of
  time. Robert Herrick.
  HaAP--WBP1
To youth. Walter Savage Landor.
  WBP1
Watching a young girl going
  alone.. Takahashi Mushimaro .
  FroC
We real cool. Gwendolyn Brooks.
  HaAP
When I was one-and-twenty.
  Alfred Edward Housman. LiHE
Youth and age, sels. Samuel
  Taylor Coleridge. WBP1
Youth and love. Philip James
  Bailey. WBP1
Youth and age, sels. Samuel
  Taylor Coleridge. WBP1
Youth and love. Philip James
  Bailey. WBP1
Yu Hsin
  Playful quatrains, sel. Tu Fu .
  GrAC
Yu-hua Palace. Tu Fu. GrAC
Yuan Chieh
  After the raiders have gone.
    GrAC
  The lesson of a former
    visit..Jang Creek. GrAC
  Pity for dissolution, sels.
    GrAC
  Rowing songs, sels. GrAC
  Thinking on high antiquity.
    GrAC
  To my neighbors on Jank Creek.
    GrAC
  Wine cup in stone hollow. GrAC
Yuan Hong-dao
  West lake. LuL
Yuan Zhong-dao
  Miscellaneous poems at three
    lakes. LuL
  "The river is white in itself."
    LuL
Yuan Zong-dao
  For three days I
    traveled...mountains. LuL
Yucatan, Mexico
  Lost in Yucatan. Tom McKeown.
Yungman, Moshe
  Don't say. VoWA
  Encounter in Safed. VoWA
  Melons. VoWA
  The Messiah. VoWA

The sacrifice. VoWA
Yuryaku (418-479), Emperor
  Song ("With a basket, a lovely
    basket"). FroC
Yuusthiwa. Simon J. Ortiz. ReE

Z (letter)
  Directions from Zulu. Daniel
    Halpern. FroA
Zacchaeus
  On Zacchaeus. Francis Quarles.
    HaAP
Zach, Natan
  Against parting. VoWA
  As sand. VoWA
  A foreign country. VoWA
  In this deep darkness. VoWA
  Listening to her. VoWA
  No. VoWA
  A peaceful song. VoWA
  Perhaps its only music. VoWA
  The quiet light of flies. VoWA
  A short winter tale. VoWA
  To be a master in your house.
    VoWA
  When God first said. VoWA
  When the last riders. VoWA
Zandoli, Valerie
  Dawn horse. YoVA
Zangwill, Israel
  Blind. WBP3
Zanzotto, Andrea
  Eclogue IV. NeIP
  From a new height. NeIP
  Lorna slope. NeIP
  The perfection of snow. NeIP
  September 13, 1959 (Variation).
    NeIP
  Subnarcosis. NeIP
  To the world. NeIP
Zapata, Emiliano
  Pentecos. Ai . TeMP
Zara's ear-rings. John Gibson
  Lockhart. WBP2
Zarchi, Nurit
  Furtively. BuAC
  Wild orchards. BuAC
Zaydee. Philip Levine. VoWA
Zeal and love. John Henry,
  Cardinal Newman. TyW
Zealot without a face. Charles
  Dobzynski. VoWA
Zeitlin (see C.Tiempo), Israel

Zeitlin, Aaron
  A dream about an aged humorist.
    VoWA